The Texas Pilgrim

20 Years of Reflection and Commentary

Jim Windham

www.TexasPilgrim.com

Publisher:
Elite Online Publishing
63 East 11400 South #230
Sandy, UT 84070
EliteOnlinePublishing.com

Editor:
Eileen Ansel Conery

Printed in the United States of America

ISBN: 978-1-956642-78-0
2nd Edition

Table of Contents

Introduction

The Texas Pilgrim began with a question from my wife, who wondered who I would talk with about the readings in history and philosophy I was consuming, the Great Books discussion sessions in which I was participating, and the periodic conferences on the humanities I was attending, none of which were high on her list of pastimes. After pondering this question for several months and borrowing some ideas from friends around the country who had pursued writing publications of personal commentary, the concept of *The Texas Pilgrim* was launched.

Blogging was in its infancy and I was computer illiterate, so the project began with my writing the monthly issue content in long hand and having a word processor transcribe it for copying and mailing by regular mail, with my wife contributing to the stuffing and mailing. In the early days it was offered with a subscription fee and at one time there were several hundred paid subscribers, but as the hassle of the regular mail edition grew burdensome and I acquired at least a minimal level of word processor capability, the regular mail print edition was dropped along with the subscription fee, and the publication went strictly online.

Now, after almost 20 years, more than 200 monthly issues, and approaching 1,000 essays, the time has come to take stock of this project and its inventory. The result is this collection comprising more than 500 of these essays and book reviews on social issues, public policy, philosophy, and American culture, all written in the spirit of the theme advanced by Richard Weaver in his classic book of the same name, that ideas have consequences.

The Texas Pilgrim has never been a "newsletter" nor has it necessarily been a political letter, except to the extent of commentary on the ideas that drive electoral politics. It has since its founding simply been a personal letter of commentary with an objective to engage readers in a dialogue on the critical issues of our time and the ideas that drive public policy and culture in America.

My sincere thanks to all who have had a part in this project and this book: to Melanie Johnson and Jenn Foster for valuable counsel and publishing expertise; to my editor Eileen Ansel Conery, who performed excellent service in compiling and structuring the essay collection; to my son-in-law Martin Wind, who has provided invaluable assistance to the publication over the years as my web master; to the hundreds of subscribers to *The Texas Pilgrim* who gave me confidence and inspired me along the way with their candid response to my work; and to "my girls," my wife Lela and daughters Victoria and Caroline, who provided suggestions and assistance in the early years with the distribution of the printed publication along with encouragement throughout this project for the past 20 years.

Jim Windham
Houston, TX
February 2019
www.TexasPilgrim.com

1
American Exceptionalism

The Tipping Point

April 2, 2010

At the close of the Constitutional Convention in Philadelphia in September 1787, a Mrs. Powell anxiously awaited the results, and as Benjamin Franklin emerged from the convention, she asked him directly: "Well, Doctor, what have we got, a republic or a monarchy?" Franklin responded, "A republic, madam, if you can keep it."

Well, after all these years, the jury is still out, but I submit that there has never been a point in time since the Civil War in which her question is more relevant, even as the words "democratic despotism," as later contemplated by Tocqueville, would now be somewhat more appropriate than "monarchy" as an alternative to a republic. For what we are witnessing is a crisis much more threatening to our constitutional order than any we have faced in over a century.

And the tipping point to which I refer is not just the reality of the consequences, both intended and unintended, of the healthcare bill, but rather the implications of the convergence of conditions in America that made such a travesty possible or even provided it with credible discussion space. And I don't want to hear that we as a people have been misled or duped by President Obama and his support base in the media and the leftist elite. We made this possible because we abdicated our duties to self-government in a long train of seduction by the lure of entitlement, of the sacrifice of freedom for security, the pursuit of consumption out of all balance with production, and the expansion of "rights" without regard to responsibilities.

So, what now? I have said before that we are at a point roughly equivalent to 1857 and the *Dred Scott v. Sandford* case in the ramp up to the Civil War. Tony Blankley recently put it at 1854 and the Kansas-Nebraska Act. The ultimate point is that, as Lincoln wisely observed, "A House divided against itself cannot stand... it will become all one thing or the other." Neither of us have in mind another civil war, but we have a situation in which a large percentage, a majority in my estimation, of opinion leadership, as well as the people at large remain committed to the principles as espoused in our founding documents, while a large percentage are convinced that these principles are outdated and should be replaced, overridden, or simply ignored. This is a collision course that has been underway for at least a century, but never has the latter group had such a leader as Obama, the most ideologically progressive President since Woodrow Wilson, who profoundly disagrees with the foundational basis of the American experiment, not to mention the entire notion of American exceptionalism.

I am an eternal optimist, and, in spite of our sleepwalking, this remains a center-right country, so I am betting on the traditionalist strains and the exceptionalist nature of our culture to rise to the occasion, but the outcome is far from certain.

Honoring Those Who Served

June 4, 2010

Recently we have heard the reports of a Connecticut candidate for the Senate who has consistently lied about his Vietnam War service and I was struck during one TV discussion of the issue by comments from Katrina vanden Heuvel, Editor of the leftist magazine, *The Nation*, who wonders why we so revere our veterans and assign their military service such a high ranking in our criteria for serving in public office in the first place. After all, she says, we are glorifying war service. Meanwhile, Pat Buchanan reminds us that of all the generals who have gone on to serve the country as President, not one led America into a new war, and only one 19th century President who had seen combat as a soldier led us into war. This may be coincidental, but I think not. Of all people, warriors hate war the most. So, in these days between Memorial Day and the anniversary of D-Day, I thought it appropriate to pass along the following anonymous observations recently sent to me that might help Ms. van den Heuvel and others understand why we honor those who served.

It is the veteran, not the preacher, who has given us freedom of religion; it is the veteran, not the reporter, who has given us freedom of the press; it is the veteran, not the poet, who has given us freedom of speech; it is the veteran, not the campus organizer, who has given us freedom to assemble; it is the veteran, not the lawyer, who has given us the right to a fair trial; and it is the veteran, not the politician, who has given us the right to vote.

Hug a veteran this week.

The New American Century

January 3, 2011

The 20th was popularly and widely known as "The American Century" for a lot of reasons, some of which are embodied in something I wrote at the end of the last century in response to a request by a publication to characterize it in 50 words or less, as follows:

"They (the Americans) reluctantly assumed the mantle of world leadership; challenged and ultimately defeated the primary instruments of totalitarianism; exported the principles of democracy and human rights to regions where those concepts were unknown; and, for better or worse, initiated popular cultural hegemony over a major portion of the world's population."

But it's a new century, and many, including our own citizens, believe we are in decline. Most point to economic factors. We are no longer the colossus of the mid-20th century in terms of economic dominance, which recently has been vividly demonstrated by the Swedish professor Hans Rosling in his fascinating portrayal of the convergence of world standards of living over the past two centuries. Other countries have dramatically closed the gap with us. Some would have us believe that this represents a loss of our vaunted exceptionalism.

But the American brand of exceptionalism is not measured in GDP; it's about our values and about who we are. No nation ever has assimilated immigrants and foreign cultures as successfully as America; no other nation has been founded by a creed, particularly one which has been so severely tested over two centuries as America's has; and no nation has so successfully embodied pluralism and tolerance in its strongly grounded religious culture. The rising economic powers and competitors cannot compete with America in these cultural foundations. These are the basis for American exceptionalism. It's incumbent on us to select leaders who actually believe in it and won't squander it.

A Waning Power

August 5, 2011

Reasonable people can and do disagree about the purposes of American power in the world. Some are close calls, for example, should we be in Libya today or is it our business what form of government prevails in Egypt? But some of the calls should be rather obvious if the premise is still valid that America has a role to play in the leadership of the free world in the interest of advancing freedom in places where it is absent and protecting it where it is under siege, in particular those places where Americans and their strategic interests are at risk One such latter place is Syria, which I would number among the two or three regimes most hostile to America and its interests, not to mention the fully documented evidence that it is more than a distant accomplice in the killing of Americans.

So, if we can't proclaim absolute moral clarity in our pronouncements that the Syrian regime should be removed and support this outcome with our military and diplomatic assets, then what is the proper use of American power in the world? Will we succumb to the liberal internationalist guilt trip that a wealthy Western nation shouldn't have national interests, much less those that it will fight for? Must there always be a well-defined humanitarian purpose for any use of American military power? Or will we return to the paleoconservative isolationism as promoted by Pat Buchanan, who evidently believes that our entry into World War II wasn't necessary? Incidentally, could we ever again conduct such a war to the finish?

These are questions that we had better be seriously considering, not to mention some others, such as what do we do when China is forced by its nationalist factions to fully assert its hegemony in what it considers its sphere of influence in the South China Sea? How far will we allow the persecution of Chinese Christians and other dissidents? What will be our response to the next uprising in Tiananmen Square or a conflict with Taiwan? What about Iran, North Korea, etc.?

If we buy into Philip Bobbitt's thesis in *The Shield of Achilles* that the world is moving from a system of nation states to one of market states, the system of alliances and interests will be transformed as they have not been since the beginning of what he calls The Long War, which began in 1914 and ended with the fall of the Soviet Union in 1990. I think I do buy into this, but I continue to believe in the need for an exceptional nation to lead the free world. Does America still have a culture with enough confidence in itself to continue in this role with moral clarity? If not us, who?

The Plight of the Essential Nation

March 3, 2013

The current thinking among many foreign policy experts, including those with particular expertise in Iranian relations, seems to be that the new foreign policy alignment in the

Obama administration – State, Defense, CIA – combined with the instincts of the President and Vice President, will have the most pro-engagement bias since the Iranian Revolution of 1979. This comes into play while Iran's leader, Kamainei, totally rejects bilateral engagement. This can't be good and might be very dangerous.

This also comes at a moment in which we don't have the will to finish the job in Afghanistan and we receive the news that Obama had vetoed the recommendation of his former top three security advisors to arm the rebels in Syria. The latter decision further highlights the weakness of his three critical security team appointments – Kerry, Hagel, and Brennan – none of whom has the standing or gravitas of their predecessors and are not likely to present Obama with views he doesn't want to hear.

Contrary to the views of Pat Buchanan, Iran is an apocalyptic regime that cannot be contained or engaged as with the Soviet Union in the Cold War. And despite the President's election year pronouncements, Al Qaeda is alive and well and actively seeking out destruction of American interests. This is a dangerous world and the U.S. remains the indispensable power, whether we like it or not. These national security appointments, particularly Hagel at Defense, send the wrong message to our friends and our enemies. What we need is moral clarity in foreign policy; what we have is reduction in means and in will, almost back to the McGovern "come home America" days of 1972. This attitude coupled with the sequestration cuts do not bode well for American security interests, much less our leadership, which is indispensable to the free world.

A Failure to Lead

May 7, 2013

In her 2002 book, *Statecraft: Strategies for a Changing World*, Lady Margaret Thatcher reflects on what the American Revolution means to the world and what America meant to her, and she writes:

"These reflections lead me to certain conclusions about the conduct of international politics:

- America alone has the moral, as well as the material capacity for world leadership,
- America's destiny is bound up with global expression of the values of freedom,
- America's closest allies, particularly her allies in the English-speaking world,

must regard America's mission as encompassing their own."
And in a previous speech to The Heritage Foundation, she said this: "America's duty is to lead. The duty of other Western countries is to support its leadership."

Pretty strong words, but they point to a significant reality: that the United States is the indispensable nation. Call it American exceptionalism if you like, that's part of it.

Lady Thatcher certainly bought into the notion. But I have plenty of doubts that the current administration does and this is playing out in its hesitancy in Syria.

Don't misunderstand me, there are plenty of reasons not to get involved in Syria, plenty of well-identified risks. But it seems increasingly clear that the risks of non-intervention outweigh those of our intervention, so as to have a role in the outcome of a sectarian civil war that is threatening to become regional, and as I have previously suggested, take on many of the characteristics of the Spanish Civil War of the mid-1930s.

In fact, we already have squandered significant time that would have been more decisive in our impact on the outcome. But more importantly, I worry that our hesitancy is based less on tactical judgments of risk and more on our lack of moral clarity, our refusal to identify our enemy, and our political fear of "another Iraq." The world and particularly our enemies are watching to see if our "red line" is purely rhetorical.

The Roots of American Exceptionalism

July 5, 2014

Dr. David Armitage, Professor of History at Harvard University, has written a great essay on the Declaration of Independence in *The Wall Street Journal* over July 4th weekend, "The Words Heard Around the World."

In it, he makes many good points, but the most insightful is the importance of recognizing and separating two distinct elements of the Declaration that often are conflated – 1) the assertion of popular sovereignty to create a new state in dissolving the political bands with Britain, and 2) the more famous element in the second paragraph, its ringing endorsement of the sanctity of the individual ("We hold these truths…").

He then goes further to trace the worldwide impact of the Declaration over the past three centuries and notes that this impact has had much more to do with the spread of sovereignty and the creation of new states than with the diffusion and acceptance of the ideas of individual rights, and that this remains one of the more pressing dilemmas of international politics. In fact, of the 120 or so declarations of independence written since ours, scarcely any of them included the self-evident truths of individual rights embodied in our Declaration.

He closes with the observation that today's authoritarians are eager to flex their sovereign muscles, but they don't like the other half of the equation, the notion that, in fact, their authority derives from the "unalienable rights" of their citizens.

As I read this essay, in particular the closing comments, it occurred to me that this is the essence of American exceptionalism. Happy Birthday!

Good for the Scots

October 5, 2014

It was encouraging that the voters in Scotland rejected the separation from the United Kingdom. Let's hope they did it for mostly the right reasons. Self-determination is a noble concept, developed and championed by Woodrow Wilson in the *Fourteen Points* that became the organizing principle of the Treaty of Versailles, and it can be applied selectively, but it can often be overly idealistic and problematic in application. Think the Balkans. Think Quebec. Or, closer to home, think the American Civil War. It occurred to me after the Scottish vote that the American notion of a country founded on and dedicated to a proposition is a modern miracle and that we almost blew it with this conflict. As Lincoln said at Gettysburg, "Now we are engaged in a great civil war, testing whether that nation, or any nation so conceived or so dedicated, can long endure…" This is American exceptionalism.

Willful Ignorance?

April 5, 2015

Lt. Gen. Michael Flynn, former head of the Defense Intelligence Agency, has described the Obama administration's policy in the Middle East as one of "willful ignorance," and it is hard to disagree with that assessment. In fact, it can be mind-boggling to watch as this incoherent strategy unfolds on a daily basis. But, as difficult as it is for a rational observer to understand, I believe that the strategy is more willful than ignorant. I believe that Obama knows exactly what he is doing and what are the likely outcomes.

First, Obama's worldview is one that does not include an exceptional America as the indispensable world power and he does not believe that this power, particularly when backed by our military, is a force for good in the world. This view is supported by almost every foreign policy initiative that he has pursued, the main thrust of which has been "withdrawal."

Further, he is clearly an anti-colonialist and believes that the role of the Western powers in history has been the primary cause of most of the geopolitical problems we now face. Closely connected to this view, when it comes to Israel, it has become increasingly clear that he is an anti-Zionist, believing that the establishment of a Jewish homeland in the State of Israel has been a mistake.

These observations are obviously open to debate, and I would welcome it, but I have watched him pretty closely for six years and have confidence in these views. So, what does this mean for his Middle East policy?

Max Boot, a senior fellow at the Council on Foreign Relations, has written an insightful analysis leading to the conclusion that President Obama's objective in the Middle East is nothing less than the most fundamental realignment of U.S. foreign policy in a generation, one that will result in the establishment of his new doctrine: Downgrade U.S. ties to Israel and Saudi Arabia while allowing our new friend Iran to fill the vacuum left by U.S. retreat.

The evidence he offers is compelling and I agree with his assessment. When the dots are connected as Boot has done, it's clear that this objective has been in evidence almost since the day Obama took office. The crowning achievement for his legacy will be the nuclear arms agreement with Iran, which will open the door for an arms race in the region and direct conflict between Iran and Saudi Arabia, Shiite and Sunni, for regional dominance, with the U.S. as a bystander. There is plenty of stupidity here, but not much ignorance, and it is almost completely willful.

And if this scenario doesn't get the attention of Congress on both sides of the aisle, they are willfully blind. There is no reason to continue to parse language and litigate the details of this pending nuclear agreement "framework" with a totally untrustworthy regime; this is a bad deal and it should be killed – now.

A Memo to the Current and Future Leader of the World of Order

January 5, 2016

If you're like me, you grew weary over the Christmas holidays of the constant droning on all the talk and interview shows about the "war on terror," the polls on whether we're winning or losing, whether Obama has a strategy to defeat ISIS or not, if so, what is it, will there be American "boots on the ground," if so, how many, etc., not to mention the increased emphasis on related national security issues in the Republican primary campaign since Paris and San Bernadino and the hair-splitting over where the various candidates would take us in this war. So, in response this is my best shot at a New Year message to whomever we elect this coming November.

Memorandum to President Obama and all those who aspire to succeed him:

- We have been at war with the ideology of Islamism since 1979, but not directly with Islam, and this is a big distinction which we should understand because we can't defeat the enemy if we can't or won't properly identify it.
- This war is in large part a major element of the reformation of Islam, which is underway, as well as a civil war to determine who speaks for political Islam, Sunni or Shiite, and among warring elements of the majority Sunni sect.
- We cannot avoid this civil war or the reformation that surrounds it and hope that they will kill each other – it has and will more aggressively come to us if we do not defeat the enemy on their battlefield.
- The alignment in this war, which has been characterized by Norman Podhoretz as World War IV, a characterization that has considerable merit, is the civilized world of order vs. the uncivilized world of disorder, and it is an existential confrontation for the world of order – we must win it.
- The current rules of engagement will not do it; in order to win, the United States must lead the world of order in all of the manifestations of that leadership, which will include the winning and holding of territory and the occupation of parts of the world of disorder for a possibly extensive period of time.

I wish it were not so, but such are the burdens of American exceptionalism and leadership of the world of order.

If you doubt the gravity of the challenge we face, simply contemplate the vast and potentially dire implications of the confrontation between Saudi Arabia and Iran sparked by the execution of a dissident cleric carried out last week by the Saudis. This could get very ugly very soon.

2
Biography

My Favorite Founder
October 2, 2002

Recently I read David McCullough's *John Adams* in order to attend as a guest at a meeting of my wife's book discussion group, and it reminded me of the qualities of this most underappreciated of our founders. McCullough's treatment has been criticized as overly admiring of Adams, overly contemptuous of Thomas Jefferson, and, as popularly written history often is, lacking in academic depth. Possibly it is some of all of this, but it was still a great character study of both John and his brilliant and devoted Abigail. As the American counterpart to the British founder of conservatism, Edmund Burke, Adams probably left more written conservative political philosophy than any American founder, and his dogged pursuit of federalism and classical republican virtue set an example that lives today. For an excellent review of his political thought in more depth, I recommend Russell Kirk's, *The Conservative Mind.* I have long believed that it is a great disservice that there is not even a small monument or memorial in the nation's capital honoring the man, but Adams himself anticipated as much, writing to Jefferson some years into their retirement, "My (conservative political treatises) were the cause of that immense unpopularity, which fell like the tower of Siloam upon me. Your steady defense of democratical principles and your invariable favorable opinion of the French Revolution laid the foundation for your unbounded popularity." A major disservice indeed!

Moynihan Remembered
May 1, 2003

Daniel Patrick Moynihan, one of my favorite liberals and public servants, recently went on to his reward. My friend Matt Ladner sent me an excerpt from Moynihan's book, *Miles to Go*, which is very instructive about him, as well as liberal thought as we have come to know it. It seems that Moynihan and a member of the Clinton cabinet were involved in an exchange of letters about a proposed and quite expensive "family preservation" program in which the then Senator was questioning the evidence that such a program would actually work to achieve its desired results, citing two studies of similar programs known to demonstrate results to the contrary. The text of the last few lines of his final letter to the official is priceless: "I write you at such length for what I believe to be an important purpose. In these last six months, I have been repeatedly impressed by the numbers of members of the Clinton administration who have assured me with great vigor that something or other is known in an area of social policy, which to the best of my understanding, is not known at all. This seems to me perilous. It is quite possible to live with uncertainty, with the possibility, even the likelihood, that one is wrong. But, beware of certainty where none exists. Ideological certainty easily degenerates into an insistence upon ignorance. The great strength of the political conservatives at this time (and for a generation) is that they are open to the thought that matters are complex. Liberals have got into a reflexive pattern of denying this. I had hoped 12 years in the wilderness might have changed this; it may be that it only has reinforced it. If this is so, current revival of liberalism will be brief and inconsequential."

This is vintage Moynihan, as he critiques the liberal mindset of our time – measurable results of government largesse are secondary, good intentions are all that matter, as it operates in the fantasy of what Thomas Sowell named the "unconstrained vision" of an insulated elite convinced of its own virtue. Although I disagreed with a substantial majority of Moynihan's votes, he was intellectually honest above all and his 1965 warning about the decimation of the black family in America and his subsequent perception of our cultural decline through what he famously dubbed "defining deviancy down" will long live as landmarks in social thought.

Person of the Year?

January 1, 2004

However well deserved, *Time* magazine's designation of the U.S. soldier as its "Person of the Year" somehow struck me as curious – a combination of intentional oversight and begrudging acknowledgement of George W. Bush's dominance of the world stage in 2003. Not that I would detract from the honor and courage with which our young men and women have served and succeeded and have helped restore the tradition of the American warrior class, but their commander-in-chief was clearly the transcending personality, a fact which I suspect *Time's* editors were loathe to admit. More than one editorialist, Tom Friedman most prominently, have compared Bush with Lincoln, at least in the degree to which he has had his greatness thrust upon him by circumstance and, more importantly, has responded by finding a higher moral purpose in the midst of war. In a seminar on the second anniversary of 9/11, Craig Stevens Wilder of Dartmouth College remarked that the attack on America that day was somewhat analogous to Lincoln's assassination, a shocking reminder and restoration of the view of America with a special destiny and mission. And it has occurred to me many times since that day that America's exceptionalism is manifest in many ways, but no more than in its valuation of human life and human freedom universally. This was a major area of political and moral conflict in Lincoln's time and it is today at the core of the war on terror. George Bush knows this. Listen to him at Whitehall in London last November: "The United States and Great Britain share a mission in the world beyond the balance of power or the simple pursuit of interest" and "It is not realism to suppose that one-fifth of humanity is unsuited to liberty; it is pessimism and condescension, and we should have none of it." Listen to him at the Coast Guard Academy last June: "The advance of freedom is more than an interest we pursue; it is a calling we follow. Our country was created in the name and cause of freedom, and if the self-evident truths of our founding are true for us, they are true for all..." And catch up with his speech on natural right at Goree Island in Senegal, the former collection point for African slaves on their way to the New World. It ranks with the truly historic. Do you hear an echo of Gettysburg here? Person of the Year? No contest.

Ronald Reagan, Godspeed and R.I.P.

July 1, 2004

If the beginning of my political initiation was the Barry Goldwater campaign of 1964, the highlight of which was "the speech" delivered by Ronald Reagan to a Los Angeles audience, the maturity of my political thought began in 1980 with Reagan's election as President. He was, along with Margaret Thatcher, my largest hero in public life, one who more than anyone else convinced me that ideas really do have consequences and that conservative values, properly understood and communicated, have strong underlying resonance in America. As I soaked up the commentary immediately following the announcement of Reagan's death last month, I was struck by the weight of the emphasis on his style over his substance. By this I mean that for most of the commentators, even many of those who were very close to him over a long period, the focus was more on his affability, his communication skills, his temperamental capacity for disagreeing without being disagreeable, his optimism, his charm, and his essential humanity, rather than the substance of his policy initiatives and his convictions. Peggy Noonan was one early exception. She went to great lengths to explain the degree to which underlying philosophical and intellectual points were very carefully woven (by him, to be sure) into most of his memorable speeches and pronouncements, and that this intended substance of them transcended even the quality of their delivery. To me, this is the core of the genius of Ronald Reagan, much of the reason he was so widely underestimated by his opponents, and why he will ultimately be grouped among the handful of great Presidents. There is here also a big reason why the mainstream punditry doesn't like the idea of acknowledging this fact, because they know that Reagan, beyond his leadership that produced victory in the Cold War, which most of them now begrudgingly admit, presided over the most significant American political transformation since the early 1930s, and it was mainly about the substance of his ideas, not simply about style.

One of my big disappointments is that his immediate Republican successors were unable and/or unwilling to aggressively defend major elements of this substance and the revolution it spawned, particularly as to the success of supply-side fiscal policy, which failure to defend provided an opening for eight years of Bill Clinton. And then there are many on the left like Carl Bernstein who seem to believe that the policy of "containment" of Soviet communism, as devised by George Kennan in the Truman years, and its derivative strategy of "mutually assured destruction," was simply brought to maturity and completed by Ronald Reagan in the fall of the Berlin Wall and collapse of the Soviet Union! Really? Who do these people think they are fooling? I don't seem to remember any period of time between the early 1950s and the election of 1980 in which the Cold War and our principal adversary in it were considered by the media and intellectual class as anything less than permanent fixtures on the geopolitical landscape, if not morally equivalent opponents. In this, as in so much else, Reagan completely changed the mindset.

Fred Barnes reminds us of Sidney Hook's distinction between an eventful man and an event-making man, the key difference being that while both may arrive at a fork in the historical road, the event-making man helped create the fork. The event-making man also "leaves the positive imprint of his personality upon history – an imprint that is till observable after he has disappeared from the scene." That's Reagan. Worthy of Mount Rushmore? You bet.

A Man For The Ages

May 2, 2005

To the volumes written and spoken about Pope John Paul II over the past few weeks, there is not much to be added. I will simply make a few personal observations. First, after reading two of his books and closely monitoring his leadership over the 27 years of his papacy, it seems to me that he came as close as one could come to the proverbial "philosopher king" – a man who combined wide-ranging and deep philosophical insights with enormous spiritual conviction, compassion, and moral courage, and who personified leadership with an acute awareness of the highest anxieties and yearnings of his constituents. Second, I was struck by Rabbi Daniel Lapin's identification of the idea that was his singular coherence – the sanctity of life, and the triumph of life over death. For him, human dignity was not only primary, it was almost everything.

Third, I agree with Charles Krauthammer's analysis of what I will call the convergence of forces and personalities, in which John Paul (along with Reagan, Thatcher, and Solzhenitsyn) was prominent, in the defeat of Soviet totalitarianism. I will quickly add that, although I am a believer, it doesn't require an inordinate amount of faith to buy into Krauthammer's suggestion that there was a providential hand at work in the choice of Karol Wojtyla as Pope at a critical juncture in history when the Brezhnev Doctrine appeared to be a permanent fact of life. And I will go further in asserting that it is not a big reach to assign a significant role for this providence to the choice of his successor at this particular time, a point to which I will soon return.

Buckley Remembered

March 7, 2008

"I believe that the duel between Christianity and atheism is the most important in the world. I further believe that the struggle between individualism and collectivism is the same struggle reproduced on another level." – William F. Buckley, Jr., *God and Man at Yale*, 1951.

Obviously, Bill Buckley had the essentials of the struggle pretty well nailed at a very young age and he pursued the battle identified in this quote with vigor and intensity, not to mention enormous success, for six decades. When he re-founded the conservative movement in the mid-1950s, it was a mess. He gave it order and coherence, a structure of ideas, relevance, sophistication, acceptability, and class. As important, he marginalized and discredited the isolationists, the John Birchers, the anti-Semites, and other radical elements.

In some ways, his recent death was timely, because it comes at a watershed moment for the movement he helped found, a time when it is badly in need of another young Bill Buckley. But it is also in need of a re-examination of what produced the success of the movement. Many say it needs new ideas, that the founding principles of the Goldwater/Reagan revolutions are anachronisms, outdated by new realities. David

Brooks, for whom I have very high regard as an articulate observer of the landscape, is one of these. He believes, for example, that supply-side economics has run its course, tax cuts can no longer be a centerpiece of conservative Republican economic policy, that the "entrepreneur is no longer king," that government must take an increasingly active role. I couldn't disagree more. The so-called "opportunity society" built on lower tax rates, supply-side economics, more competitive choices in public education and healthcare, and less punitive government regulation of business is exactly the core of the Reagan revolution that should be retained and advanced. Not that government has no role, but its role should be as enabler, not as super-nanny. If there is an ideology that is completely out of style, it is the concept of one-size-fits-all government solutions to healthcare and retirement systems, as well as monopoly management of public education. This is the Buckley legacy and it is worth preserving.

The Death of a Prophet

August 4, 2008

"Truth eludes us if we do not concentrate with total attention on its pursuit... truth is seldom pleasant; it is almost invariably bitter." – Alexander Solzhenitsyn at Harvard University, June 1978.

The death this week of Alexander Solzhenitsyn eliminates one more among the few really significant personalities who, along with Reagan, Thatcher, Pope John Paul II, and Lech Walesa, converged on the world stage at a crucial point in time to finally defeat Soviet totalitarianism. His emergence as a Russian dissident and novelist in the early 1960s provided transparency and moral condemnation to the horrors of the Stalinist regime during a period when there remained considerable sympathy for the communist model among fellow traveling leftists in the intellectual class in Europe and the U.S. Some of his most outspoken criticism, however, was of the crisis of moral courage in the West, and he continued to deliver a message of warning to the West of the need to arrest its decline into political weakness and cultural decadence.

Never was this message more eloquent or forceful than in his commencement speech at Harvard in June 1978, entitled "A World Split Apart." This is a classic analysis of what he calls the decline of civil courage in the West brought about by the primacy of materialism and consumerism, destructive and irresponsible freedom, and the dominance of a humanism, which has elevated personal autonomy to the exclusion of our moral heritage.

It is ironic that he had achieved a popular and official revival of sorts in Russia in recent years with the blessing of President Vladimir Putin, a period during which all indications are that the country is returning to autocratic rule and a tendency toward some of the forms of tyranny that he spent his entire life opposing. In fact, it would have been greatly beneficial to the Russian people and the country if he had been able to lead a "truth commission" to fully investigate, disclose, and enable some semblance of closure on the murderous lies and systematic terror of the Soviet regime. He might have been the only person with the moral authority to have led such a movement.

The Hero of the Opportunity Society

May 5, 2009

Brit Hume referred to Jack Kemp as the "original compassionate conservative" and, as much as I have always resented that term as unnecessarily redundant and wish that George W. Bush had never coined it, upon reflection, it is probably an appropriate characterization. For Kemp, more than anyone else in public life, championed conservative economic policies for exactly the right reasons – because, they are reflective of the policy underpinnings that sustain a moral economic order and they inure most significantly to the direct benefit of those on the lower rungs of the economic ladder.

If there ever was a time for reflection on the central ideas of a public figure, Kemp's passing this past week is one of those, and I am pleased that several publications have devoted space to his work, thoughts, and ideas. For those who have forgotten, he is largely responsible for the introduction of supply-side economics into public policy at the highest level, an introduction that provided Ronald Reagan with the impetus for arguably the most successful domestic policy transformation of modern times, namely the 25 percent income tax rate cuts of 1983. These cuts, along with sound money Federal Reserve policy and regulatory relief, freed the entrepreneurial spirit of Americans that produced the longest peacetime economic expansion in U.S. history, providing upward mobility for millions here and around the world.

I have long thought that it was a mistake that Kemp was not on the ticket with Reagan in 1980, and I certainly believe that he should have been there with Bush 41 in 1988. What a difference that could have made in convincing the elder Bush not to forsake the winning supply-side formula, a decision that surely helped defeat him in 1992.

An even bigger shame is that the Republican leadership has completely abdicated the policies that produced the prosperity and political success of the Reagan Revolution. Bush 43 certainly had enormous success with it, but scarcely a sound could be heard during the 2008 campaign in defense of supply-side, tax cut economics properly understood and, since then, the loyal opposition seems to have completely lost any courage to boldly defend the most successful economic policy of the 20th century. In one of his last op-ed pieces just weeks before election day last year, Kemp strongly urged John McCain to refocus his economic message on tax policy, particularly a flat tax proposal. Alas, it was too late, and McCain had shown little interest in, understanding of, or ability to articulate supply-side policy as an engine of economic growth and a moral underpinning of a just economic order. We await the successor to Jack Kemp to do so. RIP.

McNamara's Tragedy and Legacy

August 6, 2009

The recent death of Robert McNamara brought back many memories, mostly of frustration for those of my age who strained to make sense out of the Vietnam War. In many ways he embodied the essential liberal premise – that smart people from the best schools, armed with efficient systems, can apply rationality to deal with organic human problems, under the broad assumption that, as George Will characterized it, "if it can be counted, it can be controlled." McNamara exhibited this tendency both in his conduct of the war and his stewardship of the World Bank.

Similarly, Lyndon Johnson thought that if he could get enough bright people in the room he could manage the war from Washington. He also at least once said that if he could get Ho Chi Minh in a room one-on-one he could successfully make a deal to end the war. In this thinking he was the perfect leader of and complement to the "best and the brightest" of the Great Society. All of which is the epitome of Thomas Sowell's "unconstrained vision" of the elites – the Achilles Heel of liberalism in policy at home and abroad. In this particular case, the unfortunate result for America has been that the honorable purposes of the war in Southeast Asia have been discredited along with its failed execution. RIP.

The End of the Dynasty

September 7, 2009

I want to be as fair as possible in remarks on the death of Edward M. Kennedy, just as all of us will want our survivors to consider the "whole package" and defer ultimate judgment to God. I never met him, but he was generally considered to have the most effective and most competent staff in the U.S. Senate; he was without doubt a very committed liberal warrior and probably an intellectually honest man of the left; he was highly respected and well-liked by many of the conservative persuasion for whom I have high regard; and he obviously made a sincere attempt in his later years to atone for a number of egregious transgressions and indiscretions from his earlier days, the guilt from which must have weighed heavy on his soul.

He was as well the "poster boy" for everything loathsome about what 20th century liberalism morphed into after World War II. I will spare you the list here, but Jonah Goldberg covered it pretty well in his book, *Liberal Fascism.* His popular legacy will be his work in the years since the 1980 convention speech conceding the Democratic Presidential nomination, during which he worked tirelessly for the progressive agenda outlined in that speech, with considerable success thanks to Republican co-sponsorship in many cases and in spite of Republican majorities for most of that time. Some commentators applaud these measures as appropriate for the times, but I believe we will be living with both the intended and unintended negative consequences of most of them for a very long time.

My most vivid memory of Kennedy, however, will be his speech on the Senate floor during the confirmation debate on Supreme Court nominee Robert Bork, which included these lines: "Robert Bork's America is a land in which women would be forced into back-alley abortions, blacks would sit at segregated lunch counters, rogue police could break down citizens' doors in midnight raids, schoolchildren could not be taught about evolution." Nothing from the so-called "extreme right" cabal rivals these remarks for their vitriol, their dishonesty, or their subsequent negative impact on civility in the public square. RIP.

Vaclav Havel, RIP

January 5, 2012

The world lost a true hero in December with the passing of Vaclav Havel, the first post-communist president of Czechoslovakia, whose efforts on behalf of human freedom are legendary, richly deserving of the Nobel Prize, for either Peace or Literature or both. How ironic that his death coincided with that of his complete opposite, Kim Jong Il of North Korea, whom I trust will receive his just reward, but who, unfortunately, departed this life in bed.

As a colleague and soul mate of fellow dissident Natan Sharansky, Havel made a convincing case for preemptive intervention to liberate oppressed people and was an early supporter of U.S. intervention in Iraq, saying "The world could not be indifferent forever to a murderer like Saddam Hussein." The keyword for him was "indifference," which he considered a major danger in the world, and in an inspiring 1978 essay, he warned of "the attractions of mass indifference and the general unwillingness of consumption-oriented people to sacrifice some material certainties for the sake of their own spiritual and moral integrity." For him, the trump for indifference was the truth, which he considered inherently a moral enterprise. He was an intellectual of the first order and, along with Pope John Paul II and Alexander Solzhenitsyn, was hugely responsible for the intellectual leadership of the discrediting of the lies and the world's indifference to them that ultimately undermined Soviet communism.

Robert H. Bork, RIP

January 5, 2013

If you had to select a point in time or an event that was the tipping point in the trend toward incivility and almost terminal dysfunction in our nation's capital, the Senate Judiciary Committee hearings on the nomination of Robert Bork to the Supreme Court in 1987 would be a good candidate. It was so vicious that it coined a new term – to "bork" means to resort to a slanderous smear campaign to discredit and defeat a political foe or proposal, and the Democrats, led by Joe Biden and Ted Kennedy, aided and abetted by their fellow travelers in journalism went viral in their lies and distortions of his record and his judicial philosophy. It was, as now acknowledged by even many partisan liberals, a disgraceful episode in American public life. Policy deliberation in Washington, in particular the Senate advise and consent process, has never been the same.

Robert Bork was a huge figure as a teacher and a scholar and, as *The Wall Street Journal* noted, contributed far more to American law than the 58 Senators who voted against his confirmation and more than most Supreme Court justices. One of his books, *Slouching Towards Gomorrah: Modern Liberalism and American Decline*, is an outstanding survey of what significant damage has been done to the country by the ideological triumph of liberalism among American elites. His service on the Supreme Court would have been greatly beneficial to our country. Shame on those whose disservice to America deprived us of that benefit and, even worse, greatly contributed to the trend toward incivility in public life.

"The Lady's Not for Turning"

May 1, 2013

Lady Margaret Thatcher is my favorite public figure of all time, ahead of Winston Churchill and Ronald Reagan. Her motto was that "I am not a politician of consensus, I am one of conviction," and it is this moral clarity, which most appealed to me and that distinguished her from the garden variety politician of which we have become much too accustomed. Clearly, with determined political will and courage, she saved her country, and there is no doubt that she significantly bolstered the efforts of Reagan and John Paul II in finally disposing of the Soviet Union and winning the Cold War. In my estimation, she was at least the greatest peacetime British Prime Minister of the 20th century and possibly in history. While reading the many tributes to her and the recounting of her accomplishments over the week following her death, I often wondered: where is the Margaret Thatcher that we so desperately need today? RIP.

Mandela – One for the Ages

January 4, 2014

Upon the death of Nelson Mandela, *National Review* noted that he had unmatched moral authority among world leaders, a view with which I agree, and I think one would be hard-pressed to name a 20th century leader more revered in his time. In watching and listening to the coverage of his life in the week after his death, I was struck by a number of points.

First, it's important to acknowledge that he was a Marxist revolutionary who accepted significant assistance and support from the Soviet Union, Gaddafi, Castro, Arafat, et al., some of the worst players in the world and he could have easily become a Lenin-type revolutionary. Second, it's important to remember the Cold War context within which the U.S. was forced to consider policies, such as sanctions on the apartheid government of South Africa, which often put America at odds with world opinion and our own concept of human and civil rights, albeit in our interest in the various proxy wars with the Soviet Union.

Mandela often is compared to Martin Luther King, Jr., but MLK had the benefit of a foundation in the American Declaration of Independence and an appeal to the founding principles of America and related racial guilt. Mandela had no such grounding beyond the natural law. His courage was manifest in fidelity to the rule of law, the foundation of which ironically was established by the English-speaking regime dominant in the oppressive state he opposed. His campaign was not for entitlement or reparations, but for equal treatment under the law and he rejected bitterness, revenge, and recrimination.

Two of his most important decisions as President of South Africa after his release from prison were first, to call for and establish a truth and reconciliation commission, which helped to provide closure and healing, and second, his decision to step down as President after one term, which put him in the exceptional class with George Washington, because he could have easily become just another tinhorn dictator, and South Africa would then have gone the way of Zimbabwe and other tyrannical post-colonial African dictatorships.

It's true that he made selective use of his moral authority in support of human rights and he was overboard in his praise of the Castro and Gaddafi regimes and his criticism of American human rights violations. But on balance, he is deserving of the praise and adulation he has received and his revered place in history.

Scalia: A Huge Loss on Many Levels

March 6, 2016

The loss of Justice Antonin Scalia is huge – for his family, for the Supreme Court, for American jurisprudence, for constitutional fidelity, and for the country at a crucial time.

Here was a man who was larger than one Justice among nine, for the dynamic he represented with his intellectual strength and depth and his personality permeated the room and the deliberations of the Court as no other in many decades. It has been said that he was the embodiment of the conservative revolution that began with Ronald Reagan and this is no doubt true in the sense of his influence on turning Court deliberations away from what he called the "bad old days." In his almost three decades on the Court, he transformed the tradition of oral arguments and restored textual analysis to its rightful place, while demonstrating that humor, good will, and faith have a role to play even in the most intense and contentious deliberations.

His guiding judicial philosophy is probably best characterized by a quote in his dissent in *Planned Parenthood v. Casey* in 1992: "…if, in reality, our process of constitutional adjudications consists primarily of making value judgments… then the issue is properly one for democratic debate… value judgments should be voted on, not dictated."

Sanford Levinson, professor of law at UT-Austin, in an article shortly after Scalia's death, was critical of him as what he calls the Court's "trash talker" and says that the coarsening of our public dialogue will be the part of his legacy that will stand out. I couldn't disagree more strongly. This was a man of good will and good humor who reached out to those he most disagreed with on the Court. His close personal relationship with Justices Ginsberg and Kagan have been widely reported and he had the reputation of requiring that his clerks always included bright and capable liberal thinkers to challenge him on points of law and ideology. No, Professor Levinson, Justice Scalia was not the source of our problem with coarsening civility, nor was the Supreme Court as an institution. This coarsening was well underway before he arrived on the Court and grew out of the extreme politicization of the judiciary and the attacks by the left progressives and their fellow travelers on our constitutional foundations in the "bad old days" that he began to reverse.

He will be very difficult if not impossible to replace and I can assure you of this – the 2016 election moved by a big leap in seriousness with his death, particularly for Republicans.

Muhammad Ali

June 5, 2016

In the wake of Muhammad Ali's death a couple of days ago, there has of course been saturation coverage of his life and legacy, and he certainly led a life that warrants the attention. There is no doubt that he was an exceptional athlete and a world icon as a larger than life personality, about which I am of two minds. I didn't care much for Cassius Clay in the 1960s and early 1970s – the total lack of humility, the narcissism, the "Louisville Lip," and "The Greatest" routine (incidentally, much of which bluster now smacks of a certain current presidential candidate), and I resented his refusal to report for military service. However, later in life as he mellowed, even before contracting the Parkinson's disease that finally took him, I grew to respect his humane spirituality, which I believe drove his positive role as an ambassador for civil rights and as a humanitarian. RIP.

Mark White, RIP

August 10, 2017

Former Texas Governor Mark White, who died last week, was the most active correspondent with *The Texas Pilgrim* over the years. When I clicked the "publish" button for each monthly issue, I could count on his rapid response with an often lengthy email of commentary and questions on the policy issues, frequently disagreeing with what I had written or at least challenging my thinking. Of course, this is one of the purposes of a blog, so we would spar back and forth, sometimes for several days, and it became an exercise I welcomed each month, for Mark was a man of ideas and we could disagree without being disagreeable.

I first met him when he was elected Texas Attorney General in 1978 and, although we were on opposite ends of the political spectrum and I didn't support him in his campaigns for Governor in 1982 and 1986, which he fully understood, we remained friends ever since. In fact, we were scheduled to meet for lunch soon to discuss some education issues that surfaced from a recent issue of *The Texas Pilgrim.*

It has been said this week that he was the most consequential education Governor in Texas history and I think there is a good case to be made for that claim. His bold and courageous leadership in the crafting and adoption of House Bill 72 set the stage for the subsequent efforts over the past 35 years for standards and accountability-based education reform and gave Republican Governors who followed a measure of political cover for advancing the reforms.

I also have some history with Mark in commercial banking reforms. In 1986, when I was CEO of a Houston bank holding company, Texas was facing an economic crisis that threatened the viability of hundreds of Texas banks. Several of us who were involved with the state banking organizations went to him for help in changing Texas law to allow branch and interstate banking to assist with access to capital from outside the state. To his credit and against stiff opposition, he stepped up to lead the effort to do so by placing the issue on his agenda for a special session of the legislature in which the measure was adopted, no doubt saving a significant number of Texas banks and salvaging the state's recovery efforts.

His other major legacy is the leadership he provided in advancing Texas as a haven for technology development, which was critical in the diversification of the state's economy. He brought together a coalition of business interests, government, and higher education to create an environment welcoming to the "high-tech" culture that significantly moved Texas forward toward the 21st century.

A good man. Well done, Mark. Godspeed.

A Life That Mattered

July 5, 2018

The news of the impending death of Charles Krauthammer, released in the form of his noble letter to his readers several weeks ago, followed by the event itself, was a devastating blow to the intellectual community and to the quality of reasoned public discourse at a time when we most need it. This is a huge loss of intellectual honesty and civility that will leave a void not easily filled. In my experience he has no peer as a public intellectual from right, left, or center, not even William Buckley or Walter Lippmann.

Although I read him occasionally in *The New Republic* in the early 1980s and later in syndication, I first encountered his deeper philosophical thought when he was a member of the President's Council on Bioethics under George W. Bush in 2002 and wrote a comprehensive essay on the threats to human dignity of human cloning as an appendix to the final report on the subject submitted to the President. This essay is included among others in his collection of writings published five years ago as *Things That Matter: Three Decades of Passions, Pastimes, and Politics*, which was everything I thought it would be – intellectual, concise, insightful, erudite, and funny in places. And the range of "things that matter" is impressive. I skipped over some of the essays, the ones on chess, for example, but substantially all of the 80 plus essays are worth the time and are still timely. In addition to the essay on bioethics, the closing "Three Essays on America and the World," which are longer than the others, are alone worth much more than the price of the book. He will be greatly missed and right now I can't think of anyone who might even come close to filling the space. RIP.

John McCain, RIP

September 4, 2018

We have just witnessed an extraordinary week. I can't remember a longer public goodbye in such exalted national venues than was accorded John McCain. I won't make any judgment on whether or not it was warranted, but very few presidents have received such treatment. Of course, he was a hero by any definition of that term and he was a courageous and committed patriot who suffered greatly for his country and declined special treatment offers as a POW. And I have condemned Donald Trump for his outrageous and disrespectful remarks during the 2016 presidential campaign that McCain "is not a hero" and "I prefer people who are not captured."

In fact, as I think about American exceptionalism, a term I often use to describe the character and destiny of this country, it's pretty clear to me that John McCain embodies that character. As Henry Kissinger so eloquently put it at the McCain memorial service, "Honor, it is an intangible quality, not obligatory. It has no code. It reflects an inward compulsion, free of self-interest. It fulfills a cause, not a personal ambition. It represents what a society lives for beyond the necessities of the moment… Honor and nobility. For John it was a way of life." Point well taken.

But he was not without considerable faults as we all are. I have been of mixed emotions about McCain over the years and have never been a big fan. Oh, sure, I voted for him in 2008 – an easy and obvious choice for me, and he ran a terrible campaign topped by the grandstanding move to unilaterally suspend it six weeks before election day to return to Washington to help save the country from the financial crisis following the fallout from the Lehman Brothers bankruptcy filing. This was supposedly a selfless and bipartisan gesture (not matched by his opponent I might add), but one that smacked of considerable sanctimony and was no doubt a factor in his loss.

The favorite media characterization of him over the years was as a "maverick," which the left loved to use as a code for bipartisanship, or "reaching across the aisle" that usually meant frustrating a Republican majority at best or acquiescing to a Democratic position on a controversial issue at worst. And he often played his stature as a military hero as license for moral authority and shelter from criticism, leading to a certain self-righteousness. This expressed itself in many instances, none more egregious than his grandstanding "no" vote in the Senate that killed the repeal of ObamaCare, which was clearly cast purely to spite Donald Trump, not exactly in tune with his noble character as described by Secretary Kissinger and certainly not in the interests of his constituency or the country, let alone the promises of his party. I could go on to other instances in which his idea of personal honor led to other consequences, such as the Keating Five case, McCain/Feingold, his handling of the Trump "dossier," etc. But I will leave it there and choose to remember John McCain as the ultimate patriot and American original. Godspeed.

Bush 41 RIP

December 8, 2018

December has traditionally been a month of rest for *The Texas Pilgrim*, but I could not let the momentous significance of last week's tribute to President George H. W. Bush pass without comment. It has been suggested that the pomp and circumstance of the events in Washington, Houston, and College Station would not have been welcomed by the President and that he might even have been embarrassed by much of the praise heaped upon him for the life that he lived, which in his view was nothing more than what was expected of him in the spirit of noblesse oblige. I expect that might have been so.

But I have a different view. America badly needed what we experienced last week – a time of celebration of and thanks for the life of an American hero; a time of reflection on the qualities reflective of what a man should be, particularly those who aspire to leadership; a time for reverence for those values that help inform what defines American exceptionalism – faith, family, duty, country; and an extended time for renewal and open advancement of these ideas in the public square. In fact, I thought as I watched these events that there was an almost providential timing of them when the body politic seemed to need these reflections and this renewal more than ever.

There will be plenty of time to discuss his record as President, this and that decision, foreign and domestic policy, pro and con, victories and failures, and for me there is some of all of it to revisit in the coming months. My first take on it is that on balance he will be very well treated by history primarily for the way he handled the fall of the Berlin Wall, the collapse of the Soviet Union, and the reunification of Germany, and I believe he deserved the Nobel Peace Prize. But right now, let's simply hope that we have all learned something from this past week about decency and civility and have reminded ourselves of what duty looks like in a real patriot. Godspeed, George Herbert Walker Bush.

3
Business Ethics

Lessons from Enron
January 2, 2002

Clearly, there are critical lessons to be learned from the Enron debacle – about transparency in reporting, improper capital structures for derivative and commodity trading, and management hubris – all of which, and more, will be paraded before us as the regulatory and judicial process unfolds. From my perspective, one very significant lesson, or reminder, may be that there is a reason that most successful hedge funds (which, after all, is what Enron was) are not publicly owned: they are almost impossible for any but the most sophisticated investors to understand. In all that we will learn from this, however, we should keep in mind that the market worked, and this should be reported as a success. As important, we should strongly resist the tendency on the part of many to use this experience to roll back or impede deregulation and privatization initiatives. For example, the failures at Enron are not an excuse to re-regulate the energy and electric utility markets; they are not a warning not to privatize Social Security; and they are not a message for tighter controls on defined contribution (401k, etc.) plans.

Enron Follow Up
March 5, 2002

A letter from Bud Shivers in response to my January "Lessons from Enron" posed some good thoughts for follow up. There is a lot more to be learned about the true culpability as this story plays out, and much of the substance is presently being obscured by political demagoguery, but further lessons are surfacing. Enron highlights the degree to which the investment banking industry has been headed in the wrong direction since the major firms began offering their shares publicly a couple of decades ago. The concept of privately owned, general partnership governance of these firms served us well. Conversely, the perverse incentives created by the pressure for stock performance has produced conflicts of interest among corporate finance, research, and retail sales, and has certainly contributed to the quarterly earnings-driven management of client companies. As to the accounting profession, I see two problems manifest here:

1) the profession has not properly adjusted its practices to the growth and development of the "virtual" firm, such as Enron, for which the attest function is less a matter of validation of historical cost and revenue recognition and much more a validation of risk management processes, and 2) the conflict of interest inherent in the attest and management consulting functions, which has severely damaged the objectivity of the independent audit.

Alan Greenspan has made some interesting comments about the legacy of Enron. Essentially, he said that the result will be a transformation of corporate governance, which I agree is long overdue, and that the critical standard for these "virtual" companies is reputation. If he is correct, this may also mean a return to the days when investment banking, accounting, and commercial banking were conducted based on the concept of the "trustee" by partners with full liability and a significant personal financial stake in their stewardship. In the meantime, as we continue to make the conversion from "defined benefit" based to "defined contribution" based retirement funding, we are certainly in for much more government oversight and intrusion, at least until the governance and self-regulatory functions catch up with the markets.

Thoughts on Business Ethics

November 1, 2002

In the wake of the rash of corporate misdeeds for which Enron is the metaphor, it is not surprising that there has been a proliferation of op/eds, seminars, and beefed-up business school courses on business ethics. The best article I have seen so far is "Oxymoron 101," by Dan Seligman in *Forbes* magazine (it also carries the most appropriate title!). Seligman is understandably dubious of the business schools' ability to offer anything meaningful about ethical lapses in business. At the risk of appearing sanctimonious, I've never had nor felt the need for a course on business ethics, nor in my days as a CEO would I have considered requiring one for my colleagues. It's about character and the recognition of right and wrong behavior. If you need to take a course to recognize a conflict of interest, you shouldn't be running a business or any other institution. I'm not terminally naïve; I know that there are ethical and moral "dilemmas," but there is no magic about any of this.

Recent surveys reveal that lying to supervisors is rampant and that top management credibility with subordinates is seriously damaged throughout the business community. It is difficult to avoid the conclusion that much of this condition results from decades of instruction in and examples of situational ethics, moral relativity, and non-judgementalism. And we are reaping what we have sowed with the current "no confidence" attitude toward corporate governance on the part of the investing and the general public. More ethics courses and more laws and regulations never will be the answer. What we need is more of what is implied by the title of a famous early-1990s report on the subject – "obedience to the unenforceable" – the key to ethics in business and in life.

The TAB Case – Why We Should Care

October 2, 2005

For the past couple of years, we political junkies have watched, some with varying degrees of amusement, many with disdain, as Travis County District Attorney Ronnie Earle pursued partisan retribution against those who would have the temerity to exercise their First Amendment right to free political speech by exposing the voting records of duplicitous legislators in Austin. To most casual observers of the political scene, this probably has been regarded as a side show, characteristic of the pettiness of electoral politics and devoid of any significant principled issues at stake.

However, with the recent indictment of the State's largest business organization, the Texas Association of Business (TAB), by a Travis County grand jury (at Earle's instigation and at taxpayers' expense), this political intimidation and witch hunt has now reached the point of absurdity that should be given serious attention by those who value their constitutional right to political speech. For what we have here is clearly a case of a district attorney interpreting a state law to limit the freedom of speech of a private association.

In 2002, TAB created a scoring system to inform the people of Texas about the truth of the voting records of their elected officials in Austin, many of whom for some time had boasted in their home districts about their support for policies that encourage jobs, economic growth, and prosperity, but whose true legislative voting records belied their representations. This process was scrutinized as to its compliance with election law and approved by attorneys with substantial experience in the field, and at no time did the organization endorse any candidate or make any direct political contribution to, or campaign expenditure for, a candidate.

The question at issue here is whether or not there will continue to be voices independent of the mainstream news media and the "spin machines" of the elected officials that can directly and perceptively inform the voting public on the true voting records of their elected representatives without the threat of partisan, taxpayer funded intimidation.

In the interest of full disclosure, I should tell you that I am a former Chairman of the Board of TAB and continue to serve on its Board of Directors. However, regardless of whether or not we are members of TAB and/or its more than 200 affiliated local chambers of commerce, or even whether or not we are sympathetic to its mission, we should recognize that the principles involved in this case are critical not only to the viability of a venerable and leading voice for public policy that enhances the State's economic development, but to the viability of the principles of our republican system of government, and that this organization and these principles deserve our support in this battle.

Government is Still the Problem Revisited

February 4, 2006

"We're going to find out whether Republicans have an appetite for a substantial reform agenda against pork spending, out of control budgets, and deal-making politics in this town." – Rep. John Shadegg, candidate for House Majority Leader.

Well, maybe we just did, because as I write, Shadegg, the most aggressive change agent and spending reformer in the race to replace Tom Delay, has lost his bid to John Boehner of Ohio, one who seems more of a business as usual and incremental reformer. Time will tell what this means, but only a short time, because unless the Republicans return to some semblance of the revolutionary Gingrich-led "spirit of 1994" very soon, they may kiss their majority goodbye.

The Abramoff affair is not primarily about lobby reform; it's about correcting the worst abuses of the corruption of power that arise from the protection of the majority political class. More importantly, it is about the inherent corruption of big government itself, which at today's levels of intrusion in the lives and welfare of Americans, makes rent-seekers of even the most virtuous of our citizens. And it starts at the top. For all of President Bush's virtues, spending restraint isn't one of them, and his so-called "strong government conservatism" is as much an oxymoron as his "compassionate conservatism" is a redundancy. After all, he is still the only President since John Quincy Adams never to have vetoed a bill, and parts of his State of the Union messages, on the domestic side, are beginning to sound more and more like a blueprint for the Great Society of the 21st century. If I could have asked for one addition to this year's speech, it would have been the demand that Congress end, not mend, the destructive system of so-called "earmarks," along with the commitment to veto any bill that includes them. There is more to it than that, but it is central to the problem and would have been a good start and a hopeful message for this election year. Good luck, Congressman Boehner.

Harvard Refocuses the MBA

February 4, 2011

I read recently that the Harvard Business School is making major changes to its curriculum and that the changes, according to its marketing release, are aimed to "create leaders of competence and character, rather than just connections and credentials." Evidently, there is a certain concern and maybe a little guilt that 58 percent of its graduates go into financial services and consulting and, as its Dean noted, that it helped create a culture that had something to do with the financial sector meltdown and the decline in public trust of business. So a big objective now is to create more "ethical leaders." I wish them well, but I am reminded of John Wooden's admonishment that "sports do not build character; they reveal it." The same goes for business and ethics. And where do we secure a solid foundation in ethics for students beyond its principle sources in the family and religion? In the study of the humanities and liberal arts, primarily the Western intellectual tradition, and the foundations of Western civilization and American ideals. So, while we strive to correct the deficiencies of our professional schools, let's also correct the damage that has been done to the core curriculum in the liberal arts in our leading universities over the past century.

4
Cultural Issues

Creeping Boboism
July 1, 2000

David Brooks, Senior Editor of *The Weekly Standard*, has written a perceptive, but (to me) troubling book about the state of the upper middle class American ethos. Titled *Bobos in Paradise*, it posits a new ruling class, the bohemian bourgeoisie ("bobo"), that has been created by bridging the opposing cultural value systems. Briefly, Bobos are hard-working, affluent, professional, non-partisan, nonideological, moderately religious or "spiritual," and basically content, i.e., the information age elite. They have absorbed both sides of the culture war that has been raging for at least 30 years, and they almost never get outraged. Their leaders are not conviction driven; they "triangulate" and seek out the various "third way" strategies beyond left and right, such as "don't ask, don't tell." Confrontation is not their game, neither are bold policy initiatives, and they certainly do not want to make harsh moral judgments. So, if the bourgeoisie and bohemians have merged, who got the better of the deal? Brooks thinks the bourgeoisie did, because their commercial values triumphed over the bohemian complaints about capitalistic corruption of culture. In the process, however, the bourgeoisie has adopted much of the cultural value system and world view of the bohemian which essentially grew out of the European Romanticism of the late 18th and early 19th centuries: the virtues of hedonism, self-expression, creativity, and imagination. Establishment Bobos rarely present a well-grounded and consistent set of ideas and public policy initiatives based on strong conviction or worldview.

My observation of many Bobos in positions of opinion leadership, particularly in the business community, is that they could be categorized as the "don't get me hurt" coalition*f*. In other words, the avoidance of any high-profile confrontation on controversial issues, particularly of the cultural variety, is a high priority for them. While pointing out some perils, Brooks seems to take a balanced view of the world of the Bobos. I'm not so sanguine and, in fact, I deplore much of what I see in Boboland. Recently, the *Houston Chronicle* ran a syndicated article by Judy Hevrdejs entitled "Average America," which reported on the growing American tendency to exalt the mundane in life. Of course, the word mundane itself is defined as "from the secular world, distinguished from the heavenly or spiritual." The TV show *Seinfeld* is described as the ultimate show about the mundane. Today, it is trendy and virtuous to be mundane.

Am I mistaken in feeling that this is a Machiavellian trait? Is this what America is about? Have we lost the sense of exceptionalism that separated America, with its high moral ideals and unique historical mission, from other cultures? Have we become so detached and cynical that public endeavor in pursuit of the big questions is reduced to risk-free pragmatism? With encroaching Boboism, I fear the answers to these questions, as I am reminded of W. B. Yeats' famous lines, "the best lack all conviction, while the worst are full of passionate intensity."

Thoughts on Cultural Pollution

November 3, 2000

Last summer, the Federal Communications Commission released a report that was critical of the marketing practices of the entertainment industry, accusing it of, among other things, directly targeting younger children with violent TV shows, CD's, and movies. This report sparked a flurry of activity among policy makers, including hearings conducted by the U.S. Senate and chaired by Sen. John McCain. Some of the testimony was enlightening, none more so than from the industry representatives, who universally challenged any attempt to curtail or suppress media content as censorship. Another aspect of the dialogue that struck me was the fact that it focused almost entirely on the incidence of the portrayal of various forms of violence in the popular media, when the real problem with the products of Hollywood, in my view, is the consistent message of moral relativism. What is important about the portrayal of human foibles and the human experience is the moral context within which they are presented. The presentation of violence and sex per se is not necessarily corrupting; portrayal of these phenomena gratuitously or in a morally relative manner can be. And it is this relativism that permeates the popular culture, most of which accepts the worldview that any external moral authority is illegitimate and any interference with the individual's self-gratification is reactionary.

So, the problem is much broader and deeper, and the issue of content must be addressed. Am I suggesting the "C" word? Possibly, at least for the most explicit and gratuitous forms of violence and sex now being offered in the mainstream. After all, we had censorship in this country for most of our existence as a nation, some of it formal, some informal (remember the Hayes Office?). Actually, I prefer Lynne Cheney's approach. The focus should be on product content, not just marketing strategy, and we should exercise moral authority and leadership from our highest elected offices in lieu of regulation. Edmund Burke made a relevant point more than 200 years ago: "Men are qualified for civil liberty in exact proportion to their disposition to put moral chains on their own appetites. Society cannot exist unless a controlling power upon will and appetite be placed somewhere, and the less of it there is within, the more there is without."

It's the Culture, Stupid!

February 3, 2001

In my October 2000 Special Pre-Election Issue, paraphrasing Pat Buchanan, I wrote that the 2000 election was not to be about who gets what or the details of policy, but rather was to be about who we are. Now, three months after Election Day, I'm even more convinced. The post-election fight in Florida and the Ashcroft confirmation process have combined to highlight for me the opposing forces in the war for cultural hegemony that is raging in our public life at every level of policy deliberation. These opposing forces have been characterized as the beautiful vs. the dutiful, old vs. new America, urban vs. rural America, coastal vs. middle America, and the hedonistic/individualistic/secular vs. the puritanical/family-centered/religious America. However the forces are characterized, the real underlying issues that are driving our politics have become cultural ones that can only indirectly be addressed through public policy. As an example, the Ashcroft nomination fight was an impasse of the type not before experienced (with the possible exception of the Bork hearings), not of the type that the "let's make a deal," LBJ-style political processes can deal with. The left is a religion and its adherents believe that conservatives are evil and, to some conservatives, the reverse is true. These differences won't be worked out over bourbon and water in the cloak room.

Several books have helped me understand this phenomenon, notably Gertrude Himmelfarb's, *One Nation, Two Cultures*. She describes an assimilation process in which the former adversary culture of the bohemians has been democratized and popularized as a major factor in the dominant culture over the past 30 years. One of the results is that once honorific words are now pejorative, so that the worst transgressions are to be "moralistic" or "judgmental," tolerance is the only virtue, and morality itself is trivialized. The most visible element of this dominant culture, the elite, generally conforms to traditional ideals of propriety, but with no firm confidence in the principles underlying their behavior, and they find it difficult to transmit their own principles to their children. In fact, they are unable to judge what is right or wrong for themselves. I call this the "Dr. Laura syndrome" and if you've ever listened to her call-in radio program, you know what I mean.

This ignorance of the grounding of our morality and the resulting lack of conviction and assertiveness about matters that define us as a people are the sources of much of the confusion in the public policy arena. For if, as I suspect, there are no more than a small minority of energized partisans on either side of an issue in the culture war, the "diffident middle" will seem confused and disengaged, and will be subject to demagoguery.

This is a battle of ideas at the deepest level, a conflict over the foundation of the American ideal. It is a tug of war for the future of the country. Rabbi Daniel Lapin, author of *America's Real War*, believes that the basic question is whether America is a secular or religious nation and my reading of the exit polls tells me that of all the voting patterns in the recent election, religion was the most precise determinant. Whatever your views on this, it's pretty clear that the fault lines open along the division formed when modernity divorced humanity from its source and end in a God-centered universe. Shelby Steele says that George W. Bush is the first conservative on the presidential level to understand that he is in a culture war. I believe and hope so; he's going to need that insight.

The Search for the Civil Society

June 1, 2001

Among the overworked buzzwords of the past several years have been "civility" and "civil society." Civility in my context here is taken to mean the highly desirable tone and demeanor with which political discourse and debate are pursued and has even had implications for the newly created virtue of "bipartisanship." Civil society has been defined by my leading authority on the subject, Don Eberly of *The Civil Society Project*, as "a third sector of society made up of associations that operate neither on the principle of coercion nor the principle of rational self-interest." A common thread here would seem to be represented by the question (to paraphrase Rodney King), "can't we all just get along?"

I have several thoughts about these terms and their recently popularized meaning. First, I agree with Justice Clarence Thomas that, although incivility in our discourse and manner can never be excused, civility cannot be the governing principle of citizenship or leadership and that to insist on this principle has the "perverse effect of cannibalizing our civic principles." Likewise, Gertrude Himmelfarb observes "to reduce citizenship to the modern idea of civility, the good neighbor idea, is to belittle not only the political role of the citizen but also the virtues expected of the citizen – the civic virtues." The civic virtues to which she refers are those of the civic republic on which this country was founded (by fiercely partisan men, I might add).

As for civil society, Robert Bellah has written extensively on the attributes of the "good society," a closely related term originally coined by Walter Lippmann, the cultivation of which he says requires a widening of democratic participation and the accountability of our institutions to counteract predatory relations among individuals and groups. To Bellah and other communitarians, we seem to suffer from too much individualism and self-interest and need to find renewed "respect for what transcends us." Don Eberly offers the Golden Rule as a principle that might serve as the basis for the moral framework of a civil society. As he points out, there is remarkable unanimity across a broad spectrum of cultures regarding what philosophy calls "the good," defined primarily by a natural law grounded in almost all the world's religions.

I sympathize with these communitarian sentiments, and a Golden Rule movement as envisioned by Eberly would certainly be a commendable effort worthy of our support. But I wonder if the seeds for such a movement are present. In a highly litigious and procedural society closely monitored by the state that struggles with an idea as basic as the posting of the Ten Commandments in classrooms and courtrooms, I think we have some work to do with our opinion leadership and our cultural institutions. And as William Bennett has noted, "there is the belief among many of the people who have the most power and influence to shape attitudes that the most important obligation in life is to yourself, not God, country, work, or family, but to self." This attitude primarily comes from our intellectuals, our cultural institutions, and from contemporary liberalism. And, to return to Thomas and Himmelfarb, these will not be converted by an overriding commitment to civility as a governing principle.

Has Anything Changed?

May 1, 2002

In the wake of the attack on the U.S. last September, most commentators were of the opinion that a fundamental chord was struck in the collective American psyche, that our value systems were threatened in a way that would force a new sense of solidarity and community. Some even hinted that the attack and our response to it might even break the gridlock in partisan politics in Washington. Dream on!

In my October 2001 essay, "And the War Came," I suggested that our definition of "normal" had probably changed forever and expressed the hope that we will be engaged in some long overdue examining of the American idea and soul-searching about the degree to which we are truly committed to it.

What has really changed? Of course, there has been a huge outpouring of patriotism linked to unprecedented support for the President's war policy. There has been an enormously compassionate response to the victims of the 9/11 attack. And there has been the predictable response to the security lapses that enabled the success of the attack. Fundamentally, however, I wonder if we have fully grasped the enormity of the realities exposed to us on 9/11. Have we truly mobilized for the lengthy commitment to the war on terrorism that President Bush has so eloquently defined? Have we come to grips with the low threshold of war casualties that are acceptable to us? Has our collective anger at the attack on us produced the much-needed re- assessment of our values and priorities? Historically, wars have had major cultural transformational impact, on the winners as much as the losers. Think of the enormous American cultural transformations produced by the two world wars of the past century – in the role of government in our lives, in civil rights, in the role of women in society, in economic policy, and in our sense of destiny as a people.

In a recent op/ed piece entitled "Stalemate," William Schneider writes that nothing has happened since the November 2000 election to heal the divisions of that bitter experience, not even 9/11, because the gridlock is a division over values. He describes the 2000 election as a showdown between Reaganism and Clintonism that has been brewing for almost 40 years. The result: a tie. If he is correct, and I believe he is, the unity of patriotism we have witnessed over the past eight months is but a veneer that will be vulnerable to the foundational cracks underneath. In my October 2001 essay, I quoted Lincoln's phrase in the Gettysburg Address wherein he questioned "whether this nation, or any nation so conceived and so dedicated, can long endure," and I suggested that, since 9/11, we are again confronted by that question. Interestingly, I just caught up with a February 1999 speech by Charlton Heston in which he used exactly the same question from Lincoln in the context of the cultural war to which Schneider alludes. I submit that we won't completely know the outcome of the war on terrorism in all its manifestations until we break the stalemate in the cultural war.

The Post-Human Century?

January 1, 2003

Last year I invited readers to submit their thoughts as to what grand themes will dominate the 21st century, and I highlighted some of the responses in recent issues. As promised, my own views follow.

As the issues of war and peace and the defeat of totalitarianism were the dominant global themes of the century just past, there is a good chance that the war on terrorism, properly executed, with all of its repercussions, including the transformation of the Middle East, the reformation of radical Islam, and the reconfiguration of America's role in the world, will be the dominant theme of the next 100 years. Certainly, these issues will dominate the headlines for at least the first decade or two.

There is, however, in my opinion, an issue that will trump even those of worldwide war and peace. It is the looming cultural, philosophical, and religious conflict on the question of the meaning of human nature. The advances in the biosciences and neurosciences have for the first time provided man with the capability to transform his very nature. As a result, we will be forced to return to the questions of who are we? and why are we here? in a way that has been too long absent from public discourse. And, because of the enormous incentives on the so-called "progressive" side of the debate, the implications for it will make the abortion debate of the past 30 years seem mild by comparison. As Eric Cohen of the Ethics and Public Policy Center has noted, this conflict will require new political thinking and a grappling with our dependence on modernity (and its handmaiden, "scientific progress"), its failings, and its presumed superiority.

The silliness of the recent announcement (probably a hoax) of a baby cloned by the clinic founded by the Raelian cult tends to trivialize the discussion while discrediting the pro-cloning argument. Thankfully, there is responsible debate on these questions that is well underway among a number of public intellectuals, such as Francis Fukuyama and Gregory Stock, and the President's Council on Bioethics, under the leadership of Leon Kass, has published its report, which has been described as reminiscent of *The Federalist Papers* in its succinct outline of argument and counter-argument.

There will be political decisions on these issues of enormous impact and complexity under deliberation over the next several years. To hope that these decisions can be made in a morally neutral vacuum is a delusion. All due respect and sympathy for Christopher Reeve, but his comment to Barbara Walters that "religion and social conservatives should not even have a seat at the table in the debate…" is hopelessly utilitarian and totally misguided. To delegate these decisions to the scientists and professional "bioethicists" (or worse, the judiciary) is a dereliction of duty in a democratic republic.

A final thought: For those who place their faith in the rationality of man, I think of Pascal's "wager" – if you're agnostic, you'd better hope (and bet) that there is a transcendent Creator. The rationality of man doesn't have a very good record. One century of mass murder perpetrated by totalitarian regimes driven by the utopian notion of the denial of human nature should have been enough to convince us that just because man can doesn't necessarily mean he should.

The US/EU Divide

May 4, 2004

The recent addition of 10 nations to membership in the European Union is a good time to revisit the rift that exists between the U.S. and certain EU members, mainly of "Old Europe." A number of political players and commentators, chiefly those who disapprove of the foreign policy of the Bush administration, would have us believe that the problems are almost entirely driven by our persistence in pursuing preemptive war in Iraq, together with disagreements over items such as the Kyoto Treaty, the death penalty, the International Court, as well as Bush's "cowboy" demeanor. But I submit that it is deeper, much deeper, and will not improve in its essentials even after the resolution of the conflict in Iraq. In fact, as Tom Friedman has suggested, we may very well be witnessing the beginning of the end of "the West" as we have known it. He is possibly thinking in different terms, as with the post-World War II Cold War alliance, while I am suggesting something even deeper – simply that there is a wide and growing gulf between European and American worldviews and cultural values. Recent studies have shown, for example, that Americans value individual responsibility and individual freedom much higher than Europeans; that, by percentages of up to more than 70 percent, Europeans believe that the spread of American ideas is bad; and that 21 percent of Europeans say that religion is very important to them, compared to 58 percent of Americans. This prompts me to pause and ask, from where did our ideas originate, evolve, and reach maturity? To which the obvious answer is: from the many generations that preceded us in our European heritage. And this is one major reason why it is important to understand that this is not a passing fancy, it is not borne out of political opposition to one particular American administration, but represents a major divergence of historical proportions with enormous implications. In a recent essay in *First Things*, George Weigel reminds us that history is driven by culture – by what men and women honor, cherish, and worship, by how society defines the good, by how these values are expressed, and by what individuals and societies are willing to stake their lives on. As I ponder this thought, it occurs to me that we come much closer to an affinity with the new, former Warsaw Pact EU members and with some of the newly democratic developing nations than with our Old European friends.

The Necessity of Shame

March 4, 2005

Recently I was struck by an editorial exchange initiated by Dr. Joyce Brothers in Parade magazine, who suggested that the lack of respect and values seen in today's popular culture is due to a "lack of shame." This was followed by a rebuttal op/ed in the *Houston Chronicle* from Brene Brown of the University of Houston, who seems to equate shame with a lack of, or damage to one's self esteem, as in "I am a bad person." My take on this is that shame is a deeply embedded monitor, deriving from the original sin from which we all suffer, but which produces a salutary defense mechanism in us, unless it is overruled by the passions or by social pressures to be entirely "rational."

Does this mean that I agree with Dr. Brothers? Generally, yes, in that there are some things, behaviors, etc., that are simply repugnant and that this fact alone should give us pause when we encounter them. Leon Kass, Chairman of the President's Council on Bioethics, believes we should be very attentive to those things that we find "offensive" or "repulsive," because these feelings lead to deeper realities and wisdom, and he uses as an example the idea of cloning.

University of Chicago professor of law Martha Nussbaum strongly disagrees. She believes that shame and appeals to disgust have no place in public policy because they are connected with restrictions on liberty in areas of "non-harmful conduct," and that even attempts by the criminal justice system that aim to reform the whole person are too intrusive, that they tend to stigmatize people. As Roger Kimball explains in responding, Nussbaum wants to remove all stigmatization and shame from penalties, so as to completely free law from the idea of sin and disenfranchise shame from any role in public life.

If postmodernists like Nussbaum can completely free our laws and our jurisprudence from any reliance on shame, moral judgment, or our natural feelings of repugnance, indignation, and disgust, can the police state be far behind?

New Orleans after Katrina – the Good, the Bad, and the Ugly

September 1, 2005

After one week of the horror of this massive human disaster, all the returns are not yet in, but here are my immediate thoughts:

The Good – As usual, the innate and almost unlimited capacity of the American people for generosity and compassion in time of human need, , as well as the resolve and courage of the large majority of the victims of the disaster.

The Bad – Government at every level, beginning with state and local leadership. Where are the Giulianis? Nowhere to be found in Louisiana. And when will we ever learn that large public sector bureaucracies are sometimes pretty good at talking, planning, and processing, but with the exception of the military during wartime, almost always lousy at delivering?

The Ugly – When we peel back the thin layer of our social fabric, as these events force us to do, we often don't like what we see. In this case, what we saw was the fragile covering that separates us from the anarchy of lawlessness and exposes the deterioration of civil and moral order that lurks just below the surface.

The implications of this disaster are enormous, not only for New Orleans, but for that city it will prove to have been a "100-year event" and I believe will be analogous to the Galveston storm of 1900, in the sense that if New Orleans is rebuilt, it will have a much different future than anyone could imagine as recently as last week.

Defining the Enemy

April 3, 2007

As we all gather around the tube each morning to get our daily fix on the world according to Rosie O'Donnell on *The View*, many of us tend to laugh off her brand of celebrity talk show hyperventilation as grandstanding for ratings or, at worst, the innocent rantings of the lunatic leftist fringe. But when more than half of our high school seniors can't place the Civil War or World War II in the correct half-century, a significant percentage of our 20-somethings say that their primary source of news is the late-night talk shows, and scores of otherwise credible members of the engineering community actually seem to believe that the collapse of the World Trade Center on 9/11 was a government-directed inside job, we cannot so casually dismiss the pop cultural rantings of a left-wing kook. What we must realize is that this means of communication, along with the "blogosphere," is a very real, and very successful, element of the strategy of the left. We also must recognize that they don't deal in the truth, because the very concept of objective reality itself is considered by most of these people and their fellow travelers in the post-modern academic community as a construct of the Eurocentric, white, male imperialist oppressor class. I won't go nearly as far as Dinesh D'Souza in his book, *The Enemy at Home: The Cultural Left and Its Responsibility for 9/11,* which essentially blames the American secular left for enraging Al-Qaeda and its leadership to the point of attacking us. However, I do think that an indication of how far apart the opposing sides in the American culture war may be are the answers to the following questions: 1) Who is the greater threat to America, George W. Bush or Osama bin Laden? And, 2) Which represents our greatest ideological threat, evangelical Christianity or Islamic fundamentalism? To the extent that the answers to these questions indicate the assignment of anything approaching a moral equivalence in the choices of a significant number of our intellectual class, our mainstream media, and our cultural icons, folks, we have a lot more work to do in defining and identifying our real enemy.

More Election Stakes to Ponder – A Cultural Seminar

May 2, 2007

The recent Supreme Court decision upholding the federal ban of partial birth abortion should serve as a reminder of the stakes in the next election. Other than the obvious questions of war and peace that confront us, I can't think of a more important consideration. This is particularly so if you take time to read some of the excerpts from the dissenting opinion in the 5-4 decision, written by Justice Ruth Bader Ginsberg, who would have us believe that the majority decision is an "alarming" reversal of long established precedent and "reflects ancient notions about women's place in the family and under the Constitution – ideas that have long since been discredited." And these are comments about a decision upholding the ban of a gruesome procedure which almost 70 percent of Americans agree should be banned and which the late Sen. Daniel Patrick Moynihan accurately called infanticide. It is indeed chilling to consider that, to the pro-abortion left in this country, there can be no retreat from the notion of anything goes, even if, as Paul Greenberg describes it, this decision moves us only to almost anything goes. To wit, Sen. Hillary Clinton's response to the decision was as follows: "It is precisely this erosion of our constitutional rights that I warned against when I opposed the nominations of Chief Justice Roberts and Justice Alito." Need I say more about election stakes?

During a period of just over a week in the middle of April, we experienced a convergence of events that could have served as a seminar on the cultural condition of this country. In rapid succession, the firing of Don Imus, the Virginia Tech mass murders, and the dismissal of the Duke rape case, both in their actuality and the public responses elicited, were in many ways instructive on where we are and who we are in 21st century postmodern America. Let's briefly summarize and then discuss how they all fit.

Imus, of course, was an accident waiting for a place to happen in PC land, and he finally picked the wrong target, an innocent group of high-achievement college kids. In the process, the real "ho's" in his world – fawning politicos, media celebrities, elite pundits, and book pimps of every stripe – had for years lined up to appear on his show while his corporate sponsors looked away from the often rude baseness of the dialogue while the ratings held and the advertisers moved product. But anyone who believes this incident was even remotely about Don Imus isn't paying attention. It's more about a hypocritical elite, which has worked itself into the double standard of denying the cultural rot that plagues our young black people, glorifying its artists and the "street code of ethics," while enriching its purveyors and their corporate sponsors and heaping scorn on those whites who dare to cross the cultural line, thereby enabling extortion by race-baiting opportunists.

The Duke case should have ended months ago, but was kept alive because of our deference to political accountability as the ultimate legitimacy – the outlaw DA was elected, therefore "accountable" to his constituents. This is the mantra of the often oversold concept of "local control," in this case exposed only by a competitor state law enforcement agency, the *Fox News* channel, and the dogged persistence of caring parents who could afford the price of justice. Again, this was not about a particular corrupted DA, but about institutional, group, and individual cowardice in the face of demagoguery and intimidation by a lynch mob complicit with the hustlers of race and class guilt.

On hindsight, it has become clear that the Virginia Tech massacre was avoidable at several levels, both systemic and individual. From a systemic standpoint, this perpetrator was obviously disturbed and, considerations of "privacy" notwithstanding, should have been disqualified, not only from owning a firearm, but from attending a large university where he was allowed to move about freely among social and emotional pressures with which he was unable to cope. On an individual basis, we were quick to note his evident madness, but not so quick to acknowledge the evil at work, and how such tendencies can be fed by higher education faculties and their curriculum, which in far too many cases have abdicated their traditional role of in loco parentis in favor of challenging the moral grounding of the students in their care.

Is there a common thread here? Possibly a bit tenuous, but I think so. In our rush over the past several decades to elevate the status of complete personal autonomy devoid of traditional encumbrances, we have adopted a "public vs. private" argument to justify our double standards of behavior and civic norms – the use of public airwaves vs. the private choice to attend a concert or movie, public vs. private religious expression, public vs. private behavioral standards, public vs. private moral truth, etc. In other words, we have abandoned civic virtue in favor of a privatized and relativized morality and judgments of fairness in terms of due process or "procedure," wherein all considerations involving standards of public morality are off the table and all outcomes must conform to the Rawlsian concept of favoring those considered the most "disadvantaged." This didn't happen overnight, and it won't be fixed anytime soon, but we need to get on with the repair work, and maybe one or more of these illustrative events will prompt a turnaround. However, the further we stray from the foundational public belief in an objective moral truth under a natural law applicable at all times in all places, the more difficult it will be to sustain the American idea of freedom and equality under the rule of law.

Charity and Liberalism

June 7, 2008

In a recent sermon delivered by Harvey C. Mansfield at Appleton Chapel in Memorial Church, Harvard University, we are reminded of the admonition of St. Thomas Aquinas that charity is the chief of the three theological virtues of faith, hope, and charity and that charity is the common form of all the virtues because all depend on the love of God. But people have developed different perspectives on the real world implementation of charity and how it should be properly manifested in this life.

Two recent books have surveyed the various attitudes of Americans as they pertain to charitable giving and related sentiments and instincts and have produced instructive results. One of them, to which Mansfield alludes in his sermon, is by economist (and registered independent) Arthur C. Brooks who, in his book *Who Really Cares?*, notes first of all that no developed country approaches American giving. Based on the most recent data, Americans gave, per capita, amounts ranging from 3.5 to 14 times as much as citizens of other nations, and were more likely to volunteer their time by percentages ranging from 15 to 32. However, the most interesting aspect of his research shows that, by significant margins, self-described "conservatives" in America are more likely to give than self-described "liberals." In the year 2000, households headed by a conservative gave, on average, 30 percent more dollars to charity than households headed by a liberal, and this difference is not a factor of income differential; in fact, the liberal families in the survey earned an average of six percent more than the conservative families. And the trend was consistent in areas other than cash contributions. For example, in the Brooks survey, conservative Americans were much more likely to donate blood and did so more often than liberals.

The other recent survey is the subject of a new book by Peter Schweizer, *Makers and Takers*, the subtitle of which tells it all: *Why Conservatives Work Harder, Feel Happier, Have Closer Families, Take Fewer Drugs, Give More Generously, Value Honesty More, Are Less Materialistic and Envious, Whine Less, and Even Hug Their Children More Than Liberals*. The survey results highlighted here are obviously more comprehensive, but here are a few findings that have a direct bearing on charitable attitudes: 71 percent of conservatives say they have an obligation to care for a seriously injured spouse or parent, compared with 46 percent of liberals; 55 percent of conservatives say they would endure all things for the one they love, compared to 26 percent of liberals; liberals are much more likely to say that money is more important to them; they are 2.5 times more likely to be resentful of the success of others and 50 percent more likely to be jealous of the good fortune of others; and conservatives are much more likely to donate money and time to charitable causes.

Interestingly, while the single biggest determinant of one's altruism is religion, the significant differences outlined in these surveys are not simply a function of religious people's charitable giving to their churches. People of faith are clearly more charitable with secular causes as well and this is demonstrated by the Brooks surveys in particular, which found that religious people were 10 percentage points more likely than secularists to give money to explicitly non-religious charities and 21 points more likely to volunteer their time. And the value of the average religious household's gifts to non-religious charities was 14 percent higher after correcting for income differences.

In short, it is clear that there are undeniably significant charitable attitudes prevalent as one moves along the American political spectrum. What gives? Mansfield believes that the reason liberals are less personally charitable is that they believe in justice more than generosity, because the latter is "hit-or-miss," whereas justice covers everyone, at least in principle. In other words, to make sure that everyone is covered they are willing to sacrifice the voluntary aspect of virtue and go for taxes that compel everyone to be charitable. To me, the most telling survey result was the Brooks finding that people who reject the idea that "government has a responsibility to reduce income inequality" give an average of four times more than people who accept that proposition! This is the lesson learned – to most liberals, particularly those in public office, the definition of charity is redistribution funded through government programs with other people's money.

America the Fragile Idea

July 4, 2008

It's Independence Day and I'm feeling more than usually patriotic. This and other inducements have prompted me to revisit one of my old themes – the American idea. Another inducement was David Broder's article this week in which he poses the question, "is this fragile idea called America headed for trouble?" He wrote the article in response to the recent release of a report by the Lynde and Harry Bradley Foundation entitled "E Pluribus Unum," the product of a two-year study involving a number of the nation's leading intellectuals, educators, and opinion leaders on the current status of the American identity.

The Bradley study found that our young people are increasingly unaware of our founding principles and the history and meaning of our founding and, as a result, are less likely than their parents to be proud of our country and conversely, to be more susceptible to the emphasis they often receive on the more negative aspects of our history. A further consequence is that they feel less likely to be committed to our founding principles or to believe that they have provided America with a unique identity within which they consider themselves an integral part. I have read the Bradley report and recommend it.

On several occasions, I have commented on the question, "is America a culture or an idea?" This question is as old as the republic itself and has occupied many of our leading intellectuals since the founding. And it's a valid question, because Americans don't typically think of themselves as, for example, the Germans or French do, with their deep cultural roots that date from the often mythological mists of prehistory. It is our ideas that are said to be binding and that generate our cultural homogeneity, while our resulting creed always makes room for a plurality of subcultures.

In a previous issue, I made reference to my former political philosophy discussion group which was exploring the nature of man as it relates to political philosophy, which seeks to answer, among others, the questions, "how should we order our lives together?" and "what is the best regime?" It can safely be said that every important political philosophy is also a theory of human nature. If we accept this premise, it follows that it presupposes consideration of basic and timeless questions about man's nature, such as the following:

- Is man a purposeful creation and does he differ from other animals by type or simply by degree?
- Is man possessed of original sin or is man essentially good?
- To what extent is man capable of free will?
- Does man have the innate intellectual capacity to comprehend universals, as opposed to only particular objects identified by the senses?
- Is man's loyalty and commitment to a family unit a natural or conventional phenomenon?
- If there are inalienable human rights, what is their source?

When thinking through these, it becomes pretty clear that the American founding was based on a consensus as to the answers to these questions, so much so that they were "givens" in the thought of the Founders. In fact, one cannot imagine the founding document the execution of which we celebrate today without its invocations of divine providence, transcendental law, and the universal truths of human nature. True, the actuality of the ideals are still being worked out, but the underlying principles are basic to our creed and our identity as a people.

When asked to define education, G. K. Chesterton said, "Properly speaking, there is no such thing as education. Education is simply the soul of a society as it passes from one generation to another." I share the concerns expressed in the Bradley report that we are not sufficiently discharging this responsibility to pass along to our younger generations the soul of America, properly understood.

Rick Hess, who serves as an advisor to our Texas Institute for Education Reform, has this to say in the introduction of his new book, *Still at Risk: What Students Don't Know, Even Now:*

"The first mission of public schooling in a democratic nation is to equip every young person for the responsibilities and privileges of citizenship. This requires that students have the knowledge they need to be prepared for civic responsibilities, further education, or the workforce, in addition to mastering basic skills such as reading and mathematics. To do this well, it is vital that schools familiarize students with the history and culture that form the shared bonds of their national community."

Broder characterizes the Bradley report as controversial, primarily because of some of its recommendations, and he writes that the threat outlined their strikes him as a bit exaggerated. Part of his reasoning and his optimism he attributes to the fact that young people have found their way to the polling places this year in record numbers and have enthusiastically joined many election campaigns. Encouraging, yes; however, simply going to the polls is a necessary, but insufficient indicator of the quality of civic education and inculcation of the American idea in our youth, because it matters very much what principles actually inform the vote.

The Politics of the Tribe

May 4, 2010

Various pundits have been at work over the past year or so analyzing the Tea Party movement, and I don't pretend to have any better handle on it than others. In fact, I think the movement defies comprehensive characterization and is certainly not monolithic in any sense, which is why there isn't and in my view won't be a personality or identifiable "leader" of the movement, or at least in the sense that the chattering classes would like to see evolve.

Pat Buchanan has his take on it, and in his typical paleo-conservative approach, gives it a tribal designation as direct descendants of those rebels who took outrage from the trail of British tyranny leading up to 1775 and who spawned a new ethnicity – the Americans. There is some resonance in this characterization and, frankly, some of us can readily identify with it.

Peggy Noonan has a better idea. In her view the great unrest in the country is what she calls The Big Alienation – "a deep and growing alienation between the people of America and the government of America in Washington." And in her estimation this is not the old conservative "leave us alone" attitude, it is much more broadly and fully evolved, and it has a trail reaching back to two wars, Katrina, the financial meltdown, the bailouts, the healthcare fight, the deficit, the debt, bankrupt states, etc., capped recently by the new Arizona immigration law, about which more below. In Noonan's words, "the American people fear they are losing their place and authority in the daily, unwinding drama of American history… and alienation is often followed by animosity."

True enough and well said. And I would add some thoughts from the late Richard John Neuhaus who, in his seminal work of 25 years ago, *The Naked Public Square,* was even then using the alienation theme in observing that the premise of the populist movement is that "they," meaning the government and whoever is in charge of the culture, are not simply alien but are contemptuous of "us," the little people, the real people – "Millions of Americans have for a long time felt put upon. Theirs is a powerful resentment against values that they believe have been imposed upon them, and an equally powerful sense of outrage at the suggestion that they are the ones who pose the threat of undemocratically imposing values on others." Alienation indeed, and whatever your take on the phenomenon, it didn't just arrive and it isn't going away soon.

More Tea Party Analysis

July 4, 2010

It seems we're spending a lot of time analyzing the Tea Party movement, and I have previously offered some thoughts, but recently I was struck by an essay in Policy Review, "The Tea Party vs. the Intellectuals," by Lee Harris, author of a new book, *The Next American Civil War: The Populist Revolt Against the Liberal Elite*. Here is an excerpt that captures the essence of his thoughts:

The lesson of history is stark and simple. People who are easy to govern lose their freedom. People who are difficult to govern retain theirs. What makes the difference is not an ideology, but an attitude. Those people who embody the "don't tread on me!" attitude have kept their liberties simply because they are prepared to stand up against those who threaten to tread on them... The most important thing is simply to preserve this attitude among a sufficiently large number of people to make it a genuine deterrent against the power hungry. If the Tea Party can succeed in this all-important mission, the pragmatist can forgive the movement for a host of silly ideas and absurd policy suggestions, because he knows what is really at stake. Once the "don't tread on me!" attitude has vanished from a people, it never returns. It is lost and gone forever, along with the liberty and freedom for which, ultimately, it is the only effective defense.

Methinks this is wise counsel that should be heeded by the pragmatic leadership of the loyal opposition, while their "intellectuals" do the work in the think tanks to advance policy that adheres to first principles. It is the latter that concerns many of us and many of the Tea Party stalwarts. As painful as it is to admit, conservatism has forfeited its reputation as a reform movement that was earned in the Reagan and Gingrich years and must regain its reformist heritage, a branding that has been severely damaged by the profligacy of "compassionate conservatism." There is some good work underway here, such as the Mount Vernon Statement issued by leading conservative thinkers recommitting themselves to the ideas of the American founding. Great, but not enough. It will be impossible to nationalize an election without a well-documented commitment to sound policy that has been translated from these principles, in other words, policy that makes these principles relevant to today's issues and that can be understood as such by the American people.

For example, Congressman Paul Ryan of Wisconsin is one young leader who has done this with the healthcare issue, with policy details that make sense while he boils down the choices to two incompatible alternative understandings of America – one based on the principles of progressivism and rule by "experts" and the other on a Constitution with rule by free individuals under limited government. Sound familiar? This is where the battle lines will be drawn and this is where the wedge points in policy will be fought. The tea partiers, the pragmatists, and the intellectuals all have a critical role to play in advancing this model, and they need to come together and get on with it.

One more point that has been advanced by Jeffrey Friedman in *National Review*. He reports on a Pew survey that reflects a majority attitude among Americans that the central Tea Party idea, that modern government is tyrannical, fails to resonate, and he concludes that this is because Americans are by nature problem solvers and that the appeal of progressive, activist government is in solving the problems of ordinary Americans, while the tea partiers elevate individual freedom over pragmatism. This is another issue that requires careful thought and policy that correlates with principle and, as Friedman suggests, it may be that the world will belong to those who can explain why it must not be entrusted to central planners. Another role for conservative intellectuals, and let's hope this hasn't become an oxymoron.

This is Much More Than a Math Problem

March 4, 2011

As we watch the scene in the Wisconsin state capitol in Madison, we are exposed to the raw truth of where liberalism has led us – to the fraud of the "social contract" as it has evolved in the age of entitlement. The wraps are off, the facade is down, Paul Krugman for once is right – it is all about power. This budget crisis is not a math problem except at the most superficial level. It is a long overdue overhaul of the social contract, and the left did it to themselves with the final indignity of the overreach of ObamaCare. The Republicans may blow it, they have many times before, but the curtain has been raised on the great Oz of government, from Greece to Ireland to Madison – there are providers and there are takers. Every public policy has a moral basis. The Tea Party initiative and its moral basis and the crowd in the streets of Greece and the protesters in the capitol in Madison are polar opposites – the Tea Party is protesting what the crowds in Greece and Madison are demanding. The Tea Party speaks for the providers; who speaks for the takers?

Evil in Norway

August 5, 2011

The recent senseless mass murders in Norway drew the typical reaction from comments in the media that I have seen, to wit: why? Well, I have an answer in the form of a "why" question in response: Beyond motivational evidence available in a criminal investigation, why do we not recognize that, contrary to the influential teachings of Jean Jacques Rousseau, evil not only naturally exists in the human soul, but is pervasive in those souls that have not had proper nurture, a condition that has a tendency to expand in an increasingly nihilistic culture? Pending further developments, that about summarizes it for me – this guy Breivik is a nutcase, with no impulses in evidence that are either religious, conservative, or Christian, except in a corrupted millenarian sense.

A couple of references in his manifesto (which incidentally seem to be almost totally plagiarized) were to the Knights Templar and the National Association of Scholars (NAS), two organizations of which I am familiar as a member of both. In response, the national leadership of Knights Templar has issued a statement of complete denial of any relationship with this man and a condemnation of his acts, which I will not quote, but would be pleased to forward to interested parties. The NAS has been actively involved in the mitigation of the scourge of multiculturalism in the upper reaches of American higher education for several decades, an issue on which Breivik is evidently in sympathy. Needless to say, the NAS totally rejects any form of association with violence to achieve its ends in this regard and is concerned that this event will provide cover for those who disagree with its mission to imply that its advocacy incites right-wing violence of this kind.

In fact, an unfortunate by-product of this tragic event is likely to be a dampening effect on this debate on multiculturalism and the failure of Muslims to assimilate into European culture and society, a subject on which British Prime Minister Cameron, French President Sarkozy, and German Chancellor Merkel have spoken forcefully. We need more of this discussion, not less, and this event should not be allowed to intimidate this process.

Whither Europe With or Without the Euro or the Union?

November 11, 2011

"Europeans today prefer leisure to performance, security to risk-taking, paternalism to free markets, collectivism and group entitlements to individualism... Economic freedom has a very low priority here." – Vaclav Klaus, President, Czech Republic.

In this excerpt from a speech delivered last June in Berlin, President Klaus has pretty succinctly summed up the most critical of many problems facing not only the European Union, but the notion of Europe itself. In other words, it's about a lot more than "can the Euro survive" or "will the EU dissolve;" it's about who and what have the Europeans become as a people and what they want for their future as the bearer of the legacy of Western Civilization as we know it. This crisis is manifest as an economic crisis, but it is much deeper than that, as any rational observer can clearly see and as any number of thoughtful people have written and spoken about over the past couple of decades. So, where to start?

For openers, acknowledge that the welfare state and all its philosophical underpinnings have failed miserably, should have long since been totally discredited, and that the rollback must begin immediately. This is a reason why I believe that the briefly proposed national referendum on the bailout plan in Greece would have been very instructive, for the Greeks, the Europeans, and the world. It would have been a good barometer on the degree to which the Greeks, as a people and as a rough proxy for Europe, are in touch with reality and are willing to get serious.

Second, as *The Wall Street Journal* has so well noted on several occasions, the only way to salvage the Euro is to return to its founding principles which, in a few words, were to move back to a more disciplined world before the destruction of Bretton Woods in 1971 created a fiat currency world. This was a good move, but the rules were never enforced, so what survived was the notion that a sovereign nation should not be allowed to default, a moral hazard that shields profligate regimes from their incompetency.

Third, maybe most important and really in parallel with the first two steps, the opinion leaders of Europe should return to Pope Benedict XVI's September 2006 lecture at Regensburg, read it and understand it as it touches on the limitations of the human will and a most timely critique of the abandonment in the West of the interdependency of faith and reason that had provided sustenance to the development of Western Civilization over the centuries. For it is in the restoration of this interdependence that Europeans will begin to find answers to the question of what future they want for their children.

This Will Hurt

January 4, 2012

In November, I closed by indicating that I would follow up with some thoughts about our cultural trend in the direction of Europe and on how difficult our choices will be in diverting ourselves from this disastrous path. Over the holidays I revisited a 1995 collection of essays edited by Digby Anderson for *National Review* under the title "This Will Hurt: The Restoration of Virtue and Civic Order" and was reminded that we didn't just lately develop the social and cultural decay that have led us to this point. It was the second of two collections on the issue, the first being an in-depth description of the problem entitled "The Loss of Virtue: Moral Confusion and Social Disorder in Britain and America." I recommend them both. Clearly, they represent further evidence of the old adage that "the more things change, the more they remain the same."

Shortly after the publication of the second book, Digby Anderson wrote an article in *National Review* in which he summarized the essential points in both collections. Parts of it are worthy of quoting at length:

"So, what is the significance of the new talk about virtue, the reassertion of personal responsibility, the ache for order, community, ease, and goodness? It is not trivial.

Even the renewed use of moral language is very important. But it is not enough to put the clock back. That demands both an intellectual project and a revolution in human commitment. The project is to disentangle the strands of the Enlightenment legacy, to mark, for instance the proper limits of rationalistic scientific understanding, to re-anchor law in morality, to make pleasure a by-product, not a goal, to reassert the moral aspects of social problems, to redeploy social sanctions such as stigma. This will hurt. But what will hurt even more is a new human commitment and for this to ask: how much is modern man, even conservative modern man, willing to give up for virtue? The problem does not lie with the clock. Its hands can be moved in either direction. The problem is whether men want to turn its hands back, want to do so enough to suffer the consequences." Pretty strong stuff, huh? But that's where we are.

People often ask me, what have morality and all this talk about virtue to do with our enormous economic problems? My answer: almost everything. In fact, the free market cannot and will not survive without the realization of and renewed emphasis on the fact that most of the virtues required for its successful operation are those that the market itself cannot produce, and by the way, neither can science nor technology. David Brooks makes the point quite well as related to the current European crisis when he notes: "The scariest thing is that many of the people browbeating the Germans seem to have very little commitment to the effort-reward formula that undergirds capitalism. On the one hand, there are the technicians who are oblivious to values. For them anything that can't be counted and modeled is a primitive irrelevancy. On the other hand, there are people who see the crisis through the prism of some cosmic class war. What matters is not how people conduct themselves, but whether they are a have or a have-not. The burden of proof is against the haves. The benefit of doubt is with the have-nots.

Further to the point, Bret Stephens of *The Wall Street Journal* appropriately notes that "Europe's crisis is not simply fiscal and monetary; it's also a crisis of vision and character." Hmm, wonder where those things come from?

The genius of our founders provided us with a system that they hoped would protect our republic from the various tyrannies originating from our basest human instincts, and in a recent visit to the *Federalist Papers* I am reminded that arguments based on virtue, civic or otherwise, played almost no role in the debates on the ratification of the Constitution. In fact, a case can be made that the Constitution is intentionally designed to function without reference to, or even in spite of, deficiencies in human virtue. However, notwithstanding their pragmatic approach to its design there is significant evidence of their presupposition that such a system was suited only for those men of deep understanding of and appreciation for the civic and moral virtues necessary for its success. One can search history in vain for a classically liberal or conservative economic theorist, including Adam Smith (who was after all a *moral* philosopher), who could conceive of any free market system surviving in an environment of cultural nihilism and moral relativism. Folks, our country's problems are not primarily with government policy and economics.

Since Aristotle, we in the West have been instructed that, by our nature, we are directed to an end beyond our nature, the ideal fulfillment of which requires certain virtues. St. Thomas Aquinas expanded and elaborated on these virtues and identified those that require habitation – temperateness, courage, justice, and prudence – as well as instruction often reinforced by law, both natural, and human. As it has turned out, these virtues and the laws informed by them over the centuries have served us pretty well, but I would bet that if Madison and Hamilton were here to survey the current situation, they would quickly see that we have stretched their model pretty far on stored moral capital and would probably recommend that we need to significantly replenish it very soon.

The State of the Union

February 3, 2012

David Brooks thinks that this election is about averting national decline. No argument there, but he further thinks that President Obama is abandoning the larger issues to the Republicans, which I wish was the case, but I don't see the evidence. They are alarmed for sure, but except for Gingrich, I don't see the large vision or the grandiosity for sweeping reform.

One thing is certain about the Obama strategy: The wraps are off. This much has been made crystal clear by the State of the Union address and various bus tours to the election swing states. There is not even the pretense camouflaging the class warfare strategy and this represents a huge calculated risk that the electorate is as economically illiterate as I fear, that the economic anxiety factor is as pervasive as has been noted by many observers, and that the Republicans have no clue as to how to respond. And, in fact, a little of all three will contribute to Obama's re-election, which will almost certainly speed American decline.

But before commenting on how to respond, back to the question of the pending national decline. The *New Criterion* recently published "Is America in Decline: A Symposium," with essays by a number of contributors, most prominently Charles Murray with a paper adapted from his new book, *Coming Apart: The State of White America*. In it, he outlines a fascinating analysis of the trend in what he calls "the founding virtues" among non-Latino white Americans aged 30-49. Two of them are virtues in themselves – industriousness and honesty – and two of them refer to institutions through which right behavior is nurtured – marriage and religion.

The results of the study are worthy of analysis in all their complexity, but the essential finding is that as recently as a half century ago there was a civic culture that embraced all classes of Americans. Today that is no longer the case. Americans have formed a new lower class and a new upper class that have no precedent in our history, and it is not the emergence of classes that is new, but rather the fact that for the first time these divergences break on core values and behaviors. And for all four of the founding virtues, the statistical divergence breaks between those with at least a bachelor's degree and a professional background and those with no higher than a high school diploma and with blue collar or low level white collar employment. I won't go into the data, but the statistical divergence is compelling and, as Murray indicates, the divergences in the founding virtues essentially divide the two classes into two different cultures. They simply differ on some of the most fundamental dimensions of life and this is manifest in both their cultural and geographic isolation from each other. This does not bode well for the American exceptionalism that was built on a common sense of the American way of life based on the founding virtues that Murray has identified.

So, if this divergence in civic culture is a reality, how do we respond? The progressive left has a view, which is espoused by Robert Reich thusly: "Obama must show America that the basic choice is between two fundamental views of this nation. Either we're all in this together, or we're a bunch of individuals who happen to live within these borders and are mainly on their own." This is the communitarian strain that runs through the progressive worldview, and it results in the preference for only public delivery of public goods, which drives the entitlement welfare state, more government supervision of fairness and social justice, etc., a model which has proven to be a disaster.

Interestingly, another, more conservative view backed by some specific proposals, is from Rick Santorum on the Republican primary campaign trail. He understands that Reich is correct to an extent. A nation is not an agglomeration of autonomous individuals, it's an organic system of family and social relationships and he proposes a limited role for government in assisting local entities with incentives, such as increased child tax credits and other enabling initiatives to help sustain these relationships. Maybe some help here, but too much reliance on government handing out checks and not enough emphasis on the restoration of civic culture and the work ethic.

The bottom line is that there is no viable political response yet in the offing to the major dilemma of this generation, which is the solution to the structural displacement of employment and economic opportunity and the American Dream by the unrelenting competitive pressures presented by the globalization of markets. This is not just a problem for income inequality, but has implications as well for the class divergence and decline in civic culture that Charles Murray has identified. And much of the decline can be traced to the failed Great Society programs of the 1960s and some further policy mistakes in the early Nixon years of the 1970s.

We also instinctively and empirically know that this cultural and economic dilemma is largely a result of our deeply flawed public education system, but we do not yet have the political will to properly respond to it, and I don't see any of the Republican Presidential candidates talking in large enough terms about it. Thankfully, there are a number of state Governors who are talking the talk and walking the walk, however, and they deserve our attention, encouragement, and support. And remember, elections have consequences.

Romney Speaks the Truth in Israel

August 6, 2012

Maybe it wasn't the politically adept thing to say at the time and place, but Mitt Romney won some points with me and no doubt others in his truthful remarks on his trip abroad about the comparative cultures of Israel and Palestine and what this means in terms of the welfare of their respective people. He had the comparative GDP numbers wrong, but here is what he said in a speech in Israel about the reason for the significant disparity in economic vitality: "If you can learn anything from the economic history of the world, it's this – culture makes all the difference. You notice a stark difference in economic vitality between Israel and the Palestinians. And as I come here and I look out over this city and consider the accomplishments of the people of this nation, I recognize the power of at least culture and a few other things."

And in so saying, he cited the book on this subject by David Landes, *The Wealth and Poverty of Nations*, which spells out in detail the cultural attributes that define and are necessary for economic success, as well as those that hinder it. And in the latter case for the entire Arab world, those were outlined in painful detail by a team of Arab intellectuals in a 2002 United Nations report, which essentially paralleled the Landes findings. With the possible exception of Haiti and the Dominican Republic, which share an island, probably no two peoples in close proximity better illustrate the divergence of these attributes and the difference it makes in higher relief than do Israel and Palestine. And in both instances, it is all about the culture.

Of course, Romney's remarks drew an immediate response from the "Palestinians as victims" hustlers, led by a senior Palestinian official who labeled the comments "racist" and accused Romney of damaging U.S. efforts to restore America's standing in the Muslim and Arab world. There also were criticisms by a former Israeli official who bemoaned the damage to the "peace process."

These criticisms are nonsense and, in fact, are a disservice to large numbers of Palestinians, particularly the well-educated entrepreneurs and energetic workers who know that they and their people are being ill-served by their leaders. There is no peace process and will not and should not be one until we start with the truth about the respective cultures of these two peoples and the political history and geography of the Israeli/Palestinian relationship and begin to dispel the myriad of myths that surround this conflict. A couple of years ago, I reviewed *The World Turned Upside Down*, by Melanie Phillips, which describes and debunks much of this mythology very well. It's a good place to start, but in the meantime, I applaud Mitt Romney for moving the truth to center stage. We need more of that.

American Family Culture Clash

April 6, 2013

In its February 2013 edition, *First Things* magazine reports on the results of a three-year investigation conducted by the University of Virginia's Institute for Advanced Studies in Culture. The study breaks down family cultures into four categories: the Faithful, the Engaged Progressives, the Detached, and the American Dreamers. The latter two categories pretty much accept the status quo, with children of the Detached shaped by popular culture in a mindset of helplessness, and the American Dreamers somewhat more positive, but they want their children to succeed as success is defined by others.

The Faithful and the Engaged Progressives are much more assertive, raising their children on their own terms, each harboring "well-formed, confident, and comprehensive worldviews." Both categories are approximately of equal size, with the Faithful constituting 20 percent of American parents and the Engaged Progressives 21 percent.

These two cultures represent strikingly opposite worldviews. One example: 91 percent of the Faithful reject the view that "as long as we don't hurt others, we should be able to live however we want;" more than 50 percent of the Engaged Progressives affirm this view and 83 percent agree that we should be tolerant of "alternative lifestyles." The Faithful are overwhelmingly Republican; Engaged Progressives are Democrat by a four-to-one margin. And these people vote. You get the idea.

The animosity between these two categories is clearly evident in the study. The Faithful are alienated from public institutions and the dominant cultural forces at work in our society, and they largely reject the forms of social authority that are dominated by the Engaged Progressives. And for all their talk of tolerance, the Engaged Progressives are fundamentally hostile to the Faithful.

So, the culture war continues, showing no signs of abatement, and with these two well-armed and committed antagonists we're talking about more than 40 percent of the parental guidance of the country, with the balance either totally gullible or in the "whatever" column. Clearly, there is a serious divide between the two dominant family cultures in the definition of "the good life" and, even though I want my side to prevail and very much believe that it is essential to our future prosperity, I suppose this divide is to be expected in our exceptional country founded on a proposition (see the second paragraph of the Declaration of Independence). And I'm OK with that, as long as we continue to be committed to the proposition.

The worldview of the Engaged Progressives, with plenty of help from the Detached and the American Dreamers, won the last election by a narrow majority, at least on a national basis, and they are about their objective of "Europeanizing" the American political regime. They know that their chief obstacle to this mission is the traditional American family as represented by the Faithful, to which they have been hostile since the beginning of the progressive movement a century ago. This is the wedge issue that is playing out today in the same-sex marriage debate and before the Supreme Court, the decision on which will have ramifications far beyond the "right to marriage."

The very notion that this issue is debatable is problematic for the Faithful. As David Brooks has written, people everywhere have entered into what we might call the "age of possibility" and have become intolerant of any arrangement that might close off their personal options or autonomy. I have previously written about Michael Sandel's view of the "procedural republic," a regime governed by people with full autonomy, with no encumbrances of tradition or culture, no intolerance, and no judgmentalism, with all moral judgments bracketed from public deliberation. This is the opposite of the American founders' concept of civic republicanism, and Brooks himself believes that this age of possibility is based on a misconception. He writes: "People are not better off when they are given maximum personal freedom to do what they want. They're better off when they are enshrouded in commitments that transcend personal choice – commitments to family, God, craft, and country. The surest way people bind themselves is through the family." This is the worldview of the Faithful and we allow it to dissipate at our peril.

A Tale of Two Disasters

June 1, 2013

In viewing the reporting of the response to and recovery from the devastation wreaked by the tornadoes in Oklahoma, I have been struck by the contrast in the local response to this disaster with that of the 2005 Katrina hurricane and flood in New Orleans. Where is the massive evacuation of refugees, the housing of victims in squalid public facilities, the high profile pleading for public relief, and the related widespread media criticism of insufficient federal government response? Could it be that Oklahomans didn't wait for government to respond, but stepped forward to take individual responsibility for the support of their neighbors when in need? Could it be that the outpouring of support from individuals and institutions around the country is a traditional American response to such a disaster? And, perish the thought, could it be that there are cultural and, more importantly, historical dependency issues that inform the differences in the response?

I think that the comparative response on the part of the victims of these two disasters and their neighbors would be a timely subject for a study by an investigative sociologist. It occurs to me that Americans are at their best when confronted with neighbors in need and that it's possible that we could return to a day when we didn't look to the federal government to be the first source of response and primary source of restoration in the face of natural disasters.

The Dangerous Corruption of Language

March 6, 2017

In his book, *1984*, and his essays such as "Politics and the English Language," George Orwell wrote very clearly about how ideology is corrupting and how this corruption is manifest in the way we distort language to suit ideology. And to him it was clear that "…the decline of a language must ultimately have political and economic causes; it is not due simply to the bad influence of this or that individual writer." To illustrate the idea that language can corrupt thought and that ideological systems, particularly of the totalitarian bent, use it to restrict rather than broaden ideas, he invented Newspeak.

I often think of Orwell and these points when I am watching the endless political and public affairs related interviews on TV pitting left vs. right, pro vs. con, etc., on split screen with the host in the middle, with no resolution to the issue, talking past each other under a tight time restraint that ends with "to be continued" and a commercial break.

Recently, I came across another Orwell reminder, a very insightful essay entitled "Ideology and the Corruption of Language" in *The Public Discourse*, a publication of The Witherspoon Institute, by Randall Smith, professor of theology at the University of St. Thomas in Houston. He uses a 1978 essay by former Czech Republic President Vaclav Havel to discuss the distinction between "ideology" and a "principled position" as they pertain to our discourse in the public square.

So, how do we recognize the language of ideology and distinguish it from a principled position? His first clue is that those who hold a principled position welcome arguments and genuine debate testing their position, while those who hold an ideology will tend to avoid real debate or any examination of the ideology's underlying premises. For Smith, it follows that the corruption of language becomes a characteristic sign of ideology. He makes good use of the *Platonic Dialogues*, particularly the Gorgias, to define what true dialogue actually looks like and how sophistry is identified, how certain terms become "true" without explanation, the refusal to discuss terms because the point is "obvious," the use of very specialized vocabulary and "buzzwords," making highly generalized claims about groups of people, etc. As I considered these distinctions and related them to certain recent panel conversations, interviews, protests, and town hall meetings, their validity was clear, but what bothers me is how full of ideological corruption the air around us has become. Commentators talk of the First Amendment and how dear it should be to Americans, and it is. But the danger I fear is that so much of our language has been corrupted by the ideological perspective that Smith has defined that we are losing our sense of mutual respect that is necessary for honest dialogue on principled positions.

Hurricane Harvey and Houston
September 5, 2017

This will be a limited edition, because I have been temporarily displaced by our friend Harvey and related flooding in the Houston area and many of my research capabilities and resources have been curtailed for awhile. But I want to say a few words about this unprecedented calamity and the response it has produced This will be a limited edition, because I have been temporarily displaced by our friend Harvey and related flooding in the Houston area and many of my research capabilities and resources have been curtailed for awhile. But I want to say a few words about this unprecedented calamity and the response it has produced the lawn, so for us it's at least a 40-year event. But we'll get through it, which brings me to my main point.

In between calls to insurance companies, contractors, utility companies, and related over the past week, like everyone else here and abroad who have been monitoring the TV coverage, I have observed Houston at its best. From the thousands who immediately flocked to the shelters to simply do what needed done for the dispossessed, to the armada of private watercraft of all shapes and sizes manned by volunteers who boldly rushed to fill the need for help in the evacuation of refugees (including me), to the thousands of stories and scenes of neighbors who literally saved numerous lives in their respective neighborhoods, to the many millions of dollars immediately donated by businesses large and small to help fund the relief and recovery effort, we again have witnessed the true spirit of Houston, which has long been in evidence for those of us who live here.

So we'll continue to be the place that we're known for – the "can do" city with the indomitable entrepreneurial drive, the so-called "Hong Kong of the Western Hemisphere," the city that people from around the world seek out to fulfill their version of the American dream, the city in which there is no barrier to full acceptance, be it wealth, class, or race and ethnicity – but what shows most in the response to Harvey is a character that runs even deeper, and it's why I tell people in and outside Texas that if we didn't have a Houston, we would want to build one. And we will certainly immediately rebuild the one we have, even better.

The Coming Liberal Crack-Up Over Identity Politics

November 5, 2017

The clash over removal of Confederate images in Charlottesville, Virginia in August and Donald Trump's failure to specifically call out the white nationalists as the lead culprit in the melee have continued to reverberate and, as *The Wall Street Journal* has noted, it is unfortunate that most of the attention was focused on the deficiencies in the President's response rather than the underlying problem, which is the poison of identity politics in this country.

In an editorial at the time of the Charlottesville confrontation, the *Journal* reminds us that the politics of white supremacy was a poison on the right for many decades, but the civil rights movement rose to overcome it with Martin Luther King, Jr.'s leadership and message of equal opportunity and color blind justice. Alas, those principles have been abandoned in favor of a new identity politics that seeks to divide Americans by race, gender, ethnicity, and class.

This new variety of identity politics is primarily a creature of the radical left, aided, abetted, and often led by our leading institutions of higher education and executed in the field by the millennial generation, and the acknowledgment of this fact has been manifest in a vigorous debate that is underway among liberals and progressives. To wit, Mark Lilla, professor of the humanities at Columbia University and a leading liberal intellectual, has recently penned an essay adapted from his new book, *The Once and Future Liberal: After Identity Politics*, in which he suggests that liberals have lost the public's confidence by embracing the divisive, zero-sum world of identity politics and that they need to find their way back to a unifying vision of the common good.

Lilla rightly notes that, unlike the generations that found their liberal grounding in the civil rights movement, liberal political education now takes place on college campuses far removed, socially and geographically, from the rest of the country, and particularly from the sorts of people who once were the foundation of the Democratic Party. And Lilla emphasizes that these students of the Facebook age are drawn to courses focused on their identities and movements related to them. As a result, he says, the line between self-discovery and political action has become blurred and this confusion is much more pronounced in his experience as a teacher with his progressive than his conservative students, the latter of whom are far more likely to connect their engagements to a set of political ideas and principles, while the progressives are less and less comfortable with debate.

As a prominent liberal, he abhors this problem with progressivism and the liberal turn and feels that identity liberalism is misguided and counterproductive and should be condemned and replaced with an emphasis on a political consciousness grounded in our common heritage of citizenship.

In a recent response to Lilla in *The Weekly Standard* entitled "The Primal Scream of Identity Politics," Mary Eberstadt of the Faith and Reason Institute writes that the deeper question here is the elemental one: How has the question of "identity" come to be emotional ground zero for so many in America and elsewhere in the Western world? In this view, what is lacking in Lilla's analysis is "why have so many people found in identity politics the very center of their political being?" To Eberstadt, it is clear that something deeper is afoot than individualism run amok and she in fact does analogize it as something of a primal scream because its source is ultimately grounded in the fact that our macro-politics have gone tribal because our micro-politics are no longer familial, centered in the small civilization of the family unit.

In essence, she says, identity politics cannot be understood apart from the preceding and concomitant social fact of family implosion over the past five decades. And she asks, did anyone really think things would turn out otherwise – that the massive kinship dislocations produced by increases in unwed motherhood, abortion, and divorce of the past 60 years wouldn't produce increasingly visible, trans-formative effects not only in individual lives and households, but on politics and culture as well? And, of course, millennials have become the demographic backbone of identity politics, because their generation has borne the brunt of the primal urge to identify themselves.

I think Lilla and Eberstadt are both onto some perceptive thinking here, but neither leaves me with much optimism about a way out of this corrupting phenomenon. In fact, Eberstadt leaves us with the unsettling notion that, while identity politics has become an object of conversation primarily in the left-leaning circles of political thought, deliverance from this disfiguration cannot come from the same source, for a simple reason – the sexual revolution out of which much familial dislocation grew is off-limits for revision with the left. It is their moral bedrock.

The Central Liberal Truth

April 5, 2018

"The central conservative truth is that it is culture, not politics, that determines the success of a society. The central liberal truth is that politics can change a culture and save it from itself." – Daniel Patrick Moynihan.

I have referred to the quote above many times over the years, because I think it is profound on several levels. Its value and relevance do seem to me to expand over time and it has never been more relevant than it is today.

I first came into contact with the phrase in a 2006 book with the title, *The Central Liberal Truth: How Politics Can Change a Culture and Save It from Itself*, by Lawrence Harrison, who led the Culture Matters Research Project at Tufts University. He gives Moynihan's quote a central place in his thesis and his book. As he wrote in the book's introduction, "The influence of cultural values, beliefs, and attitudes on the way that societies evolve has been shunned by scholars, politicians, and development experts, notwithstanding the views of Tocqueville, Max Weber… and others. It is much more comfortable for the experts to cite geographic constraints, insufficient resources, bad policies, and weak institutions. That way they avoid the invidious comparisons, political sensitivities, and bruised feelings often engendered by cultural explanations of success and failure."

His book attempts to answer questions such as: "Which cultural values, beliefs, and attitudes best promote democracy, social justice, and prosperity?" *and* "How can we use the forces that shape cultural change, such as religion, education, and political leadership, to promote these values in the Third World and for underachieving minorities in the First World?" In his book, Harrison offers intriguing answers to these questions, many of which are controversial, contradicting the arguments of the multiculturalists by suggesting that when it comes to promoting human progress, some cultures are more effective than others. His most striking case study, which illustrates in high relief the degree to which cultures determine success, is the study of Haiti and the Dominican Republic, two countries with completely different cultures that share the geography, climate, history, and environment of the island of Hispaniola in the Caribbean, but which clearly have had remarkably different results in human progress, while politics and enormous intervention have failed to change the dynamics, at least in Haiti, the less successful of the two countries. It's a textbook case at the core of his work that has a number of current applications and deserves serious study.

Fast forward to the relevance of Moynihan's observation and Harrison's project to a couple of points I want to make. There are any number of political activists from both sides of the current divide in America who want to either drop ideological labels or advance political independence from the two major political parties in an attempt to break the stalemate and resulting gridlock in governance. Substantially all of these "movements," or at least the most significant ones of which I am aware, hold as a key to their success the set aside or bracketing of the so-called "social issues" from deliberation in their policy platforms in the belief that these issues – abortion, LGBT rights, religious freedom, etc. – are "deal killers" in almost any political conversation and which make impossible a common ground on which to pragmatically "get things done."

Such is the condition that Michael Sandel has identified in his classic, *Democracy's Discontent: America in Search of a Public Philosophy*, as the "procedural republic" that we have already become, which essentially demands that we move cultural and moral considerations off the table in our deliberations on public policy. And where has this already taken us? To *Roe v. Wade*, elimination of prayer in the schools, and other deep divisions in the body politic, because it has been denied a political resolution of many of the deep seated moral issues central to our core. As he notes, "The effort to banish moral and religious argument from the public realm for the sake of political agreement may end by impoverishing political discourse and eroding the moral and civic resources necessary to self-government."

An additional powerful point has been made by Charles Murray in his book, *Coming Apart: The State of White America, 1960-2010*, in which he identifies the domains through which human beings achieve deep satisfaction in life as only four – family, vocation, community, and faith – and proceeds to demonstrate with compelling data the degree to which these foundations have collapsed among white adults in their prime years of 30 to 49 over the past half century. And again we find that the "procedural republic," with its strictures on the moral issues that underpin our culture and prevent us from being "judgmental" about the dysfunction that has driven this collapse, is depriving us of the proper functioning of the "civic republic" that we were founded to be.

So, the profundity of Moynihan lives on and continues to enlighten, but for his politics as the central liberal truth to be effective in saving a culture, it must be allowed a free reign in order to enable the civic republic. A final thought from Sandel: "A procedural republic that banishes moral and religious argument from political discourse makes for an impoverished civic life. It also fails to answer the aspiration for self-government; its image of citizens as free and independent selves, unencumbered by moral or civic ties they have not chosen, cannot sustain the public spirit that equips us for self-rule."

5
Economic Policy

The Inevitability of Marketization

August 1, 2000

A couple of months ago, I was struck by a notice in *The Wall Street Journal* that 14 leaders of industrialized countries signed The Berlin Conference communiqué titled "Progressive Governance in the 21st Century." Among other center-left aphorisms, it states that globalization "should not just be allowed to happen" and that there should be a "return to politics" ahead of economics. They're dreaming. In 1991, former Citibank Chairman Walter Wriston wrote in his *Twilight of Sovereignty* that the days when nation-states can control economic events are numbered and that technology has produced a new "gold" standard in the form of 200,000 computers run by money managers who never sleep and who "vote" on public policy and discount its implications often before the policy pronouncements by political leaders. And this was before the explosion of the Internet! It is axiomatic that capital goes where it is wanted and stays where it is well treated. Because of this fact, I'll go one step further: wholesale privatization of the delivery of government services will be inevitable. Former Indianapolis Mayor Stephen Goldsmith, a key domestic policy advisor to George W. Bush, prefers the term marketization to privatization, but the principle is the same. The global competition for capital will force governments at all levels to subject themselves to the disciplines of delivering competitive goods, because capital is hyper-sensitive to public policies – taxes, mandates, expenditures, or regulations – that are onerous to capital formation. It will further force governments to seek out best practices on a global, not just local or national basis. They will have no choice in this move to market-driven reforms. Sure, there is and will be continuing protectionist reaction, but it will ultimately fall to the requirements of the information revolution. Jobs follow investment. The old politics of the industrial age can be obstructive if it attempts to control the variables, but cannot win in the long term. The question is, which political leaders will be able to properly articulate the risks and costs vs. benefits involved in this newer form of Joseph Schumpeter's "creative destruction?"

We must be accommodative to this phenomenon and allow the experimentation of new initiatives at the local and state level and practice the principle of subsidiarity that our Founders envisioned. And we need much less "us" vs. "them" advocacy. Business opinion leadership is key, but it must be the kind of leadership that avoids public policy considerations that are based entirely on the outdated mercantilist calculus of who wins and who loses. Marketization is not an unalloyed positive, and, as Lori Taylor of the Federal Reserve Bank of Dallas points out in a recent study, outside of public education, the jury is still out on the social benefits of public sector competition. But the competitive pressure of global capital mobility makes the outcome a matter of time. I'll have more to say on some of the cultural ramifications in future issues.

Economic Choices

April 1, 2001

There is, of course, growing evidence of a difficult period ahead for the U.S. economy, compounding the new administration's already challenging task of developing a consensus on tax and budget issues. In this environment, it is important to consider the longer-term implications of policy in the light of the new realities of the post-industrial global economy. Our economic policy gurus continue to lapse into the misguided thinking that government "runs" the economy, that it can guide and regulate its direction, pull it out of decline, or dampen "irrational exuberance." This is antiquated Great Depression-era thinking, but it persists even among many entrepreneurs who should know better, and it often leads to bad policy. Even now, the specter of protectionism that often raises its ugly head during a slow economy may be holding back several important new free trade initiatives in Congress.

There continues to be an element of opinion leadership that is fighting the old economic wars. These people evidently fail to see, or prefer not to see, the "demassification" of the economy so well described by Alvin Toffler in *The Third Wave*, the flattening of hierarchical command-and-control organizational structures, the collapsing of intermediaries that don't add value, and the explosion of productivity brought about by Moore's Law. Understandably, this revolution is a source of fear for those who can't cope or don't know how, or if, they have a place in the new scheme of things. If we're honest, we all feel some of this anxiety.

In her *The Future and Its Enemies*, Virginia Postrel identifies the opposing forces in this and related conflicts as the "stasists" and the "dynamists." In this view, the stasists are the tradition-bound reactionaries and the dynamists favor processes that lead to an open-ended future. She extols the superiority of the dynamist position across the board, in economic, as well as cultural matters. From an economic standpoint, it is difficult to deny the ultimate logic of the dynamist worldview, but I struggle with the cultural damage that often results from the "creative destruction" of markets. This trade-off is characterized by Daniel Yankelovich as the conflict between the vision of the free market vs. the vision of the civil society. I believe that, at bottom, we are now deeply immersed in this conflict in our policy choices. Where are you in this debate? Are you a stasist or a dynamist?

Voting with Their Feet

July 1, 2002

One of Houston's larger companies and the world's largest onshore drilling company, Nabors Industries, recently became the latest in a series of incorporating relocations of U.S. companies to offshore tax havens, Bermuda in this case. I have been struck by the responses to this trend from labor unions and public officials who seem to believe that they can direct public policy to repeal the laws of the fungible nature of capital throughout the world. Again, capital goes where it is welcomed and stays where it is well treated. This applies to states, as well as to nations. I have written before on the "inevitability of marketization" (August 2000) and the futility of government attempts to reverse globalization with such pipe dreams as the Berlin Conference communiqué of two years ago, which stated that globalization "should not just be allowed to happen" and that there should be a "return to politics ahead of economics." The old politics can be obstructive and are usually counter-productive, but will lose in the end to tax and trade policies that are accommodative to the competitive pressures of global capital mobility.

Voice vs. Choice

May 2, 2003

Lately I have been reminded from several directions of the efficacy in various applications of the concept of "public choice theory" as developed by economics Nobel Laureate James M. Buchanan. In a recent issue of *Imprimis*, Buchanan expounds on this theory, which to me is nothing more complicated than one that espouses a market-based system for delivery of public services. Critics of this theory seem to believe that people, when acting politically, for example, as voters or legislators, do not behave as they do in markets, that somehow they set aside human nature and become immune to the dynamics and incentives of market forces. But I believe that, after several generations of the failure of the top-down collectivist monopoly in the delivery of public goods dictated and controlled by those who have political "voice," we are finally moving toward a bottom-up "choice" model based on empowerment of the users of public services.

Two areas in which this transformation is currently playing out are education, where school choice programs of various designs are being successfully tested in a growing number of states and school districts, and healthcare, where universal, one-size-fits-all government solutions have been discredited. There are other areas in which I believe choice can and will be expanded. One of them is transportation, where it is clear that the collectivized model has failed miserably in responding to mobility problems in almost every urban area. A second is social security, which will not be viable or credible for the next generation until it is converted to something resembling a defined contribution retirement plan. Yet another is welfare services, and here it is a shame that President Bush's faith-based initiative wasn't originally structured on a voucherized basis, so that the funding would have gone directly to the person receiving the benefit who would then choose the best option for the delivery of the service from among governmental, charitable, and private providers. Likewise, the federal Head Start program, the control of which the Bush administration has proposed to transfer to the states, could be much more effective as a voucherized program rather than as block grants to education bureaucrats.

Public choice theory is not a novel concept. An early variation of it was introduced by Adam Smith in his explanation of the "invisible hand" in the 18th century, and, incidentally, his discipline wasn't economics, it was moral philosophy, which is grounded in a proper understanding of human nature. There are hopeful signs that we are returning to that understanding in our public policy.

Labor Day Thoughts on the New Realities

September 1, 2003

Each Labor Day brings the usual editorials on the concerns of organized labor and the threats of globalization of world markets, and this one was no exception. David Broder currently laments the "wasting of the manufacturing sector," and suggests it is a problem far too important to be ignored by the political class in pursuit of "some economic theory," namely, that of free trade. The classic was the line in the communiqué issued by The Berlin Conference three years ago, that globalization "should not just be allowed to happen." When I see this kind of nonsense, I often turn to Peter Drucker and his *The New Realities* for a refresher. Here are some excerpts: "the transnational economy is shaped mainly by money (capital investment) rather than by trade in goods and services… in which the traditional factors of production, land and labor, increasingly become secondary;" "manufacturing is becoming uncoupled from labor;" and the new economic policy "implies increasingly neither free trade nor protectionism, but reciprocity between regions." In this environment, he submits, management is the decisive factor of production on which competitive position must be based. Clearly, in the world of Drucker's realities, no sovereign political power, with its top-down, command-and-control compliance mandates, can dictate the investment flows that drive economic success. The challenge for us "haves" in the West is to lead the rest of the world into a system in which all the world's "have nots" can gain access to the dynamics of free trade and open markets.

Jobs and Realities

January 2, 2004

In my last issue, I commented briefly on the misguided comments of Treasury Secretary Snow in "talking down" the dollar and blaming China's trade and currency policies for the loss of U.S. manufacturing jobs. Since then, we have witnessed the domestic political payoff in the form of new U.S. quotas on Chinese textiles. Subsequently, in a wiser vein, I was pleased to read Federal Reserve Chairman Alan Greenspan's remarks in a speech to the Dallas World Affairs Council, in which he notes the futility of singling out the Chinese exchange rate as a significant cause of American job loss. In fact, the issue is much more complex, and Greenspan notes that much of our manufacturing job instability is due to the dynamic nature of global competition, which is producing greatly accelerating turnover of employment and capital equipment in order to respond to market demand (my summary of his words). In short, it's Schumpeter's "creative destruction," the lifeblood of capitalism, which, largely due to China's entry into the world trading system, is being applied worldwide for the first time in history. It is a concept that is prone to demagoguery in an election year and, without appropriate discipline, lends itself to destructive protectionist policies. Further, as former President of Mexico Ernesto Zedillo points out, China's monetary policy seems more than fair to the U.S. in the sense that it is helping to finance the U.S. fiscal deficit through large investments in U.S. Treasury bonds, and that this new interdependence in trade and finance, whether we like it or not, is positive for global peace and prosperity. Make no mistake, creative destruction is a good thing, and, as David Henderson of the Hoover Institution notes, the loss of manufacturing jobs is a sign of economic health – "the history of economic growth is the history of people making more with less and shifting into new jobs that were unheard of in the previous generation." When we talk of jobs, I worry more about our leadership in technology, innovation, and management, and the degree to which our long-term competitiveness there is directly tied to our world leadership in educating our youth. Now there is a scary thought.

More on Jobs, Outsourcing, and the New Realities

May 2, 2004

I continue to be amazed at how *CNN's* Lou Dobbs and a number of fellow-traveling politicians are consistently able to bash U.S. companies with impunity on a daily basis for their outsourcing strategies, while corporate leaders seem too cowed and intimidated to make any attempt to defend themselves. It has been called "the great outsourcing scare of 2004," and it is unfounded by any logic of market capitalism, unless, of course, one wants to challenge two of its major foundational premises, the principle of comparative advantage among nations and the faith in creative destruction. Of course, I understand that some do want to challenge these premises as outdated, namely economist Paul Craig Roberts and Senator Charles Schumer among others, but no one has an answer as to what will replace them, and some of the short-term fixes would be extremely dangerous. Probably the poster "villain" for American split-mindedness on globalization, outsourcing, creative destruction, comparative advantage, and related issues is Walmart. Recently, the residents of Inglewood, California voted to block the development of a Walmart Supercenter. Is this the tipping point? Should we care about this development? Ultimately, yes, we should, mainly because of what it represents in the failure of our elites to be honest about the issues and the realities. Tom Donahue, President of the U.S. Chamber of Commerce, was on point recently when he called on our business and political leaders to be more forthcoming, for example: Will there be more job losses from creative destruction? Yes, the next wave will probably be in land/ wire communications, the old Bells, et al, but many more jobs will be created by broadband expansion, if we don't tax it to death. The Chamber has recently released a report with some enlightening findings, such as: more Americans are working today than ever before in our history; in white collar employment, insourcing of jobs to America exceeds outsourcing; Detroit is producing the same number of autos today as it did 30 years ago with 40 percent of the workers; the unemployment rate for Americans with four-year college degrees is 2.9 percent; and the significant job growth produced by small business, particularly in rural areas, as well as by women-owned businesses, is underreported. Another point well made by Donohue is that the developing world is now doing what we told them to do over the past 50 years – get yourself educated, free your economies, free your trade, and join us in the world market. Guess what? It worked. Of course, the usual election year rhetoric won't help produce honest debate about all this because people will be told what they want to hear. (Example from John

Kerry: "My economic policy is not to export American jobs…"). And there is no doubt that the major issue for the political class is that lost jobs are an immediate problem while the jobs of the future are a leap of faith into the unknown. But hasn't democratic capitalism by its nature always presupposed a significant element of faith?

Drucker and the New Social Contract

January 2, 2006

One of my heroes, Peter Drucker, died last November, just in time to produce highlights of his work and ideas at the peak of the transformation from the old social contract to his "new realities," as illustrated by the demise of the poster child of the old contract, General Motors. GM was the model of the contract that was the post-World War II ideal – the collaboration of big business, big labor, and big government in providing sustainable dominance of American industrial leadership and steady employment for a growing workforce with collectively bargained and ever-increasing wages and benefits, supported and subsidized by Keynesian fiscal, monetary, and trade policies. This worked well during a long period of stasis in the world order, and, in "the great society" mentality, seemed to be a permanent fixture of economic life in America. But it ran head-on into Drucker's new realities of dynamism, a deregulated and market based world of low-cost global competition, the knowledge revolution, Adam Smith's principle of comparative advantage, and the free flow of investment capital and the resulting employment to venues where it is well treated.

There are wake up calls everywhere one looks, most prominently in the demise of the defined benefit pension plans, both in the public and private sectors, including Social Security, that no longer make sense in the new environment. Many of our larger U.S.-based companies, such as GM and its spin off Delphi, look more like bureaucratic healthcare and retirement benefits providers than producers of quality products, with many more beneficiaries of these plans than current employees. There is a crisis brewing here in the resolution of the unfunded liabilities of these plans that will make the savings and loan bailout of the 1980s look mild by comparison.

Fierce efforts at protection of the old social contract abound in our public discourse among policy wonks and the political class that is so heavily vested in it. And there is no better evidence of the attitude of these elites about the painful transformation to the new realities than the comparison of the mainstream media coverage of the fortunes of GM and Walmart, wherein the former is often portrayed as the loyal comrade in the preservation of the benevolence of the old contract, while the latter, the most successful model of the new contract, is portrayed as the maverick, the villain that is destroying small town America and pursuing creative destruction on the backs of exploited, under-compensated workers here and abroad.

No doubt, this transformation will be painful, but the worst we can do is attempt to protect ourselves from it, and we had best urgently move on with public policies that adapt to the new realities and advance the transformation while recognizing the human transition costs. Peter Drucker has been saying as much for many years.

No Surprises Here

March 5, 2006

In a recent article, George Will says that "Michigan Has a Problem," which is that its prosperity is withering as America's automobile industry withers. When examined more closely, the state's economy really is a microcosm of the larger problem embodied in the debate over protectionism vs. the opportunity society in coping with a globalized workplace. And, in the political response to this problem, bereft of better ideas, Democrats in Michigan and elsewhere are slowly, but surely positioning themselves as the party of protectionism and the enemy of free trade, in the mistaken belief that free trade policies are responsible for the devastation of the old industrial base, reversing the generally bipartisan free trade consensus that has sustained our post-World War II prosperity. To compound the problem, Michigan's corporate income tax burden ranks the second heaviest in the nation, and *CEO Magazine's* annual survey, which considers factors such as taxes, workforce quality, regulatory burden, and labor costs, ranks Michigan 48th on the list of the best places to do business, ahead of only Massachusetts, New York, and California. The top five in this survey were Texas, Nevada, North Carolina, Florida, and Georgia. It doesn't require much insight to determine that the states that are more attractive to business and job creation in the survey are those whose public policies favor lower taxes, less onerous regulatory burdens, and are regarded as having higher quality workers. And guess what? These states that are buying into the opportunity society are predominantly those that landed in the "red" column in the last presidential election. No surprises here.

Flat Earth II

April 1, 2007

A couple of announcements caught my attention recently. One was that Tom Freidman of *The New York Times* and "the earth is flat" fame will be releasing an update of his popular book in August; the other was that widely-followed economist and advisor to Democratic presidential candidates Alan Blinder, who has been one of the more influential free trade enthusiasts, has changed his message somewhat and is now suggesting that the downside impact of unfettered economic globalization will be deeper than we have imagined.

Why did these notices catch my attention? First, they are a continuing manifestation of the phenomena outlined by Alvin Toffler more than 25 years ago in his landmark book, *The Third Wave*, the key message of which is that we are now living in the middle of the third great transformation of the organization of work and society in world history, and there is no escape from it. Second, as will reportedly be well noted in the revised edition of Freidman's book, while seemingly 90 percent of our focus is on public policy, that's not where the action is at all. In fact, public policy is the "brain dead" arena for dealing with this transformation, to wit: there is enormous innovation underway in this country, which is adding unprecedented value and wealth, but none of it is originating in Washington, D.C. and precious little in state capitals. Third, I share Blinder's concern that the impact of this transformation and the allocation of pain now reaching the affluent white collar sector will produce heightened political action to mitigate the transition costs.

These observations taken together suggest to me that we will need enormous vision and courage in our leadership to avoid short-sighted strategies more directed toward pain protection than the urgently needed market-driven systemic reform in education rigor and delivery, healthcare finance and delivery, and the restructuring of retirement finance. Clearly, we won't get it from the Lou Dobbs wing of the Democratic Party, including House Ways and Means Chairman Charles Rangel, which will use Blinder's recent notes of caution to further their demagoguery against free trade. Nor will it come from Chuck Schumer and his allies in the Senate, who believe that the principles of comparative advantage among trading nations no longer apply in a globalized world. No, this leadership role can only be filled by our next President.

Replacing the Broken Contract

October 2, 2007

I was struck over a year ago by comments by the CEO of General Motors who, in defending the company's appeal for relief of its crushing legacy costs for healthcare and retirement benefits for its retirees, in effect said that it should not be expected to bear these costs in their entirety, because they are part of the social contract that has been in place for the past 60 or so years, in which GM has been a loyal participant. My initial reaction at the time was that, while he might have a good point, we have long known that we can no longer afford this deal, and it is his responsibility and that of his peers to provide the opinion leadership to replace this contract which has been broken for quite some time, rather than allowing the costs to be socialized by off-loading them to the taxpayers. Roll the calendar forward, and we now have a number of people talking about this broken social contract and predicting that it will likely be the most important domestic issue in the Presidential election of 2008. It's about time.

In a recent article, David Brooks brought my attention to the work of two people who have insightful things to say about this broken contract and what should be done to overhaul it. Jason Bordoff of *Democracy Magazine*, a Brookings Institution affiliate, has a slightly left of center take on the problem, which he describes as the "two-sided reality of the 21st century economy," namely that first, in an era of growing economic insecurity it must be recognized that people will not be willing or able to assume all of the inherent risks of globalization and the dynamics it produces without some assurances that there will be downside protection from job loss or dislocation and periodic non-insurability, and second, that, as companies like GM have learned, these very forces have already rendered obsolete as economically unviable the arrangements that assumed long-term employment with one employer as a significant part of the social contract. Bordoff envisions a New Social Contract that would marry economic growth and security through new and sustainable roles and responsibilities for government, employers, and individuals. Government would provide two levels of protection – basic economic security (that assumes the overhaul and resulting long-term viability of Social Security, Medicare, and Medicaid – no mean feat) and "smarter" regulations and "better designed incentives," without necessarily involving expensive new programs. I wonder. Also, employers would be required to serve as conduits for healthcare and retirement plans, but would no longer necessarily be the primary sponsors, and individuals would take more responsibility for supplementing the basic level of protection provided by the government. I fail to see how this approach will greatly alter the underlying dynamics of the current system, but given the credibility of Brookings, it will no doubt get a full hearing.

Another approach is from Stuart Butler of the Heritage Foundation, and it has the attractive distinction of taking full account of the organic nature of American society, which in no way mirrors that of European tastes for single-payer, statist systems that fail to recognize American pluralism and individualism and the fact that the primary American social relationship is not between individuals and their government.

DeTocqueville long ago recognized that the distinctive nature of American society is in its voluntary associations and social networks – churches, unions, community groups, etc. – that provide buffers between individuals and their government. It is these organic associations that Butler believes should be the conduit for the transformation to a new distinctly American social contract. He would combine this concept with state insurance exchanges allowing portability, reform of tax treatment of healthcare insurance, and phasing employers out of healthcare insurance sponsorship. His is no purely libertarian idea and he too recognizes that the new contract must have a foundational element of basic security to cover the new risk profile. However, according to Butler, the last thing we need is to get all of the smartest people in a room in Washington to build the new system.

All of these plans, proposals, and debates are on a course to collision in November 2008, and all of them assume that there is enough enlightened leadership abroad in the land to finally come to terms with the broken social contract in the first place – which, together with the prosecution of World War IV, is another reason that I believe this will prove to be the most significant national election since 1932.

Free Trade Conundrum

February 9, 2008

"Trade is a real test of leadership since its benefits are often less obvious than its downsides." – David Ranson, H. C. Wainwright Economics, Inc. in *The Wall Street Journal*, 2/6/08.

How true, and how difficult for the Republican Party, which, at least at the Presidential level, has been the leading free trade party for many decades, while the Democratic Party has essentially become officially anti-free trade. But the conundrum and the difficulty is manifest in Republican and free-trader Congressman Kevin Brady's observation that the free trade issue makes for a lot of temptation to be a populist. No problem for Mike Huckabee, who won the endorsement of the machinists union with such statements as "I'm running for President because I don't want people who have worked loyally for a company for 20 or 30 years to walk in one morning and be handed a pink slip and told 'I'm sorry, but everything you've spent your life working for is no longer here.'" This brand of populism plays well with protectionists, but that won't keep America in world trade leadership.

Recent polls show that Americans are trending against free trade – 46 percent of adults think free trade agreements hurt the U.S., 16 points more than in 1999, and 59 percent of Republican primary voters said that free trade has been bad for America. Several years ago, Sen. Charles Schumer was traveling around with economist Paul Craig Roberts, not exactly a raving liberal, making the case that David Ricardo's centuries old and widely held concept of comparative advantage among nations is no longer viable, because the factors of production that were historically relatively fixed in place are now those such as technology, ideas, and capital that can be moved with a computer click. What do we do about all of this, or more particularly, what does government do about it?

First, as always, do no harm. And one of the ways to avoid harm is to take the issue seriously, because if the debate is between those who dismiss the problem and those who have a bad solution, the bad solution folks will win. And simply to recite old maxims will not do it. We must have a serious and substantive debate about how to deal with the realities of globalization on the ground with real people – people who don't have the necessary skills for adaptation or the money or the mobility for retraining and relocation. And incidentally, this should include a debate on the continuing viability of the doctrine of comparative advantage.

Paul Samuelson, probably the leading free trade enthusiast in the economics profession, notes that Ricardo's theory, fully implemented, implies that worldwide income per capita increases enough so that the winners will more than offset the losers, but he is concerned that wealthy countries like the U.S. may be among the losers, while India and China will be the big winners. And he is probably correct in terms of traditional value-added measures, but America's value-added comparative advantage is more about ideas and innovation than things. Which is my opening to say that it will be the transformation of K-12 education in this country (or our failure to drastically transform it) that will have more impact on our success in dealing with the challenges of free trade than any other factor.

There are plenty of ideas afloat. All the Presidential candidates have issued their detailed approaches. And like most policy proposals they interconnect with other policy issues, like farm subsidies and labor and environmental regulations, for example. So, look closely and let the debate rage on.

An Idea Whose Time Has Long Passed

August 4, 2008

"It is hard in this world to do well. It is hard to do good. When I hear a claim that an institution is going to do both, I reach for my wallet. You should too." – Former Treasury Secretary Lawrence Summers, in "Notable & Quotable," *The Wall Street Journal.*

Former Treasury Secretary Summers reminds us of the folly of good intentions gone overboard without market discipline. First, the question: How can the virtuous American objective of widespread home ownership be best supported and the most adequate financing be assured? Answer: With creative capitalism, by chartering private companies as government sponsored enterprises with the mission of promoting home ownership. Give them the credibility of a public/private partnership, with a social responsibility objective for financing access to "affordable housing" balanced with the profit motive, and make it tacitly clear that the government stands behind their capital market creativity so that they have unfettered access to the markets at subsidized rates. And incidentally, allow the management of these companies unlimited lobby budgets and access to government policy makers.

If this reads like an invitation to witness a case study in terminal moral hazard facilitated by political cronyism, you're describing the outcome of the Great Society brainstorm for the restructure of Fannie Mae and the subsequent chartering of Freddie Mac. It took about 40 years for all of these good intentions to play out into the unintended consequences resulting in the inevitable bailout approved last month by Congress, but anyone with minimal insight should have foreseen the eventual outcome.

In fact, let's give some credit where it's due for the insightful and tireless reporting and editorial coverage of this looming disaster by *The Wall Street Journal* over the past six years. For a recap of this coverage and its chronology, *WSJ* Editor Paul Gigot has recently written a great article, noteworthy as much for its restraint in condemnation of the cabal of cronies who collaborated in responsibility, protection, and apologies for the perpetrators and the debacle they created, and who were so critical of his publication for calling them out. The culpability ranges across the spectrum of fellow travelers on Wall Street, in Congress, and in the mainstream media, as Gigot characterizes this crowd, "…journalists on the left, pseudo-capitalists on Wall Street, liberal Democrats and country club Republicans."

This history and this bailout are outrageous and scandalous, reflective of crony capitalism at least as bad as anything that has been witnessed in Russia since the fall of the Soviet Union, and I am disappointed that President Bush didn't veto the bailout bill, as futile a gesture as that would have been. But it will be compounded if we don't put a permanent end to these kinds of monstrosities. These two entities should be placed into receivership under the jurisdiction of a trustee beyond reproach, with authority to fully privatize them, issue a preferred security to the government so that the taxpayers are provided some possibility of recouping their "investment," and wean them off the public subsidy on a definitive timetable not longer than five years – no more government line of credit, no more implied guaranty of liabilities by either the Federal Reserve or Treasury. And then we should kill this idea of creative capitalism through government sponsored private entity forever.

Stop the Presses

October 10, 2008

Whatever the backlog of subjects I had in mind for this issue, they have been blown away by events that have overwhelmed even what is shaping up as a watershed presidential campaign. In fact, aside from their respective economic-policy strategies if elected, the two presidential nominees are pretty irrelevant to the urgency of the crisis, and both of them illustrated why this is so in their second debate.

We are certainly living through the most significant financial crisis of the past 20 years, and it will no doubt ultimately rank among the most significant in U.S. history, for several reasons: 1) since the beginning of the worldwide securitization of financial assets and the derivative segmentation of risk made possible by the warp speed development of computing technology over the past 25 years, this is the first true stress test of the management of this revolutionary risk segmentation and diffusion; 2) it comes at a time when the globalization of trade and employment and the challenges to the long-held principle of comparative advantage have given rise to worldwide anxiety about employment security and the related economic security of nation-states; and 3) because of the convergence of these forces with the current political trends, particularly in the U.S., there is the very real threat that the political response to the present crisis will result in regulatory overreach in the financial markets and other measures that will be destructive to capital formation, enterprise, and economic growth.

Many observers have blamed the financial market deregulation of the 1980s and 1990s and the failure of regulation for the crisis in the first place, but I believe that there is much more to the real story. In fact, the market, which always leads and never lags public policy, had already run circles around the antiquated 1930s financial markets regulatory system by the time the Glass-Steagall Act (which prohibited the combination of commercial and investment banking) was repealed in 1999. This was a fait accompli on the ground in the market for at least 20 years before it was ratified.

Not that I am exonerating the investment bankers or the regulators. In fact, as I wrote in the wake of the Enron meltdown in early 2002, the investment banking industry has been headed in the wrong direction since the major firms began offering their shares publicly a couple of decades ago. The concept of privately owned, self-regulated, general partnership governance of these firms served us well. As unlikely as this may be, we would probably greatly benefit by a return to the days when investment banking, accounting, and commercial banking were conducted based on the concept of the "trustee" by partners with full liability and a significant personal financial stake in their stewardship.

The late Walter Wriston, former Citicorp Chairman, had the new realities pegged in his book, *Twilight of Sovereignty*, in 1991 when he noted that the days when nation-states can control economic events are numbered and that technology has produced a new "gold standard" in the form of the then 200,000 computers (now, many multiples of that number) run by money managers worldwide who never sleep and who "vote" on public policy and discount its implications often before the policy pronouncements by politicians. And this was before the explosion of the Internet! Of course, the key is full and complete transparency of information, and that is what has obviously been left behind in the blinding speed of the effect of Moore's Law on computer capabilities to drive market innovation. And despite the diminished ability of governments to control events, they continue to have a way of pursuing micromanagement with unintended consequences.

The overindulgence in the subprime mortgage market of the past several years shouldn't have been much of a surprise after 30 years of misguided social policies in pursuit of "affordable housing," manifest in the Community Reinvestment Act and its mandated affirmative action lending practices in low socio-economic markets, compounded by the well-documented explosive growth of Freddie Mac and Fannie Mae that was directly tied to cronyism in the various Congressional relationships, the financing of which was made possible by Federal Reserve monetary policy that produced significant misallocations of resources to this high risk market. This crisis has many parents, but the real culpability should not be difficult to identify.

This too shall pass. We won't know where the bottom is until *private* capital begins to move back into the markets in critical mass. Sooner or later, this will happen. But with the change of political regimes in January 2009, I worry less about where the market bottom might be than about the movement toward the socialization of risk indicated by the tendency to cure the problem with massive asset acquisitions by the government and the resulting increase in moral hazard, along with regulatory overreach, the combination of which would have serious long-term detrimental consequences for capital formation and our competitive position in the world. We already have a Sarbanes-Oxley bill, courtesy of Enron, that is a severe overreaction and has already significantly damaged the competitiveness of U.S. capital markets; we don't need a Sarbox II for the financial institutions, nor do we need government ownership of these institutions without a definitive exit strategy and unemployment for those CEOs whose firms accept the infusions. The "too big to fail" policy also should be revisited. Someone recently said that if an institution is too big to fail, then it's too big, and I agree. We also could use some fiscal policy response, and I don't have in mind a so-called stimulus package of tax rebates, but rather a significant cut in the tax rates on capital formation, i.e., capital gains tax and the onerous corporate income tax. Good luck on that with a Democratic Congress.

So, get ready in January – at a minimum, we are certainly in for much more government oversight and intrusion, at least until the governance and self-regulatory functions catch up with the markets, and right now they are not even closing the gap.

Looming Disaster II

February 8, 2009

Last month I wrote of the disaster looming in the form of 1970's style "stagflation," as a result of a continuation of the misguided Federal Reserve monetary policy of the past five years that has disregarded its first priority – the protection and stability of the value of the dollar. Now for the second leg of the looming disaster, one that is being formulated as I write by the "world's greatest deliberative body," the U.S. Senate, as it debates the economic stimulus plan written and advanced by the left wing of the majority party and inspired and enabled by the popularity of our new President.

Former George Bush aide Pete Wehner and Congressman Paul Ryan couldn't have made it clearer for us in a recent op/ed: "We need to understand this new moment… This will reshape, in deep and enduring ways, our nation's historic sensibilities. It will lead here, as it has elsewhere, to passivity and dependence on the state. Such habits, once acquired, are hard to shake."

We were given advance notice of these transforming intentions by President Obama's Chief of Staff, Rahm Emanuel, when he said quite matter-of-factly, "You never want a serious crisis to go to waste. And what I mean by that is an opportunity to do things you think you could not do before." This is about as transparent as one can be.

In his inaugural address, President Obama was quick to depart from Ronald Reagan "government is the problem" and even Bill Clinton "the era of big government is over" with his assertion that "The question we ask today is not whether government is too big or too small, but whether it works." He ignores one very big problem – government is never benign. At some level, whether successful in its immediate objectives or not, it brings unintended consequences and becomes tyrannical in terms of its coercive nature and its tendency to create dependency and sloth. Such is the new moment that Messrs. Wehner and Ryan admonish us to understand.

Andrew Gelman of Columbia University is further instructive on this point in outlining the futility of political direction of a complex organic economy: "The law of unintended consequences is what happens when a simple system tries to regulate a complex system. The political system is simple. It operates with limited information (rational ignorance), short time horizons, low feedback, and poor and misguided incentives. Society in contrast is a complex, evolving, high-feedback, incentive-driven system. When a simple system tries to regulate a complex system you often get unintended consequences."

This is exactly what will happen with the plan currently under debate. An additional problem with this one, however, is that some of the worst consequences of the plan will not have been unintended by the perpetrators.

Recently, I revisited the 1978 classic, *The Way the World Works*, by the late Jude Wanniski. For those of you too young to remember, Wanniski's work followed on that of Art Laffer and Robert Mundell in fully developing the theories of Jean-Baptiste Say into the supply-side economics that were the platform for the Reagan Revolution of the 1980s and the Bush economic recovery of the mid-2000s, the tax policies that are consistently dismissed by the left, as recently as this week by President Obama, as the "failed policies that got us here." In response, we should forcefully remind these critics, as well as some who should naturally be more supportive of these principles, that supply-side fiscal policy, when combined with monetary policy that protects the value of the dollar, has worked every time it has been properly implemented because it relies on human nature and the power of marginal incentives to alter the functioning of the complex market systems that Gelman describes.

This is the only way out of this crisis of confidence. I don't deny that the resources of government will be necessary to enable the recovery, particularly in shoring up the financial system. But the organizing principle should be, "do no harm." And more government intervention and regulatory oversight is not and has never been the answer to such crises, nor is more Keynesian-style spending on make-work projects, nor targeted tax "rebates" to non-taxpayers. But Obama will get his stimulus bill in one form or another, because "they won" and the great "moderates" we all admire will provide the deciding votes to win the day, but it will be a day that portends much worse news down the road, because global markets will not stand still while we experiment with Eurosocialism, American-style. There will be a larger price to pay later. Remember to understand this new moment.

Protectionism Rears Its Ugly Head

March 5, 2009

One of the most insidious consequences of the worldwide recession, particularly if it persists for an extended period, will be the growing tendency toward "economic nationalism," or, to put it more bluntly, the protection of markets, industries, and jobs by home countries who feel threatened by free trade in a shrinking economy. It's a natural emotion, and one fanned by populist demagogues to their political benefit and often the detriment of their people. Of course, the worst example of this phenomenon was during the Great Depression, where the "beggar thy neighbor" trade policies spawned by the disastrous Smoot-Hawley Tariff Bill in the U.S. is generally considered to have greatly deepened and prolonged the worldwide slump.

In *A Splendid Exchange: How Trade Shaped the World*, a great book that I reviewed last year, author William J. Bernstein takes a slightly different view of the impact of Smoot-Hawley, but one that is instructive in any case. He says that, contrary to common belief, the bill did not significantly decrease overall trade flows, it probably resulted in only a one-to-two percent decrease in world gross domestic product, protectionism was already a big problem even before its adoption, and that it merely represented the peak of world protectionist attitudes. Notwithstanding that somewhat different take, he acknowledges the really significant long term damage done by the bill and the attitudes that it represented. Its most devastating impact in his opinion was the damage done to the intangibles of trade: the expansion of consumption beyond domestic goods, commerce with and living among foreigners, and understanding their motives and concerns. He believes that these damages had a significant bearing on the subsequent growth of economic nationalism and the run up to World War II.

This point is worthy of further debate at another time, but I submit that it has some relevance to our current situation. If we encourage and/or pursue the growth of the attitudes represented by economic nationalism, it will have a huge impact on our interests, but will have even a greater negative impact on those developing nations who desperately need open access to world markets for their often limited competitive products. In fact, according to Bjorn Lomborg of the Copenhagen Consensus Center, the completion of the stalled Doha Round of free trade negotiations, now in their eighth year, would represent the biggest global stimulus package that we could otherwise design, producing $120 billion per year in direct gains by 2015, $17 billion of it going to the poorest countries.

Conversely, if we continue to stall these talks and block further progress in liberalizing trade with notions like "Buy American" provisions and unrealistic labor and environmental restrictions, it will not only damage our interests, but serve to alienate our potential partners and provide ammunition for the demagogues who prey on the emotions fired by economic nationalism.

The Return of Industrial Policy

January 1, 2010

We just thought we had buried forever with the Carter presidency the notion of "industrial policy," a kind of Japanese MITI-like concept of government direction of major elements of the economy, with various aspects of "investment" in favored industries and the selection of winners to receive subsidies and targeted tax incentives. Well, guess again. The concept is not only resurrected, it is even more grandiose than could have ever been imagined by Carter's economic team. Of course, its centerpiece will be ObamaCare in whatever form it is finally adopted, but that's only the big tipping point, for to follow will be a long list of attempted intrusions into markets and private contract relationships that should keep the Supreme Court busy for many years to come. And in the face of all this, at his recent jobs summit Obama asked a room full of CEOs, "I want to hear from you, what is holding back our business investment?" Can he really be serious? And the answer is that this is what passes for economic development thinking in an administration that has no idea how jobs are created, how capital is formed, and how it is nurtured, because no one in a key policy role has ever done any of these things. How much of this can we stand? Rich Karlgaard makes the insightful point that the salvation of the 1970s was entrepreneurship and innovation, featuring many startups that are driving job growth to this day. And it's happening again. The difference is that much of it is happening offshore, and the worry is that with the anti-capital policies now being initiated in Washington, the U.S. will miss the current entrepreneurial boom.

Fixing the Global Finance System

April 2, 2010

Every pundit, regardless of their qualifications, has an opinion on who is responsible for the worldwide financial meltdown of 2008 and how to fix the problem. The majority of these fixes involve two elements – more government regulation and the early detection and prevention of "systemic risk." Each of these assume that there exists a mechanism by which systemic risk can be evaluated by public agencies and that systemic imbalances and overloads can be detected in advance. This is a dream world.

In the recent review of the book *The Big Short* by Michael Lewis, Brian Carney writes: "Under proposals currently moving through Congress, our financial regulators are supposed to sit down together to identify and head off asset bubbles before they pose a risk to the system. But a bubble becomes a systemic risk only because it is not recognized as such… it is the rare few who grasp what is truly happening when it is still possible to do something about it."

This is the problem with economics as science, of which I have been skeptical since my first encounter with college freshman economics almost 50 years ago. It's about time we came full circle to this realization that was obvious to the "economists" of the 18th century.

Adam Smith told us that his economic theories were not science, but moral philosophy, and his foundational writing was manifest in *The Theory of Moral Sentiments* at least as much as in *The Wealth of Nations*. Likewise, other foundational economic theorists, such as Friedrich von Hayek. Even John Maynard Keynes recognized the moral implications of economic theory. It was the progressives who were convinced that the laws of science could be easily applied to the social issues, beginning with Herbert Croly, John Dewey, Woodrow Wilson, et al, and extending to the 1960's intellectuals who espoused such notions as "if we can go to the moon, we can cure poverty."

The same mentality applies to the static scoring of tax rate cuts and the related resistance to the human behavioral factors embedded in the more accurate dynamic scoring of incentives to investment and growth that result from these cuts. When will we get an apology from the crowd that was so convinced of economic rationality that it could build sophisticated behavioral models with total disregard of the dynamics of human nature? The short answer is never and, in fact, what we'll get is more of the same.

A Few More Thoughts on Financial Regulation

May 4, 2010

As the Dodd-Frank financial regulation bill nears a vote in the U.S. Senate, it is difficult to fully understand its mission. Supposedly, we are responding to the "big culprit" in the recent meltdown, which has been identified as the deregulation of the financial markets over the past 30 years or so, in spite of the fact that it was the U.S. mortgage market, the most heavily regulated element of the system, that created most of the problems. I don't see anything in this bill that will address the moral hazard of "too big to fail;" to the contrary, if the $50 billion bailout fund remains, this hazard will be institutionalized. There is nothing in the bill that touches Freddie Mac and Fannie Mae, the biggest boondoggles in the entire meltdown scene, which continue to receive massive taxpayer subsidies of negative cash flow, continue to represent approximately one-half of the nation's mortgage market, continue as a huge dispenser of political patronage, and continue as the largest purveyor of "affordable housing" at any cost, the mission that got us where we are today.

I do see in the bill aspects of another version of the "search for cosmic justice" in the form of seeking social utility for derivatives, the so-called "side bets" that many believe serve no useful function. In spite of some abuses, it is a mystery to me how reasonable observers see no useful function in the market allocation of risk to those who choose to assume it at their own peril and in particular when this mechanism, properly understood, is an integral part of the ability of well-informed investors in the market to correct pricing imbalances and performs a valuable service in recognizing and sending signals on overpriced assets. If we hadn't had a John Paulson, we would have needed one, and it would have been even better if someone had shorted Fannie and Freddie before they got completely out of control.

There remains the question of failing firms and, having had considerable first-hand experience here, I favor the resolution process offered by the FDIC for failing banks, including the approach that avoids complete liquidation but wipes out shareholder equity and dismisses management, without political judgments based on which firms constitute "systemic risk" and are too big to fail.

Six months before the free fall of September 2008, I used the following quote from Allan H. Metzler of Carnegie Mellon University: "If the government underwrites all the risks, call it socialism. If it underwrites only the failures, call it foolishness." These sentiments are clearly applicable today and we are dangerously close to both outcomes with the legislation in its current form.

Common Sense Wins Every Time

July 4, 2010

"It ain't what you don't know that gets you into trouble. It's what you know for sure that just ain't so." – Mark Twain.

Nobel economist Paul Krugman is the poster boy for Twain's quote, but it runs in the ideological family as well. Krugman, of course, is a primary leader of the steady drumbeat for more government stimulus spending and regularly laments that the current problem with the economic recovery is not enough spending, to wit: "Both text-book economics and experience say that slashing spending when you're still suffering from high unemployment is a really bad idea." Wrong on both sources, of course, and history is replete with examples, which I will spare you. But it was interesting to note the recent reminder of a survey conducted by Zogby International in 2008 which tracked the relationship between economic enlightenment and a number of variables, including presidential vote, party affiliation, race or ethnic group, religious participation, union membership, household income, gender, and marital status, among others. The eight survey questions were those whose answers have long been settled by economic research and empirical results, such as: True or False – "restrictions on housing development make housing less affordable," and "mandatory licensing of professional services increases the prices of those services." The results were stunning. Using six self-selected classifications along the political ideological spectrum, from very conservative to progressive/very liberal, the number of incorrect answers from the three classifications on the left side ranged from three to six times the number from the three classifications on the right. Clearly the left has a problem with calibrating sound economic thinking with predetermined sensibilities (I've always wondered who reads Krugman's stuff). One other result was also instructive – there was no correlation between economic enlightenment and college attendance. Obviously, common sense makes a big difference, but common sense tells us that without a survey, right?

A New Legacy, If We Can Handle It

August 6, 2010

David Brooks recently outlined his view of competing visions of economic growth and vitality. He named them the Moon Shot Approach and the Unleash America Approach, the former being of the "industrial policy" persuasion, with government induced and directed enabling of economic development through infrastructure, tax credits, and subsidies, and the latter being more a project driven by American entrepreneurial spirit as outlined by Arthur C. Brooks in his book, *The Battle: How the Fight Between Free Enterprise and Big Government Will Shape America's Future*. Surely it will surprise none of my regular readers that I strongly favor the latter approach, and no one currently in a meaningful policy-making position in public life has articulated this approach better than Rep. Paul Ryan of Wisconsin. Those who believe that there are no alternative ideas being offered by Republicans should read at least the executive summary of Ryan's *Roadmap for America's Future*, initially introduced in 2008 and updated earlier this year to reflect new realities.

The three key objectives of the plan are: 1) providing health and retirement security, 2) lifting the debt burden, and 3) promoting American job creation and competitiveness. Its main components are healthcare, Medicare, Social Security, tax reform, and job training, and the measures recommended are comprehensive, aggressive, transformative, and fact and data-driven. Each provision is represented by solid proposals and legislation vetted by the Congressional Budget Office. The beauty of it is that it represents a new vision for the role of government, a new legacy, if you will, one that we thought we were building in 1980 and 1994 before the wheels fell off.

The plan represents transformative leadership in the finest sense, but surprisingly, as reported recently by Bill Murchison in *Townhall,* many Republicans are avoiding it like the plague, believing a plan offering such a drastic change in the role of government in people's lives to be politically risky and dangerous for electoral longevity. Evidently, many of Ryan's colleagues wish that he would just "cool it" on all the aggressive reform talk. To these people, friend or foe, I say: you are not the solution; in fact, you are the problem. If you are not willing to follow such leadership, not willing to pursue meaningful transformational reforms, then don't continue to seek office, step aside and, in particular, don't seek a governing majority. You have already blown it too many times.

Very Troubling Threats

October 4, 2010

Recently, I had the opportunity to participate as a panelist in a conference sponsored by the Texas Lyceum Association to explore the "problems, issues, challenges, ventures, and goals that the state of Texas should be pursuing in the public sphere." In a couple of hours, five of us and a moderator conducted a fairly spirited dialogue on our perspectives on the top priorities in this context. Of course, to no surprise, public education was at the top of everyone's list, and in second place was a variety of lesser items. But here I want to address one area that was not fully laid out that I poorly attempted to introduce late in the session, one that represents a serious threat to our prosperity, and one that is largely external, at least in the sense in which Texas policy-makers have very limited control over its impact on the state.

The threat I have in mind is the growing negative attitude toward free and open trade and the protectionist leanings that have become much too evident across the broad spectrum of public opinion. Here are some indicators: In a new *Wall Street Journal*/NBC poll, 53 percent said that free trade agreements have hurt the U.S., up from 46 percent in 2007 and 32 percent in 1999. Further, 86 percent named outsourcing as the major cause of the country's continuing economic distress, and this sentiment was consistent across party lines, job classification (professional and blue collar), and income levels. No other factor was even close in the poll, and this outcome was strongest among managers and professionals at 95 percent! Even more instructive, the "Pledge to America" recently unveiled by House Republicans, supposedly the party of free trade, doesn't even mention the subject, and in the *WSJ* poll 61 percent of those who self-identify as Tea Party members said that trade agreements have hurt the U.S.

Given these numbers and the attitudes they reflect, there is little wonder why trade agreements with Korea, Columbia, and Panama are stalled and a dispute with Mexico over trucking deregulation remains unresolved. Nor is it surprising that the Democrats in both houses have proposed significant protectionist legislation – in the Senate a bill to use tax policy to penalize companies that outsource jobs and in the House a bill passed entitled the Currency Reform for Fair Trade Act that would mandate consideration of a foreign country's currency interventions in determining unfair trade practices, a measure clearly targeting China. The fate of these proposals await the return of Congress in the lame duck session after election day, but both have bipartisan support, the message in them is clear and dangerous, and the atmosphere smacks of the days of the Smoot-Hawley tariff debacle of the early 1930s.

Some of this hostility can be attributed to the very slow economic recovery and much of it is prompted by the fact that corporate America is sitting on the largest cash horde in history and is reluctant to invest in new ventures, new facilities, and the job creation that follows. Of course this reluctance and underlying uncertainty is understandable, but why is this the case? Again, no surprises, and several reasons readily come to mind:

- Our government pursues fiscal policy, including tax, spending, and regulatory policies, that is destructive to capital and drives it offshore where it is often treated much better.
- We have pursued our monetary policy as though America is alone in the world and has no responsibility as the steward of the world's reserve currency, which must have stability in value above all other considerations.
- In trade policy, we seem to have forgotten that, despite those economists who believe it has been repealed, the Law of Comparative Advantage is still alive and well and that the American comparative advantage is the creativity, innovation, and skills of its people.
- Far too many in our education establishment are slow to recognize that this historic advantage is slipping away because of our interminable delay in drastically transforming our public education system and moving it into the 21st century.
- In spite of the lessons of recent economic history, neither political party seems to remember that economic growth trumps austerity-only as the best cure for economic distress and that supply side economic policies are the best drivers of growth

Let's hope these leading indicators are nothing more than election year temper tantrums, but if the election results do not produce a significant change in leadership and direction, we are in big trouble, and Texas, in spite of its clear advantages in people, policy, and spirit, cannot fully escape the threat.

Restoring Economic Growth

November 7, 2010

Ideas abound on what initiatives should be pursued to restore American economic prosperity. A significant by-product of the election is that a much broader range of options will be heard and hopefully, the discrediting of sound fiscal policies that has dominated the dialogue will cease and desist. Contrary to popular wisdom and the Democratic spin machine, the Republicans have rolled out a number of great ideas. Unfortunately, the one that received the most media attention, the "Pledge to America," wasn't one of them. It included a few good items, like the repeal of ObamaCare, no tax increases, hiring freezes, and spending rollbacks, but according to analysis by the American Enterprise Institute, the collective impact of the Pledge on overall spending and the deficit are negligible at best, and it makes no fundamental changes in entitlement spending or earmarks. No wonder it wasn't much of a factor in the recent elections.

As I have previously noted, the new American culture war as identified by American Enterprise Institute President, Arthur C. Brooks, will be a major battle between free enterprise and big government, read "social democracy," as the central engine of prosperity. This election has not settled that issue; it will require at least another Presidential election and the validation of the Republican majority in the House to even begin to resolve it.

But the most important aspect of this battle must begin now, and that is to put a halt to the following notions: 1) that the so-called "industrial policy" of government "investment" that was badly discredited in the 1970s has any relevance; 2) that the Reagan supply-side policies of the 1980s and the Bush tax cuts were failures; 3) that the problem that created the recent financial meltdown was under-regulation of the markets; 4) that free trade is job-destructive and that protectionist policies are the antidote; and 5) that monetary policy that ignores America's role in the stewardship of the world's reserve currency and the preservation and stability of the value of the dollar can be successful. The ideological elements of these issues must be urgently, directly, and publicly addressed if we have any hope of a recovery to meaningful economic growth. The question is, who will frame and lead the debate? And don't make the mistake of assuming that these issues break along party lines; this is not

Democrat vs. Republican, and both share in the mistakes that have moved us closer to European-style democratic socialism, not to mention the business leaders who have been complicit along the way in their rent-seeking.

In a poll conducted last April, the Rasmussen firm found that only 53 percent of Americans agreed with the proposition that capitalism was better than socialism. I am aware of the pitfalls of such polls, but we shouldn't take any comfort in this data point, nor in the obvious turn of the electorate over the past several months toward fiscal conservatism. We have a lot of work to do, and much of it involves educating opinion leadership.

Fannie and Freddie Must Go

January 3, 2011

There already is disappointing drift from Republican Congressional leadership that the privatization of Fannie Mae and Freddie Mac must be delayed or at least phased in over a longer period because of the anticipated impact on available housing finance that would result from a precipitous removal of what is, in effect, a government-subsidized floor on housing prices. Two truths emerge here: one is that, yes, government subsidies to these entities are artificially propping up housing prices, at a cost to taxpayers, so far, of $134 billion, and two, these same props are postponing the market clearance of the toxic mortgage markets and their underlying collateral and thereby greatly delaying the resolution of the problem and a return to a healthy housing market. This facade has been in place for more than three years, well known to all knowledgeable observers, including the sponsors of the new financial industry regulatory overhaul bill, which did nothing to address this problem in the slightest. There is no doubt that there will be an additional big hit to housing values when this day of reckoning comes (some observers predict as much as 20 percent), but the sooner we take it and allow the market to clear, whatever the pain, the sooner this debacle will be behind us, the uncertainty of the overhang reduced, and real recovery can proceed.

In the End, a Moral Issue

January 4, 2011

On at least a couple of occasions, I have mentioned *The Battle*, a book by Arthur C. Brooks of the American Enterprise Institute, which defines a fast-approaching pivotal moment in the form of a question that we must answer: Does America recover its commitment to free enterprise and ordered liberty or does it continue to drift toward

European-style welfare statism? This he believes is the real culture war, and I believe that he is in many respects correct, primarily because the underlying question is in essence, a moral issue. In fact, we are in constant need of reminding ourselves that Adam Smith, the traditional godfather of capitalism, was not really an economist; he was a moral philosopher and his *Theory of Moral Sentiments* is much more instructive of the underpinnings of the capitalist system than his more widely acclaimed *Wealth of Nations.*

In a recent essay in *National Affairs*, Yuval Levin points out that the two key moral features of Smith's political economy – its democratic or popular character and its disciplining effect – have been under assault in our time: the first by a growing collusion between government and large corporations, and the second by a welfare state that has expanded far beyond its needs. And the case for capitalism is a case against these two trends against the morality of the system.

So, back to the issue raised by Brooks. Can we rise above the questions involving the functionality of government and get to the underlying moral questions suggested by Levin? For it seems that the liberal vs. conservative battle has boiled down to a debate about which ideology is served by government, rather than the classic opposition between big and limited government, which is the moral debate we should be having. As former Congressman Bill Archer once asked me, "would you rather balance the budget at 40 percent of GDP or 20 percent?" This is critical, for the impact on the underlying values that we subsidize with larger government is destructive in ways that Adam Smith understood very well. Business leadership is the key. Will corporate leaders be in the forefront of this effort of moral restoration, or will they be largely rent-seekers from government?

Sweden or Greece?

August 5, 2011

I won't waste the time and space to dignify the recent deal reached by Congress and the President on the "debt ceiling crisis." Suffice to say, it can be characterized as too little, too late, not serious. But let's move on, because nothing will be settled until after the November 2012 referendum on this regime.

Arthur Brooks of the American Enterprise Institute has the issue framed well: First, it's not a party fight; it's about the 50-year trend in the role of government. Second, as I have said repeatedly, it's not an economic fight, it's a moral one. Third, even with regime change, it's not a fight that anyone can win in the 15 months until the presidential election; it will require at least 10 years of hard work. And in the end, it may very well be that there are only two possible scenarios – the Swedish model, where so few are producing the revenue necessary to support the rest that we stabilize at very high taxation and a very expensive welfare state, or the Greek model, where the welfare state collapses and we get long-term austerity financed by the productive economies of the world at very high interest rates (and, as Margaret Thatcher warned us, "the problem with socialism is that eventually, you run out of other people's money"). Frankly folks, if we want other choices, we need different leaders.

Meanwhile, I continue to wonder why we are so unwilling to frame this crisis in moral terms. Why can't we understand that the debt burden is a symptom of our decline, not the cause? Why can't we confront the socialist impulse with a reasoned response that refutes its premises in economic terms that are supported by moral instincts? Examples: incentives for economic growth are important not just to build individual wealth, but to expand opportunity for all, and lower tax rates are the correct policy not to further enrich the wealthy, but to properly reward merit and economic growth, which results in increased tax revenue. In short, this debate is not about economic efficiency, it's about the moral issues of freedom and opportunity. Again, it's not just a math problem. Free market principles have lost their moral voice and it seems that the left has commandeered the language of morality, which would be a strange scenario for our founders, who had no problem with the moral language necessary to advance public policy.

I recently came across the following passage from a short 1980 essay by Irving Kristol in *The Public Interest*, which captures this sentiment as well as anything I have seen:

Economic theory lives on... because of that bedrock of truths about the human condition: 1) the overwhelming majority of men and women are naturally and incorrigibly interested in improving their material conditions; 2) efforts to repress this natural desire lead only to coercive and impoverished politics; 3) when this natural desire is given sufficient latitude so that commercial transactions are not discouraged, economic growth takes place; 4) as a result of such growth, everyone does eventually indeed improve his condition, however unequally in extent or time; 5) such economic growth results in a huge expansion of the property-owning middle classes – a necessary (though not sufficient) condition for a liberal society in which individual rights are respected. This is not all we need to know, but it is what we do know, and it is surely not asking too much of economic theory that in its passion for sophisticated methodology it not leave this knowledge behind.

The Unraveling of the Social Contract

February 4, 2013

In December, the Michigan legislature passed and its Governor signed a right-to-work law. If there was ever a turning point in the demise of the post-World War II social contract, this is certainly it. Of all places, the citadel of union strength and solidarity and the home of the United Automobile Workers becomes the 24th right to work state and sounded the death knell for the closed shop and the requirement for a worker to pay union dues to work. This event, following the federal appeals court validation of Wisconsin's public union reforms, including limits on collective bargaining, is convincing evidence that the slow, but inevitable dismantling of the 70-year social contract among big labor, big corporations, and big government is proceeding apace.

Both of these states and their workers should welcome this transition. According to the West Michigan Policy Forum, of the 10 states with the highest rates of personal income growth, eight are right-to-work states, and between 2000 and 2010, five million people moved from compulsory union states to right to work states. It is clear that, contrary to union dogma, right to work is empowering of workers.

Globalization of markets is the culprit, but globalization was and is inevitable, and the net benefits of free trade have been in evidence for at least a couple of centuries. The question is how do we deal with the new competitive environment. Fifty years ago the tickets to the American middle class were a high school diploma and a union card. No longer. Neither one of them work as well in a dynamic and globalized market for jobs.

Frankly, we don't yet have an answer for the social contract redesign and the resulting anxiety of so many Americans whose future is threatened by the transformation currently underway. And the reason we don't yet have the answer is because of the frustration in the reform of our public education system, which is mired in the antiquated delivery system of the late 19th and early 20th centuries and the syndrome described by George W. Bush as the "soft bigotry of low expectations." We are fast replacing middle-skilled jobs with higher-skilled jobs, but every one of the latter requires more rigorous education, and we simply are not preparing enough young people for these jobs.

There is an "expectations gap" here across the board in public education that must be rapidly closed if we are to have any hope of transitioning to the new social contract while being globally competitive and maintaining our standard of living.

The Middle-Class Revolution

July 5, 2013

Francis Fukuyama, author most prominently of the provocative 1992 book, *The End of History and the Last Man*, has written an intriguing essay in *The Wall Street Journal* in which he argues that today's political turmoil all over the world – Brazil, Egypt, Turkey, the Arab Spring, China, and elsewhere – has a common theme: the failure of governments to meet the rising expectations of the newly prosperous and educated.

He writes that the global economic growth that has taken place since the 1970s has reshuffled the economic deck around the world – "The emerging middle classes in the so-called emerging market countries are larger, richer, better educated, and more technologically connected than ever before." This particularly has huge implications for China, which has developed a middle class now numbering in the hundreds of millions, and he wonders how and when these pressures will result in meaningful political change, not to mention how this will play out in terms of its impact on stability. He adds that this new middle class is not just a challenge for authoritarian regimes or new democracies and he emphasizes that no political leader should be lulled into thinking "it can't happen here."

It occurs to me that these frustrations and the inevitable transformation that will result will be messy and in many cases violent, as we are already witnessing. But I worry about the larger questions for the U.S., which are how we are positioned to defend our interests in a chaotic and violent world, and more significantly, how do we respond to the threats to our own domestic stability, competitiveness, and delivery of expectation when we are in decline in our provision of educational advancement, competency, and marketable skills in our elementary and secondary school system. We remain the indispensable nation and our leadership will be critical to world stability and prosperity, but it remains to be seen whether we will be up to the task.

The Jobs Doldrums Continue

August 4, 2013

This administration is entering uncharted territory in terms of its failure of policy for economic growth. In fact, most of what passes for policy, such as ObamaCare, the Dodd-Frank bill, and various regulatory initiatives has been destructive to job growth, while Federal Reserve monetary policy continues to misallocate and pervert the pricing of capital. Recent decreases in the unemployment rate are almost entirely the result of decreases in the labor participation rate, which is the lowest in 30 years. Moreover, more than half of recent job increases have been in the low paying restaurant and retail sectors, and approximately 20 percent of jobs added since the end of the recession in 2009 are part-time.

Much of the problem is structural, involving major deficiencies in elementary and secondary education, which are well-documented and highly resistant to reform and which have resulted in huge gaps in the skills necessary to fill the jobs that are available. But the most significant impediment is that this administration is unwilling to do what is clearly necessary to initiate growth. It's all about redistribution and President Obama's central focus on spreading the wealth as opposed to creating more of it.

No doubt, the Republican opposition needs to do a much better job in defining the alternatives, including a more robust defense of free market principles, and much of this argument is a moral one. For example, in the 2012 Presidential campaign, the Romney team did a terrible job of responding to attacks on Bain Capital and its business practices, which amounted to a full-scale assault on the underlying logic and morality of capitalism itself. This should be confronted directly and with confidence in the underlying principles, but it is more than an economic efficiency argument, it is a moral one, based on enterprise and opportunity for all, and should be argued on that basis.

Meanwhile, until a debate on this level is fully engaged, the Obama administration is well-suited for a "do nothing but repeal" Congress, because the alternative is to validate, entrench, and sustain a progressive agenda which is wrong for the country.

The Strategy of Envy

February 4, 2014

In his speech on economic inequality in early December 2013 and his recruitment of John Podesta as a senior advisor, President Obama signaled his strategy pivot to change the conversation from ObamaCare, Benghazi, the IRS, etc., to one of class warfare. I read the speech in its entirety and it is right out of Herbert Croly's progressive bible of 1909, *The Promise of American Life*, the foundational elements of which, thankfully, were rejected by the American people, in spite of the fact that many of its programs were adopted by the New Deal and the Great Society initiatives.

The sentiment of envy has never been a winning issue in America, because it is antithetical to the American character and ideal, but demagogues over the years have continued to pursue it, most out of desperation in search of a winning political formula. But this is the first President in my memory to resort to such a strategic focus as the organizing principle of a second term, along with the threat of using "a pen and a phone" to circumvent Congress and the Constitution in its implementation.

Here is what Alexis de Tocqueville had to say about inequality in 1835: "Democratic institutions awaken and foster a passion for equality which they can never entirely satisfy…(resulting in) a depraved taste for equality, which impels the weak to attempt to lower the powerful to their own level and reduces men to prefer equality in slavery to inequality with freedom." Obama would violate more than two centuries of American sensibilities on this tradeoff.

Moreover, much of the recent growth in inequality of incomes in the U.S. has been on Obama's watch and the result of his policies. The median income of the poorest 20 percent of Americans has declined in absolute terms from the height of the recession in 2009 to 2012. And the monetary policy of the Federal Reserve has distorted capital flows to the benefit of the upper income brackets. Further, now we have the nonpartisan Congressional Budget Office report that the medical insurance subsidies provided to low income brackets in ObamaCare will discourage work and result in job losses of 2.5 million over the next 10 years. Finally, unemployment rates are slowly declining, but primarily because of declines in workforce participation rates, and the current rate of seven percent, if adjusted for this participation decline since 2008, would be 11.3 percent!

So, the demagogic appeal to class warfare and envy is badly misguided and does a disservice to those most in need of policies that will promote economic growth. We know what those are, but we are unlikely to find any willingness to have a meaningful discussion on them with this administration, particularly since their turn to the hard left.

Leave U.S. Internet Oversight Alone

April 5, 2014

What could we be thinking? To abandon our role as sole overseer of the Internet domain name system is not only dumb, it's dangerous. Can you imagine how the power of sharing this oversight would almost certainly be used by China or Russia, just to pick a couple of our great friends for example? And transferring this role to the United Nations or some other world body is at least as bad an idea.

The responsibility we currently have with the Internet Corporation for Assigned Names and Numbers (Icann) is analogous to our role in enforcing freedom of the seas – we keep the sea lanes open for free trade just as we enforce an open Internet. It's part of our responsibility as the world's only superpower. No less an authority than Bill Clinton agrees. The abdication of our responsibilities here would seriously undermine the enormous capacity of this amazing technology, built under U.S. leadership, to enable and advance freedom of thought and markets throughout the world. Let many flowers keep blooming.

The Most Difficult Economic Challenge

September 10, 2015

The U.S. is now more than six years in a recovery from "the great recession," a recovery that has been the most anemic since World War II. Labor force participation is the lowest in 40 years, wage growth is slow to nonexistent, and the question of so-called income and wealth inequality is all the rage from the political left and populist demagogues. There are lots of good ideas about what to do about some of this, which await a change in the occupant of the White House, but no one seems to have an answer for the biggest challenge of all, which was highlighted in a study released last month by Georgetown University's Center on Education and the Workforce. The study tabulated job growth in 485 occupation groups sorted by the highest-, middle-, and lowest-earning thirds and measured which groups have had the most growth. The study found that the U.S. economy has added about one million more jobs since the end of the recession in occupations that rank in the top third and 800,000 more in the bottom third, while jobs in the middle third, including traditional blue-collar occupations, have collapsed, failing to recover the number of jobs lost during the recession.

Anthony Carnevale, an economist who led the Georgetown study, remarked that "It used to be recessions were pauses and people went back to the same job distribution, but that's not true anymore. A lot of the jobs in the rearview mirror aren't coming back." These results confirm widespread anecdotal evidence that the middle of the U.S. labor market is hollowing out. This is the backbone of the country, the core of the middle class.

There are no real surprises here for those who closely monitor these trends and plenty of conversation about the culprits, from the impact of economic globalization to the failure of the public education system to the over-emphasis on "college for everyone" to the rapid advances in "job-killing" technology to the lack of training for improved career transition and others. As one who is heavily involved in public education, I have my preferred culprits, but the truth is that comprehensive political leadership on this issue is sorely lacking and I believe that it is the most critical political and policy issue facing the country. It represents the highest anxiety of the American people and the political party that has the comprehensive policy solution to this problem without involving more harmful intrusion from government can stay in power for at least 20 years.

Is Faith in Capitalism Fading?

November 7, 2015

In a recent article in *The Wall Street Journal, Times of London* columnist and senior fellow of the Legatum Institute, Tim Montgomerie, reports on a survey of more than 1,000 adults in each of seven countries by a market research firm retained by the Legatum Institute to get responses to the proposition that "the next generation will probably be richer, safer and healthier than the last." The positive responses in European and Asian countries ranged from a high of 50 percent in India to 15 percent in Germany, but the most pessimistic response was a positive of 14 percent in America, with 52 percent in disagreement. Montgomerie then cites a trajectory of metrics for the world that clearly doesn't justify this pessimism. There were other responses in America equally disturbing, such as 55 percent who think the rich get richer and the poor get poorer, 65 percent who think most big businesses have dodged taxes, bought favors, or polluted, and 58 percent who want restrictions on the import of manufactured goods. Still, 49 percent think free enterprise is better at lifting people out of poverty than government and only 18 percent disagree, but the drift of the responses underscore the degree to which people think that capitalism is a dirty business. So, what's going on?

I think it's pretty simple. We have spent the last seven years listening to our national leaders and their fellow travelers in the mainstream media blaming the last recession on unregulated capitalists and the sins of globalized markets while burdening the engine of capitalism with more taxes and more regulation, which has crippled job growth and resulted in the slowest recovery from a recession since World War II. This condition, along with the underlying and not unjustified feeling that they are not being treated fairly in an environment of government-sponsored crony capitalism, has demoralized large numbers of people to the extent that they feel, rightly or wrongly, that we are a nation in decline. And as Jay Cost has noted, this unrest "amounts to a comprehensive assault on the political dispensation of the past half century. Many Americans aren't just frustrated over slow growth but now doubt the core assumptions of the postwar consensus." As I have said many times, the postwar social contract is obsolete and must be rewritten.

The explanation might be simple, but as I described a couple of months ago, the solution will be elusive until we find the comprehensive political leadership to bring the country together. Is it possible that the frustration and anger that is being demonstrated in this election cycle will be productive of that outcome? I'm hopeful, but wish I could be more optimistic.

This Land is Your Land, This Land is My Land

February 4, 2016

The citizen takeover of Oregon's Malheur National Wildlife Refuge last month led by the Bundy family of Nevada is intriguing on several levels. The Bundys came to national attention a couple of years ago in their standoff with the Bureau of Land Management. The siege they conducted in Oregon was wrong, but their grievance with the mistreatment of a ranching family by the government was valid on several counts. But to me the main issue highlighted here is the vast ownership of land by the federal government in the first place.

The federal government owns about 28 percent of the land in the U.S., but it owns more than 50 percent of the land west of the Mississippi River excluding Texas, which kept its land when entering the union. For example, the federal government owns 85 percent of Nevada, 65 percent of Utah, 62 percent of Idaho, 61 percent of Alaska, 53 percent of Oregon, 48 percent of Wyoming, and 46 percent of California, compared to two percent of Texas, which was purchased by the federal government for national parks and forests after it became a state.

There is a theory, call it an ideology, that land owned by the government is owned by "the people" in common. But there is another, in my opinion more valid theory, that ownership in common is ownership by no one, and this is the "tragedy of the commons" that individuals acting independently and rationally, according to their own self-interest, behave contrary to the interests of the whole by depleting the commons.

In the 19th century, there was a tendency to encourage settlement of the West through federal land disposal. Then in the 20th century the emphasis shifted to retention of federal land. This is a continuing debate, but I believe that we would be better served by the significant disposal of federal land to private ownership on an orderly basis of regular auctions over a period of years. This will reduce the national debt, greatly enhance the productivity of the real estate, improve environmental stewardship, and provide incentives for enormous economic growth.

The New Trade War

April 7, 2016

Donald Trump's demagoguery aside on an issue he really doesn't understand, and seems not to care to, the anti-trade issue he has raised in this campaign has resonated with large numbers of people in his support base, as well as many others, Democrats and Republicans alike, who are convinced that free trade has been a loser for the U.S., particularly in the export of manufacturing jobs to lower wage countries. For many, the North American Free Trade Agreement (NAFTA) was the original sin, considered by many as responsible for the decline in U.S. manufacturing, however strongly the evidence suggests otherwise. There is simply no evidence that imports are the primary driver of U.S. manufacturing job losses or even that the manufacturing sector overall is in decline.

No matter. The populist anti-trade crowd has pointed to a new study for the National Bureau of Economic Research by labor economists David Autor, David Dorn, and Gordon Hanson as the final validation that free trade, particularly with China, has been really bad for America and its workers, and that protectionist trade policy is the corrective.

But the reality is not so simple, as the study notes, for despite the impact of trade globalization on certain economic sectors, which is very real in terms of job destruction, there are broad-based benefits from free trade for U.S. consumers (particularly poor and middle class), businesses, and workers. The main problem that we have failed to properly address is what the study authors call U.S. labor dynamism – the natural, beneficial replacement of old jobs with new ones which is primarily a function of the willingness of workers to seek new jobs and their ability to obtain them – a factor which has decreased precipitously since 2001.

As described in a recent article in *National Review* by Scott Lincicome, the reasons for this decline in dynamism are many and include various perverse government policies, from healthcare finance to unemployment benefits to misguided job training programs to minimum wage laws. And I would add more emphasis to the role played by declining education standards as a key element in the lack of dynamism in providing worker adaptability to new job opportunities.

The bottom line for me is that, as I have suggested, the displaced middle class who are most injured by our failure to respond to these anxieties and these very real structural problems represents the core political constituency of this century.

The Dangers of Economic Populism

March 2, 2018

We now have even more firm evidence that President Trump does not appear to fully understand the importance of trade policy in sustaining economic growth, building alliances, and supporting American security. Nor does he seem to grasp the basic economics of trade, i.e., that a trade deficit is the converse, or mirror image, of a net surplus of investment capital, which provides the foreign direct investment that our trade partners use to invest in the U.S. to create growth in jobs and domestic product. It is not like a budget deficit; it does not have to be repaid.

His announcement this week that he will significantly increase tariffs on aluminum and steel imports is the one glaring element of the populism that has been so much a part of his electoral success that also could be the element that pulls down the most positive aspects of his economic policy, namely the new tax bill and aggressive deregulation that have sent the U.S. economy toward performance levels it hasn't recently seen.

It is astounding to me that he seems to have no one around him to remind him of the mistake that George W. Bush made in 2002 with his disastrous steel tariff increases that crippled the middle market companies that are the leading source of job growth, not to mention representing nothing less than the equivalent of a significant tax increase on consumers. He doesn't seem to get it that these steel users dwarf the employment base of steel makers in the U.S. by about 45 to one!

Unfortunately, President Trump has used his misunderstanding and his base supporters' ignorance on the economic basics to unfairly demagogue trade issues as if we can return to the pre-globalization days of American manufacturing dominance and the nostalgia for the U.S. Steel of the 1950s. And to compound the problem this comes shortly after messages from Treasury Secretary Mnuchin in Davos that "a weaker dollar is good for trade" sent the dollar to a three-year low against a basket of world currencies. What a plan – protectionism and dollar devaluation, a recipe for a trade war just as business and consumer confidence is booming, and the economy is growing faster than it has for more than a decade.

Our Trade Policy Resembles "Industrial Policy"

August 1, 2018

If you are of a certain age you will remember the term "industrial policy," a derisive description popularized 30 or 40 years ago to denote practices of nations, particularly Japan at the time, whose governments engaged in "picking winners" in economic competition in the private sector through subsidies or regulatory carve-outs for favored industries. It also smacks of mercantilism, or national economic policy designed to attain a favorable balance of trade by whatever means, such as China currently pursues. Both of these characterizations of national policy are anathema to free trade and, with a brief exception in the disastrous Smoot/Hawley tariff of the 1930s, have been rejected by American economic policy since the McKinley administration at the turn of the 20th century.

Until now. The most unfortunate policy development of the Trump administration to date has been the President's relentless pursuit of protectionism for purposes of chasing the false promise of favorable international trade balances, whatever its cost in terms of higher prices for U.S. businesses and consumers, the disruption of critical supply chains in multilateral trade agreements, and destructive retaliation by our trading partners.

And now, not surprisingly, this has already led to an "aid package" for one of the major victims of the new tariffs in the amount of $12 billion in government purchases of surplus farm products through the old supposedly "temporary" programs of the Depression-era Commodity Credit Corporation. This simply is fixing an economic problem of the government's own making by putting its victim on federal relief! And our Secretary of Agriculture says that this is a "short-term solution" and even indicates that part of the justification for the new protective tariffs on critical agricultural products is "homeland security." This is total nonsense and if it stands, we are headed for a situation in which every victim of these new tariffs and the retaliation that results produces a new appeal for an industry or company exemption, subsidy, or carve-out, a corporate lobbyist's dream. And although not directly related to the tariff issue, this follows on the move directed by President Trump to use federal authority to require power grid operators to buy electricity from struggling coal and nuclear plants, again supposedly in the interest of national security, to keep these plants open. If all of this is not mercantilist industrial policy, what is it?

There is no doubt that there is much legitimate work to be done in response to China's blatant violation of World Trade Organization rules that have damaged the U.S. and our allies. One important thing that Trump should pursue is to pull together the European Union along with Japan in presenting a united front against the violations of China's practices and he could have begun such a process in his recent apparently otherwise successful meeting on trade and tariff issues in Washington with EU President Jean-Claude Juncker. But across the board tariff increases followed by bailouts, carve outs, and protection of favored victims of the retaliation are not the answer, particularly since we need all the help we can get from our allies and trading partners in confronting the real culprit.

One further critical point: The robust quarterly report of 4.1 percent GDP growth along with significant increases in wages and the personal savings rate send the distinct message that policies matter and that tax reform and deregulation are much to be preferred to politically directed credit and government spending, but also come with a warning that government-directed industrial policy in trade has the potential to foster uncertainty and further retaliation that could put a damper on the sustainability of this growth. Let's hope that this message gets to the President before it's too late.

6
Environmentalism

Environmental Precaution

May 3, 2001

President Bush has been unfairly maligned by the media and the Democrats for his "reversals" on carbon dioxide emissions and arsenic in drinking water. But part of his problem is his administration's failure to confront the agenda of the radical environmental lobby with one voice in a principled way. He should start with the centerpiece of the environmental activist groups, the "precautionary principle." This principle says "when an activity raises threats of harm to human health or environment, precautionary measures should be taken even if some cause-and-effect relationships are not fully established scientifically." In other words, all new innovations are guilty until proven innocent. The "spirit" of the Kyoto Treaty, which Bush has said is "fine," is soaked with this principle. The premise is flawed and we should say so!

Radical environmentalism is a religion. It is based on the pantheistic belief that God is manifest (immanent) in nature and humans are merely intruders in an otherwise sacred environment. Unfortunately, this version of paganism has been mainstreamed, even among some Christian denominations. Most environmental activist groups are now Deep Ecology sympathizers, believing that the human species is simply one of many, not ordained by God, consciousness, or intellect to a privileged status on earth. Fighting radical environmentalism and its flawed science on purely scientific and economic terms is not enough. Bad policy based on bad philosophy must be countered in philosophical terms, head on. One place to look for some grounding is the *Cornwell Declaration*, drafted by the Interfaith Council for Environmental Stewardship (www.stewards.net), summarized as follows:

- The 20th century brought unprecedented improvement in human health, nutrition, life expectancy, and environmental quality.
- We have an opportunity, and a moral obligation, to build on these advances, and share them with less fortunate people in America and developing nations.

- None of this would be possible, were it not for the religious, economic, and scientific traditions now under assault.

A New Low for the Nobel

November 2, 2007

After Jimmy Carter, Yasser Arafat, and now Al Gore, can Michael Moore be far behind as a prime candidate for the Nobel Peace Prize? It truly makes one wonder if there are any standards for truth and objectivity in awarding the prize, or has it entirely become a form of ratification of politically correct leftist dogma.

And in the aftermath, Tom Friedman, a columnist and author for whom I have (now dwindling) respect as a professional in spite of my disagreement with him on many issues, wants to know "who will succeed Al Gore?" as a world leader. I was halfway through his article on this point before I realized that he was actually being serious.

But, hey, the demagogues are winning the global warming debate, even to the point of the successful discrediting as Holocaust denial equivalency anyone who might challenge them on the science at issue. The truly damaging part of this is that the credibility of the entire scientific enterprise is at stake, for as Patrick Basham of the Democracy Institute so well notes, at the heart of the scientific enterprise is a curious and always difficult tension between certainty and the possibility that certainty can suddenly dissolve. As a result of this age old and well-founded tension, the skeptic has a right to ask first, that the normal standards of scientific evidence are brought to the climate debate and second, to make certain there is not some politically driven and premature closure of what is a scientific controversy. Gore and his fellow travelers have failed at both, and the rush to judgment that they are pursuing is not only dangerous to our long term economic growth, but a threat to the scientific method.

The New Religion

March 4, 2011

If you are like me, there are certain "buzzwords" or phrases that enter the lexicon periodically that begin to get on my nerves after awhile. "Best practices" in education is one of these. And now the word "sustainability" is near the top of my list. Where did this term originate in its current social context? I recently read an article by Glenn Ricketts of the National Association of Scholars, "The Roots of Sustainability," which enlightened me on this irritable term.

It turns out that the word has roots in the romantic period and in the American transcendental movement (no surprise there), but more directly in the turbulent 1960s and 1970s, and its core text, according to Ricketts, appeared in a document titled "Our Common Future" published by the United Nations Commission on Environment and Development in 1987. This paper promoted "sustainable development" as the essential remedy for the interlocking crises confronting humanity and defines it as "development that meets the needs of the present without compromising the ability of future generations to meet their own needs… it involves a progressive transformation of economy and society." That last part is the kicker, for, as Ricketts further notes, while this concept smacks of radical environmentalism, it is actually much more comprehensive, because it requires that we connect with other matters of concern to social activists and submit to new structures of authority in which those who possess this new wisdom of interconnectedness will make the right decisions for us. In fact, it is this notion of "interconnectedness" as it relates to sustainability which has replaced radical environmentalism as the new religion of social justice. Just words, of course, but as we know, ideas have consequences, so beware of those who peddle "sustainability" without a very good explanation.

The New Religion of Sustainability

October 6, 2015

Are there words or phrases that you get so tired of hearing that they almost make you ill? How about "awesome?" Or "no problem," when a simple "you're welcome" would do nicely? Both of these have become obnoxious to me. But these are benign and merely irritating. A different problem is the word for the new fundamentalist religion known as "sustainability," which pops up everywhere in a multitude of contexts and, in its current ideological sense, is not merely irritating, but dangerous. My dictionary, *The American Heritage Dictionary*, has a definition for the word sustain, but no definition for sustainability. I admit that I am guilty of using the word sustainable in the context of whether or not a particular effort or policy or program can be continued or expanded in its efficacy or economic viability. But this is much different.

The notion of sustainability has become the banner under which the newest and largest pseudo-academic field travels. As George Leef of the John William Pope Center describes it, "…like the identity studies, there is no body of knowledge regarding 'sustainability;' it's just a farrago of beliefs, attitudes, and grievances centering around the general notion that most humans aren't living the right way and unless we make drastic changes, we're doomed."

The degree to which the sustainability movement has penetrated into American higher education is the subject of an extensively researched study released last summer by the National Association of Scholars (NAS), "Sustainability: Higher Education's New Fundamentalism." In it, authors Peter Wood, President of NAS, and research associate Rachelle Peterson, argue that sustainability is not really an academic discipline; rather, it's an ideology that unites environmental activism, anti-capitalism, and a progressive vision of social justice and these themes are manifest in the proliferation of courses and "studies" mainly centered around the supposedly uncontested science of global warming and the impending catastrophe. So, "sustainability" is a term that encompasses not only a particularly aggressive form of environmentalism, but also a strong attack on market capitalism and a progressive vision of social justice, a "triple bottom line," as its proponents characterize it.

In a related article on the subject, Wood writes, "The stronger claim, that sustainability is a religion, takes its warrant from the adherents to the movement who personify Earth as a deity. This claim also emphasizes the cult-like zealotry of sustainability advocates, who imagine they possess an accurate knowledge of the future that goes beyond what is actually knowable, and who regard any dissent from this orthodoxy as intolerable." This is dangerous ideology.

The findings of the NAS study have major implications. Most troubling is that sustainability has now become an academic discipline. It identified 1,438 degree programs at 475 colleges and universities focused on or related to sustainability studies, with at least one such program in each state in the U.S. The tendency that this proliferation will push downward into elementary and secondary education will be relentless, along with the indoctrination that will certainly follow.

Good Riddance to the Paris Climate Agreement

June 8, 2017

First, let's all understand that the Paris Climate Agreement has very little to add to the business case for global climate agreements. According to most reliable sources, the impact on warming would be in the neighborhood of 0.2 percent and the compliance waiver for China and India to 2030 would provide a huge competitive advantage with very little likelihood of any effective enforcement. Second, this agreement is really all about global governance and agreement for agreement's sake. But look at recent history: We terminated the ICBM Treaty of 1972, we refused to be a signatory to the

International Criminal Court, and the sky didn't fall despite warnings from the global internationalist crowd.

Barack Obama could never have obtained Senate ratification of this agreement and he knew it. It was all about appeasing the globalists and the climate change activists and was essentially designed to circumvent our democratic processes. And as for Secretary Rex Tillerson's appeal to the President based on our need to "have a seat at the table," as the indispensable nation, we will always have a seat at the table. In fact, with proper follow up, the decision to withdraw will probably reset the entire global discussion and re-establish U.S. leadership on the issue. Trump made the right decision to withdraw and it was really a no-brainer.

7
Fiscal Policy

Don't Tax the Internet

April 1, 2000

Columnist Thomas L. Friedman has written that the transformational changes being wrought by the Internet require a reconvening of the Founding Fathers, because he believes we are due for as revolutionary a period as the period between 1776 and 1787. He further predicts that the states will lead the revolution as they lose their tax base to e-commerce. Harold Furchtgott-Roth, a member of the Federal Communications Commission, feels strongly that the exploitation of telecommunications and e-commerce competition can't be centrally managed and that we should allow thousands of "flowers to bloom" and generations of archaic telecommunications regulation to be swept away in the process. I agree, and would add that a rush to tax these new revenue streams would be counterproductive to wealth and job creation that are as yet inconceivable. According to the Cato Institute, state and local governments are awash in funds, and between 1992 and 1998 state revenues grew at almost twice the rate of inflation. As Max Schulz of *The Washington Times* has written, "the Founding Fathers in their wildest dreams could never have imagined computers or the Internet. But in their wisdom they defined the regulation of interstate commerce as one of the few clearly marked responsibilities of federal authority." We should make the Internet tax moratorium permanent and let the flowers bloom.

Texas Budget Crunch

March 2, 2003

No one envies the job currently facing policy-makers at every level of government and education in the difficult task of solving the current budget imbalances. As in all such crises, the essential trade-off is about whether revenue is too low or expenses too high. Pretty basic stuff with some obvious answers for businesses and families, but governments often get confused about where to start. At the state level, there are those legislators and agency heads who immediately want to introduce new or enhanced revenue sources, i.e., taxes and fees, but Gov. Rick Perry has his priorities in good working order by refusing to talk about new funding until spending has been appropriately reduced: "Once you take your eye off of spending matters and talk about revenues, there seems to be a historical pattern of people losing their resolve to pare the budget down to where it needs to be." It could be that he remembers the difficulties of his predecessor in the legislative session of 1997, when state revenue restructuring took precedence over expense reduction, with the result that the process spun out of control in the House, forcing Senate Republicans, with the support of the Texas Association of Business, to step in to stop potentially disastrous legislation from reaching the Governor's desk.

Look no further than California for an example of what can happen when spending wish lists trump fiscal responsibility – a $35 billion budget deficit primarily created by a 14 percent increase in government employment during the period 1997-2001 compared to a six percent population increase over the same period, and a highly progressive tax system that penalizes capital formation and job creation. And Gov. Gray Davis, true to his pedigree, feels that the solution is yet another income tax rate increase for upper income taxpayers!

There is no doubt that Texas has an ill-structured, early 20th century tax system that relies too heavily on capital intensive sources, i.e., real property, plant, and equipment, and is in dire need of transformation to the service- and knowledge-based economy we have become. But, the priority should be to restructure spending patterns before arranging their financing, because it is the nature of government and its undisciplined constituencies to spend all available revenues, then ask for more.

The Next Crisis of the Moral Hazard

June 4, 2005

Who can doubt that the recent announcement that a Chicago bankruptcy judge allowed United Airlines to unload its unfunded pension liability on the federal government is potentially the break in the dam for the next crisis of moral hazard à la the savings and loan fiasco of the 1980s? Can a similar taxpayer bailout of the Pension Benefit Guaranty Corporation be far behind? The good news from this is that it may finally force us to come to grips with the antiquated nature of these defined benefit plans, both privately and publicly sponsored, including the Social Security program, and take steps to replace the entire edifice with defined contribution plans. The bottom line is that we can no longer sustain the unreasonable paternalistic retirement and healthcare commitments we have made, and we are in the third generation of this lie.

Someone, I think it was George Will, recently wrote that companies like General Motors and other members of the Fortune 500 have become giant healthcare and retirement plan monoliths, employing thousands of people who do nothing else, but handle the benefits plans of employees, retirees, and their beneficiaries, in essence as intermediaries for government. We need to get them out of this business and get them back to focusing exclusively on their core competencies. Will also noted Daniel Patrick Moynihan's comment that we, as a people, are turning away from government and "the common ethic of provision through government." If that is true, and I hope it is, it's not a minute too soon. It's just too bad that it will probably require a breakdown of both the healthcare and retirement finance systems and the pain that will follow for us to extricate ourselves from these fossils.

Looming Disaster III

March 5, 2009

With my first essay in this "disaster" series, I thought one or two would be plenty. Alas, the disasters just keep on coming. Now we have Obama's first proposed budget, and it simply takes your breath away.

First, a dose of reality. From a purely financial disaster standpoint, former Bush economic advisor Larry Lindsey put it in concise perspective recently on CNBC, as follows: The proposed budget bill when combined with the so-called stimulus package will result in a budget deficit of more than 12 percent of gross domestic product (GDP). By comparison, the 2008 deficit percentage was four percent of GDP. About half of the increase will be financed by the increased savings of Americans; the remaining four percent of GDP must be borrowed or printed. To put this in further perspective, according to the Congressional Budget Office, the largest expenditure increases by the Federal government in response to a recession since 1948-49 were just over two percent of GDP in both 1973-74 and 1981-82! Who will lend us the funds to finance this gigantic sum? Long-term bond rates have been increasing in anticipation of this unprecedented borrowing demand and inflationary expectations and, based on Lindsey's rounds among world financial centers, investors are not generally willing to finance these deficit levels for our "social transformation." Therefore, a large portion of the deficit must be monetized by our Federal Reserve, in other words, printed. This is the hottest of monetary growth, highly inflationary, and will cause the dollar to tank, thereby debauching our currency and defrauding current bond holders.

For corroboration of this scenario, look no further than liberal *Washington Post* columnist Michael Kinsley: "Even if the stimulus is a magnificent success, the money still has to be paid back… There is another way: don't pay it back. Just three or four years of currency erosion at, say, 10 percent per year would slice the real value of our debt in half… Inflation works only as a surprise or betrayal. It can never be part of any public, official plan… But if that's not the plan, what is?" At least he's being honest about the dirty little secret.

Where were you from 1966 through 1982? Remember the massive monetary growth spawned by the Johnson Great Society, which gave us 15 years of stagflation cured only by the Reagan tax cuts and the crushing monetary policy of Paul Volcker's Federal Reserve? That was a walk in the park compared to the prospects offered by the Obama recovery and budget plans.

Folks, nothing about this has anything to do with a recovery plan. It's a bold and audacious attempt to transform American society in the vision of the progressive movement of the early 20th century. The Obama budget is even subtitled, "Reviving America's Promise," a paraphrase of the *The Promise of American Life*, the progressive "bible" written in 1909 by their patron saint Herbert Croly, one of the founders of *The New Republic*. Listen to David Broder: "…a change of domestic policy of historic size… it could remake the government's relation to American society…;" to E. J. Dionne: "…he has sought, subtly, but unmistakably, to alter the nation's political assumptions, its attitudes toward collective action and its view of government;" to Robert Reich: "We can basically say goodbye to the philosophy espoused by Ronald Reagan and Margaret Thatcher;" and to Charles Krauthammer: "…the current crisis gives Obama the political space to move the still modest American welfare state toward European-style social democracy."

A few people are slowly beginning to wake up. Obviously, the financial markets have voted NO in about as loud and clear a voice as can be expected. Some of the more responsible members of the moderate wing of the Democratic Party are getting nervous. Many of Obama's upscale "left coast" financial backers in the technology and venture capital communities are having doubts about his true priorities. But there can be no false sense of security that the progressive left will heal or correct itself. They basically see this through the lens of those media fellow travelers like Dionne, Reich, Paul Krugman, and the amen corners at *The New York Times* and in the upper reaches of the elite universities. This is the opening they have been waiting for since Reagan came onto the scene, and it will require an enormous effort, including a large dose of the kind of moral courage that has been a rarity of late, to turn the tide. As Pat Buchanan has suggested, "it's pitchfork time."

The Public Sector Union Showdown

January 4, 2011

"The moral case for unions – protecting working families from exploitation – does not apply to public employment." – Tim Pawlenty, Governor of Minnesota.

Former British Prime Minister Margaret Thatcher once said that "the enemy within is much more difficult to fight than the enemy without, and more dangerous to liberty." She had referenced to the public sector unions, who at the time were holding her country hostage. Well, almost 30 years later one can say without fear of hyperbole that one of the most significant threats to self-government in America is the stranglehold of the public sector unions. In fact, it is pretty easy to make the case that we are in a position close to that of Britain when Thatcher spoke. In almost every state the primary fiscal problems are directly tied to the political and contract clout of the public sector unions or, in the case of the open shop right-to-work states, the power of their lobbies. In virtually every public policy debate, this power weighs heavily in favor of a larger role for government, less accountability for performance, and larger benefits and legacy costs ultimately underwritten by the taxpayers. In states like California, New Jersey, and Illinois it is no exaggeration to say that the public sector unions run the government. The Kellogg School at Northwestern University estimates that our 50 largest cities have combined pension underfunding of $574 billion on top of the estimated actual liabilities of their states of well over $1 trillion.

Do we have the will to turn this around? There is hope: governors in Wisconsin, New Jersey, Missouri, and Indiana are making bold steps, but much more courage is needed and should be possible during this budget crisis. In addition, there is evidence that union solidarity is breaking down as private sector union members are growing weary of subsidizing the employment protection and overly generous benefits of their brothers and sisters in the public sector while struggling with layoffs in their own industries. But this is one of the most significant policy areas in which the new Republican majority in Congress and the state legislatures will need to be very bold in the face of enormous political intimidation from a constituency that takes no prisoners.

Texas Again Has an Opportunity to Lead

February 4, 2011

The current budget crisis offers almost unlimited opportunity. I have said repeatedly over the past several months that I seldom agree with Rahm Emanuel, but I do agree with his observation that "we shouldn't allow a good crisis to go to waste." The other recent memorable quote was from Speaker John Boehner: "We can't kick the can up the road anymore, because we have come to the end of the road. Like Greece, Portugal, Ireland, Illinois, New York, and New Jersey, we have arrived at Hotel California." In a certain perverse way, this is actually encouraging.

Why? Because there is no way out except to fundamentally change the way we do business; our system of federalism encourages the states to lead the way. And Texas is uniquely positioned for this leadership. I offer one example, public education, with which I am reasonably familiar and on which Texas spends about $50 billion annually. We are besieged with woe over the prospect of what appear to be the draconian education spending reductions necessary to balance the state's budget and, while major reductions will no doubt be in the cards, the most important approach is to change the way we do business in the schools.

The Texas Education Code is chock full of opportunities for strategic transformation in the area of human resources management alone. After all, approximately 80 percent of education expense is personnel, and the Code and the rules driven by it have embedded large areas of prescriptive regulation by the state into the business of delivering education in more than 1,200 school districts, all of which a collection of activist adults, a few "stakeholders," and some policymakers (often abetted by their vested interests) at one time became convinced were absolutely necessary. These include such items as the single-salary scale, the student/teacher ratio, the tenure rules, the teacher assignment rules, the educator certification rules, the teacher dismissal process, school scheduling rules, the prohibition of salary reductions and furloughs in certain jobs, and on and on.

After serving on the State Board for Educator Certification, I know how antiquated our approach to education human resources policy has become. Our organization, the Texas Institute for Education Reform (TIER), is promoting policy recommendations that will move us away from the top-down, compliance and input-driven policy approach to one that is not only performance-based, but much more flexible and enabling of innovation in the schools. We have an accountability system; let's enforce it and allow it to work.

Several of TIER's board and policy advisory board members participated in the recent kickoff conference for the new Center for Financial Accountability and Productivity, which will offer leadership for moving Texas into transforming the way business is done in our schools. TIER's soon to be released recommendations for enhanced human resources management segue into the transformational objectives of this initiative and in many ways help lay the groundwork for a complete overhaul in the role of the state in human resources.

These approaches differ drastically from the ham-handed across the board cuts that are feared and, in fact, there are a number of strategic expenditures that represent meaningful interventions to help schools advance student success that we believe should be preserved. But business as usual is out of business, and Texas must use this opportunity to change the paradigm. We have been reform leaders before in the move to academic standards and accountability, and we can do it again.

Supply-Side Tax Policy 101

November 10, 2011

They just don't get it. Or more accurately, it doesn't meet their needs. The political left and their fellow travelers cannot seem to grasp the logic and historical success of supply-side economics, particularly as it relates to fiscal policy that gives priority to marginal tax rate cuts. To supply side guru Art Laffer it's pretty simple: There are two income tax rates that result in zero tax revenues – 100 percent and 0 percent – and the reason should be clearly obvious. The policy issue is to determine the optimum marginal rate to maximize economic growth, and this is the key – it must be scored on a dynamic basis, meaning giving effect to the adjustments in human and economic behavior induced by changes in marginal rates. The implementation of this concept in national fiscal policy has worked every time to spur economic growth and job creation.

A few months ago, I was inspired to respond to an essay in the *Houston Chronicle* by my friend Bill King (far from a leftist, by the way), who wrote "a look at the data indicates that since World War II, there has been no positive correlation between lower tax rates and stronger growth." My response was in part as follows:

Economic facts have the unique ability to support lots of differing opinions, particularly when they are used in ways that don't control for dependent factors, so I won't get into the details of a number of instances in which mitigating circumstances prevent isolation of tax policy for purposes of evaluating its impact. Suffice to say that tax rates at the margin have always had an enormous impact on the myriad of incentives which drive economic growth. Supply-side economics works, and has done, so each time it has been employed, from the Pharaohs to Kennedy to Reagan to Bush, and in the particular case of Reagan was primarily responsible for the longest sustained period of economic growth in U.S. history. For further confirmation, examine the comparison of the recovery from the 1981-82 recession to the lame recovery from the recent recession. For the authoritative work on this phenomenon, I recommend *The Way the World Works*, by Jude Wanniski, and of course the work of Arthur Laffer.

Laffer emphasizes that "all economic problems are about removing impediments to supply, not demand," and it has been a constant source of amazement to me that we have allowed the evidence of the success of policy founded on this principle to be so discredited by the failed Keynesians and their acolytes like Paul Krugman, and that the leadership of the party whose most recent success has been fueled by supply side policy has found it so difficult to defend.

The Ultimate Tyranny

June 1, 2013

"The power to tax involves the power to destroy." – Supreme Court Chief Justice John Marshall, *McCullough v. Maryland*, 1819

"In the act of appropriating taxes there is perhaps no legislative act in which greater opportunity and temptation are given to a predominant party to trample on the rules of justice." – James Madison, Federalist No. 10.

Of the various scandals currently besieging The White House, there is no doubt that the most egregious, as well as the most damaging politically for President Obama, is the IRS intimidation of conservative non-profit organizations. As important as they are in seeking the truth, not many citizens have the patience for the explanations involved in the Benghazi cover-up, and the *Associated Press*/James Rosen case is generally regarded by the person in the street as a media event. But the IRS viscerally resonates with people, as all taxing authorities have since our revolution. As the Marshall and Madison quotes indicate, this is the ultimate tyranny in a free society. And as a political issue, it has "legs" because it is bipartisan. It will also greatly re-energize the Tea Party in a way that will carry through the midterm elections in 2014.

However, I am taking the Jonah Goldberg line on this. I believe that it is important to use this issue primarily as a platform to attack the corruption of tax policy generally and only secondarily to go after individuals who might be culpable in the implementation of partisan intimidation of certain groups. Certainly, hearings should be held, investigations should be conducted, and criminal referrals should be pursued, but the primary issue here is that the taxing power of the administrative state corrupts and that overreaching government as manifest in the income tax code is the culprit that needs to be the focus of dissent. This is where efforts should be directed as a matter of principle and it will also have the most benefit politically.

The Ultimate Tyranny II

July 5, 2013

Speaking at the commencement ceremony at Ohio State University before the IRS scandal broke in May, President Obama cautioned the graduates to reject the voices "that warn that tyranny is always just around the corner," that "suggest that our brave and creative and unique experiment in self-rule is somehow just a sham with which we can't be trusted." Well, as observed shortly thereafter, it turns out that tyranny was, in fact, just around the corner and, as evidence continues to bubble up, this particular episode was about much more than a few mid-level rogue agents in Cincinnati and does seriously threaten the bonds of trust.

But, it's also becoming pretty clear that this phenomenon is about a governing philosophy that produces a culture that smacks of totalitarianism, at least to the extent that identifies the regulatory state as the embodiment of "community," or as Barney Frank has put it, "government is just another word for the things we do together."

And there are other manifestations, other ways in which this perversity metastasizes in a totalitarian culture without the necessity of direct instructions from superiors. It is inherent in the underlying principles of progressive political philosophy, with its preference for positive law and regulation (what government must do) over negative law (what government must not do).

So the IRS scandal is the high profile short-term issue, but the progressive regulatory state is the long-term problem, and it cannot be reversed until we return to our founding principles in negative law and roll back the size and intrusion of government in our lives.

The Houston Success Model

August 4, 2014

Two recent articles on my home town caught my attention recently and sent me back to some of my previous thoughts on the sources of success for one of the most unlikely of successful geographic areas. Last week, Rice University President David Leebron wrote a very insightful essay in the *Houston Chronicle* entitled "Ten Reasons Houston Attracts New Residents," in which, as a relative newcomer to the city from New York, he lists 10 characteristics of Houston that make it attractive to newcomers, even if they are at first skeptical, as many are. The key traits he identifies are: 1) this city welcomes the people who choose to come here; 2) Houston is a pragmatic, yet optimistic and ambitious city; 3) Houston is a philanthropic city; 4) Houston has great parks; 5) Houston is a vibrant cultural center; 6) Houston attracts remarkable people from other great places; 7) Houston is a tech city; 8) Houston is an international city; 9) Houston is a tolerant city; and 10) Houston is a diverse city.

I happen to agree with every trait he has suggested, all of which have meaningfully contributed to the attractiveness of Houston and many of which are well-kept secrets until a newcomer arrives.

But there is much more to it. In fact, much of what he describes is a manifestation of deeper aspects of Houston's culture, as noted by an essay in *The Wall Street Journal,* "Success and the City," by Joel Kotkin of Chapman University and Tory Gattis of the blog *Houston Strategies*. Messrs. Kotkin and Gattis posit that Houston's pro-growth policies have produced an urban powerhouse and more – a blueprint for metropolitan revival. They maintain that the growth-friendly attitude is what holds everything together in Houston and is much more than energy industry luck; it reflects a unique policy environment that will be crucial when, inevitably, the next slowdown comes.

And I would add even more, with characteristics that I have noted in previous essays that have highlighted our city's organic culture, as well as some cautions about how not to mess it up:

- The future belongs to those regions that are attractive to capital and where it is well-treated, so those attributes, particularly those that are friendly to enterprise and opportunity, that have made Houston attractive to capital should be emphasized.

- A large part of Houston's attractiveness is that there is "no price of entry" in terms of class, origin, race, or family wealth. Houston is a place where people come from all over the world to pursue whatever version of the American dream they bring with them.

- Our city's accessibility and openness should be celebrated. We don't need "image" campaigns or consultants, which often are fronts for transforming our image to one of "urbanity" and the commensurate lifestyle that fits the preference of many "smart growth" advocates.

- Houston can continue to be what *The Wall Street Journal* once called "the Hong Kong of the Western hemisphere" only if it can avoid the tendency to embrace "progressive" ideas, such as zoning and its cousins, land use planning and smart growth theories, along with publicly financed hotels and transit plans that are insufficiently user-financed.

- It will be of increasing importance to take a critical look at the role and proper functions of government at every level and to be receptive to marketization opportunities wherever they present themselves. The competition for capital will demand this.

- Race- and ethnic-based contract set asides and other group preferences, whether to correct perceived past injustices or promote "diversity," will have a long-term negative impact on social relations.

- Currently, the most threatening area of risk to our continuing success is the performance of our institutions of public education and Houston's top priority should be a model elementary and secondary education system. This will not be possible until a declaration of war is declared on childhood illiteracy and competition and accountability become fully integrated into education delivery at every level.

- If Texas didn't have a Houston, we'd want to build one, so let's take care of the one we have.

A Deal Trump Should Like

July 5, 2017

Mark Zuckerberg of Facebook fame is touting the idea of a "universal basic income," the notion that every citizen should be paid some fixed subsistence on an annual basis, and he has been joined in this thinking, for various reasons, by Tesla CEO Elon Musk and former Secretary of Labor Robert Reich. In commenting on this goofy idea, Andy Kessler quipped, "If we get universal basic income, the millennials will never leave our basements."

I have a better idea that might help achieve the same result and it came from Vernon Smith, the 2002 Nobel Laureate in Economics from Chapman University. He thinks that President Trump should advance a proposal to privatize the interstate highway system by holding a series of auctions, the proceeds of which could provide a permanent basic income for every citizen through a Permanent Citizens Fund much like the oil trust in Alaska does for citizens of that state. (Or even better, how about national debt reduction?) He even suggests broadening the asset sale to include the Bureau of Land Management's vast grazing lands and eventually oil and gas resource rights. This parallels some thinking I have had: after all, the federal government owns more than 50 percent of the land west of the Mississippi River, excluding Texas. Neither Smith nor I would include the national parks and monuments or forests, but the private sector would be a much more productive manager of these valuable resources than government and better stewards for the true owners, the American people.

Such a proposal would have the added benefit of rolling back the Progressive Era thinking of the early 20th century, which favors large-scale ownership of natural resources under management by experts in federal bureaus, and which was itself a reversal of the previously dominant classical liberal ideas that produced the successful privatization through dispersal of federal lands via the Homestead Acts.

You're probably thinking that this is either a very bad idea or a fantasy that couldn't get 10 votes in Congress, but I think it's time we had this conversation. Is there any other way that we are seriously going to begin to retire any significant portion of more than $20 trillion in national debt?

A Big Win for the Supply Side

December 2, 2017

As I write, word comes that the Senate has just passed its version of the Republican tax bill by a 51-49 vote. So, now it's off to a conference committee to reconcile the House and Senate versions. Good. This is a major breakthrough on several levels beyond the fine print in these bills. This Congress and this administration had to prove that it could do this, that it could tackle a major issue like taxes and do transformational things with it. It's been a long time, too long, and people need to see evidence that their institutions are not dysfunctional. On another level, they also need to see evidence that, particularly with a huge fiscal issue like taxes, their government is not content to accept the notion that this country will succumb to the "secular stagnation" of the past decade, that there are policy responses that can shake us out of these doldrums and give us renewed confidence and faith in ourselves. So, good for us. Let's get this completed. Now, as for the bills themselves, I received a lot of response to my essay last month on the virtues of "supply-side economics," most of it in the form of pushback on my optimism that it works. It does and has, but enough of that this month. These bills, in essence, are about one thing – significant relief in the taxation of capital, which in the long-term, if sustained, should make the U.S. much more attractive to capital, which will translate into investment, higher wages, and jobs. All the models and other stuff about individual credits, deductions, who gets what, etc., are battles that won't make any difference without the big item – business and capital tax relief. As for "paying for" tax rate reductions to avoid higher deficits, these deficits are not about insufficient taxes, they are about overspending and the urgent need for entitlement reform, which should be the next major project.

8
Foreign and Military Policy

China Watch

May 1, 2000

According to Dan Rather, appearing on *Larry King Live* last month, the "biggest, most important story unfolding now is the transformation of China into a world power on two fronts – economic and military." This may seem obvious, and it is also clear that beneath the surface, there is a huge revolution brewing in that country over human rights and the related political rights of speech, religion and consent. Typically, as with the massive repression of the Falun Dafa religious sect, as well as Christian, Muslims, and Buddhists, the Chinese Communist Party is intent on restricting spirituality, because it feels it must control all aspects of Chinese life. In the short run, they will succeed; longer term, they cannot suppress this basic human yearning and Beijing will ultimately lose the human rights debate. In the meantime, the Clinton administration continues single-mindedly to pursue permanent most favored nation trade status for mainland China without due regard for these human rights abuses or Taiwan security concerns. In fact, argues Michael Leeden in the Nov./Dec. 1999 issue of *The International Economy*, "the greatest blunder in recent history is the Clinton administration's policy, through liberalized trade, of arming the People's Republic of China." Further, Abe Rosenthal of *The New York Times* says that he has never seen the U.S. as much in the thrall of a foreign philosophy as it is now to Chinese communism. These are strong sentiments, but it does seem that the hope, or mirage, of a billion customers has overwhelmed all other motivations. I agree that trade engagement should be pursued for non-military items, but only on a year-to-year basis as to favored nation status, while keeping the heat on human rights abuses by publicizing them directly and through the United Nations. We should also visibly show our support and encouragement to the new democratically elected President of Taiwan by approving the Taiwan Security Enhancement Act and ultimately sponsoring their entry, along with Communist China, into the World Trade Organization. Sen. Jesse Helms makes an apt analogy of the two Chinese states with the former East and West Germany, which were ultimately united under democracy. This is a long-term objective for China that is worthy of our values and our support.

The Demise of the Warrior Class

June 1, 2000

In April, there was a flurry of media attention to the 25th anniversary of the fall of Saigon and the end of U.S. military involvement in Vietnam. What resonated most with me during the coverage was the degree to which the military experience and the commitment to military service have been diluted in America's leadership class. To me, military service has been the "great leveler" for American youth, primarily males, as it cut across race, class, social, and economic lines in assimilating its recruits into service to the country. The all-volunteer military isn't the same and the post-Vietnam generation missed this experience which, for most of our history, had been a "rite of passage" for us. John McCain's Presidential candidacy seemed to have an element of this generation's coming to grips with this void, with some nostalgia, some guilt, and some yearning all mixed with the repeated litany of his experience as a POW. It is also, I think, part of the fascination with movies such as *Saving Private Ryan* and books such as *Citizen Soldier* and *The Greatest Generation.* All branches of the military are falling far short of their recruiting goals and, in spite of their increased efforts, more advertising won't close the deficit.

The major factor is the growing gap between the military and American society. As the World War II generation passes on, fewer and fewer Americans feel a direct connection with or obligation to military service. In a recent article in *Duke Magazine,* Kirk Kicklighter, a former Marine Corps Captain, says that the military and the civilian culture it serves are becoming estranged, and that the problem began with Vietnam, as the students who protested the war became the tenured faculty and civilian government leaders of today and are highly skeptical of the military. Duke University is participating in a study of this estrangement, which has produced some disturbing results. Military personnel are annoyed by what they see as a breakdown in virtues, like honesty and sacrifice within civilian institutions, and they believe that civilians are in the midst of a moral crisis. Seventy-seven percent of military officers believe the adoption of such military values as honor, accountability, and teamwork would help civilian society reform itself. Eighty-one percent of newly commissioned officers feel the military's values are closer than civilian values to those of the Founding Fathers. On the other hand, the research shows that most university professors, and CEO's have never served in the military. Only about 25 percent of today's members of Congress are veterans; in 1971, 75 percent had served. Before Vietnam, neither the powerful nor the famous were exempt. There are other factors involved in this estrangement and the decline of the warrior class. The feminization of the military is one factor, as is the pattern of deployment. Most soldiers view the nonstop missions of "peace-keeping" and humanitarianism unfulfilling and unchallenging, and the "no casualties" mentality is destructive to leadership initiative. No great republic can endure without an effective, committed warrior class, properly accountable to civilian authority with a clear vision of the society's vital interests and the proper uses of power. With each passing anniversary of D-Day, I wonder whether it will be again possible for America to wage a major war and if there are vital interests for which we are willing to risk large numbers of casualties. In short, for what are we willing to die?

China Watch II

May 2, 2001

In the May 2000 issue, I noted that the Clinton administration had mistakenly pursued permanent most favored nation treatment for China without due regard for human rights abuses or Taiwan security concerns, and I highlighted the blunder of an approach defined by "strategic partnership" in thrall to the allure of the potential of a billion customers for our goods and services. It was to be expected that an incident such as the recent Hainan surveillance plane "accident" would be used by the Chinese to test the resolve of the new administration. On balance, considerable conservative commentary to the contrary, I believe President Bush acted decisively and in a measured way in dealing with the incident before it became a media "hostage" circus. This incident was instructive on several points. First, forget strategic partnership. China and the U.S. are competitors in almost every sense and adversaries on many fundamental issues. Second, as pure ideological communism has waned in China, its leaders have emphasized a virulent nationalism in order to continue their sway. As *The Wall Street Journal* has noted, the Chinese idea of sovereignty, which has been elevated to a sacred principle, is based on an outdated 19th century version that does not recognize multilateralism and emphasizes raw power. Third, the U.S. stands in the way of a major Chinese objective – military and economic hegemony in the Far East, including unification with Taiwan on their terms, as well as control of the area's shipping lanes.

Henry Kissinger has defined the two poles of American opinion on China policy as the "engagement/strategic partnership" crowd and the "adversarial/containment" crowd. I suppose I tend slightly to the latter, and I don't think this would produce a Soviet Union-style Cold War replay. Although I support trade engagement, I don't believe that our China policy can be dictated by a chamber of commerce approach that assumes that Jeffersonian democracy will necessarily follow from liberalized trade engagement. The keys are the rule of law and private property, which have historically been the determinants of the success of liberal democracy, and these, as Condoleeza Rice has noted, have a moral underpinning, which the Chinese don't yet have. In fact, as I watched the Hainan incident unfold, I was reminded of Mortimer Adler's admonition to be careful of equating Eastern and Western concepts of truth in moral philosophy. They don't mesh because the Far Eastern view is that the derivation of the truths of religion, philosophy, mathematics, science, and technology are completely different. The principle of noncontradiction, self-evident in the West, is not accepted by many Far Eastern cultures. There is a lot of work to be done to bridge this cultural gap. Meanwhile, in Ronald Reagan's words, "trust, but verify."

Thoughts On Strategic Defense

June 3, 2001

In a recent appearance on *Meet The Press*, Sen. John Kerry outlined his opposition to plans for a missile defense system as follows: That they have not been discussed on a mutual basis among nations through the United Nations and related forums, but are being developed unilaterally; that the approach of the Bush administration is provocative to potential adversaries who will respond by committing resources to finding ways around the defense; and that we should not gut the Anti-Ballistic Missile (ABM) Treaty. This, in a capsule, defines the philosophy of the multilateral internationalists as opposed to an internationalism based on American exceptionalism that should be at the heart of American defense policy. An additional objection to a missile defense system has it that we have not yet proven that it works. By this reasoning, John Kennedy was foolish in his 1961 commitment to land a man on the moon. But the most antiquated objection is the defense of the ABM Treaty, a 1972 relic with no legal standing, executed with a regime that no longer exists and which commits us to a porous "arms control" approach to nuclear threats. As usual, Lady Margaret Thatcher has it right: "On this (European) side of the Atlantic, there is a tendency to suggest that the problem of proliferation can be solved by diplomatic means and by control regimes designed to halt the flow of military technology. The possibilities were always much slimmer than the optimists thought. Now they are all but a dead letter." One source of delay in developing the system is the fear of upsetting Russia and China, the same fear that paralyzed doves during the Cold War. Thanks to the boldness of Reagan, Thatcher, and the now defunct Scoop Jackson wing of the Democratic Party, we won that one, remember?

And The War Came

October 8, 2001

"Our contest is not only whether we ourselves shall be free, but whether there shall be left to mankind an asylum on earth for civil and religious liberty." – Samuel Adams.

"Let every nation know, whether it wishes us well or ill, that we shall pay any price, bear any burden, meet any hardship, support any friend, oppose any foe to assure the survival and success of liberty." – John F. Kennedy.

"There is no security, no safety, in the appeasement of evil. It must be the core of Western policy that there be no sanctuary for terror." – Ronald Reagan

"We are not deceived by their pretenses to piety. We have seen their kind before. They are the heirs of all the murderous ideologies of the 20th century. By sacrificing human life to serve their radical visions – by abandoning every value except the will to power – they follow in the path of fascism, and Nazism, and totalitarianism. And they will follow that path all the way, to where it ends: in history's unmarked grave of discarded lies... Freedom and fear, justice and cruelty, have always been at war, and we know that God is not neutral between them." – George W. Bush

The title of this essay is from Abraham Lincoln's second inaugural address, wherein he laments the impasse that resulted in the American Civil War. Earlier, in his Gettysburg Address, he suggested the question posed by that conflict, "whether this nation, or any nation so conceived and so dedicated, can long endure." I submit to you that we are again confronted with this question.

Five years ago, in response to my friend John Andrews' request for a 50-word summary of the contribution of the Americans to humanity in the 20th century, I wrote this: "They reluctantly assumed the mantle of world leadership; challenged and ultimately defeated the primary instruments of totalitarianism; exported the principles of democracy and human rights to regions where those concepts were unknown; and, for better or worse, initiated popular cultural hegemony over a major portion of the world's population."

It is essentially this, in all its variations, for which we are hated and are being attacked in what Benjamin Netanyahu has termed "a war to reverse the triumph of the West." The

American idea is not a simple, cut and dried tautology. It is a blend of the proposition of the Declaration of Independence, the Athenian pursuit of knowledge and virtue, and the holiness of Jerusalem. This often conflicted blend is what makes it the envy of the world and the enemy of the terrorists.

I had no idea of the timeliness of my book recommendations in the August 2001 issue "A Triad On Globalization," and I have returned to them several times since the September 11 attack. Evidently, so have others. For example, in response to Fukuyama's "end of history" thesis, Jonah Goldberg has written that this thesis is not refuted by the war of terrorism, because radical Islam is not a challenge to liberal democracy in any way. He is correct in that this is not a war of ideas, because the opposition doesn't have any that are competitive. However, this doesn't mean that there is no threat to the West, as both Thomas Friedman and Samuel Huntington illustrate. Friedman's, *The Lexus* and the *Olive Tree*, calls attention to the anthropological concept of "systematic misunderstanding," which arises when your worldview and the other person's worldview are so fundamentally different that it cannot be corrected by providing more information. And the cultures of many traditional societies, including those of the Islamic world, are diametrically opposed to those of the Western tradition, even though they worship the same God. For example, in traditional societies, the collective or group has priority over the individual, and any change in this relationship represents a socially disintegrating threat.

Huntington, in his *The Clash of Civilizations* and the *Remaking of World Order*, goes further. He points out that 1,400 years of history demonstrate that the West's problems are not only with the extremist wing of Islam. He suggests that the battle with Marxism-Leninism is but a blip on the screen compared to the continuing conflict between Islam and Christianity, and that it flows from the nature of the two religions and the civilizations based on them. Both are monotheistic, universalistic, and missionary, which in his view, are invitations to conflict, and in Muslim eyes Western secularism, irreligiosity, and hence immorality are worse evils than the Christianity that produced them. I would add that this view is compounded by the often conflicted nature of the American "idea" (Athens vs. Jerusalem) to which I alluded above.

Where does this leave us? First, in my view, the attack on 9/11 was the worst and most recent of a series of acts of war. These are not crimes in the legal sense under positive law, and they should not be pursued through police and judicial processes. Justice should be delivered by economic, intelligence, and military retaliation under wartime conditions and engagement. In looking for analogies, the best is the Cold War in terms of the sustained commitment that will be necessary over a protracted period of years. And there will be ongoing retaliation from the terrorist network. We must expect it and adjust to it without sacrificing the Bill of Rights. After all, we lived under Cold War terror conditions for 45 years, before we won it and became complacent, refusing to adjust to new realities.

Second, we must properly identify the enemy. Benjamin Netanyahu put it best: "The first and most crucial thing to understand is that there is no international terrorism without the support of sovereign states. International terrorism simply cannot be sustained for long without the regimes that aid and abet it. Terrorists are not suspended in mid air." The media want a face on the enemy and the obvious lead culprit is Osama bin Laden, but if he were to be captured or killed today, the war on international terrorism would have just begun. President Bush has correctly pointed out that we must make no distinction between the terrorists and the states that support them. The entire terrorist network must be dismantled and defeated, and the American people must understand that this network includes not only the Taliban, but also very likely Iraq and others.

Third, there must be moral clarity about our mission. Terrorism is a crime against humanity and there are no "root causes" that justify it. Ask yourself how it was possible to identify evil in World War II. Nazism was a violation of natural law, not positive law. Could we conduct and prosecute the Nuremberg trials today? I've often wondered. In order to answer in the affirmative, we must be willing to invoke natural law against regimes without distinguishing among the relative "merits" of the acts of terrorists.

Having thus identified the enemy, we will be flirting with a world war between Islam and the West, which we must not allow to happen. Huntington's historical and cultural perspective notwithstanding, our ideological enemy is an extreme sect of radical Islam, not the Muslim religion, the leaders of which should loudly condemn the barbarians who have perverted their faith. They will have many sympathizers in the mainstream Muslim faith, however, and the leaders of the nation-states populated by those of this faith must understand that it is time for them to step forward and join the community of civilized nations in ending this perversion of their religion once and for all. This will be very difficult, because by so doing they will be exposed to instability in their own regimes, and it will test every skill we and our allies possess to see it through. We are talking long-term commitment here, but if we are not successful, we may get what Bin Ladin wants – a 30-year jihad.

Since Vietnam, I have wondered whether or not America could ever again prosecute another war. Not a war fought from 15,000 feet or with "surgical" air strikes on drug factories, but one with significant American casualties requiring noticeable sacrifice and commitment on the domestic front for a protracted period (see "The Demise of the Warrior Class," June 2000). We're about to find out. We are now a nation at war. Those of us who are asking when we will "get back to normal" may have a further shock – the definition of normal has changed, probably forever. Not in terms of airport bag checks, wiretapping laws, and other security measures, or even the way we go about our business and personal affairs, but in our national psyche. Gone is our feeling of invulnerability, our complacency, and probably some element of our exceptionalism.

Gone, too, may be some of our irreverence, so that some things that were humorous are now off limits for late night comedians. Hopefully, our vaunted American optimism will remain intact, for we will need lots of it in the months ahead. And hopefully we will examine again the American idea and engage in some long overdue soul-searching to determine to what extent we are committed to it. If it is, as I believe, the "last best hope for mankind," we are now called upon to defend it, and another generation now has the opportunity to be called the "greatest."

A Transforming Event

November 1, 2001

Since the Gulf War and until recently, I have agreed with and defended the decision made by George H. W. Bush not to pursue the end game with Saddam Hussein in 1991, for all the usual reasons (coalition support, the 52-47 vote in the Senate, the UN resolution, etc.). However, with the obvious benefit of hindsight, I am now convinced that this decision, exacerbated by the feckless policies of the Clinton administration, produced the enabling conditions that led to the current war. OK, maybe it took a 9/11 event to shock us to the realization that civilization is at stake and maybe the Gulf War couldn't have been fought or justified on such terms. Whatever the philosophical or practical confusion then, there should be none now. I repeat: there are no acceptable "root causes" for terrorism or its sponsorship, ever. Pluralism, multiculturalism, tolerance, moral equivalence, whatever their postmodern adaptations, don't extend to a defense of nihilism. So, I now find myself in complete agreement with Joe Lieberman – we need no more evidence; after the defeat of the Taliban, Saddam Hussein must go.

Having established moral clarity, there remain questions we have not been forced to consider at least since the end of World War II, because the nature of the Cold War gave us some comfort of clarity, except in the circles of leftist "fellow travelers." Now we face evil of the kind that is nihilistic in the same sense as Nazism, however, we face it in a world that has been structured to deal only with the East/West confrontation of the Cold War. So now we must deal with, for example, the split-mindedness and duplicity of the Saudi Arabian royal family, and we must re-examine all of the "deals" and accommodations we made over the past 50-60 years in defense of our strategic interests that were defined through the East/West prism. Even more difficult, we must do this in an environment that has been compromised by a half-century of the "hollowing" of the moral core of the West, primarily by our intellectual class.

The ultimate outcome will be transformational, for I believe there is no way to avoid the massive restructuring of the Muslim world that will follow (and parallel) this conflict. The ruling elites in these societies, friend and foe alike, must choose which future they want, and the status quo ante is not acceptable for us or them. In too many instances in the past, U.S. foreign policy has supported stability as the ultimate objective, where revolution would have been preferable, albeit messy. Might this mean transitional occupation in some instances? Possibly. A return to some semblance of colonialism, as some have suggested? Maybe. After all, we're dealing with a region with no core nation-state leadership, and societies that did not have a Magna Carta, a Reformation, a Counter-Reformation, or an Enlightenment. True, these are the unique experiences of the West, but they produced the universal values of successful civilization that most of the world is struggling to emulate in their own way. In fact, if you're watching closely, the stirrings of unrest are already bubbling in the streets of Iran. Vive la revolution!

A "Blink" for Our Clarity

April 8, 2002

In the glow of his State of the Union speech a little over two months ago, it is difficult not to feel that President Bush's April 4 message on the Israeli/Palestinian conflict dulled the sharp edge of our moral clarity in the war on terrorism. On one hand, it is impossible for the world's only superpower not to be engaged in the Middle East; on the other, it clearly works to the advantage of our terrorist enemies (the "evil ones") for the United States to be so engaged, particularly when it appears we are according terrorism some measure of moral equivalence with the civilized response to it. The unconditional response to terrorism in the wake of 9/11 has been somewhat compromised and our mission confused by our apparent return to a "peace process," which never has had credibility. We had better realize that Israel is but another front in the same war, and act accordingly.

Liberate Iraq

September 1, 2002

"Before the sun sets on this terrible struggle, our flag will be recognized throughout the world as a symbol of freedom on the one hand, and overwhelming power on the other." – Gen. George C. Marshall as quoted by Vice President Dick Cheney.

Last June I wrote of "the shakeup we need" that will prepare us for a fundamentally different kind of warfare, a kind that is in some ways alien to our value systems as they have evolved, a pre-emptive war, a total war, one that results in the complete transformation of the enemy's society. Well, we're almost there, but I am shocked that many of our opinion leaders still shrink from this reality.

Saddam Hussein must go. Now. Not after re-instituting United Nations arms inspections (a red herring); not after we prove to an international court of world opinion that he is harboring weapons of mass destruction; not after we or one of our allies has been attacked again; and not after we have commitments from a multinational coalition of allies. Certainly President Bush should make the case, forcefully and with as much candor as prudent, and he should also ask for Congressional approval, not that he needs it except as a politically unifying gesture. But the evidence is in, and I can't improve on Lady Margaret Thatcher's words: "His continued survival after comprehensively losing the Gulf War has done untold damage to the West's standing in a region where the only unforgivable sin is weakness. His flouting of the terms on which hostilities ceased has made a laughingstock of the international community. His appalling mistreatment of his own countrymen continues unabated. It is clear to anyone willing to face reality that the only reason Saddam took the risk of refusing to submit his activities to UN inspectors was that he is exerting every muscle to build weapons of mass destruction. To allow this process to continue, because the risks of action to arrest it seem too great, would be foolish in the extreme." There is no doubt that we are at the dawn of a transformation in foreign policy, diplomacy, and our role in the world. This should have been obvious since 9/11 and the enunciation of the Bush Doctrine. Steve Forbes says we are "at the creation," no less so than at the end of World War II. The first real test of the new doctrine will come in Iraq.

Unquestionably, President Bush's use of the word "evil" is unsettling to the sensibilities of the postmodern mind. We've grown accustomed to dealing with "root causes" and avoiding absolutes. To Bush, however, evil is not an adjective, it's a noun, and it exists in objective reality. The use of this terminology shows a profound understanding of how the world works, particularly the Middle Eastern world steeped in Nietzsche's "will to power."

What if the U.S. is alone in this campaign? I've written before about American exceptionalism and unilateralism and the criticism of these tendencies by our erstwhile friends and allies. In a recent *Wall Street Journal* essay, Victor Davis Hanson notes that one of the reasons we often must stand alone is that we really are different. Our Constitution alone preserves the sanctity of the individual. And I would add that our Civil War re-founding firmly established the U.S. as a culture built on the idea of the universality of certain self-evident truths about human nature, unqualified by race or nationality. And while the U.S. has interests to protect and citizens to defend, we are never without a sense of idealism and exceptionalism in our foreign policy. Most of the caution and responsible opposition to war with Iraq has come from advocates (Scowcroft, et al) of foreign policy realism, or "realpolitik" as we called it during the Cold War. This was the "balance of power" containment policy without a strong moral component that held sway before Ronald Reagan changed the objective to one of victory.

The Bush Doctrine, taken to its ultimate conclusion, will be messy, because it prefers reformation over stability for stability's sake. But it will transform the Middle East and send the message to the subjects of the authoritarian Islamic regimes that self-determination and assimilation with the modern world are realistic possibilities. Read the President's June 1 commencement speech at West Point for an indication of how the world has changed. As Michael Ledeen has noted, this is not a manhunt, it is the opening salvo of a great revolutionary war. And remember that there is no peace and no security without victory.

What Are We Waiting For?

February 4, 2003

If I hear the words "no smoking gun" one more time, I think I'll throw up. Did we really believe that the UN arms inspectors were going to discover new evidence sufficient to indict Saddam Hussein for weapons possession before a grand jury? And who is the jury, anyway? The UN, which has just appointed Iraq to chair its disarmament conference and elected Libya to chair its Commission on Human Rights? Give me a break!

What we have in Saddam Hussein is a brutal menace who has expressed the moral equivalent of Hitler's Mein Kampf about his intentions for 30 years. As David Brooks recently pointed out, this is not about this missile or that weapon of mass destruction (another term I'd like to ditch), but about the explicit objective of a madman to be known 500 years from now as the Arab who brought America down and re-established Pan Arabism by whatever means possible, including racial and ethnic genocide.

There was a time when I would have agreed with the "realpolitiks," that we must have a narrowly defined mission, a definitive and imminent threat, and a well-defined exit strategy before intervening in Iraq. The events of the 1990s, culminating on 9/11, changed this view for me. As I've suggested before, in too many instances in the past, this realpolitik has supported stability as the ultimate objective, where revolution and transformation would have been preferable, albeit messy. On the subject of this particular enemy, I'm much more a crusader in the best sense of that term, as an American form of crusading intervention for liberation, not to act as the "redeemer nation" to recreate the world in our image, as with Woodrow Wilson, but rather based on universals that are the minimal acceptable standards in an increasingly smaller and more interdependent world – the rule of law, the sanctity of each individual life, and self-determination. The ruling elites in the Arab-Muslim world, friend and foe alike, must choose which future they want, but the status quo is not acceptable for them or us. Call this type of crusading American exceptionalism if you like, but name another regime that has the moral authority to lead it.

Of Old Europe, New Europe, and U.S. Foreign Policy

March 4, 2003

With all the attention given to the confrontation on war policy between France and Germany on one hand and the U.S. and Great Britain on the other, it is useful to look at some underlying issues that do not usually make the evening news. For example, Charles Krauthammer has recently noted that the phenomenon of "old" vs. "new" Europe is not only not new, but not really even mostly about war with Iraq. We should remember that everything about the world order that we knew from the end of World War II ended with our victory in the Cold War and the disintegration of the Soviet Union in 1991, and that global institutions are slowly being transformed to adjust to this reality. Frankly, a case can be made, and Tom Friedman has made it well, that World War III began on 9/11. France, for one, doesn't like the new arrangements for dealing with such events, with the U.S. as the only remaining superpower, and is behaving, in John McCain's words loosely quoted "like the aging movie star who has gotten by on her looks for too long and they are now failing her."

So who is out of step here? Some, like former CIA official Graham Fuller, believe the U.S. is, that France and Germany represent "the coming world," that the European Union is the new model for states who are willing to give up large parts of their national sovereignty in order to join a "new civilizational project," and that America in this sense represents the old world. To me, this is internationalist utopianism to the max, but no less an authority than Bill Clinton's deputy secretary of state Strobe Talbott has written, "all countries are basically social arrangements… within the next 100 years, nationhood as we know it will be obsolete. All states will recognize a single global authority."

Robert Kagan, in his new book, *Of Paradise and Power*, has it pegged much better. He believes that there is a culture gap between the U.S. and Western Europe over a range of issues from global warming to religion to the death penalty and that Europe no longer wants to hear about issues of good vs. evil in the world, given their disastrous experiences in the previous century. This gap has enormous consequences for our relationship with Europe and it has destroyed the Cold War consensus on foreign policy, therefore, there is much work to be done to forge a new one. In August 2001 "Bush and the U.S. in Europe," I wrote of America's history as the "anti-Europe," a nation founded in opposition to the social contract theory of Thomas Hobbes and Jean Jacques Rousseau, in which the individual relinquishes his sovereignty in exchange for security and social welfare and in deference to the "general will." The nations that are being called the "new" Europe, those we freed from Soviet totalitarianism, have had quite enough of this model. I said previously, and I repeat, that President Bush's belief in American exceptionalism within the context of a shared history "reaching from Jerusalem and Athens to Europe and Washington" will enable him to craft a new post-Cold War order based on freedom, self-determination, and the rule of law.

Membership and leadership in the global institutions that supervise order (the United Nations or whatever replaces it), however, should require more than self-determination exercised by tribes with flags. This is probably too much for some, but there should be objective thresholds for determining membership in the responsible order. It befalls this generation to lead, and enforce when necessary, this transformation, which should have begun more seriously in 1991. I repeat a quote by Margaret Thatcher: "America's duty is to lead. The other Western countries' duty is to support its leadership… under American leadership, the West will remain the dominant global influence; if we do not, the opportunity for rogue states and new tyrannical powers to exploit our divisions will increase, and so will the danger to all."

Random Thoughts On The War

April 1, 2003

"However long it takes. It isn't a matter of timetable, it's a matter of victory." – George W. Bush.

It is very difficult to focus on much of anything lately except the war in Iraq, so here are some thoughts on it I have been kicking around:

- There once was a responsible anti-war left in this country, but no more. In my essay, "And the War Came" (October 2001), I mentioned Tom Friedman's reference to the concept of "systematic misunderstanding," which arises when your worldview and the other person's worldview are so fundamentally different that it cannot be corrected by providing more information. Such is the current condition of the relationship of responsible statesmanship with what passes for dissent on this conflict. It is difficult, if not impossible, to have a reasonable debate with such a cynical view of the world that presumes no good intentions on the part of the Bush administration or the unique role of U.S. leadership in the world. Even some leftists see the difference, as noted by Michael Walzer, who edits *Dissent,* a leftist magazine: "Many left intellectuals live in America like internal aliens, refusing to identify with their fellow citizens and regarding any hint of patriotic feeling as politically incorrect.
- This disconnect is nowhere more evident than in our entertainment industry, wherein its centerpiece event, the Academy Awards presentation, held on the fifth day of the war with Iraq, was almost completely devoid of any hint of patriotism, nationalism, or feeling of gratitude for the men and women in uniform who defend its enormous privileges. The cultural gap between this crowd and ordinary Americans is glaring, and would be totally harmless except for the fact that much of the world (not to mention our own youth) derives lasting impressions of our country and its values from these celebrities and their product
- In my discussions with those well-intentioned souls who sympathize with the anti-war movement, the point is made that nonviolence is not the same as pacifism, to which my response is that this is a distinction without a difference and, more importantly, that they are closely related and mainly serve as disguises for anti-

Americanism and radical cultural relativism. So all of the Green Party flower children should remember that there is no justice without freedom, and there is no freedom or security without victory.

- If, as Daniel Henninger of *The Wall Street Journal* suggests, this war "will divide the world for the better," we will know soon which way this world and the U.S. are headed, and it will be pretty easy to determine whose side you're on. In my "A Transforming Event" (November 2001), I noted: "The ultimate outcome will be transformational, for I believe there is no way to avoid the massive restructuring of the Muslim world that will follow (and parallel) this conflict. The ruling elites in these societies, friend and foe alike, must choose which future they want, and the status quo ante is not acceptable for us or them." Today, I would add that these choices also apply in many respects to our friends in Western Europe, in particular as they pertain to the mediating institutions such as the UN and NATO that were created by the victors in World War II and which have been rendered antiquated, if not totally irrelevant, by their failure of will demonstrated over the past six months.

- There is no question that the ultimate test of the success of the Bush Doctrine in Iraq will be winning the peace and, in this, the President must be very careful to avoid the American tendency to rely on quick fixes and to come home too soon. First, he must educate the American people on the necessity of a long-term commitment that could involve an extensive occupation, à la Japan after World War II. He must also heed the advice of Jim Hoagland and avoid the "Vichy French option" of relying on former Saddam Hussein collaborators in Iraq's reconstruction. There are those in the State Department who would prefer this route, believing that democracy in Iraq is a pipe dream, but they should be ignored. Steve Forbes has suggested a constitutional monarchy as a transition to democracy, with the restoration of the former royal family and someone like Newt Gingrich as a MacArthur-like high commissioner to supervise the transition to the rule of law, property rights, a stable currency, and low taxes, without the intervention of the heavy hand of bureaucracies like the International Monetary Fund. And, very importantly, Iraq's oil industry should be privatized through competitive bidding as soon as possible. Whatever the model, it should serve as an example for the rest of the Arab world.

- In winning the peace, we should be careful what we ask for, and what kind of democracy we export. The emphasis should be on the "constitutional" rather than the "democratic," and this will require lots of education in core principles. For example, if it turns out to be the American bureaucratic "procedural republic," with racial preferences and multiculturalism, we will not have succeeded. Another bad model, similarly derived from early 20th century progressivism, is the regime installed in India by the British Fabian socialists. Where is John Adams when we need him?

- Finally, for all the corporate conspiracy types who carry the "No War For Oil" placards, I love this advice from comedian and football analyst Dennis Miller: "Hire yourself a pit bull attorney and sue your school district for allowing you to slip through the cracks."

Why We Fought

May 3, 2003

My friend Stuart Schube related to me some conversations he has had recently with friends preparing for the upcoming Jewish Day of Remembrance observing the Holocaust. To one of them he commented (and I paraphrase), "If George W. Bush had been President in 1933 and available to respond to the Nazi threat in 1933-39, there would not be a need for a Day of Remembrance." And I would add, nor a Holocaust Museum. Who knows how many thousands of innocents in the Middle East and possibly other places around the world will now avoid the necessity of a day of remembrance for the continuation and possible acceleration of the genocide of the regime of Saddam Hussein in Iraq. Freedom is not cheap. And to paraphrase Churchill, "this is not the end, it's not even the beginning of the end, but it's surely the end of the beginning." Many treacherous days lie ahead in a long occupation and difficult transformation of Iraqi society. After all, Nazi Germany only lasted 11 years, while the totalitarianism of the Iraqi Baathist Party was in power for 30 years in a culture with no legacy of self-governance, and no history of a Reformation or an Enlightenment. But, however long it takes, this mission was, and is, the right thing to do – a truly transforming event with positive consequences far beyond Iraq's borders. George Bush understands this, just as he understands that freedom is God-given, not conferred by the state or any regime, and should be universal, and that there are risks to be taken and prices to be paid to create a secure environment in which freedom can advance.

In February 2002, the Institute for American Values organized a group of 60 of America's leading intellectuals to draft a declaration of the universal principles that are at stake in this war. Entitled "What We're Fighting For," they are not denominational or sectarian, but represent the received wisdom of the ages and are based on five fundamental truths, as follows: 1) all human beings are born free and equal in dignity and rights; 2) the basic subject of society is the human person, and the legitimate role of government is to protect and help foster the conditions for human flourishing; 3) human beings naturally desire to seek the truth about life's purpose and ultimate ends; 4) freedom of conscience and religious freedom and inviolable rights of the human person; and 5) killing in the name of God is contrary to faith in God and is the greatest betrayal of the universality of religious faith. These serve as valuable reminders of the heritage that must be defended and passed on.

The "Road Map"

June 1, 2003

Count me as one who is highly skeptical about the chances for success of the "road map" to peace in the Holy Land as currently conceived. In fact, I have always been troubled by any characterization resembling a "peace process" for the Israeli/Palestinian conflict, which, almost by definition, is an invention of the internationalists in the United Nations, the European Union, Russia, and certain corners of our Department of State who oppose the Bush Doctrine for the war on terrorism, recoil from the use of terms like "axis of evil" and, in fact, usually do not see a positive role for the use of American power in the world.

What is it that differentiates Palestinian terrorism from the other sources of terrorism with which we have been in a state of war for the past 10 years? When has a cease-fire without surrender ever worked in truly restoring or establishing peace? In Europe after World War I? In Korea?

There is no "peace process" in the Middle East, nor can there be one, in my opinion, until Yasser Arafat is totally removed from Palestinian leadership, Israel's right to exist is unconditionally acknowledged, and the Palestinians unilaterally and unconditionally disavow terrorism as a political weapon. In short, there is no peace and no security without victory, and for President Bush to invest his enormous prestige in a process that has no credibility on the ground is a risk that should not be taken.

Liberty, Security, Stability, and the State Department

July 4, 2003

A couple of months ago, Newt Gingrich was highly visible speaking and making the rounds of the various talk shows with his call for major reorganization of the U.S. Department of State, criticizing its institutionalized duplicity and incompetence in the process. The furor settled down, but my immediate thoughts were that it is about time a high-profile commentator gave voice to this problem. For much too long, particularly in an administration that prides itself in the primacy of freedom, when given a choice, our State Department has almost always opted for "stability" over the advance of freedom. The apparent reason is that there has long been embedded in the career bureaucracy an aversion to policies designed to encourage and assist the "messy" roll back of statism/authoritarianism/totalitarianism, often resulting in an obvious disregard for Presidential leadership. The coming transformation of the Islamic world offers a great window of opportunity to transform the State Department at the same time. I was reminded of this opportunity by a recent article by Ronald Bailey, who makes several insightful points, the first of which is the observation that the spread of liberal, free market democracy in the 20th century was largely accomplished by force of arms – mainly American. A second point is that a world that remains only half-free is inherently dangerous to liberty at home and abroad (those who feel threatened by our growing domestic security apparatus, take note). But the most important point is that we should return to the very productive Reagan Doctrine of assigning a high priority to supporting, training, and financing insurgent movements aimed at overthrowing tyrannical regimes. This is probably anathema to many senior career diplomats and policy wonks at State, but it should be an integral part of our policy for the half of the world that remains in the "not free" category. And, incidentally, a good place to begin immediately to revive this doctrine is in Iran!

Defending Moral Clarity In Foreign Policy

August 2, 2003

As we move deeper into the "funny season" of Presidential election politics, it becomes increasingly more important to stay tightly focused on the principles of moral clarity that have defined Bush foreign policy since 9/11. The strategy of those who oppose the Bush Doctrine, particularly the policy of preemption, is to attack the so-called "soft underbelly" of the rationale for such pre-emption – the intelligence that identifies the relevant security threat. By attacking the credibility of the basis for the war on terror, or its timing and selection of targets, they hope to undermine the policy. Senator (and Presidential candidate) Bob Graham said it – we need to know not only whether or not Iraq had or was developing weapons of mass destruction after the fact, but whether this should have been a reason for the timing of our strikes against it. This is second-guessing at its most irresponsible, because it has a chilling impact on bold leadership in countering terrorism. British Prime Minister Tony Blair said it best, as I paraphrase – the penalty for having been proven right and not acting will be unforgivable, many times worse than having been proven wrong and acting. Speaking of Blair, when have you heard more statesmanship or more clarity of moral purpose than in his recent address to the joint session of Congress? Dare I say that it was Churchillian or Thatcherite? It was right up there with them, and there were some memorable excerpts, such as: "September 11 was not an isolated event, but a tragic prologue;" "there never was a time when the power of America was so necessary or so misunderstood;" "our ultimate weapon is not our guns but our beliefs;" "ours are not Western values, they are the universal values of the human spirit;" "I don't believe you can compromise with this new form of terrorism;" "there is no more dangerous theory in international politics than that we need to balance the power of America with other competitive powers;" and "why us? Why America? Because destiny put you in this place in history, in this moment in time, and the task is yours to do… and our job is to be there with you."

It is amazingly ironic that this moment in history for American leadership comes at a time when we so imperfectly practice and often reject the natural right principles on which we base our liberating foreign policy. Which is why it is doubly important and timely to remind the demagogues and ourselves loudly and often that we occupy the moral high ground in this conflict. End of story.

One Down, Dozens More To Go

January 3, 2004

The title of this essay is borrowed from the headline of a review of a book by Mark Palmer, *Breaking the Real Axis of Evil*, the main point of which is that, beyond terrorism as the primary threat to the world, it is dictatorship itself that must be recognized as a crime against humanity. It follows, now that Saddam Hussein is in captivity, that we should move on to other tyrants who are the real causes of most of the miseries that plague mankind. This is not a call for making war on every non-democratic regime, but rather a "how to" guide for adopting diplomatic, economic and other policies that place a high priority on displacing dictatorships with governments of consent. I can imagine that this attitude, not to mention this book, are anathema in many corners of the U.S. Department of State, which prize "stability" and "engagement" over revolution and confrontation. The capture of Saddam ranks with the capture of the world's great tyrants (which could have included Hitler and should have included Stalin), and only a self-serving fool like Howard Dean could not consider it a positive development for American security. And is it surprising or coincidental that Col. Gaddafi of Libya chose this moment to throw in the towel? Headlines and a couple of Democratic Presidential candidates proclaimed the success of "isolation," "sanctions," and other elements of multilateral diplomacy. Who do they think they are kidding? Certainly not Col.

Gaddafi. This was purely a function of U.S. and British power and the demonstrated will to use it, and it is a vindication of the Bush Doctrine in the war on terrorism. Now let's take a page from Palmer's book, create the office of "Assistant Secretary for Ousting Dictators" in the State Department, and on to Syria, Iran, North Korea, Saudi Arabia, etc.

The Incoherent and Irresponsible American Left

June 4, 2004

The questions for the day are: Can a society steeped in postmodernism in its elite cultural institutions and that has only recently survived its first postmodern Presidency summon the moral courage for the commitment necessary to win the war on terrorism? Can we fight such a war in a 24/7 media market? Can an open society ever fight and win a total war that is considered just? Strangely enough, much of the answers to these questions depend on the "loyal" opposition, which has completely lost the grounding to be coherent and responsible and, in the process, is doing a great disservice to our mission.

In the hour of our greatest crisis since the beginning of World War II, the American left, primarily embodied in the Democratic Party, has no higher calling than to illegitimize the war effort and discredit those who are leading it. There once was a responsible left in this country, but the old leaders of that political wing would not recognize their descendants. Roosevelt, Truman, Kennedy, and Humphrey are spinning in their graves listening to Dean, Kerry, Gore, and the younger Kennedy, and where are the Scoop Jacksons of the current Democrats? Joseph Lieberman is the only one who remotely resembles him, and he was dismissed early in the Presidential primary as a result.

Not one of the present leaders on the left could credibly utter the words of JFK – "let every nation know, whether it wishes us well or ill, that we shall pay any price, bear any burden, meet any hardship, support any friend, oppose any foe to assure the survival and the success of liberty." And not one can credibly define the parameters of the purposeful use of American power in the world or the purposes for or conditions under which young Americans are to be sent in harm's way. None of them, especially their presumptive Presidential nominee, can utter anything but the platitudes of internationalizing the conflict and seeking approval and assistance from the UN, not as a means to an end, but as an end in itself. Forget about the failure to find WMDs, prison abuses, and the hawkish neo-conservative "cabal" they whine about. Those are red herrings. The real hang-up for this crowd is that they are mired in their formative

Vietnam experience, wherein any projection of American power, particularly in the national interest, is considered morally flawed.

They just don't get it. We cannot opt out of this war or delegate it to others. The leadership of the left, John Kerry in particular, needs to understand this, not as an election issue or as legitimate disagreement over tactics, but in terms of our mission as a fundamental American interest. It's about Western civilization and America's leadership of it. As Victor Davis Hanson has noted, "We are not in a war with a crook in Haiti, this is no Grenada or Panama, or even Kosovo or Bosnia. No, we are in a worldwide struggle the likes of which we have not seen since World War II. In a war such as this, the alternative is not a brokered peace, but abject Western suicide and all that it entails."

As for President Bush, this is not his Vietnam, nor is it even his Tet, but he is certainly at a tipping point, no thanks to the irresponsibility of the "loyal" opposition. The need is for a "crisis speech," as described by Carnes Lord in *The Modern Prince*, to stop the psychological and political bleeding now, and Bush is the only one who can do it. As an example, he offers an excerpt from Churchill's first address to the House of Commons in 1940: "...victory – victory at all costs, victory in spite of all terror, victory, however long and hard the road may be." The President should grab some old Churchill speeches and hit the road!

The War: What's Next?

August 1, 2004

Before getting totally consumed with the often vacuous rhetoric of Election 2004, it is important to take stock of the one truly consuming issue before the American people – the global war on terrorism. Where are we and what's next? Those who were anticipating some guidance from the recently released report of the 9/11 Commission should have been disappointed – no "smoking gun," no "red meat" for partisan consumption and assignment of blame – just an invitation to several months of bureaucratic and Congressional turf wars over the substantive equivalent of how to rearrange the furniture. So, while we deal with the almost totally politically driven response to the report, we had better be totally committed to this war for, be assured, our enemies most certainly are. I was struck by a comment in Charles Hill's recent *Wall Street Journal* essay on the Commission report: "...a platform must be found from which to explain the dimensions of the challenge. In terms of the Second World War, we are in the late 1930s. Churchill described the danger then. Today the Bush administration is understandably reluctant to talk frankly about a threat so fraught with religious, cultural, and civilizational implications." How true, but Bush and his surrogates don't have the luxury of avoiding such talk, election year or not. For the fact is that, though war talk was barely mentioned in the 2000 election campaign, we were then arguably in the seventh year of this war, and are now in the 11th! So, what's next? Here are some suggestions: It's time to launch the next offensive – Iran. Clearly, diplomatic efforts have about run their course here, the mullahs have no intention, but to buy time while they pursue their nuclear weapons objectives, and the UN is, as usual, irrelevant. So far, we have been all talk, no action. We should be pursuing regime change on all fronts – political, massive radio intervention à la Radio Free Europe, and aggressive support for the internal dissidents and revolutionaries. What if these don't work? A new test for preemptive military intervention and the Bush Doctrine.

- We should get serious about directly confronting Syria's support for the insurgents and terrorists who are killing Americans and Iraqis in Iraq. The message should be "cease and desist or else!" and should be backed by a real threat of military intervention, with which the Kurdish militia would be happy to assist!
- In Iraq, it's pretty simple: all out support for the new government's promise to "annihilate" the insurgents (i.e., no more "Fallujahs"), hold firm to the date for January elections, and begin to structure new alliances that will be more suitable for the new global realities than the tepid response we have received from our erstwhile NATO "allies" in both Afghanistan and Iraq.
- President Bush's primary responsibility in all of this, for he owns the platform, is to "explain the dimensions of the challenge," as Hill says. There will be a tendency by the "nervous Nellies" to defer any new initiatives in an election year and in the wake of the strong anti-incumbent message in the recent European Union and local European elections, particularly the big losses by Blair in the UK. The President's problems are further compounded by John Kerry's "nuanced" message on the war effort in Iraq, the anti-American sentiments of the European and American left, and their presumption of bad intent on his part. But, to paraphrase Margaret Thatcher in another crisis, "this is no time to go wobbly," and he must be even bolder on these points than he has recently shown. It is the right thing to do strategically for America and the world, as well as politically for him.

China Watch III

August 2, 2004

Very quietly, with scant notice in Western media and none in China, the 15th anniversary of the massacre of Tiananmen Square recently passed. Only in Hong Kong was there any significant commemoration. One hopes that this does not mean that this event has lost its central place in the historical struggle for freedom and human rights. Certainly, we in America shouldn't forget it, and we are remiss in not remembering it more prominently, for I believe it will prove to have been analogous to our Lexington and Concord or Boston Massacre. In the ensuing years since 1989, what we are witnessing in China is a revolution that I predict will be viewed by historians as at least the equivalent of the Industrial Revolution of late 18th and early 19th century Europe. Massive population shifts from rural villages to urban localities are taking place there – more than 300 million people since the late 1970s and a predicted additional 250 million by 2020. Needless to say, this revolution and its concomitant surge in economic growth have enormous implications for the world and present daunting challenges for U.S. economic and foreign policy. Of course, economic integration is essential, and for that reason we should support trade liberalization at every turn through the World Trade Organization and regional free trade organizations. And we should pursue domestic economic growth, job creation, and trade policies that shun protectionism and the constant bashing of China over outsourcing. All of which is to say that we need a President who understands why these priorities are important, but also, not incidentally, why the memory of the heroes of Tiananmen Square and their struggle for political freedom should be ever in the forefront of our thinking and policy deliberations.

The Citadel of Corruption

January 2, 2005

Or, as Emmett Tyrell calls it, the "tabernacle of hypocrisy." Either description will do for the United Nations, which long ago proved its unworthiness as a responsible world forum, much less as an instrument for peace, stability, and human rights, and the corruption of its mission is beyond repair. The UN Security Council validated its irrelevance during the process leading to the war in Iraq, but I challenge anyone to name one instance since its founding when the UN has played a useful role in intervening to avert conflict. Rather than preserve international law, it has almost destroyed it. On the other hand, the General Assembly long ago became a haven and pulpit for the aggrandizement of racists, anti-Semites, anti-Americans, Marxist/Leninist demagogues, tinhorn dictators, and those erstwhile U.S. allies who need legitimate cover for their lucrative deals and conspiracies. The duplicity of Kofi Annan in the Iraq oil-for-food scandal and his failure to lift a finger to stop the massacre in the Sudan should simply be the last straws. He should go immediately, of course, but more importantly, as soon as the elections in Iraq are completed, we should convene a world council of democracies and begin anew. Leave the humanitarian services capabilities of the UN in place, if necessary, but take Steve Forbes's suggestion and invite them to move their headquarters to a country, such as Haiti, that would benefit more from their presence. Then invite those nations that are committed to the rule of law and consent of the governed to organize a new forum more appropriate to the new realities and aspirations of the 21st century.

Tipping Point in Iraq

March 2, 2006

Time magazine headlines it "Iraq Breaking Point," William F. Buckley, Jr. says President Bush needs to come to terms with failure in Iraq, and even the most optimistic observer can be forgiven for seeing the beginning of devolution to civil war in the wake of the explosion of the sacred Golden Mosque in Samarra. No doubt, we are at a critical juncture in our campaign to liberate the Middle East that began with the overthrow of Saddam Hussein, and, as has come to be typical for post-Vietnam America, the biggest challenge for President Bush is to win the war on the home front. Buckley's conclusion is disappointing and gives less credence to the hope for success based on our progress to date than I would expect from him. We can engage in all of the "could haves, should haves, would haves" and "we told you sos" that journalistic license will allow, but the reality is that we are where we are, and defeat is not an option we can tolerate. I believe that the American people, at some level, understand this.

Politically, from this point forward, Iraq will be what the Iraqi people make of it. Are there any Jeffersons, Madisons, Washingtons, Adamses, or Franklins in the room? Who knows? Probably not, at least as we know them, but that doesn't mean that their own heroes won't rise to the occasion. Will the ultimate outcome be civil war? Possibly. After all, at the time of our founding we had all of those people plus a 150-year history of self-governance in the colonies in the context of the British heritage of the rule of law and still couldn't avoid a civil war with more than 600,000 casualties and a re-founding just more than 80 years after our original founding.

I have said all along that this war would be a massively (and messy) transforming event and, sure enough, it's working out just that way. To say that we should have anticipated all that has gone wrong is to be ignorant of all the history of major transformational world events, particularly those involving warfare. Think of Antietam, think of Kasserine Pass and Utah Beach – the list goes on and on. Eliot Cohen asks, "will we persevere?" and answers by suggesting that success will require the rarest of American qualities: patience. But a larger issue is the one so perceptively noted by Victor Davis Hanson, which is that Iraq is no longer a war whose prognosis is to be judged empirically. He believes, and I agree, that it has become a powerful symbol that must serve deeply held, but preconceived, beliefs – Bush's deceptions, the neoconservative cabal, blood for oil, etc. It is the insidious growth of this phenomenon that must be extracted and defeated, for the war in Iraq is, but a piece, albeit a significant one, in the larger war against Islamofascism that must be prosecuted over the coming decades and that will require much more patience and sustained commitment than has been asked or in evidence so far. In the immediate aftermath of the recent violent Islamic reaction to the Danish cartoon satire of Mohammed, Chris Matthews asked the rhetorical question: "we have a long century ahead of us; is this the beginning?" The answer is yes. Is there a Churchill in the room?

Churchill's Legacy

April 2, 2006

In response to my "Letter from London" essay and comments on Winston Churchill in the March issue, Wayne Lapham sent me a fascinating quote by Churchill from his book, *The River War*, published in 1899. It needs to be passed along in its entirety, and remember that Churchill was 24 years old at the time: "How dreadful are the curses, which Mohammedanism lays on its votaries! Besides the fanatical frenzy, which is as dangerous in a man as hydrophobia in a dog, there is this fearful fatalistic apathy. The effects are apparent in many countries. Improvident habits, slovenly systems of agriculture, sluggish methods of commerce, and insecurity of property exist wherever the followers of the Prophet rule or live. A degraded sensualism deprives this life of its grace and refinement; the next of its dignity and sanctity. The fact that in Mohammedan law every woman must belong to some man as his absolute property, either as a child, a wife, or a concubine, must delay the final extinction of slavery until the faith of Islam has ceased to be a great power among men. Individual Muslims may show splendid qualities, but the influence of the religion paralyzes the social development of those who follow it. No stronger retrograde force exists in the world. Far from being moribund, Mohammedanism is a militant and proselytizing faith. It already has spread throughout Central Africa, raising fearless warriors at every step; and were it not that Christianity is sheltered in the strong arms of science, the science against which it had vainly struggled, the civilization of modern Europe might fall, as fell the civilization of ancient Rome."

I am particularly struck by the insightful phrases, "fearful fatalistic apathy," "paralyzes the social development," and "retrograde force" and I wonder how confident he would now be that European Christianity is still "sheltered in the strong arms of science."

Little did Sir Winston know then that just more than 20 years later he would be assigned to manage the affairs of the defeated Ottoman Empire, including Mesopotamia, which produced a new map of the Middle East, making, among other inventions, a new nation – Iraq – out of a collection of tribes, decisions that continue to haunt us today as we seek to forge a "unity government" among the same tribes. Given the sentiments earlier expressed in his book, he had to know that this region and these decisions would be a continuing problem, and many historians have blamed him for not being more visionary.

But I believe we can't blame Churchill; he did the best he could do with the tools and raw material at his disposal at the time. Moreover, he was a product of his time: the Victorian notion of "progress" which had morphed into Wilsonian and Fabian Socialist "progressivism," shared by the well-intentioned, but also by the condescending and often duplicitous protectors of the perks of empire. All of this, in addition to the arrogance that we can play "czar" in dividing up the world to suit our interests and our preferences or to "teach people to elect good men" (Wilson). It is left for our generation to correct these misconceptions and the unfinished business. Freedom under the rule of law is the answer. The people of Iraq will now work it out. It will take more time and, unfortunately, more blood, but it is better than the alternatives.

Iran – Are We There Yet?

May 1, 2006

According to a few who attended a recent small gathering with Bernard Lewis, regarded as the "dean" of Islamic scholars in the U.S., he made the chilling statement that the West is today at a point with the Iranian regime almost exactly where we were with the Nazi regime in 1938. This is a striking realization, and one that we had best take seriously. In his 2002 "axis of evil" address, in which he identified Iran as one of three regimes comprising this axis, President Bush also said this: "I will not wait on events, while dangers gather… The USA will not permit the world's most dangerous regimes to threaten us with the world's most destructive weapons." Any number of our leaders from the President on down, have labeled Iran's possession of a nuclear weapons capability "unacceptable," which certainly is appropriate rhetoric.

My question is whether or not, in all of its implications, we really mean that. If we do, then we should very soon be at the "this will not stand" stage of Iranian diplomacy, à la Kuwait in 1991, and Congressional leaders, in this election year, should be called by their constituents to declare whether or not an Iranian nuclear capability is truly unacceptable. And let's face it – we won't have any more allies in this confrontation than with the war in Iraq and, while we all recognize that a confrontation with Iran would be much easier to contemplate with a significantly improved situation in Iraq, neither of these facts change by one iota the nature of the threat nor should they alter our response to it.

The Mexican Imperative

May 3, 2006

While hotly debating U.S. immigration policy, no one doubts that the public policies of Mexico are at least as important in resolving the immigration crisis in this country as any we adopt here. This is what makes the upcoming presidential election in Mexico critical for the future of this problem and at this point a beneficial outcome there seems iffy at best. If the winner is a leftist in the mold of Venezuela's Chavez, all bets are off, and a return to power of the PRI wouldn't be much better. *The 2006 Index of Economic Freedom*, published by the Heritage Foundation and *The Wall Street Journal*, is instructive in terms of the policies necessary for Mexico to close the economic gap with the U.S. and decrease the incentive for illegal immigration. The annual report surveys 157 countries, grading such things as property rights protection, regulatory environment, tax rates, fiscal policy, government intervention in the economy, monetary policy, and trade policy. Currently, there are 19 countries in the "free" category, with the U.S. ranked ninth overall. Mexico is in the "mostly free" category and ranks 60 overall (of 71 countries in the free or mostly free categories). The gap between these two categories is huge – an average GDP per capita of more than $30,000 for the former versus $13,000 for the latter – which is a big reason for the huge incentive to cross national borders illegally. So, what does this mean for American policy? Should we attempt to influence the Mexican elections? Absolutely not. However, we can and should make it clear that certain changes in their economic policies will be necessary in exchange for such things as our willingness to continue to accommodate their poor and unemployed who cross on a legal basis as guest workers, our willingness to allow the current illegal population to find a pathway to U.S. citizenship, and the degree to which we begin levying a remittance tax on their legal and illegal workers in this country. What policy changes should we suggest? That should be pretty easy – just look at the economic freedom survey and pursue policies that reverse the negative scores on the current policies that are drags on freedom and growth And I would add one more mandatory policy change, suggested by Irwin Stelzer in *The Weekly Standard* – remove the ban on foreign investment in Mexico's oil industry. Nothing would free the patrimony of Mexico's poor and underemployed to create economic growth, not to mention enhancing an alternative to Middle Eastern sources, more than opening Pemex to American capital and oil and gas production expertise. Is this a form of early 20th century "gunboat diplomacy" by other means? Maybe so, and Teddy Roosevelt would not have hesitated to use it.

What Will it Take?

August 2, 2006

"It is not clear to me what exactly the U.S. is trying to accomplish by not taking a stance in favor of an early cease fire." – Zbigniew Brzezinski, ex-national security advisor to President Jimmy Carter.

What will it take to convince world opinion leadership and the denial crowd in this country that Newt Gingrich is correct – this is World War III (or IV if you count the Cold War), it has many fronts, we have been in it for at least 15 years, and it will be a very long one? Why is it that many, if not most, Americans and Europeans understand Islamic terrorism as the disconnected actions of disparate groups of religious fanatics? What is it about the liberal internationalist mind that cannot or will not connect the dots of the sequence of events over the past quarter century? Why is it always that the world's first reaction, except in the U.S. and Britain, to the exercise of Israel's sovereign right to self-defense is accusation of "disproportionate response" with immediate calls for cease fire? Why is it so difficult for some of us to empathize with the analogy of the establishment of a state-sponsored militia just across our border launching missiles into Chicago, or at least to the comparison with our Cuban missile crisis of 1962? And why do we continue to have patience or confidence in any reliance on the inept United Nations to monitor, much less enforce, any of its resolutions?

And yet the media laments that Secretary of State Condoleezza Rice's trips to the Middle East since the Hezbollah attacks on Israel aren't really "peace missions," contrasting them unfavorably to the shuttle diplomacy of previous administrations. UN Ambassador John Bolton has it right – Hezbollah is illegitimate, incapable of commitment, and has no authority to negotiate anything, not to mention that it has killed more Americans in the past 25 years than any other group with the exception of Al Qaeda on 9/11.

Let's review: We've had Camp David, the Mitchell Plan, the Oslo Accord, Land for Peace, the Roadmap to Peace, etc., etc. All were failures. Isn't it time to win the war? No victory, no peace.

Dump the UN

October 2, 2006

What further evidence and insult do we need that the United Nations is a bad joke and should be evicted from American soil? Let the prima donnas from the tinhorn dictatorships and tribes with flags find accommodations in Port-au-Prince or some other such garden spot that will waive the parking tickets for their limos and otherwise subsidize worldwide media coverage for their anti-American ranting. The entire notion of a "world parliament of man" has been a pipe dream of the romantic internationalist elite for decades, and its futility has been clearly revealed in the complete abdication of the Security Council in its most critical moment of truth – the clear and present threat of Islamofascism joined with nuclear weapon capability. If, and it's a big if, there is a real need for a global institution dedicated to serious discussion of common security, we should organize a Congress of Democracies, or the like, to engage in meaningful dialogue about how freedom based on the rule of law and the consent of the governed can best be expanded and the real threats to world peace can be confronted and defeated.

Time for a Conversation among Grown Ups

November 2, 2006

Whatever foreign policy adjustments follow from the mid-term election results, one thing is abundantly clear to me – between now and 2008 it's time for a long and serious conversation among adults about the Long War. In fact, despite the considerable downside to the prospects for Democratic control of Congress, the configuration of a Bush White House and a Democratic Congress just might be more conducive to the seriousness of the debate. For the fact is that Bush himself has become so much of the issue that reasonable perspective among the leaders of the "loyal opposition" and their rabid left wing, anti-Bush chorus has become almost impossible. With Democrats in charge of the legislative branch, they no longer can hide behind their nay-saying, anti-Bush rhetoric and maybe some maturity and responsibility will emerge. Opinion from several for whose judgment I respect is now beginning to evolve along the lines that the situation in Iraq is so intractable that new definitions of success must be openly considered.

Charles Kesler believes that anti-Bush attitudes among Democratic leaders render them incapable of dealing with his administration in good faith and that the entire debate must be carried by the 2008 Presidential contenders. Steve Forbes is convinced that the only way Iraq can be held together without a tyrant is by establishing Swiss-style autonomous regions for Kurds, Shiites, and Sunnis, somewhat like our federal system. Charles Krauthammer says that we should make it clear to the Iraqis that we have done all we can do to deliver them the opportunity to have a democratic order under the rule of law and it's now up to them to step up and take it. And David Brooks says that it's time to adjust our plans to reality – that the country is an exercise in futility, always has been, likely always will be, and he cites the history to support this contention. Finally, and most visionary, Newt Gingrich has a step-by-step plan for how the President should proceed from here, modeled after the strategy that Abraham Lincoln chose in the dark days of 1862 when it became clear that the only viable choice for the Union was total victory.

At this point, as an approach to revised strategy, I am proceeding cafeteria-style, selecting a little from all of the above, leaning heavily toward the Gingrich plan, without the pessimism of Brooks and without abandoning the flavor of Bush's idealistic theme and sponsorship of the universality of freedom as a means of planting some semblance of democracy in the Arab Middle East, both as a foundation for lifting the region out of oppression and into modernity and as a sound investment in American security.

The President may already have sent a significant signal of strategy change to come with his replacement of Secretary of Defense Donald Rumsfeld with Robert Gates. Gates is no doubt a good man and very capable, but his reputation is very pragmatic and non-ideological, and I wonder if this change is a precursor to a move toward more war policy realism in the James Baker/Brent Scrowcroft vein. Watch closely for any policy concessions in the administration response to the report of the Baker/Hamilton Iraq study group (on which Gates is serving), as well as the Gates confirmation hearings in the Senate. I'm wary.

Of two things I remain absolutely convinced – that Iraq was at the outset and still is a major front in the Long War against Islamofascism and that any strategy that even closely resembles retreat would be a disaster for America and the West. As Tony Blair so well stated in his farewell speech to his party, "We will not win until we shake ourselves free of the wretched capitulation to the propaganda of the enemy – that somehow we are the ones responsible. This isn't our fault, we didn't cause it, and it's not the consequence of foreign policy. It's an attack on our way of life and its global… If we retreat now, we won't be safer, we will be committing a craven act of surrender that will put our future security in the deepest peril."

Lonely Joe Lieberman

March 4, 2007

"Congress faces a choice: Will we allow our actions to be driven by the changing conditions on the ground in Iraq or by the unchanging political and ideological positions long ago staked out in Washington? What ultimately matters more to us: the real fight over there, or the political fight over here?" – Joe Lieberman in *The Wall Street Journal*, 2-26-07.

"…there is a world beyond Pennsylvania Avenue that is watching and listening. What we say here is being heard in Baghdad by Iraqi moderates, trying to decide if the Americans will stand with them. We are being heard by our men and women in uniform, who will be interested to know whether we support the plan they have begun to carry out. We are being heard by the leaders of the thuggish regimes in Iran and Syria, and by Al Qaeda terrorists, eager for evidence that America's will is breaking. And we are being heard across America by our constituents, who are wondering if their Congress is capable of serious action, not just hollow posturing." – Joe Lieberman on the Senate floor, 2-5-07.

These excerpts are representative of a degree of statesmanship that have become exceedingly rare in our politics. As a result, Senator Lieberman now has worked himself into position as the last remaining Truman/Kennedy/Jackson Democrat, a position that is about as lonely as it gets in the current configuration of the Congressional leadership and the mainstream of the Democratic Party. But in the process he also has developed into the Arthur Vandenberg of the current foreign policy crisis. Senator Vandenberg of Michigan was the Republican Chairman of the Senate Foreign Relations Committee (a position occupied today by Joe Biden) who, in 1947, despite the strong incentives and desire of his party to undermine President Truman in advance of the election of

1948, strongly supported Truman in his proposals for aid to Greece and Turkey, the Marshall Plan to salvage Europe, and the founding of NATO, which spearheaded the containment of Soviet Communism that lasted until its defeat in 1991. Clearly, Joe Biden could have been an Arthur Vandenberg and hasn't chosen to be one, while Joe Lieberman already is.

Some observers have suggested that Lieberman's position on the war in Iraq represents a bias that should be expected from one of his "tribe," a deeply cynical view not worthy of the statesmanship on display here. And, incidentally, more to this point, I would ask: to what tribe do I belong?

Cold War Redux?

September 5, 2008

In his 1835 classic, *Democracy in America,* Alexis de Tocqueville was prescient in his characterization of the Russians and the Americans: "The American struggles against the obstacles which nature opposes to him; the adversaries of the Russians are men. The former combats the wilderness and savage life; the latter, civilization with all its arms. The conquests of the Americans are therefore gained by the ploughshare; those of the Russians by the sword. The Anglo-American relies upon personal interest to accomplish his ends and gives free scope to the unguided strength and common sense of the people; the Russian centers all the authority of society in a single arm. The principal instrument of the former is freedom; of the latter, servitude."

It is pretty clear from this analysis that these two cultures were on a collision course, which, aided and abetted by the assertiveness of Marxist-Leninist ideology, was manifested in the 20th century. And in spite of the fact that the West was ultimately triumphant, recent developments indicate that the conflict is re-emerging in a modified form.

In the August issue, I commented on the death of Alexander Solzhenitsyn and suggested that he would have been an obvious choice to lead a Russian "truth commission" to examine and provide transparency and a sense of closure to the Soviet Communist regime of the 20th century. What a difference this would have made in the world's response to the recent Russian invasion of Georgia. Let's be very clear – a historical accounting of the lies and crimes of the past century would put in proper context the claims that Russia is now asserting. The current aggression, conceived in the perception of U.S. weakness, because of its preoccupation with the Iraq conflict, which is acknowledged, and endemic European weakness and intimidation, which is obvious, is totally calculated to roll back American hegemony in the region, which is anathema to Russian leadership.

Russian President Medvedev has made the Russian position very clear, in part as follows: "…the world should be multipolar, a single pole world is unacceptable;… there are regions in which Russia has privileged interests." And there are a number of very influential thinkers who have sympathy for the Russian position. But let us also be clear about this pivotal point in world affairs – failing to stand up to this Russian intervention in a sovereign nation state would significantly damage every international gain since the end of the Cold War. Senators Lindsey Graham and Joe Lieberman said it well: "In the long run, a Russia that tries to define its greatness in terms of spheres of influence, client states, and forced fealty to Moscow will fail."

Obviously, the U.S. is not going to war with Russia over Georgia, but there are a number of things that should be done in response to this violation of world order, including expulsion of Russia from the G-8, the accelerated advancement of Ukraine and Georgia membership in NATO, and the denial of Russian membership in the World Trade Organization. Further, we should advance the organization of a league of democracies, which would counter the United Nations and exclude those nations, including Russia, that have not sufficiently demonstrated their commitment to rule by the consent of the governed.

American credibility is at stake here, and the presidential election campaign should give due attention to the reality of these events and their import, as well as who is best qualified to organize, articulate, and deliver the American response.

Obama in Cairo

June 4, 2009

The "amen corner" already has spoken – President Obama has delivered another masterpiece in Egypt and the relationship between the U.S. and the Muslim world will never be the same. Well, let's take a deep breath and reflect on it in more depth.

To his credit, unlike the first two legs of his international tour in Europe and Latin America, during which his remarks were littered with confessions and apologies for America's many transgressions over the past century or so and which was highlighted by a 50-minute dressing down from a Marxist thug, an insult which went totally unanswered by anyone in the U.S. delegation, the Cairo speech was much less demeaning to his country and much more relevant.

It covered the gamut of the critical issues, from democracy to economic development to Palestine/Israel to Iraq to Afghanistan to women's rights to religious freedom – a pretty comprehensive list. And he was appropriately candid in his negative references to those who deny or justify the 9/11 attack and the Holocaust, as well as those who practice "violence" (his substitute for terrorism, a word not used in the speech) in the cause of claiming moral authority. And naturally all of this was couched in terms of "a new beginning" for U.S./Muslim relations (meaning post-Bush, of course).

So far, so good, and everyone is talking about the numerous applause interruptions. And there were many, but a review of their prompting phrases reveals an interesting pattern – not one was prompted by a reference to a call for change in the behavior of the Muslim world; every applause line was a reference to what America will do to change its policies in and attitudes about the Middle East or to further support economic development in the region or to stop the growth of Israeli settlements or to close Gitmo or to a commitment that America will never go to war with Islam. In fact, I could find no significant challenge to the Muslim world to modify its behavior or to condemn global terrorist jihad (another word that was not used) in any way. The only possible exception was a suggestion that each culture should resist negative stereotypes of the other, a line that was heartily applauded.

So, what we had was vintage Obama – plenty of style points, smooth delivery, well articulated to convey the sense that things will be OK now that he is in charge. We'll see. But conspicuously missing from the speech was the truth about U.S./Muslim relations in any real depth, which he briefly could have outlined as suggested recently by Charles Krauthammer: Five military campaigns in the past 20 years engaged by Americans on behalf of Muslims resulting in the liberation of the people of Bosnia, Kosovo, Kuwait, Iraq, and Afghanistan. These efforts brought little gratitude, it should be noted, but were accompanied by hatred, assassination, mass murder, and economic attack, to wit: the assassination of our ambassador in Sudan, the Arab oil embargo, the murder of our ambassador to Lebanon, the attack on our embassy in Teheran and the holding of our hostages for 14 months, the bombing of our embassies in Nairobi and Tanzania, the attack on the USS Cole, and ultimately the attack of 9/11.

There is plenty of evidence here that a state of war has existed between America and radical Muslim jihadists for about 30 years, for most of which time the mainstream Islamic world has been at best ambivalent and at worst complicit and enabling.

Likewise conspicuously missing from Obama's presentation was any reference to the difficult choices that responsible Muslim leaders must make to bring the Arab Middle East into modernity. He could have referenced Pope Benedict's Regensburg Lecture of 2006, much maligned in the Muslim world for its alleged blasphemy, but in fact a textbook outline of how the choices made by Islamic intellectual and theological leadership over the centuries have resulted in an inability to reconcile the truths of their religion with those of reason, a critical ingredient that has produced the dominance of the West in scientific and economic development. He briefly mentioned the Muslim role in paving the way for the European Renaissance and the Enlightenment, but the Muslim world was not a participant in either transformation, nor did it experience a Reformation or the Scientific Revolution.

Nor was there any emphasis in the speech on the responsibility of Muslim leadership, particularly in the Middle East, to use its vast oil wealth to leverage its development, both economically and culturally, through the education of its young people and the cultivation of the minds of its women.

Beyond these omissions, there was the typical implication moral equivalence of Israel's defense of its right to exist vs. the Palestinian right to its own state and the equivalence of U.S. installation of the Shah in the mid-1950s as a protection of American Cold War interests with 30 years of serial acts of war by Iran on the U.S.

I wish the President well in his campaign to "change the image of America around the world," whatever that means beyond "we're not George Bush," but the large majority of Americans still believe in American exceptionalism, which among other things means that, as George Weigel has so well noted, there is no alternative to U.S. leadership in the war against global jihadism, not only because the U.S. has the resources for the job, but because it is, or ought to be, the repository of the ideas, drawn from both faith and reason, that must shape that struggle. I hope, but wonder if, Barack Obama understands or believes that or really knows the people he is leading.

The War of Necessity

October 8, 2009

"This is not a war of choice; this is a war of necessity. Those who attacked America on 9/11 are plotting to do so again... So this is not only a war worth fighting; this is fundamental to the defense of our people." – President Barack Obama, speech to the Veterans of Foreign Wars, August 17, 2009.

Well, that was then. Now it appears that we are rethinking that bold commitment and conviction. For almost eight years, Afghanistan has been the "good war," particularly for the left, and was used by Democrats as the abused policy stepchild for continuing criticism of Bush's Iraq venture, even after the surge in Iraq turned defeat into victory. I'm not cynical by nature, but forgive me if it now appears that this "good war" rhetoric was never anything more than a facade for the true passion of the left to avoid any assertion of American military power. Now we hear that a re-evaluation of the strategy announced last March is being conducted before responding to the commanding general's request for additional resources, including troops, to complete the mission. And what is the mission? I can't remember hearing a clear answer from the Obama administration, particularly one that includes the word **victory**.

Professor Fouad Ajami reminds us that it was not Afghans who struck America on 9/11. It was Arabs, and their terrorism was informed by the pathologies of Arab and Muslim political life. Therefore, it was important to take the war into the Arab world. George W. Bush did this, not without a number of mistakes, but also with a number of important victories, and the key thing to remember is that this is a war with many fronts that must be waged over a protracted period of time with persistence, a trait not exactly one of America's great virtues since the Vietnam experience.

President Obama is on the eve of a watershed policy decision. Success is absolutely necessary, but will require a sustained commitment of many more years, the implementation of which will require the best of his exquisite skills of eloquence in articulation in the face of a political base that will be a very difficult sale at best. He was correct in his August remarks to the VFW – any bets that he will re-confirm those convictions on the ground in the war zone?

Another Bailout

October 8, 2009

This bailout was of a different kind, and potentially much more serious. In meeting with Iran President Mahmoud Ahmadinejad's representatives in Geneva, the U.S. and other major powers allowed his regime a legitimacy and rehabilitation that no amount of imagination could have perceived following the fraudulent June elections. President Obama characterized the talks as a "constructive beginning." A beginning to what? And to what end? We've been talking to this regime for 30 years to no avail under conditions tantamount to a state of war perpetrated by them. This regime has no credibility, zip, nada, no grounds for trust in any form.

Now we have sold out the Czechs and the Poles on our commitment to a missile-defense security agreement in order to appease Russia and entice them to help put pressure on Iran. Result? Nyet! No less a hawk than French President Sarkozy was even shocked that Obama could be so naive, not to mention being insulted that he was forced to scratch his remarks before the UN Security Council on the revelation of an illegal uranium enrichment facility in Iran so that Obama could release the news the next day to the G-20 in Pittsburg and not have it serve as a "distraction" in his later remarks at the UN. You can't make this stuff up.

This administration obviously is reconciled to the conclusion that a nuclear armed Iran is inevitable and can be contained much in the manner that the Soviet Union was contained during the Cold War. How utterly naive and misguided. How can Obama possibly not realize that he is pushing Israel into a direct strike on nuclear facilities in Iran? And does he believe that the U.S. would not be held almost entirely responsible for such a strike? How can he not realize that the asymmetrical threat posed by Iran is of a nature totally different from the symmetrical threat represented by the Soviet regime?

Israeli Prime Minister Netanyahu has made it clear that, for him, it is "1938," and that there will be no second Holocaust on his watch. Methinks that he is dead serious and that there is not much time left to perform our duties as the world's only superpower.

Obama at Oslo, West Point, and On Iran and the "Overseas Contingency Operation"

January 1, 2010

Hold the thoughts of Victor Davis Hanson in mind while contemplating the Obama war (or "unwar") strategy. In Oslo to accept the Nobel Peace Prize, he at least acknowledged that "evil exists in the world" and that there is such a thing as just war, a major concession for him to the obvious consternation of his Norwegian hosts and his base on the left. In announcing the Afghanistan troop increase at West Point, he made a point to emphasize freedom and human rights as universal birthrights, a page out of George Bush's doctrine. Good for him. But can someone please explain his detached demeanor and absence of outrage, moral clarity, and resolve at the continuing Islamic jihad against America as manifest in the terrorist attacks at Fort Hood and the commercial airline flight to Detroit, and most egregiously, the continuing acts of war perpetrated by the regime in Iran? Everyone with any common sense understands that these are not isolated "criminal" events subject to Constitutional rights and presumption of innocence and that we continue to be engaged in a multi-front war against various elements of radical Islam. Why has this escaped an administration that seems oblivious to the threat to Americans and our allies worldwide and refuses to even use the correct terminology? When will we get serious about profiling the Islamic jihadist terrorist threats that make a mockery of homeland security? And why can't Obama bring himself to express unconditional support to the now certainly genuine Iranian democratic revolution, a move which could tip in our favor the most transformational event possible in the Middle East – regime change in Iran? I'll attempt some answers later.

The Russia – U.S. "Reset"

March 3, 2010

At the dawn of the Obama administration, the mission of U.S.-Russian relations was characterized by "reset," even to the point of a silly reset button visual aid presented to Russian leadership by Secretary of State Hillary Clinton. What reset means to the Russians was described by Russian President Dmitry Medvedev as "to move beyond Cold War mentalities and chart a fresh start in relations between the two countries." One of my problems with all of this reset talk has been that we have never really told the truth about the Cold War or the relative ideological positions of its major antagonists, nor has there been the transparency of a "truth commission" to introduce the full reality of the failed Soviet regime to the Russian people. On the other hand, we have heard former Russian President Putin describe the collapse of the Soviet empire as "the greatest political catastrophe of the 20th century." and we have witnessed aggression on the part of the Russians that could serve no purpose other than to restore their hegemony over the sovereign states that once constituted this empire. Reset? Whose Cold War mentalities?

In a recent issue of *Cato's Letter*, former Soviet political dissident and author Vladimir Bukovsky has some interesting things to say, such as: "The Cold War was a confrontation between liberal democracy and totalitarian socialism. It was an ideological battle, a war of ideas. And a war we never won. We never even fought it… Because we didn't win it, it isn't over. To do it we need a Nuremberg trial, but not a trial of people; it isn't about judging individuals, it's about judging the system."

Bukovsky spent considerable time and effort trying to persuade the Yeltsin government to conduct such a trial, to no avail. Why not? Yeltsin was under tremendous pressure not to do so, mainly from the West, as he reports, as a result of the deep collaboration between left-wing parties in the West and the former Soviet Union. This extended to the leadership of the movement for the European Union, which believed that the disclosure of the total failure of the socialist experiment in Russia would discredit the left in Europe. It is painful to note that Bukovsky believes, with some credibility since much of it is well documented, that the U.S. was complicit in supporting the Soviet Union in its attempt to prevent the breakup of its empire.

This is useful perspective from one who witnessed this monumental transformation from the inside out. Now think back to President Obama's Russian summit of July 2009. In her reporting on the meetings, Liz Cheney described them primarily in terms of a comparison of two different versions of the end of the Cold War – the Russian version and the truth – with President Obama endorsing the Russian version. In characterizing the conflict, Obama couched the confrontation in terms better suited for an athletic, business, or scientific competition, implying a moral equivalency between the two systems that belies the worldwide battle between freedom and tyranny that was actually the case.

The point is this: if by "reset" the Obama administration has in mind some form of revisionism of the history of the ideological conflict that was the Cold War that implies any moral equivalency between the two systems, as it evidently does, or if there is any intention to have another generation of young Russians be sheltered from the truth about that conflict and the evil Soviet regime that waged it, the American people, who financed and won a hard-fought 46-year war, should completely reject this aspect of U.S. foreign policy and those who implement it.

Speaking of the New Start With Russia

May 4, 2010

This is more dreamworld. We won the Cold War by being willing to think the unthinkable. The Soviets were not stupid and they understood cost/benefit analysis. They also knew that U.S. nuclear retaliation in response to something dumb on their part was a very real probability under every American President since Truman. Was this realistic? No one knows and thankfully, we haven't been forced to learn, but it kept us safe for more than four decades and it's a good reason to conclude that the utopian notion of "zero nukes" is not healthy for the U.S. and our allies and only benefits outlaw regimes. The New START exposes a very disturbing aspect of President Obama's worldview. About a year ago, he previewed his strategy when he said "as the only nuclear power to have used a nuclear weapon, the U.S. has a moral responsibility to act." Well, I have a different take: The moral authority to remain the world's only nuclear superpower trumps any moral responsibility stemming from its only historic use. This treaty weakens America and its allies, it undermines our flexibility to employ strategic defensive weapons, it plays into the hands of the world's rogue states, and it should be rejected by the Senate.

Know Your Enemy?

June 4, 2010

The Deputy National Security Adviser to President Obama is John Brennan, who first came to my attention in the aftermath of the Ft. Hood shootings and the almost successful Christmas bombing of an airliner in Detroit. Here is a man who is on the front lines of a war that has been underway in its most intense phase for almost nine years and, in reality, for more than 30 years. One would think that he has the enemy pretty well identified, right? Well, not quite, and he seems to have a tendency to think out loud in his deliberations, as evidenced by recent appearances. In a speech at the Center for Strategic and International Studies, he repeated the administration's argument that our enemy is not "terrorism," but then said that the word "jihad" should not be used either, as follows: "Nor do we describe our enemy as jihadists or Islamists, because jihad is a holy struggle, a legitimate tenet of Islam, meaning to purify oneself or one's community, and there is nothing holy or legitimate or Islamic about murdering innocent men, women, and children." This despite the fact that enemy leadership itself describes their struggle with the West as jihad, that the word almost always connotes war, and that Osama bin Laden and other Islamic radicals commonly use the word to call for war against us. And this guy is one of the administration's principal spokesmen on national security?

Alas, these remarks are consistent with the characterization of the perpetrator of the shootings at Ft. Hood by the Army Chief of Staff on the scene and later by the Attorney General before Congress. They also fall in line with the initial identification of the intended airline bomber as a "lone wolf." New York Mayor Bloomberg speculated that the recent Times Square bomb might be the work of someone unhappy with the healthcare bill, and our Attorney General again avoided the obvious by saying "there are a variety of reasons why people do these things." How can we continue to prosecute a war without properly identifying the enemy? It's people like these who are aiding and abetting our real enemy by refusing to face the truth and misleading us from clarity on the objective.

Vindication in Iraq

September 6, 2010

In September 2002, I wrote this: "Saddam Hussein must go. Now. Not after re-instituting United Nations arms inspections (a red herring); not after we prove to an international court of world opinion that he is harboring weapons of mass destruction; not after we or one of our allies has been attacked again; and not after we have commitments from a multinational coalition of allies. Certainly President Bush should make the case, forcefully and with as much candor as prudent, and he should also ask for Congressional approval, not that he needs it except as a politically unifying gesture. But the evidence is in, and I can't improve on Lady Margaret Thatcher's words: 'His continued survival after comprehensively losing the Gulf War has done untold damage to the West's standing in a region where the only unforgivable sin is weakness. His flouting of the terms on which hostilities ceased has made a laughingstock of the international community. His appalling mistreatment of his own countrymen continues unabated. It is clear to anyone willing to face reality that the only reason Saddam took the risk of refusing to submit his activities to UN inspectors was that he is exerting every muscle to build weapons of mass destruction. To allow this process to continue, because the risks of action to arrest it seem too great would be foolish in the extreme.'

There is no doubt that we are at the dawn of a transformation in foreign policy, diplomacy, and our role in the world. This should have been obvious since 9/11 and the enunciation of the Bush Doctrine. Steve Forbes says we are 'at the creation,' no less so than at the end of World War II. The first real test of the new doctrine will come in Iraq."

It has been a long and deadly, mistake-filled road from that point until President Obama's announcement of "the end of combat operations." Was it worth the effort and price? Yes, but only if we sustain the effort to its satisfactory conclusion, which is the transforming presence of a working democracy (no, not by American standards) in what has been called "the Germany of the Middle East," the economic and cultural linchpin of the region, and one that is a peaceful and mostly reliable ally of the U.S. What will it take to reach this conclusion? Probably what many Americans don't want to hear, but what most believe will be necessary to finish the job and validate the price we have paid, and that is nothing less than what was required to ensure a peaceful, independent, and friendly Japan, Germany, and South Korea.

And wouldn't it be an honorable gesture for Obama to at least acknowledge the vindication of his predecessor in making the politically bold, courageous, and unpopular, but ultimately successful decision to launch the military surge that produced the victory that made this day possible?

A Major Disconnect

October 5, 2010

Quite a lot has been written about the disconnect that obviously has widened in recent years between the so-called "elites" who populate the governing classes in politics, the media, and academia, and the rest of the citizens who must find a way to get through the day in dealing with the results, while keeping their lives and fortunes intact. Peggy Noonan has been particularly good at describing this phenomenon and senses that this gulf has never been as wide as it is right now. I agree, and one particular aspect of this gap that is especially worrisome is the one between those who have some connection to past or current military service and those who have not.

In a recent article, Gary Schmitt and Cheryl Miller note that, despite the fact that we have been at war for almost 10 years continuously, and although Americans hold military service and sacrifice in very high regard, they do so increasingly from a distance, and they believe that this trend is a threat to America's civic ethic of equal sacrifice. The latest figures show that veterans now represent nine percent of the total population, a percentage that continues to decline, and that less than one percent serves in any of the military services, active duty or reserves. The data also shows that our soldiers come from an increasingly narrower segment of society – geographically and culturally. Not surprisingly, Southerners disproportionally populate all the military branches, while the middle-class suburbs surrounding the largest cities produce relatively few service members compared to their large populations of young people.

The all-volunteer military has served our country very well, and I am certainly not suggesting the return of the draft. But we should be concerned about many of the attitudes among our opinion leaders and some of its resulting policy that smack of a certain dismissiveness of the willingness and commitment of our young people to serve their country. To wit, several weeks ago, during a discussion about the "end of combat operations" and pending troop reductions in Iraq on the MSNBC program *Morning Joe*, commentator Lawrence O'Donnell made the comment, "If you want to end U.S. involvement in wars, reinstate the draft; that will do it instantly." Commentator Doris Kearns Goodwin said that she was struck by the reaction at a party in New York when she mentioned that her son had chosen to enter the military. There was disbelief among those at the party, as though they could not imagine why he would do that. To which O'Donnell then replied "That's because the elite understand the burdens and risks of war as others don't. The volunteers are full of a lot of naivete." The final comment from a discussion participant from *Rolling Stone* magazine was "And they volunteer, because they need the employment." If this dialogue doesn't represent the ultimate in elite condescension, I don't want to hear anything worse. Is there any doubt about how out of touch this crowd is with the warrior class and the patriotic sense of duty of the kids who defend this country and the families from which they originate?

More than 10 years ago, in the June 2000 issue, I wrote of "The Demise of the Warrior Class" in which I noted that it is clear that, as the World War II generation passes on, fewer Americans feel a direct connection with or obligation to military service. I also quoted Kirk Kicklighter, a former Marine Corps Captain, who said that the military and the civilian culture it serves are becoming estranged, and that the problem began with Vietnam, as the students who protested the war became the tenured faculty and civilian government leaders of today and are highly skeptical of the military.

Coincidentally, Duke University was then conducting a study of this estrangement, which produced some disturbing results. Large percentages of military personnel reported being annoyed by what they saw as a breakdown in virtues like honesty and sacrifice within civilian institutions, and they believed that civilians are in the midst of a moral crisis. Seventy-seven percent of military officers believed the adoption of such military values as honor, accountability, and teamwork would help civilian society reform itself. Eighty-one percent of newly commissioned officers felt the military's values are closer than civilian values to those of the Founding Fathers. Of course, this survey was completed before 9/11 launched us into our current conflicts and it would be interesting to know how these attitudes would compare 10 years later, but my guess is that they would be fairly consistent. They are certainly worthy of our attention.

I repeat: The attitudes and sensitivities of our elites to the contrary notwithstanding, no great republic can endure without an effective, committed warrior class, preferably one that is representative of the body politic, properly accountable to civilian authority with a clear vision of the society's vital interests and the proper uses of power. God help us if we ever forget this.

Egypt: The Army or Qutb?

February 3, 2011

"The formula that triggered a democratic revolution in the Soviet Union had three components: people inside who yearned to be free, leaders outside who believed they could be, and policies that linked the free world's relations with the USSR to the Soviet regime's treatment of its own people... It will work anywhere around the globe, including in the Arab world." – Natan Sharansky, *The Case for Democracy*.

This is the ultimate article of faith among foreign policy idealists, and it formed the organizing principle for the Bush Doctrine. In fact, George W. Bush was known to have spent quite a bit of time with Sharansky and his thought, which served as an inspiration for what will no doubt be a central legacy of his administration. I believe that there is little doubt that the aspirations at least partly inspired by this doctrine are playing out in Egypt as I write – credit or condemn it as you will, but the Bush Doctrine is alive and well in the Middle East.

Unfortunately, at critical times since the formulation of this doctrine, we blinked and hesitated – in Iraq when Bush felt obliged to de-emphasize freedom as the primary mission as the conflict bogged down in the dark months of 2005-06 before "the surge" won the day; in Iran in the summer of 2009 as we watched without encouragement and support as freedom fighters took to the streets in opposition to an evil regime and its fraudulent re-election; and in Egypt as we continued to defer to an authoritarian regime that ostensibly protected our interests in the region, while consistently denying economic freedom and civil rights to its own people, thereby building rage and animosity over denied aspirations that finally burst into revolution.

At this point, there is no way to know how this will end, but it figures to be one of the most transformational events in the Middle East since the fall of the Ottoman Empire and the Caliphate at the end of World War I. My reference to the choice of Qutb refers to the late Sayyid Qutb, an Egyptian and the intellectual founder of the Muslim Brotherhood, and in fact an inspiration for much of the ideology of Islamic jihadism as it is currently practiced, with a large following throughout the Arab world. On the other hand, the Egyptian army is generally pro-Western and is clearly preferable in the interim as a transitional stabilizing element. Question is, transition to what? Are there any Jeffersons, Madisons, Adamses, or Washingtons in the street? No one knows, haven't seen one yet, but if not, the void is partly our fault, and we must deal with it as best we can. Freedom is messy and, needless to say, the stakes are pretty high. If Qutb wins, we're in big trouble.

It's 1989 in the Middle East

March 4, 2011

"For the first time in 1,000 years Arabs are taking control of their own affairs." – Farheed Zakaria.

Dare we say that the explosion of freedom in the Middle East and North Africa might be the equivalent of the fall of the Berlin Wall? We can pray that it is at least as eventful and we should be doing everything in our power to ensure that it is so. We can do a lot worse than be guided by two references: one, George W. Bush's second inaugural address of January 2005 and two, Natan Sharansky's classic *The Case for Democracy*. Bush essentially invoked the criteria established by Jeanne Kirkpatrick in her *Dictatorships and Double Standards*, the gold standard in distinguishing between totalitarian and authoritarian regimes and why it matters. This makes a significant difference in the current cases when determining which messages to send to the respective regimes in the region. Sharansky, of course, makes the case for the fact that the desire for freedom is universal and that a regime must ultimately be judged and dealt with based on the way in which it treats its own people.

This is a major watershed event, world historical, a huge opportunity, but our response to this combustion has been mixed at best. We were slow to recognize the scope of the revolutions across North Africa and worse, very tentative in standing with the insurgents in the streets. The response in Libya has been particularly disappointing. Here we have a brutal dictator and enemy of long standing and the administration cannot even bring itself to acknowledge these facts in spite of direct questioning. And while we have now at least demanded that Gadhafi leave the country, we have a situation in which this delusional tyrant is murdering his own people and we are relegated to appeals to the United Nations and its committee on human rights on which Libya serves!

I have repeatedly emphasized since 9/11, the absolute necessity of moral clarity in dealing with and defeating the forces arrayed against us in the Islamic world. Why is this so difficult for this administration? Why the relativism? Why the confusion when identifying the enemy, even when it has clearly exposed itself, as in the case with the Fort Hood shootings and other terrorist attacks and attempted attacks on Americans over the past two years? Say what you want about the mistakes of George W. Bush, but moral clarity was not a problem for him, and I suspect that Gadhafi would be as well aware of that as he was during his encounters with Ronald Reagan.

We know that revolutions often do not end well for the people, and we have only to look at history to confirm this. Of the major revolutions of the past 250 years only the American resulted in a better deal for the people, and the reason was that it alone was a battle for the acknowledgment and restoration of rights that are God-given, not a battle for rights to be granted by the state. The French, Russian, and Iranian revolutions were disasters for their people, and we would be well-served to help the struggling freedom fighters of the Arab Middle East and North Africa understand the difference.

Exit Gates

June 22, 2011

As Robert Gates plans his exit from distinguished service as Secretary of Defense, he has made a number of public appearances involving provocative comments on foreign and defense policy. His remarks in a speech that any President who considers committing significant ground troops to a land war in Asia or the Middle East "should have his head examined" received considerable attention, as did his comment that he has grown wary of "wars of choice" as opposed to "wars of necessity." He leaves to our speculation precisely what criteria should be applied to this distinction, but the implication is that our engagement in Iraq would be in the former column. Presumably these details will surface after he is comfortable in retirement.

Two of his points in particular deserve considerably more attention than they have so far received. One is that NATO has become a "two-tiered alliance," with diminishing abilities to mount operations and that unless Europe increases its commitment, NATO faces "collective military relevance" and a "dim and dismal future." The other is his reminder that history clearly shows that when America turns inward, big wars often result, the message being that we should avoid across the board defense budget cuts that will damage our response capability and our preparedness. The convergence of these two contingencies would be devastating for world order.

Granted, NATO is a Cold War relic, but unless and until a better configuration of the Western democracies surfaces, it is the primary instrument of collective Western response to military threats and intimidation, and Europe should be on notice that the days are numbered for the current level of American subsidy of its defense responsibilities.

As for defense budget cuts by the U.S., it is increasingly clear that a growing tendency toward isolation is underway, from both the political right and left, and given the already well advanced public frustration with our military entanglements it would not be surprising to hear a McGovernite call to "come home America" from significant voices in next year's election campaign. To the extent that this sentiment infects budget deliberations, it will represent a dangerous prospect for us and the world. And I might add that the "Dennis Kucinich Republicans" are no help with their newly minted isolationism and their cynical attacks on Obama's policy in Libya based on the War Powers Act of all things!

Let's hope that, before he leaves office, Secretary Gates will devote considerable time and effort to making these points loudly and clearly, both publicly and privately to the President.

It's Bush's Fault

September 26, 2011

All critique of the delays, the means, the mission itself, and the American role in the effort aside, to be rid of a murderous tyrant like Moammar Gadhafi of Libya is a blessing for the world and a major victory for American interests. What follows there is another discussion, but whatever the prognosis it shouldn't detract from this victory and President Obama deserves credit for "leading from behind," for America's role was obviously decisive in the outcome. Meanwhile, we should not lose sight of what provided the catalyst for these momentous events, which include more broadly the entire phenomenon of the "Arab Spring" uprisings. The elements of the Bush Doctrine that called for the priority of freedom over stability deserve enormous credit, and the overthrow of Saddam Hussein's Iraq regime was clearly the proximate event that sent a chill down the spine of the tyrants of the Arab world while instilling hope and encouragement in the hearts and minds of the Arab street. These seeds spread from Iraq to Egypt, Sudan, Darfur, and Libya, not to mention Syria and Iran, where we should be doing much more to assist with the replacement of those regimes. All of this is vindication, as well, for the principles of freedom and democracy enunciated by Natan Sharansky, whose life and work inspired President Bush and his policies in the Middle East. It will be many years before we know how all of this will play out, but I am betting that history will record that, thanks largely to George W. Bush, freedom ultimately trumped the authoritarian stability of tyrants in the Arab world.

Political Retreat

January 4, 2012

We are witnessing a slow, steady retreat from victory in the Middle East and, I fear, a prelude to significantly more conflict down the road and the unfortunate loss of more American lives. Why? Because of the political imperative of troop withdrawals to accommodate the political timeline of the Obama administration.

Is there another possible rationale for an announcement now of additional withdrawals in Afghanistan in 2013? This policy flies in the face of the pressing need for a more assertive stance with Pakistan and will clearly result in the latter's further questioning of America's will in the region. Yet we get the following comment from a White House spokesman: "We have been very clear that we do not seek permanent bases in Afghanistan or a long-term military presence there that would be a threat to Afghanistan's neighbors." What does this mean? Look at the neighborhood – Central Asian states plus China, Iran, Pakistan. How can it not be in our strategic interest to have a long-term commitment there, particularly when there is a very high risk of their return to failed-state status?

Then there is our premature and unwise military departure from Iraq. Here we have the obsession of Obama to atone for the sins of the original engagement and for its implications for him of the image and legacy of colonialism. Again we provide evidence of our fecklessness and lack of will in the region, severely damage the progress that has been made to establish a viable state, invite Iran and other subversives to foment civil war, and worse, we show complete disdain for the sacrifice of thousands of American troops who produced victory when all seemed lost before "the surge." And, as John McCain has pointed out, this withdrawal will have serious consequences for Afghanistan, as well, providing plenty of doubts on the part of both friends and enemies about our willingness to honor our commitments there.

The announcement this week of the administration's plan for "a leaner, cheaper military" only compounds the problem and further confuses the message with phrases like "the tide of war is over" and "the question this strategy answers is what kind of military we will need after the long wars of the last decade are over." Is this the President's "mission accomplished" banner?

Of course, this flawed policy is designed to appease the American left (along with Ron Paul and his followers who can be disruptive within the GOP) and any downside will be laid at the feet of the "original sins" of the Bush administration, but I wonder how much longer this President can avoid ownership of and accountability for what is very likely to be a failed Middle East policy. The answer probably depends on the immediate prospects for the threat from Iran, and after the recent policy decisions we should know the answer very soon.

Fool Me Three Times?

March 7, 2012

There is an old saying: fool me once, shame on you; fool me twice, shame on me. Well, what happens the third time? That's where we are with North Korea. In fact, they have now fooled three U.S. administrations, dating back to the Agreed Framework of 1994 negotiated by Jimmy Carter for Bill Clinton. This time it's food for… what? Another promise, this time to suspend nuclear tests. Secretary of State Clinton called it "a modest first step in the right direction." After 60 years with this criminal regime and we're into modest first steps? All this does is once again buy this murderous regime some time, when we should be pursuing every step possible to bring it down. This would be much preferable to its suffering people than buying time with food most of them will never see.

China Watch IV

May 4, 2012

In a January issue, the lead article of *The Economist* was "The Rise of State Capitalism," featuring China as its leading example, of course, with comparisons with the recent problems in the world's free-market systems suggesting that "the era of free-market triumphalism has come to a juddering halt." But in all objectivity, after careful analysis, in the end the long essay arrives at the wise conclusion that state capitalism's biggest failure has to do with liberty.

I would add that we certainly are seeing serious problems in China as a result of this void in liberty, both in human and economic terms, and the most significant deficiency in the state economic model is the absence of Joseph Schumpeter's principle of "creative destruction," the bane of all state capitalistic models, which deprives the system of the natural function of rewarding success and disposing of failure and replacing old technologies with new ones, thereby rationalizing the allocation of capital. In fact, *The Economist* admits this in an indirect way, when it says "By turning companies into organs of the government, state capitalism simultaneously concentrates power and corrupts it." A related deficiency is that this concentration severely limits the free flow of ideas which drive innovation. So, as long as China disallows creative destruction to work its will, the days of its economic miracle are numbered, and when the bust comes and its corrupt system of crony capitalism hits the wall, as it most assuredly will, the good news will be the further discrediting of the state capitalism model one more time.

And it will further signal the day when it will no longer be possible to segregate the dynamics of the liberty of markets and human liberty, which is the elephant in the room in our diplomatic relationship with China. The Chen affair is but the most recent manifestation of their moral dilemma and the tradeoff between human rights concerns and the need for open U.S. – China diplomatic dialogue. President Obama says that "human rights are on the table in every conversation" with China. Yes, but they are not pushed, and the elements of our relationship with China need not be mutually exclusive. Ronald Reagan advanced both elements of our relationship with the Soviet Union forcefully and vocally – "the evil empire," "tear down this wall," etc. It can and has been done successfully.

The leadership of the Chinese Communist regime has serious legitimacy problems, they know this, and they don't know how to respond to the human rights issues as framed by a dissident like Chen without further undermining their legitimacy, but it's only a matter of time until this facade crumbles.

Team Obama's Middle East Mess

August 6, 2012

"We do not get to choose if a freedom revolution should begin or end in the Middle East or elsewhere. We only get to choose what side we are on." – George W. Bush in *The Wall Street Journal*, May 18, 2012, from a speech to the Bush Institute at SMU.

The Bush Doctrine has become a forgotten relic, dismissed by today's White House, but I continue to believe as Bush 43 does that it or a very similar doctrine will be necessary to free the Muslim Middle East to join the civilized world. What will or should replace it? For awhile, Barack Obama was forced by circumstances to continue various elements of it, primarily those involving American security, and he certainly deserves credit for taking out Osama bin Laden. But the balance of Obama's record in the Middle East has been miserable, and this is most recently reflected in the utter failure, to the surprise of almost no one, of the U.S.-backed United Nations approach to Syria and the obvious backsliding of democracy and increase in terrorist activity in Iraq as a result of premature withdrawal of American troops. These trends highlight the indispensable necessity of presidential assertion of direct American leadership, which has been sorely lacking in this administration, and the President himself seems not to have the inclination for hands on involvement, instead preferring to "lead from behind."

There is no lack of reasoned strategy advice from an informed group of foreign policy experts outside the administration, most prominently a recent report from the Hudson Institute addressing the overall threat of Islamic extremism. This report makes the point that, contrary to the Obama administration's statement that "we are at war with a specific network, al-Qaeda and its terrorist affiliates," the U.S. is taking a much too narrow approach to the definition of the enemy. It maintains that the Bush administration's broader characterization of the threat remains true, that "the principal terrorist enemy confronting the U.S. is a transnational movement of extremist organizations, networks, and individuals and their state- and non-state supporters, which have in common that they exploit Islam and use terrorism for ideological ends."

So defeating al-Qaeda in Iraq is not enough. The essence of the problem is ideological and we cannot solve it by focusing our efforts on a single organization and its affiliates.

And according to the study, the key is to stimulate and influence debate among Muslims in order to promote interpretations of Islam that do not assert the legitimacy of terrorism. Will this strategy work? Not without a definitive plan and certainly not without the committed leadership of the President of the United States.

But, this President is not committed to any strategy except for one that favors a worldview dominated by transnational consensus based on the judgment of international organizations. Meanwhile, there have been more than 10,000 deaths among the rebel forces in Syria, Iran continues on the path toward a nuclear capability while assisting in the killing of Americans on every front, democracy in Iraq is deteriorating, and Russia and China continue to block any serious UN response to any of this. The President has said that "the tide of war is receding." Is he looking at the same Middle East map that I am?

The Syria Decision

September 5, 2013

The most incredible fiasco in modern foreign policy management and the strangest and most blatant abdication of a U.S. Commander in Chief in American history has now come down to a monumental gamble on the willingness of a fickle Congress to provide the political cover to prevent a President from vacating the role of the U.S. as the indispensable leader in enforcing world order. And make no mistake, once vacated, the damage to American credibility will not be reversible for decades, if ever. We're talking about a tipping point here.

Don't misunderstand. As I have said before, there are plenty of reasons not to get involved in Syria, plenty of well-identified risks and unknowns. And the in-competency of this administration over the past two years has put the U.S. in a position with dwindling choices that can make a difference in the outcome. But it is clear that the risks of non-intervention outweigh those of intervention so as to offer any chance to have a role in the outcome of a civil war that is threatening to become regional and, as I have previously suggested, take on many of the characteristics of a proxy war like the Spanish Civil War of the mid-1930s. And the winners in such a scenario, without our decisive intervention, would clearly be Russia, Iran, and Hezbollah, giving these enemies a dangerously dominant position in the region to the detriment of our allies, our interests, and world order.

So what is decisive intervention? Well, it's certainly not a "shot across the bow," a symbolic act, or even an attack aimed at deterrence of future use of chemical weapons or "changing the momentum" of the war. These efforts would be worse than no intervention. The problem is Bashar Assad and his family and the only intervention that makes sense at this point is to take out the ruling regime and be prepared for almost certain retaliation. But support for intervention must start with a President who is serious about his and America's badly damaged credibility and exceptional role in the world. So far, this President hasn't been, and without this level of seriousness, he has not earned our support.

America Continues to Shrink

November 9, 2013

Norman Podhoretz has called it "Obama's successful foreign failure," Peggy Noonan has described "a new kind of credibility gap" and "a small President on the world stage," and Fouad Ajami says that "Obama is lost in the Mideast bazaar" and is operating like "a lawyer lost in a region of thugs." The common thread that runs through the analysis of this administration's Middle East policy by these and other observers is that, contrary to what one might think, President Obama is playing out a script exactly to his liking with an end result that he believes is a winning one, namely, American withdrawal from world leadership and influence in that region.

So, as a result of a series of blunders going back at least to the blown opportunities during the so-called Arab Spring and now culminating in badly misguided deal-making with Iran's new "moderate" President, who is playing us like a cheap violin, we have the strange scenario in which Saudi Arabia is chastising us for our credibility gap and, along with France, is taking the moral high ground in the region! We will be very fortunate to have any credibility left with friend or foe when this crowd leaves office and it might take at least a generation to restore it.

"Russia Will Always be Russia"

March 5, 2014

"*The collapse of the Soviet Union was the biggest geopolitical catastrophe of the (20th) century.*" – Vladimir Putin, April 2005.

George Kennan, the father of U.S. containment policy in the Cold War beginning in the late 1940s, continually reminded us that the soul of Russian leadership would never stray very far from the czars and that "Russia will always be Russia in the pursuit of its strategic interests." We have been reminded of this on numerous occasions over the past 10 years, but seem not to be able to deal with its reality.

The current manifestation of this reality in Ukraine is the most threatening since the fall of the Soviet Union in 1991. President Putin obviously is unreconciled to the loss of Russian empire and, in fact, plans to restore it. If we are naive enough to believe that he is not serious, it will have very troubling consequences for the U.S. and world order. We think this is not a chess game? Not a zero sum contest? Maybe not to President Obama, but certainly to Putin. This is a battle between a community organizer and a KGB thug who has outwitted him at every step.

Putin's march into the Crimea is an act of war, under auspices reminiscent of the Nazi march into Czechoslovakia to "rescue" the Sudetenland Germans, a brazen act which led to the capitulation of the West at Munich in 1938. You know the rest.

But what do we expect from a feckless leader who draws a meaningless "red line" at every trouble spot and then does absolutely nothing when it is crossed except give another speech warning of consequences that never materialize. This weakness has clearly emboldened Putin and don't think the Chinese are not watching closely as they plot their next move in the South China Sea.

I'm not suggesting that we go to war over the Crimea, but there are a number of well-identified measures we should already have taken to inflict economic pain on Putin and his cronies, with or without European support. And we should have immediately terminated Russian membership in the G-8 and the World Trade Organization and boycotted the upcoming G-8 meeting in Russia.

Meanwhile, Obama conducts a 90-minute phone call with Putin. For what? This should have been a two-minute call in which Putin was informed that, in the words of Bush 41, "this will not stand." And in public pronouncements he should have spoken in past tense, as in "I have ordered these things."

You have to wonder if Obama knows what American strategic interests are. He doesn't seem to think that we have any in this showdown. He certainly didn't mention any in his very weak statement on the situation. America must lead, in concert with the UN and Europe, but alone if necessary. That is the burden of the world's only superpower and leader of the free world. Meanwhile, the administration announces major cuts in military readiness in order to reallocate resources to its domestic wealth redistribution strategy and the cause of "social justice" in the world. Great timing.

Daniel Henninger reminds us of a speech by Ronald Reagan in Chicago in 1980, in which he said that "a realistic hope for peace is possible only if the U.S. maintains the 'vital margin of safety.'" Henninger adds that this is not about public threats of war, it's about maintaining the marginal advantage in diplomacy and the belief on the part of our adversaries that we might act militarily. If friends and enemies reach the conclusion that no one believes it, the margin is gone.

A Dishonorable Transaction

June 8, 2014

Some people are calling the Sgt. Bergdahl exchange for five Taliban killers imprisoned at Guantanamo a "fiasco" or a ham-handed misjudgment of anticipated popular feedback by a bunch of political hacks who seem to be in charge of the Obama foreign policy team. It was certainly that, and I wish that was all it was, but knowing this crowd and its record, I'm pretty sure that it was a well-calculated decision, purposely circumventing Congressional input, to change the subject from the VA and other current scandals and make good on Obama's commitment to close Gitmo, with total disregard for the consequences of the release of enemy combatants, who will almost certainly return to the battlefield as a threat to Americans.

Other observers, such as Charles Krauthammer, would have approved the exchange, because the underlying military policy of "leave no soldier behind" is what separates the West from its barbarous enemies – the value of each individual life – and the West always comes out on the short end in these transactions, but must do so in the interest of its values, although he thinks that the swap represents a "defeat for a clueless President." I agree with Krauthammer on the latter point, but disagree with him on the approval of the exchange itself. The President made the point that "this is what happens at the end of wars," but this war is not over; the Taliban and al-Qaeda missed the memorandum – they are not leaving the battlefield and they are still killing Americans!

Further, some commentator made the point that the reason these particular five killers were still at Gitmo is that there was insufficient evidence to try them in the U.S. criminal justice system. That point is problematic in the first place – we should have never pursued or allowed access to that system by imprisoned enemy combatants; they should have been held until hostilities ended, however long that takes.

Finally, the "leave no soldier behind" policy is not unconditional. The behavior of Sgt. Bergdahl has been erratic and spooky at best, traitorous at worst, and it is pretty clear that he deserted his unit, probably more than once. Otherwise, I will reserve judgment, but to characterize his service as with "honor and distinction," as Susan Rice asserted on one of her favorite Sunday talk shows, simply speaks for itself. Whatever the final assessment of Bergdahl's actions, however, do we really believe that the exchange of these five "worst of the worst" Taliban killers and war criminals was a balanced transaction? Think of the Nuremberg trials of the Nazi war criminals – Rudolph Hess, Hermann Goering, et al. These five are analogous. If we are going to honor "leave no soldier behind" unconditionally, how about the four dead Americans at Benghazi, the U.S. Marine in jail in Mexico, or the beleaguered veterans having to deal with the fraudulent and dysfunctional VA? Where is the similar urgency here?

And if we are going to have a Rose Garden photo/op victory lap with Bergdahl's parents to congratulate ourselves for freeing him, how about including the families of those soldiers who died searching for him over the past five years?

There is much more to be known about this transaction, including the degree to which the discussions leading up to the exchange had wider objectives, such as a negotiated cease fire with the Taliban, and we need many more facts, but at this point the whole thing is not only a fiasco, but a dishonorable one.

A Moment of Truth with Putin

August 4, 2014

The attack on Malaysian Airlines Flight 17 is a watershed moment, analogous to the shooting down of the Korean Airlines plane by the Soviets in 1983. It is truly a moment of truth for Vladimir Putin, but even more for President Obama, the West, and the American people, who are now face-to-face with the consequences of their collective "fatigue" with the world and its bad guys and the implications for American security of our withdrawal from Western leadership. The evidence of complicity and direct responsibility for this murderous act on the part of Russia is incontrovertible, so now what?

The increased U.S. sanctions on Russia, Putin, and his cronies will not stop them. Putin feels more pressure from his own people than he does from the U.S. and the West. At a minimum, we should arm and provide intelligence support to Ukraine, reinstate our objective to shore up defense systems in Poland, and publicly reassure the Baltic states that we will assist them as well. As for our European friends, it's time to get serious. Thankfully, British PM David Cameron has called out Western Europe and urged it to "fundamentally change its approach to Russia," specifically singling out France for continuing its "unthinkable" plans to sell naval assault ships to Russia. But, so far, no other meaningful response.

As for the American people, the polls are upside down on this issue, with large majorities adamantly opposed to aggressive assistance to Ukraine (or any other foreign involvement, for that matter). Well, this is where American presidential leadership comes in. Obama needs to get off the cutesy domestic political fundraising talking points and coffee shop photo ops and get serious about leading the American people to a cure for their "fatigue" and into the right frame of mind. This is what Presidents are supposed to do – not read the polls, but drive them.

We are close to a tipping point in the failure of foreign policy leadership by this administration. Will this team ever be held accountable for anything?

Gaza and Moral Clarity

August 4, 2014

A resolution adopted by the United Nations Human Rights Council on July 23 tells you about all you need to know about the fecklessness of our allies, mainly those in Europe, and the worthlessness of the UN. By a vote of 29-1, with the U.S. being the only "no" vote and with 17 abstentions, including European nations, the Council's resolution calls for the establishment of an international commission of inquiry to probe allegations that Israel has committed war crimes and violated international law in the defense of its homeland from attacks by Hamas originating from Gaza. In fact, it "condemns in the strongest terms" the conduct of this defense with no mention of the inhumane tactics of Hamas and scarcely a reference to its rocket attacks on Israel.

At least the U.S. stood with Israel on this vote, but not much else can be said in favor of Secretary of State Kerry's shuttle diplomacy, which has emphasized immediate "ceasefire" conditions equally applied to both sides over a sustainable resolution of hostilities that recognizes Israel's unequivocal right to defend itself and destroy Hamas and its military capacity. This is not the level of moral clarity that is needed from U.S. leadership.

- Anyone who wants to assign any level of moral equivalency to both sides in this conflict should "Google" The Covenant of the Hamas and read a few pages of this 1988 covenant of the Islamic Resistance Movement, also known as HAMAS. Here are a few tidbits:
- The Islamic Resistance Movement is a distinguished Palestinian movement, whose allegiance is to Allah, and whose way of life is Islam. It strives to raise the banner of Allah over every inch of Palestine.
- Palestine is an Islamic land. Since this is the case, the liberation of Palestine is an individual duty for every Muslim wherever he may be.
- In the face of the Jews' usurpation, it is compulsory that the banner of Jihad be raised.
- Peace initiatives and so-called peaceful solutions and international conferences are in contradiction to the principles of the Islamic Resistance Movement… There is no solution for the Palestinian problem except by Jihad.
- The Day of Judgment will not come about until Muslims fight Jews and kill them.

And this is a group with which we expect to conduct a "peace process?" When do we get serious? No victory, no peace.

Destroy the Islamic State

September 1, 2014

The title of this essay is borrowed from the title of a recent article by John Bolton in *National Review* in which he lays out the challenge we now face in the Middle East from the latest personification of radical Islamist jihad in the form of the Islamic State, commonly known as ISIS or ISIL. He makes it clear, as others have, that our strategic objective must be to destroy this menace, not contain it, not simply protect constituents and other interests in the region, but unconditionally destroy it. The question is when or if we will ever hear this mission enunciated by our President.

In 2006, Norman Podhoretz wrote a controversial book, *World War IV: The Long Struggle Against Islamofascism*, in which he outlined the history of the conflict that culminated in the attack of 9/11, the various responses to that attack, and suggestions about the way forward. He referred to the current conflict as World War IV because he believes as I do that this war is every bit as global in reach and will require at least the level of commitment for success as the first three in the series (the Cold War being number III). And he recognizes that, as he writes, "the question of whether and to what extent the American people of this generation can or will discharge the responsibility that 9/11 imposed on us will ultimately be answered by the outcome of [the] great war of ideas at home… nothing less than a kind of civil war." Eight years later, this internal debate rages on, while the case for Podhoretz's thesis continues to grow, and the threat posed by ISIS may be its ultimate validation.

From her recent interviews, Hillary Clinton seems to get it, suggesting that "jihadist groups are governing territory; they will never stay there, though; they are driven to expand… this jihadism shows up in many contexts, but whether in Gaza or Syria or Iraq, it is all one big threat." Meanwhile, as former Secretary of Defense Robert Gates notes in his revealing book, "for Obama, it's all about getting out." He made this pretty clear in a major speech at the National Defense University in May 2013, saying that the "perpetual wartime footing" and "boundless war on terror" that had permeated American life since 9/11 should come to an end. "This war, like all wars, must end."

Well, ISIS didn't get the memo, and the premature and unwise withdrawal of troops from the region and the vacuum in American leadership in confronting the challenges in Syria and Iraq provided them the opportunity to galvanize their message and resolve into a dangerous new brand of extremism unlike any we have seen since this war began in 1979. And they leave no mystery about their mission. It is well-documented in sophisticated publications that are published online in English. Much as *Mein Kampf* spelled out Hitler's world view 10 years before he took power, these people have explained to us in no uncertain terms what they have in mind.

Returning to Podhoretz, he closes his book with a quote from George Kennan from his famous "X" essay written at the beginning of the Cold War: "…the thoughtful observer of Russian-American relations will experience a certain gratitude for a Providence, which by providing the American people with this implacable challenge, has made their entire security as a nation dependent on their pulling themselves together and accepting the responsibilities of moral and political leadership that history has plainly intended them to bear." Podhoretz suggests that to substitute "Islamofascism" for

"Russian-American relations" in this statement makes every word of it apply to us as a nation today.

What's Next?

January 1, 2015

President Obama has two years left in his administration, so it is difficult to be overly optimistic, but I tend toward the view that he won't or can't be as destructive with domestic issues as he has been in his first six years because of the control of both houses of Congress by Republican majorities. Certainly, there is more damage to be done with his "pen and phone" and the Republicans can badly misplay their hand, as they have done from time to time, but I think the worst is behind us.

Foreign policy is a different matter. Because of the fecklessness and incompetence of this administration, there are reasons to believe that the next two years will be the most dangerous period since the end of the Cold War. There are any number of possible flash points, from Russia to China to ISIS to the revival of the Taliban in Afghanistan to North Korea to cyber warfare from anywhere – you name it. But, I believe with Israeli Prime Minister Benjamin Netanyahu that Iran is the highest risk threat that we face. And this is true today primarily because of a combination of the messages of retreat and concession we have sent over the past six years and the choices we have made in dealing with Iran on the development of their nuclear arms capability. To wit, here is Obama's approach to the nuclear negotiations with Iran, as stated in a recent interview: "I believe in diplomacy, I believe in dialogue, I believe in engagement" and he added that Iran can be "a very successful regional power," one that is "abiding by international norms and rules." And he even has refused to rule out the possibility of a renewal of normal diplomatic relations with Iran, including the reopening of our embassy. This is naive to the max and recklessly hopeful. Iran is our most prominent and committed enemy, the biggest single cause and supplier of Islamic terrorism in the world, responsible for thousands of American deaths, and with which arguably we have been at war since 1979.

Beyond the specifics of the Iranian threat and other particular hotspots is the worst part. This is the overarching problem of the core of the Obama worldview, which is that America is not a positive force in the world, it's a problem for the world and should withdraw. It's like a big neon sign over the door – we're in a withdrawal mode with two years left, so act accordingly. A great example of this view was coined early in his administration by one of his foreign policy advisors – "leading from behind." Nothing better fits the mindset of this President and his progressive foreign policy strategy than this phrase and no message could be more dangerous for America and the world.

They Simply Don't Get It

March 5, 2015

In an essay entitled "Our Plan for Countering Violent Extremism" (a title which should immediately give its reader some pause) Secretary of State John Kerry writes, "Eliminating the terrorists of today with force will not guarantee protections from the terrorists of tomorrow. We have to transform the environment that gave birth to these movements… This means building alternatives that are credible… The most basic issue is good governance." This had been preceded a few days earlier by comments from State Department spokesperson Marie Harf, who responded to a question in a press briefing that "We cannot win the War on Terror, nor can we win the war with ISIS, by killing them. We need to find them jobs. We need to get to the root cause of terrorism, and that is poverty and lack of opportunity in the terrorist community."

You can't make this stuff up. This is total nonsense. It's Peace Corps language. This kind of thinking can only come from an environment in which we have completely forgotten who we are and how this evil world of disorder that we face differs so drastically in kind from the world of order. This is a battle and a critical time of decision about which direction the West will pursue, while the Islamic world fights over who speaks for Islam and who defines it. In many ways we find ourselves in the midst of an Islamic Reformation and the outcome will be existential for a lot of people – millions of them.

America is uniquely qualified to lead, but we must first shake the multicultural blinders of our leadership for long enough to remember who we are and what our role should be as the indispensable nation. And it starts with properly identifying the true nature of the enemy, establishing moral clarity, and recognizing that, in addition to a killing war, this is a war of ideas and worldviews, and the fact that we have yet to fight on this basis is a strong indication that we don't get it. Or do we?

The Deal with Iran: A Monumental Mistake

August 7, 2015

"Don't be fooled. The battle between Iran and ISIS doesn't turn Iran into a friend of America. Iran and ISIS are competing for the crown of militant Islam. One calls itself the Islamic Republic. The other calls itself the Islamic State. Both want to impose a militant Islamic empire first on the region and then on the entire world. They just disagree among themselves who will be the ruler of that empire..."

"So when it comes to Iran and ISIS, the enemy of your enemy is your enemy... I'll say it one more time – the greatest danger facing our world is the marriage of militant Islam with nuclear weapons. To defeat ISIS and let Iran get nuclear weapons would be to win the battle, but lose the war. We can't let that happen."

These words of Israeli Prime Minister Benjamin Netanyahu from his address to the U.S. Congress last March are worth repeating, because they represent the proper identification of the enemy and moral clarity that are badly missing in the rhetoric from this administration.

Approval of the pending nuclear agreement with Iran will return an outlaw state, the leading state supporter of Islamic terrorism, to the community of nations with a restoration of their economic viability that will enhance their capacity for worldwide mischief, while assuring that they will join the list of nuclear powers in a minimum of 10 years even if they fully comply with every word of the agreement, which is a pipe dream.

We should have never sat down at the negotiating table with this evil regime for any purpose other than to discuss the timetable for the complete dismantling of all vestiges of their nuclear weapons capability and potential development. As I have previously noted and Henry Kissinger has recently reminded us, these talks with Iran began as an international effort, supported by six UN resolutions, to deny Iran the capability to develop military nuclear weapons. Now we find that the agreement is essentially about the scope of that capability and, in Kissinger's words, "the impact of this approach will be to move from preventing proliferation to managing it."

Contrary to what this administration would like to offer as an analogy, there is no similarity whatever with our arms limitation talks with the Soviet Union during the Cold War. These were talks between two world powers with symmetrical incentives, risks, stakes, and fears, none of which applies here. A better analogy is with the agreement reached with Nazi Germany in Munich in 1938 and even there the full intentions of evil on the part of our adversary then were not yet as obvious as they are with the current Iranian regime. But the stupidity and fecklessness of this deal will top even that one because as a result of it we should know better.

The Consequences of American Retreat

September 10, 2015

We are witnessing the largest mass migration of refugees and oppressed people since World War II and it is only the beginning. If decisive action is not taken soon to arrest the causes of this migration at its source, it will reach tens of millions in very short order. Without doubt, over time this will produce a major economic and cultural calamity for Western Europe, one that it cannot afford.

What should be done? First, we should deal with the immediate humanitarian crisis as America always does – with compassion, medical attention, food, shelter, and sanctuary for those who are truly refugees from oppression. But, we must also recognize that our failed policy of retreat in the Middle East has been a significant cause of the problem. All wars create refugees, but this problem could have and should have been mitigated by maintaining a significant U.S. presence in Iraq and by American intervention in the Syrian civil war at a time when it would have been decisive in taking out the Assad regime and reducing the threat of ISIS. Now we face the additional consequence of announced Russian support of the Assad regime in Syria, making any decision to intervene much more problematic.

In a recent *Wall Street Journal* essay by Bret Stephens, he references a 2003 book by Robert Kagan, *Of Paradise and Power*, in which Kagan noted the philosophical divide between Americans and Europeans. He wrote that Americans occupied the world of Thomas Hobbes, in which "true security and the defense and promotion of a liberal order still depend on the possession and use of military power." By contrast, Europeans, according to Kagan, live in the world of Immanuel Kant, in which "perpetual peace" is guaranteed by a set of cultural conventions, consensually agreed rules, and a belief in the virtues of social solidarity overseen by a redistributive state. The problem now, as assessed by Stephens, is that Barack Obama has adopted the Kantian view so that America and Europe have been in concert on most of the critical foreign policy issues – get out of Iraq, stay out of Syria, negotiate with Iran – retreat, retreat, retreat.

The primary overall consequence of this is world disorder and it will not end until America returns to its proper role in world leadership. And after eight years of the

Obama administration, we will have a lot of work to do to restore our credibility with both our allies and our adversaries.

Obama and Putin at the UN

October 6, 2015

There couldn't have been a more striking juxtaposition of diametrically opposed leadership styles than the split screen of Barack Obama and Vladimir Putin in their respective remarks to the UN General Assembly on Syrian and Middle Eastern policy.

This administration has orchestrated a disaster in foreign policy that will require decades to overcome, if at all. Obama thinks that there will be some kind of settlement of the civil war in Syria on favorable diplomatic terms (a "managed transition away from Assad"); Putin knows that there hasn't been a civil war settled by compromise in at least three centuries. His plan is being backed by force; Obama thinks Putin will get bogged down as the Soviets did in Afghanistan in the 1980s. My prediction, and I hope I'm wrong: Putin and Russia will win in Syria and, combined with the Iran/Iraq/ Russian deal to defend Iraq, will be dominant in the Middle East for the first time since the Soviets were forced out of Egypt in 1973, relegating the U.S. as a fringe player; what a legacy.

Meanwhile, the "how did we get here?" crowd, both in and outside the Beltway (including Donald Trump), continues to reference the Iraq war initiated in 2003 as the decisive disruptive moment that ultimately led to ISIS, the mess in Syria, and the migrant and refugee crisis we now face. Granted, many mistakes were made by the Bush administration after victory in Iraq – the occupation was botched there and in Afghanistan as well. But it was bailed out by the surge of 2007; Obama was handed an Iraq and Afghanistan that represented victory.

One of the organizing principles of progressivism is the notion that history is inexorably relentless in its evolutionary movement and that we must be on the "right side of history," a phrase that Obama has used many times in a variety of contexts. He obviously believes that this principle is at work in the Middle East and that he is on the right side. Putin isn't buying it.

Pounce on me as a discredited neoconservative if you will, but I agree with former Russian dissident Natan Sharansky that the disruptions of freedom and struggling democracy are preferable to the so-called stability of the "strongman" authoritative regime. That was the core of the Bush Doctrine, which I believe was the correct approach to the Middle East after all these years of support for the strongman and various proxies in the region, such as Saudi Arabia and, at one time, Iran. Our victory in Iraq set the stage for the further disruption in Egypt, Libya, Syria, and spawned the Arab Spring. Contrary to the view of both Putin and Donald Trump, these were positive developments, albeit messy, as revolutions always are. But the U.S. under Obama lacked the vision and leadership, not to mention the sympathy for the spirit of the Bush Doctrine, to take advantage of our victory across the region and we pursued a doctrine of retreat resulting in a vacuum reversing 70 years of U.S. Middle East policy which has directly led to the disruption we have today – total chaos without the hope of freedom or democracy for the oppressed in the region.

Obama's "Arc of the Moral Universe"

June 5, 2016

In one of his better recent columns, Charles Krauthammer provides good working definitions of an "idealist" and a "realist" in foreign policy and how to distinguish the two. Essentially, in my words not his, realism is a conservative notion, while idealists have a conservative wing and a liberal wing, generally represented by the so-called neo conservatives and the internationalists, respectively. The key differentiation for Krauthammer is the answer to one question: Do you believe in the arrow of history? Both wings of the idealists believe in the notion of perfectibility, if not of man, at least of the international system. Both believe in the arrow of history.

This leads me to one of President Obama's key speech lines: "The arc of the moral universe is long, but it bends toward justice." This is the arrow of history. I believe he really believes that and that he has built his entire foreign policy mission on that phrase, beginning with his world "apology tour" at the beginning of his administration through his recent trips to Hiroshima, Japan and Vietnam. I will credit him for one thing on the recent trip. At least he departed from the apology routine in Hiroshima, but it would have been appropriate to have rounded out his visit there with an invitation to the Japanese Prime Minister for a visit to the U.S.S. Arizona Memorial at Pearl Harbor.

His idealism surfaced, however, with remarks like "Among those nations like my own that hold nuclear stockpiles, we must have the courage to escape the logic of fear, and pursue a world without them," the pipe dream of all liberal internationalists, and "We must change our mind set about war itself. To prevent conflict through diplomacy and strive to end conflicts after they've begun. To see our growing interdependence as a cause for peaceful cooperation and not violent competition. To define our nations, not by our capacity to destroy, but by what we build. And perhaps above all, we must reimagine our connection to one another as members of the human race." To do this, he suggests, will require a "moral revolution." These are noble sentiments, but they represent the height of idealism of the liberal international mindset.

Meanwhile, when we survey the real world, we find either current or looming disasters in Iran, Russia, Syria, Iraq, North Korea, and China, all of which have grown more ominous under this administration. I've been accused, with justification, of being somewhat of a George W. Bush/Natan Sharansky neoconservative, but I suspect that what Obama is leaving behind for his successor around the world will require a pretty full dose of realism.

The Tragic Obama Legacy

January 3, 2017

As we count down the final days of the eight-year reign of the Barack Obama administration, it has become increasingly clear that his primary legacy will have been sealed by the events of its final weeks, and it isn't pretty. I am referring to two shameful decisions that will live in infamy – the abdication of moral and strategic leadership in the Syrian civil war and the abandonment of Israel in the abstention vote on the UN Security Council resolution condemning the Jerusalem settlements. With a possible exception noted below, nothing else he has done or failed to do will be close – not ObamaCare, which will be unrecognizable in a few months and not even a blip on the screen of history, not any of several dozen executive orders which will be reversed by the stroke of Trump's pen, and certainly not the "shovel ready" infrastructure projects, which were to have saved us from deep depression and provided impetus for economic growth, neither of which will stand historic scrutiny.

It will be very interesting to read in his memoirs how he spins the moral and strategic failure in Syria. I can't imagine how, except to say that he used all his political capital to get a nuclear deal with Iran, but this would be nothing more than to substitute a deal that might be a fairly close third in terms of his historically disastrous decisions for one that outranks it. With the fall of Aleppo, it is now simply a matter of Russia and Turkey mopping up in Syria and dividing the spoils, and it will be decades, if ever, before the U.S. regains its relevance; we're not even invited to the peace talks!

The refusal to veto the UN resolution on the Jerusalem settlements is a betrayal of the worst kind, because it was dishonorable, very likely done in spite of Israeli Prime Minister Benjamin Netanyahu, and it is probably irreversible in terms of its damage to our only reliable ally and the only democracy in the Middle East, not to mention the severe damage done to any hope of peace. The resolution substantively changes diplomatic agreements going back to 1967 and it denies Israel legal claims to the land, including Jewish holy sites such as the Western Wall, while reversing the land-for-peace formula that has been in place for five decades, and yet Secretary Kerry refers to East Jerusalem as "occupied territory." Someone should remind him that there has never been a Palestinian "people," nor has there ever been a Palestinian state or any state in the geographic area known as Palestine that was not Jewish. Anyone with the slightest insight into this issue knows that the primary barrier to peace is the refusal of the Palestinians to recognize Israel as a Jewish state within any borders. But at bottom this decision was vintage Obama because it reflects his worldview. He is an anti-Zionist progressive internationalist who is anti-U.S. and Israeli exceptionalism to the core and this was thus a defining act of his presidency. A tragic and shameful legacy.

The Inevitable Showdown with North Korea

August 5, 2017

A clear consensus has finally formed that we are at the point of a showdown with the Kim regime in North Korea. The inexcusable torture and death of student Otto Warmbier on top of the continued provocation and advancement of its nuclear weapons program has left us with no choice, but to confront this dangerous threat to the U.S. head on, and, in fact this conclusion is long overdue after at least 25 years in which hope has reigned supreme over experience in our appeasement.

And there are no good strategic choices, as we have constantly been reminded, but that is no longer an excuse. We must act now, and **every** option must be on the table, including the military. I'm a long way from any level of expertise or intelligence here that would qualify me as a resource, but I favor regime change as a top priority, hopefully followed at some point reasonably soon by a reunification with South Korea. This psychotic dictator must go, and China must be convinced that this outcome is in its best interest, as well as ours, but even without that help, we should proceed. And it would be helpful if our leadership was less confusing in its messaging, with recent mixed signals on regime change as an objective coming from Secretary of State Tillerson and CIA Director Pompeo.

Meanwhile, as the diplomatic strategy is redesigned, we need a much tougher policy right now and there are some additional pressure points that could immediately be applied that will send a message to friend and foe alike, such as banning any travel to North Korea without government approval, adding serious sanctions on all banks and businesses that do business with North Korea and its banks, having the Navy stop ships suspected of transporting North Korean military equipment, and establishing a policy of shooting down missiles launched by North Korea. The time for patience and appeasement is over.

Trump at the UN

October 3, 2017

On September 19th at the United Nations, Donald Trump made the most important foreign policy speech of his term to date, probably his most impressive utterance of any type, when he hit most of the right notes in explaining to the world what to them has become an inconvenient truth that they needed to hear from an American President. This message is essentially the gravity with which he views the threat from North Korea in a morally clear and unequivocal way and that the U.S. reserves the right to use nuclear weapons to pre-empt a first strike from an adversary and its weapons of mass destruction. During the Cold War we called this "deterrence," but we were then dealing with rational players and it seemed not so necessary to make such threats publicly. And of course it was reported that there was shock in the room, because such blunt talk irritates the sensibilities of the world's diplomatic corps at Turtle Bay and is a rude, but refreshing alternative to the doublespeak we normally get from the UN podium.

But, this is a different ball game. After 25 years of more or less standard diplomacy, we're dealing with one reckless regime that is possibly within months of reaching the capability of launching an ICBM and another adversary with whom we have signed a very misguided treaty that will almost certainly result in its becoming a nuclear power within a few years. It's time for a new approach and that is what Trump was all about at the UN.

One other part of his speech was also instructive. He has clearly moved the U.S. back to realpolitik and away from nation-building, but he placed significant emphasis on the importance of sovereignty. He made it clear that, while he will always put America first, as other leaders will put their people first, and in spite of the degree to which the free flow of goods and people are making traditional national identities obsolete, "the nation-state remains the best vehicle for elevating the human condition" and "nations and borders matter no less in the era of globalization."

If I had one quibble, it would be that he should have mentioned that sovereignty is about more than borders and interests; it's also about the people's rights and the methods by which they are governed. But I will leave that for another day. The speech was well done and very important.

Bergdahl Walks

November 5, 2017

"The decision on Sergeant Bergdahl is a complete and total disgrace to our Country and to our Military." – Twitter quote from President Donald Trump.

I couldn't agree more with the President. In fact, these were almost exactly my thoughts when I heard the news that U.S. Army Sgt. Bowe Bergdahl was spared any prison time for his desertion from duty in Afghanistan, receiving only a dishonorable discharge, which will almost guarantee that he will appeal to have his case totally dismissed.

Former Vice Chief of Staff Gen. Jack Kean explained it well. There is a reason that the U.S. military has a criminal justice system separate from the civilian system and part of it has to do with the charge of desertion. When a civilian walks off his or her job, their continued employment might be at risk, but it is not a criminal act. When a member of the military deserts from duty, it is a criminal act, because of the necessity of preserving the discipline that is critical to the defense of the country and the lives of those serving with you. This judge, Col. Jeffery Nance, has undermined that principle with a gut punch to every currently serving and veteran of U.S. military service. And to remember that in this guy's last email before he was captured by ISIS he wrote "the horror that is America is disgusting" and "I am ashamed to even be American" and that our government traded five Taliban prisoners for his release, not to mention the serious injuries suffered by those who went out to search for him, makes this ruling even more disgusting.

A final point: Our country is getting by very well with voluntary military service and our military institution itself is one of the only government entities that is held in high esteem by the American people. But I fear that, partly as a result of the volunteer nature of service and the fact that fewer and fewer of our country's civic and political leaders have experienced military life, there is a growing disconnect between our civilian and our military life such that we no longer really understand, much less identify with the military culture. I can't help but believe that decisions like this one are part of the result.

Trump Foreign Policy – A New Direction

December 2, 2017

There is no doubt that foreign policy under President Trump is taking a different direction, one that represents a break from the post-World War II worldview and presidents of both parties since then that has been based on institutions fashioned by the victors in that conflict and a world order enforced by U.S. leadership. A lot of establishment types are nervous about it, but what did they expect from a candidate who clearly expressed his view that this old order is outdated? There are a range of views on this transformation. One camp that can be represented by Robert Zoellick, who has spent a career shaping and sustaining this institutional order under multiple presidents, takes the position that the undermining of this system is mistaken and that the Trump administration's move toward a "populist" approach is not supported by the American people who, according to polls, tend to favor the current architecture of alliances and institutions. He and other observers further believe that Trump's core supporters are moving dangerously toward protectionism and against alliances and a confrontation between nationalists and internationalism. On the other hand, Walter Russell Mead of the Hudson Institute, while characterizing Trump's foreign policy as a "high wire" act, takes the view that much of the international institutional network needs updating and that our post-Cold War policies no longer can be politically sustained, that there are new realities, primarily China, that must be dealt with, and that our policy format must be redesigned. As he writes, "for the foreseeable future, foreign policy is going to be less about making dreams come true and more about keeping nightmares at bay." As a Bush 43 and Natan Sharansky neoconservative, I share a vision for making dreams like freedom and democracy come true, but I now tend to side with Mead that current realities dictate a more realistic view that will necessitate an updating and restructuring of the institutions of world order and I don't fear giving Trump his chance to lead this transformation.

Of significance, Zoellick and Mead agree as do I that Trump does not appear to fully understand the importance of trade policy in building alliances and supporting American security. Nor does he seem to grasp the basic economics of trade, i.e., that a trade deficit is the converse, or mirror image, of a net surplus of investment capital, which provides the foreign direct investment that our trade partners use to invest in the U.S. to create growth in jobs and domestic product. So, a trade deficit is not necessarily a bad thing, but unfortunately President Trump has used his misunderstanding and his supporters' ignorance on the basics to unfairly demagogue trade issues. It is not like a budget deficit; it does not have to be repaid. This is particularly important in considering the North American Free Trade Agreement (NAFTA), which is arguably the most successful trade agreement in U.S. history. As Kevin Williamson of *National Review* has noted so well in a very good essay on the subject, one of the strongest aspects of NAFTA has been the enhancement of economic efficiency, which comes from comparative advantage, another term that Trump doesn't seem to understand. The complexities of this concept are enormous, but Williamson notes that one very significant result of NAFTA is that American companies enjoy tremendous benefits from being part of a continental supply chain that is enabled by the agreement and would not otherwise be possible if it were not in place. Does it need some tweaks? Sure, most obviously, because of updates needed to take into consideration the world wide web and its impact on digital commerce. But to dismantle it or to make unreasonable demands on Canada and Mexico based on benign "trade deficits" or silly domestic origin rules would, as *The Wall Street Journal* has noted, be the "worst economic blunder since Nixon."

Obama Couldn't Have Been More Wrong About Iran

January 3, 2018

Anti-government protests in Iran are now a week old and showing no signs of abating. This will no doubt get very ugly when the crackdown by the mullahs comes, which it certainly will. So, what are we learning about the assumptions about Iran and policies applied by the Obama administration and their results and future prospects? Quite a lot, and it isn't pretty:

- Obama's people peddled the notion that a much firmer approach to Iran by Trump would unify the Iranian public in opposition to the U.S. Wrong. This protest is all about the resentment of the regime by the people in the streets who have been badly misled.

- The nuclear deal was projected by Obama and his people to have the result of "evolving" the behavior of the Iranian regime toward the U.S. and strengthen the standing of more moderate factions. Wrong. This isn't happening.

- The previous administration sold the bill of goods that the billions in resources we released to the Iranian regime in exchange for the nuclear deal would be used "for butter, not guns." Wrong. Substantial sums are being spent through the Iranian Revolutionary Guard to back our enemies all over the region and to prop up Syria's Bashad Assad

What should we be doing? First, we should understand that the Iranian Republic is a leftover relic from 20th century historicist ideologies that needs to go. Obama didn't get this; I sense that Trump does and he also gets the fact that they are a profound threat to American security. And in his own inimitable way, he is taking the appropriate lead by expressing his support for the oppressed Iranian people in the streets and recognizing the difference between them and their government. The Europeans and the Democrats should be doing the same and loudly supporting this fight for freedom, but don't hold your breath.

The Long Overdue Recognition of Jerusalem

January 3, 2018

Good for President Trump in defying what was probably the majority of opinion among his advisors in his foreign policy administration in his recognition of Jerusalem as the capital of Israel. After all, at least his last three predecessors have made the commitment to do so, but he is the only one who made good on the promise, which in fact is, as he called it, "a recognition of reality." And to no one's surprise, the professional street mobs in the Middle East and elsewhere dutifully hit the streets in protest over the damage done to the "peace process," and of course the United Nations responded in kind, with a resolution condemning the recognition by a vote of 128 to nine, with 35 abstentions. UN Ambassador Nikki Haley had some very appropriate words in response to this vote, including a pledge to the General Assembly that we will remember those who voted "yes" when it comes time for UN funding or other favors requested by our "friends" in the organization.

More on the continuing joke that the UN continues to be another time, but suffice to say that the constant criticism and condemnation of Israel by UN resolutions of the General Assembly and Security Council over the years have done considerably more damage to the so-called peace process than anything contemplated by this recognition. In fact, one of the most shameful episodes took place just as Barack Obama was on his way out the door in December 2016, when the U.S. abstained in the vote on a UN Security Council resolution condemning the Israeli settlements in Jerusalem.

As I wrote at the time, the refusal to veto this resolution was a betrayal of the worst kind because it was dishonorable, very likely done in spite of Israeli Prime Minister Benjamin Netanyahu, and it is probably irreversible in terms of its damage to our only reliable ally and the only democracy in the Middle East, not to mention the severe damage done to any hope of peace. The resolution changed diplomatic agreements going back to 1967 and it denied Israel legal claims to the land, including holy sites such as the Western Wall, while reversing the land-for-peace formula that has been in place for five decades, while then Secretary of State John Kerry referred to East Jerusalem as "occupied territory." Obama, Kerry, and their crowd should be reminded that there has never been a Palestinian "people," nor has there ever been a Palestinian state or any state in the geographic area known as Palestine that was not Jewish. Anyone with any insight into this issue knows that the primary barrier to peace is the refusal of the Palestinians to recognize Israel as a Jewish state within **any** borders. Any damage done by our symbolic recognition of Jerusalem pales in significance to this shameful chapter. We should get on with moving our embassy to the legitimate Israeli capital city.

Cold War II Enters a New Phase

January 2, 2019

Last May, I wrote of the importance of transformational leadership in negotiating the long-term strategic relationship between the U.S. and China in order to avoid what Graham Allison has named the "Thucydides Trap" in his compelling book, *Destined for War: Can America and China Escape Thucydides's Trap?* In October at the Hudson Institute, Vice President Mike Pence significantly turned up the urgency of this question with a speech that seemed to take what already has been characterized as Cold War II to a new level. Walter Russell Mead, who was in attendance, said the speech sounded like something Ronald Reagan could have delivered against the Soviet Union, a "tear down this wall" kind of broadside.

Here are some key phrases: "Through its Made in China 2025 policy, the Communist Party has set its sights on controlling 90 percent of world's most advanced industries… Beijing has directed its bureaucrats and businesses to obtain American technology by any means possible… America had hoped that economic liberalization would bring China into a greater partnership with us and the world. Instead, China has chosen economic aggression, which has in turn emboldened its growing military." In another part of the speech, he alleged that China is embarked on a comprehensive effort to "interfere in the domestic policies of this country," including the 2018 elections and the re-election of Donald Trump. And he made it clear in no uncertain terms that the U.S. would remain the Pacific's dominant power and identified China as the challenger.

These allegations have had the immediate effect of putting the trade disputes between the two countries in a much broader and more ominous context, and it has been very surprising to me that there hasn't been more attention paid to this speech and its ramifications for the U.S. beyond the analytical class. Frankly, I welcome this new rhetoric; the heat needed to be turned up and the emphasis needed broadening well beyond a dispute based on balance of trade to the geopolitical conflict that is has become. And there is growing evidence that the Trump administration is positioning itself to allocate resources for serious follow up on Pence's assertions. Meanwhile, the President has agreed to a 90-day "truce" in implementing tougher tariffs on Chinese imports pending China's response to the most serious violations and threats.

The critical need now is that this be an "all hands" effort on behalf of America's interests, and I wonder what can truly be expected from U.S. corporate interests when the heat really gets turned up on policies that might conflict with Chinese market access. And, needless to say, the national security implications are huge, even existential, and totally dependent on support from the private sector – are you listening Google?

Transformational, indeed. We won Cold War I and we can't afford to lose this one. I hope we're up to it.

On the Syria Pullout

January 2, 2019

As always with President Trump, if you don't like one of his announced decisions, wait a couple of news cycles and he will have rethought, regrouped, and often changed course. And this now appears to be the case with his surprise announcement that all U.S. troops immediately will be pulled out of Syria, so stay tuned.

I didn't like the decision in the first place, and the way he managed the announcement made the decision itself much worse. No one doubts his authority as commander-in-chief to have made the decision, but he probably violated every rule of management and leadership protocol in the process, alienating allies, senior staff, and Pentagon military leaders. It will cost him in ways not yet visible, particularly in the humiliating resignation of Secretary of Defense James Mattis, a major loss. And I might add that his resignation letter was a masterpiece, especially in describing the necessity to be "resolute and unambiguous in our approach to those countries whose strategic interests are increasingly in tension with ours" and that "our strength as a nation is inextricably linked to the strength of our unique and comprehensive system of alliances and partnerships."

The pullout decision itself was a mistake for many of the reasons that have been aired by knowledgeable observers – the abandonment of our Kurd allies, who at a minimum we owe protection and support for their self-determination; the creation of a vacuum that will be filled by Russia and Iran; the prospect of Turkey using our departure to inflict brutalities on Syria's Kurds it sees as terrorists; and the risk that ISIS, although severely crippled, is not yet completely defeated.

So where are we now? Expect a complete review of Trump's irrational knee-jerk decision and I predict at least a significant delay, but who knows? The bottom line for me is that America is the only honest broker in the region and our presence there at some level will be essential for some time to come, in Syria, Iraq, and Afghanistan. Call me a neoconservative if it fits, but I still believe that our power in all of its instruments has a role to play not only in protecting American interests, but in maintaining order, and that our policy also should continue to have space for support of self-determination and a "freedom agenda" without "nation-building." And in case you're wondering, yes, we must maintain a close and undiminished strategic alliance with Saudi Arabia, although I am not pleased with Trump's insufficient condemnation of the Saudi crown prince's murder of Jamal Khashoggi.

This is a very difficult and dangerous neighborhood and Trump was left a mess by Barack Obama – the "red line" legacy in Syria, the terrible Iran nuclear agreement, premature withdrawal, etc. – and frankly so far he hasn't altered the strategic balance of forces, so it remains an area in which American exceptionalism as the "indispensable nation" is most essential.

9
Healthcare

Patient "Rights"

July 3, 2001

The debate in Congress on the Patients' Bill of Rights legislation sent me back to my notes on a Rice University lecture series of several years ago on ethics in today's society. The subject then was "Hillary Care," but the questions remain. The most basic one is "is there a right to healthcare?" You may suggest that the American people have already answered this question in the affirmative. I'm not so sure. A corollary question railed in our lecture group was "of all the unfortunate circumstances in the world, which ones constitute unfairness and generate a set of rights, therefore claims on society?" After all, you can't have a right without a legitimate and enforceable claim to satisfy that right. The rights that our founders believed government were instituted to secure included life, liberty, and the pursuit of happiness (the latter generally considered to include property rights). They were also very clear about the source of these rights ("endowed by our Creator") and they agreed with President John Kennedy who said, "The rights of man come from the hand of God, not the state."

So, how have we arrived at this notion of a right to healthcare? I suggest that this perversion of the Constitution began with Franklin D. Roosevelt's 1944 State of the Union message, in which he proclaimed a second bill of rights because, he said, the original set "proved inadequate to assure us equality in the pursuit of happiness." These new rights included "the right to adequate medical care…" which, of course implied a claim on society. I mention this, because I believe it is important to have more of a national dialogue on these philosophical questions before we proceed to adopt universal healthcare. And make no mistake: Hillary Clinton and Ted Kennedy have every intention of succeeding with incrementalism where they failed with the comprehensive plan in 1994.

In my view, the pending legislation (as I write, it has just been approved by the Senate) is a good place to start refocusing the dialogue, with a veto by President Bush. Then we can get on with the business of transforming healthcare policy by empowering individuals with Medical Savings Accounts, making insurance premiums tax deductible by individuals, providing for coverage portability, phasing all employers out of the health insurance business so that the insured own their policies, and returning individual responsibility and cost/benefit considerations to the system. Healthcare is a contractual relationship between providers and consumers, not a right.

An Instructive Healthcare Survey

April 8, 2002

In February of this year, the Texas Association of Business and Chambers of Commerce surveyed Texas voters on their attitudes on healthcare issues. The results were instructive to me, but maybe not in the same way that they were to the TABCC. For instance, healthcare, along with jobs and the economy, was the most important issue facing the families of those surveyed and the most important thing the voters would change about health is the cost. About 62 percent believe the most important healthcare issue facing the Texas Legislature is holding down the cost of healthcare. Not surprising, but I was struck by the degree to which the respondents assign to government the responsibility for controlling these costs. Voters rank government regulations and the pharmaceutical companies as the top two sources of responsibility for healthcare costs, but only five percent believe that patients have the primary responsibility and four percent believe employees do, significantly less than doctors, hospitals, and HMOs. More than 65 percent of respondents report that their employer pays more than half their health insurance premiums. Am I wrong in discerning a direct correlation between the perception of responsibility for cost control and the fact that most patients/employees are covered by their employers? I think not. I have said before that I believe we have come too far down the road toward leading our citizens to view healthcare and insurance as a "right" primarily financed by someone else. We can begin to restore balance in responsibility by phasing employers out of the business of providing employee coverage, by providing full deductibility of premiums for individuals, portability of coverage, and full authorization of medical savings accounts.

Medicare "Reform" Only the AARP Could Love

January 4, 2004

Does anyone really believe that the American Association of Retired Persons would have supported the Medicare/Prescription Drug bill if it represented true market-based reform? The only reason for their support is that they know it is inevitable that the originally projected $400 billion cost will be greatly expanded, and they will be back with Tom Daschle and Ted Kennedy working on "fixing it" as soon as Congress reconvenes. The Democrats and their allied protection racket are adamantly opposed to any reform that introduces the dynamic of competition to the delivery of public goods, which is precisely the dynamic that will ultimately necessary to insure quality and control healthcare costs. As Stephen Moore of the Cato Institute points out, there are only two industries in America today that suffer from rampant inflation, healthcare and education, and in both cases the government plays the dominant role, either in delivery or finance or both. This is not coincidental. The only saving grace in this bill is the provision for Health Savings Accounts, which will afford individuals the same tax treatment for their deposits to these accounts as are now only available to employer-paid health insurance premiums. This is an empowering idea that could be revolutionary. Let's hope it gets off the ground in a big way before the "non-compete" crowd "fixes" it.

Healthcare Fixes – Do's and Don'ts

March 3, 2007

If the states are to serve as laboratory models with guidance on how to fix healthcare finance, there are already some models to avoid. One is in California, which is essentially proposing a plan to tax, spend, and regulate the state's path to universal coverage, with an enormous additional subsidy from the Federal government. I'm sure there are many in the new Democratic majority in Washington including a few Presidential candidates, who welcome this leadership as a possible precursor to a national plan. It's a recipe for disaster. A slightly better, but still flawed plan, is the one Massachusetts adopted early last year, which is too heavy on regulation and mandates, but does offer a way to equalize tax treatment of insurance premiums. In Texas, the lawsuit reform measures that cap non-economic medical malpractice damages already have improved the health insurance market, and the Texas Association of Business has some productive recommendations for Texas policy-makers that include expansion of consumer-directed health plans, increased information on cost and quality of plans, prohibition of so-called "balance billing," reforms to physician referrals, and expansion of Medicaid managed care. In his State of the Union message, President Bush proposed a plan that has merit, particularly in ending the preferential tax treatment for employer-provided medical insurance that is a relic of the World War II wage and price control system. This, along with continued expansion of Health Savings Accounts, represents progress, but still isn't bold enough.

For a bolder and better path, let's listen to the late Milton Friedman in a Hoover Institution interview for the World Health Congress a year before his death. In answer to the question as to how he would reform the U.S. Healthcare system, other than getting the government entirely out of the healthcare business, which he favored, he responded with two additional suggestions:

- Eliminate the tax exemption of employer-provided medical care insurance, because there is no reason to treat medical care differently from other essential goods, and businesses could then use the money to increase direct wages so that employees could then make their own healthcare insurance decisions.
- Nationalize the health insurance market by eliminating regulatory barriers to purchasing insurance across state lines, which are protectionist measures that are probably unconstitutional violations of the commerce clause.

The Next Major Battle

July 4, 2007

Get ready for the next major battle, and it will be at least as potentially divisive for the Republicans as the immigration divide. The issue is universal healthcare, and the forces of this "one size fits all" system are in full stealth mode, with the lead element being the massive expansion (to $75 billion over five years) of the State Children's Health Insurance Program (SCHIP). What makes this vehicle so insidious is that it emphasizes children's health and the underinsured condition of so many of them, while infiltrating families, including coverage of large numbers of adults, whose annual income is as high as more than $80,000. It goes without saying that once a program this broad takes hold, it will be virtually impossible to reverse such a middle class benefit, and from there it will be only a small step to universal "cradle to grave" coverage and a complete socialization of the nation's healthcare system, Hillary Clinton's dream. Some observers feel that the Democrats may overplay their hand with the very expensive SCHIP expansion and be forced to significantly cut other popular programs to pay for it, such as the subsidy for Medicare Advantage, the private Medicare program. But don't bet on it. More likely, it's time to get talk radio geared up again and for President Bush to dust off the veto pen, in the middle of an election year to boot.

The Healthcare Debate

August 6, 2009

After all that has been written and said about healthcare reform over the past six months, it is virtually impossible to offer much that is original. Much of the editorial commentary in favor of the various concepts floated by the left reflect such an ignorance of the realities of economics, human nature, incentives, and markets that it is not worth the time and space to refute them. I'll just throw out one question involving their organizing principle that to any rational analyst should undermine the entire basis: How can we adopt a new system of financing healthcare that supposedly will add 47 million new insured people while reducing the cost of the system on a budget-neutral basis without rationing of care and disastrous increases in taxes? It violates the law of non-contradiction on its face, and if the American people ultimately buy into anything close, they will have fooled me (again).

There has been one unique take on the debate that is the best I have seen, coming from the school of thought that I had believed to have been totally silenced, which is the one that asks: Is equality of healthcare a fundamental right? I have previously attempted to make the case that it isn't, and I continue to believe that there is a strong case there, but I am no doubt in the minority, and certainly so since at least the time of Franklin Roosevelt's enunciation of his "Second Bill of Rights" in the early 1940s.

In this vein, I was struck by the commentary of Dr. Thomas Szasz, author and emeritus professor of psychiatry at Upstate Medical University in Syracuse, New York. Rather than paraphrase his premise, I will simply quote the critical passages from his recent essay in *The Wall Street Journal*:

"The idea that every life is infinitely precious and therefore everyone deserves the same kind of optimal medical care is a fine religious sentiment and moral ideal. As political and economic policy, it is vainglorious delusion. Rich and educated people not only receive better goods and services in all areas of life than do poor and uneducated people, they also tend to take better care of themselves and their possessions, which in turn leads to better health. The first requirement for better healthcare for all is not equal healthcare for everyone, but educational and economic advancement for everyone.

We must stop talking about healthcare as if it was some kind of collective public service, like fire protection, provided equally to everyone who needs it.

If we persevere in our quixotic quest for a fetishized medical equality we will sacrifice personal freedom as its price. We will become the voluntary slaves of a 'compassionate' government that will provide the same low quality healthcare to everyone."

A final thought. I have previously written about "public choice theory" (May 2003), a concept which is applicable in the current debate. This theory was originally formulated by Nobel Laureate James M. Buchanan and in simplest terms is nothing more complicated than the espousal of market-based principles and systems for the delivery of public services. Critics of this theory seem to believe that rational people, when acting on certain desires or needs normally delivered publicly, do not behave as they do in markets; that somehow they set aside human nature and become immune to the dynamics and incentives of market forces. The sooner we rid ourselves of this nonsensical policy thinking, the sooner we can come to grips with the realities of the market and incentive systems that will be necessary to rationalize our healthcare finance system.

Big Time Systemic Misunderstanding

November 8, 2009

Tom Friedman's notion of what he calls "systemic misunderstanding" is a condition of debate or conflict between or among parties in disagreement wherein the conflict cannot be resolved with more facts or information. With Thomas Sowell, among my favorite essayists, such a condition is even more deeply seated in what he has named "a conflict of visions," which is also the title of his great book of 20 or so years ago. For Sowell, the intellectual origins of the sides of debate on essentially all public policy issues can ultimately be traced to the degree to which the opposing parties are of the "constrained" or "unconstrained" vision. Consequently, the very meaning of words like "freedom," "rights," "equality," and "power" may be drastically different, depending on their context within different worldviews, or visions of man.

Without getting too mired in the details of Sowell's thought, the two key criteria for distinguishing the constrained and unconstrained visions are: 1) the locus of discretion (who decides?) and 2) the mode of discretion (what is the decision process?). Both visions acknowledge inherent limitations in man, but the nature and degree of these limitations is different. Put simply, the unconstrained vision allows for considerably more knowledge, morality, virtue, and fortitude on the part of human nature to successfully accomplish its objectives than are thought humanly possible by the constrained vision.

I have been thinking of Sowell and his thought on these issues throughout the healthcare debate over the past year, and it occurs to me that nothing so vividly illustrates the validity of his theory, as well as Friedman's, than the profound policy differences in evidence here. Examine closely the comments from noted commentators from the left and you get the picture: Thomas Frank writes that the left is "reclaiming freedom" from the right in this debate and he points to FDR's Four Freedoms, particularly the one about "freedom from want," as the foundation for government intervention in the provision of healthcare. Most people of the constrained vision would respond that freedom is not defined as a taxpayer-funded entitlement. In his book, *The Future of Liberalism*, Alan Wolfe writes that "the welfare state is an institutionalization of the moral idea of empathy," while most of us of the constrained vision are wary of those who seek power under the guise of government delivery of empathy. Then there is our President, who, in response to a question by *The New York Times* on how we will deal with a healthcare system that will potentially allocate 80 percent of its resources to the chronically ill and those near the end of life, said "it is very difficult to imagine the country making those decisions just through the normal political channels." You get the point – with universal healthcare we have the ultimate in unconstrained vision proposed by those who are convinced of the efficacy, morality, virtue, and intentions of rational elites and their bureaucracies to deliver it. The result so far is that our House of Representatives has just passed what *The Wall Street Journal* has called "the worst bill ever."

Finally, there is another way to define the struggle at work here, ably noted by Arthur Brooks of the American Enterprise Institute, but entirely consistent with Sowell's conflict of visions. Brooks notes that the healthcare debate is part of a larger moral issue over the free enterprise system (a constrained vision, by the way), and that it will be replayed in every other major policy area in coming months. It comes down to competing visions of America's future based on the same notions about the nature of man and his limitations – will we strengthen freedom (properly understood), opportunity, and enterprise, or will we expand the role and power of the state? A source of systemic misunderstanding big time, and the stakes couldn't be higher.

The Debacle of a Progressive Con Job

November 5, 2013

"Of all tyrannies, a tyranny sincerely exercised for the good of its victims may be the most oppressive. It would be better to live under robber barons than under omnipotent moral busybodies. The robber baron's cruelty may sometimes sleep, his cupidity may

at some point be satisfied; but those who torment us for our own good will torment us without end for they do so with the approval of their own conscience." – C. S. Lewis.

The ObamaCare debacle is far beyond website failure, rollout "glitches," or even broadly the incompetency in its implementation. It will go down as a classic case of progressive ideological hubris, or as Daniel Henninger describes it, "...the failure of the very idea of progressive government. Not liberal government. Progressive government." It goes far beyond the typical partisan warfare of such as the so-called shutdown crisis and other similar inside the Beltway spectacles. This is watershed stuff. The Obama phenomenon was about the revival of the progressive movement of the early 20th century, beyond 1960s liberalism, and made particularly distinctive by the mandates of the ObamaCare legislation, which are consistent with the spirit of the "general will" of the social contract of Jean Jacques Rousseau – you will be forced by mandate to be "free." This has never worked in America and it won't work now.

Beyond the obvious lies from the President and the con job about retaining existing insurance coverage, there has been expert reporting and at least tacit acknowledgment that the Obama administration knew months in advance of the rollout that the enrollment systems were not ready. They refused to admit this and proceeded with the rollout as scheduled, because they did not want to succumb to Republican pressure to delay the implementation or to undermine their political position in the face of opposition proposals to postpone implementation, as well as the individual mandates, which would have amounted to a political defeat and capitulation during the budget showdown. This is what you get when political hacks are making policy, and it is an abdication of leadership accountability of the first order.

Given the magnitude of the economic impact of a failure to launch an undertaking of this size, while covering up the knowledge of a defect of this magnitude represents a subordination of the public interest to partisan political interest that, when fully vetted, could border on grounds for impeachment. In a parliamentary system, the government would be forced to resign. Accountability to the truth should trump political calculation without exception.

The Ultimate Progressive Mindset

March 5, 2014

For a brief moment before it reached the light of day, the Federal Communications Commission planned a major study of journalism newsrooms designed to define

"Critical Information Needs." The idea was to send out agents to media outlets around the country to inquire about such things as "who decides which stories are to be covered," "news philosophy," "responsiveness to underserved populations," "the demographics of news management," defined by race and gender, etc.

I assume that the left, having given up on the legislative and judicial branches, was attempting to use the regulatory arm of the FCC to reinstate the Fairness Doctrine or to achieve the same result – the stifling of media outlets with, shall we say, views inconsistent with those of the current regime.

Nothing exposes the true mindset of the progressive left more than clear evidence of its proclivity for the rule of experts, and this project could be exhibit number one. The arrogance is stunning, and I am almost sorry that it was canned immediately upon public scrutiny and not allowed to play out for awhile longer, if only to further expose this hubris for what it is, the fascism of the left.

No Surprises in Supreme Court Rulings

July 9, 2015

Did anyone really believe that the Roberts/Kennedy court would rule any differently on the same-sex marriage and ObamaCare cases? Is there any doubt that the Supreme Court not only reads election results, but responds to opinion polling? Unfortunately, however adverse to the intent of the founding, this is the state of affairs to which we have evolved in the constitutional balance of powers among the three branches of government.

Let's consider the two most prominent decisions in turn. First, the same-sex marriage case, *Obergefell v. Hodges*, in which the Court held in a 5-4 majority that the 14th Amendment requires a state to license and recognize in all respects a marriage between two people of the same sex. This decision was no doubt reached substantially in response to polling that reflected the most sweeping transformation of public opinion in history and in spite of a relatively recently adopted federal defense of marriage act and significant voter disapproval of same-sex marriage in several states.

It is interesting that all four dissenting justices wrote their own separate opinion. For example, Chief Justice John Roberts attacked the majority's substantive due process argument (a 19th century invention that gave us the right to abortion decision in *Roe v. Wade*), writing "the majority's approach has no basis in principle or tradition, except for the unprincipled tradition of judicial policymaking that characterized discredited decisions such as *Lochner v. New York...* but this court is not a legislature. Whether same-sex marriage is a good idea should be of no concern to us. Under the Constitution, judges have the power to say what the law is, not what it should be." Exactly on point in my judgment, but I wish Roberts had been as true to these principles in his two opinions, which bailed out ObamaCare!

I also like Samuel Alito's dissenting opinion, joined by Scalia and Thomas, which states, "Today's decision usurps the constitutional right of the people to decide whether to keep or alter the traditional understanding of marriage… It will be used to vilify Americans who are unwilling to assent to the new orthodoxy. If a bare majority of Justices can invent a new right and impose that right on the rest of the country, the only real limit on what future majorities will be able to do is their own sense of what those with political power and cultural influence are willing to tolerate."

If there is some hope in this decision, it is in Justice Kennedy's majority opinion, as follows: "…it must be emphasized that religions, and those who adhere to religious doctrines, may continue to advocate with utmost, sincere conviction that, by divine precepts, same-sex marriage should not be condoned. The First Amendment ensures that religious organizations and persons are given proper protection…"

And herein lies the rub, for already we have florists and bakers being charged and fined for refusing to participate in same-sex ceremonies and the left will not relent until the principle of religious freedom as understood in the Constitution has been completely gutted. And they will not stop there. Based on this decision, we can look for attacks on tax-exempt status of religious organizations, accreditation of religious colleges and schools, contracts with faith-based service organizations, etc. This is the next phase of this battle and it almost certainly will be back in front of the Court.

In *King v. Burwell*, we have possibly an even more egregious violation of the clear intent of the law under review. Here, in a 6-3 decision, the Court upheld the outlay of premium tax credits to qualifying persons, whose health insurance is subject to the Patient Protection and Affordable Care Act, better known as ObamaCare, in all states, whether or not the state established an exchange for this purpose as clearly stated in the statute and as aggressively described by advocates on numerous occasions in promoting its adoption. Yet in the majority opinion written by Chief Justice Roberts (no surprise here), the Court found the disputed clause concerning the exchanges to be ambiguous, and that it ought to be interpreted in a manner "that is compatible with the rest of the law." A total fabrication.

I always hate to say "I told you so," but in March of this year I wrote "I hope I am wrong, but I'm betting that the politics will win out and that the Chief Justice will once again bail out this abomination in "compassionate" deference to the resulting impact of the elimination of the subsidy for 10 or so million people and the damage he thinks will be inflicted on the institution of the Court."

What should our response be to these landmark cave-ins? Well, I like Lincoln's approach, who, when responding to questions about the infamous 1857 Supreme Court decision in the Dred Scott decision on slavery, said this: "If the policy of the government upon vital questions affecting the whole people is to be irrevocably fixed by decisions of the Supreme Court, the instant they are made in ordinary litigation between parties in person actions, the people will have ceased to be their own rulers, having to that extent practically resigned their government into the hands of that eminent tribunal."

10
Higher Education

Historical Amnesia

January 3, 2001

The American Council of Trustees and Alumni (ACTA) was founded in 1995 under the leadership of Lynne Cheney and Joe Lieberman to promote improved academic standards and greater accountability in the higher education community. Ms. Cheney, long one of my heroes for her tireless work in education and the arts, now serves as ACTA's Chairman and has been an outspoken advocate for active governance on the part of university trustees and alumni in attacking the status quo of lower standards and lax accountability. Last summer, the ACTA released its report, "Losing America's Memory: Historical Illiteracy in the 21st Century," which among its shocking findings, revealed that 81 percent of 556 randomly chosen seniors at 55 top-rated colleges and universities received a D or F on a high school level American history test, and the average score was 53 percent. I've seen the test and I can say without equivocation that these results should be worse than embarrassing to anyone associated with these schools. And yet, complacency was the word used to characterize the response by most of the administrators.

Thomas Jefferson admonished us long ago that "if a nation expects to be ignorant and free, it expects what never was and never will be." And the worst place in which to exhibit ignorance in a democratic republic is in the transmission of our common heritage and founding ideas. G. K. Chesterton defined education as simply the soul of a society as it passes from one generation to another. The Council on Civil Society has declared that a "basic responsibility of the school is cultural transmission, particularly a knowledge of the country's constitutional heritage, an understanding of what constitutes good citizenship, and an appreciation of the society's common civic faith and shared moral philosophy."

A recent *Portrait of America* survey found that roughly one-half of American adults would vote for the U.S. Constitution if it was on the ballot today. To me, this is a frightening statistic, but not surprising, given the fact that Americans as a whole seem to have only a remote understanding of American civilization and our best and brightest have no sense of our history. How can we be knowledgeable critics of public policy or even sustain this experiment in self-governance in this environment?

Anti-Americanism and Higher Education

May 4, 2002

"Since the 1960s, anti-Americanism has flourished on college campuses, in Hollywood and among the chattering class. Anti-Americanism is the conviction that our history is one long chronicle of crimes against humanity – slavery, segregation, dispossession of the Indians, exploitation of labor, and suppression of dissent. It is blind to America's greatness – to our unparalleled contributions to the advancement of human liberty, the development of representative government, and the march of progress... All of this is a far cry from legitimate disagreement over policy." – Don Feder.

To those of us who are serious about cultural renewal, the front lines are our leading institutions of higher education, which are the breeding grounds and laboratories of anti-American and cultural relativist nonsense. In addressing the problem, however, often the most difficult thing to do is develop an awareness among opinion leaders from the private sector. Most of these leaders are highly visible corporate types with their own public relations concerns who do not want conflict and would rather be sycophants to the university administrators and trustees and their sphere of influence. To them, peace and harmony come with appeasement.

Recently, it was gratifying to witness the response of President Larry Faulkner of The University of Texas in rebuttal to UT Professor Robert Jensen's anti-war on terrorism editorial after the September 11 attack. Unfortunately, this type of response is an exception on our campuses. However, thankfully, there are some very capable people at work to reverse the long trend of irresponsibility. David Horowitz's *FrontPageMagzine.com* and his Think Twice campaign are busy exposing the anti-American rot in many of our universities. Recently, I read a great piece in *FrontPage* by Robert Locke in which he outlines the very systematic means by which the left in American academia works it indoctrinating mischief and suggests some steps that can be taken to restore balance and true diversity to our college classrooms. The American Council of Trustees and Alumni has just released the revised and expanded version of its report, "Defending Civilization: How Our Universities Are Failing America and What Can Be Done About It." In its words, there is "a striking divide between our intellectual elites and the mainstream American public." The report makes clear that our colleges and universities are failing in the task of equipping our civilization's ability to defend its core beliefs, because they have abandoned these beliefs as a required staple of the curriculum. And don't think it isn't happening or can't happen at your alma mater. The ACTA is busy marshalling support from trustees, donors, and opinion leaders to reverse this condition. These efforts are worthy of our encouragement and involvement.

The SAT, Diversity, and Cultural Literacy

April 8, 2002

Bending to criticism of cultural bias from the University of California, the College Board is planning significant changes to the SAT college admissions test. Evidently, the "diversity police" at Berkeley have determined that the test is biased against minorities, an argument that has been raised many times before, but which has reached new intensity in the wake of Proposition 209 outlawing racial preferences in admissions. No one should be fooled by the cynical motivation here. It is purely a circumvention of the ban on racial preferences in the name of "diversity." In fact, it is a flawed approach that will allow a more "comprehensive" review of an applicant's background in addition to the SAT changes, which are likely to eliminate or reduce the analogy section of the verbal portion of the test in lieu of a "fairer" means of testing literacy, particularly cultural literacy, the means by which we communicate our shared history and values. As E. D. Hirsch made clear in his groundbreaking 1987 book, *Cultural Literacy*, these changes will further impoverish our young people in an area in which American children have shown consistent decline over the past 40 years.

"Order" In Higher Education

August 3, 2003

Former Houstonian John Moores, currently Chairman of the University of California Board of Regents, hit upon an age-old problem in a recent op/ed essay, one that has vexed any number of Texas Higher Education Coordinating Boards and "blue ribbon commissions" – how to bring strategic order to the State's system of higher education. There have been various plans advanced over the years by well-intentioned people, probably the most ambitious of which was developed by a commission led by Larry Temple in the 1980s. It offered two alternatives – a functional and a geographic structure for higher education institutions. But, like all other such proposals, it went nowhere. Why? Several reasons seem prominent (all of which I encountered when serving a six-year term on the board of one of our four-year universities): 1) intense regional competition for economic development and research, 2) board appointments are largely driven by school loyalty, 3) board members are or soon become provincial in their outlook and "boosterism" is the expectation of the alumni, 4) let's face it – a certain level of anti-intellectualism is alive and well in Texas, and 5) politically, higher education access always trumps excellence. I could give many examples of these, but you get the point.

Rather than spend more time and effort with top-down restructuring plans, we should be making bold moves toward marketizing the system, as some have suggested and as some other states are piloting. Market-based tuition is a good start, but we should be much bolder, as in spinning off entire departments and/or colleges of university systems as stand-alone schools, with certain services provided by the "parent" institution on a contract basis. Over time, this would produce a much better allocation of resources based on customer demand and preferences (and in the process probably eliminate much of the nonsense that now passes for meaningful curriculum), ultimately result in a restructuring of delivery systems commensurate with the needs of the customers, and I would bet that much of this would eventually align itself along functional and geographic lines. The trade-off, of course, is state support, but why should the state bureaucracy dominate the governance of our flagship universities in exchange for 20 percent of their total funding? And when 75 percent of the parents of students at the University of Texas at Austin earn more than $100,000 annually, why do they need the state subsidy anyway?

Frankly, I believe marketization is in many respects inevitable, because it will be forced by economics, not just in Texas, but throughout higher education, particularly the "flagships." On a per student basis, the state appropriation to the University of California at Berkeley is three times that at the University of Texas and Texas A&M, and there is no way the gap can be closed without unacceptable concessions in excellence, which, ironically, would run counter to the primary reason for closing the gap! And the bottom line is that there is no long term economic growth without centers of excellence in higher education.

The Tipping Point For the Left in Higher Ed

February 4, 2005

The domination of the left in the higher reaches of our elite institutions of higher education may have reached a tipping point with the eruption of Ward Churchill at Colorado University and his characterization of the 9/11 bombers as "combat teams," the Pentagon victims "military targets," and the World Trade Center victims "little Eichmanns." This might just do it – this might finally command the attention of mainstream opinion leadership to the abrogation of responsibility on the part of higher education leadership that has been much needed since the total capitulation of university administrators to the militant left 40 years ago. Add to this the remarks of none other than the President of Harvard University, Lawrence Summers: "One of those disturbing tendencies in academic life is that there is a desire on the part of many in the name of open-mindedness to fall into a kind of relativistic denialism in which all positions are equally legitimate, all positions must be respected, and compromise must be entered into no matter what the starting point or reasonableness of the two parties." This strikes me as an astounding statement from one in his position, and a major breakthrough for common sense. Academic freedom and the cover of tenure can and should be set aside in the case of moral turpitude, and a clear case for it can be made here as with those continuing comments of Robert Jensen of my alma mater, The University of Texas, among many others. We may be bound by freedom of speech to tolerate their ideas, but we aren't obligated to pay to hear them.

As Edward Feser states so well in his essay, "The Opium of the Professors," "the de facto function of the modern university is precisely the opposite of the traditional idea of education, which was to socialize the young by instilling into them, at a higher intellectual level, the culture they have inherited from their forebears. The professor was the guardian of a tradition greater than the student and greater than himself, a tradition which it was his duty to impart – not uncritically, to be sure, but at the same time with a reverence and humility appropriate to the grandeur of a civilization that has existed for more than two and a half millennia, and for the wisdom that its institutions embody and its thinkers have articulated." Dare we hope for a comeback of this mission in its fullest?

Tuition Costs

April 4, 2005

If you think healthcare costs are out of control, check out their comparison with college tuition – over the past 20 years, according to the Bureau of Labor Statistics, price growth of 191 percent for medical care and 289 percent for college tuition! With the growing trend in deregulation of tuition and costs among the nation's top state-supported institutions, many blame this explosion, at least recently, on what they call this "student tax" as a way of shifting costs from stingy governments to the education consumers. Patricia Kilday Hart of *Texas Monthly* magazine shares this view, and feels that worthy students from moderate income families are being squeezed out of an opportunity for an excellent education at the top tier schools. Not so, says Richard Vedder in *The American Enterprise*, who writes that colleges and universities are increasingly like hospitals and doctors – they depend largely, directly, or indirectly, on third parties for payment of their bills. So when government subsidizes low-interest student loans, it increases the demand for higher education at existing tuition levels, leading to higher prices, as well as more kids going to college. This third party payment system makes the customer less sensitive to price, allowing the schools to raise prices dramatically without adverse enrollment effects.

I have previously (August 2003) suggested that we should be making bold moves toward marketizing the system, with market-based tuition as a good start, but also by spinning off entire departments and/or colleges of university systems as stand-alone schools, with certain services provided by the "parent" institution on a contract basis. Vedder has an even better idea: states should provide their support in the form of vouchers or scholarships to the students directly, which could be made both progressive and performance-based. Progressive in that the vouchers would vary inversely with family income, more to the needy than the affluent, and performance- based in that the voucher amount could be tied to student performance, more to the high achiever than the laggard. Over time, these changes would produce cost efficiencies and a much better allocation of resources based on customer preferences. (As a useful by-product, I wonder if the likes of Ward Churchill would be able to keep their jobs in such a system.)

American Higher Education: Issues and Questions

November 2, 2005

"We have a responsibility to make sure our higher education system continues to meet our nation's needs for an educated and competitive workforce for the 21st century." – Margaret Spellings, Secretary of Education.

In this excerpt from the announcement of the Secretary's appointment of a commission to study and make recommendations on the future of American higher education, I have emphasized "educated," because while we are appropriately very concerned with our nation's competitive strength, its research and technological leadership, and providing its succeeding generations with the tools to excel in a globalized environment, we should also be concerned with the education of our youth, properly understood.

G. K. Chesterton understood education this way: "Properly speaking, there is no such thing as education. Education is simply the soul of a society as it passes from one generation to another. Whatever the soul is like, it will have to be passed on somehow, consciously or unconsciously, and that transition may be called education."

Continuing in this context of defining education, when we contemplate the mission of higher education, I am attracted to the statement recently adopted by Students for Academic Freedom: "The central purposes of a university are the pursuit of truth, the discovery of new knowledge through scholarship and research, the study and reasoned criticism of intellectual and cultural traditions, the teaching and general development of students to help them become creative individuals and productive citizens of a pluralistic democracy, and the transmission of knowledge and learning to a society at large.

Free inquiry and free speech within the academic community are indispensable to the achievement of these goals. The freedom to teach and to learn depends upon the creation of appropriate conditions and opportunities on the campus as a whole, as well as in the classrooms and lecture halls. These purposes reflect the values – pluralism, diversity, opportunity, critical intelligence, openness, and fairness – that are the cornerstones of American society."

The American Council of Trustees and Alumni, in its 1998 booklet, *What Every Educated Person Should Know*, reminds us that the foregoing principles underscore a belief that a shared understanding, a shared knowledge, help unify and advance civilization, and that, indeed, the American system of self-government is uniquely premised on the need for a citizenry so educated in order to sustain it.

Regrettably, over the past several decades, there has been a breakdown in this commitment to a shared common core of learning and understanding – of our culture, our ideas, our ideals, our history – in short, of the foundations of our civilization and how we can sustain them.

It is in a spirit of hopeful revival of this commitment that I suggest the following questions and the issues raised by them for serious consideration by the commission:

- How should academic freedom be defined, and how has the concept evolved over the past century, particularly as to its intersection with intellectual diversity and free speech, properly understood? Has this evolution been beneficial?

- What should be the future of academic tenure?
- In the wake of the Gratz and Grutter Supreme Court decisions on affirmative action at the University of Michigan, absent legislative or judicial correctives, what should be the future of race-neutral admissions, enrollment diversity, and minority access to highly selective public institutions?
- What has been the value of the trend toward the "elective system," and should we return to a universal core curriculum grounded in the Western intellectual tradition?
- What should be the obligation of higher education for the standards and accountability of elementary and secondary education to produce college readiness?
- How can we establish a system of K-12 teacher education and preparation in our public universities that will produce a sufficient quantity of highly qualified teachers necessary to revitalize elementary and secondary education?
- Considering the significant criticisms in the 2001 Knight Commission Report on Intercollegiate Athletics and its predecessor 10 years earlier, what should be the proper relationship of major college sports with the mission of the NCAA Division I universities?
- What are the major drivers of the accelerating costs of higher education, and what can be done to mitigate them and slow the growth?
- How should the cost of publicly supported higher education be allocated among its primary constituents – students, the public sector, and the private sector?

Secretary Spellings has selected an outstanding group of scholars and education policy veterans for the commission, with a visionary leader as Chairman in my friend, Charles Miller. The subject matter could not be more urgent, and it is my hope that this group will produce a product that will engage all of us in an overdue and much-needed dialogue on the future direction of this institution that is so critical to the continuing success of the American experiment.

Texas Higher Education Overhaul

February 3, 2007

There have been a number of recent appeals to Texas policy makers from business-related groups, such as the Governor's Business Council and the Build Texas Program to overhaul the structure and enhance the accountability and funding of the State's publicly assisted institutions of higher education. In addition, the leadership of the two flagship universities, UT-Austin and Texas A&M, have appealed to opinion leaders and policy makers to recognize their combined economic and research impact on the state and acknowledge their value-added in considering their respective appropriations.

All of these appeals are well taken, and Governor Rick Perry has now responded with his own policy recommendations to the Texas Legislature. There is a lot to like about his proposals, particularly the accountability measures that will require some type of "exit exam" for graduation and hold institutions responsible for the graduation rates of their students with incentive funding.

But there are at least three items of emphasis that seem to be missing. The first is illustrated by the advice offered to his successor by departing UT-Austin President Larry Faulkner in his State of the University Address in September 2005: "Your greatest challenge will be to work out a new, stable financial model for the long-term sustenance of the university. For decades, we have been drifting away from a model built on public higher education as a public good toward one that treats all higher education, even in the public sector, as a private benefit… we are approaching a point of no return. Will the university be forced to become essentially private to sustain its quality?" I have my own thoughts about the public-private issue which I have previously expressed (August 2003, April 2005), but President Faulkner is implying the need for a long-term strategy for Texas higher education, one that has eluded us for many years too long. Maybe the recent appeals will prompt the necessary vision to come together, but I don't see it in the Governor's proposals.

Second, if higher education is to fully return to its role as a driver of the public good, this criterion should be defined in terms beyond simply economic impact. The American Council of Trustees and Alumni, in its 1998 booklet, "What Every Educated Person Should Know," reminds us that the principle espoused by G. K. Chesterton, that "education is simply the soul of a society as it passes from one generation to another," underscores a belief that a shared understanding, a shared knowledge, help unify and advance civilization, and that, indeed, the American system of self-government is uniquely premised on the need for a citizenry so educated in order to sustain it. Regrettably, over the past several decades, there has been a breakdown in this commitment to a shared core of learning and understanding – of our culture, our ideas, our ideals, our history – in short, of the foundations of our civilization and how we can sustain them. There appear to be some initiatives underway directed toward the revival of a required core curriculum, and these should be greatly encouraged.

Third, we need much more accountability for the role of our higher education institutions in the preparation of teachers for our K-12 public school system. There are islands of excellence here, but generally speaking, the traditional colleges of education are in bad need of overhaul. Our organization, the Texas Institute for Education Reform, has developed detailed policy recommendations on how to accomplish this enhanced accountability, but it needs much more attention from state political leaders and the leaders of these institutions, and the best way to get this attention is through tying accreditation and state funding to the value-added to enhanced student achievement by their graduates.

Again, I applaud the Governor for these initiatives; on balance, they are a big step in the right direction, but we need much more.

Students as Customers

February 8, 2009

It was recently reported that a large majority of faculty members at three Texas A&M University campuses declined to participate in a cash bonus program based on student evaluations, which is part of a group of proposals by Gov. Rick Perry designed to increase accountability in higher education. This was déjà vu for me. While serving on the Board of Regents of Stephen F. Austin State University in the early 1990s, I proposed a somewhat similar program there, and the response was about the same. Listen to what Robert Kreiser of the American Association of University Professors had to say about the TAMU plan: "Students are attending colleges and universities to be educated; they're not there as customers; they are not there to get a product as one would in a supermarket or a department store." This is very similar to the response I received 15 years ago, and my response to Mr. Kreiser is this – many of us have had quite enough of this arrogance, and you and your colleagues had better take a longer look at the changing configuration of the K-16 continuum in education, as well as the latest customer-driven college cost/benefit analyses lest you become obsolete.

But What Will They Learn?

January 1, 2010

The American Council of Trustees and Alumni has recently released two reports, *Protecting the Free Exchange of Ideas and What Will They Learn?* The former identifies concrete measures recommended by ACTA and taken by 40 universities to ensure that students are learning how to think and not what to think. The latter demonstrates that our institutions of higher education are doing a poor job preparing the next generation for citizenship and the global marketplace. It also explains why a core curriculum is so important, what a good core curriculum should include, and why so many of our universities are deficient in this regard. The following quote from former Harvard College Dean Harry R. Lewis cuts to the heart of the issue: "At its best, general education is about the unity of knowledge, not about distributed knowledge. Not about spreading courses around, but about making connections between different ideas. Not about the freedom to combine random ingredients, but about joining an ancient lineage of the learned and wise. And it has a goal, too: producing an enlightened, self-reliant citizenry, pluralistic, and diverse, but united by democratic values." In a closely related effort, I am proud to be part of a movement in Texas called the Coalition of American Traditions and Ethics, which is strongly advocating for core content in Western Civilization and American traditions in state supported colleges and universities, and I am pleased that we have been successful in the approval of an interim study of the issue by the Higher Education Committee of the Texas House of Representatives. I believe that the future of our country may very well depend on the restoration of the core liberal education, and it will almost certainly be necessary for the revival of conservatism, properly understood as classical liberalism. Stay tuned.

The Coming Tsunami in Higher Education

August 5, 2012

The advance of technology in delivery is transforming higher education in America. Approximately one-third of current higher education students are enrolled in at least one online course, and the number is growing at a significant rate. Ron Trowbridge of the Center for College Affordability and Productivity thinks this trend will expand into radical reform and what he calls "disruptive innovation" in higher education, much like Schumpeter's concept of "creative destruction." I agree and I applaud this phenomenon, because I see the absolute necessity of expanding distance learning for a variety of reasons, not to mention its inevitability, but I am concerned about two aspects of this trend: one, its growing emphasis on the purely vocational attributes of postsecondary education and two, the decline in many of the benefits offered by the traditional higher education experience, particularly in the liberal arts.

In the first instance, we who are heavily involved with elementary and secondary education are in a continuing debate with those who would predestine many of our students to a vocational pathway that is void of the rigor necessary for success in the 21st century workplace, which is synonymous with postsecondary success on either pathway – college or career education leading to industry certification. The motto on this issue for my organization, the Texas Institute for Education Reform, is "one standard, multiple pathways, equal rigor."

In the second instance, higher education is about much more than vocational preparation. A purely vocational curriculum deprives our students of the necessary grounding in many of the verbal, analytical, and communications skills that are honed by an immersion in the liberal arts, not to mention the study of the founding principles and cultural literacy of America, which are necessary for responsible citizenship. These groundings are best absorbed in exchanges with other students and mentors in an interactive setting.

So, I am supportive of the initiatives to enhance the accountability of higher education for the progress of its students and the advancements in technology and productivity in its delivery, and I am hopeful that the hybrid online/classroom capabilities and the enhancement of interactive content quality in online delivery proceed at a pace that will mitigate my concerns.

The Undermining of History Standards in Texas Higher Ed

February 4, 2013

(Note: A version of this essay was previously posted to www.seethruedu.com, an initiative of the Texas Public Policy Foundation focused on higher education reform. I am pleased to be a contributor to this site and I invite Pilgrim readers to visit the site for enlightened commentary on higher education issues from a number of knowledgeable contributors.)

Congratulations to the National Association of Scholars (NAS) and its Texas affiliate on the release of a very instructive study of the American history curriculum at The University of Texas (UT) and Texas A&M University (A&M) and for the initiative to shed light on the required foundational American history courses at the state's two flagship institutions. Credit is due to these schools for requiring these foundational courses and to state lawmakers for requiring the transparency that all course syllabi, course reading assignments, faculty backgrounds, and research priorities be made easily available.

However, the results of the study, *Recasting History: Are Race, Class, and Gender Dominating American History?*, are very disappointing and confirm growing suspicions that Texas is not immune to the national trend in the insidious growth of multiculturalism in higher education curriculum, the insular nature of the target audience for research priorities, and the growing politicization reflected in the heavy concentration in the various cultural identity "studies," particularly those of race, class, and gender.

To briefly summarize several key points of the study:

- Seventy-eight percent of faculty members at UT and 50 percent at A&M were "high assigners" (more than 50 percent of the assignments) of readings focused on race, class, and gender.
- Of the 100 foundational "milestone documents" of American history as identified by the National Archives, only 23 were assigned, and 89 percent of the faculty members assigned none of these documents.
- Three of the top four research priorities for faculty members were race, class, and gender, and these included 78 percent of the UT faculty and 64 percent of the A&M faculty.

I repeat the principle espoused by G. K. Chesterton, that "education is simply the soul of a society as it passes from one generation to another," which underscores a belief that a shared understanding and a shared knowledge help unify and advance civilization. The American system of self-government is uniquely premised on the need for a citizenry so educated in order to sustain it.

There has been considerable response to the study and, of course, much of it from the circled wagons within the halls of the subject institutions. But, I was encouraged by the commentary of Richard Pells, an American historian who taught at UT for 40 years, who reported that, "based on my own experiences there, I believe the report's main arguments are largely correct." He further wrote that "what UT historians need to do is stop railing against the report and start re-examining their hiring practices and expand their far too limited intellectual horizons."

Good advice. Let's hope that this study, available at http://www.nas.org/articles, and its wide distribution will help spark a serious conversation among higher education and elected officials on this critical point and how the most damaging of the trends reflected therein can be addressed.

The Humanities Wars

October 6, 2013

We are besieged by commentary in the battle over the humanities curriculum in higher education – do we need more emphasis? Do we need less? Is it all about jobs? Is it all about competency in a skill set? What about critical thinking? What about making good citizens? What about the pursuit of meaning in life? etc.

Partly in response to all of this, the American Academy of Arts and Sciences formed the Commission on the Humanities and Social Sciences, co-chaired by Duke University President Richard Brodhead and retired Exelon CEO John Rowe and comprised of a blue-ribbon group of 50 scholars, business executives, lawyers, judges, university presidents, and cultural celebrities. After more than two years of careful study, the report of the Commission, named "The Heart of the Matter," was released in June. It contains some interesting and useful recommendations for reviving interest in the study of the humanities. For example, the creation of a "Culture Corps" in communities across the country to convey humanistic expertise and interest to the next generation, a concept, incidentally, that G. K Chesterton believed was the central purpose of education.

But nowhere in the report was the recognition that the major deficiency in what now passes for the study of the humanities is the denigration over the past several decades of its core intellectual foundation in Western Civilization. As noted by Peter Berkowitz, the report never really gets to "the heart of the matter," which is the illiberal nature of liberal education at our leading colleges and universities.

In a recent essay in *The Wall Street Journal*, Jonathan Jacobs, Chairman of the Department of Philosophy at John Jay College of Criminal Justice has this to say:

The primary concern shouldn't be how American students rank in international science and math scores (though that is certainly relevant). It is whether the U.S. can be a prosperous, pluralistic democracy if higher education fails to require students to think, inquire, and explain. A liberal democracy requires a certain kind of civic culture, one in which citizens understand its distinctive principles and strive to preserve them.

And more than 50 years ago, Leo Strauss delivered an address entitled "What is Liberal Education?" In it, he said:

Liberal education is the counter poison to mass culture, to the corroding effects of mass culture, to its inherent tendency to produce nothing but "specialists without spirit or vision and voluptuaries without heart." Liberal education is the ladder by which we try to ascend from mass democracy to democracy as originally meant. Liberal education is the necessary endeavor to found an aristocracy within democratic mass society. Liberal education reminds those members of a mass democracy who have ears to hear, of human greatness.

We need much more of this, properly understood, not less.

The Real Issues with Boko Haram

May 11, 2014

The kidnapping of hundreds of Nigerian girls by the radical terrorist organization known as Boko Haram has aroused the outrage of all civilized people and has become a particular cause for the cultural elite in the U.S. My first reaction was, where have they been? This behavior is consistent with that of radical Islam at every flash point where it clashes with civilized states around the globe, and it is not coincidental that it most often attacks Christians. Why does the West ignore this reality? And why do we constantly hear that the average Muslim wholeheartedly rejects terror and holy war, while we hear nothing from these "average Muslims" and their leaders when confronted with these outrages?

As a refugee from radical Islamic oppression, Ayaan Hirsi Ali has written and spoken courageously and forcefully about this issue. In the first place, she translates the name Boko Haram in terms more revealing about the group's mission – "The Fellowship of the People of the Tradition for Preaching and Holy War" – and explains that the mission is no different from that of the Taliban and other jihadists – the oppression of women. They sincerely believe that girls are better off enslaved than educated. Ali has been carrying the message to anyone who will listen.

Incredibly, not everyone in the West wants to hear her message and her wake up call. This spring, she was to have received an honorary degree from Brandeis University, but last month, after protests by students, faculty, and some outside groups, the University revoked its invitation. Those who protested accused her of being "Islamophobic" in her advocacy for the rights of women and girls. Folks, this is what passes for liberalism in many of our elite institutions of higher education.

To her credit, she wrote an essay for *The Wall Street Journal* entitled "Here's What I Would Have Said at Brandeis." It represents the best of what classical liberalism, properly understood, should be about. I hope the Brandeis trustees read it and were duly ashamed. They should have been. As for the rest of us, there are two messages here. The first is that we had better get very serious about the continuing threat of Islamic radicalism, and in particular, the complicity of "average Muslims" in its mission. The second is that we need to take a hard look at the upper reaches of American higher education and its mission and how this mission is being corrupted in far too many instances among our so-called elite institutions.

A Bright Spot for the Liberal Arts at UT-Austin

May 11, 2014

For many years, there has been considerable angst over the severe decline in the study of the humanities in American higher education. This decline has been particularly precipitous since the mid-1960s, and in fact, studies show that bachelor's degree completions in the humanities nationwide declined from 14 percent of the total of all degrees in 1966 to just seven percent in 2010. The reasons are several, not the least of which has been the drift in the core curriculum so well noted by Allan Bloom in his 1987 classic, *The Closing of the American Mind*, compounded more recently by the accelerated emphasis on vocational grounding in the curriculum and the pressure for more faculty research productivity, particularly in the larger public research institutions.

In the midst of these problems and trends in the liberal arts, there are a few bright spots around the country, and one of them is at The University of Texas at Austin, where, under the leadership of Tom and Lorraine Pangle, the Thomas Jefferson Center for the Study of Core Texts and Ideas, on whose Advisory Committee I serve, is providing a refreshing alternative and an island of excellence for students who want much more meaningful foundational grounding in the core curriculum, regardless of their major course of study.

Founded six years ago to foster a restoration of the Western intellectual tradition to the core curriculum at UT, the Center offers all students the opportunity to meet six of their 14 course university-wide core requirements through a coherent, rigorous sequence of six courses in the great books and ideas that have shaped Western Civilization. These courses take students through a close study of the Bible and other foundational religious texts; major works of literature and philosophy from ancient Greece; the history of political thought from ancient times to the present, including the original proponents and major critics of modern liberalism; and the founding documents and principles of the American Republic.

Recently, the Center has launched its Jefferson Scholars Program, which will offer to exceptionally motivated freshmen and sophomores the opportunity to study these texts in small classes providing access to leading faculty and lively interaction with their peers. The response to this offering has been overwhelming across a range of majors from business to engineering to the natural sciences to the liberal arts and, in fact, is oversubscribed, which is a good problem to have and reflects the hunger for this kind of meaningful content. Here is a sample letter from among similar ones from almost 500 applicants:

"I would like to be in this program because as a person I want to be more insightful. I want to learn things in college that I can take with me throughout life, things that cannot be measured by a piece of paper. I feel that this program will allow me the opportunity to learn more about myself and humanity from some of the people who have had the greatest influence on humanity. I want my life to be one spent learning and growing. Through the Jefferson Scholars Program I know that I can develop skills that will prove invaluable for the rest of my life."

There is much more to be done, but this is a very good start at the state's flagship, and the University's president, provost, and dean of liberal arts are to be commended for their support of this initiative.

No More "Studies" Courses

May 11, 2014

The Texas State Board of Education voted last month to approve a modified rule that will advance the development of public school course offerings in Mexican-American Studies. This is a mistake. We already have far too much curriculum content focused on cultural "studies" in our higher education institutions. In fact, based on a 2012 study by the National Association of Scholars, approximately 78 percent of the emphasis in American history courses at The University of Texas at Austin, in terms of assigned readings, is concentrated on race, class, and gender; at Texas A&M, this emphasis is 50 percent. We don't need more emphasis on these multicultural "studies," we need less, and we don't need to introduce this concept in our secondary education curriculum. What we do need is a heightened focus on Western Civilization, the founding of the

American Republic, and the contribution to it made by all cultures and all Americans, without hyphenation and without cultural relativism.

The College Graduation Rate Conundrum

June 8, 2014

Every college and university, particularly those that rely heavily on taxpayer support, is striving to improve the four-year graduation rate of their students. And it makes sense as a high priority objective – many knowledgeable observers consider the four-year graduation rate a critical measure of institutional success and a low four-year rate of graduation is a very costly proposition to all stakeholders: taxpayers, contributors, students, and families.

The University of Texas at Austin, for example, has as its objective an increase in the four-year graduation rate from the current level of approximately 52 percent to 70 percent by 2019. This is a pretty tall order, particularly since the rate has been flat for about 10 years, but it can be done, given the enormous resources at its disposable. A major issue, however, is the perverse incentives that might come into play in order to achieve the objective, particularly in terms of the possible lowering of standards. The problem of grade inflation in higher education across the board is widely acknowledged, and in the absence of an external objective assessment, there could be unintended consequences from increased pressure on graduation rates. This is why many observers, including me, support independent assessments such as the College Learning Assessment and/or the various competency exams that are coming into use to measure what students have learned and what value has been added over four years. In fact, it seems to make sense to expect these institutions to show overall growth in average scores on the exit exams, while also increasing graduation rates.

Another issue of concern with graduation rates is the issue of "mismatching" students and their college choices, because of affirmative action in order to achieve racial and ethnic diversity. This practice no doubt has a dampening impact on graduation rates in highly selective institutions that admit significant numbers of students who do not meet the achievement and postsecondary readiness standards of their peers. Many of these students, although they have good high school grades, are 200-300 SAT exam points below the average admission standard at places like UT-Austin and Texas A&M and are not ready to succeed there, producing discouragement, requiring more support and remediation, lengthening degree completion time, and increasing the chance of failure. They would be much better served by a less selective school.

Finally, one of the best solutions to the problem of low college graduation rates is to continue the push for higher standards in our elementary and secondary education system. Currently, 51 percent of Texas high school graduates who choose to attend community colleges are required to take remedial courses due to the failure of our schools to prepare them for postsecondary success. This percentage must be drastically reduced and our institutions of higher education have a responsibility to work closely with public school educators to assure that curriculum is aligned with higher education requirements and that the standards for rigor are strengthened.

More Mischief at the College Board

July 5, 2014

Previously I have commented on the announcement by David Coleman of the College Board of the new SAT to be released in 2016, without much good to say about the so-called "improvements" that supposedly are designed to better reflect what students have actually studied in high school, but appear to be simply more "dumbing down" of standards.

Now comes the release of the Board's new AP U.S. History Framework, a document that dictates how teachers should cover the required history topics with America's brightest high school sophomores and juniors. In a comprehensive analysis entitled "The College Board's Attack on American History," Jane Robbins of the American Principles Project and retired U.S. history teacher Larry Krieger pull back the covers of this Framework to find that it is woefully deficient in a grounding in the lives and character of our founders, in our founding documents, and generally in the facts about our country's development. Instead, according to the analysis, "The redesigned Framework inculcates a consistently negative view of American history by highlighting oppressors and exploiters while ignoring the dreamers and innovators who built our country." In addition and maybe even worse, beyond the leftist slant, Robbins and Krieger write that the new Framework reflects "the general view that academic historical knowledge is unnecessary."

G. K. Chesterton wrote: "Properly understood, history is a chronological map that shows us not only where we have come from, but also where we are, and how we got here… history also can be a prophet… This, however, is only true if the chronological map is accurate. If it has been drawn by those with prejudiced perceptions or a prejudiced agenda it will only succeed in getting us lost. There are few things more dangerous than an inaccurate map, especially if we find ourselves in perilous terrain."

For those who wonder where this kind of thing comes from that pollutes far too many of our public school classrooms and our so-called elite institutions of higher education, it primarily comes from the institutions held responsible for professionally training our teachers and with organizations like the College Board that should represent the gold standard for the criteria of the curriculum. As renowned classics professor Donald Kagan recently said in response to a related question, "…the barbarians are not at the gates, they run the place… there is no choice, but to fight it, to fight it every way you know how as hard as you know how."

Short-Changing a Lot of Bright Kids

October 5, 2014

A recent article by Harold Levy, executive director of Jack Kent Cooke Foundation, highlighted what seems to me to be a glaring oversight. A study by his foundation using data from the Department of Education to track talented students found that only 59 percent of smart children from low-income households, defined as those who scored in the top 25 percent on standardized exams, graduate from college. This compares with 77 percent of similarly bright children from affluent families who complete an undergraduate degree. In addition, it found that high-achieving students from low-income backgrounds graduate from college at about the same rate as low-scoring students from affluent families.

Further, as recently reported by *The New York Times*, in 2006, at the 82 schools rated "most competitive" by *Barron's Profiles of American Colleges*, 14 percent came from the poorer half of the nation's families, according to a study of the data by Georgetown University and the University of Michigan. This percentage was unchanged since 1982. At a more elite group of 28 private colleges including the Ivy League, researchers found that between 2001 and 2009, a period of explosion in financial aid at these schools, enrollment of students from the bottom 40 percent of family incomes increased from 10 percent to only 11 percent. I suspect that a significant number of these kids are high achievers.

Doesn't there seem to be a disconnect here? While we are piling up astronomical amounts of student debt and ever-increasing aid to these institutions, which arguably drives tuition and fee escalation, and while we continue to pursue discriminatory admission policies based on the so-called state interest in "diversity," it appears that a large number of the deserving students we ostensibly are trying to help are falling through the cracks, not only to their detriment, but to the country's.

No doubt, tapping this pool for the more highly selective schools is difficult for a variety of reasons, but it is hard not to at least some extent agree with Anthony Carnevale, director of Georgetown University's Center on Education and the Workforce, who said, "Higher education has become a powerful force for reinforcing advantage and passing it on through generations." We need to take a hard look at the perverse incentives that are sustaining this outcome, and thoughtful university trustees and alumni are the people to do it.

The University of Houston and the TIER I Conundrum

October 5, 2014

The recent dustup between University of Houston Chancellor Renu Khator and Texas Senator John Whitmire over the school's proposed requirement that, with some exceptions, all freshmen would be required to live on campus, poses some interesting questions about the role and aspirations of this and other similarly situated universities.

Under Khator's inspiring and impressive leadership over the past several years, the University of Houston (UH) has made great strides toward its mission to become what is known as a "Tier I" institution of higher education. Why is this objective considered important? For a couple of reasons, aside from the prestige it brings. The widely accepted opinion is that Houston should have such an institution for its beneficial impact on economic growth and other research and intellectual property by-products and that Texas is trailing other states, notably California, in its pursuit of higher education excellence due at least in part because California has nine universities with such designation, while Texas currently has only three – Rice University, The University of Texas at Austin, and Texas A&M University.

In furtherance of the objective to correct this competitive imbalance, the Texas Legislature has offered incentives to seven state institutions to, in effect, compete for the designation, which admittedly is a better approach than simply politically anointing the candidates, and UH has been aggressively involved in this competition. The problem for UH is one that I anticipated and is partly illustrated by the recent flap over freshman housing and that is that the school has almost, since its inception, been identified as largely a commuter college primarily serving the needs of an urban, often part-time student constituency and this role has entrenched itself as a primary element of its identity. In fact, many years ago an observer once suggested that UH will be "the City College of New York of the 21st century." This is the crux of Sen. Whitmire's objection to the new freshman housing policy. And frankly, while this historic role is an important one not to be disrespected, it might not be consistent with the aspiration for Tier I status as a major research institution.

There is another somewhat related issue that is almost certain to come into play. In Texas higher education philosophy and policy, "access" will almost always trump "excellence." For UH to reach Tier I status, it will no doubt be required to increase admission standards and move toward a more highly selective admissions policy. This will cut against its role as an urban part-time student institution serving large inner city and often minority constituencies and no doubt will bring additional pushback of the nature of Sen. Whitmire's objections from these communities.

Senator Whitmire makes a great point, and in a way, it is my point as well. Texas has long struggled with a master strategy for higher education and has resisted almost all attempts to develop one in a grand top-down manner, which means that the 34 state-supported institutions and the 15 appointed boards of regents, are relegated to fighting politically for their roles and support from one legislative session to the next based on regional clout and provincial interests. We have two flagship research university systems in the state that are of Tier I status and are highly recognized centers of excellence. Why do we need more of these? Why should we diffuse available funding in pursuit of them? Why shouldn't we pursue a strategy of concentrating our investment in these centers of excellence as research institutions while designating strategic and market-based roles to be filled by the other public institutions that serve important regional and/or functional needs for the state? It has been a long time since we attempted to address these questions. I think it is time to revisit them.

A Huge Challenge and Dilemma for Texas Higher Education

January 1, 2015

Texas has made good progress and the Texas Higher Education Coordinating Board has provided good leadership on the 15-year strategic plan implemented by the Board in 2000, significantly increasing the number of people enrolled in higher education and meeting the objectives for the number of undergraduate degrees or certificates awarded, as well as the increase in the number of nationally recognized programs and services at Texas institutions. And the Board expects by next year to meet most of the other goals of the current plan, which has been revised as the state met the benchmarks.

But, as the Board finalizes and begins to implement the next 15-year phase of the plan through 2030, the standards must be significantly higher to meet the need, while the challenges mount. For example, based on a draft of the plan discussed in a recent meeting, the proposed target for educational attainment in Texas calls for increasing the percentage of Texans aged 25-34 with a postsecondary degree or credential to at least 45 percent by 2020, 52 percent by 2025, and 60 percent by 2030. Currently, it is 38 percent, compared to 43 percent for the overall U.S. population.

To put this challenge in perspective, note that, based on research conducted by the Coordinating Board and Houston Endowment on the fall 2000 cohort of Texas eighth graders, only 19 percent of them earned any sort of postsecondary credential within six years of expected high school graduation, and for the economically disadvantaged segment of this cohort the result was nine percent. This statistic represents the current status of the "pipeline" of those ready for college and the 21st century workplace that will feed the ambitious objectives that the Coordinating Board has in mind. Further to this point on "readiness," we know that 51 percent of Texas high school graduates entering community colleges need remediation and that very few of these kids ultimately graduate.

So, my first thought when seeing the preliminary draft of the 2030 higher education plan was, given the current state of PreK-12 education in Texas, how in the world can these objectives be met. The answer is, they can't, which is why our state's future is in the hands of those responsible for leading our elementary and secondary system of schools. They are the only ones who can fill the "pipeline" with the postsecondary ready students we will need for the state's prosperity, and they should be held accountable for doing so. Yet as the 84th Texas Legislature convenes in a couple of weeks, we know that there are a number of bills already filed that are intended to go beyond the destructive provisions of House Bill 5 from the 2013 session, further roll back the standardized assessments necessary to measure the postsecondary readiness of our pending high school graduates, and undermine the very accountability for the college and career readiness of our kids that we know we must have. There is a big disconnect here.

As those of us who are involved with education reform have said numerous times since the adoption of the accountability system embodied in House Bill 3 in 2009, unlike the succession of all previous accountability assessments, the new one (STAAR) moved the achievement bar from "passing" to "readiness," a big leap that almost no one in the education establishment was prepared for. The question is, how long to we allow them to get ready? And do we really want to use the new alternative pathways to "track" students and sort them into two or more groups and label their high school diplomas, as many well-meaning leaders seem to want?

These are the questions we need to address, and as important as this visionary work on the part of higher education leadership is, we truly need a PreK-16 approach so that we are fully in touch with the realities and are properly addressing and resolving these issues in PreK-12.

Are College Students Customers?

June 6, 2015

I was struck and conflicted by an insightful article by Larry Hubbell, Director of the Institute of Public Service at Seattle University, in the current edition of Academic Questions, entitled "Students Aren't Consumers." In it, he makes some very penetrating points that seem to be of the "wedge" variety in the ongoing discussion on the transformation of higher education mission and delivery.

Basically, he contends that, although in many areas of the economy higher standards work to improve sales, in academia, it's the reverse, and therefore, the student as consumer has become part of academic decline. He then proceeds to outline the basis for this argument by citing the undermining trends in grade inflation, student evaluations of faculty, the evolution of the demands made on faculty for much more detailed course syllabi into something of the sort of a contract, and the significant increase in student demand for study guides that seem to be analogous to the "teach to the test" phenomenon in the high schools.

He then closes with this:

"As students are presented with more choices throughout their young lives, it is inevitable that colleges and universities will embrace the practices of the private sector as they vie for their education dollars. The college experience should be focused on the pursuit of learning, not customer satisfaction. That pursuit is hindered when professors become purveyors and the students become buyers. Now that unabashed consumerism has infiltrated the college experience – from extravagant dining options to elaborate dormitory living – it may seem inevitable that classrooms across campus will subscribe to the pervasive customer consciousness. Nevertheless, those loyal to the cause of learning must resist that pull."

For the past 20 years since I have been heavily involved in education – as a business leader, as a university trustee, as an elementary and secondary education reformer – I constantly have preached the notion of students as customers much in the sense of the business model, while preserving a reverence for the student in the pursuit of learning and self-fulfillment. So I have a lot of sympathy for Hubbell's point of view here, but I am conflicted by my commitment to an education system that must be accountable for student achievement that delivers responsible and contributing, as well as economically productive citizens.

Everything we know about where the higher education mission is headed today, tells me that the notion of the student as a customer is becoming dominant in this trade off and a big part of me is pained by the fact that, for example, the humanities and liberal arts are the losers, and with them, the pursuit of learning for its sake. But it seems impossible to head off this overwhelming demand for measurable value-added in the credential and the almost totally consumer-driven approach to postsecondary study, with its Massive Open Online Courses, competency-based credit, the $10,000 BA, etc. Can we have it both ways? Is this simply the C. P. Snow conflict of the two cultures updated to the 21st century? The resolution of this issue may very well be the leading problem for higher education leadership in this century.

Affirmative Action in College Admissions and Its Conflict with High-Achieving Students

July 9, 2015

Recently Jason Riley of *The Wall Street Journal* gave us a somewhat different take on the perverse arguments for affirmative action in higher education admissions with his very provocative essay, "The New Jews of Harvard Admissions." A new take, because unlike the experience of other minorities, it is a perspective from the point of view of alleged admission discrimination against Asian-American students who are consistently at the top of the applicant pool in almost every measurement of student achievement.

The complaint, based on the appeal of 64 groups to the Department of Education, is that Harvard University is discriminating against Asian-American applicants by holding them to higher standards to keep them from growing as a percentage of the student body, a charge that is analogous to similar charges levied against elite institutions early in the last century for discrimination against Jews.

In a recent interview of Florida businessman Yukong Zhao, one of the organizers of the groups making the appeal, by Kate Bachelder, it appears that their case is a pretty good one. The share of college-age Asian-Americans in the U.S. population has risen from three percent in 1990 to five percent in 2011 and members of this five percent make up approximately 30 percent of National Merit semifinalists, while Harvard admissions do not come close to reflecting these gains. In fact, this spring 21 percent of the students admitted were Asian-American; in 1993 it was approximately 20 percent.

Harvard, like many institutions (which unfortunately include my alma mater, UT-Austin) that are pained to live with convoluted affirmative action court rulings that continue to allow racial considerations, uses a "holistic" approach, meaning consideration of a number of subjective factors in addition to grades and exam scores, which of course can include racial and ethnic considerations in the interest of the claim of "diversity" as a compelling state interest. What is interesting in the interview with Mr. Zhao is the comparison with those institutions that do not permit any consideration of race or ethnicity in admissions. For example, Cal Tech's share of Asian-American students rose to 42.5 percent in 2013, double Harvard's and a large increase from 26 percent in 1993. At Cal-Berkeley, the share is more than 30 percent, and it is instructive here to note that California banned its state schools from using racial preferences in 1996. Similar comparisons appear very consistent across the board and it's pretty hard not to sense what Mr. Zhao calls a "de facto quota system," however difficult it might be to prove.

Even more compelling is a 2009 study by Princeton sociologists noted by Riley that found that Asian-Americans have the lowest acceptance rate for each SAT test score bracket, having to score 140 points higher than a white student, 270 points higher than a Hispanic student, and 450 points higher than a black student to be on equal footing with these ethnic groups. If this isn't a flagrant double standard, how would we define one?

In an exchange of letters to the editor commenting on Jason Riley's essay, one reader writes of an acquaintance who defended affirmative action policy by stating, "We must have some kind of affirmative action, otherwise Cal-Berkeley will end up 90 percent Asian!" To which his reply was, so what? Exactly my sentiments.

Just this week, the Department of Education dismissed the complaint from the 64 groups, citing pending litigation on the issue. But the only pending suit is one against Harvard and the University of North Carolina and now these schools have filed motions to halt the suit until the Supreme Court rules on the reconsideration of *Fisher v. University of Texas*, which won't be until well into 2016. This is obviously another attempt to drag out the process until the schools get a blessing for race-based admissions. At this point it should be clear that we should end this charade and terminate these perverse admissions practices now.

Out of Control Tuition Isn't the Major Problem and Free College Tuition Isn't the Solution

March 6, 2016

Politicians get a lot of mileage out of support for "free" college tuition; it plays really well with the millennial crowd and aspiring college students who are facing significant financial barriers to college entry, and if anyone is listening to proposals coming from the current presidential campaign, there are actually some pretty good ideas, primarily from Republicans, on plans to make higher education more affordable. The core of these proposals is the reduction and simplifying of the federal government's role in it.

These proposals include plans ranging from allowing private investors to finance college costs in exchange for a share of future student income, to more transparency on linkage between colleges and the success of their graduates, to the deregulation of the accreditation of higher education institutions, to the replacement of the various college loan programs and tax credits with a new federal line of credit plan with repayment tied to a percentage of income.

These and other ideas should be considered seriously and they, as well as education issues generally, are not getting much play in these sandbox fights that pass for presidential debates, but I want to make another point: the major problem is not the control of the growth of tuition, because this is not the primary barrier to student access to higher education and success once they get there.

The primary barrier is student postsecondary readiness. Our PreK-12 public education system is simply doing a miserable job of producing college and meaningful career readiness. In fact, in Texas, more than 50 percent of high school graduates must take remedial courses when applying for community college. And we have a new ambitious higher education completion plan for the state called "60x30," which means 60 percent college graduates by the year 2030, but the elementary and secondary school readiness pipeline to move this percentage from its current 38 percent simply is not in place, and this deficiency applies generally across the nation. This lack of readiness is the barrier to success that should be our primary focus, not so-called "free" college.

Researchers from the Center for American Progress released in January a study examining the effects of a state's commitment to standards-based reform (as measured by clear standards, assessments aligned to those standards, and whether a state sanctions low-performing schools) on low-income student test scores measuring reading and math achievement on the National Assessment of Educational Progress (NAEP) exams from 2003 to 2013. Not surprisingly, the results indicated that states ranked highest in commitment to standards-based reform had stronger gains in NAEP scores, while low-income students in those states ranked lowest in this commitment did worse.

And yet, almost everywhere you look we are busy lowering standards and expectations in our public education accountability system! Go figure.

Good for ACTA and the University of Chicago

May 5, 2016

Over the past several years, in examples like the *Charlie Hebdo* killings in Paris, there has been no shortage of righteous indignation in this country by people who are quick to champion those who satirize or condemn the views and religion of Islamists in places like France and Denmark. But most of these same people seem to forget that if these people had made an attempt to publish the same satire in almost any prominent American university publication or campus newspaper, it would have immediately been brought down under accusations of hate speech by administrators, faculty, and students. The dirty little secret fact is that the citadel of intolerance of free speech is in the upper reaches of higher education in America. And this extends most prominently to the shouting down or forced "disinvitation" of campus speakers who are not acceptable to the leftist point of view.

To be fair, there is a fine line here between standards of civility and respect for all views and the maintenance of proper decorum and order. But finely tuned legalistic guidelines that turn out to be codes attempting to define hate speech are nothing more than lightly veiled and often ham-handed censorship of speech, and this approach is doing more harm than good.

So, it is refreshing to note that in 2015 the University of Chicago released its "Report of the Committee on Freedom of Expression" drafted by a group of professors led by law professor Geoffrey Stone appointed by the University's President and Provost. Here is an excerpt:

"The University's fundamental commitment is to the principle that debate or deliberation may not be suppressed, because the ideas put forth are thought by some or even by most members of the University community to be offensive, unwise, immoral or wrong-headed. It is for the individual members of the University community, not for the University as an institution, to make those judgments for themselves, and to act on those judgments, not by seeking to suppress speech, but by openly and vigorously contesting the ideas that they oppose... To this end, the University has a solemn responsibility not only to promote a lively and fearless freedom of debate and deliberation, but also to protect that freedom when others attempt to restrict it."

Good for Chicago in their leadership. And good for the American Council of Trustees and Alumni (ACTA), which has now followed up on Chicago's leadership by conducting a nationwide campaign among university trustees and alumni to have this resolution adopted broadly throughout the higher education community. Let's hope that this resolution will be widely adopted and strictly enforced. As for accountability for those institutions whose leaders don't adhere to these principles, particularly those that are public, how about denying federal and state funding to those who restrict freedom of speech through "speech codes" and other obstructions to free exchange?

Who is Killing the Liberal Arts?

January 3, 2017

The Texas Association of Business and the U.S. Chamber of Commerce are touting a new resource to add significant transparency to the costs and benefits of various degree plans in higher education. The name of the initiative is Launch My Career, a website built and maintained by College Measures. The site calculates how much time and money is necessary to earn a certain degree or industry certificate from Texas colleges and universities, as well as compares this information with average salaries for the available jobs for each credential, cost of living information, and job satisfaction surveys. I have spent a little time on the site and it does provide quite a bit of data that will be useful in the deliberations of college-bound students and their families in their post-secondary choices. Check it out at www.launchmycareertx.org.

I don't have a problem with more transparency, particularly with an issue like this that is suffering from such a shortage of it. My problem is the accelerating trend over the past decade or more to relegate the quality of substantially all post-secondary academic pursuits to their economic and vocational value alone, as well as the resulting denigration of the liberal arts and humanities. This trend has reached the point that many university educators are experiencing increasing parental pressure against the liberal arts, so much so that large numbers of students are going to double majors – one to satisfy their interests and one for the demands of their parents.

The cost/value issue is certainly a key consideration that is easy to understand for those who must foot the college bill. The larger question is what has so undermined the perceived value of the liberal arts curriculum? Heather MacDonald of the Manhattan Institute recently dug into the question, "Who Killed the Liberal Arts?" in a post for Prager University. As she sees it, the evolution of the liberal arts curriculum over the past couple of decades "seeks to infuse the humanities curriculum with the characteristic academic traits of our time: narcissism, an obsession with victimhood, and a relentless determination to reduce the stunning complexity of the past to identity and class politics." Roger Kimball of *The New Criterion* identifies the primary culprit as the basically anti-Western ideology of multiculturalism: "Multiculturalism is a moral intoxicant; its thrill centers around the emotion of superior virtue… Wherever the imperatives of multiculturalism have touched the curriculum, they have left broad swaths of anti-Western attitudinizing competing for attention with quite astonishing historical blindness. Courses on minorities, women's issues, and the Third World proliferate… The key issue is not partisan politics, but rather the subordinating of intellectual life generally to non-intellectual, i.e., political imperatives."

So, we get such absurdities as English majors without any requirement for courses in Shakespeare, history majors without any serious study of American history other than race, class, and gender studies, and recently a report that George Washington University has eliminated its requirement for history majors to take a course in American history at all! And the list goes on. Parents have had it – they aren't buying this liberal arts product and neither are the students, other than those who are lucky enough to attend a quality great books program grounded in a Western intellectual core.

And, as my daughter has added after reviewing a previous draft of this essay, there are three culprits here with varying degrees of culpability: the parents/students, the college trustees, and the employers – none of which demand with any serious moral suasion or vehemence that the curricula resist the poison of multiculturalism. Each of those three have had their hand in allowing liberal arts as a pursuit of knowledge, wisdom, truth, and a reasonable means of problem-solving to disintegrate slowly over decades. No wonder we are polarized; we are actively being taught polarization and are teaching our young citizens how to "group" people, divide them into factions, define them for their political power rather than for their potential as rationally thinking humans.

So who is killing the liberal arts? It is simply a case of suicide for those institutions that didn't stay ahead of the relevance curve and then sold out to the postmodern, multiculturalist, identity-study junkies.

UT Folds Houston Expansion Plan

March 6, 2017

The announcement last week that The University of Texas System has ended its planning for development of its proposed 332-acre Houston "intellectual hub" to focus on so-called Big Data in energy, healthcare, and education left me with mixed emotions. First, the rollout of the land acquisition transaction left a lot to be desired, with poor advance notification of the Higher Education Coordinating Board and a number of interested parties, not least the University of Houston, and the strategic planning seemed dysfunctional in terms of advance planning of purpose and use of the property. After noting these mistakes by UT Chancellor William McCraven, however, I commend his boldness and visionary thinking that led him to the project and I didn't then and don't now believe that such a project in Houston has no place in the mission of UT, as some have suggested. After all, UT is the state's flagship university and has a statewide charter in our constitution already manifest in a major presence and investment in research, service, and teaching in the Houston area. The notion expressed by several who should know better that this plan was an "invasion" of Houston by UT was hyperbolic nonsense.

As I wrote shortly after the original announcement in late 2015, the turf battle that emerged and the furor that was caused more than anything else was further manifestation of the lack of a coherent strategy for Texas higher education governance and the roles that each of our public institutions should play. Every effort in my memory to bring coherence to this issue, which dates to a proposal more than 30 years ago by a commission to design either a functional or a geographic approach to higher education in Texas, has failed because of parochial politics. I see no resolution to that situation in the immediate future, given the current race among seven of our institutions, including the University of Houston, to achieve national "Tier One" status and given the treacherous political terrain for any statewide official or legislator who tackles the issue. It is not a political winner.

Meanwhile, however, as well noted by a *Houston Chronicle* editorial in the wake of the decision to end the project, we have a need for boldness and big ambitions that should transcend parochialism and small bureaucratic thinking, and I wonder along with the *Chronicle* whether or not this failed plan sows doubt about our openness and capacity for big ideas and bold strategic thinking.

The Middlebury Follow Up

April 3, 2017

The silencing of social scientist Charles Murray at a scheduled speech at Middlebury College in Vermont and the response to it seem to have legs unlike most recent free speech violations. Daniel Henninger has called it "a major event in the annals of free speech" and there have been several very striking essays in response indicating that we may truly be at the tipping point on college campuses that I described a couple of months ago after the outbreaks at Cal-Berkeley and NYU. Why is this so? I think Steve Hayward is correct in his essay "Free Speech is Not Enough," in which he argues that perpetrators are immune to First Amendment appeals and have embraced the idea that America is so profoundly beyond repair and so corrupt that appeals to reason under our principles are simply more examples of "tools of oppression" subject to overthrow by any means necessary in pursuit of "social justice."

In a recent *Wall Street Journal* article by Crispin Sartwell, he suggests that one evolving force behind what he calls this new wave of the culture wars is a theory of truth, which holds that we don't merely describe or represent the world in language; language creates the world and ourselves. In other words, "we are the stories we tell." These ideas hark back to one of the leading postmodern intellectual figures, Richard Rorty, who held that reality was a matter of widely accepted narratives – in particular narratives of social progress. Again, progress toward what Tom Sowell has nicknamed "cosmic justice."

This notion of a "narrative" reminds me of the concept of "poetic truth," as defined by Shelby Steele in his great book, *Shame*. This is a form of truth that disregards the actual truth in order to assert a larger essential truth that supports one's ideological position. Poetic truths defend the sovereignty of one's ideological identity by taking license with reality and fact.

So, the birth and nurture of this campus phenomenon has grown out of the ideology of the mid-20th century postmodern left, but in the process even the responsible left has been transformed. As recently as a generation ago, social justice was defined by equality of opportunity; now justice demands equality of outcomes. As social critic Jonathan Haidt has noted, according to the academic left, everyone is racist, because of unconscious bias and systemic racism, which makes justice impossible to achieve.

What is the answer? It's pretty simple, but it will also be difficult. Simple, because the solution is a return to the pursuit of truth through the Western intellectual tradition that begins in our elementary and secondary schools and is consistently applied in postsecondary work. Difficult, because we have a lot of rewiring to do and a lot of garbage to take out. And, mainly we need more serious adults at the governing level throughout the education food chain to take charge of the academic cultural overhaul that is long overdue. There are some positive signs of movement here, but we need much more, and very soon.

Civic Ignorance

May 6, 2017

Several years ago, former Supreme Court Justice David Souter spoke at the New Hampshire School of Law on the subject of what he called "civic ignorance," in which he said, "I don't worry about our losing our republican government in the United States, because I'm afraid of a foreign invasion, I don't worry about it, because I think there is going to be a coup by the military, as has happened in some other places. What I worry about is when problems are not addressed, people will not know who is responsible… There is not a more critical issue facing us than the pervasive civic ignorance of our constitution and structure of government." What he had in mind was the gaping void in our civic education, which is obvious across the full elementary, secondary, and post-secondary spectrum.

In my essay "America the Fragile Idea" a while ago, I wrote of a 2008 report by the Lynde and Harry Bradley Foundation entitled "E Pluribus Unum," the product of a two-year study involving a number of the nation's leading intellectuals, educators, and opinion leaders on the current status of the American identity. The study found that our young people are increasingly unaware of our founding principles and the history and meaning of our founding, and as a result, are less likely than their parents to be proud of our country, and conversely, to be more susceptible to the emphasis they often receive on the more negative aspects of our history. A further consequence is that they feel less likely to be committed to our founding principles or to believe that they have provided America with a unique identity within which they consider themselves an integral part.

When examining other aspects of this issue, it is not very surprising how we arrived at this point. An American Council of Trustees and Alumni (ACTA) study, "No U.S. History? How College History Departments Leave the United States Out of the Major," based on requirements and course offerings at 75 leading colleges and universities, found that "the overwhelming majority of America's most prestigious institutions do not require even the students who major in history to take a single course on United States history or government."

The University of Texas at Austin (UT) and Texas A&M University (A&M) were not among those who didn't have such a history requirement, but a 2013 study by the National Association of Scholars (NAS) entitled "Recasting History: Are Race, Class, and Gender Dominating American History?" in which I had some involvement, reflects considerable concern about the quality of their course offerings. To briefly summarize several key points of the study:

- 78 percent of faculty members at UT and 50 percent at A&M were "high assigners" (more than 50 percent of the assignments) of readings focused on race, class, and gender.
- Of the 100 foundational "milestone documents" of American history as identified by the National Archives, only 23 were assigned, and 89 percent of the faculty members assigned none of these documents.
- Three of the top four research priorities for faculty members were race, class, and gender, and these included 78 percent of the UT faculty and 64 percent of the A&M faculty.

Finally, in another study of trends in how American higher education teaches civics entitled "Making Citizens," released early this year, the NAS found that traditional civic literacy is in deep decay. What has become known as the "New Civics," a movement devoted to progressive activism, has taken over civics education. "Service-learning" and "civic engagement" are the most common labels used, but the movement also calls itself global civics, deliberative democracy, and intercultural learning and it focuses on turning students into progressive activists. So, obviously, Justice Souter is justified in his worries, but I think he should be equally if not more concerned about the willful abuse in evidence here as about the ignorance that results.

In his book, *Still At Risk: What Students Don't Know, Even Now*, Rick Hess has this to say in the introduction: "The first mission of public schooling in a democratic nation is to equip every young person for the responsibilities and privileges of citizenship. This requires that students have the knowledge they need to be prepared for civic responsibilities, further education, or the workforce, in addition to mastering basic skills such as reading and mathematics. To do this well, it is vital that schools familiarize students with the history and culture that form the shared bonds of their national community." Amen.

11
Immigration

Immigration and Assimilation

March 3, 2002

Prior to the War on Terrorism, immigration policy was a front-burner item for the Bush administration, having been given heightened visibility by the President's early September 2001 meeting with Mexican President Vicente Fox and the floating of various amnesty and guest worker plans. Understandably, the events since 9/11 tabled these proposals temporarily, but concurrently gave immigration policy new impetus and new perspective. Then came Pat Buchanan's popular book, *The Death of the West,* around which the issues of assimilation, nativism, and cultural decline received much visibility. Whether or not one buys Buchanan's complete argument, and I don't, it is difficult to disagree that our current immigration policy is flawed and that we are trending toward a double standard of citizenship. Serious attention is warranted to the points he raises.

Clearly, President Bush's vision is based on a determination to recognize U.S.-Mexico interdependence by placing the American relationship with Mexico on a par with the Atlantic Alliance with Great Britain. The centerpiece of this interdependence and this vision is, of course, free trade leading to hemispheric economic prosperity, but it has huge consequences for our culture, not to mention domestic politics. The cultural implications should be of great concern. Buchanan's thesis that current immigration policy leads to the death of American culture will be true only if it is assumed that assimilation is not possible.

Michelle Malkin has correctly noted that our founding fathers didn't envision the naturalization process as a means to boost the labor supply or voting rolls. The ultimate end, she writes, the purpose of granting citizenship is to help create one people who share a common allegiance. I would add that this allegiance ultimately is to more than an abstract universal idea, although it may begin there.

In the first half of the 20th century, the primary job of assimilation into the American social fabric was assumed by our public schools. This began with our language and proceeded to our history, our heroes, and the founding ideas that are essential to the sustenance of allegiance to a common sense of the good. Unfortunately, over the past several decades, our schools have lost this sense of the common culture and have taken on a multicultural approach, as though instruction can be adjusted to the ethnic composition of the neighborhood. This is part of the popular notion of "celebrating diversity," but in fact, is cheating our children and undermining the distinctive American culture.

The War on Terrorism has added a dimension to the immigration issue that transcends Bush's North-South vision. We should now have in high relief the necessity for clarity in our convictions and the importance of our founding ideals, not only to the sustenance of our republic, but to human freedom throughout the world. In re-thinking immigration policy, let's not squander the opportunity to re-establish assimilation as a top policy priority.

Is E Pluribus Unum Out Of Style?

October 1, 2002

When I asked last May for reader thoughts on the defining themes of the 21st century, my friend Van Ballard responded with the challenge to "merge the ever growing number of minority groups in this country with our existing political, economic, educational, and religious culture without losing our democratic system of government and simultaneously avoid open conflict." It would be difficult to argue that this is a daunting challenge and one that certainly belongs high on the list of American priorities. But, as with many of our "wedge" issues, I wonder if we have the political will, or as important, the institutional fortitude to confront it. I read the reports of the cultural fault lines that are surfacing in the Netherlands and Germany, for example, as a result of the huge influx of people from non-Western cultures, and I share Van's concerns about the growing multicultural ethos in the U.S. and what it means for our unique republican institutions.

The debate over whether America is essentially an idea or a culture has raged among our leading intellectuals for well over a century (see "A Culture Or An Idea?" *The Texas Pilgrim*, April 2000), but whatever the answer, there is no doubt that, until recently, there had been a consensus in the expectation that immigrants to our country should be assimilated with our values and foundational beliefs. Consistent with this has been the expectation that immigration should be as beneficial to the host country as to the incoming immigrants, which at a minimum implies the loyalty of the new arrivals to the host nation. This consensus and its intellectual grounding have apparently collapsed. As John O'Sullivan notes in a recent article in *National Review*, there is a series of new assumptions and related rules around the world concerning the obligations to assimilation and loyalty. These assumptions would transfer the obligation to change from immigrant to host nation. Accordingly, in the interest of the immigrant's autonomy and self-actualization, it is the responsibility of the host to accommodate its practices and institutions so that the immigrant can remain his "old self." If you think this is far-fetched, consider that a former general counsel for the U.S. Immigration and Naturalization Service remarked that assimilationists repeat "the old error of seeing America as fixed and placing the needed adjustment on the immigrant's side. A more accurate understanding pictures America as a contract under constant renegotiation." In a previous issue (June 2000), I posed the question, "is the American proposition still valid?" If we answer this question in the affirmative, we need to come to grips with the fact that this proposition is totally incompatible with our current immigration policy and our growing reverence for the gods of multiculturalism and cultural relativism.

Thoughts On Immigration Policy

February 5, 2004

There will be much more to say later as it plays out in Congressional deliberation and the election campaigns, but for now President Bush deserves credit for putting into play the thorny problem of illegal immigration. There is much not to like about his proposal, but what better time to debate it than during an election year? It seems to me that this issue as much as any presents a convergence of often conflicting American passions – our compassion for the underdog, our heritage as an immigrant nation, our free market idealism, and our commitment to the rule of law. I would like to believe that we will resolve it with due respect for all these instincts, but I know that some parts of all of them will suffer. I am not a "restrictionist" as that term has been defined, but I come down on the side of those who believe that we will not solve this problem without first committing to a policy of restoring the value of citizenship and strictly controlling our borders, while requiring assimilation to this culture by those we choose to admit.

The Minutemen Should Be Heeded

May 5, 2005

Of all the current national policy issues, the one on which I find myself most at odds with the President is immigration, and I believe that those who dismiss the sentiments embodied by the "Minutemen" on the Arizona border do so at their political peril. The issue is often expressed in terms of its implications for national security, but to me it's about much more – it's about the credibility of the rule of law in a society that preaches it consistently to emerging democracies, but looks away as it is snubbed with impunity by those in this country who hire illegal labor; it's about fundamental fairness to law-abiding legal immigrants; it's about the unreasonable burden on our taxpayers of the welfare and education of illegal immigrants; it's about whether a nation can practice one of the most basic acts of sovereignty – the control of its borders; and it's about preserving our culture in the face of its undermining by the ravages of multiculturalism. And I agree with Congressman J. D. Hayworth – enough is enough, Mexico! His message to President Vicente Fox: If you want to work constructively for immigration reform in general and a guest worker system in particular, you must start by becoming a partner in securing our border instead of being an accomplice in overrunning it. And I would add to that: you must transform your monopoly based slow growth economy so that you can wean yourself off the black market in annual remittances from those who are in this country illegally.

What Multiculturalism Hath Wrought

April 1, 2006

At this point, there is not much to add to the cacophony of voices currently very loudly expressing themselves on the immigration reform issue, nor to my views on the matter previously expressed in these pages. So, for openers, I will repeat some thoughts, and then add a few new ones: It seems to me that this issue, as much as any we face, presents a convergence of often conflicting American passions – our compassion for the underdog, our heritage as a nation welcoming of immigrants, our free market idealism, and our commitment to the rule of law. I would like to believe that we will resolve it with due respect for all these instincts, but I know that some parts of all of them will suffer. I am not a "restrictionist" as that term has been defined, but I come down on the side of those who believe that we will not solve this problem without first committing to a policy of restoring the value and the priority of citizenship and strictly controlling our borders, while requiring assimilation to this culture by those we choose to admit. In other words, immigration should be first about citizenship, not about new voters or new workers.

In a book by Noah Pickus of Duke University, as recently reviewed in *First Things*, the author makes the excellent point that the current debate is largely about different ideas of what it means to be an American citizen, and he insightfully observes that we now "…face the difficult task of sustaining a civic nation in the absence of a dominant culture, ethnic identity, or consensus on the meaning of constitutional values…" making the challenge of forging unity much more difficult than in the founding era or even in the Progressive Era of unlimited immigration. Why is this the case? I submit that it is, because the assault of the ideas of multiculturalism and postmodernism by our cultural and educational institutions over the past several decades, as well as the advent of market globalization, has undermined this consensus on what is meant by American citizenship. Can it be restored? We're about to find out, with far-reaching consequences for our future as a republic, and a major leading indicator will be the way we resolve this issue.

So where does this leave us on the immediate immigration questions? First, we can no longer just "muddle through;" we must find a long-term solution. Second, the rule of law should be the top priority, meaning that our borders must be strictly enforced and the "don't ask, don't tell" sanctuary policies of local law enforcement authorities must end. Third, I agree with Theodore Roosevelt who, in effect, said that we have no room for "hyphenated Americans" or dual citizenship; there is only room for those who want to be completely Americans. Fourth, the notion of temporary "guest" workers is unworkable – it creates a separate and un-American caste and it is unreasonable to expect them to honor the expiration of their guest permit. Let's decide how many immigrants are required on an annual basis to meet the ever growing workforce needs of our economy and increase our immigration quotas to meet the need from those who want to become Americans in every sense or at least on a permanent visa basis. This can include those who are now here illegally, but only if they return to their country of origin, get certification from their home country that they do not have a criminal record, apply for permission to come here and work, receive an authenticated identification card, and sign a contract for work, as well as a commitment to pursue citizenship or permanent visa. Finally, to remove the major incentive for illegal immigration, serious employer penalties for hiring them should be enforced as a felony, so that over time and in combination with the other measures, the number of them will drastically shrink. These measures are true to our values and true to our instincts and will send the message that we have begun to restore the consensus on what it means to be an American citizen.

When is Enough Really Enough?

September 1, 2007

The execution-style schoolyard murders of three college students in New Jersey should have once and for all convinced all clear-thinking Americans that the "don't ask, don't tell" sanctuary policies we tolerate in our cities should end now. There should be no bail ever for an illegal immigrant and every judge and district attorney should be required by law to determine the immigration status of apprehended criminal suspects, who should be deported immediately with no chance of returning in any capacity. Michelle Malkin has asked the right question: "Are we a sovereign nation or a sanctuary nation?" Government at every level is failing miserably at the most important duty of government – to protect its people. And I would add to that one that is a very close second – protect the sovereignty of the nation.

OK, so we didn't get "comprehensive" immigration reform. Now it's on to the next step, which is to strictly enforce the laws already on the books by securing the border, cracking down on outlaw employers, reminding state and local authorities that they have the constitutional authority to make arrests for violations of federal immigration laws, and penalizing sanctuary cities, as well as visitors who overstay their visas. I cannot agree with the Texas Association of Business, an organization I once served as Chairman, or my favorite editorial page at *The Wall Street Journal*, that state and local authorities have no responsibility for immigration enforcement or that these measures will result in long-term devastation to our economy or our relations with legal immigrants, whom we should certainly continue to welcome. The lengthy national debate on the proposed legislation had the beneficial effect of alerting Americans to the current woeful state of practice and neglect in our immigration policy, and they didn't like what they saw. Now maybe we can proceed to answer Michelle's question with authority.

Immigration, Sovereignty, and Sanctuary

June 4, 2010

The new Arizona immigration law continues to resonate around the country and now figures to become a tipping point for advocates on all sides of this issue and a level of activism that has now risen to a fever pitch. In a recent edition of the *Houston*

Chronicle, my friend Bill King wrote an insightful piece on the term "sanctuary" in lamenting the degree to which it has become laden with such negative connotations and the designation as a "sanctuary city" so subject to derision, and he wonders how such a noble idea became so scornful.

In an exchange of emails, I responded to his article as follows:

I share your concern that the traditional "sanctuary" represented by the beacon of America has become a pejorative for many otherwise charitable, generous, and welcoming Americans, but we need to consider what made it so: the complete abdication of our political leadership in fulfilling the most basic responsibility of stewardship – the protection of our sovereignty.

We have been able to accommodate the "tired and huddled masses," because we have been and remain the exceptional nation, the only one in world history based on a proposition. But there was always a catch – that, as Teddy Roosevelt so aptly put it, "there is no such thing as a hyphenated American who is a good American. The only man who is a good American is the man who is an American and nothing else." In his forthright manner, he was referring to complete assimilation, one of the great miracles of the 20th century, and I don't believe he had in mind a disavowal of cultural heritage.

The American cultural mosaic produced by late 19th and early 20th century assimilation was a model to be applauded, but over the past several decades the ideology of multiculturalism has gone far beyond healthy cultural pride to divided loyalties. What we have today in far too many cases is a new proposition, one that contemplates dual citizenship, dual loyalties, multiculturalism, bilingualism, and yes, often sanctuary from enforcement of the law, while our leadership class does nothing. It's not about cultural holidays, it's the ethnic nationalism, primarily initiated by the radical advocacy groups and aided and nurtured by the "open borders" crowd and their fellow travelers. All of this causes many otherwise well-intentioned people to become cynical and to reach for the lesser angels of their nature. This, and the total disregard for the law and American sovereignty, is what has sullied the honorable concept of sanctuary.

We can fix this problem and restore the word sanctuary to its traditional meaning, but it will require political courage that I don't see in place in either major party, and the American people already have been fooled once by a "comprehensive" solution that made the problem worse.

Compounding Lawlessness

July 6, 2012

"Those who would change a culture, corrupt its language, particularly by hiding the reality of an evil they desire behind a less revealing name." – *Politics and the English Language*, George Orwell.

I thought about Orwell's quote when I recently caught an exchange between two friends and fellow CNN contributors on the terms we use in discussing illegal immigration. One of them, Charles Garcia, had written that the phrase "illegal immigrant" is "biased" and "racially offensive," also implying that it is a "slur" and invoking Orwell with the term a "worn-out and useless phrase." His friend, Ruben Navarette, responded that the term is none of these; rather, the term is an accurate representation of reality, however difficult it is for some people to accept.

Further, Navarette rightly adds that those who have trouble with the term are really bothered by something deeper – the fact that, in the final analysis, by supporting a pathway to earned legal status, they are defending a group of people who engaged in unlawful activity.

So where does this position our chief law enforcement officer? Very simply, the President compounds the original lawlessness by concocting schemes that involve selectivity of enforcement and instructing the Department of Homeland Security to no longer enforce immigration laws against illegal immigrants who meet certain criteria, mainly those between the ages of 16-30 who meet other criteria, referring to them as "Americans for all intents and purposes." Really?

And if you read the Supreme Court decision in *Arizona v. United States*, this was exactly the point in the 8-0 decision by the Court to allow Arizona police to verify the legal status of people who come into contact with law enforcement, which the Obama administration had argued was in conflict with "its enforcement priorities" in spite of its compliance with federal law. Amazingly, the administration's response to this decision was even more lawlessness, when it announced that it would suspend cooperation with Arizona on immigration enforcement.

Arizona should be prepared for an onslaught from swarms of attorneys watching every move of law enforcement officials for the slightest bobble in the way in which their newly confirmed authority is implemented.

Meanwhile, Mitt Romney responded to all of this very tepidly, simply saying that Obama is advancing temporary stopgap measures in lieu of leadership on a long-term solution. True, but he should be much bolder, and here again we see the intimidation of the left, which knows that conservatives will pander and moderate on this issue, because of fear of perceived political damage in the Hispanic community. This is a misguided path that accepts the view of the left that the Hispanic community is a monolithic special interest group rather than fellow citizens who should be dealt with as such with bold provisions for a long-term solution, while scoring Obama for undermining the rule of law.

Immigration Disconnect

July 5, 2014

On July 4th, President Obama made ceremonial remarks to a class of new U.S. citizens in which he indicated that we want America to continue to be accessible to the "best and brightest" of those who strive to become Americans. How true this should be, but he is either disingenuous or obviously totally out of touch with the reality on the ground, for current policy encourages and provides incentives for just the opposite.

We should be expanding our legal immigration quotas through incentives for those who want to come to this country for citizenship who are educated, innovative, and want to assimilate to our culture. Meanwhile, we should strictly control our borders and admit only those we choose to admit. Immigration policy should be first about citizenship, not about new voters, new guest workers, and certainly not about a priority for family reunification.

As for the current disaster at the border with the refugee children, this has very little to do with immigration policy, and nothing that has been proposed in the cause of so-called "comprehensive" immigration reform would have done anything to prevent this debacle. Anyone with a heart will sympathize with these kids, but don't buy into this notion that all of a sudden the conditions in Central and South America have become so repressive that these children were induced to risk their lives for this treacherous trip. The economic and political conditions in these countries haven't changed in decades. The current incentives have recently been supplied by the messages from the

Obama administration that, if the children can get here, they can stay, and sure enough probably 90 percent will never return. It was not a huge step for the coyotes to step in and take advantage of their plight and false hope. And where are our friends in Mexico on a solution to this disaster and our President in demanding one? But, of course, we can't even get an innocent U.S. Marine out of a Mexican jail after three months!

Milton Friedman often said that "you can't have open immigration and a welfare state." How true and I would add, particularly with a third world country on your border.

Sanctuary and Sovereignty

July 5, 2017

Texas Senate Bill 4, recently adopted by the Texas Legislature, and related federal initiatives designed to penalize so-called "sanctuary" jurisdictions who give cover to illegal immigrants, have produced a firestorm of reaction. Some of it is understandable. Most credibly, local law enforcement needs communication links in the illegal population that are undermined by the threat of deportation. I get that. But beyond that appeal, although I have compassion, I lose sympathy with those who simply believe that we should be an open border and I certainly am not persuaded by the corporate interests who speak in terms of the damage they feel the new anti-sanctuary laws will inflict on the economy, either by boycott or by disruption of labor markets.

And I know that there are many who disagree, particularly my friends in the business community on the latter point on the economic impact. But we must retain the sovereignty of our people to decide who gets to enter our country. Our founding fathers didn't visualize the immigration process as a means to boost the labor supply or voting rolls. To maintain the integrity and sovereignty of the nation-state and the rule of law, immigration policy must be first about citizenship, not about new voters, new guest workers, and certainly not about a priority for family reunification.

As I have written before, this issue presents a convergence of often conflicting American passions – our compassion for the underdog, our heritage as an immigrant nation, our free market idealism, and our commitment to the rule of law. I would like to believe that we will resolve it with due respect to all of these instincts, but I know that some parts of all of them might suffer.

The current confrontation across the country, highlighted in Texas by the SB 4 reaction, serves to emphasize the enormous difficulty in unwinding the tangled legacy of the

1986 amnesty under Ronald Reagan. This well-intentioned, but failed solution to what was then a relatively modest problem has now mushroomed into an illegal immigrant population of 11 to 15 million or more people who are entangled in our workforce, our education system, the criminal justice system, and our social services system, not to mention the family and institutional connections that advocate for their interests. This is a mess and the resolution of this entanglement will be very painful on many levels, but it must be done in a way that is true to our sovereignty and the rule of law.

12
Leadership

Old Thoughts on Leadership

July 2, 2000

Recently, in thumbing through some old files, I rediscovered copies of a speech and an article I authored on two occasions in the mid to late 1980s. I was honored to be invited to deliver the commencement address to the Spring 1985 graduating class at Stephen F. Austin State University, and in 1989, I was asked to write an article for *The Texas Lyceum Journal*. The subject of both was Leadership and I was struck by how relevant they still are to my thinking, so I decided to share critical passages from them with Pilgrim readers, as follows: With the possible exception of love, leadership is probably the most discussed and least understood topic in our society. There are very few definitive studies on it that are in popular use, yet leadership is a term that we use almost indiscriminately. In his 1978 book on leadership, James Macgregor Burns defines two basic types:

- *Transactional leadership* – this is by far the most common type. It is one in which the leader and the follower exchange one thing for another – jobs for votes, for example – and is basically the traditional power relationship that often connotes dominion or control wielded by a holder of power. It is a bargaining, manipulative kind of leadership very often based on trade-offs among competing interests.
- *Transformational leadership* – this is more complex, because it employs vision and a sense for the needs, motives, and anxieties of those who would be followers, and it provides a means for converting followers into leaders. It is based on mutual understanding between leader and follower, mutual trust, a sense for responsiveness to societal changes, and a commitment to the building of consensus on the critical issues.

It is the subtle differences in these two types that are so important today and that have produced a desperate need for this rarest type of leadership, the transformational variety. Never in our history has there been such a void and a need, and conversely, such an opportunity. In the past 25 years, we have seen an amazing erosion of true transformational leadership. Our relationship with leadership seems to have been replaced by the cult of personalities, and our leaders by celebrities. We seem to have a devotion to trivia about people centered on the private lives of our leaders – we seem to know a lot about our leaders, but place on them far too little demand for true leadership. And most of the time, we get just what we want, or should expect.

Opportunities for leadership skills abound; we have a proven need for it. So what do we do?

This, I believe, is step one: we must develop an understanding of the basic differences in the types of leadership we produce. Our society has plenty of transactional leaders – plenty of power brokers, plenty of people who would lead by celebrity cult or by exchanges of one favor for another. We must understand and seek to provide a higher degree of transforming leadership – the type that produces fundamental growth and develops new leaders for the future, the type that provides moral leadership, seeks consensus, provides mutual stimulation, and does not shy away from the occasional leap of faith. The type of leadership that truly values statesmanship, stewardship, and integrity of purpose highly above partisanship.

For too long, the more common type of leadership has been acceptable, based on the traditional power relationship and often a bargaining, manipulative style. And in the private sector we confuse true leadership traits with good management skills, or those attributes that produce efficiency, order, and often success in business, at least by the traditional standards. Don't misunderstand me, good management we need, and good management skills are in short supply, but the leadership we need has very little to do with the functional aspects of managing.

Step two is simply getting involved. We in this country have a responsibility for individual commitment. It's part of our heritage. The responsibility for the stewardship of our values is ours – yours and mine. We have spent much of the last 50 years transferring leadership to entities far detached from those who need it and whose expectations are to be fulfilled. In the past few years there have been signs that this trend is reversing itself through private sector and personal initiative and a return to volunteerism. It is crucial that this trend continue and that these initiatives succeed – in our schools, our communities, across the nation, so that a sense of "neighborhood" is cultivated once again. This is the necessary active involvement that Professor V. O. Key spoke of when he concluded, "the critical element for the health of a democratic order consists in the beliefs, standards, and competence of those who constitute the opinion leaders and activists. If a democracy tends toward indecision, decay, and disaster, the responsibility rests there, not in the mass of the people."

Our nation is in the midst of watershed transformation – the "third wave," as Alvin Toffler has called this period. We have the future shock of the ever increasing pace of technology, the globalization of communications and markets, new definitions of values and lifestyles, new and more difficult tests of the old systems of evaluation and standards. Business as usual is out of business. This transformation in our society demands leadership to match, leadership that has vision, that exercises power prudently and for the right purposes, that is not afraid of the quantum leap in pursuit of excellence. Henry Kissinger once said: "true leadership involves taking people from where they are to where they have never been." This is the leadership it is our responsibility to develop.

A Revolutionary Century?

August 2, 2002

In response to my request for comments from readers on their ideas for the prominent themes of the 21st century, I received a particularly provocative response from Dr. John Fieler, which follows in part:

"This century will either be noted for the rise of a third party into a position of prominence in this country, or the demise of our form of government into just another socialist country. The Republican Party is now nothing more than another entitlement generator. They have abdicated their basic principles in order to win election and they brag about the permanence of their proposed entitlements. I don't know where the new party will come from, but it will be the only chance for a revolution within the framework of the Constitution… When the ruling class takes from the producers to give to the non-producers, society eventually unravels. Ours will be no different."

Coincidentally, and consistent with John's theme, David Brooks for *The Weekly Standard* editors produced a lead editorial on June 24, entitled "The Problem With K Street Conservatism," in which he bemoans the tepid response of conservatism as practiced by the Republican Party to the current range of opportunities for transformational leadership. As he puts it, "instead of a fundamental debate about ideas, conservative politics becomes transactionalism." I have written before about the difference between transformational and transactional leadership and the difference it makes for our country. With K Street corporate priorities dominant, we get transactional leadership tied to the here and now, devoid of transformational ideas, with no strategic vision and plenty of cynicism. Where are the Gingrich-era insurgents? It makes one wonder why it is important for conservatives to elect Republicans, for they have done very little to differentiate themselves from the other party. Ramesh Ponnuru of *National Review* points out that the Democrats have been successful in frustrating the Republicans, because the latter have refused to politicize the war. It seems that they hope that homeland security will drown out debate on domestic issues and allow them to avoid such debate. This is a strategy that will doom them to minority status.

July 11, 2002 was the 21st anniversary of the Kemp-Roth bill, the legislation most responsible for completely transforming the terms of policy debate and launching the Reagan Revolution. And how did he do it with Democratic majorities in both houses of Congress? He went over their heads to the people and won with Democratic support. The economic boom that is just now taking a breather began then. Properly understood and properly articulated, limited government and conservative policy wins. The tragedy of the 1990s, beginning in 1988, is that we allowed the Reagan economic policies to be discredited without lifting a finger to defend them philosophically or with the facts of their success.

President Bush should forget about the K Street crowd and use his high approval rating now in the same way Reagan used his popularity. Otherwise, maybe John Fieler is right, that a third party revolution is the wave of the future.

The "C" Word

July 2, 2005

An editorial lead in the current issue of *Chief Executive Magazine* caught my attention. It essentially suggested that CEOs of the major companies are finally waking up to the realization that a renewed and primary emphasis on competitiveness is the key to the restoration of business credibility on a range of issues, including the multiple threats of globalization, and that a sense of urgency on this renewal will help to repair the damage that has been done to their image and standing in the body politic. It struck me that, aside from the fact that this is almost self-evident, this theme is common to many of our other beleaguered institutions, and that business opinion leadership is critical to the restoration of these as well.

For example, I speak quite often on issues related to public education reform, and I am often questioned and, in fact, sometimes chastised on my frequent use of the word "competition" to describe a solution to many of the perverse incentives that plague the delivery of education. And this critique comes not only from members of the education establishment, among whom the word itself is anathema, but often from business owners and CEOs, the constituency that should understand the concept better than most. As so well explained by Caroline Hoxby of the Hoover Institution's Koret Task Force on K-12 Education, there is an obvious 30-year old productivity crisis in public education, and a major key to a turnaround in student achievement is competition among education delivery systems. Why this age-old concept is lost on the many business leaders who want to continue to pour more money into an underperforming monopoly is a mystery to me.

Other examples are healthcare and retirement benefits programs. Business leaders who truly respect and want to defend the power of the dynamics of competition and free markets to enhance productivity, expand availability, and lower costs should be at the forefront of leadership in demanding the deregulation of medical insurance finance through such innovations as Health Savings Accounts and the conversion of Social Security to defined contribution plans, but often seem to fear the invocation of the "c" word in addressing them. Again, it remains a mystery that business opinion leadership on these initiatives, particularly among large corporate CEOs, has been tepid at best, and completely missing at worst.

It is well accepted that business leaders have responsibilities that transcend the purely parochial interests of maximizing the profitability of their economic units, but even if this is their only concern, it is long past time for them to "wake up and smell the coffee," for many of these public policy problems have a direct impact on their economic viability, their leadership is absolutely critical, and the solution to them in many cases can be found in the same place – enhanced competitiveness.

The Threat to America's Leadership

March 4, 2010

No less an authority than Lech Walesa (you remember him, the former electrician who stood up to the Soviet puppet government in Poland, which ultimately, with a little help from Ronald Reagan, Margaret Thatcher, and the Pope, led to the fall of the Soviet empire) recently made an insightful observation: "The world has no leadership. The U.S. was the last resort and hope for all nations. Today, we have lost that hope; they don't lead morally and politically anymore."

Why is this the case? Well, in my estimation, for a couple of reasons. First, large segments of our institutional opinion leadership are dismissive of the notion of American moral leadership in the first place, particularly as it pertains to American interests or the pursuit of American exceptionalism. Second, and more currently, we have so undermined our financial solvency and economic viability with our reckless profligacy that we have become beholden to our creditors and are less capable of delivering the leadership the world needs from us.

These threats were essentially echoed by James Piereson in *The New Criterion*: "I wonder whether the ideology underpinning the welfare state is antithetical to the kind of ideas and citizens that are required for a strong national defense. The welfare state is based upon dependency and entitlement, while national defense needs to be based on something like duty as the price of citizenship."

Western Europe has had an answer to this problem for about 60 years – let America handle it. Lech Walesa and I are wondering – how much longer can America handle it?

The Limits of Competence and Its Frustration

June 3, 2010

The political class and all of its groupies in the punditry industry just can't stand it. They cannot abide a major disaster of the nature of the Gulf oil well blowout that doesn't have a political solution. This frustration is manifest in every media update on the well and every White House press briefing – the 21st century expectation of government, particularly one in the hands of the "chosen one," is that it should "take charge," be more "hands on," demonstrate that it is in control, that it "cares," that it is enraged, etc. Finally, at long last there is the reality expressed by Coast Guard Admiral Thad Allen: "The government doesn't have everything we need to solve this problem." Thanks for the belated understatement, Admiral. He could have and should have added, "and it is not the role of government to assume the on-board technical or management expertise to solve such a problem," that the solution is far beyond the core competencies of government at any level.

David Brooks recently has suggested that the systems that run our world are based on technologies that are so complex that no one person can or should be expected to understand them or the risk they present, let alone government bureaucrats. There may be some truth to that as we continually are reminded in crises such as the mortgage finance meltdown of the past couple of years. But these risk assessment failures are compounded by the hubris of government intervention and its very often disastrous unintended consequences. In fact, no evaluation of the role of government in this particular event will be complete without considering the consequences, intended and unintended, of the misguided environmental and energy policies that have placed energy abundant areas in Alaska, the western U.S., and shallow offshore areas off limits for oil and gas production. These policies have pushed the companies into deeper, more expensive, much more complex, and higher risk environments, which should be reconsidered in light of the recent disaster.

Over recent history, we have created the unfortunate environment in which no elected official is willing to admit or level with the American people as to the competency limits of government. And, in fact, in many corners of the left wing of the political class there is the incredible belief that government should have the on-board capability to directly solve such problems and be prepared to deal with disasters such as once-in-a-lifetime oil well blowouts. Is there a role for government here? Sure there is: assurances to the public that government is monitoring progress, making its public facilities available to the private sector effort, and helping to explain the difficult complexities involved are all parts of that role. No doubt that there was significant human error on the part of British Petroleum here and there will be ample time to assess the damage and the accountability. But self-serving statements of blame such as "we're keeping a boot on the neck of BP," criticizing the previous administration for "gutting regulations and putting insiders in charge," and, above all ridiculous moves, launching a criminal investigation against the very people who are in the midst of the ongoing efforts to shut down the well flow have made this administration's response to this disaster a complete disaster in itself. There won't be a political solution here, but there will no doubt be huge political fallout.

Leadership and the "Swarm"

June 8, 2014

A couple of months ago, David Brooks wrote an article lamenting the fact that based on recent polling, including a recent Pew Research Center survey, many Americans no longer have faith in top political figures or the military to keep the U.S. on top in world affairs. My first reaction was, does he think we should be surprised, given the cast of characters currently in charge? But then a friend asked me what I thought of the essay and what Brooks was attempting to convey, and I gave it more thought.

Brooks says that what is happening can be more accurately described as follows: Americans have lost faith in the high politics of global affairs. They have lost faith in the idea that U.S. political and military institutions can do much to shape the world. The real power of the world is not military or political – the power of the state can pale before the power of the swarm of individuals. He calls this "global affairs with the head chopped off."

Well, if you keep a close watch on world affairs, it certainly appears this way. My take of what he is saying is somewhat a form of what Bill Clinton said – "the era of big government is over" – but it is deeper psychologically in that Brooks senses that popular support for and trust in government at every level is over. This may be well-earned and healthy at some level, but it is troubling from the standpoint that people have lost any confidence that we can do great things, such as go to the moon or win a world war (or any war, for that matter). And the cynicism is so deep that there are no heroes, and when one potentially appears, he or she is subject to immediate destruction. One particular data point in the Pew study is most troubling – 40 percent of baby boomers believe most people can be trusted, but only 19 percent of millennials believe that. I don't know how we turn this around easily, particularly in America, without a complete overhaul of some of our institutions, particularly in education across the board. And it is not primarily an economic or even a political issue, it's a moral one.

The U.S. and China: The Mandate for Transformational Leadership

May 3, 2018

"No relationship will be as important to the 21st century as the one between the United States, the world's great power, and China, the world's rising power" – Richard N. Haas, President, Council on Foreign Relations, April 2007.

"Let China sleep; when she wakes, she will shake the world" – Napoleon, 1817.

The world is faced with so many challenging issues that it is difficult to determine which is most critical and which talents will be in highest demand in addressing them. However, there is very little doubt that the future relationship between the United States and China will be the central geopolitical consideration of the 21st century. And it is further evident that the most critical challenge of all will be to develop the appropriate leadership style necessary to insure that this relationship is sustained in goodwill and recognition of human dignity.

This outcome will require the development of exchanges at the highest level of opinion leadership that acknowledge the cultural differences and barriers that exist while recognizing the common threads that will lead to understanding and goodwill. The idea of leadership is probably one of the most discussed and least understood topics in our society. It is a term that we use almost indiscriminately, yet the subtle differences in the types of leadership are so important and produce a need for that rarest type of leadership, the transformational variety.

At its core, transformational leadership is moral leadership and, as George Will has noted, statecraft and political leadership, properly understood, are "soulcraft." This type of leadership does not shy away from the occasional leap of faith and it truly values statesmanship, stewardship, and integrity of purpose, above all else.

I previously have expressed many of these thoughts on leadership in this publication and in an essay I wrote a few years ago for the Confucian Lyceum Institute of Texas which was focused on cultural exchanges with China, and I was reminded of them by a book recently given to me by a friend involved with that organization, which put them into contemporary context like nothing I have read before. The book is *Destined for War: Can America and China Escape Thucydides's Trap*, by Graham Allison.

What is the Thucydides Trap? Very simply, it is that when a rising power threatens to displace a ruling power, alarm bells should sound: danger ahead, and it is the author's contention that China and the U.S. are currently on a collision course for war – unless both parties take difficult and painful actions to avert it. The name is derived from a concept first identified by the ancient Greek historian Thucydides writing about the Peloponnesian War that devastated Athens and Sparta 2,500 years ago as a result of, as he explained, "…the rise of Athens and the fear that this instilled in Sparta that made the war inevitable." As further evidence of this phenomenon, Allison, who directs the Thucydides Trap Project at Harvard, has identified and studied 16 comparable cases in history in which a major nation's rise has disrupted the position of the dominant state and the existing world order, 12 of which resulted in war.

The cultural differences between China and the U.S. are critical to understand and the author does a great job of explaining the significant tensions and dynamics, including the key philosophical ways in which Western and Confucian societies tend to differ, but there are many characteristics common to each, all of which he submits are shared by the current leadership of China and the U.S. Both:

- Are driven by a common ambition: to make their nation great again, which for China means returning to the predominance in Asia it enjoyed before the West intervened.
- Identify the other nation as the principal obstacle to their dream.
- Take pride in their own unique leadership capabilities.
- See themselves playing a central role in revitalizing their nation.
- Have announced daunting domestic agendas that call for radical changes.
- Have fired up populist nationalist support.

Is war inevitable? Of course not, but neither was it necessarily inevitable for Athens and Sparta nor the other examples Allison has studied. But of one thing the author is certain and would get Napoleon's agreement – the return to prominence of a 5,000-year-old civilization with 1.4 billion people is not a problem to be "fixed;" it is a chronic condition that will have to be managed over a generation or more, and I would add that transformational, not simply transactional, leadership absolutely will be crucial to survival.

William Galston has noted that the next several weeks possibly will shape American diplomacy for years to come and he describes three major tests ahead – trade negotiations with China, the fate of the nuclear deal with Iran, and the coming summit meeting with Kim Jong Un of North Korea. He probably is not underestimating the gravity of the issues involved, but this is a multi-generational project and I am struck by the degree to which they, along with the mess in Syria, are all in certain ways interconnected with the long-range prospects for the U.S. in its relationship with China.

And make no mistake, this is not a zero-sum proposition that can be approached as though each issue for negotiation is one that produces winners and losers. That is transactional leadership. This is bigger than that; it is about much more than "the art of the deal."

13
Legal and Judicial Issues

The "End of Democracy" Debate
September 4, 2000

Unfortunately for the republic, one of the most critical issues that energize both sides of the Presidential election is the prospect that the new President will likely appoint several Supreme Court Justices, not to mention scores of Federal judges on lower benches. I say "unfortunately," because our Founders could not have conceived of the current policy domination of the judicial branch and the degree to which the legislative branch has abdicated its role in the development of public policy in many crucial areas, particularly social policy. Some have gone as far as to suggest judicial hubris in the conduct of the Supreme Court, particularly in its view of the U.S. Constitution as a document authoritative only as to questions, not answers. It is as though the Court feels that some hot-button issues cannot be peacefully handled by the democratic process. To some, republican democracy is not an institutionalized process, but a list of substantive results based on universalistic principles of equality and justice as they define them. The potential backlash is damaging to the institutional integrity of our constitutional system which is based upon balance among the three branches. David Broder has warned of the "derailing" of democracy in his recent book that discusses the growing trend toward the use of initiative and referendum, which he says is driven by the power of money, because it can dictate the success or failure of issues in a referendum. I'm no fan of I&R, because it is antithetical to our republican system of legislating, but it fills a void because it is customer-driven and offers an opportunity for real debate on issues that are often perverted by the legislative process or deferred to the judiciary. In 1996, the journal *First Things* conducted a symposium on this issue, entitled, strangely enough, "The End of Democracy?: The Judicial Usurpation of Politics," in which the participants condemned recent judicial activism as both procedurally undemocratic and substantively immoral or unjust. I read most of the proceedings and came away feeling that there is, in fact, serious cause for concern about the integrity of our republican system and our ability to govern ourselves if we continue to allow the judiciary to usurp the legislative process and balance of powers.

Defending the Rule Of Law at Home

April 3, 2003

While we're grappling with exporting our constitutional principles to those less fortunate in the world, it is important to note that some of them are under siege here at home. In an important book, *The Case Against Lawyers*, former Texas judge and current host of Court TV Catherine Crier makes a bold statement about the current condition of the rule of law in this country: "Our great cornerstone of democracy, the rule of law, has become a source of power and influence, not liberty and justice. I resent the insidious manipulations of those entrusted with such authority and, even more, I despise our deliberate ignorance and passive acceptance of those shackles on the American spirit." Ben Stein lists a dozen suggestions on how we can completely ruin American competitiveness and innovation, among which prominently is "to encourage the making of laws by trial lawyers and sympathetic judges, especially through class actions." I would add to these observations that these tendencies also will destroy American exceptionalism, undermine its world leadership and its moral authority, and eliminate it as a beacon of hope for the world. Thankfully, there are statesmen on the job. Common Good is a national bipartisan initiative launched in 2002 to overhaul America's lawsuit culture, return us to the essential idea of the law as defining the boundaries of legal action, and depart from the concept of using the law as a tool for various theoretical "value" judgments without evidentiary proof. Another group that has done yeoman work in restoring common sense is Texans for Lawsuit Reform, and it is currently guiding tort reform legislation through the Texas Legislature that will serve as a model for other states in curbing the abuses of the law and the judicial system. These groups deserve our support. Oliver Wendell Holmes defined law as "prophecies of what the courts will do." Without arguing the validity of his statement, we should at least agree that, in a society governed by the rule of law, "what the courts will do" must be predictable.

Judicial Tyranny

July 1, 2003

At the beginning of this nation, the Founders had in mind that, of the three branches of government based on Montesquieu's idea of the separation of powers that evolved into the American concept of "checks and balances," the legislative branch, as representative of the sovereignty of the people, would be dominant and the judicial branch would be inferior. Of course, this balance was altered significantly with the decision in *Marbury v. Madison* in 1803, which, in effect, made the Supreme Court the final arbiter of the constitutionality of laws. With this ultimate power over the years since, the Court has produced some shocking results, many of which (the *Dred Scott* decision and *Plessy v. Ferguson*, for examples) were later corrected by the Court itself, by constitutional amendment or by legislation. However, the recent Supreme Court term has made it abundantly clear to me that we have now reached the point where judicial overreach is a serious threat to representative democracy (see "The End Of Democracy Debate," September 2000). Possibly not since the *Dred Scott* decision of 1857 confirming a property right in owning slaves has there been more ominous language written by a Supreme Court majority or language more at variance with the ordered liberty envisioned by the Founders than that in the University of Michigan affirmative action cases (more on this below) and the *Lawrence v. Texas* sodomy case. Again, ideas have consequences, and, as Robert Bork warned in his book, *Slouching Towards Gomorrah*, the ideas of a general and undefined right of privacy and to "personal dignity and autonomy" have now morphed into the radical individualism embodied in the now famous "mystery passage" in the majority opinion in *Planned Parenthood v. Casey*: "At the heart of liberty is the right to define one's own concept of existence, of meaning, of the universe, and of the mystery of human life." Really?

At issue here is much more than the particular facts of the cases. What is at stake is the sanctity of constitutional law and the sovereignty of representative government, particularly when they come into conflict with the current "political correctness" of the underlying issue. Columnist Jonah Goldberg has noted that the entire culture is now soaked with the moral relativism implicit in postmodernism, the central assumption of which is that independent moral judgments are impossible. Most people would prefer it otherwise, but the reality is that we are in a war over the future of our culture. There are values at stake here that will determine the fate of the American idea. The public square, i.e., the legislative and political process, is the proper arena in which to fight the battles of this war, and to relegate them to the judiciary is a complete failure of leadership on our part.

The Continuing Attack on the First Amendment

February 2, 2004

"Congress shall make no law... abridging the freedom of speech." What part of this passage is so difficult to understand? In a continuing dismantling of the founding principles underlying the First Amendment, the U.S. Supreme Court confirmed a direct hit on free speech in upholding the Campaign Reform Act of 2002. Much as the

Court has emasculated the concept of the establishment and free exercise clauses as they pertain to religious practice in this country, it has now completely transformed the original meaning of free speech as envisioned by the Founders. And in so doing, it constrains and targets for regulation the specific type of speech that the Founders deemed most important to protect – the type that is political, partisan, and is used during the heat of election campaigns. This, of course, is consistent with the "John Rawls approach" to public policy deliberations, which, in terms of the right to free speech, is to "protect" the less affluent from the views of those who can afford to broadcast their opinions. As Thomas G. West sadly notes, the prevailing progressive mindset is that, if you publish or broadcast "too much," government has the duty to silence you, and free speech in effect becomes a right dispensed by government only when it meets certain standards of fairness and justice. Of course, in the end, the intent of the law will not be realized, and the political class already has begun to devise ways to circumvent the new restrictions. And I must add that President Bush was AWOL on this issue by not vetoing this legislation that he clearly opposed, hoping that the Court would bail him out. Surely by now he should realize that the majority on this Court cannot be considered reliable in defending the Constitution.

The Battle Over Marriage

March 2, 2004

I hate to say "I told you so," but I did. The battle over gay/lesbian "rights" has spilled into the public arena and the Presidential election, because the American people will not allow four Massachusetts judges to throw out several thousand years of natural law, and they shouldn't. This is not about equal rights nearly as much as it is about whether or not we can sustain a federal republic under the rule of law, or whether we will allow the critical issues involving who we are to be determined by judicial fiat. Lincoln said it as well as anyone in his first inaugural address, referring to the Supreme Court decision in the *Dred Scott* case: "…the candid citizen must confess that if the policy of the government upon vital questions affecting the whole people is to be irrevocably fixed by the Supreme Court, the instant they are made in ordinary litigation between parties in personal actions, the people will have ceased to be their own rulers, having to that extent practically resigned their government into the hands of that eminent tribunal." President Bush didn't start this war by endorsing a constitutional amendment on marriage, but by so doing he did introduce it into the appropriate arena – the court of public opinion in an election year – which hopefully will produce a solution by the people through democratic processes, as the Founders intended.

The Culture and the Courts

June 1, 2004

It is universally recognized that one of the subliminal factors that will play a significant role in the Presidential election will be the great cultural divide that provided the primary separation between the "red" and "blue" states of the election of 2000. I say subliminal, because neither candidate to date appears to have assigned high visibility to the importance of the issues that feed into this divide – the usual suspects, of course, being abortion, homosexual marriage, the role of religion in public life, bioethics, etc. But, the most critical aspect of these issues, aside from the substance of each, which is important, is the means by which American society resolves them. Quite simply, I believe that the future of the republic rests on the answer to the question of whether or not the legislative and executive branches will cease to abdicate their responsibilities and rescue the democratic process from the willful disregard of the Constitution by the judiciary. Many of the Supreme Court decisions of the 1950s and 1960s, such as those on civil rights, were considered fairly radical at the time, but were basically restorations of rights. After all, Martin Luther King's revolution was about living up to our principles, not inventing new ones. But the courts have long since gone past the protection and restoration of rights and have extended their power down to the minutiae of public policy, even to the point of referring to judicial precedents from other countries in Supreme Court decisions! This has enormous implications for self-governance, and should be a major factor in this election, however radioactive the underlying issues may be. In fact, George Bush should make it one – it would be a big winner for him. As Michael Novak has noted, "It is a constant struggle to maintain free societies in any of their three parts, economic, political, or cultural. Of these three, the cultural struggle, long neglected, is the one on whose outcome the fate of free societies in the 21st century will depend. We will have to learn, once again, how to think about morals, and how to argue about them publicly…" No better time than in an election year.

The Latest From Our Imperial Judiciary

March 3, 2005

Meanwhile, in the Supreme Court decision in *Roper v. Simmons* to arbitrarily set an age limit on the assessment of the death penalty to juvenile criminals, once again our imperial judiciary has completely disabled state legislators and juries in a decision that preempts the value judgments of the people. And again I repeat – the critical issue is not the substance of the underlying case or the moral issue involved, but rather the question of who decides.

To compound this particular decision, we have reliance on "evolving standards of decency" and "national consensus," the evidence for which is questionable at best, not to mention another instance of reliance on "the overwhelming weight of international opinion." Where in the U.S. Constitution is the authority for the Supreme Court to impose its moral values as the law, determine the national consensus, or rely on international opinion to overturn an American jury?

Representative democracy is being further undermined, and we need to get very serious about this very soon. We should start by demanding of the Republican Senate leadership that the Democrats be stopped from perverting the constitutional advice and consent doctrine in the confirmation of judicial appointees, regardless of the potential fallout for other legislative priorities, all of which are secondary to this one. We should also demand that our legislative leaders take charge of the jurisdiction of the federal judiciary, as they are empowered to do by the Constitution, and reassume policy leadership on any number of issues on which they have abdicated their responsibility. A good guide to thinking about all of this is *Men in Black: How the Supreme Court is Destroying America*, by Mark R. Levin.

The World's Greatest Minority Party Folds Again

June 2, 2005

Question for the day – what is the most important issue of our time in America, except for national defense? Is it gasoline prices or energy policy, education, stem-cell research, immigration policy, Social Security reform, universal healthcare, or any of the other weekly hot buttons of the polls and focus groups? No, it is none of these. I submit that the most urgent strategic issue of our time is the restoration of the constitutional order and ending the assault on representative democracy. Why? Because without this restoration, none of these other things will matter. This is the disheartening part of the deal forced upon and accepted by the Republican Senate leadership by the "gang of 14" assembled to avoid the showdown over judicial confirmations, ostensibly in the interests of Senate tradition and "comity." This showdown has been brewing for more than 40 years, and it is past time to have it. Now, just when we seemed finally to have gathered the courage to consummate it, the party granted the mantle of leadership and the obligation to govern by majorities expanded in three consecutive elections folded. It capitulated to forces that have spent every waking hour over four decades undermining the constitutional rule of law in favor of a postmodern ideology grounded in the concept of the "living constitution." If Republican control of the Senate doesn't count for judicial confirmations, it doesn't count for anything. Many have said that this deal was essentially an agreement reluctantly accepted to buy time to confront the issue on another day. Hope springs eternal, but often overcomes experience.

Bush's Historic Opportunity

October 3, 2005

As I write, John Roberts is about to begin his tenure as the 17th Chief Justice of the U.S. Will he preside over what can be described as the "Roberts Court?" This remains to be seen, but the critical next step is for President Bush to solidify Roberts' leadership with a bold appointment of another Justice in the same mold, or even better, one that is more of a "movement" natural law enthusiast similar to Clarence Thomas. Would this result in the use of the so-called "nuclear option" in order to break an expected Democratic filibuster? Maybe, but bring it on. If not now, when?

After the Roberts hearings and the confirmation vote, the bright dividing line in competing judicial philosophies is absolutely clear. The Senate Judiciary Committee Democrats on the left of this line were totally revealing on this point, as evidenced by their inquiries. Listen to Richard Durbin: "…beyond loyalty to the law, how do you view the law when it comes to expanding our personal freedom?" Beyond loyalty to the law, Sen. Durbin? Are you kidding? (I wish that had been Roberts' response). And Dianne Feinstein, in announcing her "no" vote, said she was disappointed when, with respect to the issues surrounding end of life decisions, she asked him how he "feels" as a husband, father, or son, and received only a "detached" answer. (Much like we should expect of a judge, Sen. Feinstein?). These inquiries epitomize the jurisprudence of the left and the captivity of the Democratic Party to it – total constitutional incoherence.

In fact, the most striking phenomenon throughout the Roberts confirmation hearing was the degree to which it seems that our entire public discourse is being driven by the fealty to complete personal autonomy and a generalized "right to privacy," the concept that was created by the Supreme Court out of "the emanations and penumbras" of the Constitution, in other words, out of whole cloth, and which later drove the *Roe v. Wade* decision. As a result, as so well noted by Hadley Arkes in his book, *Natural Rights and the Right to Choose*, the Democratic Party has become the party of the courts, has completely prostituted itself to the privacy/abortion lobby, and demands that the judiciary continue to alienate itself from a central mission of the jurisprudence of a republic – the protection of human life.

As a follow up to one of Sen. Durbin's questions on loyalty to the law, Roberts made an instructive statement. He said that he had been asked, "Are you going to be on the side of the little guy?" His answer was, in effect, that whether the little guy or the big guy wins a case will depend on which one the Constitution says should win, because his loyalty is to the Constitution. This is a refreshingly direct affront to the philosophy of John Rawls and his *A Theory of Justice,* the liberal "bible" of distributive justice for almost 40 years. You want to know whether John Roberts will preside over a "Roberts Court?" He will if he has a sustained majority on the Court for the point of view embodied in his answers to Durbin, Feinstein, Schumer, et al., and this is why it becomes even more imperative that Bush follow up boldly on this once in a lifetime opportunity to transform our jurisprudence.

The Long Overdue Debate

January 4, 2006

In a *Wall Street Journal* essay last fall, in advance of President Bush's nomination of Samuel Alito to fill the vacancy on the Supreme Court created by the retirement of Sandra Day O'Connor, Robert George wrote this: "Here is my proposal: To fill the seat… Bush should nominate an intellectually distinguished and articulate judge willing to set forth and defend a sound understanding of the constitutional limits of judicial power in the confirmation hearings. Give up the stealth strategy… Let the nominee make the case for true constitutional government to the American people. Let us have a national debate…"

Well, President Bush complied with the first part of this proposal; now, he and Judge Alito's handlers should let the nominee get on with the second part, a long overdue confrontation with the proponents of the "living constitution." Let's have the "teaching moment" the country deserved and was so frustratingly deprived with the Harriet Miers mistake, the debate that will take to the people the real issues underlying the corruption this process has endured since the Bork fiasco in 1987, which was probably the low point of reasoned debate in the proud history of this country. Properly understood, this is a process that is so essential to self-governance, when we get to hear the competing philosophies of constitutional jurisprudence discussed openly and when nomination and confirmation is about not only who is appointed, but why their judicial philosophy was preferred and was decisive.

In such a scenario, how many Democrats will want to stake out the ground of the hard left that could care less about the rule of constitutional law or which judicial philosophy prevails as long as they get their desired results? My guess is, not many, at least explicitly, but many will do so duplicity, which is the height of intellectual dishonesty, and should be exposed as such to the American people. Let the debate begin.

Lessons from Enron Revisited

June 1, 2006

A couple of months ago, Daniel Henninger of *The Wall Street Journal* had the following striking headline to his weekly essay – "Barry Bonds, Please Meet Andrew Fastow" – a clear reference to the common thread that runs through the fraud manifest in both cases. The point is that there is a condition that transcends enforcement and prosecutorial methods such as drug testing in professional sports and Sarbanes-Oxley laws in corporate governance, which is the breakdown in the code that has restrained private vices and sustained the moral order of successful societies over the centuries. What happened to this code which defined and disseminated our common sense of right and wrong? That's a long story, but the end result has been the relegation of morality to matters of personal choice and "privacy" and its removal from instructional methods that once were widely available in the public square, but that have been slowly eliminated by the politics of tolerance and relativism. This is probably the most instructive lesson of the Enron case. At its outset four years ago, I noted that the market had worked its discipline and exacted its penalty in the Enron collapse, and that the case should not be used as an excuse to roll back or impede deregulation, re-regulate the electricity markets, halt the privatization of Social Security, or spawn tighter controls on 401k plans. Well, what we got was Sarbanes-Oxley, which has already produced ample evidence of the usual Congressional over-reaction, and is showing signs of a dampening effect on U.S. capital formation due to its onerous compliance burden on management, particularly of small- and mid-size growth companies. Another lesson, and one we should have learned long before Enron.

A third lesson should be the warning signs from the prosecution methods used in this case, which have been touted by the *Houston Chronicle* as innovative "new tools to defeat corporate felons." Characterized as enhanced "cooperation" by corporate management with federal prosecutors, these new tools include waiving attorney-client privilege, refusing to pay attorneys fees for individual suspects, and appointing independent monitors who participate in corporate strategy, while reporting to the government. The quid pro quo for this cooperation is supposedly the avoidance of the fate of Arthur Andersen & Co., the venerable firm which was destroyed by its indictment (later thrown out by the courts) by prosecutors as a by-product of seeking out individual culpability among its partners in the Enron debacle. To me, this new approach smacks of serious prosecutorial overreach, and will have further chilling impact on corporate innovation and capital formation over time. We would be better served by having more of the time and effort of this bright legal talent applied to the legal and political means by which a strengthened moral code can be restored to the public square, but in the current climate that's pretty naïve thinking.

Judicial Restraint

November 3, 2006

A recent poll conducted by Opinion Research Corp. on behalf of CNN shows that 67 percent of those surveyed say that federal judges and the decisions they make should not be subject to more control by politicians. I haven't seen the phrasing of the question, and this is often crucial with polling, but to the extent it was not biased and that the respondents understood the meaning of "control," we have an obvious conflict here, not only with the intent of the Founders, but with the written words of the Constitution itself in Article III, Section 2, which gives Congress the authority to establish rules for federal appellate jurisdiction. Former Supreme Court Justice Sandra Day O'Connor had previously weighed in with an opinion essay complaining about attempts to discipline judges, as with the South Dakota ballot initiative called a "judicial accountability initiative law" and efforts by Congress to "police" the judiciary, and she worries that these and other activities might serve to damage the independence of the judiciary and/or intimidate judges. In a subsequent interview with CNN she laments, "As I went through the last few years of service here at the court, I saw increasing indications of unhappiness with judges." Justice O'Connor may have justification for her concern, but she shouldn't be at a loss for the reasons for the unhappiness with judges. In a response to her essay, retired Fifth Circuit Court Judge Charles Pickering has it pegged: "Some in America today seek to win in a court of law that which they cannot win in the court of public opinion, at the ballot box. Americans do not want "sympathetic" judges, they want impartial ones… justices are now asserting that they have the power to exercise their independent judgment to determine the "sense of decency" of modern, evolving society… the thought process for political, not judicial decisions." The end result of the judicial overreach described by Judge Pickering is the removal of many of our "wedge" issues from their proper home in the give and take of the democratic process, however messy it might be, producing an environment that is largely responsible for much of the sense of frustration and incivility that prevails in our public policy discourse.

The Real Bush Legacy

July 1, 2007

Talk all you want about Iraq, the Bush Doctrine, "compassionate conservatism," or other remnants of the Bush Presidency, but its lasting legacy is likely to be the beginning of the reversal of judicial activism led by the John Roberts Supreme Court. There are significant signs in the term just ended that the 50-year trend in looking to the Court for redress of every social grievance will soon be reversed, however incrementally and however closely divided in numerous 5-4 decisions.

And, for those of us who would have preferred bolder sweeping reversals in some of the key decisions recently rendered, there is a lot to like about this incrementalism. For example, I would have preferred a completely stricken McCain-Feingold campaign finance law, but the significant restoration of political speech in the last days of an election campaign severely guts it. Likewise, I would have preferred much more clarity in the decision involving student free speech, including Justice Thomas's recommendation that the traditional in loco parentis legal doctrine be restored and a reversal of the Tinker decision of 1969 that started us down the path to near anarchy in many of our schools.

Of course, the decision generating the most controversy was the ruling in multiple opinions that at long last substantially ended the use of voluntary plans to create racial balance among students in public schools. Here again, we had an incrementalism that was gratifying, but not completely fulfilling, in that, contrary to Justice Kennedy's muddled concurrence, we should have had a complete declaration that, in the true meaning of the 14th Amendment and Dr. King's legacy, our constitution is color blind.

But I won't let the perfect be the enemy of the very good, for the real message from this term is that Presidential elections have consequences that are truly transformational, and Bush's appointments of Roberts and Alito may indeed begin to direct us away from much of the judicial tyranny of the past several decades and take us back to, as Roberts himself put it, "a modest approach to judging, which is good for the legal system as a whole."

Whither Marriage?

August 6, 2010

Now at least there is a pathway to a resolution to the same-sex marriage issue. With the district court decision overturning California's Proposition 8 prohibiting such marriages, the stage is set for a process almost certainly leading to the Supreme Court. Again, as I have noted any number of times, the judiciary has decided to impose its will to circumvent the democratic process, a habit that, beginning most notably with *Roe v. Wade*, has been the single most destructive element to civil discourse, coloring, and often poisoning almost every area of deliberation of domestic policy. When will we ever pay due attention to the damage that has been done to our republican system by the imperial judiciary and the abdication of our elected officials? As for the institution of marriage, David Blankenhorn, lead witness for the defense of Proposition 8, said it best: Historically, marriage has been a child-centered social institution, and "same-sex marriage would accelerate the deinstitutionalization of marriage and weaken the family by mainstreaming alternative family forms." And, make no mistake, these additional "forms" and their consequences would certainly follow.

Americans Can Handle It

March 4, 2011

Two issues in the news lately once again have highlighted our propensity to judicial activism. One, the Obama administration announced that it will no longer defend the Defense of Marriage Act; the other involves the Supreme Court decision in favor of Westboro Baptist Church in its public desecration of military funerals. I won't spend much time on the underlying merits of each, except to say that, in the former, it seems that an oath to execute the laws implies the defense of them in court and, in the latter, it seems that the First Amendment is primarily about political speech, properly understood, and not about grandstanding for publicity.

The primary issue for me in both of these instances is that they should be settled by political and democratic processes, not by the judiciary. This is a mature country of fairly well-settled values, with a republican form of government in each of 50 state jurisdictions with a total of more than 7,000 legislators, and with vast numbers of citizen associations that form the voluntary mediating powers and institutions highlighted by Tocqueville that make America exceptional. This is the "civic republic" well-described by Michael Sandel in *Democracy's Discontent*, but it has been corrupted by what he calls the "procedural republic," which essentially demands that we move cultural and moral considerations off the table in our deliberation on public policy. And where has this taken us? To *Roe v. Wade*, elimination of prayer in the schools, etc., and deep divisions in the body politic, because it was denied a political resolution of the issues nearest and dearest to our core. It is time for the procedural republic to step aside and let the civic republic take over. We can handle it.

The ObamaCare Decision

July 5, 2012

In the first 48 hours after the surprising Supreme Court decision in the ObamaCare case, after recovering from the initial shock, I was prepared to give Chief Justice John Roberts a break, the benefit of doubt about his intentions and rationale. I drank some of the Kool-Aid from the conservative bloggers about the genius, the liberal baiting on the Commerce Clause, how he was "playing chess while everyone else was playing checkers," and the underlying conservative instincts involved in the strategy and reasoning of the Chief Justice. But I have since read every analysis I could get my hands on and I have changed my view: While not entirely without merit in some of its by-products, this was a deeply flawed and disturbing decision, and not mainly because of the final outcome, but because of the manner in which it was reached.

I won't get into the arcane nature of the tax vs. penalty issues in the insurance mandate; the dissent signed by Kennedy, Scalia, Thomas, and Alito and a brilliant analysis by *The Wall Street Journal* have performed a complete hatchet job on any credibility in this gambit. The big problem with this sleight of hand is that it results in a complete rewrite of the law, for the Roberts version with its massive tax on the middle class would have had no possibility of passing even the Democrat-controlled Congress that adopted it. So much for a non-activist judiciary!

But the disturbing part of all of this is the calculation, the cleverness itself, more lawyer trickiness than sound judgment, which smacks of political opportunism from a man who was supposedly the paragon of judicial rectitude, prudence, and Federalist Society fidelity to the Founders' legacy, for clearly, Roberts had to reimagine this monstrosity to find it constitutional. Why did he do this?

Several people have identified what I believe to be the main reason, probably best described by Michael Gerson in *The Washington Post*. Gerson writes that there are two types of judicial conservatism – institutionalism and constitutionalism – that can lead to very different outcomes, and he believes that Roberts is emerging as the great institutionalist, primarily concerned about the reputation of the Supreme Court and its place in American life. In this view, the Court should take great pains to defer to the legislative branch, lest it violate a duty to continuity and avoidance of partisanship, as with *Bush v. Gore and Citizens United* cases, for example.

The leading constitutionalists, of course, are Scalia, Thomas, and Alito, who are totally focused on rigorous application of the words in the document, whatever the political consequences or partisan appearances. Gerson himself is a self-described institutionalist, but he believes Roberts blew it in this decision because of lack of fidelity to any credible application of the law in this case. To me, this is the most disturbing aspect of this decision.

But there is more to this, and it involves a phenomenon that has been persistent at least since the New Deal, and that is the vulnerability of conservatives to intimidation from the left, of which there was an avalanche from all directions leading up to this decision, and I believe that the Chief Justice, in his role as protector of the institution of the Court, at least partially bent to this intimidation.

Why is it that conservatism is the wing of our political spectrum that is consistently vulnerable to this intimidation of the left wing? Why is it that the left's "good intentions" are almost never questioned in terms of clearly documented bad consequences from the resulting policy? Why is it that conservatives consistently feel the need to accommodate the left, to be the conciliators, to be those most concerned with the civility of the body politic and, in the particular context of the ObamaCare case, intimidated by the threat that the integrity of the Supreme Court would be damaged by a close decision against the President's signature initiative by a conservative majority of the Court?

Is there any instance in recent memory in which the reverse was true, in which the left was in any way hesitant or subject to intimidation not to overturn a precedent or a democratically established policy, however adverse to constitutional scrutiny? I certainly can't think of one. The reasons are many, but chief among them are, because in spite of the fact that this remains a center-right country, the left occupies the high ground in almost all elements of the popular culture, the news media, most of our non-profit institutions, and the upper reaches of higher education, to the extent that conservatives are considered duty-bound to answer for any objections to the "progressive" agenda in all of its manifestations, while the left is almost never held to any such corresponding duty by our mainstream institutions. And this situation won't change until we change these civic and cultural institutions.

These are questions and considerations to ponder as we deliberate how we will respond to this decision in this election year; meanwhile, painfully, but no doubt appropriately, John Roberts has left us with our last resort – the ballot.

The SCOTUS Rules

July 5, 2013

The Supreme Court got a few big things right in its current term, but also added further confusion in a couple of places. Here are some thoughts on a few of the most prominent cases.

With the decision in *Koontz v. St. Johns River Water Management*, the Court again validated the constitutional takings clause in reversing the Florida Supreme Court ruling in a wetlands case that extended two previous rulings that prevent government from using development permit denial as a way to extort property without actually condemning it. A big victory for private property rights. Hopefully, the Court soon will revisit and reverse its abuse of eminent domain in its terrible *Kelo v. City of New London* decision of a few years ago.

In *Shelby County v. Holder*, the Court struck down the section of the Voting Rights Act of 1965 that prescribes the coverage formula for federal preclearance of states that want to change their voting laws. This is big and long overdue. Anyone who looks objectively at the voting records of states operating under the scrutiny of this law today compared to the situation in 1965 must conclude that this is a federal civil rights initiative that actually worked. Now let's move on.

A 7-1 majority in *Fisher v. The University of Texas at Austin* rejected a lower court decision upholding how the University considers race in admissions on grounds that it didn't meet the "strict scrutiny" test for using race. Unfortunately, the decision left standing the 2003 decision in *Grutter v. Bollinger* that allowed the continuing use of race in admissions in pursuit of a compelling state interest in "diversity." I share the disappointment of many who wish that Clarence Thomas, who concurred with the majority, could have written its opinion. In his concurrence, he forcefully said that he would have preferred to overturn *Grutter* and the entire convoluted mess created by the Court's tolerance of racial preferences beginning with the 1978 *Bakke* decision as a violation of the equal protection clause of the 14th Amendment. They will get another shot at it when the Court hears a case on the constitutionality of the ban on racial preferences passed by Michigan voters in 2006. Here's hoping that, at long last, they will finally "end it, not mend it."

The biggest muddle of the term involved the decisions on same-sex marriage. In two 5-4 decisions, the Court overturned the Defense of Marriage Act (DOMA), defining marriage as between a man and a woman, and left California's lower court decision intact in support of the repeal of its Proposition 8, which featured the same marriage definition, the latter case decided not on substantive grounds, but rather for lack of standing to sue on the part of the plaintiffs, a group of private citizens who supported Prop 8. So, same-sex marriage is legal in California, and with the decision on DOMA, the battle will now be fought out in the states, except that the equal protection language used by Anthony Kennedy in the DOMA opinion threatens to subvert that process. So, this leaves a mess, and I think possibly the most damaging aspect of these rulings is the lack of standing ruling in the Prop 8 case, which could have the effect of undermining initiative and referendum and other forms of direct democracy across the country. The cleanup work here will take years.

This was a consequential term of the Court, and these cases in some ways illustrate the difference in the liberal and conservative philosophy of judicial review. The conservative tendency more often is to be in restraint of sweeping and disruptive changes and to focus on tightly worded adjustments and fine tuning to current law that often fail in overall satisfaction of resolution and sometimes add to the confusion. So, for example, the conservative majority gave Congress two chances over a seven-year period to fix the Voting Rights Act before striking the section on the coverage formula and then left it to Congress to revisit those provisions for repair. Likewise, it once again tinkered with race-based affirmative action in a further attempt to respect precedent and legislative prerogative, as opposed to abruptly ending a policy with which it basically disagrees. The DOMA decision could be considered sweeping, but the majority here, except for Kennedy, seemed to be searching for a legislative and political way out in dumping the issue back on the states. On the other hand, the liberal tendency has been to sweeping and disruptive change over the years, particularly with the cultural issues, in the mold of *Griswold v. Connecticut, Roe v. Wade, Lawrence v. Texas, Brown v. Topeka*, etc., in a manner that foreclosed democratic processes and exacerbated cultural conflict. And is there any doubt that, if there was a liberal majority on this court, it wouldn't have hesitated for an instant to strike down in one fell swoop the 35 state laws banning same-sex marriage? It often frustrates me that a conservative majority won't be more sweeping in its opinions, particularly in reversals of badly misguided precedents, but my better judgment says that some restraint and deference to the political process is the better route.

More to the point in a currently unfolding issue in the special legislative session in Texas considering the imposition of limits to abortion, a *Houston Chronicle* editorial said this: "...the abortion issue doesn't belong in the political sphere. As *Texas Monthly's* Paul Burka noted last week, 'it's a fight that cannot be resolved. There is no middle ground. When there is no middle ground, politics cannot work.'" Burka and the *Chronicle* are wrong. That's exactly where it does belong. The fact that it was removed from the political process by the *Roe v. Wade* decision in 1973 is why it has so corrupted our politics since then. Politics is the only resolution of moral issues. We should have learned this from our Civil War.

No Surprises in Supreme Court Rulings

July 9, 2015

Did anyone really believe that the Roberts/Kennedy court would rule any differently on the same-sex marriage and ObamaCare cases? Is there any doubt that the Supreme Court not only reads election results, but responds to opinion polling? Unfortunately, however adverse to the intent of the founding, this is the state of affairs to which we have evolved in the constitutional balance of powers among the three branches of government.

Let's consider the two most prominent decisions in turn. First, the same-sex marriage case, *Obergefell v. Hodges*, in which the Court held in a 5-4 majority that the 14th Amendment requires a state to license and recognize in all respects a marriage between two people of the same sex. This decision was no doubt reached substantially in response to polling that reflected the most sweeping transformation of public opinion in history and in spite of a relatively recently adopted federal defense of marriage act and significant voter disapproval of same-sex marriage in several states.

It is interesting that all four dissenting justices wrote their own separate opinion. For example, Chief Justice John Roberts attacked the majority's substantive due process argument (a 19th century invention that gave us the right to abortion decision in *Roe v. Wade*), writing "the majority's approach has no basis in principle or tradition, except for the unprincipled tradition of judicial policymaking that characterized discredited decisions such as *Lochner v. New York*... But, this court is not a legislature. Whether same-sex marriage is a good idea should be of no concern to us. Under the Constitution, judges have the power to say what the law is, not what it should be." Exactly on point in my judgment, but I wish Roberts had been as true to these principles in his two opinions, which bailed out ObamaCare!

I also like Samuel Alito's dissenting opinion, joined by Scalia and Thomas, which states, "Today's decision usurps the constitutional right of the people to decide whether to keep or alter the traditional understanding of marriage... It will be used to vilify Americans who are unwilling to assent to the new orthodoxy. If a bare majority of Justices can invent a new right and impose that right on the rest of the country, the only real limit on what future majorities will be able to do is their own sense of what those with political power and cultural influence are willing to tolerate."

If there is some hope in this decision, it is in Justice Kennedy's majority opinion, as follows: "...it must be emphasized that religions, and those who adhere to religious doctrines, may continue to advocate with utmost, sincere conviction that by divine precepts, same-sex marriage should not be condoned. The First Amendment ensures that religious organizations and persons are given proper protection..."

And herein lies the rub, for already we have florists and bakers being charged and fined for refusing to participate in same-sex ceremonies and the left will not relent until the principle of religious freedom as understood in the Constitution has been completely gutted. And they will not stop there. Based on this decision, we can look for attacks on tax-exempt status of religious organizations, accreditation of religious colleges and schools, contracts with faith-based service organizations, etc. This is the next phase of this battle and it will almost certainly be back in front of the Court.

In *King v. Burwell*, we have possibly an even more egregious violation of the clear intent of the law under review. Here, in a 6-3 decision, the Court upheld the outlay of premium tax credits to qualifying persons, whose health insurance is subject to the Patient Protection and Affordable Care Act, better known as ObamaCare, in all states, whether or not the state established an exchange for this purpose as clearly stated in the statute and as aggressively described by advocates on numerous occasions in promoting its adoption. Yet in the majority opinion written by Chief Justice Roberts (no surprise here), the Court found the disputed clause concerning the exchanges to be ambiguous, and that it ought to be interpreted in a manner "that is compatible with the rest of the law." A total fabrication.

I always hate to say "I told you so," but in March of this year I wrote "I hope I am wrong, but I'm betting that the politics will win out and that the Chief Justice will once again bail out this abomination in "compassionate" deference to the resulting impact of the elimination of the subsidy for 10 or so million people and the damage he thinks will be inflicted on the institution of the Court."

What should our response be to these landmark cave-ins? Well, I like Lincoln's approach, who when responding to questions about the infamous 1857 Supreme Court decision in the *Dred Scott* decision on slavery, said this: "If the policy of the government upon vital questions affecting the whole people is to be irrevocably fixed by decisions of the Supreme Court, the instant they are made in ordinary litigation between parties in person actions, the people will have ceased to be their own rulers, having to that extent practically resigned their government into the hands of that eminent tribunal."

Gov. Abbott's Ambitious Constitutional Revival Plan

February 4, 2016

Gov. Greg Abbott wants Texas to lead the call for a constitutional convention to amend the U.S. Constitution in the interest of states' rights and he is not without details, having released a 70-page plan, which if nothing else, is a great teaching guide in American civics, that outlines nine proposed amendments that would roll back the half century or more federal power grab and return the country to its constitutional roots in a balanced federalism.

Of course, this is a great idea, and if he were czar for a day, I would love to see him pull it off. But it obviously represents a gargantuan task with overwhelming odds stacked against it, and I am not aware of anyone who thinks it is possible in any timely fashion. I do believe that it has significant value, however, in sparking a national conversation on the long overdue need to restore the founding principles to our governing structure.

One of the things that immediately occurred to me when I first read of his plan is that most of the problem he is addressing, if you think about it, has been facilitated if not directly caused by a dereliction of duty by the U.S. Congress over the years, either by abdicating their constitutional responsibilities and/or deferring critical issues to the jurisdiction of an imperial judiciary. So, if Congress were to begin to restore itself to its proper constitutional role, many of the issues Gov. Abbott is addressing could be resolved without a constitutional convention.

It happens that Christopher DeMuth, Distinguished Fellow of the Hudson Institute, has offered some suggestions along these lines in a speech delivered in September 2015 at Hillsdale College entitled "Reviving a Constitutional Congress." To begin, he suggests that our system of government depends on a reasonable balance of power among the three branches, and we are losing that balance with a dramatic power shift over the past several decades, primarily to the executive branch, but also to the judiciary. And, as I have suggested, a large part of this drift is the relinquishment of its powers voluntarily, by its abdication to the other two branches and by delegating broad policy-making authority to a plethora of commissions and agencies of the executive branch. The result has been a violation of the balance of powers foundation of the founders' design, which has had the effect of violating states' rights as well through the undermining of our system of federalism.

To begin the constitutional restoration, DeMuth has a five-step plan, highlighted as follows:

- Congress should retrieve the taxing, spending, and borrowing powers it has delegated to executive agencies and place all agencies on annual appropriations regardless of their sources of revenues.
- Congress should exercise its appropriations power under the procedures of the Budget Act of 1974, passing individual appropriation bills on a regular basis.
- Congress should relearn the arts of legislating by recovering many of the lawmaking powers it has handed off to the regulatory agencies. This will require a return to "regular order," strong leadership, and tough choices, but it must be done.
- Congress should reconstruct an internal policymaking hierarchy that was dismantled for good reason in the 1960s and 1970s as overly obstructionist. This reconstruction should feature a strong meritocracy that complements partisanship, but emphasizes mastery of policy fields and skills in negotiation, with leadership accountable for results.
- The Senate should cut back to near abolition the "filibuster" and the "hold," both of which have become frequent, costless, and routinely employed.

Needless to say, there has not been a rush to sign on to his plan, for all the obvious reasons, but I believe it is a great first step, if very difficult, toward restoring constitutional governance of the type our founders intended and would move us toward the objectives that Gov. Abbott has in mind without the need for constitutional amendment. In fact, if we don't soon advance something close to this level of comprehensive Congressional reform, our republic is headed for some severe damage.

A Minimalist Supreme Court? How Convenient for the Left

June 5, 2016

It's really very interesting and ironic that no less a progressive than Harvard law professor Cass Sunstein now finds solace in the fact that, with the death of Justice Antonin Scalia, which has basically produced a 4-4 Supreme Court on any seriously contentious issue, the Court might in the interim get used to being less activist and more minimalist in its rulings. How convenient for him and his fellow travelers on the left, now that about 50 years of liberal activist jurisprudence is on the books as so-called "settled law." In a recent op-ed, he even quotes Chief Justice John Roberts in what he calls "the cardinal principle of judicial restraint – if it is not necessary to decide more, it is necessary not to decide more." And, according to Sunstein, that principle contains two ideas: that decisions should be narrow rather than wide and that they should be shallow rather than deep, and he adds that such rulings reflect one virtue above all: humility. Another benefit he highlights as almost equally important is that minimalist rulings have the advantage of keeping major issues open for debate.

Really? When has the left ever expressed an interest in either one of these virtues? Where is the humility in the numerous decisions that have "discovered" rights that are nowhere expressed or implied in the Constitution and where is the deference to the democratic process in a Court whose progressive wing has repeatedly removed momentous national issues from deliberation with a broad "one size fits all" stroke. Both lists are long.

So, now we are supposed to welcome a minimalist Court? If that means not reversing a number of atrocious decisions by what has too often been an activist and imperial Court, no thanks.

The SCOTUS Rules

July 4, 2016

There were only a couple of bright spots for me in the recently announced rulings from the Supreme Court; overall, the decisions were very troubling. Here are some comments on a few of the most significant cases.

- In *U.S. v. Texas*, the Court split 4-4 on the challenge by 26 states to President Obama's executive order legalizing several million undocumented aliens. At least this no-decision validates the lower court's decision and kills the order. But, because of the split vote, the Court did not elaborate the underlying views on the issue, which is a disappointment. I just can't imagine how anyone with common sense about our constitutional system could support such a flagrant abuse of power, but four justices did just that. And we wonder why the rise of Donald Trump?

- In a surprisingly unanimous 8-0 decision, the Court reversed the corruption conviction of former Virginia Governor Robert McDonnell, basically saying that however distasteful the facts, the gifts he accepted from a constituent did not rise to the level of a bribe. This is a good outcome, for it refutes the view of campaign finance reformers who want to make substantially all campaign contributions synonymous with bribery, so as to ultimately remove all private contributions and turn campaign funding over to the government.

- In *Fisher v. University of Texas*, the long-running affirmative action in college admissions case, the Court surprisingly ruled 4-3 in favor of the University, supporting its so-called "holistic" criteria review of applicants that might use race as a factor under strict scrutiny in the interest of diversity in the student body. Surprising, because Justice Kagan an almost certain vote for the University's position, had recused herself from the case. This is a horrible decision, made even more so by the fact that Justice Anthony Kennedy, who wrote the opinion, in effect reversed himself on the issue from his statement in the first appearance of *Fisher* before the Court in 2013, in which he wrote "judicial review must begin from the position that any official action that treats a person differently on account of his race or ethnic origin is inherently suspect." But in this case, he was almost totally deferential to the university's judgment, with scant evidence that there were any strict scrutiny criteria in place. Kennedy obviously is struggling with his convictions, particularly now with Antonin Scalia not around to prop him up. What a tragedy.

- In *Whole Woman's Health v. Hellerstedt,* Justice Scalia would not have changed the outcome except with moral suasion. In a 5-3 decision written by Justice Breyer, the Court struck down the Texas law that had added regulations to abortion practices in the state. The basis for the decision was that the law posed an "undue burden" on a woman's right to an abortion, a legal test of state regulatory authority that was added in the 1992 abortion case, *Planned Parenthood v. Casey*, in a majority opinion written by Justice Kennedy. This decision had left open the authority on the part of the states to develop measures that would offer additional health and safety protections to women seeking abortions. The decision in this case seems to eliminate this authority and it drew a scathing dissent from Justice Thomas, who wrote "The Court should abandon the pretense that anything other than policy preferences underlies its balancing of constitutional rights and interests in any given case." Amen. If you want to find something positive here, I read this week that the number of abortions performed in Texas decreased by 14 percent during the time the law at issue in this case was in effect.

- Finally, in what Justice Alito calls an "ominous sign" for religious freedom, the Court decided not to hear a case challenging a Washington state law that would force a family owned pharmacy to dispense emergency contraceptives. Chief Justice Roberts and Justice Thomas joined Alito in voting to hear the case, but four votes are required, which is why Alito issued his warning in his dissent that "if this is a sign of how religious liberty claims will be treated in the years ahead, those who value religious freedom have cause for great concern."

Need I remind you that elections have consequences?

Thoughts on the Mission of the Special Counsel

July 5, 2017

I have refrained from commenting on the various "investigations" involving the Russian influence on the 2016 election and Trump campaign collusion in same, former FBI Director Comey's testimony, alleged "obstruction of justice," and related circuses, because that is exactly what this has become. And I am certainly not going to attempt any explanation let alone defense for President Trump's various responses to all of this or any other aspect of his management style or temperament, much of which is unprofessional, possibly pathological, and adds to the circus element. But as *The Wall Street Journal* recently has noted, you don't have to be a Trump partisan to have concerns about where all of this is headed, even though it is clear that the President brought much of it on himself with his careless conduct. And there are valid concerns we should all have about the mission of Special Counsel Robert Mueller having to do with the scope of his work and the people he has so far chosen to carry it out. I won't repeat the details that have been widely reported, but suffice to say that there is at least the potential of conflict, as well as prosecutorial overreach.

As for the investigation itself, for all the bluster and smoke, where is the fire? There is no evidence, no laws broken, no Russian collusion; so far, it's all about leaks of bad information and it's very destructive to the country and instructive about the tactical level to which the left will sink when they have no other message. The only issue that begs for a real investigation here is the corruption of U.S. intelligence agencies, which has been almost the sole source of the false evidence and anonymous leakage that is driving this circus, all in the name of undermining the Trump administration. This never has been a partisan letter, but this process has long ago reached the level of the ridiculous and reasonable people should know it. The world is on fire and this charade is dangerous to American interests.

The Supreme Court and the Kennedy Succession

July 5, 2018

The Supreme Court has just completed one of the more consequential terms in recent memory, with significant victories for constitutional liberties. Probably the most significant was with *Janus v. Afscme*, wherein the Court ruled 5-4 to overturn a deeply flawed precedent in the 1977 *Abood* decision that allowed states to require workers who aren't union members to pay "agency fees" to support collective bargaining. As Justice Alito wrote in the majority opinion, "The idea of public-sector unionization and agency fees would astound those who framed and drafted the Bill of Rights." This is a long overdue at least partial correction of a problem that should not have been created in the first place; in fact, as President Franklin Roosevelt noted in a famous letter to a labor leader in 1937, "All government employees should realize that the process of collective bargaining, as usually understood, cannot be transplanted into the public service." The next step for complete reform on this issue is to repeal John F. Kennedy's Executive Order No. 10988 which recognized a right for federal workers to bargain collectively, but that is a debate for another day.

Other first amendment victories in this term included the previously announced Masterpiece Cakeshop decision, which struck another blow for religious liberty, and *National Institute of Family and Life Advocates v. Becerra*, which struck down a California law which singled out and required pregnancy service centers that offer an alternative to abortion to notify clients of the availability of low-cost abortions from the state and provide contact information. What is very interesting in *Becerra* is the strong comments by Justice Kennedy in concurrence with Justice Thomas's majority opinion: "It is not forward thinking to force individuals to be an instrument for fostering public adherence to an ideological point of view they find unacceptable… It is forward thinking to begin by reading the First Amendment as ratified in 1791; to understand the history of authoritarian government as the Founders then knew it… Freedom of speech secures freedom of thought and belief. This law imperils those liberties."

Whatever problems traditional conservatives have had with Justice Anthony Kennedy over the past three decades of his service, and I have several (*Planned Parenthood v. Casey; Obergefell v. Hodges; Boumediene v. Bush*; the affirmative action cases, to name a few), one cannot doubt his dedication to the First Amendment, particularly free speech, and these recent opinions are further evidence of that. Now he is retiring, so what next? Based on President Trump's short list, I expect we'll get another Federalist Society-vetted candidate out of the Neil Gorsuch mold, which will move the Court slightly to the right, but it will no longer be the "Kennedy Court" in the sense that he was the swing vote on so many 5-4 decisions. Time and cases will tell whether or not there will be such a swing vote on the new Court.

Of course the left is now in full scale scare campaign mode to enliven their base over the possibility of an overturn of *Roe v. Wade, Obergefell*, the ObamaCare decisions, and other favorites of progressive activism. I wish it weren't so, but as badly reasoned and decided as these decisions were, I don't think they will be overturned by a post-Kennedy court, and not entirely because of *stare decisis.* Why? Because I think that the new court finally will become the "Roberts Court" whose majority under his leadership will protect, above all considerations other than the Constitution, the integrity and consistency of the institution. Of course, some of this thinking is about *stare decisis,* but it's more about the notion of "settled law" that has in many ways become organic together with some deference to the intent of the legislative branch (dare I include a touch of public opinion?). I don't happen to agree with these sentiments when they prevent some necessary repair work on serious mistakes, but on the evidence so far the Chief Justice is less inclined to be disruptive than I might be.

With at least one aspect of this possible shift in emphasis I would agree. That is to make the Court much less consequential in our lives by returning it to its proper role in judicial review and leaving the activism and its drama to the other two branches, the states, and the people. In this respect, the left has much more to worry about than the reversal of a few hot button cases, even *Roe*, for with another appointment of the quality of Gorsuch, Trump has an opportunity to put an end to five decades of judicial activism and law-making that really began in *Griswold v. Connecticut* in 1965 with a right to privacy leading to *Roe* that Justice William Douglas somehow found in the "penumbras formed by emanations" of the Bill of Rights, whatever that means.

In any event, we're at another milestone and turn in the road, and we should thank Justice Kennedy for his service and for his timely retirement.

Big Data on the Edge

September 4, 2018

I will make no attempt to hold myself out as one with expertise on the "big data" models of Facebook, Google, You Tube, et al. I barely know what an algorithm is, but it is pretty clear that these monster near-monopolists are very near the edge of a major regulatory pushback in their attempt to "have it both ways." What do I mean? The Communications Decency Act of 1996 says this about the role of internet platform companies: They offer "a forum for a true diversity of political discourse, unique opportunities for cultural development, and myriad avenues for intellectual activity." They are talking about the companies that recently banned hard right commentator Alex Jones, censored conservative PragerU posts, shut down an online storefront selling gun designs, and increasingly patrol their sites for what they consider "hate mail."

In a recent article, law professor Glenn Harlan Reynolds explains that if these platforms were publishers, none of these actions would be a problem, because publishers are responsible for their decisions and can be held liable. But under the current law they are treated as conduits, vehicles that others use to spread their own ideas, and they aren't legally responsible for what other people publish on their sites. Back to my point – they want it both ways: complete control over content without liability as publishers. So far, they are getting away with it, but they are on the edge, particularly when it comes to the First Amendment.

In *Matal v. Tam* in 2017, the Supreme Court unanimously reaffirmed that there is no "hate speech" exception to the First Amendment. Justice Samuel Alito put it this way in his opinion: "The idea that the government may restrict speech expressing ideas that offend… strikes at the heart of the First Amendment. Speech that demeans on the basis of race, ethnicity, gender, religion, age, disability, or any other similar ground is hateful; but the proudest boast of our free speech jurisprudence is that we protect the freedom to express 'the thought that we hate.'" Granted, this reaffirmation applies to government restrictions, but the fact that these near-monopolistic tech giants play such a dominant role in controlling what views get aired and published will put enormous pressure on Congress to act. And if they do, this won't end well. Better to have these companies accept the fact that this phase of their model has run its course and that they must decide what they are – publisher or conduit – and act accordingly.

The Kavanaugh Ordeal

October 4, 2018

As I write, one of the most shameful public episodes of my lifetime is slowly grinding to a conclusion, except that whatever the final outcome, when the U.S. Senate finally votes on the Kavanaugh Supreme Court appointment during the next few days, it will not represent anything resembling closure for the American body politic because the damage that has been done will reverberate for at least a generation.

This has been a disaster ruthlessly initiated and carried out by the worst instincts of the far reaches of the left wing of the Democratic Party and their fellow travelers in the media and the cultural institutions in the interests of power. And it has been orchestrated without the least regard for the devastating impact on a good man and his family, the time-honored principle of the presumption of innocence, the institutional integrity of the U.S. Senate, and common fairness and decency.

And to what end? It's all about the fact that the progressive left has no prayer of advancing their agenda without a Supreme Court amenable to a "living Constitution" and they know it cannot abide a Court comprised of a constitutional "originalist" majority from "central casting" at the Federalist Society. So, for them this is war, no holds barred, and for the left the holy grail to be protected starts with Roe v. Wade.

I have maintained for many years that the 1973 *Roe v. Wade* decision was our generation's *Dred Scott* decision of the Court on slavery in 1857, which led directly to the Civil War, in that it removed the abortion issue from the democratic process and deprived the people through their local and state assemblies to have the final word on a moral issue of extreme intensity. And our politics and deliberative processes have not been the same since – *Roe v. Wade* is lurking just under the surface of almost every issue that involves direct or indirect control of the judicial branch and it has now provided the incentive to poison the advise and consent authority for decades.

The late Justice Antonin Scalia had some interesting thoughts on this in his dissent in *Planned Parenthood v. Casey*: "If the Supreme Court is simply to be a vehicle for choosing among competing values, in a democracy it should be the values of the voters that prevail… confirmation hearings for new Justices should deteriorate into question and answer sessions in which the Senators go through a list of their constituents' most favored and most disfavored alleged constitutional rights." That's not what the founders had in mind, as Hamilton expressed in Federalist 78 in describing the judiciary as the "least dangerous" branch, but it might be an improvement over the currently dysfunctional process we now have created.

14
Media

Of Biases, Right and Left

March 1, 2003

One of my favorite liberal columnists, E. J. Dionne, Jr., wrote several months ago, "It took conservatives a lot of hard and steady work to push the media rightward. It dishonors that work to presume that – except for a few liberal columnists – there is any such thing as the big liberal media." Aside from the fact that he conveniently ignores the three major television networks, almost every major daily newspaper, and most of the very large foundations that support leftist causes, he is correct that the right has made significant media inroads in recent years.

It has happened mainly, because people in the so-called "red" electoral regions or "flyover country," finally, and over time, grew tired of the condescending attitude of the media elite of the two coasts. The de-massification of the media so accurately predicted by Alvin Toffler more than 20 years ago in, *The Third Wave*, also has helped. Radio talk shows and cable TV competitors brought an unbundling of the message, and with it, more unvarnished news and analysis. As a result, the mainstream outlets, plus CNN, were forced to respond by at least attempting to appear more accommodating. In the final analysis, Americans essentially have conservative instincts, our regime is grounded in conservative political philosophy, and our cultural levers of power – media, academia, and philanthropic institutions – have been too long out of step. Some healthy competition was long overdue. As Limbaugh often says, "we are equal time." Eat your heart out, Phil Donahue.

Big Media Comeuppance

October 2, 2004

David Broder said it well: "Once upon a time, the media knew better. The first sign of wavering confidence came when news organizations began offering their most prestigious and visible jobs, not to people deeply imbued with the culture and values of newsrooms, but to stars imported from the political world."

In the wake of the Dan Rather/CBS/National Guard memo scandal, one wonders with Broder, in effect, how CBS would have conducted their due diligence on the story or responded to the egregious error in judgment in the age of Edward R. Murrow and Ernie Pyle, et al.? We can speculate, but unfortunately there are fewer and fewer of us around who remember when the major news organizations were staffed by people who had been tested on city hall and local police beats under severe scrutiny from experienced and skeptical editors. More importantly, these were people who primarily came from the American experience themselves, before the proliferation of schools of journalism and public affairs where they are more likely to be advised that their mission is to change the world, not report it, and, in too many instances, that loyalty to their profession and to "history" trump loyalty to their country.

More than anything else, the CBS story is one of the terminal arrogance of the old 20th century institution of mass communication that is in steep decline and of the liberal/left dominance of that institution. And as Bernard Goldberg has so well described in his two recent books on the subject, big media leadership is completely oblivious to its own bias and arrogance. I believe this blindness lies in a condition deeply embedded in the pathology of the left that allows and condones a duplicity and double standard in the processing of reporting and the shaping of messages in the public square that they don't even recognize, because they are so seldom exposed to voices of introspection from their peers. This is, I think, primarily based on the presumed sanctity of their good intentions and is manifest in any number of examples, wherein the service of well-intentioned ends justifies almost any means (think of the Al Sharpton/Tawana Brawley case, Clinton's lies about "personal matters," Michael Moore's "documentary" film, and the characterization of George Bush as a "divider" on "wedge issues," among many others).

The triumph of the underground media, the bloggers, the talk shows, the small opinion journals, and generally, the "counter-establishment" media in this instance has been heralded as a watershed, a revolution in news, a "big cultural moment," as *The Wall Street Journal* described it. But Alvin Toffler predicted it more than 20 years ago in his book, *The Third Wave*, wherein he describes for us the inevitable loss of influence of mass media in what he called the "demassification" of information, beginning with the decline of the major newspapers, mass market magazines, and even the major television networks, in favor of niche publications and other delivery systems aimed at special interest, regional, and local markets. And this was before CNN, the explosion of cable TV, talk radio, and certainly the Internet! Most importantly, what all this means for the big media elites is that they no longer can manage images, shape content, and presentation, as well as control opinion with impunity, which is a refreshing and long overdue development.

Oprah and the Truth

February 3, 2006

The recent tribulations and mea culpa of Oprah Winfrey over her endorsement of James Frey's *A Million Little Pieces*, a book of fabrications sold as a true story of triumph and redemption, brought together for me several strands related to the current state of truth and objectivity in our culture. For example, the movie *Munich*, Steven Spielberg's account of the events leading up to the murder of Israeli athletes by Palestinian terrorists at the 1972 Olympic Games. I haven't seen the movie and don't plan to, because I am persuaded by a number of in-depth reviews that it is fiction with a political twist masquerading as history. Spielberg could have done better, and has (think of *Schindler's List*), but he obviously chose to make a political statement involving the moral equivalency of the basis for the Palestinian plot that led the murderers to the heinous deed. No surprise here when one considers that the co-author of the screenplay is Tony Kushner, who has written and is known to believe such mythology as that Ethel and Julius Rosenberg were innocent of spying for the Soviets and were "murdered, basically. He and E. L. Doctorow, the author of *The Book of Daniel*, supposedly loosely based on the Rosenbergs, have made joint public appearances challenging the Rosenberg guilty verdict as a product of "a Puritan, punitive civil religion" and Cold War paranoia.

There are any number of other examples, but my point is that we are constantly presented with works that, when truly exposed, really seem to be designed to offer and impose on us a kind of cultural therapy, as though we need to have our values reworked and our history restated and cleansed of all their prejudices and other baggage of our "oppressive" nature. I don't have a problem with this, as long as truth in advertising is practiced with all of this historical fiction and public therapy. As suggested by Joseph Rago in a perceptive editorial, "when the aesthetics are pointless bathos and the opinions are the whole point, politics ought to be taken into account," and I would add that a disclaimer should be clearly in view of the consumer. At some point, however, we need to get to the root of our disconnect from truth in labeling, which will be almost impossible until we engage in some serious repair of the main fount of our postmodern shaping of truth for political purposes – our institutions of higher education, particularly the elite colleges of liberal arts and journalism. As for Oprah's eventually coming around to her public mea culpa and dressing down of Frey, good for her. We need more of that humility and commitment to truth from those who occupy large public pulpits. I want to believe she reversed herself for the right reasons.

Ferguson and Related

January 1, 2015

After reflection on the events following the grand jury no-bill in the Ferguson, Missouri case, and its aftermath, it occurs to me that the main culprit in the story is the media, which desperately must fill its voracious news cycle with provocative material. The media predominantly is not interested in balanced coverage, preferring instead coverage that features the theme of racial conflict and often promotes the narrative of the aggrieved and the oppressed. As suggested by Jason Riley of *The Wall Street Journal*, the Ferguson case and others like it fit this narrative and are covered wall to wall, while Chicago, with its rampant black on black crime, does not.

When the media suggest that we need a "conversation on race," what they really mean is a politically correct conversation, one limited to the analysis of oppression of minorities by the system, regardless of evidence and moderated by the likes of Al Sharpton and other race hustlers who have no credibility as contributors to this conversation at any level and whose inclusion as an advisor to President Obama is an outrage which severely damages the credibility of his office on the issue. However tragic his demise in Ferguson, Michael Brown wasn't the victim in this story, he was the bad actor, primarily responsible for his fate. The unfortunate victims are: 1) the true status of race relations in this country, which is in much better shape than was portrayed by the media coverage of this case and the subsequent "protests," and 2) police protection in urban areas, which will suffer as police officers become more reluctant to respond to potential crime threats as a result of the lack of support from political leaders such as New York City Mayor DeBlasio. And the ultimate losers will be responsible blacks in heavy crime areas.

15
Monetary Policy

The New Market Risks

September 2, 2007

As a former refugee of the commercial banking meltdown of the mid-1980s, I can't help but hear some echoes of that period in the current fallout from the collapse of the subprime mortgage market bubble. Hopefully, we won't repeat the mistakes that were made then in adopting the selective bailout procedures, the "too big to fail" strategies, the moral hazard practices, and the "we know it all" attitudes assumed by the regulators of that era that converted a $10 billion problem into an $800 billion debacle, much of it centered in Texas. I am pretty far removed from all of the surrounding issues now, but it seems to me that, so far, Federal Reserve Chairman Bernanke has played his cards just about right, supplying liquidity through open market operations, signaling support as a lender of last resort through the discount window, and refraining from lowering federal fund rate targets. And the last thing we need to do is increase the size cap for mortgages purchased by Fannie Mae and Freddie Mac, institutions, which are a large part of our problem in the first place.

As some have noted, this may be the first real test of the "new marketplace" of securitized debt obligations and segmented risk tranches that, however efficient in terms of allocation of risk, are very complicated to analyze from an underwriting standpoint and even more difficult to track in terms of ownership. In effect, in large measure we have separated the underlying business transaction from its ultimate financing source, thereby increasing the risk of metastasizing the problem. In the end, there will no doubt be more pain and some major corporate failures, but such is the price of the market discipline necessary to prevent a much larger meltdown.

Been There, Done That

February 8, 2008

Recently, as the mainstream media pounded away in its coverage of the subprime mortgage "crisis" and the political class scrambled to "do something," I looked back to the most recent replay of such moments, the 9/11 and Enron scandal induced, pre-tax cut recession of 2001. At that point, just as Federal Reserve Chairman Alan Greenspan rendered his judgment that the recession had run its course and expansion was well underway, the then Republican-controlled Congress gave us an economic stimulus plan whether we needed one or not. Of course, none of this had any impact on the economy until the Bush tax rate reductions of 2003 put us on the growth track that has persisted until this very day.

"We are all Keynesians now" is a quote that has been variously attributed to Milton Friedman, who says he was quoted out of context, and Richard Nixon, who threw in the towel on fiscal and monetary policy discipline in 1971 and ended the Bretton Woods accord on the gold-backed dollar while resorting to wage and price controls in a disastrous attempt to control inflation. Actually, the British economist John Maynard Keynes would be appalled at much of the irresponsible monetary and fiscal policy that has been pursued in his name, and once said "There is no subtler, no surer means of overturning the existing basis of society than to debauch the currency." Yet here we are, almost seven decades later, resorting to demand-side stimulus plans for feel-good solutions to economic slowdowns that have nothing to do with demand-side problems. For Keynes would be the first to say that we can't consume what we don't produce and the idea that government can deliver something for nothing is a pipe dream.

We have such short memories. Remember when Ronald Reagan took office in 1981? The national psyche at the time was that stagflation was embedded in the national economy, that industrial planning was the order of the day, and that the Phillips Curve mandating an inverse relation between inflation and unemployment was inviolable. Then two things – the Reagan supply-side tax cuts and the monetary policy of the Paul Volcker Federal Reserve – changed the mindset. Was there pain? Sure there was, but the pain was a necessary price to pay to squeeze moral hazard out of the market and send the message to our risk analysts and our foreign investors, including central banks, that the U.S. was serious about breaking the inflation cycle and preserving the value of the dollar.

For about 15 years we maintained fealty to this discipline. Then, beginning with the Rubinomics of the Clinton administration in the late 1990s (devotees of the Phillips Curve) and the Alan Greenspan Federal Reserve, we "fell off the wagon" and allowed the money supply to grow too rapidly and rates to remain too low for too long, feeding an overinvestment in high risk assets, devaluing the dollar to the detriment of our credibility with foreign central banks and investors, and defaulting in our discipline in maintaining price stability.

To turn things around, we need an immediate change in course. The Federal Reserve should announce that, henceforth, it will have as its top priority the enhancement and preservation of the value of the dollar and it should abandon its short-term management of the overnight Federal funds rate and allow the rate to float, while focusing on reducing the money supply and lowering the price of gold to reverse the inflationary psychology that is creeping back into the commodity markets and the mindset of investors and foreign central banks. Then we need real stimulus in the form of the permanence of the Bush tax cuts, accelerated depreciation of capital expenditures, and reversal of the most onerous provisions of the Sarbanes-Oxley regulations that are stifling capital formation and sending American business to foreign capital markets for their investment banking needs.

A recession is not inevitable. With responsible and determined policy changes, it can be avoided. Not without pain, but with the re-establishment of our credibility in foreign markets and the avoidance of a return of the inflationary mindset and undermining of the currency, which should have the highest priority.

It's the Currency, Stupid!

March 7, 2008

"The elephant in the living room – the topic Washington won't broach – is the dollar itself as a powerful, but unused monetary policy tool... probably the most important economic and investing variable in the last decade. The best stimulus policy is a sound currency." – David Malpass, Chief Economist, Bear Stearns, *The Wall Street Journal.*

No less an authority than Lenin well understood the importance of a sound currency in the stability of economies and societies, and in fact, said that there is no surer means of overturning the existing basis of a society than to debauch the currency. We may not be near debauchery, but the trend is clear and the results are becoming traumatic. In the last week of February, the dollar reached a new record low against the Euro, a six-year slide during which it has depreciated 40 percent versus the European currency and more than 20 percent against a broad index of currencies. And what was Federal Reserve Chairman Ben Bernanke's response in testimony before Congress? To point to the weak dollar as a rare bright spot in an otherwise gloomy economic picture because of its impact on exports, jobs, and the trade deficit! Further, he indicated that the Fed will do whatever it takes to stop the subprime mortgage-induced credit squeeze from becoming a recession. He couldn't have been more clear in confirming that he has completely abrogated the Fed's number one responsibility – the stability of prices and the value of the currency.

And more recently, evidently believing that voluntary loan restructurings arranged between borrower and lender are not enough, he strongly urged lenders to begin discounting the principal balance of distressed mortgages to their borrowers, thereby restoring equity in the underlying collateral and the incentive to remain in the home. Since when did the Federal Reserve, which has considerable responsibility for the soundness of the banking system, become the coercive supervisor of bank loan workout policy? This puts him in virtually the same policy position as Congressman Barney Frank, except that the latter would then have the government refinance all the distressed mortgages, a path to the same disastrous "solution" that we reached in the savings and loan debacle of the late 1980s with the Resolution Trust Corporation that converted a $10 billion problem into a $500 billion problem. This is madness.

The dual strategies of ignoring the restoration of the value of the dollar as a primary foundation of monetary policy and pursuing coercive credit restructuring procedures that infringe on the sanctity of contract and subsidize moral hazard are very dangerous for our economic health and will produce major unintended consequences.

Looming Disaster

January 4, 2009

It is comforting to think that the worst of the economic meltdown may be behind us, that hopefully the extreme volatility of the markets has abated somewhat and they have found their bottom for the time being, but I fear a more profound and longer lasting negative impact from the "cures" that have been applied and proposed. The most destructive policy has been the Federal Reserve's failure to honor its most important responsibility – to preserve the value of the dollar.

Believe what you will about the causes of the recent crisis, but the political corruption of Fannie and Freddie, the failure of regulatory oversight, and the overreach of Wall Street product engineering would have produced relatively controllable aberrations were it not for the enabling availability of oceans of excess dollars that financed the debacle. Aside from this role played by the Fed's monetary policy over the past five years in misallocating capital in excessive amounts to the subprime mortgage market, the policy that has been pursued over that period has been destructive in a number of other respects. It has used a cheapened dollar as an instrument of trade protection, thereby significantly damaging U.S. credibility in world markets, which for the country that manages the world's reserve currency is absolutely critical to world order. It has undermined the world's pricing discipline, for our markets can operate to clear themselves only in an environment of rational pricing based on the value of underlying goods and services without the manipulation of exchange rates by central banks. It has destroyed the anti-inflation discipline of the past 25 years, and with the prospect of new "stimulus" plans proposed by the Obama administration, which can only be financed by the creation of many billions of additional dollars along with the expected tax increases, it will be the accomplice for what I fear will be a renewed round of 1970s-style stagflation. This will have repercussions for entrepreneurial activity far beyond its immediate impact on inflation and prices.

My hope is that, as a principal advisor to President Obama, Paul Volcker will speak forcefully against this continued misdirection in Fed policy, although it appears that he may be in the minority on the new economic advisory team. As for the longer term, we need a revived Bretton Woods type compact among a new league of democracies, one that will restore gold backing to the dollar and tie the dollar to the world's currencies. Our role as the keeper of the world's reserve currency and our stewardship of order in world financial markets is much more than a good strategy, it is a moral obligation and we have failed to uphold it.

The End of Entrepreneurial Banking

June 5, 2009

It appears that we finally have reached the tipping point at which commercial banking is headed toward becoming a cost-plus monopoly, with rate-based assets much like a public utility and very close to a nationalized industry. Maybe not for all institutions, but I can envision a two-tiered system in which the 20 or so "too big to fail" entities fit the mold just described, with second tier status for regional and community banks. What this will mean is a much different culture, temperament and mindset, much less oriented to capital formation, entrepreneurship and innovation.

I predicted such an outcome more than 20 years ago when I left commercial banking as a "refugee" of the banking debacle of the mid-1980s. All that was necessary was another major crisis of the kind we currently are experiencing at a time when the political left is positioned to reconfigure the regulatory environment. So, now the planets are aligned for the next step, and you can see it coming in the discussions about the carryover Bush administration proposal for a single federal bank regulator with virtually no role for state authorities. This would be a huge mistake, a violation of the principle of federalism that has served us so well for so long, but one can see a compromise in the making – a sole federal role for the "too big to fail" and shared federal/state regulation for everyone else. The result will be a significant majority of commercial banking assets in the hands of what would soon evolve into a cost-plus public utility. Let's hope that's the worst outcome and that there remains a largely deregulated and innovative second tier of independent banks under state supervision, and by all means reject what would be an even worse outcome, a much discussed *global* bank regulatory agency, heaven forbid.

Inflation Watch

June 5, 2009

"Throughout history, what the political class has done is they have turned to the central bank to print their way out of an unfunded liability. We can't let that happen. That's when you open the floodgates. So, I hope and pray that our political leaders will just have to take this bull by the horns at some point. You can't run away from it." – Richard Fisher, President, Federal Reserve Bank of Dallas, as quoted in *The Wall Street Journal.*

This kind of talk is obviously not what the nation's current financial management wants to hear, which is why it's a great idea to have an independent Federal Reserve with independent regional reserve banks and boards along with independent executives like Fisher who have a voice in monetary policy. I hope he gets some help with this message, because I believe that all the signs point to inflation as our next big worry – not today or next week or maybe even next year, but certainly in the next two or three years.

Look at some leading indicators of concern – a sharp uptick in Treasury bond rates as we prepare to sell $2 trillion (that's with a "t") in Treasury bonds this year; the prospect of a $1 trillion deficit with no conceivable way to finance it without the monetization of debt by the Federal Reserve; comments by Treasury Secretary Geithner that he wants China to exercise "greater exchange-rate flexibility," which means a cheaper dollar vs. the yuan; the price of gold recently has bumped $1,000 per ounce; and comments by no less an authority than German Chancellor Angela Merkel rebuking the world's central banks, most prominently our Fed, for "being too politically accommodating."

Federal Reserve Chairman Bernanke recently has made some pointed remarks himself, cautioning Congress about the ever growing projected federal deficits. But let's face it: the Federal Reserve severely has undermined its independence from government fiscal policy over the past six to 12 months, and its involvement with the various bailouts makes it increasingly difficult to restore this independence. It has a big decision to make at its upcoming meeting as to whether or not and by how much to increase its purchases of Treasury bonds. It really seems to have no choice, given the market response to the recent auctions, which means that the monetization of the debt will continue as long as we continue to write hot checks to finance the Obama regime. Not a great prognosis.

Bad Fed Policy Made Worse

October 8, 2011

Congressman Barney Frank has another flawed idea – somehow he thinks that the Federal Reserve has too much independence from political guidance, so he has a plan to reduce the representation of the regional Fed bank presidents on the central bank policy board and replace them with political appointees. We have enough problems with monetary policy as it currently is being managed without further politicizing it.

Congressman Ron Paul may be a borderline kook on many issues, but one he understands very well is the role of a sound reserve currency in the maintenance of growth and stability around the world and the importance of such a mission to American prosperity. Earlier this year, Paul asked Federal Reserve Chairman Ben Bernanke, "what is your definition of a dollar?" The answer, not surprisingly, was "My definition of the dollar is what it can buy," in other words, its purchasing power, which conforms to the currently popular understanding, but bears no relationship to the traditional definition or to the Constitutional intent of the role of the Congress in maintaining the value of our currency.

Seth Lipsky, Editor of *The New York Sun,* has written a masterful essay in the Summer 2011 edition of *National Affairs* entitled "What is a Dollar?" in which he describes how we came to this point in defining the dollar in these terms, the damage it has done to our economy and order in world trade, and what we should do about it. In brief, we should start by restoring some semblance of the Bretton Woods accord that provided the foundation for stability in the dollar as the world's reserve currency from 1944 until Richard Nixon dismantled the system in 1971.

In *Forbes* magazine, Charles Kadlec catalogues where we have been since that dismantling in terms of economic growth, inflation, and unemployment. I won't bore you with all the numbers, except to pass along one startling point he makes that is clear from the data – that "the whole notion of an energy crisis since 1973 becomes a grand illusion created by the fall in the value of the paper dollar against gold!"

Needless to say, our purchasing power valuation policy has been a disaster for growth and prosperity and has been possible to sustain only because we have somehow maintained the dollar's position as the world's reserve currency, a luxury that may not last much longer if we remain tied to current monetary policy, and much less so if we buy into the further politicization of it with loony ideas like Barney Frank's latest.

At Last – A Sound Dollar Act

May 5, 2012

A couple of years ago, I wrote a brief review of a very good book, *Econoclasts*, by Brian Domitrovic, a professor of economics at Sam Houston State University. The book outlines the formulation, rationale, and history of the application of supply-side economic theory, with emphasis on the people who sparked the supply-side revolution beginning in the 1970s. Essentially, the story is about monetary policy at least as much as fiscal policy, because the policy mistakes there have been the primary culprit in most of the crises of the past century, including this one.

In a recent article in *Forbes* magazine entitled "The Weak Dollar Caused the Great Recession," Domitrovic returns to this latter point, explaining very convincingly that the rush to invest oceans of capital in housing, energy, and commodities between 2003 and 2008 was sparked by one thing – people lost trust in the value of the dollar. And history tells us that when this happens, people rush to hedges against superfluous dollar production, which incidentally is still underway. Domitrovic describes it in cause/effect terms: Cause – comprehensive devaluation of the dollar on the part of its government masters (the Fed); Effect – major investment shifting into hard assets corresponding to fear for the dollar's soundness. And as the flight from the dollar proceeded, the financial sector whiz kids were prevailed upon to provide products to accommodate the new opportunities and niches.

I have been writing about this for several years, and adding that the real problem is that the Federal Reserve has long since abandoned its primary mission, which was the preservation of the value of the dollar as the world's reserve currency.

So, what's new? Finally, some members of Congress are responding in a realistic way to the underlying problem. Rep. Kevin Brady (R-TX) and Sen. Mike Lee (R-UT) have filed counterpart bills in each house that will simply give the Federal Reserve a single mandate: to maintain price stability. This would eliminate the dual mandate established by Congress during the Carter administration that included maintaining full employment, an unrealistic mission both now and then for an agency whose role never was contemplated to include micromanaging the economy as it has attempted to do in recent years.

More work will be needed, but this legislation will be a good start toward returning the Fed to its historical mission and possibly begin to restore the credibility of the dollar as the world's reserve currency.

The Bank Regulatory Dilemma

June 2, 2012

As a retired banker and one who struggled mightily through the Texas banking debacle of the mid-1980s, the current debate over the "too big to fail" problem resonates with me. I served as CEO of a sizable banking organization, but one that was not considered too big to fail, and I watched other banks that were so anointed receive preferential treatment from regulators who were woefully deficient in competency to deal with the massive asset valuation collapse of the time.

Tom Frost, of the venerable San Antonio banking franchise that bears his family name, has recently written a perceptive essay in *The Wall Street Journal* in which he decries the "too big to fail" moral hazard that plagues the banking regulatory environment, and suggests that the solution to the dilemma is to separate the two business cultures in commercial banking – the basic business of intimate depository and credit relationships with local and regional customers and the higher risk business of proprietary trading in global financial markets which threaten the first culture if they are allowed to exist within the same institution.

There was a time, 25 years ago, when I was supportive of the integration of these two cultures in the belief that the market was a corrective to abuses, but my experience in the 1980s and the continuing concentration of commercial banking assets in institutions that are so dominant as to represent a compelling moral hazard have changed my view. An institution too big to fail is too big, and we compound the problem by attempting to identify those institutions, bank and non-bank, that embody "systemic" risk, as the

Federal Reserve is attempting to do, thereby signaling that these will have priority with government assistance in the event of impending failure. This won't do. It actually increases the problem of moral hazard and is a further perversion of the regulatory overkill already embodied in the Dodd-Frank law.

As Allan Metzler of Carnegie Mellon University has noted, we need more capital in banks, not more rules, which are an inadequate substitute. Bankers can't add value without taking on risk, but commercial banks need to be able to respond to their customers without the burden of regulatory micromanagement, and with clear capital requirements that penalize them for excessive risk.

In addition, we need deposit insurance reform. Thirty years ago, FDIC insurance was $40,000 per account, and it was increased to $100,000 on a stealth basis in 1982. Now it is $250,000. The insurance of depository accounts was never intended to cover more than the funds of a modest household. Bank deposit reform has been elusive, but we should take it on, and it should require that institutions pay a risk-adjusted premium for insurance of accounts, in addition to introducing a sliding scale of coverage for depositors beyond a modest minimum coverage per account.

The bottom line is that Dodd-Frank should be recognized as a gross regulatory overreaction to a crisis and repealed. Then we can start over with the proper recognition of the characteristics of the two banking cultures, as well as revised capital requirements and deposit insurance reform that provide the proper incentives and consequences for risk management.

The Fiscal Mess, the Fed, the Dollar, and Gold

October 7, 2012

A chorus of pundits, experts, and opinion pieces is growing around the need for a completely overhauled monetary and fiscal policy infrastructure for the country. I say that we cannot move too fast to get about it.

Five senior fellows at Stanford University's Hoover Institution, including former cabinet level government officials involved in fiscal and monetary policy, recently collaborated on an essay in *The Wall Street Journal* in which they wrote, "The next Treasury Secretary will confront problems so daunting that even Alexander Hamilton would have trouble preserving the full faith and credit of the United States," and went further to describe current problems that are so bad that they are "close to being unmanageable now, and if we stay on the current path they will wind up being completely unmanageable, culminating in an unwelcome explosion and crisis."

One underlying current in this dialogue is the realization that a significant part of the problem is the U.S. system of fiat money, and this has moved talk of a return to the gold standard out of the shadows. In fact, the Republican Party platform includes a new provision that calls for a commission to examine "possible ways to set a fixed value for the dollar," and this wasn't added simply to appease the Ron Paul wing; there were some other serious thinkers pushing it as well. Steve Forbes believes that this issue and this commission will take on an importance over the next couple of years that will totally surprise the policy establishment, and for good reason. The world's economic and political realms are in disarray, and the one indispensable nation in turning it around is the U.S., whose current policy structure and priorities are an abysmal example of leadership. Thoughtful and serious people know this and will take action to correct it.

I recently attended a forum sponsored by Hillsdale College, which featured a panel on the history of and arguments for and against returning to a gold standard, and the arguments "for" were quite compelling. Given the daunting challenges described by the "five wise men of Stanford," it seems to me that we cannot begin to address these problems unless we cease and desist in debauching the dollar, the world's reserve currency, and defrauding the holders of dollar-denominated debt. I am persuaded that the only way to protect us from these ravages is to anchor the dollar to an external standard of value that has historically served as a pricing signal for policy correction. Whether this means a return to something like the Bretton Woods model that governed the international monetary system from 1944 to 1971, I'm not sure, but we need to give this idea serious and urgent consideration.

Regardless of the outcome of the gold standard debate, there certainly should be a major restructuring of monetary policy as currently practiced by the Federal Reserve. Under Ben Bernanke, it has been a disaster. The continuing policy of "quantitative easing" and managing interest rate levels at close to zero has destroyed the reliability of the pricing mechanism for borrowing and lending money, which is essential for the proper evaluation of risk and financing economic growth. This has resulted in a misallocation of available credit toward government and large corporate entities, not the best sources of innovation and job creation. There are trillions of dollars available for lending, but the destruction of a credible pricing mechanism has distorted the market for available credit and introduced uncertainties for both borrowers and lenders. Then Fed Chairman Paul Volcker faced the same policy options in the early 1980s, but opted to manage the money supply and let market rates adjust accordingly, which, along with Reagan's supply-side fiscal policy, produced very high interest rates and a very painful, but short-term recession followed by a clearing of the markets, the defeat of inflation, and 20 years of solid economic growth.

We need a return to this discipline and it begins with a commitment by the Federal Reserve, backed by Congress, to abandon its mission creep and return to its primary mission – the preservation of the value of the dollar. And a return to some form of a true gold standard would help make this possible.

More Misguided Fed Policy

January 5, 2013

Monetary policy continues in disarray and the Federal Reserve continues to act as though it can micromanage the economy by fine-tuning interest rates. Following its October announcement that it expects to keep rates low until at least 2015, it recently announced adoption of a policy that it will not increase interest rates until unemployment falls to 6.5 percent or inflation increases to 2.5 percent. This represents a return to monetary policy based on the Phillips Curve, the notion in economics that there is an inverse relationship between the rate of unemployment and the rate of inflation in the economy. This theory was refuted 30 years ago when the Volcker Fed crushed inflation, defeated "stagflation," and, along with Reagan's supply-side fiscal policy, launched the longest peacetime economic expansion in our history. And it was done without "managing" interest rates, but rather by managing the money supply to protect the value of the dollar and allowing rates to move with the market. It's incredible that we are going back to such an outdated theory. Tying monetary policy to unemployment doesn't work and is also dangerous for the economy. But what else is new for this administration?

David Malpass on Misguided Federal Reserve Policy

June 5, 2016

David Malpass, a research and consulting economist, is a former Treasury Department official under Ronald Reagan and a former State Department official under George H. W. Bush. In a recent hearing before a subcommittee of the House Financial Services Committee, he delivered a devastating and valuable critique of Federal Reserve policy over the past seven years that should have received more attention than it has. Certain passages are worth quoting:

"I think the Fed has been hurting growth and causing income inequality by misallocating capital to bond issuers. By constantly replenishing its giant long-maturity bond portfolio, it biases the credit system in favor of bond issuers (who are responsible for 75 percent of U.S. credit growth over the past five years) at the expense of smaller borrowers, notably the small new businesses that are critical to U.S. dynamism. The Fed should change direction, including downsizing its balance sheet, reducing its $2.4 trillion in bank debt, reducing the interest rate it pays banks, and shortening the maturity of it $4.2 trillion bond portfolio. These steps would increase growth and income, especially for the middle class which has seen an unprecedented decline in real income during the recovery. These steps would also reduce the fiscal deficit..."

I want to make clear that I support the Fed as an institution. The problem is that Fed policies aren't working. Its concept of its mission has grown way too large and is not sufficiently focused on maintaining a strong and stable dollar. It has created a huge balance sheet and regulatory apparatus that hurt growth, and it is allowing itself to house inappropriate executive branch functions, such as the Consumer Financial Protection Bureau."

This is about as profound and concise explanation of a major part of the reason for our economic doldrums and weak recovery over the past seven years that I can imagine, and yet we continue to persist, as though somehow we hope that doing the same thing will soon provide a different result. In fact, Malpass goes further to remind the Committee that since former Fed Chairman Ben Bernanke explained his theory on which these policies are based in a lengthy op/ed in November 2010, the Fed has been projecting that fast growth based on these policies will start working, but that it has had to slash its forecasts in every single year since. Isn't this close to a working definition of insanity?

16
National Security

The Shake Up We Need

June 3, 2002

The recent reorganization of the FBI in the wake of allegations and much evidence that it did not properly respond to serious warnings of terrorist activity last summer is long overdue, but probably not enough. I expect another round, possibly including much higher level terminations.

These preliminary steps at the FBI are but the first of many that will be necessary to transform our thinking. We need a major shift in our collective mindset and it will not be easy for Americans to absorb. For too long, we have lived with a false sense of security behind two oceans without fear of war on U.S. soil. To be sure, the Cold War was real, but psychologically, a potential nuclear conflict between two superpowers, each with much to lose in the exchange, is a much different threat than terrorism, which in many ways, is more insidious.

Compounding the challenge is that a primary role of our domestic investigative agencies will now of necessity be prevention, not apprehension after the fact. This means a transformation to a culture that allows for pre-emptive strategies that will no doubt conflict with many of our civil liberties. The American Civil Liberties Union already has expressed dismay at some of the recent policy changes. They haven't yet seen anything like what will be necessary to get the job done, and this conflict will almost certainly produce visitations to many of the liberals' most cherished judicial precedents of the past 40 years. Can you imagine the reaction in this country if we were subjected to a handful of suicide bombings like those in Israel? How fast do you think the prohibition of "profiling" would end? How quickly would vigilante groups be organized? How fast would airline pilots be armed?

In a recent *Wall Street Journal* essay, former Reagan undersecretary of defense Fred C. Ikle talks of the "political asymmetry of ends and means," by which he means that our current enemy, like the 19th century anarchist, seeks not conquest and expansion of his nation-state, but complete destruction of ours.

We need a shakeup (and wake up) that prepares us for a fundamentally different kind of warfare, a kind that is alien to our value systems. As Jonah Goldberg has suggested, this will also require "total war," a type that not only defeats the enemy's military capability, but forces a complete transformation of his society, as with Japan and Germany after World War II. Can we handle it?

Truth in Labeling

July 2, 2002

In a world so steeped in postmodern confusion that a U.S. President must resort to a spin on the definition of the word "is," it is not surprising that we have difficulty defining our enemies. Kathleen Parker has illustrated this confusion well in a recent essay in townhall.com in which she advises "you can't cure a disease without proper diagnosis, and you can't win a war without naming the enemy." Further to the point, a past president of the Southern Baptist Convention was roundly criticized for his characterization of Islam as a warrior religion that breeds terrorism. And, of course, we have the endless debate over "profiling" as a means of identifying possible enemies. In a great essay, Walter Williams points out the idiocy of the FAA's air travel security procedures, which "assign an equal probability that anyone who boards a plane is a potential hijacker." He recommends a multiple-choice test covering every significant terrorist attack against Americans over the past 30 years. (I will email the complete test upon request.) In every case, the perpetrators have been Muslim male extremists between 17 and 40 years of age. Duh? Is there a distinct profile here? The ACLU and FAA, take note!

As one Supreme Court justice (I've forgotten which) has said, "the U.S. Constitution is not a suicide pact." We are at war, and our defense must be preventive, and where necessary, pre-emptive. The editors of *National Review* have offered that the worst effect of creating the new Department of Homeland Security would be to create an atmosphere of activity without facing the difficult choices: profiling, arming airline pilots, pre-emptive strikes on the enemy abroad, and changing regimes in places like Saudi Arabia. But mission clarity begins with truth in labeling, and there are two parts to this in my mind. One is the question of what *The Weekly Standard* calls the "law-abiding terrorist," the true enemy whose acts we have traditionally treated as a law enforcement problem. The other is the cultural issue raised so eloquently by Roger Scruton: can we live with the Muslim next door, and can he live with us? Or, in other words, can we assimilate with a culture and creed that has had no Reformation and has no concept of the secular nature of government we inherited from Christianity and Roman law?

These are not easy questions for Americans to deal with, particularly in the procedural republic we have become. Even to pose them is to risk being denounced as xenophobic, racist, or (the worst postmodern sin) intolerant. Hollywood itself is guilty of ducking the issue as illustrated by the altering of Tom Clancy's novel in the screenplay for *The Sum of All Fears* to avoid Muslim stereotypes. But deal with them we must, and soon. What do you think? I would appreciate your thoughts.

Thoughts on the 9/11 Commission

April 1, 2004

While we are engaged in the typical American habit of self-flagellation and assignment of blame for the attacks of 9/11, I am reminded of an only partly facetious rule of thumb from the private sector in the form of the "five stages of a project:" 1) excitement and euphoria, 2) disenchantment, 3) search for the guilty, 4) punishment of the innocent, and 5) distinction for the uninvolved. Not a pure analogy, but close. Actually, prior to the prostitution of almost everyone involved in the ongoing pandering to the duplicity of former anti-terrorism "czar" Richard Clarke, there was some hope of productive work from the Commission, but the expectation that we can "get to the bottom of it" with conversation about what we knew and when we knew it is hopelessly misguided. The "bottom of it" is that there are two types of thinking about the War on Terror – pre-9/11 and post-9/11 – and there is absolutely no objective way to put ourselves back in the pre-9/11 thought box, because everything, and I mean everything, changed on that day.

Why can't we understand this? When will we grasp the fact that we must have a new way of thinking about U.S. engagement in the world, new ways of thinking about preemption and just war theory, about whether or not there must be an identified nation-state as the enemy in a state of war, about our long-standing relationships with our Middle Eastern "friends," about the degree to which we must merge domestic law enforcement and intelligence, about how much legal "due process" is owed those who intend harm to Americans, indeed, about whether or not the U.S. Constitution is being treated, as some have suggested, as tantamount to a suicide pact? (For an instructive view of the pre-9/11 mindset, I recommend Richard H. Shultz's article in the January 26, 2004 issue of *The Weekly Standard*, wherein he outlines nine reasons why, for example, a "seek and destroy" mission against al Qaeda prior to that day was considered strategically unthinkable and politically unpalatable.)

Even more importantly, we must think seriously about why we can't openly discuss these issues in an atmosphere of presumed good intentions. Have we lost this capacity for intellectually honest introspection? Have we become so cynical and so acclimated to the presumption of bad faith that we cannot expect integrity? For example, am I in the minority in being disturbed by the apparent fact that a large number of people actually believe that the Iraq war was "a scheme hatched by Bush down in Texas for political purposes," that the war is mainly about control of Iraq's oil and war profiteering by Bush/Cheney's corporate friends, or that Osama bin Laden already has been captured and Bush is merely waiting for the politically opportune time to announce it? I am reminded of the late Christopher Lasch's 1979 book, *The Culture of Narcissism*, in which he laments "American life in an age of diminishing expectations," and I fear that the most devastating loss of expectation is that of the capacity for mature republican citizenship in the face of a significant challenge to our civilization.

Hurricane Watch

October 4, 2005

There is now a second event to be added to the one on 9/11 that will dominate George W. Bush's place in history, dictating as it will the future of "small government conservatism," the concept of federalism as we have known it, and as a result, the future shape of the Republican Party. No less an authority than Bill Clinton has remarked that the aftermath of Hurricane Katrina will force a debate on three questions: 1) what is our obligation to the poor, 2) what is the role of government, and 3) how do we pay for it? He is correct, and the answers will determine the future of the electoral revolution began by Ronald Reagan in 1980 that has been sustained for 25 years.

Those first two days after Katrina landfall of images outside the New Orleans Superdome – the teeming masses of the primarily black, poor, and dispossessed that have reportedly been "seared" into the memory of Americans – should be a condemnation and refutation of 40 years of the Great Society social engineering experiment, images of big government dependency that should also be a wakeup call to finally bury this experiment on the ash heap of utopian fantasies. Will it be so? We will know very soon. It's all about expectations, their management, and the choices we make, on two levels.

On the first level, the New Orleans restoration, the President has set the expectation level pretty high with his statement that "there is no way to imagine America without New Orleans; this great city will rise again." The added question on this point, however, is what kind of New Orleans? To this I simply say that no rational investor, public or private, should invest a nickel in the restoration of this clearly dysfunctional city under the jurisdiction of current management. We should have seen enough incompetence and corruption, and regardless of how much or how little of the city is restored, there should be a trusteeship appointed to manage its affairs until there is satisfaction on the part of the public investors that it can be responsibly returned to local elected officials, after a new election to determine who those will be. Nor should anything, but the minimally necessary public infrastructure be rebuilt that cannot be privately insured. Let's put an end to the moral hazard of government indemnity and subsidy for below sea level homes and businesses.

As to the second level, the future of disaster response, in the wake of 9/11 and the creation of the Department of Homeland Security, performance expectations have been totally disconnected from reality and deliverables. Our system of federalism doesn't contemplate a primary role for the Federal government in natural disaster preparedness and recovery, nor should it. Large public sector bureaucracies are still bureaucracies, with all the inefficiencies, perverse incentives, and biases against decisiveness that come with that designation. They are by nature risk averse, not decisive. As Daniel Henninger has so well noted, the forces that have caused the deterioration of performance across the public sector spectrum, from education to welfare to disaster recovery, are now eroding the one most essential function of government – providing for the citizens' personal security. It follows that the one thing we don't need is more of the same in response to this disaster. So, it's time to choose, and the electoral base that has sustained the Republican revolution for the past 25 years will be watching.

It's Time to Stop the Nonsense

June 2, 2006

"The upshot of the changes ahead is that Americans are now, and increasingly will become, less secure than they believe themselves to be. The reason is that we may not recognize many of the threats to our future... They may consist, too, of an unraveling of the fabric of national identity itself... Democracy may be hollowed out from the inside... The growing sense of power that will accrue to many individuals... could corrupt moral balances and erode moral disciplines... It could threaten the balance of healthy civic habits that have long sustained democratic communities." – Excerpt

from the Report of the U.S. Commission on National Security/21st Century, chaired by former Senators Warren Rudman and Gary Hart.

I wonder how many Americans took the time to reflect on this report or on these words as they pertain to our future as a community with a shared sense of purpose. Probably not very many, about the same number who have taken time to read and reflect on the Bush Doctrine, the most sweeping transformation of U.S. foreign policy in more than 50 years. I think about these points as I watch and listen to the daily grind of "us vs. them" talk shows, partisan bickering and posturing, CIA, and other agencies leaking for advantage, as well as other nonsense emanating from our political leadership class. I wonder if we really understand what is at stake here. As our reigning dean of Islamic culture, Bernard Lewis, expressed to *The Wall Street Journal*, "In 1940, we knew who we were, we knew who the enemy was, we knew the dangers and the issues… It is different today. We don't know who we are, we don't know the issues, and we still do not understand the nature of the enemy."

Jean-Francois Revel, recently deceased, described as France's most prominent intellectual, often remarked on the dilemma of Western democratic societies, which have a tendency to self-destruction and, in fact, in his 1983 book, *How Democracies Perish*, he described democracy as "the first system in history which, confronted by a power that wants to destroy it, accuses itself… The distinctive mark of our century is the humility with which democratic civilization agrees to disappear and works to legitimize the victory of its mortal enemy." These words were written with primary reference to the Cold War with Communism, but are appropriate as well in our current confrontation with Islamofascism.

Why is this so? Revel seemed to believe it is a trait inherent in a regime which pursues liberalism and its tolerance to the point of undermining its own foundations. In his recent essay, "White Guilt and the Western Past," Shelby Steele has another idea, and I believe he is on to the core of the problem. To him, our tendency to hesitation and restraint in defending our civilization is the result of a minimalism growing out of the late 20th century collapse of white supremacy as a source of moral authority in the world. For this he blames white guilt from the perceived sins of racism and imperialism and notes that white leaders struggle, above all else, to distance themselves from these sins for which they have been stigmatized. As a result, any military action, however noble or justified in terms of the defense of our civilization, must be defended on two fronts with two separate victories – on the battlefield and on the front of dissociation from guilt. He further believes, and I agree, that this guilt is a major reason why we cannot truly confront the need for control of our border with Mexico. And it is this guilt for the historical sins of white moral authority, real or perceived, that is the primary source of anti-Americanism.

So, how do we stop the nonsense and turn this around? It won't be easy. Return to Bernard Lewis – we don't know who we are, we don't know the issues, and we still do not understand the nature of the enemy. Lynne Cheney often has said that it is difficult to defend what you do not understand or no longer believe. We are living off the accumulated capital built over almost four centuries of commitment to core beliefs, which were encapsulated by our founders in the political institutions that have provided our continuity. This continuity has produced enormous power and affluence and a lifestyle that is the envy of most of the world, but the degree to which we understand or still believe in the core tenets of our founding is questionable in my view, let alone whether we have the strength of our convictions necessary to overcome the guilt that Steele describes and to successfully export these beliefs.

In addition to the realization that we are engaged in the equivalent of World War IV, we also need to understand that we are one of the catalysts for and are in the midst of an Islamic Reformation from which it will be impossible to extricate ourselves, that it will no doubt continue for several decades and that a lot of people, including many Americans, will be badly hurt before it has run its course. This is a part of the uncertainty and anxiety that Rudman and Hart allude to in their report, and the jury on the final resolution of these anxieties will be out for a long time. The urgency of these points has been insufficiently explained to the American people, and if an when they finally resonate there is sure to follow the mother of all national political debates about the future of this country. So, we had better put a halt to the nonsense and begin the process of rediscovering who we are.

Can We Handle the Truth?

February 8, 2009

In all of the debate over the accusations of torture by the Bush administration, the alleged violation of civil rights perpetrated by abusers of the Patriot Act, the alleged mistreatment of prisoners and world condemnation of our detention facility at Guantanamo Bay, I am often reminded of the famous challenge issued by Jack Nicholson as Col. Nathan Jessup to his interrogator played by Tom Cruise in *A Few Good Men*: "You can't handle the truth!" Jessup was clearly in the wrong, but his plight was not without some sympathy in the context of our present predicament and that of those on the picket line manning the outer edges of our defense of freedom, as well as those who command them. I suspect that President Obama has a significantly more refined appreciation of the tradeoffs today than before he began receiving regular security briefings shortly after election day. So, when he said in his inaugural speech, "As for our common defense, we reject as false the choice between our safety and our ideals," he probably now has a much different perspective on this choice than the luxury of the campaign trail would allow. Closing Gitmo was a pander to buy a year's time with the anti-war, anti-American left, both at home and in Europe, and his apology for the past 20-30 years' treatment of Muslims over Arab TV, extremely disappointing and misguided on its own, will appeal to the same sensibilities. But these gestures also will send a message of weakness to a world that understands only one thing – power and the will to use it. Obama is a lot closer to the truth and the realities than he was a couple of months ago. Let's see if he can handle it.

An Instructive Convergence

May 6, 2013

I was struck during the past several weeks by an interesting and instructive convergence of events – the 10th anniversary of the invasion of Iraq by U.S. forces, the terrorist bombing at the Boston Marathon, and the dedication of the George W. Bush Presidential Library. Remembrances of the Iraq invasion returned us to the commentary and debate on the wisdom of that decision and the relative success of the mission. This commentary segued into a retrospective on the Bush presidency in the context of the ceremonies surrounding the opening of the Bush library. And the Boston bombing drew attention to probably the most significant aspect of the Bush legacy to date – that whatever his deficiencies, this is the first terrorist attack on American soil since 9/11, a testimony to the efficacy of his much maligned homeland security policy.

These converging events involved a lot of conversation about Bush 43. Whatever else you might want to say about him, he was a President of character and conviction, and although the outcome of the Iraq invasion will not be fully conclusive for quite some time, it is conclusive that he kept us safe and that President Obama would do well to reinforce the homeland security policies he left in place.

From the Bush Doctrine to What?

June 1, 2013

I often said during the George W. Bush administration that whoever succeeded him would be hard pressed to find a better strategy for the defeat of radical Muslim jihadism than the Bush Doctrine. And, in fact, President Obama has used significant elements of it to great advantage during his term, without directly crediting its author, of course. But now, with his May 23 foreign policy speech at the National Defense University, the Bush Doctrine appears finally dead.

What will replace it? Bret Stephens of *The Wall Street Journal* characterizes what he heard in the President's speech as "The Retreat Doctrine," and a good case for this terminology could be made in the obvious gradual and intentional withdrawal of American power and commitment to the principles outlined in the Bush Doctrine and the Congressional war authorization following 9/11. And why not, if the President can simply and unilaterally declare that "the war on terror is over?"

But there is abundant evidence that this war, which arguably began in 1979, is a long way from over, and what I heard and read in the speech was a misguided return to the mentality of 9/10, when terrorism was considered a widely diffused threat conducted by disparate individuals that could be managed with law enforcement, good intelligence, and civilian courts, without the weapons and mindset of wartime footing.

This mindset also ignores the best analogy to the current conflict, the Cold War, which we waged for more than 40 years and which was declared over when our opponent dissolved and we won! In his 2007 book *World War IV*, the name he gives to the current conflict, Norman Podhoretz writes that the proper name for the Cold War should be World War III. And in making the analogy, he offers comments by Eliot Cohen of Johns Hopkins University in his description of the characteristics shared by III and IV: "That it will in fact be global; that it will involve a mixture of violent and non-violent efforts; that it will require mobilization of skill, expertise, and resources, if not vast numbers of soldiers and a conventional front; that it may go on for a long time; and that it has deep ideological roots."

Likewise, the Truman Doctrine, which gave substance to our policy in response to the worldwide Soviet threat in 1947, is analogous to the Bush Doctrine in response to 9/11.

We forget this history, abandon a doctrine that has worked, and revert to a pre-9/11 mindset at our peril.

France Has Its 9/11

February 4, 2015

From all the many responses that I read to the January 7 terror attack and massacre at the *Charlie Hebdo* offices in Paris, I will highlight a few and add my own thoughts.

First, in a *Wall Street Journal* opinion piece by Ayaan Hirsi Ali, who knows a thing or two about real terror, she leads by writing that "perhaps the West will finally put away its legion of useless tropes trying to deny the relationship between violence and radical Islam… in too much of Islam, jihad is a thoroughly modern concept. The 20th century jihad "bible," and an animating work for many Islamist groups today is "The Quranic Concept of War," which argues that, because God, Allah, himself authored every word of the Quran, the rules of war contained in the Quran are of a higher caliber than the rules developed by mere mortals, and… the key to victory taught by Allah through the military campaigns of the Prophet Muhammad, is to strike at the soul of your enemy through terror." She finishes by instructing us that we must acknowledge that today's Islamists are driven by a political ideology embedded in the foundational texts of Islam, and act accordingly.

As we have seen, she is not welcome to speak at a number of our best universities, which is unfortunate for us on several levels, not least because she is blessed with a wealth of courage and the moral clarity we need to hear.

The second response that resonated with me most emphatically was the speech delivered by Newt Gingrich at the Iowa Freedom Summit on January 24. In it, he like Ms. Ali made a number of clarifying points about radical Islam and then closed with two compelling instructions: 1) we must have the same commitment and the same concerted effort to confront and defeat radical Islam that we did in confronting the threat of Soviet Communism beginning in the period 1945 to 1950, and 2) you Iowans must demand that every candidate for President who comes to Iowa between now and the primary caucuses has a definitive answer to the question – how will this be done?

In the previous week, Gingrich had written an op/ed outlining specific work that should begin immediately by the Congress to evaluate the worldwide scope of the Islamist threat and the foundations of its ideological thinking and strategy, no matter how controversial the response. He followed by analogizing this threat and the necessary analysis to the famous "Long Telegram" written by George Kennan in 1946, which shaped the transition of American policy in dealing with the Soviet threat, and he suggests that we need an equivalent "Long Telegram" on the nature of radical Islam. This is great advice.

There were other good responses. From former Senator Joe Lieberman, who acknowledges that we are in a global war with radical Islam and says that the civilized nations of the world must accept this reality and the need for a global alliance against it, and from Bernard Henri-Levy, who insightfully characterized this as "the Churchillian moment of France's Fifth Republic, the moment to face the implacable truth about a test that promises to be long and trying."

What was missing? Most prominently, any coherent response from our commander in chief and leader of the free world. Not just because he was missing in action at the unity parade in Paris, but because he basically can't, or more likely, won't even identify the enemy. And we can't defeat an enemy we haven't identified.

Henri-Levy is correct, this struggle will be long and trying indeed, for as I have suggested before, Europe has for some time been in dire need of a wake-up call from its multicultural malaise of the past several decades. I was encouraged several years ago by German Chancellor Angela Merkel, who announced that attempts to build a multicultural society in Germany had "failed, utterly failed," and had the courage to relate the truth that there should be no immigration without assimilation, which begins with learning the native language. Now maybe there is hope that Charlie Hebdo is a real turning point for Europe, but it will be painful, not to mention impossible without considerably more moral clarity and room for the truth than has been in evidence.

As for the U.S., we are pretty far down the same pathway and in need of the same introspection and damage control. I repeat, we are the product of a long trail of classical liberal values dating from the Reformation and the Enlightenment that help us distinguish between our version of reason and that not only of radical Islam, but of the core beliefs of Islam itself. This heritage has been corrupted by the postmodern notion of multiculturalism to the point of confusion about who we are. Our intellectuals have failed us in this regard and they should repent and repair the damage, the sooner the better, before we develop a terminal case of the European disease. Let's hope this doesn't require a *Charlie Hebdo* event or God forbid, another 9/11.

Paris 11/13/15: A Game Changer

November 15, 2015

As I monitored the coverage from Paris over the past weekend on the terrorist attacks around the city and processed what this means for the future of the conflict with Islamic extremism, I felt compelled to write an addendum to the November 2015 edition. Without jumping to unreasonable conclusions, the following points are clear to me:

- This attack must dispel any notion that we are not at war with radical Islam and arguably have been since 1979. They hate us for who we are and what we stand for. No, Mr. President, this isn't an "attack on all of humanity and the universal values we share;" it is an attack on the slice of humanity and its values that calls itself Western civilization, which built modernity.
- We must abandon any sentiment that to identify Islamic extremism as the root ideology of our enemy is "Islamophobic" and that there is any moral equivalency with "religious extremism" generally. There are no Baptists, Methodists, or evangelical Christians who are blowing up restaurants and randomly shooting up concerts. This ideology must be attacked loudly and specifically.
- The view that the U.S. should allow the Islamic civil war now raging in the Middle East to be regarded as an avoidable involvement or one in which we can "lead from behind" with sporadic air strikes is naive at best. ISIS will come after us directly, whether or not we intervene.
- The leader of the free world needs to wake up and realize that the top priority for world leadership from the U.S. is not closing Gitmo or climate change, it is to lead the defeat of Islamic jihad in all of its manifestations. I wish I could be optimistic.

More of the Same from ISIS and Obama

July 4, 2016

Last November, in response to the ISIS sponsored terrorist attacks in Paris, I wrote a special post in which I referred to the date, November 13, 2015, as one we will remember as a "game changer" in our war with radical Islam. Then in December came San Bernadino and in March came Brussels. Now on June 12, we had yet another such event to remember in Orlando which was even more devastating and my first thought was, has the game really changed since Paris? The answer is absolutely not – ISIS is on the march around the world and President Obama is still in denial as to the threat we face and even to the religious and ideological sources of the enemy's legitimacy.

When will we accept the fact that we are squarely in the middle of an almost worldwide civil war for the soul of Islam that will play out over many years much like the Reformation in Europe? The view that the U.S. should allow this civil war to be regarded as an avoidable involvement or one in which we can "lead from behind" with sporadic and surgical air strikes is naive at best. It will require the active involvement of NATO, as well as virtually every element of our vast intelligence, military, and diplomatic resources.

The leader of the free world needs to wake up and realize that the top priority for world leadership from the U.S. is not closing Gitmo, climate change, or transgender rights in the military forces, it is to lead the defeat of radical Islam in all of its manifestations.

President Bush made his share of mistakes in the Middle East, but he was right about a lot of things, primarily that our choice is to defeat the enemy there or be forced to defeat them here. And I should add that the two presumptive nominees to succeed Obama must get much more serious about what they will do to accomplish this mission come January. Right now, neither one of them is close to rising to the threat. The American people deserve much better.

How Many More "Enough is Enough?"

June 8, 2017

After Manchester and London again, this almost 40-year-old war is at a new level, and it's fair to ask when we will really get serious about global Islamic terrorism. Not the "we will defeat ISIS" pronouncements, but the kind of commitment that will be necessary to root out this evil from its sources. Islamic terror will not be defeated by military action alone. UK Prime Minister Theresa May came close to this kind of commitment after the most recent London attack, certainly far beyond her European counterparts, when she outlined a new strategy that goes directly to the Islamic ideology and will involve "difficult and often embarrassing conversations" with the Muslim community about the evil in their midst.

This is what we have needed for years and it will be very difficult, even more now because of several decades of coddling the "moderate" Muslims who, along with the ACLU and fellow travelers, consider any such talk deemed critical of Islam

Islamophobic and because of the failure of immigration policy and assimilation, especially in Europe. As Chilton Williamson notes in his book, *After Tocqueville*, Muslim immigrants and their offspring are demanding not integration with the natives on equal terms but acceptance by them on terms favorable to, and dictated by, Islam. And "when a weak and uncertain majority culture – like that of Europe – lacking confidence in itself and in its past is challenged by an assured, self-confident, and aggressive minority – such as Islam – the consequent conflicts are likely to by settled in favor of the minority." But in spite of these liabilities, these difficult conversations must begin soon, along with much else, political correctness be damned.

More broadly, we need to immediately rally the West against the Islamic ideology and its propagation, whether in mosques, madrassas, or the internet, and we should demand cooperation in this effort from our Middle Eastern allies. We should also require that Facebook, YouTube, Twitter, and other outlets of social media join in fighting the radicalization for which they serve as a conduit, even if it means some censorship, either voluntarily, or if necessary, involuntarily. Our Constitution and First Amendment are not suicide pacts. We should not allow people to come to this country to preach and foment violence against our people.

We must also return to our roots, as Pope Benedict so well outlined more than a decade ago in his lecture at Regensburg. For if we have forgotten who we are, we will lack the moral clarity to deal with this crisis. And I would remind you that the enemy suffers no such confusion with a quote from Osama Bin Laden: "There are only three choices in Islam: either submit, live under the suzerainty of Islam, or die."

17
Politics

Special Pre-Election Issue
October 1, 2000

This edition will be devoted entirely to thoughts I have been collecting over the past several months about the Presidential election. First, I should come clean with my bias. None of you are likely to be shocked by my admission that I am a supporter of George W. Bush. So what else is new? But far beyond partisanship, the critical point is that this election is not about who gets what; it's not about the minutiae of policy; it's about who we are.

What do I mean? No less an authority than Bill Clinton has said that this election is the most ideological since at least 1980. For one of the few instances, I agree with him. For the political left, if the Democrats cannot keep control of the executive branch, the ideological foundation of statist policy that has dominated political discourse since the Great Depression is at stake. For those of us who saw the Reagan Revolution as a watershed return of conservative values, it is a test of the validity of that optimism. I believe we are entering a transforming period in our country's existence during which we will be forced to answer some defining questions about ourselves. Will we continue to be a society that is guided by morally ordered liberty under the rule of law? Can people who have learned that they can vote themselves prosperity sustain a republic? Is civic republicanism worth saving? Can it be saved? Do we care? Can we still reach for that distinctive American idealism that says it's more important to live nobly than to live well? Frankly, as I have observed the events of the past several years, I am fearful of the answers to these questions.

Having said all that, there are major ideological issues at stake and huge differences between Al Gore and George W. Bush that should be made clear. After Gore's acceptance speech at the Democratic convention, commentator Chris Matthews said that Gore's platform was "a program designed for the special pleaders about the particulars of what's in it for me, a policy wonk speech with no great themes." Peggy Noonan commented that the speech could have been given by Walter Mondale in 1984 or Edward Kennedy in 1980. On the other hand, Bush's convention speech, if you listened carefully, acknowledged that politics at its most basic level is a duel between competing belief structures, a clash of cultures. And he's right. Gore would have us return to the progressive ideology of the early 1900s espoused by Herbert Croly and John Dewey, a collectivized marshaling of government power as the only bulwark of the weak against mysterious "powerful forces." George Melloan has called this tendency of the Democrats the socialization of risk and the politics of fairness (as they define it). The Republicans at their best have traditionally countered with the politics of individualism, grounded in the Christian teaching that each person is a unique creature with inalienable rights, answerable only to God. Bush has to an extent melded the two with his theme of compassionate conservatism. I must add that I find this term redundant, because conservatism, properly understood, is compassionate, but Bush's point is that there is no inherent conflict between individualism and compassion. This will sell as long as he keeps the primacy of property rights the centerpiece of the campaign and remembers the huge investor class that has been created by the democracy of the market.

This clash of collectivism (or paternalism) vs. individualism (I prefer empowerment) in all its nuances, however simplified I have made it here, works its way into almost every domestic policy difference between the candidates. Take one example, income taxes. The difference in Bush's tax rate cut proposal and Gore's targeted tax cuts involves much more than the details of how to distribute a projected surplus. The argument is a moral one, and so far, it has been entirely debated on economic terms. Bush's version, based as it is on supply-side economics, wins the economic argument, but the more important argument is that tax policy helps determine the nature and character of civilized society and whether private property will have primacy over statism. Gore's tax proposal pits constituent groups against each other and puts the government even more in the business of doling out favors. I could go on to Medicare and Social Security, school choice, and other domestic issues – paternalism vs. empowerment.

Another key ideological divide concerns what many have called "honor" in public life. Here we have one candidate (Gore) who believes that honor and moral authority reside in the policies a leader advocates and one (Bush) whose conviction is that honor means duty to the law, the truth, and the integrity of the office aside from policy preferences. For one, policy and politics trump morality, for the other, the reverse is true. Another unfortunate legacy of Clintonism that should be defeated is the concept that politics trumps honor. Some journalists have written that this election is shaping up as a ratification of Clintonism no matter who wins. I hope not. In fact, I believe Bush can win only if he successfully draws a sharp distinction between his philosophy and style of leadership and that of the Clinton/Gore years. Large portions of the Republican Party, particularly business interests, are not comfortable with culture clashes and ideological crusades, but this remains an essentially conservative country, and he must make the case for individualism/empowerment over collectivism/paternalism, responsibility over victimhood, excellence over mediocrity, and morality over politics.

The idea has been floated that the party that loses the 2000 Presidential election will be subjected to massive reorientation. Both parties have "crazy aunts in the attic" in terms of issues that dare not dominate their campaigns at the risk of alienating their respective bases. In a parliamentary system, there would probably be half a dozen contending U.S. political parties. A truly "big tent" for each means that they must meet in the middle to get elected. As a result, gridlock may be with us for awhile yet. The problem is that we have a tendency to defer to the judiciary on many of the contentious domestic issues (see "The End of Democracy Debate," Sept. 2000) and muddle through on the economic issues (globalization, etc.). Unfortunately, this makes Supreme Court appointments a major issue in Presidential campaigns, never more crucial than in this one, given the current configuration of the Court and the prospect of what four to eight years of Gore appointments would do to the rule of constitutional law. Again, it's all about who we are.

Reflections on the Election

January 1, 2001

It is difficult to find much to add to the saturation of commentary on the almost surreal election "overtime" period, but I will hit a few points that stood out for me.

The most instructive aspect of the conflict in Florida was the U.S. history and civics lesson, primarily a refresher, as follows: 1) this country is (or was founded as) a federal republic, not a majoritarian democracy, of which the Electoral College is a central feature, 2) Article II, Section 1 of the Constitution makes the selection of Electors a state legislative responsibility, which not only makes this a political process, but a partisan one, as the Founders intended, 3) the notion that we can avoid partisanship through the arguing of legalities before the courts is a myth of the same type that permeated the Clinton impeachment hearings.

In a previous issue (Sept. 2000), I commented briefly on "The End Of Democracy Debate" and the degree to which we have abdicated the political process to the judiciary on many of our most critical policy matters. Lincoln cautioned us on this in his first inaugural address, warning that a people who so abdicate "will have ceased to be their own rulers." The U.S. Supreme Court, using appropriate judicial restraint, gave the Florida authorities every opportunity to get it right, and in the end, had no choice, but to overrule an overreaching Florida Supreme Court. My only wish was that Article II had been invoked by the majority opinion, requiring the Florida Legislature to do its job.

I will take some other lessons from this experience, primarily from those on the political left in this battle. Only the left, with its saturation by postmodernist "no truth" dogma, could factor into every deliberation sufficient cynicism to discredit the motives of every duly elected official involved with this process. Only the left, with its disdain for the objectivity of the law and the strict construction of the Founders, could dismiss the authority of the Florida Legislature as the "ultimate partisan act" and a "blatant attempt to go around the will of the voters." This is highly irresponsible rhetoric. Only the left is dominated by the view that power trumps principle and that the rule of law is a license to manipulate the law to your best advantage, regardless of the by-product. And the worst of it is that we are led by a complicit media to believe in the moral equivalency of the posture of every demagogue, regardless of the merit of their argument, to the detriment of civil discourse in the body politic. If you want a primary reason why people are turned off by the political process, start right here.

A Clinton Retrospect

August 2, 2001

A part of me had hoped to allow Bill Clinton to go away with good riddance and without editorial comment and to simply accept his eight years in our faces as an unfortunate mistake on the part of a large number of well-intentioned people who were duped by the best political con man of the 20th century. And I have always begrudgingly given credit to Clinton where it is due – his amazing political instincts, his intellect, and his accurate perception of the transforming power of the technology-driven globalization of markets and culture. But the dominant part of me realizes that what we have witnessed is not, unfortunately, a passing fancy.

During the later months of Clinton's term, a number of prominent talking heads persisted in the notion that nothing Clinton did approached the level of culpability of Richard Nixon. I disagree. Nixon was paranoid, insecure, and darkly neurotic. But Clintonism will prove to have been much more insidious, because it undermines truth and promotes duplicity as a way of public life. It corrupts the process. Clinton perfected the "permanent campaign" and made it an acceptable governing style, and the reasons we will "miss" him are the traits and legacy that make Clintonism so dangerous – the demagoguery, the duplicity, the solipsism, and the innate ability to be the chameleon, to morph into whatever one needs to be to please the immediate audience – a psychologist's dream!

Clinton often has been described as our first baby boomer President, but more importantly, he was our first postmodern President – the truth is totally situational. As John O'Sullivan has noted, he is a different person for everyone he meets, and in the process, he fulfills every fantasy of the postmodern elites, because they can never repudiate him entirely or permanently. I'd like to think this was an aberration, that Clintonism will pass along with Bill Clinton. I'm not optimistic. The American people gave him a pass; we succumbed to the notion that morality and core principles are manifest only in public policy initiatives, that tolerance is the greatest virtue and that to judge is the greatest sin. "An ignoble moment for a great people," in Bill Bennett's words. Quite a few of his former "enablers," primarily Democrats who no longer need him, have now surfaced to condemn various aspects of his tenure in office. Many have said that this or that transgression "must never happen again." What must never happen again is to elect as President someone with as deeply flawed character as Bill Clinton. George Will said it best: "he is not the worst President the republic has had, but he is the worst person ever to have been President."

"Let's Have an Argument"

April 8, 2002

I am borrowing the title of this essay from one written by David Brooks of *The Weekly Standard* in August 2001, wherein he chides the Bush administration for being too defensive in policy initiatives and "strategically crippled" in pursuit of the centerpiece of the Bush Presidency, compassionate conservatism. Of course, this was pre 9/11 and a different Presidency. It would be difficult to characterize Bush's leadership in the war on terrorism as anything but masterful, at least until his April 4 message on the Israeli/Palestinian conflict, about which more below. Having said this, there have been serious mistakes lately. Last month, I mentioned the steel import tariffs and the farm bill. These were damaging enough, but now we have a whopper – the campaign finance reform bill. If there will ever be a case made for a veto, this was it, not only on constitutional grounds, which are obvious, but because the legislation is contrary to the principles on which the President campaigned and won, against the primary supporter of the Legislation!

In September 2000, I wrote briefly of the "end of democracy" debate, which is primarily about the undermining of the integrity of our republican system by an over-active judiciary. Unfortunately, the new campaign finance law does further damage, not only by deferring to the judiciary on a clear constitutional issue, but by its terms constricting issue advocacy and thereby adding a measure of incumbency protection.

It has been suggested rather harshly that the approach of the Bush administration to domestic policy legislation is, in many respects, "intellectually dishonest." That may be a strong indictment, but it seems to me that the approach does ask that we believe that people cannot be expected to understand the logic and merit of conservative public policy in the light of Democratic/liberal/media-driven efforts to demagogue and discredit it. It further assumes that this liberal cabal has won in the market for ideas and that the electorate cannot be expected to cut through the demagoguery to know what is the public interest and who represents it. I strongly disagree and, even if I'm wrong, the fight and the argument are worthy of the risk.

Government is Still the Problem

August 3, 2002

"If the choice is between doing too much and nothing at all, I'll choose the latter every single time." – Jonah Goldberg.

"If you see 10 problems rolling down the road, nine of them will roll into the ditch before they hurt you." – Calvin Coolidge.

Thank God Congress soon will be in recess! Maybe back in "flyover country" members can listen to some common sense about the frenzy over corporate misdeeds and what to do about them. When I hear people like Sen. Paul Sarbanes declare, "we're out to restore capitalism," and the bill to increase regulation of the accounting profession is approved by the Senate on a 97-0 vote, I fear for the republic. Even the vote to declare war on Japan was not unanimous.

Where do we get this idea that it is the business of government to intervene in every instance where there is tragedy or economic loss? The political class has been led to believe that there should be a government answer for every misfortune, including those that are the result of the vagaries and over-indulgence of the market. It reminds me of the old comic strip, "There Oughta Be A Law." Why is this the case? Because the people expect it and the political class, both Republican and Democratic, is only happy to accommodate. I submit this came from an entitlement culture that grew out of the progressive philosophies of the early 20th century and was given impetus by FDR and his four freedoms. If entitlement doesn't drive greed and deceit, it gives them a big push.

Do we need some corrective measures to shore up corporate governance? Sure. Do we need to correct the glaring conflicts of interest in the accounting/consulting and investment banking industries? Absolutely. And the crooks should go to jail. But the markets will punish substantially all the non-criminal bad behavior and have done a pretty good job of it already, with U.S. market losses of about $1.5 trillion since the first of July alone. In my opinion, we have now reached the point where the markets now fear regulatory overkill most of all. More regulation and more government is not the answer. More integrity is. Rules are never a substitute for ethics.

There is nothing new here, but as one analyst on CNBC pointed out, people are watching and want to know what behavior will be rewarded and what will be penalized. And while we're on the subject of ethics, who gave us our most recent lesson? Which teacher-in-chief (President) of the past 22 years was most instructive on this subject? Was it the "decade of greed" of the 1980s that produced this phenomenon? No. It was the "irrational exuberance" of the 1990s, during which we were pondering the definition of "is" and wondering whether character counts! And, by the way, does anyone care to compare business waste, fraud, and abuse with those of government? No contest.

Meanwhile, President Bush and the Republicans have joined the push to find a government solution. I just hope we can get past the November elections before permanent damage is done.

Domestic Timidity

October 5, 2003

In my view, President Bush's re-election prospects depend less on our success in Iraq than on his success on the domestic front, read broadly to include the economy of course, but also spending and other aspects of domestic policy. Frankly, although they have been relatively muted in their criticism, much of it so far has been a disappointment to his core base of movement conservatives. The litany of obvious mistakes has been well documented – the steel tariff, the agriculture subsidy bill, etc. – but there have been at least as many mistakes of omission as of commission. My concern is that the President has not used the "bully pulpit" and his position as "teacher-in-chief" nearly to the extent that he should. There are numerous examples:

- The Supreme Court decision in the University of Michigan affirmative action case that effectively entrenched the concept of diversity through racial preferences as a compelling public interest was, in effect, applauded by the White House.
- The tax cut was a big victory, but was sold by the administration simply as a stimulus package, without any reference to the validity of supply-side fiscal policy or its long-term impact on the size and role of the government in people's lives.
- The most significant reason for the return of budget deficits is the largest non-defense discretionary spending spree since the Great Society of the 1960s, mostly for education, healthcare, and transportation, which was largely condoned by the administration.
- Bush is the first President since John Quincy Adams not to have vetoed a single bill at this point in his term in office.
- The Senate Democrats get away with blocking Bush's judicial appointments without a serious fight and without even a real filibuster, allowing advice and consent to be completely subverted into a partisan contest requiring a supermajority for confirmation.
- Aggressive leadership on the wedge cultural issues that are crucial to social conservatives is avoided except for glancing references in occasional speeches.
- Spending on "corporate welfare" has reached record levels, almost three times the amount that will be spent on the war in Iraq this year, and, in the case of the agriculture subsidies, undermines our credibility in world free trade negotiations.
- The plan to privatize Social Security has taken a back seat, and the priority of marketizing prescription drug benefits and Medicare has obviously been subordinated.
- Legislation to provide school choice for the District of Columbia, which would provide a major breakthrough for the concept nationally, is languishing in the Senate without significant vocal support from the White House.

Does this resemble the party of Ronald Reagan? Is this all that is left of the Gingrich Revolution of 1994? Has "compassionate" conservatism become "big government" conservatism? Bush has already proven himself as a transformational foreign policy and wartime leader and, unless the Democrats significantly improve on their current message, he probably will be re-elected provided the situation in Iraq does not become a disaster and the economy continues to rebound, but I remember a line from his acceptance speech in 2000 – "they did not lead, we will," and I believe he and his advisors are underestimating the latent political support for much more aggressive advocacy of conservative domestic policy. He should use his 2004 State of the Union message to aggressively re-launch such an agenda.

If this is Governance, I Prefer Gridlock

January 5, 2004

As much as he deserves credit for his bold foreign policy, the President deserves criticism for a total lack of restraint in domestic spending, and as much as they wish, administration apologists cannot lay it off on wartime spending as the culprit. As the Heritage Foundation reports, since 9/11, 55 percent of the total federal spending increase of $296 billion has been in areas totally unrelated to defense and homeland security, discretionary in the sense that lawmakers have control over them. And this is before any impact of the prescription drug benefit bill. Some Republican leaders have responded that this, as *The Wall Street Journal* calls it, is "the price of governance" as the majority party in order to be responsive to voter concerns and "getting things done." But overall spending grew by 21 percent over the past two years, under a government whose legislative and executive branches were both under Republican control for the first time in 50 years, and George W. Bush is the first President since John Quincy Adams not to have vetoed a bill at this point in his term. Is this the party of Reagan and the party of the Gingrich Revolution of 1994 and the Contract with America? Maybe divided government isn't so bad – let's hear it for gridlock!

Swift Boats and Old Scars

September 1, 2004

Of all the heat and light sparked by the campaign of the Swift Boat Veterans to discredit John Kerry, I have been struck most by two perceptive essays written one day apart by David Broder of *The Washington Post* and Daniel Henninger of *The Wall Street Journal*. Essentially, both of these pieces cut through the daily hair-splitting over the particulars of the events of Kerry's Vietnam service to the crux of the issue

– the "cauldron of memory," as Henninger calls it, of the culture war that grew out of the 1960s and that has divided the baby-boomer generation ever since over the war in Southeast Asia and the cultural revolution for which it became a metaphor. Broder harks back to Marilyn Quayle's speech to the 1992 Republican Convention in Houston: "Remember, not everyone demonstrated, dropped out, took drugs, joined in the sexual revolution, or dodged the draft. Not everyone concluded that American society was so bad that it had to be radically remade by social revolution…Though we knew some changes needed to be made, we did not believe in destroying America to save it." I was present at that speech and it resonated with me, for I was a borderline baby boomer at The University of Texas supporting Barry Goldwater in 1964 and soon afterward watching closely as the "make love, not war" groups were in formation along the West Mall and The Drag on the UT campus. I was in hot debate with the John Kerrys of my world then, and very little has changed.

Kerry's testimony before the Senate Foreign Relations Committee in 1971, which has been rerun several times recently, brought back old and painful memories, and old anger. For his testimony was not just about the accusations of military atrocities committed in the field of battle that has the Swift Boat Vets so ballistic; it was about his condemnation of what he and his wing of his generation considered the atrocity of U.S. foreign policy in its entirety, not to mention the American society that had produced it, i.e., America is the problem. In many ways, this is the pedigree of Michael Moore.

A number of my friends and I have wondered, how could Kerry and the Democrats have been so misguided as to allow all these ghosts to be awakened by having his Vietnam War record become the centerpiece of this campaign without apology for his denigration of the country and its heroes who fought it? Henninger has the answer: it's a matter of principle – opposition to the Vietnam War is the moral foundation of the modern Democratic Party, and Kerry thought he could have it both ways. Condoleezza Rice made the same point when she noted that Vietnam is the lodestar of 1960's protest and Democratic Party principle – we were wrong and America is to blame.

Broder completes his essay by predicting that this aspect of the cultural divide will not rest until all of my generation has passed on. He may be right, but it's about more than a war, it's about a worldview, and until then, it's "us versus them," and we know who is on our side.

Special Post Election Edition – Perspectives on the Outcome
November 4, 2004

Surprise, surprise! Character and moral values count. One of these days I will learn to have more confidence in the judgment of the American voter. On the eve of the election, I was very concerned that the electorate was about to set aside its natural conservatism and basic value judgments and be fooled again by an opportunistic charlatan. My thinking was that a country that can elect a Bill Clinton twice could certainly elect a John Kerry. O ye of little faith! Obviously I had an unwarranted lapse of it, because the American people, in their largest turnout in history, penetrated the façade and made the final determination that, particularly in a period of crisis, character and conviction matter most, and voted their deepest held values.

Contrary to most analyses, which placed the war and the economy as the top issues for voters, both were edged out by moral values, and of the 22 percent of voters who emphasized these, Bush won 80 percent – 85 percent in Ohio! In fact, in retrospect, it can now be said that Kerry lost this race the night he attended the big Hollywood celebrity Bush bashing in New York, featuring Whoopi Goldberg and friends, and announced afterward that their presentation represented "the heart and soul of America." And don't forget the debt owed to the Massachusetts Supreme Court, which handed Bush a big wedge issue with its decision imposing gay marriage on the state. Not to mention Michael Moore, the poster boy for backlash from the cultural traditionalists. The bottom line here is that the left just doesn't get it – in determination of values, liberals emphasize the moral obligations of society, while conservatives reject this view in favor of personal morality and the obligations of the individual. Tom Friedman frets that this election not only reflects a disagreement over what we should be doing, it reflects big differences in what America is. I have news: that's what elections are about. At this point, the Democrats have ceded to Republicans the language and habits of the moral and spiritual sources of American public life, particularly those informed by religion. And there is more to come, because this phenomenon, as much as anything else, has resulted in a structural shift in party registration, from a 20-point Democrat advantage to a 37-37 percent tie in a generation.

Beyond the culture war, the election was a referendum on Bush and the Bush Doctrine, and here it is not an exaggeration to say that Kerry was almost irrelevant. Whatever the misgivings and disagreements over the pursuit and conduct of the war in Iraq, and there are many even among Bush's staunchest supporters, the American people were unwilling to return to the appeasement of liberal internationalism and the "nuanced" approach to the war on terror and Islamofascism.

A final point on tactics: I thought I would never see an election that turned on voter turnout won by Republicans. They have just never been as good at it as Democrats. Congratulations again to Karl Rove and the masterful organization that out-registered and out-hustled the vaunted Democratic machine in almost every precinct and overcame the longest and most vicious attack against an incumbent in recent memory, which was aided and abetted by almost every mainstream media outlet.

Implications

In a word – enormous. It is as big a watershed as any election at least since 1980, when we can only shudder to think of what a Carter re-election would have meant. Think now what the election of John Kerry would have meant – in terms of its messages to our allies and our enemies abroad, in terms of economic and trade policy, the direction of the judiciary, the restructuring of Social Security, entrepreneurship, tax policy, tort reform, not to mention again the cultural issues that drive policy, and on and on. There were big differences at stake here, more so even than in the days of Clinton, because as duplicitous as he was, at least he was a New Democrat, shamelessly willing to "triangulate" with the center-right on such issues as trade and welfare reform, whereas Kerry and his primary support base were clearly from the Old Democrat mold of internationalist appeasement abroad, big government, and one-size-fits-all solutions to domestic problems, protectionist trade policies, and pandering to the wide range of "victims" groups and their special pleaders through their allies in the plaintiffs' bar.

Of course, the biggest implication is likely to be the vindication of the Bush Doctrine, which is the boldest and most significant transformation of foreign policy since Reagan dumped containment and detente as the primary instruments of restraining the Soviet Union and decided to win the Cold War. A victory by Kerry would have meant a major course change, not necessarily in the short term in Iraq, but rather in a gradual return to the mindset of conducting the war on terror – defensively as a homeland security issue and offensively as a law enforcement and intelligence gathering function primarily carried out by international agencies, now popularly known as the "September 10th" approach. Whatever your sentiments about the implications of some of the Wilsonian aspects of the idealism embedded in Bush's worldview, this reversal of foreign policy under Kerry would have been a disaster for America and the world.

What Next?

"There's an old saying: Do not pray for tasks equal to your powers; pray for powers equal to your tasks." – George W. Bush in his acceptance speech on November 2, 2004.

What a striking contrast is this comment to what I can imagine Bill Clinton might have said in similar circumstances. This struck me as characteristic of Bush, the man – comfortable about who he is, humble about his capacities, confident in the sources of his strength, and resolute about his mission.

In the days since the election, we have been immersed by the analysts in the notion of Bush's responsibility to unite the "deeply divided country, "reach out" to his political opponents, "move toward the center" to govern, in other words, concede ground to the opposition on many of the issues on which he has just won the election. Not a word yet about any responsibility on the part of the defeated party to make similar gestures. I am again reminded of John F. Kennedy's remark on the day after his election in 1960, an election, incidentally, that was much closer, and in fact, was probably stolen: "The margin of victory was narrow, but the responsibility is clear." After all, Bush is the first President since his father to receive more than 50 percent of the popular vote, and only two Democrats since Franklin Roosevelt have done so. So, what else is new about close elections? There was or should have been no doubt about Bush's priorities nor how he would pursue them upon re-election, so anyone who voted, and more did than in any election in U.S. history, cannot plead ignorance. Also, as I have quoted Henry Kissinger many times, leadership is about taking people from where they are to where they have never been, and I would add that it is also about defining the governing priorities, not waiting to be told what they are. It has been noted this week that this election was the first truly "us" versus "them" election. Well, guess what? "Us" won. But don't think for a moment that "them" will abandon their causes, miss any opportunities to fight back with every tactical and political resource, obstruct where possible, and give Bush more than he wants in terms of a "loyal opposition" to his policy priorities.

Having said all that, Bush was on point in his post-election press conference that he will "reach out" to the reasonable opposition who want to assist with his mission, but that he feels vindicated in this mission by the election results and will use the resulting political capital to pursue it, and so he should. Does that mean "mandate?" What an overworked and misunderstood term, but this election comes as close to one as any in this century since FDR. So, what does this mean in terms of his immediate priorities? Aside from the war, at least six:

- Move quickly to document the "ownership society" with Social Security Personal Retirement Accounts, universal Health Savings Accounts, making the income tax cuts and estate tax elimination permanent, and replacing John Snow as Secretary of the Treasury with someone who identifies with entrepreneurship, such as Don Evans or Steve Forbes.
- Revive "compassionate conservatism" by aggressively moving to voucherize the faith-based initiatives he championed early in his first term.
- Push for early Senate approval of major reform of Federal tort law to attack the "tort tax" on small business and innovation.
- Take education accountability to the next level beyond the No Child Left Behind Act by aggressively supporting comprehensive school choice, beginning with voucherizing Title I funding.
- Return to the Reagan motto of "government is too big and spends too much," beginning with an early and significant veto of excess discretionary domestic spending.
- Send the distinct message that judicial appointments will be consistent with his worldview and that Senate obstruction will not be tolerated (he could, but probably won't, start here with signaling his disapproval of Arlen Specter as Chairman of the Senate Judiciary Committee). And, by the way, no David Souters!

Longer term, it obviously should go without saying that he should complete the mission in Iraq and deal decisively with the nuclear threats in Iran and North Korea, as well as keep the pressure on the Saudis and Syrians in order to further transform the Middle East and encourage the responsible Muslim community around the world to engage themselves in the reformation and/or elimination of their fascist components.

A large agenda, but, after all, a President's political capital is to be spent, not saved.

The New Governing Majority

January 1, 2005

In the approximately 40 years of my political consciousness, two events stand out as watersheds – the election of Ronald Reagan in 1980 and the election of the Newt

Gingrich-led Republican Congressional majority in 1994. The first represented the culmination of the maturity of the conservative movement, beginning in the mid-1950s, from a fringe, reactionary backwater, to a truly competitive, policy-based governing alternative. The second represented the consummation of the conservative revolution against the New Deal/Great Society legacy of overreaching 20th century liberalism. Both of these events set the stage for what now can be the advent of a new governing majority that, if properly led and managed, can last for several generations. From all appearances, it seems that George W. Bush is at the right place at the right time, with just the right temperament, to lead this transformation. It remains to be seen, however, whether the other necessary ingredients will be in place. These are, in no particular order of importance, as follows:

- The necessity of what George Will and Jonah Goldberg have called the use of "dogma and rhetoric over demagoguery." Relieved of the damaging demagoguery, dogma, and rhetoric are necessary elements of our political speech used for outlining priorities and policy boundaries. It is more important to know the "why" of policy than to know "what" and "how," for we should do things for the right reasons, and conservatives, Bush in particular, haven't been as adept with this skill as they need to be. The high ground on enlightened rhetoric and dogma must be captured and held.
- Avoid the diseases of incumbency and arrogance of power. The new governing majority will be short-lived if it fails to reject the sense of entitlement and perpetuation in office that were the diseases it was elected to cure. In the 10th year of conservative Congressional ascendancy, there are quite a few symptoms of these ailments now in evidence. Whither the Revolution of 1994? Its spirit needs to be revived very soon. Bill Clinton was fond of saying that you cannot love your country and hate your government. Maybe not, but you can and should want much less of it, particularly its corrosive tendencies to coercion and dependency.
- Have no fear of boldness. The forces of "progressive" opposition and the vested interests of the liberal status quo will be no less strident and vicious against half measures or "reform-lite" proposals on such issues as permanent tax rate cuts, Social Security reform, Health Savings Accounts, judicial appointments, and tort reform, so the motto should be to "go for the whole loaf," and don't buy into the "no mandate" nonsense.
- Trust the people. Clearly, this President has enormous capital with the American people, he says he will use it, and he should, early and often, by appealing to

them over the heads of the Beltway insiders. The liberal/left is back on its heels in disarray, greatly misunderstanding the innate and unique brand of American conservatism that is congruent with Bush's, and it's time to "close the deal."

- Most second-term Presidents are preoccupied with building or preserving a legacy and are leery of bold new initiatives. This one has an opportunity to be very different, in obvious ways by successfully completing the mission in Iraq and firmly installing the Bush Doctrine in U.S. foreign policy, but also by laying the groundwork for ending 20th century liberalism as we have known it, launching the "opportunity society" century and, as a result, a new governing majority. Go for it!

The New Governing Majority Revisited – Issues Big and Small

May 3, 2005

It appears that predictions of a new- and long-lasting Republican governing majority may have been premature, and in fact, if they don't start acting like a majority party pretty soon on a range of issues, they won't be one for very long! Of course, in any evaluation of policy priorities, there are big issues and small issues, issues that are transformational and those that are transactional. And it is the transformational issues that require principled leadership, significant expenditures of political capital, and in many cases, absolute party discipline; here are some examples:

- *The Bolton nomination to the UN* – to lose a nomination such as this would send the message that aggressive reform initiatives on behalf of a conservative President and outspoken critique of the liberal international order represented by a corrupt and incompetent institution in dire need of serious reform are out of line and detrimental to one's career.

- *Social Security reform* – there is a limited window of opportunity to completely change the 70-year-old social contract mindset from one of entitlement to one of ownership and move the national retirement system from an antiquated one based on defined benefit to a defined contribution system more aligned with the aspirations of ownership and inheritability. Personal accounts are transformational, salvaging the current system isn't; let's get on with it.

- *Judicial appointment confirmations* – capitulation here will serve to perpetuate the perversion of the constitutional principle of advise and consent, enshrine a super-majority precedent for judicial nominees, send the message that elections have only limited consequences, and condone and accelerate the trend toward judicial supremacy in matters involving core moral and social issues.

- *Permanent tax cuts* – in the face of all the accumulated evidence of its success, it is amazing that we still are debating the wisdom of supply side economics as a primary driver of economic growth, and continue to subject ourselves to the intimidation and demagoguery of the various "fairness" arguments.
- *Life and death issues* – it is time to put to rest the questions of the creation of embryos for cloning and stem cell research and move forward on the implementation of the recommendations of the President's Bioethics Council before the rapid advances of our science present us with a fait accompli and a perversion of what it means to be human.
- *Tom Delay* – his defense may seem marginal as a transformational issue, but if one of history's better enforcers of party discipline for the conservative cause can be eliminated from leadership because of indiscretions, that however unsavory, are fairly typical and of minor consequence, it will have a chilling impact on like-minded legislative leaders who, as a result, might be less inclined to confront or ignore the liberal media elite and their fellow travelers for many years to come.

All of these have a price, and some say a few of them exact a price too high in terms of "comity" and political fallout, but my response is that the bigger price will be paid for failure to aggressively pursue the wedge issues that are critical to the base of the majority, as well as the welfare of the country.

Presidential Resolutions

January 1, 2007

All the cuddly overtures in the spirit of bipartisanship on the part of the new majority that permeated the immediate post-election period will dissolve before the swearing in of the 110th Congress. In fact, most of that talk is disingenuous in the first place, because bipartisanship in the current usage only means one thing – you must see things my way and move toward my position on the issue at hand. Give me a break! What we have in this country is a major case of what Tom Friedman calls "systematic misunderstanding," which arises when your framework, or worldview, and the other person's framework are so fundamentally at odds that the impasse cannot be resolved by providing more information or facts. Since the end of the Reagan era and the Cold War, this nation is essentially a 50/50 split politically and the stalemate will not be resolved in the next 18 months, which is the length of time before the party conventions, the culmination of the nominating campaigns that already have begun. So it's on to 2008, which will be the next watershed event and in my estimation will be the most defining election for this country since at least 1980 and possibly since 1932.

What President Bush should resolve to do now is, first, remember that for all the talk on the left about "mandate," this election was not a repudiation of conservatism; to the contrary, there is abundant evidence that the results were as much punishment for the abandonment of conservative principles as anything else; second, he should establish the following objectives and resolve to "push the envelope" on them with the Democratic Congressional majority at every opportunity:

- Win the war
- Protect life
- Appoint strict constructionist judges
- Shrink government
- End Congressional "earmarks"
- Advance free trade
- Marketize healthcare and retirement finance
- Control the borders
- Expand the "opportunity society"

Third, he should make the principles that underlie these objectives clear to all and veto any bill that violates them.

What Kind of Leader?

April 2, 2007

What kind of leader can fill the role that America and the world need? Although many of us probably feel we already have heard enough presidential politics, at least in the unattractive style in which it is presented to us, it's not too early to get a fix on those qualities we want in a successor to George W. Bush. I will spare you my final critique of President Bush until later, but suffice to say, the low points of his term in office suggest that we will be looking for a much different type of leader, and that competence might very well be a leading theme. These things seem to run in cycles. I remember Michael Dukakis' remark during the 1988 campaign that "this election is not about ideology, it's about competence," and how far off base he was in that perception at the time. For 2008, it may be a different story. In a recent article, David

Brooks suggests we might be in the market for a wily, effective leader, one who has more of the cunning that our foreign enemies have exhibited, and a certain cleverness more than Gary Cooper-like simplicity and virtue. Rich Lowry of *National Review* thinks in terms of detail orientation, toughness, particularly in judgment of people, and proven management skills.

All of this is well taken and probably on point. But let's not forget two very important considerations: first, when the new President takes office in January 2009, we still will be a nation at war with an enemy determined to seek out and kill as many of us as possible by whatever means and who represents a form of totalitarianism at least as threatening as those we faced and defeated in the 20th century; and second, as historian Paul Johnson reminds us, America will sometimes need to play Leviathan at the risk of blood and treasure when there is a void in the rule of law, and we do so because we are a country founded on idealism. And in that role, we are the indispensable nation. If we elect leaders who forget these points, competence won't save us.

The Search for Relevance

July 5, 2007

It's time to discuss seriously the means by which President Bush can maintain some sense of order and mission to his remaining time in office or, as Bill Clinton found necessary in his dark days of 1994-95, the pursuit of relevance. Clinton found it in a gift from Newt Gingrich in the budget impasse over the government shut down. I have no good answer for Bush. In the wake of the immigration defeat, he will almost certainly have to find relevance to some extent in obstructing the various Democratic domestic schemes, but must also necessarily have some help from the war effort. In fact, so much depends on external events and the situation on the ground in Iraq, and almost no one hasn't made up their mind on that, or is open to be persuaded, or is even paying much attention to progress reports. In addition, it is clear that the administration is obviously tired and frustrated and the arguments for victory in Iraq are now fewer and even less often heard or heeded. The President is to be greatly commended for his persistence and determination and I continue to hold out hope that his mission will be vindicated in the end. The problem is that the conservative movement and the party that carries its banner may be irreparably damaged in the meantime, and many of its stalwarts have already bailed out.

It is one of the great tragedies that the mission in Iraq, as well as the broader mission against Islamofascism, has failed to gain traction on the points that were absolutely critical:

- the ability to achieve total moral clarity,
- success in identifying the enemy, and
- convincing enough opinion leaders of the magnitude of the threat, the consequences of defeat, and the necessity of pre-emption.

To compound the problem, all of these were undermined by 50 years of encroachment by the insidious ideologies of multiculturalism and moral relativism in our cultural institutions. But I continue to assert that, whatever the outcome of the election in November 2008, the President who takes the oath of office in January 2009 will be the President of a nation at war, and, if not the Bush Doctrine, had better have something pretty close to it ready for implementation. If nothing else, this fact will continue to sustain his relevance.

The Long Campaign: Are We Having Fun Yet?

January 6, 2008

I know I share the sentiments of many in the vapidity of the "audition" now in its 13th month that will ultimately decide who will succeed George W. Bush. Newt Gingrich had the right idea last year with his in depth sessions with Mario Cuomo to illustrate how a meaningful dialogue could produce real value for voters in a very short time frame, but no one was listening, so we are getting more of the same daily and nightly droning about who's up, who's down, who's "going negative," etc., to the point that, no matter how hard one listens to the candidates themselves, it becomes very difficult to have matters of substance fight their way through. And I admit that I am still undecided on my support in the campaign, but I have given considerable thought to the criteria for selection. Even this has been no easy task for, as Charles Kesler of the Claremont Institute has noted, conservatives face a particular dilemma that they have not had to grapple with recently, which is, in effect, to reinvent conservatism for our times and then identify the most appealing messenger for the concept.

Why is this so? Well, primarily, because the Reagan coalition that was fused among social conservatives, fiscal conservatives, and Cold War hawks has been in part rendered obsolete by our victory in the Cold War and in part undermined by "compassionate" (read big government) conservatism as practiced by George W. Bush and the former

Republican Congressional majority, as well as fractures in the conservative foreign policy establishment caused by the implementation of the Bush Doctrine. These divisions will not be healed overnight and the leadership for the transformation has not yet even begun to surface. And time is short, because as I have indicated previously, what we now see is what we get in November, and frankly I don't see anyone on the scene who has thought long enough or deeply enough about the issues to lead this transformation. Remember, Ronald Reagan's revolution began with the Goldwater campaign in 1964 and he had been formulating and honing his ideas for many years in dialogue with a number of policy advocates such as the Heritage Foundation, Arthur Laffer, et al.

Of one thing I am sure: this will not be a "post war election," in the sense that there is a feel that the war and security issues will take a back seat to domestic issues, as David Brooks has suggested. He may be right that there has been a shift in values and there is little doubt that there is an attitude of "what can my country do for me?" One look at the recent crisis in Pakistan should convince even the most casual observer that we will still be a nation at war in a very dangerous world in January 2009, which means that my criteria number one for U.S. leadership in that world will be a person who will endorse the continuation, in whatever name is chosen, of a foreign policy very close to the Bush Doctrine.

A Watershed Moment for the Conservative Movement

February 9, 2008

John McCain's almost miraculous comeback from near death as a viable candidate to the point of being the presumptive Republican Presidential nominee has put the American conservative movement in its most difficult spot since the rise of the right propelled Barry Goldwater to the GOP nomination in 1964. How the movement responds to this challenge will have very far reaching consequences for the next several decades. I have said that this election just might be the most critical since 1980 and possibly since 1932, and it is playing out just so, but the stakes are much higher for the Republicans and the conservative movement than for the Democrats and the left.

How did we get here? Well, in the first place, we conservatives have only ourselves to blame for painting ourselves into this corner. We allowed the revolutionary and euphoric election of 1994 to degenerate into a struggle to protect the perks of partisan power and the spoils of the majority. We looked the other way when our "compassionate" conservative President signed the campaign finance bill restricting political speech co-sponsored by John McCain, a bill creating a massive new drug entitlement program, an executive order expanding tariffs on imported steel, and an embarrassing farm bill that in effect repealed the revolutionary Freedom to Farm Act of 1996, among other projects of "big government conservatism." We didn't seem to notice or care when Tom Delay replaced the Democratic lobby teams on K Street with Republican teams representing the same special pleaders in the misguided and unprincipled Republican "K Street Strategy" that resulted in total complicity in the more than quadrupling of "earmarks" that has totally undermined the credibility and historic GOP reputation as the party of fiscal responsibility and limited government.

Secondly, although the conservative movement suffers from the absence of a coalescing leader, the problem is more about ideas than personalities. Reagan came to town with two organizing principles – shrink government and win the Cold War. He then infused us with enough renewed confidence in the American experiment of the "city on a hill" that we accomplished the second objective and temporarily succeeded with the first one. But the issues now are more diffused, most of them don't break out neatly along ideological lines, and don't as readily lend themselves to movement politics. Enter a moderate maverick with a mixed conservative record who is a favorite of the talk shows and the favorite Republican of most liberals. The conservative movement gags – is this the guy who will preside over the reconstitution of the conservative movement and redefine the organizing principles?

My short answer is NO. But it is what it is, and I believe we must recognize that we are in a transition period during which the movement will need some time to sort things out and identify the next generation of principled leaders around whom to coalesce. They are out there (a good example from the left is Barack Obama – where was he six years ago?). Meanwhile, conservatism has been the movement of ideas for the past 50 years, but recently has lost its edge and needs to regain it, so the gritty work of issue development must kick into high gear. And everything, but core principles should be on the table.

What about 2008? To me, it's not pretty, but it's simple: conservatives don't have the luxury of accepting a loss to Clinton or Obama in hopes of a "cleansing" effect of the electorate in preparation for another revolution in two or four years. As Daniel Henninger of *The Wall Street Journal* has noted, it's "McCain or the wilderness" and possibly for a long time to come. So whenever I get the urge to be passive about this election and the choices, I remind myself of the only possible answer to this question: Who do you want as Commander in Chief and to appoint the next two Supreme Court justices? All else is at least debatable and we can fight about it on another day, but if we get the answer to this question wrong there might not be another day for a very long time. Watershed moment, indeed.

Obama in Berlin: Citizen of the World

August 4, 2008

If John McCain somehow defies the current odds and defeats Barack Obama in November, analysts might look at a particular moment as the turning point. At no time and in no appearance has Obama revealed his worldview more vividly than in his appearance and speech before a reported 200,000 or more during his stop in Berlin on his recent grand tour of the Middle East and Europe. I was so struck by a couple of the bites on TV that I printed and read the full text of the speech, and it was most revealing, not so much for any policy pronouncements, of which there were none of any significance, but rather because of what it revealed about the man and his disingenuous and dangerous message.

This speech could have been the transnational progressive manifesto, because it reflected the worldview, not simply of a liberal internationalist of which there are many in America across the political spectrum, of one who has no concept of how American power and purpose has shaped and led the free world we have known since 1945, and no appreciation of how American led power and politics will be necessary to insure free world leadership in this century. From there, it goes without saying that he has no appreciation for the concept of American exceptionalism, which has informed and provided moral context for our foreign policy for more than two centuries. In short, there was in evidence no appreciation of the realities that make his "can't we all just come together and get along" appeal a trip through fantasy land. (David Brooks called it a "Disney" moment.)

Does he really believe in "global citizenship" as an objective reality? Does he think that the Berlin wall came down because "there is no challenge too great for a world that stands as one?" Does he really think that the success of the Berlin airlift of 1948-49 to which he referred was a testament to anything other than the stubbornness of an American President, a Democrat no less, along with this country's prowess and perseverance? And does he truly believe that "this moment," to which he refers on almost every campaign stop as a metaphor for his election as President, is the equivalent of a Godsend for the people of the world he addressed from Berlin? If so, such naivete, such arrogance, such presumption and demagoguery, is fraudulent to his base of supporters, and even worse than that, it may succeed.

POST ELECTION ROUNDUP

November 9, 2008

It has taken a few days to decompress and collect my thoughts on the election results, and I must admit that there really weren't many surprises, because in hindsight this one was pretty well determined some weeks ago, particularly after the market meltdown that began in mid-September. Many of us had hoped until the end that the polling would prove flawed, but let's give some credit there – it was remarkably accurate, particularly given the new internal polling dynamics created by the Obama phenomenon. In deference to those who just want it all to go away, I won't make an attempt to rehash the trite and the obvious, but will rather offer a potpourri of ramblings on where we might be headed.

What Does A President Obama Mean for This Country?

First reaction – who knows? It really depends on who shows up on inauguration day. Will it be the protégé of Jeremiah Wright and the colleague of Bill Ayers, the one who counts Warren Buffett and Paul Volcker as key advisors, the post-partisan healer and uniter, or the instrument of patronage for the menagerie of leftist interest groups? Or maybe it will be a composite of these. At this point, my guess is that we can be sure that it will not be a repeat of the Clinton era, because the dynamics are much different now. We are at a tipping point at which we are literally being forced into re-thinking the American idea, and the answers could take us in several directions. Folks, I am not being overly dramatic here – fasten your seat belts.

Back to the Future

A number of observers, mostly prominently Jonah Goldberg and Tony Blankley, have noted that there is nothing new in the Obama rhetoric, and they are correct. Aside from a "new" New Deal and Great Society, in this administration we will be consistently dealing with the underlying notion first articulated by the progressives of the early 20th century, led by Woodrow Wilson and surrounded by intellectuals such as Herbert Croly and John Dewey, who believed that the Constitution of the Founders was hopelessly antiquated for the needs of a democratic society. Heed the words of Barack Obama in a 2001 interview on National Public Radio: "…the (Warren) Court never ventured into the issues of redistribution of wealth and the more basic issues of political and economic justice… It didn't break free from the essential constraints that were placed by the Founding Fathers in the Constitution… an enormous blind spot that carries on until this day… the fundamental flaw of this country." We had best pray that Obama doesn't have an opportunity to replace Roberts, Alito, Thomas, Scalia, or even Kennedy on the Supreme Court.

The Center/Right Holds

I was greatly encouraged by several developments on election day that were directly counter to the surge from the top of the ticket, primarily the rejection of same-sex marriage in California, Florida, and Arizona, and the elimination of race and gender preferences in government employment in Nebraska and Colorado. The California result was particularly gratifying in view of the fact that Obama opposes the Defense of Marriage Act and he carried the state by 24 points. These results should provide additional caution not to pursue an aggressive advancement of the culture war through the appointment of activist judges, not that I expect the hard left to heed the caution.

It was also instructive that not one Republican governor was defeated for re-election. There are some good ones in office and they will be the core leaders of the revival of the ideas that will be necessary for a Republican comeback.

From Camelot to Grant Park

There is of course the real possibility that the Democrats will overreach, with or without the full support of the President, due to the zealotry of the party's Congressional leadership, which is far to the left of the American people and totally beholden to the various special pleaders who are the core constituency of the party. And this could turn ugly, depending on the degree to which Obama accommodates the more extreme elements of the left in his party. If he mishandles the elements that will demand immediate radical change, there will be a backlash from a body politic that remains center-right in its basic sentiments. In effect, there is the dilemma for Obama that he now presides over a governing majority that has a choice between being at odds with its base or with the nation it governs. Think of the relatively short distance from the early days in "Camelot" under Kennedy to the total meltdown of the Democratic Party in Grant Park, Chicago in the summer of 1968. Obama has been widely credited with a first rate temperament well suited for the awesome responsibilities of the office. We will soon learn whether or not this credit is misplaced.

Biden Was Right – There Will Be a Quick Challenge

Of all of George W. Bush's potential legacies, the one that I think will ultimately have the most resiliency is the one that is anathema to Obama's core leftist constituency –

the Bush Doctrine. This is the wake-up call that he probably already is receiving in the context of the daily security briefings in which he is now included. We are a nation at war. And, as such, there are various options available to a commander-in-chief, but in order to win this war, which must be done to maintain the security of this country, most of the options look a lot like the Bush Doctrine. He can call it what he wants, but the fact is that there has not been an attack on this country in more than seven years, and I strongly suspect that this has been due primarily to the success of this doctrine and its related provisions, such as the Patriot Act. Welcome to the real world, Mr. President.

The Great Anxiety

Last month I noted that the current market crisis comes at a time when the globalization of trade and employment and the challenges to the long-held principle of comparative advantage have given rise to worldwide anxiety about employment security and the related economic security of nation-states. This is particularly true in America, which historically had always felt itself somewhat protected by two oceans and a certain sense of exceptionalism. This is much less the case now, and I believe that this is one of the reasons that Obama is now President-elect, as well as one of the larger issues that needs to be addressed by both parties. But in this anxiety and the Obama response to it there is a caution, and it has to do with what Fouad Ajami of the Hoover Institution calls an underlying "sense of unease" that is manifest in the "politics of charisma" practiced by Obama, with the huge adoring crowds mesmerized by the soaring sense of expectation. This is not the American style, he says, but more the style of Arab and Muslim societies that has left them disappointed and frustrated over many years. This observation struck me as one that should give us pause – beware the earthly messiah/redeemer and promises of "salvation by society."

Meanwhile, to the Wilderness

Shortly after John McCain was nominated by the Republicans, I suggested that he was not even close to my preference, but that the only choice then remaining was "McCain or the Wilderness." Well, we got both. Furthermore, the Republican Party had best retire to a comfortable wilderness retreat very soon and engage in some deep soul-searching about its future. I will have more on this later, because it is worthy of much more space. Actually, the Republican Party itself is not, nor has it ever been my concern; it is important only to the extent that it serves as a successful vehicle for political conservatism. And on this point, for now it will suffice to express my scorn for those cowardly McCain staff members who have been anonymously scapegoating and undermining Gov. Sarah Palin (incidentally, without one word in her defense to date from McCain). Message to these small and petty nuisances – Sarah Palin has a future in the conservative movement; you and John McCain never really did and certainly don't now. Please go away quietly.

Finally, above all political considerations, I consider myself a patriot, and we have only one President at a time in America. So, while some of us might find disappointment in many of the results of the recent election, we should immediately find pride in and be profoundly thankful for the wisdom of the system that will again allow us to perform one of the miracles of the American experiment – the peaceful and relatively seamless transition of political power in the most powerful nation on Earth. That's pretty awesome.

More Nobel Thoughts

November 8, 2009

A number of additional thoughts have come to mind since the early October announcement of the Nobel Peace Prize for 2009 and my brief October posting on it "The Nobel: Are They Serious?"

First, it seems obvious that the award was entirely predicated on President Obama's disavowal of American exceptionalism, a view that he has repeatedly confirmed in interviews since his election. The notion that America has a special role in the world, a kind of providential destiny, is simply anathema to him. Even Bill Clinton subscribed to the long-standing notion of America as the "indispensable nation." This President seems to think we owe the world an apology for our presuming any such role.

Second, this tendency is part of a larger one noted by John Bolton that characterizes Obama as the first "post-American" President. Not *anti*-American, just one that is "above" all of that so-called jingoism. As *Newsweek* editor Evan Thomas said, "Reagan was all about America; Obama is 'we're above that now,'" meaning we stand for something not so parochial, so chauvinistic.

Third, we shouldn't be surprised at the shallowness of the award. After all, as Bret Stephens notes, the Peace Prize always goes to a "Goodist," the people who believe all conflict stems from avoidable misunderstanding and that all evil springs from technologies and systems, anything but the hearts of men. Certainly no warrior would ever be eligible (think Roosevelt, Churchill, Reagan, Bush) although it has been warriors who have been responsible for more lasting peace and saved more innocent lives than all the Goodist world leaders one can name.

Fourth, to follow on the last point, Tom Friedman had the best suggestion I have heard for those truly deserving of a peace prize in 2009 – the men and women of the American armed services.

Fifth, you would think that the Nobel Peace Prize winner and the leader of the free world would have taken time to acknowledge with his presence the 20th anniversary of the fall of the Berlin Wall, one of the most significant events in the march of freedom from tyranny of the past century and certainly an event that greatly enhanced the cause of world peace, while also giving recognition to those who were responsible for its collapse, particularly one of his predecessors who was the first post-World War II President whose objective was to actually win the Cold War. But of course he's above all that.

What's Not to Like?

November 7, 2010

I suppose that Election Day 2010 was about all I could ask for. OK, Barney Frank, Barbara Boxer, and Harry Reid all survived, and the best California can do in its dysfunction is to resurrect Governor Moonbeam, but we need a few poster children as continuing reminders of the threat from the goofy left. The bottom line here is a major repudiation of the Obama regime, a rejection unlike any in almost 80 years, and the best part for me was that we can take hope from the fact that the American people, for all their gullibility in putting these people in office in the first place, stood up and said STOP!

So now what? First, the exhilaration is not the same for me as were the watershed elections of 1980 and 1994. The first of these represented the culmination of the maturity of the conservative movement, beginning in the 1950s, from a fringe, reactionary backwater to a truly competitive, policy-based governing alternative. The second represented the consummation of the conservative revolution against the New Deal/Great Society legacy of overreaching 20th century liberalism. This wave was much more a return to the norm, a recognition that the progressive binge is over, a reminder that this remains a center-right country, and that the death of conservatism predicted just two years ago by Sam Tanenhaus and James Carville was delusional.

Second, this is not the same caliber of event, because the party that serves as the principal vehicle for political conservatism has been there before, has blown the opportunity before, and still suffers from critical brand damage as a result. In the wake of George W. Bush's re-election in January 2005, I wrote that the new governing majority must avoid the temptations of incumbency and arrogance of power and "will be short-lived if it fails to reject the sense of entitlement and perpetuation in office that are the diseases it was elected to cure." Well, guess what? They couldn't stand the prosperity, they succumbed to these vices, and paid a terrible price, along with the people they were elected to serve. This election merely represents a temporary reprieve, and Republicans should not suffer any delusions about their anointment – they were by and large the "default" choice.

Third, I want to return to some insight from Peter Berkowitz of the Hoover Institution on the role of conservatism in America in the 21st century. He builds on the work of Edmund Burke in his view that the essence of modern conservatism is the balancing of the claims of tradition and liberty, or showing how liberty depends on tradition. Further, he adds that the divisions within contemporary American conservatism – social conservatives, libertarians, and neoconservatives – arise from differences over which goods most urgently need to be preserved, to what extent, and with what role for government. And I would add: at what cost, both in terms of the use of scarce material resources, as well as the unintended costs in social and moral order. As we move ahead to the enormous challenges of this exceptional experience, the need for this balance is more crucial than ever.

The Field is Set, But Who has the Answers?

October 7, 2011

What you see is what you get. The Republican field for the nomination for President is set and it's on to the main event, so quit looking for the knight on a white horse – he or she isn't coming. Can one of the candidates measure up to the challenge? We'll see, and one of them will obviously be nominated, but so far I don't see any one of them rising to the occasion in a way that is convincing to the electorate. And what is the occasion? I can't put it any better than *The Wall Street Journal*: "America's problems reflect a philosophical gulf far more than they do technocratic policy differences. The country is sharply divided over the role of government as a driver of economic investment and redistributor of wealth." The one who can articulate that divide and boldly suggest both practical and moral solutions will rise above the others. Again, as I have said a number of times, this isn't a math problem, it's about the deepest values that we hold dear, and the current regime has failed miserably in addressing this challenge.

But that failure is not enough to ensure its removal from power. And recent polling provides a sense of the battle ahead. As reported by Henry Olsen of *The Hill*, the Pew Research Center identified eight distinct voting blocs beyond party membership that help to define voting preferences. The critical one for Republicans is "Disaffecteds," made up primarily of whites without a college degree who are political independents, a bloc without a majority of which the Republicans likely cannot win the Presidential election. And here is the problem: This bloc is significantly at odds with the mainstream Republican priority on the importance of reducing the budget deficit, on major cuts in government programs, and on tax increases. They are significantly more likely to want to cut defense spending and are adamantly opposed to altering entitlements, including majorities among them who oppose Congressman Paul Ryan's entitlement reform plan.

For conservatives, this is a real problem. If the Obama administration continues to slide in popularity, there is a slight chance that he can be beaten without resolving these differences, but one thing is certain: the country cannot be repaired or even governed without a resolution of these core issues going forward, regardless of who is in the White House. And aside from Ryan's efforts I don't see the kind of messaging and boldness from the loyal opposition that will carry the day for these "disaffecteds;" certainly I am not seeing it on the campaign trail, and if what we see now is all we get, it won't get the job done.

Mario Loyola of the Texas Public Policy Foundation has written of the 21st century version of "a tale of two cities," featuring the dramatic differences in the fates of Detroit and Houston in the period since World War II and the difference made by public policy. Michael Barone has written similarly about "The Fall of the Midwest Economic Model" and how, in 1970, the future seemed to belong to Michigan's example of big companies and big unions. Not anymore. Both now seem to agree that, in Loyola's words, "In the degree of collusion between business and government, in the power of labor unions, in the method of economic development, in the burden of taxation and regulation, in the tolerance of diversity – in all these ways and more, the two cities (Detroit and Houston) stand as diametric opposites in the choices a society can make."

Stark differences in models, no doubt. But back to the "disaffecteds" and we find that, as David Brooks notes about this class, voters in the region described by Loyola and Barone "face structural problems, not cyclical ones… Intensely suspicious of government, they are nonetheless casting about for somebody, anybody, who can revive their towns and neighborhoods. Disillusioned by big government and big debt, they at least want to see their government reflect their values of discipline, order, and responsibility… American politics are volatile, because nobody has an answer for these people. They will remain volatile until somebody finds one."

What will it take to find this answer and to break out of a cycle wherein conservatives are periodically able to roll back the excesses of the left, but have apparently lost support of the core of middle and working class independents, who obviously feel threatened, in significantly reversing the entitlement regime? This is the major challenge of the 21st century and a subject for another essay, but suffice to say that it cannot be accomplished without significant improvement in elementary, secondary, and higher education leadership and productivity.

They Don't Get It

February 2, 2012

I'm sure you are getting more than you want of the constant dribble of the triviality of much of the interplay among Republican primary candidates and I don't want to add to the frustration, but I can't avoid a few shots. First, I have been appalled at the demagoguery from several candidates, primarily Perry and Gingrich, with their attacks on the "job destruction" and "vulture capitalism" involved in Bain Capital's generally successful corporate restructuring and turnaround strategy under Mitt Romney's leadership, a strategy which in many cases saved companies from total failure and ultimately preserved many times more jobs than were displaced. This is a textbook example of creative destruction, a core principle of capitalism best characterized by Austrian economist Joseph Schumpeter, and without which there is no long term economic growth. It is an essential component of classical liberal economics, of which we need more, not less. It is difficult enough to defend free market capitalism in this environment without a circular firing squad among people who should know better. And the notion that several so-called conservative Republican Presidential candidates are reduced to an attack on these practices is beyond negative campaign tactics, it is an embarrassment and it gives Barack Obama cover for similar attacks with impunity in the general election campaign.

But Romney doesn't get it, either. He doesn't know how to respond to the unfounded attacks on the Bain record, because he seems to want to account for the validity of the Bain business plan with individual anecdotes or case studies. This is a failed approach. And he compounded the problem when he drew an analogy between his work at Bain with Obama's bailout and layoffs at GM and Chrysler, implying in effect that these practices approach some sort of equivalence! An instinctive conservative would have a natural response to such attacks grounded in a defense of creative destruction on its face based on the principles of capitalism and the dynamics and underlying morality of the free market system.

Another example: Romney's recent comments on his concern, or lack thereof, with the poor and working class and his policy emphasis on the middle class were probably well-intentioned, but a conservative would never think of couching his remarks on economic policy in terms of who among the various classes or income quintiles might or might not be targeted or benefit from policy. Similarly, his previous misguided comments on favoring tax-rate cuts only for those below certain income levels. And now we learn that he supports an increasing minimum wage indexed for inflation – digging the hole deeper! This is industrial policy talk, this is redistributionist thinking, this is the thinking of the left and it will be a dangerous trip down the class warfare trail that overwhelmingly favors the Democrats. A conservative thinks instinctively in terms of the dynamics of markets, economic mobility, and opportunity that benefit all Americans who work hard and are incentivized, as well as supported by consistent and fair taxation for all along with unobtrusive government regulation.

Romney doesn't seem to be instinctive about these issues. These are not responses that one learns on the campaign trail; they come naturally to a conservative. So far, he is all about his résumé, which is the best of the field by far, his "inevitability" as the nominee, his funding, and his organization in the field, but "movement" conservatives want much more than that. They want a President who defends creative destruction on its merits; they want a President who defends capitalism as the most moral of economic and societal orders; they want a President who is immersed in the moral principles outlined by Michael Novak in *The Spirit of Democratic Capitalism* and who understands, as well as articulates the validity of supply-side fiscal policy; they want a President who knows and says that the primary role of the Federal Reserve is to maintain the value and stability of the dollar; and they want a President who understands that Barack Obama is not just a "nice guy who is in over his head," but who means what he says when he declares that he wants to transform America. Finally, they want a candidate who understands that this election is about much more than policy or competency, but is about defeating a regime whose mission is to fundamentally redefine our founding.

A bruising primary fight should have been productive in making Mitt Romney sharper in his proposals and more energizing to a Republican base that is hungry for this bold agenda, and maybe I have missed some messages, but it seems that all it has done so far is to toughen his negative character attacks. Newt Gingrich has more baggage, volatility, and ego than most people can stomach, and would be a very high risk nominee, but he moves people. Reagan could do that, Thatcher could do that, and however deeply misguided in content, Obama can do that, but Romney hasn't done that and it's the reason he hasn't closed the deal. It's not about the resume, it's about the instincts.

Hopefully, the Real Battle is Being Joined

August 5, 2012

One gets the distinct feeling that this presidential election is about to blossom into a very serious and substantive debate about voter choices on the future of this country. Unfortunately at present, there are only hints of this meaningful battle beneath the surface of the frivolity involving such inanities as Bain Capital's outsourcing, the "made in China" U.S. Olympic Team uniforms, the continuing mind-numbing demagoguery about how to "pay for" the continuation of the Bush tax rate cuts for "the rich," and Mitt Romney's tax returns.

Several astute observers (not to be confused with what passes for mainstream coverage of the issues), including Yuval Levin in *The Weekly Standard* and Jay Cost in *National Affairs*, have recently written that, in effect, the entire American social contract that has been in place since World War II is now up for grabs, and I agree. Levin says it this way: "We have a sense that the economic order we knew in the second half of the 20th century may not be coming back at all…We are on the cusp of the fiscal and institutional collapse of our welfare state, which threatens not only the future of government finances, but also the future of American capitalism." Cost offers this take on it: "The days when lawmakers could give to some Americans without shortchanging others are over; the politics of deciding who loses what, and when, and how, is upon us… Neither party yet fully understands the implications of this shift…"

Finally, in a thoughtful essay in *The New Criterion*, James Piereson makes the point that we may very well be on the verge of what he calls "the fourth revolution," after the first three American political revolutions – the election of 1800, the Civil War, and the New Deal – because the crisis we now face is far deeper than the overhang from the recent "great recession." Rather, as he says, almost parroting Levin and Cost,

"The deeper causes lie in the exhaustion of the postwar system of political economy that took place in the 1930s and 1940s… That system now is unwinding for several reasons, not least because the American economy can no longer underwrite the debt and public promises… The urgent need to cancel or renegotiate these debts and public promises on short notice will ignite the fourth revolution."

Beyond a few well-intentioned and courageous individual initiatives (Congressman Paul Ryan comes to mind), as a body politic we haven't come anywhere close to engaging these issues and their ramifications with the depth and intensity that they deserve. Nor do I think that we have yet come to grips with what the answer will mean for our republic and our constitutional order. Needless to say, there are very different worldviews at odds in this debate and very different ideas about the future of the current model, which is clearly no longer sustainable. Whether or not the American people are willing to face that reality and make the necessary transformation to a new model will depend on the quality of the coming debate and the skill of the opposition party and its leader in making the case. A fourth revolution? I don't know, but I do know that this is a very big deal.

Finally, the End of the "Narrative?"

October 7, 2012

When I previously used the title phrase "The End of the Narrative" in January 2011, after the 2010 election rout by the Tea Party, it was accurate to an extent, but largely premature. Here is what I said then:

"As we welcome the new year and a new political season, having given considerable time to analyzing the meaning of the November elections, one thing is abundantly clear: the mystique of the Obama narrative is over and the reality of governing has finally overtaken this administration. Until now, President Obama has been significantly aloof, above it all, possessed of his own exceptionalism (not to be confused with the truly American brand) based on the strength of his unique personal narrative, that he is not only different from those "ghosts," as he has called them, pictured on U.S. currency, but somehow immune to their burdens. Well, the people didn't buy it. In fact, they soundly rejected it, and any notion that it would have been different if the unemployment rate had been two points lower or GDP growth a couple of points higher is moot, but nonsense. The basic underlying themes of domestic policy pursued by this regime are alien to the American psyche. A student of history should have known this."

I stand by this analysis, but what I didn't recognize then is the depth of the fraud, or to use Bill Clinton's characterization, "the biggest fairy tale I've ever seen," embodied in the mystique of Barack Obama's narrative, nor did I understand the extent to which he and his fellow travelers in the media could completely mask the reality of the fraud. But, now finally, thanks to Mitt Romney's performance in the first presidential debate, the real Obama has been exposed on a stage and in a directly confrontational way that no amount of spin could mask.

Basically, there is no "there" there. Obama is not serious, having conducted no important policy work for quite some time. In contrast, for example, Hillary Clinton is serious. Whatever one thinks about her, she is doing serious work. Paul Ryan is serious, doing serious work. Obama is not. It's been all about him and the permanent campaign, all about this narrative. And he uses only the media outlets that maximize his advantage – *Letterman, The View*, and other trivialities – again not serious, which reflects badly on our priorities as a people. And if he succeeds, which he still might do, he will be justified regardless of substance, and will have confirmed for many that this is the only important objective. And if so, this is where we will have arrived – the politics of narrative devoid of substance; a sad outcome for a noble nation historically led by serious people that desperately needs extraordinary leadership from very serious people now more than ever.

What Now?

November 8, 2012

To paraphrase former President Gerald R. Ford, with apologies – our long national nightmare continues.

Did we actually just spend a reported $6 billion for this, to move two states from one column to the other, leaving all else virtually intact? And did we leave the same guy in office as CEO, after having presided over what was arguably the most incompetent and damaging presidential term in my lifetime? Do the people in the majority on this decision really believe that this man learned anything or that there will be any change in strategy or priorities? What's the definition of insanity?

You'll get more than you want of analysis of what went wrong for Romney, where the GOP campaign management failed, that the demographics now substantially favor the Democrats, that the national media is biased to the left, that "superstorm" Sandy was an October surprise that worked, etc., but I will spare you all of that.

What I will say is this – that we will not effectively address the enormous problems this country faces, fiscal, as well as social, until we have a generation of leaders from both the public and private sectors who are willing to risk significant political capital to get serious about telling the truth about them and about the pain that will be necessary to resolve them. And I mean truth in all of its manifestations without calibrations for preferred constituencies. There were scant occasions during this long campaign that anything approaching this happened.

One of the most interesting and provocative phrases since election day was the theme of an essay by Kyle Scott, who teaches politics and constitutional law at the University of Houston: "The key to political victory is figuring out how to tell the most people 'yes' and the fewest people 'no.'" Well, my friends, that's not the solution, that's the problem. For it represents the underlying strategy for the role of government since the 1930s that has corroded every corner of our lives and produced a sense of entitlement, dependency, and coercion that has crippled our souls and undermined civil society to the point of dysfunction. This is where the truth must start. If I am naive, please correct me.

The Second Term

February 4, 2013

President Obama's inaugural address was arguably the most ideological such speech in American history – a litany of progressive dreams, devoid of any recognition of the current realities, the most significant of which is the bankruptcy of the post Great Society social contract and the crisis of the entitlement state, about which more below.

We're a society almost equally split between two different planets and worldviews, as illustrated by this quote from White House communications director Dan Pfeiffer shortly after the inauguration: "There's a moment of opportunity now that's important; what's frustrating is that we don't have a political system or an opposition party worthy of the opportunity." Ah yes, of course, that old problem with the Constitution and the messy separation of powers, the 100-year-old dilemma of the progressive movement in achieving its moral destiny.

In a commercial for the MSNBC cable channel, Chris Matthews talks of the ongoing so-called "civil war" in this country over liberty and rights, in which, of course, he paints conservatism as the enemy of both. The key ingredients he omits are the source of these rights, which come from our Creator, not the state, and the nature of them in our Constitution, which are negative (what government cannot do) vs. positive (what progressives believe government should do to greatly expand rights read as entitlements).

So, what does a good progressive do to overcome these institutional obstacles? More of the same – executive orders to circumvent Congress, for which Obama already holds the record, more regulation dictated by the executive branch, and a final strategy fully enabled by a second term: what Rep. Paul Ryan has characterized as the "delegitimization" of the opposition, the Republican Party, through a campaign to discredit any opposition to progressive ideals as regressive, illegitimate, and out of mainstream conversation.

Not exactly Lincolnian, Reaganesque, or even Rooseveltian, but this is what now passes for presidential leadership in Obama's progressive world.

Some Thoughts on the Elections

November 6, 2013

Some interesting results from around the country in the past week, a few of which might have implications for the midterm elections in 2014 and the Presidential race in 2016. Here are a few odds and ends:

New York City: The recent trend toward renewed prosperity in the Big Apple has probably just peaked with the major turn to the left in the election of Bill de Blasio as Mayor. And I mean hard left. This guy is at least a borderline Marxist with a record to prove it. Good luck on avoiding major negative reversals in crime, education, city finances, job growth, and city services, along with general living conditions and progress in many of these areas that had been made over the past 20 years under Giuliani and Bloomberg.

Virginia: A big blown opportunity for the Republicans that could certainly have implications for 2014 and 2016. Holding the Governor's office in a key swing state like Virginia is critical and they had every opportunity to do so with the right kind of help from the party regulars and the insurgents in the Tea Party. In the end, they lost it to a carpetbagging political hack.

New Jersey: I don't yet have settled opinion on Chris Christie, but it's becoming clearer to me that he now is the leading GOP name for 2016 and possibly could win if he can get nominated! What is not clear is whether or not Republicans will adhere to the "Buckley Rule," which is to aggressively support the most conservative candidate who can be elected. If not, they will blow it again.

Colorado: Voters soundly rejected, by almost 2-1, the highly touted Amendment 66, which would have represented a major overhaul of the state's education finance system and resulted in a $950 million tax increase. The outcome came in spite of well-funded support by the Governor, various progressive leaders nationwide, and celebrities such as New York City Mayor Mike Bloomberg, as well as Bill and Melinda Gates. The message here is that people are fed up with the constant demand from the education bureaucracy for increases in funding while pushing back hard on the necessary reforms in expectations and accountability. Let's hope this message is heard loud and clear around the country, particularly in Texas.

Texas: No national implications here, but close to home and at long last after more than five years of failed political leadership on the issue, the voters of Harris County have spoken and defeated the proposal to "repurpose" the Astrodome. Supporters of the referendum to spend $217 million on the project are blaming "bond fatigue," but that's a cop-out. The County proposal, like many others submitted by private interests over the past several years, was not economically viable and there has been no demonstrated need other than to satisfy the emotional attachment to this iconic structure, which has been condemned for more than four years. The only realistic option is demolition, and the Harris County Commissioners' Court should get on with it right away. After all, despite the great memories, as *The Wall Street Journal* has noted, this isn't the Alamo we're talking about.

The Donald

August 7, 2015

This has never been a letter about electoral politics – who's in, who's out, who's up, who's down, etc. – and I'm not about to change that. But I can't pass on the Donald Trump phenomenon, because of what it represents about our politics early in the 21st century.

I think his popularity with Republicans ultimately will fade, but there are a couple of things to like about the Trump candidacy and I am generally a fan of non-traditional candidates, particularly those from the private sector who have no experience in elected office, like Carly Fiorina. He obviously has hit a nerve with GOP voters who are frustrated with the establishment and the gridlocked system that is dysfunctional on a number of critical issues, and I have a level of sympathy with that. And I like the idea of a guy who doesn't worry about what people think about his non-politically correct bombs and who disrupts the spin-doctored management of the traditional candidates.

But Trump is of a different order because he is a product of our reality TV celebrity-saturated culture and I fear that his popularity is driven by a policy that is increasingly ignorant of the implications of their choices. I don't want to come off as elitist, but you don't need to watch many segments of the Watter's World interviews of people on the street to be horrified, and Trump is at least partially a product of this culture, which should give all of us pause. And as for his policy positions, he is all over the map over the years, most of it lacks any real depth, and a lot of it is anathema to the movement conservative base, which is damaging. But as I have said many times, with an electorate that twice voted for a charlatan like Barack Obama, anything is possible.

The Reality of the Trump Wave

January 5, 2016

One of my favorite liberals is William Galston, who offers his insights on politics and social issues in *The Wall Street Journal*. Over the past couple of months he has written about the demographics and underlying economic and social issues driving the Trump phenomenon.

In one article, he notes that much of Trump's support grows out of what he calls "an angry, disaffected U.S. white working class that, for the first time in decades, has found its voice." He also notes that xenophobia, nationalism, and bigotry are dominant tones, which tempts many of us to turn away, but he cautions that this would be a mistake, because underneath these noises are real problems, many of which are tied to the failure of government to provide a sense of prosperity and economic security.

I agree, and this is the crowd that I have previously identified as the key to any realistic political consensus in America and have suggested that the political party that finds some answers that capture their allegiance can stay in power for several decades.

In another article, Galston reports the results of a recent survey released by the Public Religion Research Institute and the Brookings Institution, which identifies with more precision the sources of Trump's support. Some highlights: 55 percent of his supporters are white working class, compared to 35 percent for the rest of the Republican field;

the most likely demographic group to support him is composed of men ages 50-64 with no more than a high school education; this group is the most likely to believe that immigrants are taking jobs away from American workers; 30 percent believe that immigrants strengthen the country compared to 51 percent of whites with college degrees; and possibly most striking, 62 percent believe the country has changed for the worse since the 1950s, only 42 percent believe that America's best days are ahead, and 68 percent believe that hard work and determination are no guarantee of success for most people.

These findings confirm anecdotal evidence that has been pretty obvious for some time now. It reflects the frustrations of mainly white working class men who no longer recognize their country. This is the core of the sentiments to "take our country back!" and "make America great again." But I submit that before we dismiss or ridicule them and their leader as inarticulate buffoons, we should remember that the last leader who captured this crowd was Ronald Reagan (remember the Reagan Democrats?) and he carried 49 states. I'm not suggesting that Donald Trump is anything close to Ronald Reagan, but what I am suggesting is that there are very real problems here in what represents the backbone of our country in many ways that are not being adequately addressed by any message other than Trump's demagoguery and we had better wake up.

Uncharted Territory

May 5, 2016

Clearly, the notion of Donald Trump as the Republican nominee for President, with all that he brings and doesn't bring to the table, has sent the Republican party into a frenzy of soul-searching. We are truly in uncharted territory here and there is simply not yet an identified pathway. The only thing reasonably certain from my perspective is that the Reagan Revolution, which began with "the speech" in the 1964 Goldwater campaign, is over.

Some have commented that this necessary soul-searching will be broader than the future of the Republican Party, and I don't disagree that the current disarray is not limited to the conservative movement. Bernie Sanders has produced almost as much frenzy for the left as Trump has for the right, and Hillary Clinton doesn't have an answer there either.

Where I disagree with the commentary, primarily from the center-right so far is with David Brooks and his comment that "we'll probably need a new national story," because "that story isn't working for people anymore, especially for people who think the system is rigged." No, the national story is still valid, it's the failed policies that have been advanced and the failure of our intellectual and political leadership in properly communicating the national story that has failed us.

As I have written before in connection with the birth of the Tea Party, as painful as it is to admit, conservatism has forfeited its reputation as a reform movement that was earned in the Reagan and Gingrich years and must regain its reformist heritage, a branding that was severely damaged by the profligacy of "compassionate conservatism" and led to the disaster of Obama's "hope and change." The result has been an undermining of the spirit of American exceptionalism, the basis on which Trump masterfully demagogued his way to the nomination for President.

Regardless of the outcome in November, severe damage has been done and the repair work will be painful.

The Election

November 10, 2016

To paraphrase former President Gerald Ford at the end of the Watergate crisis, "our long national nightmare of a presidential campaign is over." And the tradeoff that the American people have made is to accept the gamble on a politically inexperienced, often vulgar and undisciplined, and multi-flawed narcissist in exchange for finally ridding the nation of what is arguably the most corrupt self-serving political machine in U.S. history. A worthy bargain in my view. In addition, four to eight more years of assertive progressive rule would have so entrenched the federal Leviathan in every corner of civic and personal life as to make this country unrecognizable.

How did this happen? As for the defeat of the Clinton machine, the critical mass of more than 25 years of cronyism, political webs, sinister private/public networks, well-documented lies, topped off by the recent email dumps and foundation "play for pay" conflicts took its toll – the country finally had enough of the Clintons.

And the Trump phenomenon? I don't want to say that I was among the first to notice, but I wrote of the "Trump wave" more than a year ago, being prompted by a series of articles by William Galston about the demographics and underlying economic and social issues driving the Trump movement.

In one article, he noted that much of Trump's support grew out of what he called "an angry, disaffected U.S. white working class that, for the first time in decades, has found its voice." He also noted that xenophobia, nationalism, and bigotry are dominant tones, which tempts many of us to turn away, but he cautioned that this would be a mistake, because underneath these noises are real problems, many of which are tied to the failure of government to provide a sense of prosperity and economic security.

This is the crowd that I had previously identified as the key to any realistic political consensus in America and about which I have suggested on a number of occasions that the political party that finds some answers that capture their allegiance can stay in power for several decades.

In another article, Galston reported the results of a survey released by the Public Religion Research Institute and the Brookings Institution, which identified with more precision the sources of Trump's support. Some highlights: 55 percent of his supporters are white working class, compared to 35 percent for the rest of the Republican field at the time; the most likely demographic group to support him is composed of men ages 50-64 with no more than a high school education; this group is the most likely to believe that immigrants are taking jobs away from American workers; 30 percent believe that immigrants strengthen the country compared to 51 percent of whites with college degrees; and possibly most striking, 62 percent believe the country has changed for the worse since the 1950s, only 42 percent believe that America's best days are ahead, and 68 percent believe that hard work and determination are no guarantee of success for most people. All of this evidence has of course now been validated by numerous additional surveys, not to mention the election results themselves.

It seemed to me that these findings confirmed anecdotal evidence that had been pretty obvious for some time. It reflected the frustrations of mainly white working class men who no longer recognize their country. This formed the core of the sentiments to "take our country back!" and "make America great again."

In describing this phenomenon, Arthur Brooks of the American Enterprise Institute, in a *Wall Street Journal* article the day after the election, has a slightly different take on the progressive emphasis on the income inequality that threatens the body politic. He thinks that the critical gap is not an income gap, but a "dignity gap," that the country is separating into a nation of economic winners and losers, the latter of which are predominantly working class men, and he cites data that show the percentage of working class men outside the workforce having increased to 22 percent from 10 percent since 1965. This, says Brooks, is producing significant problems beyond economics created by a life without the dignity of work. Trump spoke to and resonated with these people in a way that none of our elites, from the right or left, has done.

For those who wonder about the Obama legacy, it is now pretty simple – the Obama legacy is Donald Trump. And he comes to office with legislative majorities that have resulted in the Republican Party being the national ruling party. How ironic it is that only a few weeks ago, the conversation was about what seemed almost certainly the post-election Republican collapse and the necessity for the GOP to be completely rebuilt from the ground up. No doubt it will be a different party transformed by the Trump ascendancy, but it is now the Democrats who must totally reorganize and soul-search.

At the end of the day, Daniel Henninger said it best: "What we learned on November 8, 2016, was that voters looked past or through all the atmospheric debris of this campaign and focused on what mattered – the direction of their country, its economy, its politics, and the state of the culture."

The country has many problems, but there are numerous opportunities for revival. The incoming President will need all the help he can get, as he soon will learn.

Let us pray.

Election Afterthoughts

November 18, 2016

We've now had about 10 days to process the earth-shaking presidential election, time enough for some afterthoughts and observations on Trump's amazing victory and the reaction so far:

- Trump won primarily because of the failure of the Obama policy priorities and governing performance and the glaring weaknesses of Hillary Clinton as a candidate. As Karl Rove has noted, when voters were asked if they wanted the next president to continue Obama's policies, 28 percent said "yes" and they voted 91 percent for Clinton, while the 48 percent who said they wanted more conservative policies voted 83 percent for Trump. Obama/Clinton have left the Democratic Party in a shambles bordering on collapse. It is clearly now the Sanders/Warren party, almost entirely based on group identity politics, and if its leadership reacts to this defeat by moving even further to the left, it will disappear as a nationally competitive party.

- The mainstream media coverage of this election was a disgrace to whatever is left of professional journalism in this country. The leadership of what passes as the mainstream outlets had better take a long look into their collective souls, because their credibility is at rock bottom.

- The street and campus protests of Trump's election around the country are simply additional manifestation of the fraud and bankruptcy of the left and its mantra of "tolerance." The children of the 1960s should be ashamed of this ignorant, pampered generation, many of whom other than the pure thugs seem to have no idea why they are in the streets. The most disappointing aspect of this development is the complicity in and often the leadership of this nonsense ("safe spaces," cancelled classes and exams, etc.) by education leaders, in both K-12 and higher education, who in doing so are in dereliction of their duty as educators.

- There is no doubt that Hillary Clinton already is culpable for a number of personal transgressions and I predict that the Clinton Foundation will probably not survive the coming investigation of its "pay to play" practices. She would, in all likelihood, already have been indicted under normal circumstances. And it would not surprise me if President Obama pardoned her before he leaves office. If I were Donald Trump, I would not instruct my Attorney General to prosecute, but rather I would wait for the upcoming congressional investigations to run their course and produce a possible criminal referral and/or the appointment of a special prosecutor. The rule of law absolutely must be maintained, but Trump's time and his administration's preoccupation for the next several months are better directed to other priorities. The Clintons are history. Good riddance.

- For the fifth time in U.S. history, the popular vote leader for President will not be elected, and once again, the Electoral College has reflected the genius of the Founders. Those who would destroy it would subscribe to a notion of popular majoritarianism that was no part of the republican constitutional design. A letter to *The Wall Street Journal* this week lamented that the presidency is the only elected office for which this can happen. Well, yes, and this is as it should be. The President alone must be representative of a broad and diverse electorate, devoid of the tyranny of the "factions" feared by James Madison in the *Federalist Papers*. The

Electoral College tends to force national candidates toward the center, requiring broad-based coalitions to govern. We disturb this venerable institution at our peril.

- The opportunities for the Trump administration are many and the priorities must be carefully selected, because the honeymoon is short and the window is always narrow in a two-year election cycle. Beyond the appointment of a successor to Antonin Scalia to the Supreme Court, which should be the top priority, my other priorities would be those that would have the most impact on economic growth, which is the grounding of Trump's electoral constituency. These would include broad deregulation, beginning with the reversal of substantially all executive orders that Obama used to circumvent legislative prerogative in law-making; repeal of ObamaCare and its replacement with a system grounded in the market for healthcare; the overhaul of Dodd-Frank, which has stifled the allocation of bank credit and job creation; and the repeal of a number of stifling EPA regulations. Finally, tax-rate reductions are important, particularly corporate rates that would incentivize repatriation of trillions of dollars parked overseas for domestic reinvestment, resulting in enormous job creation.

- The wild card with Trump will be foreign affairs, particularly how he might respond to a crisis or provocation early in his term, which is almost certain to occur somewhere in the world he has inherited from the failed Obama foreign policies. He just needs to surround himself with the right people and listen. I like Gen. Michael Flynn as national security advisor. Rudy Giuliani would be OK as Secretary of State, but John Bolton would be better, and he actually already has a plan to restructure the outmoded international institutions, beginning with the UN, which are in need of major reform.

Bottom line: Just keep praying.

A DC Whirlwind

February 5, 2017

We've not seen anything quite like it, at least in my lifetime. The Trump transition has been like a drink of water from a fire hydrant and we're just two weeks into it. I said all along during the election year that I could see no really good outcome regardless of who was elected, but on balance I must say that I think there is much to like so far. In fact, the very serious nature of it aside for a moment, I can't think of another time when I've had more fun than with the political and policy disruption that Trump has brought to Washington. The Reagan transition of 1981 was a lot of fun and certainly the Gingrich revolution of 1994 was exhilarating and transforming, but probably largely, because the election was such a surprise, this transition tops both.

Of course, there have already been both highs and lows. The appointment of Neil Gorsuch to the Supreme Court was virtually perfect, the rollout of the immigration and refugee policy, while well-intentioned, was a disaster; putting Iran "on notice" was long overdue, the humiliation of Mexico's President was bad manners at best, damaging diplomacy at worst. And it would be nice if Trump had a lot more of Reagan's grace and humility, but let's face it – his style is a big part of what got him there, and frankly, some of the bluntness is refreshing. There will be much more of all of this, so relax and roll with the punches. And maybe the best part of it for me is that the Democrats and the left have no clue how to respond, except through futile resistance and obstruction along with support of mobs in the street. And I wonder if they realize how goofy and embarrassing much of their pandering to the loonier elements of their base makes them look. All of this nonsense about the fear engendered that Trump's appointees (which have overall been surprisingly very good, incidentally) will move the country to the hard right, the boycotting of committee votes on nominees, etc. They need to get this straight: Trump's election, however narrowly decided, is a mandate to immediately move away from the eight-year trend in progressive left ideology domestically and the liberal internationalist/blame America first mode in foreign policy. His government should and will reflect that. To quote Obama in 2009 – "I won!"

There is, of course, a major risk that all of this aggressiveness will be too hastily initiated and/or overdone and result in overreach, particularly if Trump gets too far ahead of his Congressional majority on key issues like trade and ObamaCare overhaul. Another risk is in the streets, and although a leftist Tea Party as successful as the 2010 populist right version is probably not in the cards, these anti-Trump marches and event protests are not going away and there is at least some chance that they could spell trouble if capable leadership steps forward. But for the time being, the not so loyal opposition doesn't have a leader or a playbook.

Of Investigations and Partisanship

January 3, 2018

This letter has never been about partisan politics or about electoral politics generally, except to the extent of commentary on the ideas and policy priorities that drive electoral politics. No doubt regular readers over the years should have no difficulty in identifying my political philosophy, but I abjure partisanship. Consistent with this commitment, I have avoided commentary on the daily spin cycle of partisanship that dominates what passes for journalism in this highly polarized environment that has been supercharged by the election of Donald Trump as President.

Having said that as a disclaimer, I must say that what we are witnessing now in the daily pursuit of possible culpability of Trump and his family, campaign staff, and supporters by the special counsel appointed to investigate alleged Russian influence in the 2016 elections has reached the level of conflict of interest and prosecutorial tyranny that is dangerous to the integrity of the rule of law in this country. Already we have seen the resignations or otherwise removal of several FBI and special counsel staff attorneys for partisan conflicts due to their documented opposition to Donald Trump and/or support of Hillary Clinton. Further, the FBI's reluctance to release significant documents to the House investigating committee and the stonewalling of senior FBI management in testimony before this committee, which is at this point the only item of obstruction that is fully in evidence, betrays a predisposition to protect Hillary Clinton and an embarrassed FBI. I had hoped for better from this agency and from Special Counsel Robert Mueller, but obviously I was mistaken. In spite of the thousands of dedicated and professional law enforcement officers in this venerable agency, there is obviously a credibility problem at the higher levels of management.

I have my own problems with a number of aspects of Donald Trump as President, but he is our constitutionally elected president and to me overwhelmingly preferable to the alternative that was available. My problem is that I have continuously underestimated the vitriol and defiance of the radical left, the Democratic Party, and their fellow travelers in the holdover Obama administrative state in their willingness to go to any length to invalidate and discredit his election, and that this extends to the undermining of the rule of law, which many of them evidently consider secondary to the protection of the country from a successful Trump administration. This has become even more abundantly clear in this biased investigation and I fear that, regardless of the outcome, it ultimately will do great damage to the republic. The only way I see out of this mess and provide the necessary transparency and impartiality is for Congress to take charge of all aspects of the investigation into outside influence in the 2016 election under its constitutional oversight role, which should immediately include strict enforcement of its contempt of Congress authority under the law.

Not a Bad Year After All

February 5, 2018

Love him or hate him, and I have found very few who are indifferent, Donald Trump had a pretty good first year as President. How much of what has been accomplished can be directly attributed to him is debatable, but the same can mostly be said of any President. As Ramesh Ponnuru notes in *National Review*, "People who voted for Trump in November 2016 on the theory that he would deliver policies radically different from what other Republicans would do should be disappointed. Those who voted for him because he would usually line up with conservatives and sign Republican bills, on the other hand, have reason to be pleased." This is a pretty fair assessment, but I would add that signing executive orders has been at least as important to this latter group as the bills signed, for all things considered, this past year has witnessed a massive reversal of the Obama progressive agenda.

Let's look at the list:

- Withdrew the U.S. from the Paris climate agreement.
- Rolled back the mandate that employers provide employees with contraception and abortifacients.
- Recognized Jerusalem as the capital of Israel.
- Adopted a much firmer policy on Afghanistan and in effect defeated ISIS in Iraq.
- Led a bold assault of deregulation on the regulatory/administrative state in almost every area.
- Signed legislation to open up oil drilling in the Arctic National Wildlife Refuge.
- Signed the most significant overhaul of the tax code in more than 30 years.
- Appointed Neil Gorsuch to the Supreme Court and a significant number of appellate judges.
- As previously noted, issued numerous executive orders reversing the Obama legacy.
- Released a new National Security Strategy that offers realism with no hint of isolationism and reverses the past eight years of withdrawal.

There is a lot here to like, but of course there is much more to be done, and one hopes that serious restructuring of Social Security and Medicare will be on the short list soon after the immigration issue is resolved. There is also a lot to worry about, high on the list for me being Trump's misguided rhetoric on trade, particularly the North American

Free Trade Agreement, a collapse of which would be a disaster for the country. And, of course, with Trump, there is the constant threat of big mouth overload and the out of control twitter attacks, which will not be disciplined, a risk that cannot be quantified, but what you see is what you get, and so far on balance that has been pretty good and better than we had a right to expect.

The SOTU According to Trump

February 6, 2019

Pundits go into big stage events like the State of the Union address looking for headline "takeaways," specific proposals that provoke or those that can guarantee surviving at least one news cycle. In this particular one last night, President Trump's second, most were looking for a major pronouncement on the immigration stalemate and/or the declaration of a national emergency on the border situation, neither of which happened. The two issue-related comments that resonated with me had to do with the President's commitment to the sanctity of life in the context of recent news about third trimester abortion bills and the pronouncement that "America will never be a socialist country" (as if that should need confirmation). But to me the main thrust of this speech and his message was embodied in the last couple of paragraphs, which will probably not be remembered beyond the end of this week, but which deserve more attention. I quote them in full:

What will we do with this moment? How will we be remembered? I ask the men and women of this Congress, look at the opportunities before us. Our most thrilling achievements are still ahead. Our most exciting journeys still await. Our biggest victories are still to come. We have not yet begun to dream. We must choose whether we are defined by our differences – or whether we dare to transcend them. We must choose whether we will squander our inheritance – or whether we will proudly declare that we are Americans. We do the incredible. We defy the impossible. We conquer the unknown. This is the time to reignite the American imagination. This is the time to search for the tallest summit and set our sights on the brightest star.

This is the time to rekindle the bonds of love and loyalty and memory that link us together as citizens, as neighbors, as patriots. This is our future – our fate – and our choice to make. I am asking you to choose greatness. No matter the trials we face, no matter the challenges to come, we must go forward together. We must keep America first in our hearts. We must keep freedom alive in our souls. And we must always keep faith in America's destiny – that one nation, under God, must be the hope and the promise and the light and the glory among all the nations of the world.

Yes, I know – he didn't write this. But that's OK; neither did our previous Presidents craft many of their most memorable lines. After all, we haven't had many Lincolns. But he spoke the lines and the words, and I believe he sincerely meant them, and along with the introductions of his guests for the evening in the gallery, they were the highlights of the event worth remembering and taking to heart.

It was interesting to hear the results of the immediate post-speech polling on the public response. CNN's poll of those who watched reflected a 59 percent approval of the speech; a similar poll by CBS reflected 76 percent approval of the speech and 72 percent approval of the points on immigration. Say what you want about this guy, but the Democratic left and their fellow travelers in the mainstream media have thrown everything in the book at him for three years, and he is not only surviving, but on balance, he is winning.

18
Political Philosophy

The American Proposition: Still Valid?

June 1, 2000

During the second half of 1999, my monthly political philosophy discussion group took on an exploration of the nature of man as it relates to political philosophy. Political philosophy, as our group defines it, seeks to answer the questions: "how should we order our lives together?" and "what is the best regime?" In fact, it can be safely said that every important political theory also is a theory of human nature. If we accept this premise, it follows that political philosophy presupposes consideration of basic and timeless questions about man's nature, such as:

- Is man a purposeful creation and does he differ from other animals by type or by degree?
- Is man possessed of original sin or is his nature essentially good?
- To what extent is man capable of free will?
- Does man have the innate intellectual capacity to comprehend universals, as opposed to only particular objects identified by the senses?
- Is man's loyalty and commitment to a family unit a natural or conventional phenomenon?
- If there are inalienable human rights, what is their source?

As we discussed these and related questions, I was reminded that the American founding was based on a consensus as to the answers to these questions, so much so that they were "givens" in the thought of the Founders. One cannot imagine our founding document, the Declaration of Independence, without its invocations of divine providence, transcendental law, and the universal truths of human nature. True, the actuality of the ideal, "all men are created equal," had to be worked out over most of our history as a nation, after Abraham Lincoln began the reconciliation by merging this ideal with the U.S. Constitution. But recent trends and anecdotes lead me to wonder whether or not we still broadly accept the founding consensus. Two recent examples: In New Jersey, the state legislature was unable to pass a bill requiring public school students to recite the "We hold these truths..." paragraph of the Declaration each day, and the American Civil Liberties Union recently succeeded in judicial voidance of Ohio's state motto, "With God, all things are possible." I will have more to say in future issues about our reverence for the gods of multiculturalism and diversity, two problems of postmodernity whose currently popular definitions are deeply at odds with our cultural heritage. For now, consider this question: Could the language of the first two paragraphs of the Declaration of Independence be adopted word for word by Congress today?

Truth and Consequences

August 2, 2000

"Truth is something outside yourself, something to be discovered, and not something you can make up as you go along." – George Orwell, 1944.

"There are no facts." – Michael Foucault, 1968.

The two quotes above illustrate both the wide divergence of views of truth that have come to prevail and the drift in the conception of truth from the respect for objective truth that undergirded everything from religion to science to the postmodern view that there is no truth other than claims made by the powerful to justify their power. *The American Enterprise* magazine devoted an entire issue in 1999 to the examination of the destruction of truth in Western society and the impact on our culture, politics, and governance. It is not a pretty picture. You know the recent history of the celebrated fabrications, such as the Tawana Brawley "rape," the Rigoberta Menchu book on *Guatemala*, the falsified journalism of *The Boston Globe's* Mike Barnicle and *The New Republic's* Stephen Glass, not to mention the stream of dissembling and prevarication from the Clinton White House. The amazing and disheartening thing about these cases, and many others, is the absence of outrage and the fact that in many instances, the person who exposed the lie bore the brunt of the criticism. As Christopher Hitchens has noted, "there is a tendency in our postmodern discourse to inquire first about whose truth and which power stands to gain, and only then to take an interest in things like verification. Lying and perjury and neat evasions and sordid double talk are not just excused but praised and justified by many elites." In the culture wars of the past 30 years, truth has been a casualty, not only particular truths, but allegiance to the very ideal of truth as an indispensable component of a just and moral life. Noted philosopher Richard Rorty approvingly describes American pragmatism as our "refusal to believe in the existence of truth in the sense of something with authority over human beings." How did we get here?

Recently, I read *Time for Truth*, by Os Guinness, a senior fellow at the Trinity Forum. He targets the casual acceptance by much of contemporary American society of the idea that it is legitimate to create an entirely fictional self-image and pass it off as the truth. He blames philosopher Friedrich Nietzsche for setting in motion "perspectivism" (there are many kinds of truth, therefore there is no truth) as a wholesale assault on truth. And, as postmodernists argue, if there is no truth, then nothing is left, but a struggle for power. It doesn't take long to figure out that most of the past century's brutalities were perpetrated by regimes that believed this. Guinness further identifies "a profound crisis of cultural authority in the West, of beliefs, traditions, and ideals."

Unfortunately, much of this crisis has been aided and abetted by our elite institutions of higher education, particularly in the humanities, where truth is not always explored or celebrated, but is criticized or "deconstructed." Fortunately, however, although too many Americans find it necessary to debate whether or not character and fidelity to truth in our political leaders really matters, pure moral relativism, and disregard for truth has not yet spread widely and deeply. Let us hope it doesn't spread much further, for without respect for objective truth in our institutions and opinion leadership, it will be impossible to sustain justice or freedom.

A Culture or An Idea?

April 4, 2001

Is America a culture or an idea? This is a question that has occupied many of our leading intellectuals at least since the re-founding of our country beginning in the period immediately preceding the Civil War. We don't typically think of ourselves as a single people as the Germans or French do (although my friends in the paleoconservative movement would take issue with this). It is our ideas that are said to be binding and that generate our homogeneity, and our creed always has made room for a plurality of subcultures. But as I pointed out in my June 2000 essay on "The American Proposition," there are reasons to worry about whether or not we can sustain a consensus on the critical ideas that have produced the distinctly American culture. According to census results, California soon will become the largest proving ground for our experiment in assimilation, for it is now the first large state in which non-Hispanic whites are no longer a majority, a real test for the region from which many of our social and political trends originate. Many thoughtful people feel strongly that we can't have immigration from non-Western countries on the scale the U.S. has received over the past 30 years and get assimilation as a result, even if we don't discourage it with bilingual education, affirmative action, and the multicultural agenda, which we are doing. There is much more to be said about multiculturalism as the antithesis of the ideas that have sustained this culture, but for now we need to consider that when new immigration, coupled with multicultural ideology, undercuts these ideas, it's time for a pause.

Conservatism and the Moral High Ground

July 5, 2001

My instincts, political and otherwise, have been conservative for as long as I can remember (Goldwater '64, etc.), although, at least until lately, my definition has not always been as clear as I would have liked. For me, conservatism consists in dispositions and habits of mind and heart encompassing the accumulation of experience and wisdom over many generations, enlightened and guided by God. What is it that this conservatism wishes to conserve? Many tried and true virtues and traditions, but mainly self-governance, both individually and institutionally. Why has this been so difficult? Because the competition with self-governance in its several facets is so fierce. There are many competing options that are attractive to human nature in its fallen state. In spite of the competition, and an almost complete lapse into statism and relativism over most of the past century, I believe that self-governance, conservatively understood, is in ascendancy. In preparing this essay, however, I was struck by two pieces in *The Wall Street Journal* written about 10 months apart by Shelby Steele. In August 2000, he announced that for the first time American conservatism is going on the offensive in the culture war through "compassionate conservatism" (a term I have always thought redundant; conservatism is compassionate by definition). In June 2001 he writes that the greatest limitation on conservative political power in America is a gap in moral authority, primarily on the issues of poverty and race. The left, he says, has failed miserably in addressing these issues, but retains the moral high ground because it took responsibility for them in the 1960s and it will retain it until conservatism takes the same moral risks in addressing them soon. We conservatives know that our principles, properly understood and applied, are clearly superior and have stood the tests of generations, but it's difficult to argue Steele's point that more principled boldness and political risk will be necessary to capture the moral high ground from the left.

The "Public" vs. "Private" Debate

April 3, 2004

Most Pilgrim subscribers know that I am pretty heavily involved in public education reform, and in my work in this arena, at least one Texas teachers' union has described me as a proponent of education "privatization." An interesting characterization, no doubt intended as a pejorative in my case, and I assume it is assigned to me, because I am a long-time proponent of school choice. But it caused me to think more deeply about the ideas underlying much of the debate on reform of the delivery of public services generally, whether healthcare, education, social services of various types, postal services, etc. Basically, where is it written that high quality public goods cannot be delivered by market-based delivery systems, and what is the reason for the seemingly innate aversion to this innovation? As TV personality John Stossel has noted, the media consistently attempts to convince us that the public, non-profit world is warm, caring, and totally devoted to the public good, whereas, the greedy, for-profit world is involved with exploitation of the weak. (To quote the head of the American Federation of State, County, and Municipal Employees: "we refuse to be marketized…" and Ted Kennedy: "What we will not tolerate is the Republican efforts to privatize Medicare.") One of Stossel's favorite illustrations is to juxtapose Mother Teresa and financier Michael Milken, and pose the question, which one really helped the most people? Think about it. A good treatment of this debate is by Frederick M. Hess, in his "Making Sense of the Public in Public Education," in which he defines the various conceptions of "public," and refocuses the question on the best way to deliver the public goods intended by a particular service, so that the basic concern of public consensus becomes the objective of the service, not its method of delivery. This is a debate that will not go away, and will become more heated as globalization continues to drive down costs and place increasing pressures on governments at all levels to compete for capital and human resources. Only fools, Luddites, and the protectionist left can rest assured that they will not ultimately be subjected, directly or indirectly, to the dynamics of competition.

Freedom for What?

May 3, 2004

Notwithstanding the talk show debates ad nauseum about the reasons for the U.S. intervention for regime change in Iraq, WMDs, etc., it cannot be denied that a high priority, maybe the highest priority, for George Bush is the expansion of freedom in the world and the introduction of democracy in the Arab Middle East. As the war continues, it has occurred to me that we should take a moment to examine our own version of these concepts, what has become of them since our founding, and what exactly we hope to export. An insightful publication for me has been *Propositions,* published by the Institute for American Values. Recently, I revisited the Fall 2001 edition, which speaks to this question. In it is this passage: "We are the only country in the history of the world defining itself and organizing its affairs principally on the basis of an abstract and universally invitational philosophy. No other fact about this country is more amazing." Similarly, I am reminded that Lady Margaret Thatcher once said of America that it is the only country with a culture defined by an idea. This idea, of course, is freedom. But, if we are honest, we must admit that our concept of freedom has morphed itself into a certain libertinism, a value-neutral, consumer-driven autonomy without rules. And we should also admit that this perception, as much as anything else about us, helps feed the hatred that many in the Islamic world feel toward America. As Graham Fuller explains so well in his *The Democracy Trap*, the first brand of freedom introduced by America was the "freedom to do" as ultimately embodied in our Bill of Rights. The next phase was "freedom from," as we sought to spare the public from want, hunger, disease, etc. Today the issue we confront as we advance the exportation of our values is "freedom for," and it is likely to be the most difficult phase of all, for freedom is an instrumental good, not an end. Answering the question, 'freedom for what,' will force us to examine our very existence and who we are, as well as hopefully renew our own ideas and ideals in the process. It is this that I believe will be the most enduring legacy of 9/11.

The Battleground – in the War and the Election

July 3, 2004

The use of the word "evil" continues to surface, in remembering Ronald Reagan's pronouncements on the Soviet Union and in characterizing our current enemies in the war on terror, particularly in the tactics they employ, such as beheadings of innocents. *The New Yorker* columnist Hendrik Hertzberg would like us to believe that this term, as Reagan used it, is a political one, meaning simply "bad" behavior subject to correction, and not a true description of the condition of fallen human nature. He is misguided. Evil is a religious distinction, and the concept of evil is one wing of the age-old Manichean struggle within the human soul, which happens to be playing out in extremely violent ways in the Middle East. If we can't talk about evil in this context, we will never have the moral clarity to win this war on global terrorism. Ronald Reagan understood this, notwithstanding his son Ron's comment that he never wore "religion on his sleeve." George Bush understands this. And so does Sen. Joseph Lieberman, who said that Reagan would understand the parallels between the Cold War and the war on terror, because he would have recognized the parallels of evil involved and that our adversaries in both conflicts did not respect the God-given right to human freedom. Anyone who has any pretensions about leading this country had better understand this. Yes, there is much to do in getting at the psychological roots of the hatred that drove 9/11, but this is a fight to the death between two irreconcilable forces, and one of them is evil. The capacity and willingness to understand and to make this moral distinction are as much the battlegrounds of this war as those of actual combat, as well as critical points of contention in this election year, which is fast becoming a referendum on the nature of radical Islam. No victory, no peace.

Two Speeches for the Ages

February 3, 2005

It was called the most philosophical inaugural address ever, and I thought it was Bush's best ever, until he at least equaled, and might have topped it with his State of the Union speech. One would be hard pressed to find more comprehensive pronouncements of natural right conservatism (some might add neo-) this side of Leo Strauss, and it was blended with his own particular style of Christian political philosophy. Peggy Noonan, surprisingly, said the inaugural contained "too much God," Joseph Bottum said it had "just the right amount of God." Whatever your preference, and I lean more toward Bottum, there was plenty of Lincoln and a whole lot of Bush's favorite new friend and author, Natan Sharansky (whose book, *The Case for Democracy*, I am now reading and highly recommend). And no one can say that they were not bold, visionary messages from a President who will not be satisfied with anything less than changing the course of world history. These are big ideas – "ending tyranny in our world," "no one is fit to be a master, and no one deserves to be a slave," "self-government relies, in the end, on the governing of the self," "when you stand for your liberty, we will stand with you," and "there is no justice without freedom, and there can be no human rights without human liberty" – and no bigger ideas have guided an administration since the days of Lincoln.

Overreaching in some respects? Possibly, and as Noonan suggests, some of Bush's objectives are not possible in this world, only in the next, but we live in a world in need of more, not less, bold vision of the type that is restorative of our founding ideals and less, not more, of the "laundry list" of government commitments of favors to the special pleaders on the right and left.

There is in the insular world of American political life an extreme bias against initiatives that are not absolutely politically necessary as a last resort to respond to a crisis, and there is a void in incentives for strategic thinking that is firmly embedded in D.C. culture. In these two speeches, Bush has confronted these biases with rare choices – conviction over calculation, transformation over transaction, event-making over event-managing, and risk-taking over legacy-building.

Whither Europe?

June 3, 2005

"This constitution is in its way, a daughter of French thought." – French President Jacques Chirac.

A very perceptive quote, for, in fact, the document in its essence is a direct derivative of the ideals of the "general will" as embodied in the thought of the French philosophes who formed the ideology that led to the French Revolution, an ideology that peaked in 1789! Margaret Thatcher was even more perceptive when she wrote, "During my lifetime most of the problems the world has faced have come, in one fashion or another, from mainland Europe, and the solutions from outside it." And if you think about it, she is correct – the nihilism of World War I, Nazism, even Marxism – all have European roots.

Hopefully, as a result of the resounding defeat of the European Constitution by French and Dutch voters (even if many of the reasons for the rejection were not the right ones), reasonable heads can prevail in returning to first principles and rejecting the whole concept of a transcendent European superstate. This would be the best news for Europe, America, and the world, but I am not optimistic, for reasons that have much to do with the source of Europe's underlying problem and the unwillingness of its elites to recognize or confront it. For the problems are not primarily economic or political, but cultural and moral, and grow out of the rejection of these first principles and the very essence of French thought to which Chirac alludes, as well as to a somewhat lesser extent, German ideas.

It is clear from all indications – economic, political, demographic, and spiritual – that Europe suffers from a severe crisis of confidence. A society that will not even reproduce itself suffers from a malaise that cannot be explained by the gross national product or unemployment numbers. For an analysis of the true underlying crisis, I suggest George Weigel's book, *The Cube and the Cathedral*, in which he submits that, possibly, Europeans are at least finally beginning to ask the deeper question about their future – European unification for what? He further notes that, in this cradle of Western Christianity, the underlying constitutional debate must ultimately answer the following question: Is it possible to construct and sustain a democratic political community absent the transcendent moral reference points for ordering public life that Christianity offers the political community?

I recently wrote that it is not difficult, even for people with very little faith, to recognize a providential hand at work in the choice of Karol Wojtyla as Pope John Paul II at a critical juncture in history to help liberate Eastern Europe from totalitarianism. Is it a bigger reach to suggest that same providence at work in the selection of his successor? After all, the very name he chose, Benedict XVI, is a throwback, not so much to the last Benedict of the early 20th century, but to St. Benedict, one of the patron saints of Europe and the founder of Western monasticism, which was greatly responsible for creating what we have known as European culture. Might this mean, as some have suggested, that he will call for a revival of the Benedictine movement to restore the foundational premises of this culture? We'll see. He will make his first big splash at World Youth Day in Germany in August. That's not a bad place to start the campaign to save Europe from itself – again.

Freedom and Its Legacy

May 1, 2007

"China Approves Property Law Strengthening Its Middle Class" – March 2007 *The New York Times* headline of article announcing China's first law protecting private property.

"The whole theme of the last century and of Einstein's life is about people who fled oppression in order to go places to think and express themselves." – Walter Isaacson, author of *Einstein: His Life and Universe.*

"The case for trade is not just monetary, but moral. The case for freedom creates habits of liberty. And habits of liberty create expectations of democracy." – George W. Bush.

What is all of this about? It is about the theme of the 21st century, which I think, far beyond Einstein's 20th century, will prove to have witnessed the liberation of more people than in all of world history to date. China's announcement was but a validation of what already had become a fait accompli on the ground with many millions of its people, and the party elites there will not be able to avoid the continuing march toward the consent of the governed in their public life. Likewise, although it is very difficult to be optimistic at this point and it will be a bloody road, Islamofascism will join the 20th century forms of totalitarianism in the dustbin of history, ultimately falling before the relentless pursuit of freedom.

Who has set this example? No contest – Western civilization, primarily the English-speaking peoples, as explained by the moral philosophy of Adam Smith: pursuit of self interest, division of labor, and freedom of trade. And, as P. J. O'Rourke explains so well in a recent *Forbes* article on Networks, Smith saw clearly that the free market answered liberty's need for a larger network of voluntary associations. And he also understood that these networks are what make the free market moral, as well as free. He may not have imagined Amazon and Google, but he knew that everything would depend on freedom.

This is the reason I cannot understand why so many reasonable people are so inclined to bash Walmart. Sure, I understand their concern with the encroachment on traditional distribution systems and the disruption they can bring to communities. But the history of human freedom is paved by disruption and Schumpeter's "creative destruction." Walmart has become the world-wide model for the creative destruction of state run monopolies and the liberator of the dispossessed, and it has probably already saved more lives and lifted more people out of poverty than the United Nations could dream of. We need much more of this model, not less, and places like Russia could stand a large dose right now!

Whither Conservatism in the Obama Era?

January 4, 2009

Happy New Year! As I indicated in the close of the November letter, as Americans we should begin the new year and the prospect of a new era in our politics with enormous pride in and thanks for the wisdom of the system that will again allow us to perform the true miracle of the American experiment – the peaceful and seamless transition of political power in the most powerful nation on Earth. And as patriots, regardless of our partisan leanings, we should also wish our new President Godspeed and every success in the best interests of the American people.

As for those of us in the loyal opposition who tend toward the traditional and conservative on the political spectrum, we are presented with a set of challenges that haven't confronted our movement for at least a generation. This will require some deep soul-searching, for all is not well in the great land of political conservatism and significant damage has been done to the brand of the party that has been its vehicle, most of it self-inflicted. It has been suggested by several that much of the introspection needed by the Republican Party about its future and that of the conservative movement will be largely determined by the result of a lengthy debate about the Bush administration. That may be true, and I will have my own thoughts about the outgoing President soon, but at this point I will leave all of the party introspection to others, because as I have previously written, the GOP is important to me only to the extent that it serves as a useful vehicle for political conservatism.

So, whither conservatism in the new era that is upon us? Peter Berkowitz of the Hoover Institution at Stanford University, building on the work of Edmund Burke, has written that the essence of modern conservatism is the balancing of the claims of liberty and tradition, or showing how liberty depends on tradition. Further, he adds that the divisions within contemporary American conservatism – social conservatives, libertarians, and neoconservatives – arise from differences over which goods most urgently need to be preserved, to what extent, and with what role for government. There is much more to his analysis about how the hotly contested debates among these divisions over the competing goods play out, but this is about as concise a modern definition as I have seen.

In the wake of recent election defeats, conservatives have been counseled by a range of observers to build a "bigger tent," adopt a more "moderate" stance on a number of issues, particularly those that are considered "social" in nature, to be more "inclusive" and more "tolerant." We are told that there is a creeping "anti-intellectualism" in the movement and a turn to populist demagoguery cultivated by its principal media spokesmen, Rush Limbaugh and Sean Hannity, and personified by the new conservative star, Sarah Palin. We are advised that the demographic and generational changes in our country demand that conservatism be "modernized" to reflect the new notions of procedural fairness and social responsibility, as well as enlightened government activism to realize the goals of "positive liberty," as opposed to the "negative liberty" conceived by the Founders.

Some of this advice may be well taken, although I don't buy into a lot of it, and all of it should be included in the mix of discussion about the future of conservatism as a political movement in America. And I agree that conservatism needs new faces and that it should rethink and develop new applications for its traditional values as they apply to contemporary issues in addition to the priority of goods to be preserved. But I am troubled by those who preach "moderation" as the answer for the problems of conservatism. What is a moderate? Is it someone who splits the difference on policy issues? Is it someone who is "middle of the road?" What does that mean in the context of specific issues?

I suspect that most who use the term "moderate" have in mind its application to the issues that are usually most important to traditional or social conservatives. Should these be off the table entirely as some suggest? Why should consideration of our most deeply held values, those that are foundational to who we are as a people and as a culture be left off the table of policy deliberation? And can we and our public policy really be moderate or neutral on these foundational beliefs? Can we be neutral on the validity of the ideas espoused in the second paragraph of the Declaration of Independence? Can we be neutral on the foundational belief in a moral order undergirded by natural law? Can we be neutral on the degree to which the freedom and equality we champion can be sustained only within this moral order? What is moderation in these contexts? If we adopt a neutral stance on these issues and their implications, or bracket them out of public discourse, then our civic republican ideal of ordered liberty under the rule of law cannot survive. In the right ordering of the priority of goods, these goods must have the heaviest weighting; otherwise, all the other goods treasured by conservatives will be moot.

In a more recent article, Berkowitz suggests that a successful compromise among the divisions in conservatism can be built around a commitment to our constitutional order and its underlying principles, much as I have indicated here, but that the demand for purity by the partisans of the two major blocs – social conservatives and libertarians – will be destructive. I agree, for the reality of simple electoral math is that neither wing can be successful without the other.

This is not a rhetorical exercise, for the hopefully revived and enhanced conservative movement will be immediately challenged by a new regime that has a drastically different worldview, including that of America's foundations, as well as its future role. It ultimately will reveal itself as the most radically leftist regime in American history and one that is Eurosocialist and multicultural to its core. What will follow is a battle for the political soul of the country. So, let the debate proceed with considerable urgency.

The Cult of Fairness

March 4, 2010

For as long as there has been an American party of the left, it has been associated with an obsession with the notion of "fairness" and a related hatred of social and economic inequality of condition, which is often closely allied with envy and even hatred of the "rich." This began long before the late John Rawls, but he was one of the more recent and most articulate philosophers of fairness, and his *A Theory of Justice* (1971) is a classic in the field. One of the signature principles for which he is best known is the "difference principle," which provides that inequalities in distribution of social and economic goods should be allowed only to the extent that they directly improve the condition of the least advantaged members of society. This has grown to be the left's underlying basis for a definition of "fairness" in public policy. A current devotee of Rawls is Ronald Dworkin, whose views on distributive justice can be summarized by a quote from his book, Sovereign Virtue: "a distribution of wealth that dooms some citizens to a less than fulfilling life than others, no matter what choices they make, is unacceptable, and the neglect of equality in contemporary politics is therefore shameful."

Does this resonate with any rhetoric that we have heard lately? Well, it should, because essentially all of the Obama administration's domestic policy is drenched in it. It is not far from the surface in almost every pronouncement and proposal, from taxation to budgets to financial regulation to energy to employment policy to education to healthcare.

There is an antidote to this madness and, as usual, Thomas Sowell is here when we need him. He has recently written a series of essays under the title, *The Fallacy of Fairness* in which he totally discredits the notions of distributive justice described by Rawls and his followers and goes even further in illustrating the futility of the pursuit of fairness by describing the ways in which the discrimination of nature itself dwarfs any form of discrimination conceived by man. His conclusion is that fairness as equal treatment does not produce fairness as equal outcomes, and that the confusion between the two meanings of the word has created enormous mischief, much of it at the expense of the lagging groups of people in our society. Much more of Sowell on the subject can be found in his 1999 book, *The Quest for Cosmic Justice*, which historically shows how confused conceptions of "fairness," equality, and justice consistently end up promoting injustice and inequality.

Studies conducted in recent years and reported by Arthur C. Brooks of Syracuse University reveal that, contrary to the claims of the fairness cult, to focus public policy on inequality instead of opportunity is to make a serious error, one that will worsen the problem we hope to solve. In fact, the survey data tell us that economic mobility, not equality, is associated with happiness among the population. These findings and the common sense analysis of the historical development of cultures and political economy are pretty conclusive on the means by which opportunity and mobility are enhanced, but some people will never learn and some don't want to.

No Labels or No Convictions?

January 3, 2011

I am constantly bemused by the very large crowd of political activists who wants us all to "just get along" or "get things done" or drop the partisanship or avoid "going negative" in policy or electoral debates. My sense is that most of this comes from the pragmatic, "whatever works" people who are only casually or periodically involved with either electoral politics or public policy advocacy, but it's an attitude that I consider to be both naive and non-productive. Moreover, it represents an essential misunderstanding of our republican system, which was not designed for ease in "getting things done." It was built and thrives on an inescapable condition – the ongoing clash of interests and ideas.

The most recent manifestation of this sentiment is the "No Labels" movement, which is comprised of some very capable, knowledgeable, and well-intentioned leaders from around the country and the full ideological spectrum who are circulating a petition urging our political leaders to drop the "labels," presumably the ideological or partisan ones, to come together to solve the crisis of governance.

I'm OK with dispensing with labels of the kind that bind us to an ideological pigeon hole or blind party discipline. What bothers me is that many of these people seem to expect that we can dispense with our deepest held convictions in the interest of compromise and "getting things done," or even the fantasy of bipartisanship. There are quite a few things that shouldn't get done and many more that have been done that should be undone. As I have often written, there are some issues on which we cannot be neutral or even moderate. For example, how about the second paragraph of the Declaration of Independence? The overriding causes are ordered liberty and freedom from tyranny from whatever source, whether internal or external. What's the moderate or "no labels" position on that?

"The Unhealthy Soul of Liberalism"

February 3, 2011

The quote in the title is from *National Review* magazine and I thought it apropos to the knee-jerk reaction across the board in the liberal establishment to the Tucson shooting rampage by the deranged, drug-addled kook Jared Lee Loughner.

I suppose that Richard Hofstadter is credited with beginning the current genre with his, *The Paranoid Style in American Politics*, in 1964, an update of Charles Mackey's 19th century classic, *Extraordinary Popular Delusions and the Madness of Crowds.* These people and their camp followers are so ill that they must really believe that the conservative mindset and worldview leads one to be innately susceptible to violence and murder by metaphorical suggestion. This pathology was given credence when the American political right wing was charged with complicity in the assassination of John F. Kennedy by "creating the atmosphere" in which he was killed. And in fact, Jackie Kennedy lamented bitterly when she learned that her husband was killed by a warped leftist and said, "He didn't have the satisfaction of being killed for civil rights; it had to be some silly little communist. It even robs his death of any meaning." As James Piereson so well describes in his book, *Camelot and the Cultural Revolution,* this view, widely held by many in the liberal establishment, fed ultimately into the beginning of what he calls "punitive liberalism," the assumption that conservative America was responsible for numerous crimes and misdeeds throughout its history.

All of this sentiment comes to fore when some nutcase goes on a rampage, *except* when the perpetrator's ethnic or cultural background precludes condemnation for reasons of political correctness, such as with the shootings at Fort Hood by a confirmed Islamic jihadist sympathizer, and only when there is an opening to condemn Palin, Limbaugh, Beck, Fox News, the Tea Party, and the other usual suspects.

This country is in big trouble when loyal Americans are painted with an extremist brush while merely vigorously expressing their frustration that we have seriously drifted from our founding principles and who loudly demand that we return to them. To demonize and delegitimize these sentiments as hateful and paranoid seems to be the only remaining weapon of the progressive left, which has proven once again to be devoid of successful ideas.

The Last Bastion of Multicultural Mythology

March 4, 2011

First, it was German Chancellor Angela Merkel, then French President Nicolas Sarkozy who denounced the philosophy of multiculturalism as a failure, and finally the most ringing critique of all from British Prime Minister David Cameron who, in a recent speech to the Munich Security Conference, not only denounced it, but put the issue squarely on the table as a primary element of the security agenda of the West. But he did even more by suggesting antidotes, including what he called "muscular liberalism," by which he means that a genuinely liberal country, as opposed to one that is "passively tolerant," believes in certain values and actively promotes them and "it says to its citizens, this is what defines us as a society; to belong here means to believe in these things." This kind of talk in the European public square is long overdue. Maybe it represents the first stirrings of a wakeup call for the European malaise of the past several decades. Let's pray that it does. But also let's hope that we can see and hear this sentiment expressed loudly and publicly by our own leaders, beginning in the White House, and it would help if we could have more pressure applied by trustees and alumni to those last bastions of multicultural mythology, the upper reaches of our leading colleges and universities.

We are the product of a long trail of classical liberal values dating from the Reformation and the Enlightenment that help us distinguish between our version of reason and those not only of radical Islam, but of the core beliefs of Islam itself. This heritage has been corrupted by the postmodern notion of multiculturalism to the point of confusion about who we are. Our intellectuals have failed us in this regard and they should repent and repair the damage, the sooner the better, before we develop a terminal case of the European disease.

Islamic Voices in the Wilderness

July 10, 2011

Several months ago, David Brooks raised the question as to whether or not the events of the past year in the Middle East, which seem to represent a yearning for freedom on the "Arab street," truly undermine the ideas expressed by Samuel Huntington in his landmark 1993 essay, "The Clash of Civilizations" and his book of the same name which followed. Huntington's thesis is that the clash between the alien cultures of Islam and the West is inevitable and that the more the two cultures intermingle, the worse the conflict will be. Given the trend in events since 1979, this certainly has appeared to be the case. But the recent uprisings have given pause to this argument, and only time and events will tell.

Previously, in defending Rep. Peter King's decision to conduct hearings on the risks of domestic infiltration by radical Muslim jihadists, I have recommended the book *The Closing of the Muslim Mind*, by Robert Reilly, which addresses in much detail the essence of what Pope Benedict was saying in his major lecture in Regensburg in 2006 and what Muslim intellectuals are not yet discussing in the open as forcefully as they should be – that Islam must return to the ideological choices it made in the period from the mid-ninth to the 12th century that began its divergence with the West. In another speech that year, the Pope was clear in his reference to "a clash of civilizations… made more acute by organized terrorism. Its causes are many and complex, not least those to do with political ideology, combined with errant religious ideas…"

As Reilly makes clear, these ideas are not simply a radical perversion of Islam, they are part and parcel of Islam itself and have been imbedded for a millennium, and I am not talking about radical jihadism, but rather the core philosophical underpinnings of the Muslim faith, which are inimical to reason. They will not overcome this without a major reformation of their faith and, for better or worse, we cannot avoid being in the midst of, if not the catalyst for, this reformation.

Lately, there are glimmers of hope from some Muslim corners, to wit: Malaysian Prime Minister Abdul Razak gave an encouraging speech at Oxford University in which he exhorted Muslim moderates to speak out forcefully against terrorism, and he used Burke's famous quote, "all that is necessary for the triumph of evil is for good men to do nothing." Even more provocatively, Muslim writer Irshad Manji called out Muslim "moderates" as the problem, and said that what Islam needs is not more moderates, but more true and outspoken reformists who are willing to admit that their religion is used to incite Islamic radicalism and that a core problem for reform is Muslim "identity politics." This is rare courage and there must be much more of it. Remember, the Christian Reformation lasted about 175 years, so they are just getting started, and the notion that America will not be a participant is a fantasy. And I might add that the political correctness, multicultural ideology, and inordinate fear of "Islamophobia" that is pervasive on this subject in American intellectual circles is detrimental to the advancement of the dialogue.

The House Divided

May 4, 2012

Two fundamentally and diametrically opposed interpretations of the origin of American rights:

"We hold these truths to be self-evident, that all men are created equal, that they are endowed by their Creator with certain unalienable rights, that among these are life, liberty, and the pursuit of happiness, that to secure these rights, governments are instituted among men, deriving their just powers from the consent of the governed..." – Second paragraph, The U.S. Declaration of Independence.

"The Declaration of Independence discusses the problem of government in terms of a contract. Government is a relation of give and take, a contract, perforce, if we would follow out of which it grew. Under such a contract rulers were accorded power, and the people consented to that power on consideration that they be accorded certain rights. The task of statesmanship always has been the redefinition of these rights in terms of a changing and growing social order." – Commonwealth Club Address, Franklin D. Roosevelt, September 23, 1932.

Much as Lincoln described in his "house divided" speech of 1858 as it pertained to slavery, the nation cannot continue half under one concept of the derivation of rights and half another, as represented by these two totally opposed interpretations; it will proceed all one or all the other.

FDR compounded the problem with his annual message to Congress in 1944, in which he outlined his "Second Bill of Rights," adding wide-ranging rights to "security" to the rights of life, liberty, and pursuit of happiness, which he described as inadequate without the underlying economic security in the new self-evident rights to a job, a home, a fair wage, education, and medical care.

Herein lies the conflict between the negative rights embodied in our Constitution, which prescribes limited and enumerated powers for government, versus the progressive notion of positive rights as expressed by FDR. This positive rights concept was recently suggested by Alan Blinder in the context of the healthcare debate when he writes, "Our country was founded on the idea that the rights to life, liberty, and the pursuit of happiness are unalienable. Access to affordable healthcare is surely essential to two of these rights, maybe to all three." This is the house divided in a nutshell.

The implications of this gross misunderstanding of our grounding reach into every public issue and, as I have previously suggested on this conflict of visions as with many other issues, we cannot be neutral – there is no "moderate."

Restoring Constitutional Government

November 8, 2012

For most of the past 100 years we have been engaged in an intense debate on the purposes of government, particularly the concept of constitutional government. This debate originated earlier in the aftermath of the Civil War, continued through the growth of an industrial America, was energized by the Progressive movement of the early 20th century, and peaked in the crisis of the Great Depression of the 1930s. During this period a number of our founding principles were compromised, but the consensus of the American people in their commitment to constitutional government remained intact. However, this consensus began to unravel in the 1960s and has reached a level that is threatening to our American exceptionalism as a constitutional republic.

Why is this so? Primarily, because we have become what Michael Sandel of Harvard University describes as a procedural republic, more concerned with rights and process than with substance, where moral considerations are set aside in favor of "fair" procedures. What does this mean? It means that substantive and objective considerations in public policy are subordinated to what is considered fair, regardless of the consequences, and moral considerations are off the table.

How must we respond? First, by reminding ourselves that our founding principles embodied in the Declaration of Independence and codified in the Constitution are moral principles. Next, we must demand that our education system teach these principles and require them as part of the core curriculum necessary for graduation from our high schools and colleges.

We have re-elected an administration that has announced its commitment to "fundamentally transform the United States of America." This means nothing less than an endorsement of the progressive agenda of the early 20th century and the undermining of the constitutional principles of our founding, codified in part by Roosevelt in the 1930s and expanded by LBJ in the 1960s. The only way to counter this effort is to return to constitutional government and this will only be possible with a significant commitment to the education of our people in our founding principles.

No institution is doing a better job of this than Hillsdale College of Michigan, and their outreach is nationwide. I have been a long time supporter and I invite you to visit their website at www.hillsdale.edu and review their national outreach offerings, particularly the lecture series on the U.S. Constitution. They deserve our help in expanding this very important initiative.

Has Democracy Had Its Day?

June 1, 2013

"Our purpose is to cultivate in the largest possible number of our future citizens an appreciation of both the responsibilities and the benefits, which come to them, because they are American and they are free." – Harvard University President James Bryant Conant in the preface to the 1945 report, *"General Education in a Free Society."*

Concerns about the fragility of democracy are coming from across the political spectrum, as illustrated by the appearance of essays and interviews in the last several weeks from representatives of both ends of it, for example, Donald Kagan of Yale University from the right and columnist E. J. Dionne from the left. And they both have points well-taken in lamenting the trend, with the obvious dysfunction in evidence throughout the Western democracies, but they also have different perspectives.

Dionne sees the problem as a weakness in the ability of governments to deliver on the common goods that people want and need, and says that, "since World War II, bouts of economic growth have allowed the democracies to buy their way out of trouble. One can hope this will happen again – and soon." This seems to me a utilitarian approach. But he quotes from a recent report by the Transatlantic Academy, a global partnership of think tanks, entitled "The Democratic Disconnect," which begins with the opening statement, "Democracy is in trouble; the collective engagement of a concerned citizenry for the public good – the bedrock of a healthy democracy – is eroding."

In my reading, Kagan has a more fundamental view of the issue grounded in the failures of our education system to define this public good. In a recent *Wall Street Journal* interview, he says, "Universities are failing students and hurting American democracy. Curricula are individualized, unfocused, and scattered. I find a kind of cultural void, an ignorance of the past, a sense of rootlessness and aimlessness. Rare

are faculty with atypical views. Still rarer is an informed understanding of the traditions and institutions of our Western civilization and of our country and an appreciation of their special qualities and values."

Democracy, he has written, is "one of the rarest, most delicate and fragile flowers in the jungle of human experience." It relies on "free, autonomous, and self-reliant citizens and extraordinary leadership to flourish, even survive," and he notes that these kinds of citizens aren't born – they need to be educated. He is exactly on point and it is in this role that our intellectual community, largely represented by our elite universities, has failed us.

It is not as though we haven't been warned over the years, beginning most prominently by Allen Bloom in his 1987 bestseller, *The Closing of the American Mind*, and we don't have to look very far to see new evidence in the form of two recent studies by the National Association of Scholars, one on the prominence of race, class, and gender studies in the American history curricula of The University of Texas and Texas A&M University, and the other a scathing across the board expose' and indictment of the moral corruption and political intimidation at Bowdoin College. And I suspect that these cases are but illustrations of much deeper problems throughout higher education, despite the islands of excellence that persist against all odds.

Has democracy had its day? Are the foundations of self-government in our education system crumbling? The trend doesn't look promising, and we had better get about the business of turning it around. In a recent issue of *First Things*, R. R. Reno describes civic friendship as "possible across any number of disparities and inequalities if they are encompassed by a larger common purpose, commitment, or belief." In other words, a sense of the common good. But you can't defend what you haven't been taught and don't understand and, unfortunately, it seems that we have spent the past half century in disarming ourselves.

The Chimera of "Cosmic Justice"

May 11, 2014

Beyond any U.S. President, in his demagoguery on the fairness/inequality issue, Barack Obama has employed the pursuit of egalitarianism and the politics of envy to an extreme degree, to the point where we are rapidly becoming what Bill O'Reilly has called the "grievance nation." America never has been susceptible to such notions on a large scale, but the premise that this is an oppressive, unfair, bigoted, racist, sexist society has been fanned very effectively by Obama and his fellow travelers in the media, and the effect has been exacerbated by the failed economic policies of this administration over the past five and a half years.

Early in his first term, in his speech on Abraham Lincoln's birthday in Springfield, Illinois, Obama noted that "justice and fairness – the sense of shared sacrifice and responsibility for ourselves and one another" – is "the very definition of being American." That may be Obama's take on it, but it wasn't Lincoln's definition of justice, which was thoroughly grounded in the rule of law, not outcomes. In fact, he noted many times that the chief curb on power was not "fairness," but law, and that injustice is not corrected by displays of well-intentioned power, but by strict adherence to law. And he knew that the genius of the American system was opportunity, not "fairness." As he said, "Inequality is certainly never to be embraced for its own sake" and it should be no sanction for "the pernicious principle that no one shall have any, for fear that all shall not have some."

My use of the term "cosmic justice" is from the title of Thomas Sowell's book, *The Quest for Cosmic Justice*, which was a follow up to his classic, *A Conflict of Visions,* an essential analysis of the ideological origins of contemporary political struggles. In it, he describes cosmic justice (the type of social justice contemplated by Obama) as being of a much higher order, requiring vastly more knowledge and much more concentrated power than traditional justice. The great danger of this pursuit, according to Nobel economist Friedrich Hayek, is that it undermines and ultimately destroys the concept of a rule of law. Sound familiar?

Shortly after receiving the Nobel Prize in 1976, Hayek wrote this: "I have come to feel strongly that the greatest service I can still render to my fellow men would be that I could make the speakers and writers among them thoroughly ashamed ever again to employ the term social justice." He and his protégé Tom Sowell have made a valiant effort but, unfortunately, thanks to the current administration, this deeply misguided concept is making a comeback.

The Reformation that Awaits

October 5, 2014

The irony is almost poetic: We now have a deeply troubled and humbled Presidency the historical legacy of the incumbent of which will now rise or fall based on his success as a war President! That is if and when he ever really admits that he in fact is a war President. You can't make up this stuff.

And as I have said before, when one takes the long view backward and forward, we have really only been focused on the tactics of war, the various terrorist "groups" and the compartmentalization of the battlefield, and insufficiently on the global strategy to defeat the ideology. This is what has been missing since the inception of this war, at least since 9/11 and arguably since 1979. This is World War IV – one threat, one war, many battles, global commitment. For Obama, this notion, this worldview is totally alien, for the facts on the ground don't fit his narrative of anti-colonialism and the priority of American withdrawal. Israeli Prime Minister Benjamin Netanyahu gets it, as evidenced by his recent speech to the United Nations; Obama does not, and neither does the substantial majority of our intellectual class.

Why not? We refuse to deal directly with the threatening ideology, because of the cultural relativism that has become embedded in our institutions. We don't want to be accused of waging war on or even being critical of Islam. But the unwelcome fact and inconvenient truth is that it is in Islam itself that is embedded the ideology that must be reformed or defeated. This is the reformation that awaits and it is a deeply philosophical problem that is centuries old and that will require decades to resolve. After all, the Christian Reformation lasted more than 150 years; the Islamic one is just beginning.

No one has understood this better than Pope Benedict XVI, who expressed it in no uncertain terms in his controversial Regensburg Lecture in 2006. Without getting deep into the philosophical weeds, in essence, the problem is the nature of Islam itself, which holds that God or Allah is pure will (sola voluntas), implying a Godhead whose power is not limited even by the foundational principle of noncontradiction, the principle that governs reason. Without that, there is no philosophy and science is impossible, which is a significant reason why Islamic societies did not participate in the scientific revolution and the Enlightenment. Once this is understood, one can understand that the ultimate threat comes not simply from a perversion of Islam, but from its core.

There are voices attempting to break through on this issue, with much difficulty. One is the persecuted Somali-born American activist Ayaan Hirsi Ali, who very courageously is defying death threats to explain the true nature of the issue. Recently, she had this to say: "The core idea of Islam is submission, specifically submission to the will of Allah… the West has been exercising restraint in dealing with the metastasis of that demand for submission… And we seem to be gearing up to go after the new brand name called "Islamic State." But we have failed to challenge the underlying reality, the core idea, that makes Islam a threat."

She is exactly right and we had better listen: military action is a necessary, but insufficient response to the problem. More importantly, so-called moderate Muslim leaders and the Islamic intellectual class had better listen to the implied call and need for reformation of a religious faith that went off track a long time ago.

The Brits and the EU

March 6, 2016

After some preliminary concessions worked out by UK Prime Minister David Cameron, the stage is now set for a June British referendum on the continuation of Britain's membership in the European Union. This is a long overdue reassessment of a failed experiment in my opinion, and I would strongly suggest that every British voter get a copy of Lady Margaret Thatcher's 2002 masterpiece, *Statecraft: Strategies for a Changing World* and go immediately to the chapters on "Europe – Dreams and Nightmares" and "Britain and Europe – Time to Renegotiate" for a primer on the principles that should apply.

She starts with a quote from 19th century German Chancellor Otto von Bismarck, who, when commenting on appeals to European idealism in pursuit of the "European Idea," said "I have always found the word 'Europe' in the mouths of those politicians who wanted from other powers something they did not dare to demand in their own name." In other words, in his, as well as her view, the idea of Europe has always lent itself to a large measure of humbug because, as she notes, "not just national interests, but a great array of group and class interests happily disguise themselves beneath the mantle of synthetic European idealism."

The truth is that, after flirting with the European Idea herself early in her political career, she came to realize that "the drive to create a European superstate" is "perhaps the greatest folly of the modern era." For her, the principle flaw was that democratic accountability would be impossible across a wide array of nationalities with varying histories, cultures, values, and languages. This fear has been realized and the European Idea has become simply synonymous with bureaucracy, which she says is "the ultimate bureaucracy because it is sustained by nothing else."

She is cautious in her book about the details of how she would have renegotiated UK membership in 2002, but with her obvious pessimism about the possibility of EU democratic reform and an additional 14 years of hindsight, I suspect she would come to a recommendation to end it, not mend it.

The Brits Vote to Take Their Country Back

July 4, 2016

"We have not successfully rolled back the frontiers of the state in Britain, only to see them re-imposed at a European level with a European super-state exercising a new dominance from Brussels." – British Prime Minister Margaret Thatcher, "Speech to the College of Europe," Bruges, September 20, 1988.

In a previous issue, I recommended Lady Thatcher's book, *Statecraft: Strategies for a Changing World*, particularly its chapters on the European Union. It appears that large numbers of British voters shared her sentiments in the winning Brexit vote.

Count me as one who, on balance, applauds this result. It is a positive for the longer term, however, this will not be an easy transition and Britain has made its share of the mistakes that led them here, but it will not result in a "lesser Britain" as some have asserted. Most importantly, the U.S. must pay close attention to the support that will be needed to maintain the important "special relationship" between the U.S. and the UK, which is so critical to world order, and cut this nonsensical "go to the back of the queue" talk.

The European Community was a good idea at the outset as an economic community, particularly for a continent coming out of two devastating world wars over a 30-year period, but as it evolved into the EU after the Maastricht Treaty in 1992, as usual, the natural inclination of the state in its arrogance is to more centralization and more aggrandizement, eventually leading to tyranny. And Lady Thatcher told them so, for after initially supporting the so-called "European Idea," she came to realize that "the drive to create a European superstate" is "perhaps the greatest folly of the modern era."

So the EU elites (some of whom govern at Westminster) brought this on themselves, and dismissive, condescending, overreaching progressivism has been overthrown by populist ethnic nationalism yelling Stop! And this is primarily not the bigotry of the masses as many observers would have us believe, but mainly a healthy nationalism proud of the good things in its heritage. Can it happen here? Is Brexit a form of Trumpism? Stay tuned.

A Trump Movement?

January 3, 2017

President-elect Donald Trump says that his victory was grounded in a "movement." Is it a movement? If so, what's it about? Like a lot of folks, I have spent considerable time since election day and read and heard tens of thousands of words by various analysts investigating this and related aspects of the Trump phenomena.

The best answers I have found are in revisiting a book I read and reviewed more than six years ago, *The Next American Civil War: The Populist Revolt Against the Liberal Elite*, by Lee Harris. I had previously come into contact with Harris when I commented on an essay he had written in Policy Review entitled "The Tea Party vs. the Intellectuals." He contacted me and offered a copy of the book and I accepted. The book is in many ways an expansion of his theme in the essay, but it is also a broadening of the description of the cultural conflict and the history of American thought that has brought us to this point. I highly recommend it.

The conflict, of course, has all the elements of a populist revolt, of which, as he points out, there have been several in our history. But he adds, "Today's popular revolt is different from earlier populist revolts, because it is a rebellion against a new kind of elite. It is an elite that is a product of the modern system of education-based meritocracy that has come to dominate not only the U.S., but all the advanced nations of the world." And this cognitive elite, he says, can exclude ordinary people from deciding who gets to be a member, even though they might have access through merit, and to that extent it is self-selecting and self-perpetuating, anathema to the populists.

Another element that is different is that, in the past, the anti-elitism of American populism positioned it in conflict with the American conservative tradition; in fact, one could say that the term "populist conservative" historically has been an oxymoron. But no longer, for they have now largely merged their key cultural issues and work closely on the political stage. And as Harris notes in extended discussion, what most agitates the populist conservative is a conviction that America is losing it historical uniqueness, well-known to them as "American exceptionalism," as that term has come to define America's status as "chosen by divine providence to play a uniquely benevolent role in the general history of mankind."

So to sum up his analysis in overly general terms, what we have on one side of the cultural divide are those who believe they are entitled to govern by virtue of their superior knowledge and expertise and on the other side we have those who resent being governed by anyone at all and are fully convinced that they are best equipped to control their own lives. Current economic anxieties are certainly part of the mix for the latter group, but it is far more motivated by a sense of cultural alienation with the cognitive elites, and it is this spirit which won the day for Trump. Does this revolt make a movement? Can Trump lead it to a major turn for America? No one knows, but it will be a bumpy ride.

Are We Witnessing a Global Tea Party?

March 6, 2017

Ever since the Brexit vote in Great Britain last summer followed by Donald Trump's victory in November, coupled with the strengthening of political movements on the populist right in other European countries, we are besieged by analysts left and right who wonder whether we are witnessing a massive move to populist nationalism in the West. Then Trump continued using "America First" as a major theme of his administration and added to the paranoia in the U.S. media by hiring a notorious bogeyman to the left, former Breitbart executive Steve Bannon, as one of his top strategic advisors in the White House. The speculation about what this means for America, the West, and world order has since intensified, but several have at least given it some calm and considered thought, helped along by Bannon, who recently came out into the open for the first time since the inauguration with an appearance at the Conservative Political Action Conference.

In this appearance, he seemed to very helpfully offer somewhat of a creed in his view of nationalism, possibly even of Trump's view of America First, although those words were not used. Here is what he said:

"The center core of what we believe, that we're a nation with an economy, not an economy just in some global marketplace with open borders, but we are a nation with a culture and a reason for being."

If this is the core of American nationalism, there are a lot of folks who will buy into that, and many obviously already have. But he says more:

"This movement is the working men and women in the world who are just tired of being dictated to by what we call the party of Davos."

Sounds like the makings of a global tea party to me, but President Trump has made it clear that he has no interest in being "global president." And whether or not he has fleshed out all the implications of America First is questionable, but I'll bet Steve Bannon has, along with the nationalist, anti-globalist playbook that goes with it. We almost certainly can't all agree about the nature of our culture and reason for being, even though the founders did a pretty good job of spelling it out and, in spite of a civil war, at one time there was a fair amount of consensus on that, but after all that's what the current debate is about, isn't it?

There is a lot more to come on this discussion and it won't be resolved soon. One of the best comments I have seen came from an essay entitled "Why Historians Get It Wrong" by Jeremy Black in *The New Criterion:*

"There is no greater gulf than that between, on the one hand, those who identify primarily with their nation, and are concerned at what globalization might be doing to it and to them personally, and, on the other hand, those who identify with wider abstractions and are more concerned with retaining the benefits that globalization has brought them."

China's Puzzling Recognition of Karl Marx

June 5, 2018

China's recognition of the 200th anniversary of the birth of Karl Marx is strange on several levels. First, it comes during what many believe and the facts support in large measure, which is a capitalism-inspired economic miracle for the country. Second, it honors a man whose economic theories were largely discredited and whose philosophical grasp of human nature misguided, the human cost of which have been the deaths of untold millions, and counting, in the regimes that were and still are beholden to Marxism and its closely related socialist ideology. And, in fact, it was under the leadership of Chairman Mao Zedong, founder of the Chinese communist regime, that Maoism, a close relative of Marxism, produced human death and suffering that dwarfed most others, including those of Hitler and Stalin. Yet China's supreme leader for life, Xi Jinping, seems to be promoting Marx as some kind of rallying symbol for the nation in all kinds of celebrations.

When I was in China with a group about 10 years ago for a cultural exchange and meetings with several Politbureau-level leaders, I had the sense that they somehow know that they are living a lie which is on borrowed time. And they probably feel threatened by a rebound of Confucianism, the rapid growth of Christianity, and the fear of another Tiananmen Square debacle, which would no doubt doom the regime. So, maybe it isn't too surprising that they would use Marx's bicentennial as a focal point to remind the nation that in their adopted form his ideas have enabled it to return to greatness and as a way to demand loyalty to the ruling party.

Chinese historian Daniel Leese describes it this way: "The posthumous cult of Marx these days serves to legitimize the present leadership and whatever it claims Marxism to be, and only Xi Jinping is said to be capable of synthesizing classical doctrine with present realities."

It remains to be seen how long this lie can hold out.

The Perversion of Truth

November 11, 2018

"Not only do women like Dr. Ford, who bravely comes forward, need to be heard, but they need to be believed." – Sen. Maize Hirono (D), Hawaii.

One of the most troubling aspects of the Kavanaugh nomination debacle, aside from the refutation of the jurisprudential presumption of innocence and the burden of proof, was the exposure of the ongoing perversion of truth in our public discourse. Victor Davis Hanson said it well: "Truth, due process, evidence, rights of the accused. All are swept aside in pursuit of the progressive agenda. George Orwell's 1949 dystopian novel, *1984,* is no longer fiction. We are living it right now." And Secretary of Education Betsy DeVos identifies the culprit: "The pernicious philosophy of relativism teaches that there is no objective truth. Nothing is objectively good or objectively evil. 'Truth' is only personal point of view – you have your truth and I have mine – fleeting circumstance and one's own desires. And those views, those experiences, those desires can be understood only by those who live them. Nothing else and no one else matters."

And this kind of truth has taken on several forms. One is "poetic truth," so well defined by Shelby Steele in the context of racial politics as a narrative that disregards the actual truth in order to assert a larger essential truth that supports one's ideological position and that defends the sovereignty of one's ideological identity by taking license with reality and fact, in this case that America is an intractably racist society. This brand of truth is manifest throughout our elite universities as students and left-leaning faculties interpret every issue through the prism of identity politics, social justice, and the essential truths of progressive ideology.

Another kind is "therapeutic truth," much in evidence in the Kavanaugh hearings, in which the therapist's job is, according to psychoanalyst Erica Komisar, "to emphasize and believe the patient's story, not test it against objective reality, and in which in many cases therapy leads patients to change the stories they tell themselves to heal their emotional wounds."

Of course these diversions grow from relativism's primary product, the 20th century notion of "postmodernism," the philosophical concept that there is no universal truth and, in particular, no moral truth and no natural law, a concept which is anathema to the Western intellectual tradition. It is nihilistic to its core and totally destructive of the foundation for the rule of law so necessary for the survival of a democratic republic. Without this foundation, we can't run a country, a judiciary, or a Senate. We must stop this post-truth cancer before it completely seeps into and corrupts our jurisprudence and social order.

Surprise, Surprise: We're in a Culture War

February 6, 2019

A couple of weeks ago, Gerald Seib wrote, "The border wall fight is more than a border wall fight. It has crystallized a deep cultural divide, between those happy with the evolving face of America and those alarmed by it." Well, duh, this has been the obvious state of affairs for the past 50 years, Gerald, but thanks for the update. And, by the way, in case you've missed it, the left has been winning pretty consistently.

My friend Greg Stachura sent me a piece by the late American jurist Robert Bork from *The Wall Street Journal* in October 1997, the key phrase of which deserves to be quoted in full: "The growth and intrusiveness of governments and the vitality of our economy are important conservative issues. But in our current state of affluence, social and cultural issues are more important to the good life. They are also where the votes are. To get these votes and restore sanity and morality to our lives, we must do nothing less than refight the battles of the 1960s – battles over educational curricula, the content of popular culture, the feminization of the military, the understanding of the family, the proper spheres of reason and emotion, and much more. This long countermarch through the institutions will not be easy. The resistance of the cultural elite will be furious. But until it makes that fight, conservatism will continue to fail."

This about sums up the nature of the fight and the sentiments still loudly resonate today. So, how is the "countermarch" coming along? In a recent issue of Imprimis, a publication of Hillsdale College, Charles Kesler describes the current clash as "America's Cold Civil War" and it basically boils down to a conflict of visions about our Constitution, which has been going on for more than 100 years – the conservative/originalist vision that views the document based on its original meaning as amended, the other that views the document as a "living" instrument to be adjusted for the progressive needs of the 21st century. Again, in its current form this is already a 50-year war and shows no signs of abating, and Kesler doesn't seem to be very optimistic about the countermarch.

I recently caught up with an interesting take on what conservatives should do to regain the momentum, and how to do it, in an article for *The American Mind* entitled "Our House Divided: Multiculturalism vs. America," by Thomas Klingenstein, Chairman of the Claremont Institute. He writes that "conservatives have been dazed by Trumpism" and are not quite certain what is to be learned from Trumpism that might inform the future of the conservative movement and maybe even provide impetus to the countermarch.

For Klingenstein the lesson is this: get right with Lincoln. What does that mean? Lincoln made opposition to slavery the non-negotiable center of the Republican Party. He was prepared to compromise on all else, because for him the public's understanding of justice was the single most important political issue. Klingenstein is suggesting that conservatives should do likewise with multiculturalism, which threatens our understanding of justice. He believes that, in effect, Trump already had framed the 2016 election as a choice between two mutually exclusive regimes – multiculturalism (including "identity politics" and "political correctness") and America, with its fully formed exceptional culture.

And the other way to "get right with Lincoln," he believes, is to relearn what Lincoln knew, that the purpose of higher education, in particular elite higher education, is to train future citizens on behalf of the common good. And this common good is being undermined by the multiculturalism that is currently pervasive in these institutions.

I think that Klingenstein is on to something here that just might begin to turn the momentum and jump start the countermarch, and who would have thought that Donald Trump's America First might be the catalyst.

19
Public Education

No Excuses

May 1, 2000

The Heritage Foundation recently has published a report entitled "No Excuses: Lessons From 21 High-Performing High-Poverty Schools," based on research conducted by Samuel Casey Carter, a Bradley Fellow at the Foundation. I strongly recommend it to anyone remotely concerned with the state of public education in this country. Carter's research comprised a nationwide survey of the best practices used by successful schools that serve above average "at-risk" populations. For all the differences in these schools, they share certain core beliefs and traits. Seven traits are common to all: 1) principals are free to run their schools, 2) principals use measurable goals to establish a culture of achievement, 3) master teachers bring out the best in a faculty and effective principals turn their schools into schools for teachers, 4) rigorous and regular testing leads to continuous student achievement, 5) achievement is the key to discipline, 6) principals work actively with parents to make the home a center for learning, and 7) effort creates ability, or time on task is the key to success in school. These traits translate into a set of practices common to all the successful high at-risk schools.

The two most common themes throughout the study are the importance of leadership from the principal's office and the high expectations for all students held by these schools. Universally, these successful schools dismiss the popular wisdom that poor or otherwise socially disadvantaged children are doomed to lag behind their peers or that only "developmentally appropriate" instructional models should be used with these children. To these principals, this is a cop out that has been used to blame the children, the family, or the society for the failures of the schools. Of the hundreds of U.S. schools surveyed, 21 were selected to be profiled in the final report. It has been my privilege to have worked closely for several years with the leadership of one of these schools, Thaddeus Lott and Wilma Rimes of Houston's Wesley Elementary, in the development of an early intervention reading initiative in Houston sponsored by the Houston Livestock Show and Rodeo. From this experience, as well as close observation of practices, methodologies, and results in a range of environments, I can testify as a layman that we know what works. We know how to be successful in high-poverty, low socioeconomic environments. We have known these things from research and common sense observation for years. So why is it that, as indicated in the Heritage study, 58 percent of low-income fourth graders can't read? There are many culprits and not enough room here to give them their due, but the malpractice of the education establishment is staggering. Friends, there are no excuses.

Teacher Education Reform

May 4, 2001

William Raspberry asks in an August 2000 editorial why more administrators of mediocre public schools aren't learning from the practices of models and methodologies in their midst that are proving successful, particularly in very high "at-risk" environments. Good question. I wonder why best practices in reading instruction, in which I have been very active, are not more readily adopted by educators who are failing in their mission to teach children how to read. In my case, I've been heavily involved in attempting to convince several colleges of education of the clear superiority of Direct Instruction reading methods in high at-risk elementary school populations, where it is well demonstrated that even mediocre teachers can be successful with proper application of the process. The response has been frustrating at best, tragically slow at worst.

Colleges of education have been mired in the progressive education ideologies of John Dewey since the 1920s. Some of these are fine for those children who come from an educationally and socially enriched family environment, but disastrous for the children who do not and for their teachers, many of whom are of marginal competence and need a more structured approach. In these environments, teachers must teach, not facilitate. Meanwhile, pedagogical change in teacher training remains on hold, while the latest National Assessment of Educational Progress report shows that two-thirds of the nation's fourth graders lack proficiency in reading. And of all the factors contributing to these results, research shows that class size, ethnicity, location, and poverty levels all pale to triviality compared to teacher competence.

In all of the talk about accountability in education, I hear very little about holding our colleges of education accountable for these results. Contrast this with our top colleges of business, which are totally accountable to the employers (customers) who hire their product. The difference is incentives. In a monopoly industry in which a unionized workforce that controls entry and certification delivers the primary service, even well proven innovation doesn't stand a chance.

This is why empowering parents with school choice and enlightened school administrators with alternative training and certification of teachers must externally drive education reform. The former is ultimately inevitable and the latter is a growing trend, as more schools grow weary of the often mediocre product of traditional teacher education.

Arrogance in Education

April 8, 2002

In my travels among education policy-makers I am constantly amazed at the arrogance of some public educators who, unfortunately, comprise a large portion of what passes for industry leadership. There are two recent examples among many I could cite. In one, the Austin ISD Board rejected proposals from "outside" entities to manage woefully under-performing schools. Board members said they want the district to find ways "on its own" to fix the problem, and teachers' groups were fearful that a successful private school solution would serve as a model for more widespread parental school choice, anathema to them. The other example comes from recent comments by several members of the Texas State Board of Education along with Lt. Gov. Bill Ratliff, to the point that people who do not have children in public schools should not have a role in education policy as members of the SBOE. The latter example flies in the face of all philosophical grounding of our constitutional basis in the truth of objective reality and the rule of law, and both examples are evidence of the arrogance of the current system in the face of massive failure to serve our children.

Dr. Paul T. Hill is Director of the Center on Reinventing Public Education at the University of Washington. In his excellent 1998 book, *Fixing Urban Schools*, he outlines the roots of disagreement among school reform advocates as between intrinsic and extrinsic reforms. Simply put, intrinsic reformers are those totally protective of the prerogatives of the education establishment and highly skeptical of any external reform motivation, particularly economic. Extrinsic reformers, on the other hand, are typically not professional public educators and do not believe that public education can "heal thyself" without significant external motivation, particularly from reforms that introduce competition and "marketization" of the system.

No doubt there are deep-seated ideological and cultural groundings for these respective approaches that in many ways transcend education policy, and they surface in almost every policy forum in which I participate, bringing me to one more example of arrogance. At a recent policy meeting of an education reform organization to which I belong, it was suggested to me, as an extrinsic reformer, that the burden of proof for our reform proposals is on us to show that they would not work to the detriment of the stakeholders in the status quo. With this attitude prevalent even among many who call themselves reformers, bold systemic public education reform and hope for our underserved children in failing schools are still pipe dreams.

A Time to Choose

July 4, 2002

When I served as Chairman of Texas Business Leaders for Educational Choice during the 1998-99 Texas legislative biennium, I began most of my speeches and debates across the state with the following opening:

"Let's start with a basic premise about the school choice debate: No child should be left behind because of failure of the education distribution system to deliver the best possible opportunity. If we cannot deliver on this commitment, we are failing in our public education responsibility, and no historical attachment to a particular delivery system should prevent our making the necessary changes. We are talking about lives, about our future as a society. This debate is about children, not about a system. School choice is a public policy whose time has come."

With the Supreme Court decision in the Cleveland school choice case, a huge "red herring" has been removed and we can now move to the next level of what I believe will be the civil rights revolution of the 21st century. Church-state considerations have never really been the critical issue with school choice opponents. Their opposition is all about power and protection of the perks of the status quo for the entrenched vested interests of the educational establishment. Now we can get on with the more substantive elements of the debate without the First Amendment smokescreen. What are these? Most prominently, the opposition has done a great job in shaping the debate into a focus on "draining" funds from the public schools. My response here is that, first, it is very difficult to make the case that public education is underfunded, but, more to the point, in an truly competitive system, the ultimate accountability is the power of the customer, parents and their children, to "vote with their feet" and have the funding follow the child. Remember that school choice already exists for those who are privileged to be able to afford a private school or a home in an affluent neighborhood with a high quality public school. The substantial majority of those left behind without such choices are relatively poor, inner city, and often minority children. We owe them the same opportunity.

The biggest hurdle in my school choice advocacy has been the reluctance among many to understand and accept the dynamics of competition and how, in a choice environment, these dynamics will produce a supply of quality education alternatives to meet the demand. So well entrenched is the static one-size-fits-all delivery system with its top-down mandates and accountability that we fear the dynamics of a deregulated market for education. Will there be failures? Sure, but there are numerous failures in the current delivery system that cannot begin to be rectified by the existing perverse incentives favoring compliance over performance. School choice in Texas can supplement the state's top-down accountability system with a bottom-up accountability system, and the resulting competitive environment will drive improvement for all.

In Rod Paige's final "State of the Schools" address as Superintendent of the Houston Independent School District, he outlined a very bold strategy to have HISD become "the K-12 education system of choice for the citizens of Houston." This is a commendable objective for Houston and Texas that can only be achieved if there is a truly competitive alternative to the present delivery system. Let's give choice a chance.

The Teacher Preparation Challenge

September 2, 2002

As we begin the new school year and, in Texas, look toward the next level of school performance accountability, I believe it is important that we look beyond the test-driven accountability system, as useful as it has been, for more instructive leading indicators of progress toward excellence in public education. As Texas Education Commissioner Felipe Alanis said in a recent appearance in Houston, "it's not about where we are, it's about where we are going." And I suggest we even look past the new, more rigorous Texas Assessment of Knowledge and Skills (TAKS) test as such an indicator. As anyone reasonably conversant with education performance knows, the success of the students in the classroom can be directly correlated with the quality of the teacher in the classroom. This has been confirmed by numerous studies, most particularly those that focus on value added for individual students after controlling for background characteristics like socioeconomic status. What this means for those of us who are concerned about "where we are going" is that the quality of our teacher preparation system is the absolutely critical element in the enhancement of the quality of our children's education.

So, what is the quality of our teacher preparation system? For a current status report, I recommend "Meeting the Highly Qualified Teachers Challenge: The Secretary's

Report on Teacher Quality," recently released by Secretary of Education Rod Paige. To be blunt, it isn't a pretty picture on a national basis, and Texas is no exception. The report describes teacher preparation generally as "a broken system" that is "failing to produce the types of highly qualified teachers that the No Child Left Behind Act demands." There are many specific criticisms in the report, the most glaring of which are the very low academic standards for teachers. For example, on one widely used teacher certification test, only one state out of 29 set its passing score near the national average (50th percentile) in reading. This is particularly discouraging when we realize that studies have consistently documented an important correlation between a teacher's verbal and cognitive skills and student achievement, particularly in the early formative years. In my experience with reading intervention in the Houston area, I have found that almost none of the teacher preparation programs are properly preparing their teachers to teach at-risk children how to read. More than 50 percent of Houston area fourth graders do not read at grade level and in 129 of the Houston ISD's 177 elementary schools, the average third grade reading level is below the 50th percentile in national norm-referenced testing. You would think that the curriculum of area colleges of education would be highly focused on the research-based methodologies that have been proven to work with these children, but, sad to say, they remain mired in the constructivist, "reading comes natural" mindset.

The Secretary's report is especially critical of the present system of teacher certification and the degree to which it is overly beholden to the traditional route to preparation through the colleges of education with their emphasis on pedagogical instruction versus academic content. It applauds the expansion of alternative routes to certification that bypass the traditional system, but laments the fact that often these are still loaded with too many non-academic content requirements.

The No Child Left Behind Act requires that all teachers be "highly qualified" by the end of the 2005-06 school year in order for their schools to continue to qualify for Federal Title I financial assistance. The exact definition of "highly qualified" is still being refined, but there is no doubt that the bar has been raised for teacher preparation programs and, based on the current status of these programs, there is a huge challenge ahead. As a member of the Texas State Board for Educator Certification, I have more than a passing interest in this problem, but anyone who has a stake in public education – parents, taxpayers, employers, public officials – should be asking what we are doing to meet this daunting challenge. We hear a lot about the teacher quantity problem, but not enough about the quality problem. If we fail to meet this challenge, all our progress in public education accountability will have been for naught.

Lessons from California

October 3, 2002

The latest word from California education officials is that they are discussing whether to postpone the enforcement of the state's new high school graduation exam, because so many students (evidently up to 50 percent) are failing the test. The president of the state education board has stated that a low pass rate could leave the exam open to legal challenges about its fairness, and he suggested that a legally defensible pass rate would be above 90 percent!

I have a suggestion: the parents should sue the public school system for its complete failure to honor its contract to educate the students. For what we have here is the reaping of what California has sowed in its public education policies for the past 40 years – constructivist curriculum, whole language reading instruction, and the primacy of the pursuit of Rousseauite self-esteem. The answer is not to back down on standards, defer accountability, and "dumb down" the curriculum, but to tell the truth about the current state of the educational preparation of our children. Then maybe we can really get serious about truly meaningful reforms, such as school choice.

More rude awakenings are in store: The No Child Left Behind Act will not be kind to those states that do not meet the "highly qualified teacher" mandate (California is already on notice), and the new SAT college admission test is reportedly much more rigorous and, hopefully, will call further attention to the deficiencies of many more public schools, including rampant grade inflation and the huge disconnect between K-12 and higher education. And in Texas, the new Texas Assessment of Knowledge and Skills (TAKS) test will be in use at the end of this school year, coinciding with the new law limiting social promotion in public schools. Hopefully the State Board of Education will resist the call of many school administrators to set the TAKS passing score at a minimal level so that we can properly assess true student preparedness.

Recently, I agreed to participate in the Texas textbook selection process by reviewing a high school economics textbook. In addition to the overall "value neutral" tenor of the textbook, I was shocked at the lack of depth of discussion of the issues and concepts and the general lack of rigor in the text. The presentation was right out of MTV – lots of color, graphs, charts, sidebars, and flash – like watching an action TV show. Folks, if this is the standard, we have a long way to go. I hope we're paying close attention to California; it may be instructive for us.

The College of Education Disconnect

November 2, 2002

Recently, I had the opportunity to speak to the fall teacher education conference of the Consortium of State Organizations for Texas Teacher Education (CSOTTE). It was quite an experience, primarily because, probably needless to say, much of my evaluation of colleges of education is at extreme variance with the audience of approximately 400 deans, associate deans, and education curriculum directors.

What strikes me most as a disconnect with the teacher education establishment (and I must be careful here not to overly generalize) is that it seems to recognize no real connection between teacher preparation and student performance, nor any responsibility for the under-performance of public education. The collective attitude, usually implied, but often expressed, is "we do the best we can with the raw material we're given to work with." The truth is closer to this: Traditional educator preparation leadership is totally immersed in the shibboleths of "discovery" or "learner-centered" philosophy in learning, "academic freedom" in pedagogy, resistance to "teaching to the test," and opposition to competitive value-added evaluation of performance and accreditation of programs.

I have been repeatedly reminded that a public school is not a business and cannot be managed as such. I accept that there are major differences, but I am equally sure that public education and the institutions and programs that supply its management are not immune to the incentives that drive human nature and performance in business and other walks of life. I am further convinced that the next phase of education reform must include radical reform of teacher preparation and teaching methods inside the classroom. This will require a re-evaluation of many of the most cherished "sacred cows" of the education establishment. It is long overdue.

"A Nation at Risk" at 20

June 4, 2003

In April, there was quite a lot of attention given to the 20th anniversary of "A Nation at Risk," the 1983 report of a blue-ribbon task force on the state of education in the U.S. Almost anyone vaguely familiar with the report remembers the oft-quoted finding that "The educational foundations of our society are presently being eroded by a rising tide of mediocrity that threatens our very future as a nation and a people…

If an unfriendly foreign power had attempted to impose on America the mediocre educational performance that exists today, we might well have viewed it as an act of war. As it stands, we have allowed this to happen to ourselves."

Over the past few weeks, many have asked what has been done in response to this challenge, and what has been the result. Of all the commentary, the best I have seen came from the Hoover Institution's Koret Task Force on K-12 Education, which published a follow-up report entitled "Our Schools and Our Future – Are We Still At Risk?" In it, the message is more shocking than the original report: after 20 years of reforms requiring vastly increased expenditures and effort, the performance of the U.S. public education system remains virtually unchanged. Why is this so? The authors primarily identify three powerful forces, underestimated by the commission in 1983, that have converged to thwart true reform: 1) the organized interests of the K-12 system, including teachers' unions, school administrators, colleges of education, state bureaucracies, and school boards; 2) the tenacity of the "thought world" of the nation's colleges of education, which see themselves as owners of the nation's schools and the minds of educators; and 3) the large number of Americans, particularly in middle-class suburbs, who believe that their schools are basically sound. To overcome this resistance, the 11 members of the Task Force unanimously concluded that "… fundamental changes are needed in the incentive structures and power relationships of schooling itself. Those changes are anchored in three core principles – accountability, choice, and transparency."

Put simply, we have an institutional problem that cries out for massive restructuring, but we are hamstrung by vested interests and powerful constituencies that can effectively veto structural change. There is hope, however, and I see it in the growing anger and protests among parents over so-called "high stakes" testing. Already in Florida and Massachusetts, as well as possibly other states (probably soon to include Texas as the new TAKS test becomes fully effective), there are serious challenges to a system that fails to prepare large numbers of children academically, then denies them high school graduation and access to higher education. Some feel that the testing itself is the problem, but I am encouraged that most will avoid that cop out and that this may be the beginning of a powerful revolt at the grass roots that will demand systemic reform. If so, it is not a minute too soon, and it deserves the support of our business and opinion leadership so that we don't condemn another generation to educational mediocrity.

The Civic Education Debate

February 1, 2004

"Properly speaking, there is no such thing as education. Education is simply the soul of a society as it passes from one generation to the next." – G. K. Chesterton.

I am reminded of the above quote, which is among those taped to my desk, by numerous articles and commentary highlighting the debate over civic education in America's public schools, to wit: what is the proper role, if any, of the teaching of civic virtue in our system of public education? Lately, the answer to this question essentially has boiled down to a tug of war between the political right and left, not about whether to teach civic virtue, but which values to teach. In spite of the claims of partisans on both sides, most professional educators seem to subscribe to the view that, since there is much broader consensus on the so-called intellectual virtues than the civic and moral virtues, public education should confine itself to the former while the latter should be left to the home and religious institutions. A corollary to this view is that the schools should focus more on training the mind toward the pursuit of knowledge than on the transmission of a specific body of knowledge. To me, this is a constructivist cop out. Public education cannot be value-neutral and, to paraphrase Rabbi Daniel Lapin, depriving children of grounding in America's civic virtue and belief may be a form of child abuse. Of all forms of government, a liberal democratic republic is most vulnerable to failure when it cannot, or will not, transmit its founding values from one generation to the next.

A Modest Step Toward Educator Preparation Reform

March 1, 2004

Last November, the Texas State Board for Educator Certification (SBEC), on which I was appointed to serve by Governor Rick Perry, narrowly approved a very controversial rule authorizing probationary certification to aspiring teachers who want to be licensed to teach using an alternative to the traditional certification route, typically through the colleges of education. Recently, the State Board of Education (SBOE), in effect, ratified the new rule by failing to veto it. There is nothing particularly revolutionary about this new rule; in fact, there are more than 60 so-called alternative certification programs in Texas, and approximately 25 percent of the new teachers licensed in the state last year used an alternative route. What is deemed by its opponents as so radical about this new route, and what made it so controversial, is the fact that, unlike the other alternatives, it circumvents the traditional "gatekeepers" to the profession – the state education bureaucracy and the colleges of education – and gives the school district superintendents the flexibility and discretion to manage their human resources by determining who is qualified to teach in the classrooms under their jurisdiction.

There has been much confusion and misrepresentation in reporting about the new rule itself. Basically, its provisions are as follows: If a prospective teacher who has a baccalaureate or advanced degree in an academic major other than education passes the appropriate certification exams and background checks and is hired by a school district to teach in the subject area of preparation in grades eight to 12, the candidate will be granted a probationary certificate for a maximum of two years, at the end of which time the school district decides, based on the teacher's performance, whether or not to recommend the issuance of full standard certification. The school district must provide evidence that the teacher has been provided intensive support during the probationary period through mentoring and pre-service training.

When this concept was proposed (unsuccessfully) as legislation in both the 2001 and 2003 regular sessions, it seemed pretty reasonable to me, and I have consistently supported it. But from the loud protests of the various constituencies who have a vested interest in the status quo, one might have thought that it was the ruination of public education in general and the noble calling of the teaching profession in particular. At the public hearing conducted by our Board on the proposed rule, there was testimony from 50 witnesses, the large majority in opposition, primarily representing the teachers' unions and advocacy groups, colleges of education, and assorted education activists. While much of the opposition came from groups to which this new alternative represents a healthy competitive threat, it is instructive to note that significant support for the new rule came from organizations representing school boards and school administrators and personnel directors, who are, after all, the primary customers of SBEC and the teacher preparation system.

In the final analysis, I believe that public policy in teacher preparation should be guided by several priorities as follows, all of which should have as their primary objective the advancement of Texas student achievement:

- We should fully define "highly qualified teacher" for Texas not just in regulatory terms, but in terms of the qualities and performance that are expected, which will necessitate a re-evaluation of the strategic policy document, "Learner-Centered Schools for Texas: A Vision of Texas Educators," adopted in 1997, as well as the transformation of educator employment terms from "contract" to "at will," with enhanced compensation based on performance tied to student achievement.

- We should demand the transformation of educator preparation programs into customer-driven institutions by developing assessments of them that are grounded in output- and performance-based criteria, so that Texas becomes the model for value-added evaluation of such programs.
- We should emphasize regulatory rule making that allows for the maximum prudent flexibility for school district administrators to manage their human resources, and demand accountability for student achievement results.

It is my hope that this new rule will represent a truly new route to standard certification for many prospective teachers in Texas and a useful tool for districts to meet a portion of their personnel needs, and not be used simply as a "quick fix" for the widely reported teacher shortages, as some have suggested. To the extent that it is at variance with the existing top-down, compliance- and input-based system of certification governed by the traditional monopoly routes to teaching, it is a small step toward what some have called "competitive certification," a concept I believe we should embrace and expand.

Special Edition: Education Reform in Texas – The Next Phase

May 5, 2004

In speaking and writing about the current status of Texas public education reform, I am often torn, in the metaphor of the drinking glass, between the half full and half empty portions and sometimes criticized for my emphasis on the half empty portion. So let me start with the half full portion. There is no doubt that Texas has led the nation in public education reform and has served as a model for other states in the advancement of standards and accountability. In fact, the centerpiece of President Bush's education initiative, the No Child Left Behind Act, is almost a carbon copy of the Texas model. And Houston, under the former leadership of Bush's Secretary of Education Rod Paige and an enlightened board of trustees, has been a beacon for urban school reform, having achieved well-deserved recognition as the best urban school district in America. This is the half full part, and it has been accomplished by the dedication of a statewide coalition of educators, administrators, and legislative and business leaders in a consistent effort over a period of 20 years.

However, I submit that the easier phases of reform are behind us in Texas, that we are at a critical juncture, that there is some evidence of backsliding, and that the most difficult phase lies ahead. I offer two examples of many available to illustrate why the easy part of reform is behind us. One involves the level of reading achievement, and I will use Houston ISD reading scores as a proxy. On the 2003 SAT-9 reading test, a nationally norm-referenced test, more than 60 percent of Houston's third graders scored below grade level, and on the 2002 National Assessment of Educational Progress test of reading achievement, 52 percent of Houston's fourth graders and 41 percent of eighth graders scored below basic achievement level, while only 18 percent and 17 percent, respectively, were at or above proficient level. It is also noteworthy that Houston's average SAT-9 reading scores for 2003 peaked in the first grade at the 51st percentile, and consistently declined beyond that point to the 27th percentile for ninth grade students, a level at which a student has almost no comprehension of the assigned textbooks.

At this late date, and 20 years after the publication of "A Nation at Risk," these results represent a tragedy, and the fact that they were better than other major U.S. urban districts (remember, this is the best urban school district in America) is little consolation when one considers that, ultimately, the dropout odds are stacked heavily against any child who cannot read at grade level by the end of third grade. To compound the tragedy, we can't plead ignorance. We know "what works" and how to fix the problem – the education establishment knows how to teach the vast majority of at-risk children how to read, as well as read to learn at a very early age, which is in itself a subject for another essay.

The other example illustrating the more difficult task ahead involves access to higher education by racial and ethnic minorities. Based on surveys over recent years of the potential college applicant pool of African Americans and Hispanics of typical college entrance age in Texas, the following picture emerges: Of the total of approximately 135,000 minority 18-year-olds in a given year, roughly 55 percent are high school graduates, 16 percent have taken a college entrance exam, and three percent have scored the equivalent of 900 on the SAT exam and ranked in the top 40 percent of their high school class. Not only does this describe an uphill battle, but it serves to illustrate the puzzling priorities we often emphasize – one half of minority children don't complete high school, over one half of third graders cannot read at grade level, and our policy and media attention are focused on affirmative action to achieve diversity in admissions as a compelling objective at our two flagship universities! One would think that a much higher priority should be the expansion of the pool of qualified candidates produced by our public schools. Go figure.

Given these two examples of many available indices of the daunting challenge ahead, where are we on the reform front and how do we get to the next level? In Texas, there is good news and bad news. The good news is that we have government policy and legislative leadership with the most aggressive reform orientation in history, and there are in fact some good reform initiatives in motion. In addition, we boast a wide range of well-intentioned reform organizations and intervention initiatives of business and education leaders. But the bad news is that we are mired in reform "incrementalism" and we continue to suffer from the inertia of the structure of public education and the resistance to true reform from well-entrenched vested interests.

Dr Paul Hill of the University of Washington describes two types of education reform – intrinsic and extrinsic. Basically, intrinsic reform is driven by those who believe that good intentions and the inherent attractiveness of good ideas will make schools more effective. Proponents are primarily those dedicated to the education profession and confident of the morality of education as a public enterprise free of commercial or economic motivation and incentives. Extrinsic reform, on the other hand, is driven by those who believe that external motivating and competitive factors have a primary role to play in more effective schools, and proponents of this type are typically not professional educators. Essentially, in layman's language, intrinsic reform is the "heal thyself" variety, and I believe we have taken this type about as far as it can take us, with top-down standards and accountability. Why is this so? Because, for all the progress we have made, we still have not fully addressed the perverse incentives embedded in the structure of public education, which remains primarily driven by inputs and compliance when it should be driven by outputs and performance. That is why the easy part of reform is behind us – because the next phase involves major changes in adult behavior. And this can only come, in my opinion, through the dynamics of deregulation and marketization of delivery systems and of educator preparation and compensation. Many consider this a last resort. I believe we are there now.

It is long past time to move to the next level of reform and accountability – the extrinsic type – and this is the trend we must and will see over the next several decades in what I believe will be the civil rights revolution of the 21st century, which I think will play out simultaneously on the two tracks I have just mentioned: the delivery system for education and the means by which we prepare and compensate educators, primarily teachers.

Since the end of the 2003 regular session of the Texas Legislature, we have been struggling with the overhaul of Texas public school finance and searching for a successor to the flawed "Robin Hood" system. In this debate, many of us have taken the position that finance reform should be closely tied to, if not preceded by, comprehensive structural reform. The Texas Education Reform Caucus said it best: "Texas has a great opportunity to take a giant step forward in K-12 school reform. The Texas Legislature should tie to a new school finance system that meets the needs of equity and adequacy bold, comprehensive reform legislation to take Texas to the next level of accountability. The Legislature must make it possible for school districts to drive accountability into the classroom and every corner of district operations." I couldn't agree more, but what will be necessary to overcome the embedded perverse incentives and drive such a massive cultural shift in public education?

First, as to the reform of delivery systems, this certainly will entail a range of alternatives to the current system, the growth and development of some of which already are underway, including charter schools, contract schools, home schooling, and expansion of online education and "virtual" schools, among others. But the centerpiece of delivery system reform must be the full introduction of competitive dynamics to the incentive structure through the adoption of comprehensive school choice, at least in our larger urban districts. This is the ultimate accountability system, and it would have the additional benefit of completely transforming school finance.

What are the primary objections to this child-centered reform? Most prominently, the opposition to choice has done a good job of shaping the debate to focus on "draining" funds from the public schools. My response is, first, it is difficult to make the case that public education is underfunded. Total annual public education operating expenditures in Texas approximate $7,000 per student and aggregate spending increased by 43 percent over the five years ended in 2002, more than twice the sum of enrollment growth and inflation over the same period. As significant, this average annual cost per student is approximately twice the amount of the average annual tuition of all private and parochial schools. So, the funding already exists to finance competitive options to the current delivery system. More importantly, in a truly competitive system, the ultimate accountability is the power of the customer, parents and their children, to "vote with their feet" and have the funding follow the child. We should remember that school choice already exists for those who are privileged to be able to afford a private school or a home in an affluent neighborhood with a high quality public school. The substantial majority of those left behind without such choices are relatively poor, inner city, and often minority children. We owe them the same opportunity.

Over the years, one of the mysteries of my school choice advocacy has been the reluctance among many, including a large number of supposedly market sensitive business leaders, to understand and accept the dynamics of competition and how, in a choice environment, these dynamics will produce a supply of quality education alternatives to meet the demand while driving improvement in the public schools. So well entrenched is the static one-size-fits-all delivery system, with its top-down mandates and accountability, that we fear the dynamics of a deregulated market for education. And the concept has never been fairly tested in Texas, because religious schools, which comprise the vast majority of private schools, have never been included in the available universe of options.

In the school choice debate, we should start with a basic premise: No child should be left behind because of failure of the education distribution system to deliver the best possible opportunity for every child. If we cannot deliver on this commitment, we are failing in our public education responsibility, and no historical attachment to a particular delivery system should prevent our making the necessary changes. This debate is about children, not about a system.

A competitive delivery system is a necessary, but not sufficient, reform, because any delivery system is only as good as the educators in the school building. As Secretary Rod Paige so well noted in his first annual report to Congress on Meeting the Highly Qualified Teacher Challenge in June 2002, the teacher preparation system is "broken" and, although Texas has done a better job than most states in raising teacher preparation standards and accountability, we are no exception to this generalization. So, we must also transform the means by which we manage the human resources of our public education system, and this will require that we examine every aspect of the way in which we prepare, certify, mentor, retain, evaluate, and compensate educators, so that this entire chain and all of its links will be assessed based on their value added to Texas student achievement.

Gone is the paradigm, outlined in the landmark Coleman Report of 1966, wherein it was assumed that the impact of an educator in the classroom was to a large extent limited by the socioeconomic and cultural environment from which the children came. This assumption has been superseded by the wealth of data and research that demonstrate the primacy of the skill sets that the individual educator can bring to bear on individual student achievement regardless of background. The problem is that our teacher preparation system remains largely mired in the constructivist, learner-centered, input-driven mold, with licensing primarily governed by the traditional college of education and regulatory compliance dominated routes, both to the classroom and the administrative offices.

There is currently a heated national debate over the means by which educator quality can be enhanced, highlighted by the conflict between those who espouse "professionalization" and those who favor "deregulation." Although I tend to fall into the latter camp, I do not believe that these two approaches are necessarily mutually exclusive, but that is beside the major point, which is that we must establish as an objective the transformation of educator preparation programs into customer-driven institutions with assessments grounded in output- and performance-based criteria, so that Texas becomes the model for value-added evaluation of such programs. To do this will require that teacher preparation programs, particularly the colleges of education, adopt the attitude and strategy that the leading business schools were forced to adopt a number of years ago to avoid irrelevancy socio-economic become customer driven, which for the colleges of education means becoming primarily student achievement driven. In my experience, this is rarely the case.

To facilitate this educator preparation transformation, several things need to be done:

- We should fully define "highly qualified teacher" for Texas, not as a mandated regulatory term, but in terms of the qualities and performance that are expected (this will necessitate a re-evaluation of the 1997 document, "Learner-Centered Schools for Texas: A Vision of Texas Educators" as well as the HOUSSE standards adopted in response to the No Child Left Behind Act).
- We must aggressively encourage the creation of a competitive critical mass of privately and publicly sponsored alternative preparation and certification programs, as well as other non-traditional routes to the profession so as to "let many flowers bloom" and create an atmosphere of competitive certification, with value-added assessment of the graduates tied to student achievement.
- We should adopt teacher certification standards that place increasingly more emphasis on academic content, particularly in grades 5-12, and verbal and cognitive skills, particularly in grades PreK-4.
- We should adopt administrator certification standards that place more emphasis on management and leadership skills, education, and experience, and seek out means by which more entrepreneurial talent can be recruited to education administration from non-traditional backgrounds.

- Teacher compensation should be restructured to provide more incentives tied to performance, first by significantly reducing the number of steps on the salary scale, and then by phasing in a performance-based system as the value-added assessment model evolves to the individual classroom level.
- A high-level public/private sector task force should be appointed to lead a cross-jurisdictional effort to attack the teacher retention problem in Texas in all of its aspects.
- Our education agencies should emphasize regulatory rule making that allows for maximum prudent flexibility for school district administrators to manage their human resources.

Old entrenched habits and vested interests die hard and, again, the easy reform steps have been accomplished. Moreover, none of the steps of the next phase will be possible without fighting and winning some major battles at the attitudinal, ideological, political, legislative, and policy levels, and without breaking down some long-standing barriers of distrust among education stakeholders. And none of this will be possible without the complete support of the state's major opinion leaders, primarily from the business community. In fact, the current situation is analogous to the beginning of the furious debate over tort reform in the early 1990s, when business leaders were finally energized and organized to take on and win a protracted battle against a threat that had seriously jeopardized the state's economic viability. This necessary opinion leadership is not yet sufficiently energized for this next phase of education reform, but I submit that the current state of and prognosis for our public education system represents a threat even more onerous to our economic and cultural future and it is one that is worthy of a similar long-term commitment to overcome.

Reviving and Advancing the Texas Education Miracle: Where Do We Go From Here?

March 6, 2005

There is very little doubt among sophisticated observers that Texas has led the nation in public education reform over the past decade or so and that it has served as a model for other states and the nation in the advancement of standards and accountability. This has been accomplished by the dedication of a statewide coalition of educators, administrators, and legislative and business leaders in a consistent effort over a period of 20 years.

However, there is mounting evidence that the easier phases of reform are behind us in Texas, that some of the more intractable student achievement problem areas have not been reached by the reforms while serious backsliding is underway in others, that more of the same accountability and standards will not produce the results we want, and that a much more difficult phase of reform lies ahead.

When we examine the education priorities of the State's political leadership as evidenced by the policy initiatives of the 79th session of the Texas Legislature, we find a policy mix dominated by three priorities: property tax relief, fixing the broken "Robin Hood" system of school finance, and providing more funding for public education. As for additional reform, in fairness, there are a number of well-intentioned and well-crafted proposals directed toward incremental improvement in the current reform model, but with few exceptions, there seems to be little sentiment for serious introspection or candid appraisal of the current status of the reforms that have produced what has been dubbed "The Texas Miracle."

The current reform model, as it has evolved over the past 20 years, is based on the curriculum standards embodied in the Texas Essential Knowledge and Skills (TEKS) document adopted in 1997, on which the entire edifice is built – the curriculum, the assessments, the teacher preparation, and the incentive system. The assessment vehicle, the Texas Assessment of Knowledge and Skills (TAKS), is a criterion-referenced assessment subject to all of the possible pitfalls of such an examination, particularly when used as the sole determinant of all aspects of accountability for student achievement.

During the period since the adoption of the TEKS and the implementation of the assessments that have evolved into the TAKS, the improvement in the performance of Texas schools, as determined by the state assessments, has been remarkable. However, upon close analysis, one can begin to detect deficiencies in the standards- and accountability-based model and problems for its future as the primary determinant of progress in student achievement.

In research-based analyses of such indices as college readiness, reading ability, the rigor of curriculum, and the credibility of assessment, there is mounting evidence of the need to revisit the Texas reform model and the foundations on which it is based, and to have the objectivity and courage to make course corrections where they are warranted by the facts.

This process can only begin with complete candor about the current status of public education in Texas, the progress of our reform efforts to date, the prognosis for achieving the essential universal educational proficiency of our children, and the daunting challenges that we face in doing so. And this will involve confronting the enormous vested interests that sustain not only the "one best system" that has been in business for almost a century, but the model that has been chosen as the Texas reform vehicle. Total honesty and transparency is a must, a difficult principle to enforce when even the most well-intentioned of us are often intimidated by the inertia of the current structure of education and the natural reluctance to be introspective.

Armed with an objective analysis of where we have been and where we are, and keeping in mind that everything we do or don't do should be evaluated in terms of its impact on Texas student achievement, there are specific actions that can be taken in key areas that would immediately begin to revive and advance the "Texas Miracle" in public education, as follows:

- *Academic Standards* – Return to the premises of TEKS, refine and strengthen it to identify explicit, objective grade level expectations for all core subject areas, and revisit and reject the foundational "constructivist" philosophy of education.
- *Assessment* – Replace or supplement criterion-referenced testing with national norm-referenced testing and add end-of-course exams in high school, as well as value-added assessment throughout K-12.
- *Academic Accountability* – Significantly increase the State standards for K-12 district and campus performance, add college readiness as a standard, measure it with the SAT or ACT exam for high school exit, and install urgent and serious consequences for underperforming campuses.
- *The Reading Crisis* – Because everything about student achievement follows from the ability to read, we should declare the moral equivalent of war on the illiteracy of our children, beginning immediately in our urban areas.
- *Empowerment Through School Choice* – The centerpiece of delivery system reform must be comprehensive, child-centered school choice in all of its manifestations, including vouchers, charters, online, homeschooling, etc., beginning with aggressive expansion of open enrollment charter authority and voucherizing special education and students in failing schools.

- *Educator Quality* – Aggressively expand alternatives to educator preparation and certification, lead the movement to national standardized certification, significantly expand new teacher mentoring, aggressively recruit non-traditional leadership to school administration, and introduce performance-based compensation for all educators based on value-added evaluation.
- *Financial Accountability* – Develop a more robust reporting and management system that will bring improved transparency and productivity to education finance down to the classroom level.
- *Structural Deregulation* – Dump the age old "one best system" and allow wide-ranging authority for deregulation of human resource management, as well as innovations in scheduling and delivery that will certainly involve significantly more "time on task" and use of technology.

The current situation in Texas is analogous to the beginning of the furious debate over tort reform in the early 1990s, when business leaders were finally energized and organized to take on and win a protracted battle against a threat that had seriously jeopardized the State's economic viability. This necessary opinion leadership is not yet sufficiently energized for this next phase of education reform, but the current state of and prognosis for our public education system represents a threat even more onerous to our economic and cultural future and it is one that is worthy of a similar long-term commitment to overcome. In addition, and more importantly, it represents the civil rights revolution of the 21st century.

Responsible Citizenship

November 4, 2006

In my current speaking travels on education reform around the state, I am often asked about the purpose of the phrase in our organization's mission statement that, in addition to college and workplace readiness, our high schools should produce graduates fully prepared for "responsible citizenship." In a recent research report commissioned by the Intercollegiate Studies Institute entitled "The Coming Crisis in Citizenship," the explanation should be very clear. Called the largest statistically valid survey ever conducted to determine what our colleges and universities are teaching their students about America's history and institutions, the results are not only that these institutions are failing to increase knowledge about these basics, but that the most prestigious of our colleges are often at the low end of the "value added" scale on them. So you ask, what does this have to do with our high schools? Here's what: as bad as our higher education institutions are in adding value, the base knowledge from which entering freshmen begin is even more embarrassing. On 60 questions asked of entering college freshmen and seniors in four subject areas – history, government, world affairs, and the market economy – the average of the freshmen scores was an appalling 52 percent! So the fact that higher education added an average of only 1.5 percent over the next four years (to 53.5 percent) is terrible, but it is clear that the cultivation of civic literacy, the foundation of responsible citizenship, must begin much earlier if we are to have any hope of sustaining a free republic.

Drucker – Final Thoughts

March 2, 2007

Recently, I commented on one of my favorite thinkers, Peter Drucker, who died late last year. More recently, I read a review essay by Adrian Wooldridge on Drucker's thought as described in a new book on his life and was struck by the following fact: seven of the 10 companies that have seen the biggest growth in share value over the past five years did not exist 20 years ago! What more significant evidence of Joseph Schumpeter's "creative destruction" is there? And what more evidence of the wisdom of Drucker's opinion that the challenges facing companies now are more dramatic than anything seen in his lifetime? These points served to remind me of his most critical advice, which is that these new realities demand that institutions completely rethink everything. And by everything, he meant just that, but primarily a fierce focus on core competencies. My anecdotal reflection on how well American institutions "get it" and have accomplished this over the past couple of decades is fairly positive, at least in the private sector.

The major failure in adopting this mindset has been with government at all levels, and especially those government institutions that deliver K-12 education. Note the following comments (unusually Drucker-like coming from an educator) by Joel Klein, New York City school chancellor, to a CEO summit on education: "Other than global security, I don't think there's a more important issue facing our nation – and I don't think as a nation we're remotely serious enough about the issue… there needs to be a profound shift… the whole educational system is run on the myth that we can figure out through a compliance-based model a way to manage ourselves to success... if there was ever a set of dysfunctional incentives, it's in public education…" Drucker would be pleased, and we need more of this attitude, but I frankly don't hear enough of our education or business leaders talking in these terms.

"A Nation at Risk" at 25

May 6, 2008

During the past couple of weeks, there have been a number of articles and features marking the 25th anniversary of "A Nation at Risk," the groundbreaking 1983 report on the dismal status of American public education, wherein the most famous line was the one that served as the national wake-up call: "If an unfriendly power had attempted to impose on America the mediocre educational performance that exists today, we might well have viewed it as an act of war." Pretty bracing words, indeed.

Of the half dozen or so of these pieces I have read, interestingly enough, the best is a joint statement from a group of center-left organizations that commends the national commission that authored the report for recognizing that "the twin goals of equity- and high-quality schooling have profound and practical meaning for our economy and society, and we cannot permit one to yield to the other either in principle or practice," while lamenting the fact that "in 25 years, our country hasn't gotten this part right, not even close."

George Will makes the point that in 1976, for the first time in its 119-year history, the National Education Association, the teachers' union, endorsed a presidential candidate, Jimmy Carter, who repaid it by creating the Department of Education, and education policy never has been the same. This act has been the bane of most true reformers ever since, which makes it ironic to note that one of the primary planks of the Republican "revolution" of 1994 was to close this department, while the crowning domestic achievement of the administration of George W. Bush has been the No Child Left Behind Act, the most sweeping federal education program since the original Elementary and Secondary Education Act of 1965!

In fairness to President Bush and my friends who helped him craft this bold experiment in standards and accountability-based reform from the federal level, it has accomplished much in the way of significantly raising the national consciousness that our expectations for all of our children are much too low and that we are not asking nearly enough from either our children or our educators. It has its flaws in engineering and many more in its implementation, but let's give credit where it is due, to a bold and warranted effort to shake up the education establishment. It is now highly unlikely that the NCLB Act will be reauthorized prior to the end of this term, and I don't hear much from the presidential candidates about their education priorities.

I am not a big believer in top-down, compliance-based and prescriptive reform, particularly from the federal level, and I was sympathetic with the revolutionary platform of '94, but it is unrealistic to assume that we can entirely rid ourselves of deep involvement by the federal government in K-12 education. Let's just hope that President Bush's central message of the "soft bigotry of low expectations" has reached the desired audience with enough impact that a new administration can now proceed to restructure the federal role in the system into one that sets very high standards and accountability with consequences, but with much more flexibility for implementing the standards at the state level. It remains the central civil rights issue of our time.

Texas Education Update

April 2, 2009

The Texas Legislature is now in full swing and, of course, the Texas Institute for Education Reform (TIER) is at every table on every significant public education issue at stake, hopefully providing meaningful policy advocacy leadership. We have a comprehensive agenda for the session, but I am often asked – if I could get only one major thing accomplished in this session, what would it be?

That is not an easy question to answer, but I think it goes something like this. Texas has been at this thing called standards and accountability based education reform for about 25 years, with substantial results in terms of student achievement and national leadership. This has been an all-hands effort on the part of elected officials, educators, business leaders, and parents. It has also been incremental in nature in the sense that, as we have progressed in our standards, we have ratcheted up the expectations for our kids and our educators. This has produced fairly consistent incremental gains, but also some frustration about where we are and where we are going. So now we are at the point, after all these years, that we owe it to the kids, their parents, our educators, and the taxpayers to define the "end game" – what should be our expectations for our children and what should be the value of a Texas high school diploma?

In response, as state policymakers began about a year ago to consider significant revisions to the state education accountability system, our organization and its allies established what we believe should be the organizing principle of the new system, a hybrid between college readiness and workplace readiness we call *postsecondary readiness*. This is defined as follows:

"The range of academic, workforce, and social proficiency that high school students should acquire to successfully transition to skilled employment, advanced military training, an associate's degree, a bachelor's degree, or technical or industry certification, without the need for remediation."

A proxy for this definition is community college readiness without remediation. This we believe is the minimally acceptable standard of expectation for all Texas students who pursue the recommended curriculum to a high school diploma, regardless of the postsecondary path they choose.

From this organizing principle flows grade level benchmarked standards along a K-12 "ramp" leading to the postsecondary readiness exit; vertically scaled assessments with value-added capability measuring growth along the way; criteria holding schools accountable for student progress; and interventions to help those educators and students in need.

So, this is my answer to the question "if I had only one wish" – that the Legislature would embed in law this organizing principle, for which the motto would be "one standard, multiple pathways, equal rigor." Frankly, to do so would greatly simplify filling out the remainder of the system and its execution and would provide all the players in the chain the necessary clarity of mission and expectations.

Education Reform Update

November 8, 2009

I hope at least my Texas readers will be interested in an update on the efforts by many of us to advance standards and accountability based reforms in Texas K-12 education. We made good progress on our objectives during the 82nd Texas Legislature this spring and are hard at work in assisting with the implementation of the resulting legislation and other aspects of regulatory oversight and advocacy.

The centerpiece of the work of the Texas Institute for Education Reform (TIER) and our coalition, the Texas Coalition for a Competitive Workforce, was House Bill 3, a hard-fought overhaul of the Texas school accountability system. The bill was more than 200 pages in length and there are many moving parts, but the major breakthrough from which all else flows is that for the first time in Texas a high school diploma at the recommended curriculum level will represent "postsecondary readiness," defined as a melding of college and 21st century career readiness without the need for remediation.

Folks, this may appear elemental, but it is big. What follows is that from this graduation standard, there will be benchmarked standards at every grade level, assessments that are vertically scaled so that we can track each student's pathway toward the ultimate exit standard, and accountability on the part of educators for student progress along the "ramp" to this postsecondary readiness objective.

As you might imagine, it is one thing to have such standards and accountability in place in the law, but quite another to properly implement them. And that is the phase of our work in which we have been heavily engaged since the end of the legislative session in early June. In fact, we have developed the following agenda for our program of work over the interim period leading to the next legislative session:

- Work with the Texas Education Agency (TEA), the Commissioner of Education, the State Board of Education, and other appropriate officials to ensure that the discretionary aspects of the reforms embodied in HB 3 are implemented in accordance with our recommendations and legislative intent.
- Assist the appropriate officials in their work to upgrade the state's education data systems in order to provide the necessary infrastructure to accommodate the enhanced accountability system.
- Work with the TEA to ensure appropriate standards for the use of the new Texas Projection Model, which tracks student growth toward proficiency on the postsecondary readiness "ramp."
- Assist the TEA in developing more rigorous and relevant career, as well as technology courses that will improve the options for students who choose to pursue a high school pathway to industry or commercial certification.

And, while the implementation of new legislation is important, we also will be working hard on other policy developments with a view toward the next legislative session, as well as policy enhancements through the various rule-making authorities in the interim:

- We will work closely with the Texas charter school association to develop policy to strengthen charter schools as competitive alternatives by closing ineffective charters, providing equitable funding for successful charters, and increasing or eliminating the cap on charters.

- We will continue to advocate for measures that will enhance educator quality, partly through the implementation of new legislation and partly through working with the TEA, the State Board for Educator Certification, and the Texas Higher Education Coordinating Board to develop rules that will lower barriers to entry; more properly evaluate and compensate teacher effectiveness; assess and improve teacher preparation and professional development programs; and improve the quality of campus leadership.
- We will be actively engaged as a policy resource on such interim legislative study issues as expansion of pre-kindergarten and public school finance.

If all of this seems ambitious, it is. But we must pursue these policy deliberations and enhancements with all deliberate speed and we cannot delay them any longer, because to do so would be a disservice to our kids and our future.

And while all of this is proceeding at the state policy level, let me add a point about federal initiatives. I have been critical of the Obama administration in a number of deserving respects in terms of major policy disagreements, but I must say that his public education policy pronouncements and those of his Secretary of Education, Arne Duncan, have been right out of TIER's "play book." The Race to the Top competition that has been established for the states encompasses a number of priorities that are absolutely essential, namely:

- Creating common, internationally benchmarked standards, as well as holding educators and students accountable for meeting them.
- Nurturing effective teachers who are supported by effective leaders and removing those who are proven to be ineffective.
- Generating statewide longitudinal data systems to support the necessary sophistication of the accountability systems.
- Turning around or reconstituting chronically failing schools through aggressive intervention.

Our organization applauds the Obama team for its leadership in this initiative, we support these objectives and this competition for funding among the states for their implementation, and we have encouraged our state's leadership to aggressively pursue this funding.

Now a short commercial – this is a never-ending battle and we need your help, including your financial support, so please visit our website at: www.texaseducationreform.org and sign up.

Back to the Future?

February 5, 2010

I don't often disagree with George Will, but I must take issue with parts of his recent essay "Unlike China, U.S. has a future rooted in the past" that closes with the following: "While China increasingly invests in its future, America increasingly invests in its past, the elderly… America's destiny is demographic, and therefore is inexorable and predictable, which makes the nation's fiscal mismanagement, by both parties, especially shocking."

I certainly don't disagree with the remark about our fiscal mismanagement, the current manifestation of which was begun by a Republican administration and greatly expanded by the current Democratic one. And I find the current distribution of healthcare costs badly skewed toward the later stages of life, although I don't have a solution, short of government-mandated care and price controls, which are anathema to most Americans. But I refuse to believe that demographics is destiny, because I continue to have confidence that the American tradition of common sense will ultimately prevail in the policy arena. One might say this is naive. Maybe, but it's not cynical.

Will notes the enormous investment that China is making in education. Well, no nation spends more on public education than the United States, more than $10,000 per student annually. We may complain about the results, and no one does more of that publicly than I do, but these resources are allocated based on the consent of a free people expressed through their chosen representatives, an important point. I have been to China, have had dialogue with some of its top leaders, and read extensively of their thoughts and strategies. They are scrambling fast to maintain control and deliver success to their people, mostly because it's the right thing to do, but also because they know that theirs is essentially an illegitimate regime that must produce results at almost any cost. The Chinese also know that, ultimately, to produce the kind of results they need, they must adapt the success factors of the West to their culture, keeping the ideas that are useful, while rejecting the ones that are subversive to their control (witness the current conflict with Google). In the long run, this is a losing battle and I believe they also know that.

Contra to Will, Joel Kotkin writes that demographics is actually an advantage to America, particularly given the differing demographic trajectories of the U.S. compared to the Western European countries and Russia. As for China, he suggests that their xenophobia is so embedded in their worldview that demographics can be a disadvantage in their ability to function successfully as a world and economic power.

In the end, America remains the only nation that, as Chesterton said, is "founded on a creed." I am evidently somewhat more confident than George Will that the next generation can sustain that exceptionalism and all that it means for our world economic leadership, while not abandoning us in our advancing years.

The Rest of the Story on Texas High School Graduation Rates

September 3, 2012

Early in August we were treated to news from the Texas Education Agency that Texas high school graduation rates have reached an all-time high of 86 percent. Regardless of the qualifications one might add to this number, this represents the continuation of an increasing trend in graduation rates over the past 20 years of standards and accountability based reform in Texas public education, and we should applaud educators across the state for this achievement. And incidentally, these results confirm the fact that accountability doesn't drive an increasing dropout rate, as is suggested by some who oppose high stakes accountability.

However, while we should welcome this news, let's take a closer look at the rest of the story, as highlighted by the recent release of the Condition of College and Career Readiness Report, based on scores on the ACT exam popularly used for college admissions. Of the 39 percent of 2012 Texas graduating seniors who took the ACT, only 24 percent met all four benchmarks for postsecondary readiness in English, mathematics, reading, and science, a result that is below the national average of 25 percent and that has been relatively flat for a number of years. And in fact, 32 percent of Texas graduates didn't meet any of the benchmarks!

There is even more to the story: 51 percent of Texas students entering community colleges need remediation and, more significantly, based on a recent study sponsored by Houston Endowment, only 20 percent of Texas students are earning any sort of postsecondary credential within six years of expected high school graduation. The latter statistic represents the "pipeline" of those ready for college and the 21st century workplace and is a more realistic measure of educational success and the challenge we face than any "dropout" calculation or graduation rate might indicate.

Over the past year, we have been besieged by a firestorm of protest from the education community about the "oppression" of the high stakes standardized testing of students under the Texas accountability system, including resolutions adopted by approximately 500 school district boards of trustees calling for rollbacks in assessments and accountability. These complaints have been coupled with the usual demands for more funding, to the ludicrous suggestion that "we can only justify as much accountability as the funding will allow."

Well, it seems that the ACT report card and the other data represent a validation of educator performance independent of the dreaded and vilified TAKS and STAAR assessments, including the significant disconnect with the graduation statistics. Should we continue to put more money into this system? Consider this: according to Education Resource Group and data from the Texas Education Agency, aggregate public education funding from all sources over the past 14 years has increased by $70 billion more than the increase necessary to fully fund the growth in enrollment and inflation combined over this period, even when adding a factor for the increase in special needs students. It's pretty clear to me that a continuation of this growth in funding is not sustainable and certainly not justified by the productivity of the system.

Our organization, the Texas Institute for Education Reform (www.texaseducationreform.org), has identified the primary challenge to Texas public education by 2020 to produce 80 percent postsecondary ready high school graduates without the need for remediation – a very tall order. How do we do this? With a serious commitment to the following fundamentals: 1) demand and defend accountability, 2) innovate and deregulate the delivery system, 3) enhance choice and competition, and 4) emphasize efficiency and productivity in funding. All four of these areas of reform must "hang together" as an interdependent and comprehensive whole, but it begins with the completion of the implementation of the new state system of accountability, for without the infrastructure provided by this system the other pieces have no coherence.

The Elusive "Skills Gap"

April 6, 2013

The recent release of the March employment data reflecting the pitiful growth in net new jobs for the month of 88,000, while almost half a million more Americans left the labor force during the month, sent the experts scurrying once again to explain why, four years after the technical end of the so-called great recession, we have such dismal growth in the economy and jobs along with the lowest workforce participation rate since 1979. The reasons that I have seen and heard offered range from: the federal budget sequestration; to the restoration of the two percent payroll tax cut; to the overburden of federal regulation; to the lack of bank financing; to slack consumer demand; to the failure of Federal Reserve policy; to the dysfunction of Congress; to the implementation of ObamaCare; and to the fear and anticipation of more of all of these. Certainly, all of these factors are playing some part in the failure of recovery.

There also is another factor that is discussed and debated, primarily in the business trade media – the "skills gap," the notion that there are large numbers of jobs available for which there are no candidates who have the necessary skills required. Unlike the other factors, with the exception of our flawed fiscal policy, an issue for another day, the skills gap problem is largely structural. Basically, we haven't yet resolved the issue of adapting our deeply flawed public education system into one that can cope with the intense dynamics of economic globalization.

Chief Executive magazine editor J. P. Donlon writes that the most prevalent answer he gets when asking CEOs what single thing, apart from the general economy, is holding them back from growing their businesses is the inability to find people with the right skills. In the current issue of the magazine, it is reported that a study by the American Enterprise Institute reflected that the shortage of skilled workers is a "serious challenge that needs to be addressed." In September 2011, Deloitte and the Manufacturing Institute surveyed 1,123 U.S. companies and found a "moderate to severe" shortage of skilled workers that translates into approximately 600,000 skilled positions then unfilled. And the article further notes that, due to the aging of the current employment base, this gap is likely to widen.

Recent data from the Bureau of Labor Statistics reflecting the education levels needed for workplace entry, as analyzed by the Economic Policy Institute, shows that approximately 43 percent of available jobs projected in 2020 will require a high school diploma or equivalent, roughly the same percentage as in 2010. This is a lower percentage than other analyses I have seen, but will suffice to make my point, which is that the issue in question here, when we consider the skills gap problem, is the quality of the high school diploma in terms of the rigor of the curriculum and the skill sets it represents. For example, if we use community college readiness without the need for remediation as a proxy for postsecondary readiness, including a meaningful 21st century job, we know that less than 25 percent of Texas high school graduates taking the ACT exam score at this readiness level. Further, based on a study by Houston Endowment, only 22 percent of Texas students in the eighth grade cohorts of 1996-1998 have secured any type of credential, college degree, or industry certification, within six years after their expected high school graduation. And, we know that 51 percent of Texas high school graduates entering community colleges require remedial courses. These results are not appreciably different in other parts of the country, better in some areas, worse in others. At a minimum, this should give us cause to look more closely at the entry level skills and true competencies delivered by our education system and represented by the high school diploma.

My take on this is that the current and growing skills gap is a very real structural impediment to job creation and economic growth, with enormous consequences for the prosperity of generations to come and the security of our country, and that we (and here I refer primarily to business leadership) need to get much more serious and urgent about the structural changes in our education delivery system that are necessary to attack the problem.

Special Edition – Education Reform for the 84th Texas Legislature

February 9, 2015

The 84th Session of the Texas Legislature is in full swing and no policy issue under consideration is more important than education in general and PreK-12 education in particular. In fact, it could be said that Texas is at a crossroads in determining in which direction it wants to go, furthering its public education reform progress that has been slowly, but surely moving forward for 20 years until recently when the rigor of the accountability system took a significant hit in the last session.

The organization that I chair, the Texas Institute for Education Reform (TIER), is involved with every aspect of the reform agenda, and we recently completed a "road show" in several major cities around the state to discuss our policy priorities with business and education leaders. Following is a synopsis of our message.

Since the beginning of the Texas commitment to public education standards and accountability based reform in 1993, the state has made remarkable progress in student achievement. Based on results measured by the National Assessment of Educational Progress (NAEP), improvements in accountability have significantly raised achievement in reading and math among all student groups. In addition, high school graduation rates have steadily increased over this period.

However, significant problems remain: 51 percent of high school graduates entering community colleges need remediation, and more significantly, based on studies sponsored by Houston Endowment, only 20 percent of Texas students are earning any sort of postsecondary credential within six years of expected high school graduation. The latter statistic represents the "pipeline" of those ready for college and the 21st century workplace and is a more realistic measure of educational success and the challenge we face than any "dropout" calculation might indicate.

TIER has identified the primary challenge to Texas public education by 2020 to produce 80 percent postsecondary ready high school graduates without the need for remediation – a very tall order.

How do we do this? With a serious commitment to the following fundamental points:

- Expand education choice for families
- Increase school district autonomy
- Attack the reading and literacy crisis
- Emphasize funding efficiency and productivity
- Defend and demand accountability

Let's take these one at a time.

1) Expand education choice for families. We should enhance school choice and competition and allow the evolution from a "school system" to "a system of schools," with robust choices for parents and students that meet their needs, and with funding that follows the student. To begin, we should adopt comprehensive public school choice throughout the state, subject to capacity. But more capacity for choice is needed. We should expand and improve the charter school system with more co-location of charters with traditional schools, equalized funding, and a more robust "parent trigger" to authorize parents to change the management of unacceptable schools. Further, we should provide a state-funded scholarship for students in chronically failing schools to transfer to any school of their choice and we should adopt a scholarship program for special education students based on the successful MacKay program in Florida.

2) Increase school district autonomy. We must adopt policies that enable deregulation and innovation in the schools and move away from the top down, compliance, and input-driven system to one that is output and performance based. The role of the state beyond accountability should primarily be to enable and encourage new teaching and learning methods through the use of technology and innovations in scheduling and delivery. Schools should be free from unnecessary state bureaucracy and the time-honored management principle of "authority commensurate with responsibility and accountability" should be the prevailing operational model. This should include eliminating the role of the state in managing local human resources, including compensation of educators and arbitrary class size restrictions. And we should expand truly alternative routes to the teaching profession and hold teacher preparation programs accountable for the effectiveness of the product they deliver measured by their value-added to student achievement.

3) Attack the reading and literacy crisis. Only 28 percent of Texas fourth graders performed at or above the proficient level on the 2013 National Assessment of Educational Progress (NAEP), about the same as a decade ago. And the average reading score for Texas fourth graders is lower than the scores for 30 other states and jurisdictions. The problem is not due to lack of know-how. Extensive research provides clear direction on the most effective ways to teach reading and writing, but practitioners seem to have willful indifference to what this research has shown. This must stop.

It's time to get serious about this crisis. We must immediately do the following: 1) raise standards for reading proficiency in the early grades (PreK-2) and incorporate early reading measures into the school accountability system; 2) require all schools to provide effective reading programs for all students in every grade, PreK-12; 3) ensure that teachers are identifying struggling readers early and connecting them with the intensive help they need; 4) guarantee that state certification tests evaluate teachers' knowledge of reading science, including a stand-alone test for those who teach reading; and 5) provide ongoing training through summer reading academies focused on science-based reading instruction and rigorously evaluate that training to determine its efficacy.

4) Emphasize funding efficiency and productivity. We must spend education dollars much more efficiently. In all of the current litigation on school finance, we must ask ourselves, which is the most important consideration – adequacy, equity, or efficiency? We submit the following response: 1) aggregate statewide funding is adequate and, in

fact, public education funding from all sources over the past 15 years has increased significantly more than the increase in enrollment and inflation combined, even when adding a factor for the growth in special needs students; 2) equitable funding is questionable in many ways, including between administration and the classroom, between and among many rural and urban areas, and between traditional and charter schools; 3) the "Robin Hood" finance system is a failed attempt at equity; and 4) the constitutional mandate for school "efficiency" should have priority in driving the school finance debate.

Let's face it – the current education delivery system is not sustainable. We cannot continue to finance this top-down, compliance and input-driven system. Only when we replace it with a more competitive, deregulated, and innovative system that incentivizes educators and enables productivity with true financial accountability will we know what funding adequacy and equity really mean.

5) Defend and demand accountability. Postsecondary readiness should be the organizing principle of PreK-12 education. What does this mean? We define this level of readiness as follows: The range of academic, workforce and social proficiency achievement that students should acquire to successfully transition from high school to skilled employment, advanced military training, an associate's degree, bachelor's degree, or technical or industry certification, without the need for remediation. The proxy for this standard is community college readiness without remediation.

In addition to college and career readiness, postsecondary readiness must also mean "one standard, multiple pathways, equal rigor" in the Texas default high school plan, so that students must have multiple pathway choices to college or a meaningful career represented by industry standards, with equal rigor of curriculum.

Accountability must have three components: 1) diagnostics to assist educators in determining the intervention needs of students; 2) transparency for parents and taxpayers; and 3) consequences for educators in terms of compensation and continuing employment; as well as for students in terms of promotion and graduation.

How do we assess postsecondary readiness? Texas is committed to an assessment that measures student achievement against the standards at each grade level that indicate what students should know and when should they know it, leading to the postsecondary readiness standard at graduation. In addition, we should have the capability to measure the value-added to each student's achievement on an annual basis, as a diagnostic measure of annual progress of the student and the effectiveness of educators.

As to the debate on standardized testing, it is difficult to cut through the rhetoric and paranoia on the subject, except to say that every meaningful pursuit in life involves an assessment of achievement related to a standard. The abuses alleged in the testing process appear to be more a problem related to constant practice and benchmark testing at the school district level than problems with the requirements of the state accountability system, which are benign by comparison. The anti-standardized testing firestorm is misguided and misinformed.

Finally, all five of the fundamental points of reform must "hang together" as a comprehensive whole, but it begins with the state system of accountability for results, which provides the infrastructure for the entire public education system and is the key element enabling education reform. Without it, the other pieces have no coherence.

The Forbes Education Challenge

May 5, 2015

In a very interesting and ambitious project, last year *Forbes* magazine challenged experts in business and education philanthropy to single out five big ideas over the next 20 years that could make American students the most highly achieving in the world and had research and modeling specialists with no stake in the outcome analyze the returns on a cost and benefit basis, a kind of GDP return on investment plan for education reform. They called it "America's Education Moon Shot."

As reported in December 2014, the top five big ideas that surfaced were as follows, along with my off the cuff comments:

- Teacher efficacy (probably the most difficult of all to achieve)
- Universal pre-K (lots of movement in that direction already)
- Common Core standards (not a favorite of mine nor in Texas)
- Blended learning (incorporating technology into teaching, very important)
- School leadership (critical and an area of major weakness)

The resulting numbers were very big – a required investment over 20 years of $6.2 trillion, $310 billion annually in today's dollars, with a payoff to GDP of $225 trillion over 80 years.

So why don't we do this? The easy answer is that we lack the stakeholder consensus and political will to do it, and that's true, but not complete. My answer is more foundational: it is that fixing public education is not a scientific and engineering project like a moon shot, it's a social good that is analogous to the poverty problem that was so unsuccessfully attacked by the Great Society. And because of the different nature of these social goods and their entanglement with cultural norms, they cannot be successfully addressed by a top-down, compliance-based, one-size-fits-all approach by government, particularly at the federal level. Government's role should be to set high standards, assess results, and require accountability to the public.

This was a productive exercise with discussion and analysis of the problem that added significant value, but please, no "moon shots" in education.

A Duplicitous Tantrum by Texas Educators

October 6, 2015

Over the past three legislative sessions, the Texas public education accountability system, once rated by national organizations as the best in the country, has come under relentless attack by a firestorm of misguided opposition to standardized and so-called "high stakes" testing, so that by the end of the 2013 session, the system had essentially been gutted. The result has been a lowering of expectations, relaxation of accountability, and dilution of rigor in the curriculum. And I believe that this, more than any other factor, is producing the disheartening decline in the achievement of our kids as reflected in the SAT scores released last month, as well as recent trends in the Texas National Assessment of Educational Progress scores.

In the wake of this news and in spite of these developments, just last week we got an outburst of supreme irony from Texas educators that should be embarrassing to them all. At the joint annual conference of the Texas Association of School Administrators (TASA) and the Texas Association of School Boards (TASB) in Austin, these education "leaders" gave a scorching earful to Education Commissioner Michael Williams on the state accountability system from top to bottom – questioning the validity of the assessments, criticizing recent education agency intervention initiatives, dismissing the new A-F school rating system as a "gimmick," and in general, roundly criticizing the more rigorous academic standards and the plans to prudently and steadily enhance these standards in order to reach student postsecondary readiness.

I have previously written about the ambitious goals of higher education in Texas, in particular the commendable new 60x30 Plan, and the obvious disconnect between the trends in K-12 readiness and these ambitious goals. The bottom line here is that our state's future is in the hands of those responsible for leading our elementary and secondary system of schools. They are the only ones who can fill the "pipeline" with the postsecondary ready students we will need for the state's prosperity, and they should be held accountable for doing so. Yet all we hear from them are demands for more funding and less accountability, and most of the people in the room in Austin last week beating up on the Commissioner represent the more than 600 school districts in Texas that are currently suing the state for more funding.

It is disingenuous to the max that the people who are suing the state for more funding supposedly in order to comply with the additional demands of higher rigor and more accountability are the very same people who have succeeded in gutting the accountability system and watering down the curriculum standards and value of a Texas high school diploma over the past two legislative sessions.

Standardized Testing is not the Problem

November 7, 2015

President Obama now has succumbed to the firestorm in opposition to standardized and "high stakes" testing that has swept the country over the past several years, even picking up on the talking points – "Learning is about so much more than just filling in the right bubble." So, now he wants a cap on standardized testing at two percent of classroom time. Really. The Middle East is blowing up and the leader of the free world is micromanaging school-time distribution.

Let's look at the data and an interesting survey. The Council of the Great City Schools just released a study of the nation's 66 largest school districts that revealed that students spend approximately 20-25 hours per school year taking these standardized tests, which amounts to 2.3 percent of classroom time for the average 8th grader who will take about 112 of them between PreK and 12th grade, approximately eight per year. In Texas, students spend the equivalent of two full class days taking these tests, exclusive of retakes, about 1.1 percent of the 180-day school year. Doesn't sound too onerous, but that's only part of the story, because most of the abuses of the testing are with the constant practice testing by the schools and "benchmarking" of students to prepare for the tests, none of which is mandated by the accountability system, but that gets lost in the demagoguery.

The Great City Schools study has other interesting findings. One of the most intriguing is that in their poll of parents, 78 percent of the respondents agreed or strongly agreed that "accountability for how well my child is educated is important, and it begins with accurate measurement of what he/she is learning in school." Yet this support declines significantly when the word "test" appears in the question and parents respond more favorably to the need for improving tests than to references to more rigorous or harder tests. To me, this is pretty clear evidence of the success of the anti-testing advocates in demonizing any form of assessment that will provide the independent data that we need for diagnostics and to drive the accountability system. The sentence, "It is important to have an accurate measure of what my child knows" is supported by 82 percent of public school parents. Language about "testing" is not. Very instructive, don't you think? In Texas, we are about to have a major statewide conversation about this issue as we address the next generation of public school accountability and assessment through a 15-member commission created by the Legislature to study the relevant issues and report findings by December 2016. This is an extremely important undertaking that will have implications for the state for at least a decade or more. We have been on a march for the past 25 years that had led us to what was rated as the best public school accountability system in the country, one that, when fully implemented would measure progress to postsecondary readiness at every grade level culminating in a high school diploma signifying college and 21st century career readiness. Over the past two legislative sessions, this system has been gutted by the anti-testing zealots, so this new commission will try and determine where we should go from here. Whether or not you now have or will have children or grandchildren of school age, this process is important to you, because it's very important to Texas and the country, so please pay attention.

The Ongoing College Readiness Debate

September 4, 2016

Who should go to college? Obviously, those students who aspire to and those who are seriously prepared or who at least believe they are and are ready for the challenge. But what do we owe those students who either don't have those aspirations or are not prepared to be successful? The truth. And often, according to an insightful essay of several months back by my friend Michael Petrilli in *Education Next*, large numbers of students are not getting the truth from their elders or at least don't believe it, and he cites compelling data to back this up.

Consider what he calls the "college preparation gap," defined as the gap between the college enrollment rate, the percentage of high school graduates in the trailing 12 months who enrolled in college, and the percentage who were prepared to be there, based on reading scores from the National Assessment of Educational Progress. From 1992 to 2013 this gap ranged from 21 percent to 32 percent. And sure enough, recently published data reflects that only 53 percent of the students who began higher education in 2009 had earned a degree six years later.

Petrilli believes that most ordinary people are fully aware of this gap in student capability, but are either too "politically correct" to admit it publicly or, in the case of college administrators, are admitting far too many unqualified students by withholding the truth in the interest of maintaining tuition revenue.

We have been having this conversation for as long as I have been involved with education issues. And there is no doubt that, as Petrilli makes clear, we are not going to set high school exit exams at four-year college readiness levels, which would deny a majority of 18-year-olds a high school diploma. Many leading analysts have suggested a two-tiered high school graduation standard and diploma, and most states have a basic diploma option, one with less rigor, but we must be very careful here that we do not engage in "tracking" kids by lowering standards and expectations, which is a risk and a tendency when dealing with high stakes accountability.

In fact, in Texas this lowering of expectations is exactly what has been happening over the past several years, to the point that in 2015 more than 12,000 waivers were requested from students who failed the required recently watered-down, end-of-course exams necessary for high school graduation, and 52 percent of these applications were approved by local "graduation committees" under new legislation. And according to a survey by the Texas Association of Business, the waiver approval rate among seniors in the 100 largest districts was 86 percent! This is certainly not the answer.

So what is the answer? Well, more of the truth, for sure, but I would add another element. I am not yet ready to give up on the policy of "one standard, multiple pathways, equal rigor" for all students. In Texas several years ago, a state commission on which I served attempted to answer the question "what defines success" in a high school diploma, and in our deliberations, the term "postsecondary readiness" was chosen to reflect the conviction that success in college and the workplace require the same level of rigorous preparation, and the following definition was adopted:

"Postsecondary readiness is the range of academic, workforce, and social proficiency that high school students should acquire to successfully transition to skilled employment, advanced training in the military, an associate's degree, a bachelor's degree, or technical certification, without the need for remediation."

The proxy for this standard is community college readiness without the need for remediation. Should this be the minimum graduation standard for a high school diploma for 100 percent of students? Of course not, but we can certainly set the bar higher than it currently stands and I would hope that we could make this expectation the default standard and incrementally increase expectations to meet it to a level of at least 60 percent in a decade or so. Am I dreaming? Maybe, but the alternatives are not pretty.

Should We "Track" High School Students?

June 5, 2018

We are about to arrive at the 10th anniversary of a document of which I am proud to have been a co-author named "Common Ground: A Declaration of Principles and Strategies for Texas Education Policy." This paper was the product of 10 months of intensive discussion in periodic sessions held in three cities during 2008 by five of us, including Sandy Kress, Don McAdams, Mike Moses, David Thompson, and me, in an attempt to lay some groundwork for the 2009 session of the Texas Legislature, during which a new public school accountability system was to be debated. Some of us and the institutions we represented had been on opposite sides of several issues in the accountability advocacy discussions for several years, so the paper certainly represented a number of compromises, but all five of us signed off on the final product and then appeared together before business, education, and civic leaders in several cities to discuss its proposals. I am certainly not totally objective, but I think it fair to say that a number of our recommendations found their way into the Texas standards and accountability system adopted by House Bill 3 in 2009, a system that, when fully implemented, was judged to be the best such system in the country by several national education advocacy organizations.

I refer to this history as a reminder and for some context, because to me it's hard to believe that it has been 10 years since the paper was written, and because, 1) for a variety of reasons the new system was attacked and diluted almost "in the crib" and certainly long before it was fully implemented, and 2) we in Texas and around the country are now struggling mightily to determine the future of standards and accountability based reforms in the wake of years of dismantling the premises and consensus on which that system and most all other reforms were built.

Foremost among these premises was the idea that the organizing principle of PreK-12 public education should be the advancement of postsecondary readiness, a term that was defined in Texas in early 2008 by the Texas High School Completion and Success Initiative Council on which I served as "the range of academic, workforce, and social proficiency that high school students should acquire to successfully transition to skilled employment, advanced training in the military, an associate's degree, a bachelor's degree, or technical certification, without the need for remediation." A proxy for this standard we determined was community college readiness without remediation.

To implement accountability along the K-12 continuum, we devised what we call the postsecondary readiness "ramp." Standards from K through 12 and their accompanying assessments would be aligned with curriculum so that at any grade level in any subject passing the relevant assessment meant that the child has met the standard and is "on the ramp" to postsecondary readiness. An important corollary was that there would be postsecondary options other than college, known as Career and Technology Education pathways to a diploma, but that the motto was to be, "one standard, multiple pathways, equal rigor."

Ten years later, substantially all of the implications of these premises have been challenged and undermined, we are adrift in seeking a new consensus, and that leads me to the title of this essay. In Texas in recent years we have celebrated consistent increases in the four-year high school graduation rate, which now is about 87 percent. Yet, when postsecondary readiness standards are applied, the readiness percentage of these students drops to around 40 percent, depending on the subject matter, and more than 50 percent of those graduates who apply to attend community colleges are required to take remedial courses. Texas has adopted an objective called "60x30," which is that 60 percent of 25-34 year olds will hold an associate's degree, a bachelor's degree, or an industry certification by the year 2030. Currently that percentage is about 40 percent.

Some of us are responding to these disappointing facts by supporting the reversal of the damage that has been done to expectations and advocating a return to the standards and rigor of the system adopted by HB 3 in 2009. This is not likely in the current political atmosphere. But, there are others in a growing crowd, including a number of my reform colleagues, who want to take a different approach, one that seems designed to acknowledge that “one standard, multiple pathways, equal rigor” is no longer a realistic objective.

A good example is Oren Cass of the Manhattan Institute, who in recent articles advocates for increased emphasis and resources for vocational education in the recognition that all students won’t, and shouldn’t attend college, and that the stigma of second-class status currently assigned to vocational pathways should be eliminated. He says that the problem is that schools refuse to “track” – to separate high school students into different educational programs that target different outcomes. Further, he thinks that treating everyone equally in high school harms students for whom the college track is not appropriate. Not too many years ago, this “tracking” would be condemned as inegalitarian at best and even racist at worst by some. The question of course is, who decides? To be fair, he emphasizes that the choice should be with the parents and students, but I wonder and worry about the potential moral hazard for coercion to duck accountability.

My response to this suggested tracking is twofold: First, in most places we already have begun the development of multiple pathways that include vocational choices and many of them have dual completion opportunities with the traditional curriculum sequence.

Second, we obviously know that college isn’t for everyone, but research shows that more than 60 percent of students will need some form of postsecondary education to meet the demands of the 21st century workplace and the rest of them will need the chance for a basic high school diploma that qualifies them for meaningful work and responsible citizenship, which is an opt-out from the default pathway that is widely available to parents and students.

This debate will rage and grow as we restructure the next consensus, but until we do, I prefer to stick with the principles we outlined in Common Ground, that the best education we have to offer should be available to all, and that the motto “one standard, multiple pathways, equal rigor” is worth defending. The excuse I hear too often from educators is “we do the best we can with what we have to work with.” This should not be acceptable. All students can achieve; it’s our job to expect that and to enable them to do so.

The Texas Education Challenge

January 2, 2019

As we begin the new year from a public policy standpoint, most politically observant eyes in Texas will be on the opening of the Texas Legislature under a new Speaker of the House, and many of those same eyes will be once again focused on what is to be done about public education finance, the issue that has received most of the preliminary analysis and emphasis. It would be great if among proposals currently under review – from the Commission on Public School Finance, from Governor Abbott and others – there was a solution in sight that would fix the glaring deficiencies of the flawed "Robin Hood" system that the state has been struggling with for many years and in numerous court decisions, but very few are optimistic that the result will be much more than continued tweaking.

My view is that, as important as finance reform might be for taxpayers and regardless of the prospects for success in systemic finance reform, our most significant time and energy should be invested in a much larger challenge – how to restore the consensus that once existed among education opinion leaders that propelled Texas to national leadership in education standards and accountability reform.

For approximately 25 years, from the early 1990s through 2009, Texas business and education leadership was committed to a long-term strategy that called for steady and incremental advancement of PreK-12 standards and expectations for students and educators, with appropriate assessment and accountability, leading to the establishment of a Texas high school diploma as emblematic of post-secondary readiness, which should be the organizing principle of PreK-12 public education. This was defined as the range of academic, workforce, and social proficiency that high school students should acquire to successfully transition to skilled employment, advanced training in the military, an associate's degree, a bachelor's degree, or technical certification, without the need for remediation. A proxy for this standard is community college readiness without remediation.

Currently, in spite of consistently higher high school graduation rates, which are almost totally meaningless, more than 50 percent of Texas high school graduates require remedial courses when entering a community college. So, granted, this post-secondary readiness objective was very ambitious, and by 2009, the Texas system was described by national organizations as the most rigorous in the country. So rigorous, in fact, that there was enormous pushback from a range of "stakeholders" in and outside the education community over testing, local control, and other issues. The result over the last several legislative sessions has been a significant rollback of standards and accountability, and there is compelling evidence that this rollback has been largely responsible for flat to declining scores on national assessments of Texas student achievement since 2011.

In 2016, Texas higher education leadership developed its second 15-year plan for post-secondary achievement, called 60x30, which calls for 60 percent of 25- to 34-year-olds to have in hand an associate's degree, bachelor's degree, or industry certification by the year 2030. Currently, that percentage is about 42 percent, so this is a tall order, particularly since only about 22 percent of the 2008 cohort of eighth graders have any of these credentials six years after anticipated high school graduation, and for minorities this percentage is around 13 percent.

Texas Aspires, the education reform organization on whose board I serve, is fully committed to the 60x30 objective as an overall guiding principle and is tailoring its objectives for the legislative session accordingly. See www.texasaspires.org for details. We hope to be able to rally a critical mass of like-minded leaders and organizations to advance this agenda and there is encouragement that more active reform leadership on a regional basis is developing around the state. But we must be realistic: There is not a prayer for accomplishing the 60x30 plan without a renewed consensus on a statewide commitment to rigorous PreK-12 standards and accountability and a concerted effort to repair the damage that has been done by misguided policy over the past several years. As a policy and strategic issue for the future of the state, I believe it's the most important challenge we face.

20
Race and Ethnic Issues

The God of Diversity

March 4, 2001

"...nor shall any State... deny to any person within its jurisdiction the equal protection of the laws." – Amendment XIV, U.S. Constitution.

"I have a dream that my four little children will one day live in a nation where they will not be judged by the color of their skin, but by the content of their character." – Dr. Martin Luther King.

After the Adarand and Hopwood court decisions of the mid-1990s and the passage of Proposition 209 in California, many of us were encouraged that our nation was finally on a path toward the realization of the ideals embodied in the two passages above. Alas, the vested interests of race-based preferences in hiring, college admissions, and contracting have mounted aggressive counterattacks that have taken several forms, in and outside the judicial process. These efforts, to me, are particularly egregious in our elite institutions of higher education, which ostensibly have as their mission the pursuit of truth but which have practiced a considerable degree of intellectual dishonesty in fighting to preserve race-based admissions preferences. As a result, we get the various "X percent rules" that guarantee admission to a certain top percentage of each high school graduating class, proposals to replace standardized tests such as the SAT with more "holistic" admissions criteria, and the promotion of "diversity" in admissions as a compelling public interest. Of course, diversity is defined for this purpose in terms of color or ethnicity, not thought or ideas or political philosophy, and, at least in the top business schools, is said to be driven by the demands of the market and prospective corporate employers. Most of these companies have been shaken down by the affirmative action establishment, and they seem to lack the moral authority to insist on true excellence from minority students. Shelby Steele of the Hoover Institution believes this is the reason that the white leadership of American institutions keeps trying to engineer results rather than asking for development. It's as though they feel they must seek racial moral authority by proving a negative – that they are not racist.

The problem for Steele is that this moral authority comes at the expense of minority development.

The corruption this promotes is pervasive. We are led to believe that diversity initiatives have nothing to do with racial quotas and that they are crucial to learning, academic excellence, and the pursuit of truth. In fact, there is ample evidence that many in higher education leadership believe that achieving a certain racial mix on campus is more important than maintaining educational standards.

There are any number of strategies that we should emphasize in lieu of this deeply flawed approach. As I have written in a previous issue, enrollment parity for economically and socially disadvantaged students will come only when these students are much better prepared for higher education by our public school system. Some of our leading universities are beginning to pay more attention to this seamless "K-16" nature of education and develop initiatives to address the college preparation problem. This is a much better use of talent and resources than worshipping at the altar of engineered diversity, but it will require a different brand of moral authority to succeed.

PC and The Alamo

June 4, 2002

The ultimate Texas shrine was injected into the political correctness wars a few days ago when an official of the Houston Independent School District announced a change in the way the siege at the Alamo will be treated in history classes, so as to make the dialogue less of an "us vs. them" confrontation and supposedly not be as offensive to the large and growing number of HISD students of Latino descent. We await the rewriting of the textbooks to see what revision of the facts will be proposed. This follows the huge annual Cinco de Mayo parade and celebration of Mexican cultural pride and a March debate between the two Texas Democratic gubernatorial candidates that was conducted entirely in Spanish (to his credit, Dan Morales protested loudly, to no avail; he lost the argument and the election).

The Alamo incident is producing a backlash, much of it, I am pleased to say, from students of Latino ancestry who said they simply want to be taught the truth and the facts. After all, the siege at the Alamo was about a lot of things – courage in the face of long odds, the human will to freedom, property rights, and America's manifest destiny – but not about race or ethnicity. Similarly, most Hispanics I know believe that the only successful route for their children is through assimilation with American culture, beginning with a mastery of English. But the flap brings to mind reports on articles and commentary coming from the National Council for Social Studies, a large organization of teachers of history, geography, and political science, who have the responsibility for teaching civic values to our young people. If their pronouncements are to be believed, this group sees its mission to "de-exceptionalize" the United States and promote the idea of the cosmopolitan citizen without allegiance to a particular history, culture, or locality. Nothing could be further removed from the Founders' ideal of civic education as a prerequisite to self-governance. Is there any wonder why there is moral confusion about our role in the world?

On Affirmative Action and Misplaced Priorities

February 3, 2003

It has been instructive to me that one of the leading stories on the domestic front recently has been the University of Michigan affirmative action cases pending before the U.S. Supreme Court, the briefs filed on them by the Bush administration, and the related question of racial and ethnic diversity in college admissions as a compelling public interest. Who are we fooling? Almost one-half of minority children don't complete high school and over one-half of third graders cannot read at grade level. And our primary focus is on diversity in our elite institutions of higher education? Recently, I participated in an education conference in which my friend, Dr. Matt Ladner, presented some interesting statistics on the potential Hispanic college applicant pool in Texas. Starting with approximately 93,000 18-year-olds in 1997, 54,000 graduated from high school, 13,000 took a college entrance exam, 5,800 scored more than 900 on the SAT, and 2,600 of those were in the top 10 percent of their graduating class. This tells me that, in order to meet their "diversity" objectives, the top public colleges in Texas (mainly The University of Texas and Texas A&M) are relegated to fighting over the three percent of Hispanic kids who could possibly succeed at that level. Yet I read this week that Texas A&M admissions officials, after announcing the creation of the office of Vice President for Diversity and making ethnic diversity a top priority, are convinced that, without racial preferences in admissions, little can be done to "entice" more black and Hispanic students to the school. Not a word suggesting measures to increase the pool of candidates who are qualified.

Count me as one who is disappointed in the Bush administration's brief in the Michigan cases. A much stronger stand should have been taken by not only rejecting the particular Michigan racial preference plans, but also in disavowing ethnic diversity as a compelling public interest justifying racial discrimination in admissions (see "The

God Of Diversity," March 2001). However, the much more compelling issue here is the abject failure of the public schools to produce more qualified candidates, for while only a lucky few will benefit from these misguided "diversity" quotas, large percentages of our minority youth are being condemned to permanent second class status.

Finally Getting the Message

November 3, 2003

More and more I sense that black journalists and commentators are seeing the light, removing the racial blinders, and recognizing that the huge and seemingly intractable educational achievement gap between minority and white children isn't a function of racism. People like syndicated columnists William Raspberry and Clarence Page, as well as Andrea Georgsson of the *Houston Chronicle* have been noting consistently the need for what I call the "Booker T. Washington approach" of hard work and education as a personal responsibility, in addition to the demand for higher expectations from parents and the education establishment. The Thernstroms, Abigail and Stephan, have spelled it out well in their book, *No Excuses: Closing The Racial Gap In Learning* – a big part of the achievement gap problem is in attitudes toward academic achievement that are prevalent in the black community. I'm not saying that the conversion is complete, and it will be awhile before the NAACP and the race hustlers pick up on this theme, but it is encouraging to see some typically liberal black opinion leaders put away the "race card" and the "insufficient funding" mantra when discussing the low minority achievement levels. The true reality also has surfaced for black political leaders like Mayor Williams of the District of Columbia, and the real test for this new attitude and the willingness to buck the entrenched protectionism of the education establishment and its "amen corner" in the Democratic Party is underway right now in the U.S. Senate debate over a school choice plan for DC schools.

UT Back in Court on Affirmative Action

March 7, 2012

It appears that my alma mater will be on the leading edge of what could be a watershed decision by the Supreme Court on affirmative action in the use of race-based criteria in college admissions. They have been there before – in breakthrough segregation cases like *Sweatt v. Painter* and the previous affirmative action case of *Hopwood v. Texas* – but this one, *Fisher v. The University of Texas*, has the potential to end, once and for all, the notion of race-based admissions, either as a remedy for previous discrimination or, more importantly, to achieve diversity in admissions as a compelling state interest going forward. This latter manifestation of affirmative action, diversity as a compelling interest, was established by Justice Harry Blackmun in 1978 in the *Bakke* decision in California to continue to justify race as a factor in college admissions, and this concept was sustained in the *Grutter v. Bollinger* decision in 2003, when Justice Sandra Day O'Connor was the deciding vote in a 5-4 decision.

There are supposedly educational benefits for students in this compelling interest of diversity, in the form of the unique viewpoint contributions that the students so admitted bring to the institution, but all of those contributions typically identified are racially stereotypical, and therefore racist. In fact, the very benefits claimed come as a result of using these students as a means to the ends of others. Furthermore, extensive studies have shown not only that these preferential admissions do not benefit powerless minorities, but that they very often do harm to the groups they are designed to help. Interestingly, in the face of this evidence and the pending Supreme Court review, the Obama administration has issued new guidelines for enhancing diversity in college admissions and proposing new ways in which colleges might factor race into their admissions process.

We have a much different court now than in 2003 and there is reason to hope and believe that it will finally come to the conclusion that this definition of diversity is an open-ended objective and serves as a continuing cover for discrimination that violates our sense of merit and racial equality and that neither serves a compelling state interest nor benefits the people it has been designed to help. Let's quit mending it and end it.

This is an excerpt of what I had to say just before the Grutter decision in 2003 about the alternatives to the flawed approach of discrimination to achieve diversity, and it's still valid today:

"It is clear that enrollment parity for economically and socially disadvantaged students will come only when these students are much better prepared for higher education by our public school system. When almost one-half of minority children do not complete high school and more than one-half of all third graders cannot read at grade level, the lucky few who fit into the "diversity" quotas are insignificant in number compared to those condemned to permanent second class status by failing public schools."

The New American Majority

June 2, 2012

Recently, the news cycle was captivated by the report from the U.S. Census Bureau that, for the first time in U.S. history, whites of European ancestry account for less than half of newborn children, supposedly marking a tipping point for the economy, the workforce, and politics. Commentators marked it as a major turning point for American society, and it might well be, but it shouldn't.

In fact, this milestone should not be of much significance at all. For if we are the America in which race and ethnicity aren't decisive in the distribution of public goods; if we are the America in which assimilation into American life, language, citizenship, and founding principles has top priority; and if we are the America that, as Teddy Roosevelt said, has no room for what he called "hyphenated Americanism," this recent trend in demographics shouldn't matter.

Unfortunately, in the America that we have become, these statistics do matter. In the multicultural America and the welfare entitlement state America, we count by race and ethnicity to allocate the intervention of government into the various racial and ethnic group grievances advanced by hustlers with vested interests; in the affirmative action America we discriminate in employment, public contracting, and college admissions based on the "compelling state interest" of racial and ethnic diversity; and we continue to disaggregate accountability for student achievement in public education based on racial and ethnic groupings. Moreover, we filter every public decision, such as decennial legislative redistricting and the use of voter ID to protect the sanctity of the rule of "one man, one vote," and many private ones, such as the allocation of credit by financial institutions, through the judicial scrutiny of the perceived "disparate impact" on racial and ethnic minorities, whether or not there is any malevolent evidence or intent, while ignoring such blatant abuses as the observed intimidation of voters at polling places by leftist thugs.

So we reap what we sow, and race does matter… to racists. As Thomas Sowell has so well noted, "demography is not destiny, but unless this fashionable Balkanization of America is stopped soon, along with the growing double standard in the rule of law, demography will become destiny and a tragedy for all."

The 50th Anniversary of "The March"

September 5, 2013

Count me as disappointed in the overall message and theme of the celebration of the 50th anniversary of The March on Washington, when it could and should have been an event worthy of the commemoration of a significant turning point event in American history.

First, the celebration had all the earmarks of a partisan Democrat rally. Not one Republican was on stage. President Bush 43 was invited, but couldn't attend. Where was Sen. Tim Scott? Where was Justice Clarence Thomas? Just to name a couple of those inexplicably missing.

Second, what would Dr. King think about the messages and the commentary? Where was any mention of the tragic disintegration of the black family, of the 73 percent of black births out of wedlock, of the cultural rot of the rap industry, of the disaster in the urban education system and the teacher union veto on the truth about it, of the disgraceful failure to socialize black male youth? These are themes that I suspect Dr. King would have brought to our attention. And the commentary from spokesmen and reporters in the days ahead of the celebration was derelict in its failure to address any of these questions. Instead, it was all about the voter ID laws, the Trevon Martin verdict, the "attacks" on affirmative action, the "rollback" of the Voting Rights Act, the perpetual grievance message in general, the appeal for more government programs, for unending "conversations on race." One example – Colin Powell on *Face the Nation* – some credit acknowledged for the enormous racial progress that has been made since 1963, but not a word about the current pathologies in the black community or taking personal responsibility for any of them.

Finally, most disappointing was the appearance of President Obama as the headline speaker of the day. He appropriately celebrated the courage and perseverance of the civil rights leaders of the March, who deserve their place in history. But he could have greatly improved on the overall theme of his remarks, which were filled with the politics of polarization, critical of "entrenched interests" who benefit from an "unjust status quo" predicated on greed and resistant to government efforts through redistribution to give working families a "fair deal," etc. Is this the message of a uniter, not a divider? Does this message accord proper recognition of the many millions of Americans of all races and ethnicities who still revere Dr. King's words from that day a half century ago that asked us to judge not by skin color but by content of character? King's dream, as he said, was rooted in the American founding documents, in the classical liberal tradition grounded in negative liberty, or freedom from government tyranny. But this concept of liberty is anathema to the progressive left, which wants positive rights to material things, and this is the ideology from which Obama originates. We've come a long way from the true meaning of Dr. King's eloquent words on that day.

The Moynihan Report at 50

May 5, 2015

In a recent review of the new book by former World Bank economist Joseph Stiglitz entitled *The Great Divide*, reviewer Brian Wesbury writes this:

"A running theme of the book is that the American dream is dead, because policymakers have failed to implement truly liberal policies. But for the past 50 years, liberals have gotten almost exactly what they wanted. Between 1950 and 1965, government spending outside of defense was just 7.8 percent of GDP. Liberals weren't happy with that, so they proposed to make America a "Great Society" by creating the modern welfare state along with Medicare and Medicaid. After five decades of growth in these redistribution programs, nondefense government spending is now 16.8 percent of GDP… Liberals are like the dog that finally caught the car. Now what will they do?"

Good question. And, as we recognize the 50th anniversary of the release of the U.S. Department of Labor report titled "The Negro Family: The Case for National Action," better known as "The Moynihan Report" after its author Daniel Patrick Moynihan, particularly in light of the recent series of events in Ferguson, Charleston, and Baltimore, it is more than fair to expect some accountability and to wonder what we have gained from this transformation of American society. The amount of treasure expended in the various Great Society programs originally dubbed the "war on poverty" now totals approximately $12-15 trillion, depending on whose numbers one uses, yet Stiglitz and his fellow travelers on every channel of communication call for even more funding, a "national urban strategy," a "conversation" about race, etc.

When the report was released in 1965, 25 percent of black births were to unmarried mothers and this was characterized as a looming disaster. Today, that number is 72 percent. The comparable numbers for whites are five percent in 1965 and 36 percent today, so the disaster is well past the looming stage, and the meaning of single motherhood has changed, making it even worse. In 1960, 95 percent of unmarried mothers had been married at some time in the past; by 2003, only 50 percent had ever been married. These numbers alone are plenty of evidence that, in spite of some progress in lifting the worst burdens of poverty, this massive experiment has been an abject failure in terms of the societal dysfunction that has been the result. Again, liberals caught the dog a long time ago, and have no plan about what to do now.

One of the helpful things they could do right away is to stop listening to people like Stiglitz and start reading and listening to people like young black leader Jason Riley of *The Wall Street Journal*, who, in his book, *Please Stop Helping Us*, suggests that they could do better to focus much less on racial grievances and much more on prevalent ghetto attitudes towards school, work, marriage, and child-rearing. For this is not about race, it's about the creation, through a half century of misguided government intervention, of a culture of dependency that is in its third generation. They also could pay attention to David Brooks, whose writings have lately taken a spiritual and moral direction, to his credit, and who recently has noted the social cost of the moral relativism that permeates our society. He writes: "The first response to these stats and to these profiles should be intense sympathy… But, it's increasingly clear that sympathy is not enough. It's not only money and better policy that are missing in these circles; it's norms. The health of a society is primarily determined by the habits and virtues of its citizens… Reintroducing norms will require, first, a moral vocabulary. These norms weren't destroyed, because of people with bad values. They were destroyed by a plague of non-judgmentalism." Amen.

There are any number of other changes in approach that would be helpful, but first will be required the realization on the part of liberal elites that more government is not the answer and, despite all its best intentions, the unintended consequences of the Great Society have done much more harm than good. I would like to think that most of the responsible among them will have the intellectual honesty to do so.

Here We Go Again – Texas Back in Court on Affirmative Action

February 4, 2016

"There are those who contend that it does not benefit African-Americans to get them into The University of Texas where they do not do well, as opposed to having them go to a less-advanced school, a slower-track school where they do well. One of the briefs pointed out that most of the black scientists in the country don't come from schools like The University of Texas, they come from lesser schools where they do not feel that they're being pushed ahead in classes that are too fast for them." – Supreme Court

Justice Antonin Scalia in oral arguments in *Fisher v. University of Texas at Austin*, December 9, 2015.

Justice Scalia is on to a key point here, but has been pilloried for these comments and, to be fair, he could have been much more artful in the way he expressed these views, but the fact is that there is good evidence based on credible studies that shows that he is correct in a number of ways that go to the heart of the efficacy of race-based discrimination in college admissions.

Most recently, in October 2015, the National Association of Scholars released a report by Gail Heriot, a professor of law at the University of San Diego and a member of the U.S. Commission on Civil Rights, entitled "A Dubious Expediency: How Race-Preferential Admissions Policies on Campus Hurt Minority Students." This study confirms in many respects the studies performed by Richard Sander and Stuart Taylor, Jr., the results of which are detailed in their 2012 book, *Mismatch: How Affirmative Action Hurts Students It's Intended to Help, and Why Universities Won't Admit It,* and adds significant new analysis that is compelling. There is little doubt that it is the evidence presented in these works that Scalia referenced and which provides the backbone of his remarks at the hearing.

Since the oral arguments before the court, Sander has written that the gaps in academic preparation are wide, with mean SAT scores among freshmen admitted to The University of Texas outside the state mandated top 10 percent class rank admissions system reflecting a gap of 390 points higher for whites than for blacks. This is indicative of a large preference, not to mention a huge competitive disadvantage for blacks, lending to the credence of the mismatch problem, however, as he points out, not enough data has been made public to study the matter properly. It's clear that the lack of transparency is an issue that clouds credibility and that there exists a pattern of denial.

The larger question in *Fisher* is, how long will we continue to hide behind the smokescreen of a "holistic" (whatever that means) approach to college admissions as a camouflage for discrimination based on race and ethnicity in order to achieve the elusive so-called "compelling state interest in diversity?" As these studies reveal, the more we know about the effects of these programs, the more fraudulent they appear, in spite of the recurring theme of the proponents that a "critical mass" of students from certain groups is necessary to reap the educational benefits attributable to this diversity, an empty claim of the type identified by Shelby Steele as "poetic truth."

In her report, Professor Heriot makes the statement, "But if anything can cause good-faith supporters (of affirmative action) to stop and reconsider, it is the mounting empirical research showing that race-preferential admissions policies are doing more harm than good even for their intended beneficiaries." The critical condition here is good-faith, and I don't want to accuse her of naiveté, but I wish it was this simple.

Justice Kennedy Adds to the Confusion on Affirmative Action

August 5, 2016

Last month, I commented briefly on *Fisher v. University of Texas*, the long-running affirmative action in college admissions case, on which the Supreme Court ruled 4-3 in favor of the University, supporting its so-called "holistic" criteria review of applicants that might use race as a factor under strict scrutiny in the interest of diversity in the student body. Because of the implications of the decision, I want to expand my commentary on the case and return to some comments on it that I have previously made over the past couple of decades.

This is a horrible decision. It is made even more so by the fact that Justice Anthony Kennedy, who wrote the majority opinion, in effect reversed himself on the issue from his statement in the first appearance of *Fisher* before the Court in 2013, in which he wrote "judicial review must begin from the position that any official action that treats a person differently on account of his race or ethnic origin is inherently suspect." But in this case, he was almost totally deferential to the university's judgment, with scant evidence that there were any strict scrutiny criteria in place. Kennedy obviously is struggling with his convictions, particularly now with Antonin Scalia not around to prop him up. What a tragedy.

After the *Adarand* and *Hopwood* Court decisions of the mid-1990s and the passage of Proposition 209 in California, many of us were encouraged that our country was finally on a path toward the realization of the ideals embodied in the equal protection clause of the 14th Amendment and Dr. Martin Luther King's "I Have a Dream" speech. Alas, the vested interests of race-based preferences in hiring, college admissions, and contracting have mounted aggressive counterattacks that have taken several forms, in and outside the judicial process.

These efforts are particularly egregious in our elite institutions of higher education, which ostensibly have as their mission the pursuit of truth, but which have practiced a considerable degree of intellectual dishonesty in fighting to preserve race-based admissions preferences. As a result, we get the various "X percent rules" that guarantee admission to a certain top percentage of each high school graduating class, proposals to replace standardized tests, such as the SAT with more "holistic" admissions criteria, and the promotion of "diversity" in admissions as a compelling public interest. Of course, diversity is defined for this purpose in terms of color or ethnicity, not thought or ideas or political philosophy, and, at least in the top business schools, is said to be driven by the demands of the globalized market and prospective corporate employers. Most of these companies have been shaken down by the affirmative action establishment, and they seem to lack the moral authority to insist on higher expectations from minority students. Shelby Steele of the Hoover Institution consistently has made the case that this is the reason that the white leadership of American institutions keeps trying to engineer results rather than demanding higher achievement. It's as though they feel they must seek moral authority by proving a negative – that they are not racist. The problem for Steele is that this moral authority comes at the expense of minority development.

The corruption this promotes is pervasive. We are led to believe that diversity initiatives have nothing to do with racial quotas and that they are crucial to learning, academic excellence, and the pursuit of truth. In fact, there is ample evidence that many in higher education leadership believe that achieving a certain racial mix on campus is more important than maintaining educational standards. In other words, access trumps excellence, even when it has been clearly shown that the "mismatches" in admissions often result in frustration and failure for minority students.

There are a number of strategies that we should emphasize in lieu of this deeply flawed approach. First, it is clear that enrollment parity for economically and socially disadvantaged students will come only when these students are much better prepared for higher education by our public school system. Thankfully, some of our leading universities are beginning to pay more attention to this seamless "K-16" nature of education and are developing initiatives to address the college preparation problem. This is a much better use of their talent and resources than worshipping at the altar of engineered diversity. More importantly, however, we need to transform the entire delivery system for public education through extrinsic reforms that include comprehensive school choice for every child and the overhaul of teacher preparation and certification that will loosen the monopoly of the colleges of education.

All the easy education reform has been accomplished, the more difficult and challenging elements are ahead. But when less than one-third of our high school graduates are postsecondary (college and career) ready, one-half of them must take remedial courses to enter community college, and almost one-half of urban third graders cannot read at grade level, the lucky few who fit into the "diversity" quotas are insignificant in number compared to those condemned to permanent second class status by failing public schools. The continuation of affirmative action in college admissions is not a cure for this problem.

21
Religious Issues

Faith, Reason, and Wisdom

May 1, 2000

One of my heroes of the 20th century is Pope John Paul II. He not only has been a great leader for his church and his faith, but a significant statesman and one who provided critical political (yes, political in the philosophical sense) and moral conviction during the momentous final years of Soviet and Eastern European Communism. His 1994 book, *Crossing the Threshold of Hope*, offers insight on the great theological concerns of our times on an accessible level: the existence of God, the dignity of man, pain and suffering, evil, as well as the relationship among the various Christian faiths, between Christianity and other faiths. Most of all, it is about hope for all mankind in his motto, "be not afraid." Recently, I completed a second reading of his September 1998 encyclical to the Catholic bishops, Fides et Ratio, on the relationship between faith and reason. Here is his magnum opus, a broad sweep of 90 pages of distilled wisdom from a life of philosophical and theological study. In it, he traces the historical relationships between and among faith and reason, philosophy, science, revelation, and empiricism, pointing out many of the false philosophical idols and sophistries along the way, many of which are with us today in the forms of the various postmodern ideologies. Finally, he calls for a return to true, speculative philosophy as "an inquiry that can help greatly to clarify the relationship between truth and life, between event and doctrinal truth, and above all between transcendent truth and humanly comprehensible language." I often have thought that our intellectuals have failed us in leading us away from this inquiry over the past century. Hopefully, John Paul II has helped redirect us.

Thoughts On Faith-Based Initiatives

February 2, 2001

Of all President Bush's proposals to date, the most difficult and potentially most transformational is the centerpiece of his compassionate conservatism, the plan for Federal support of faith-based social programs. Fully competitive school choice and full privatization of Social Security would certainly be more dramatic, but these aren't in the cards for awhile and don't represent as bold a leap into the unknown. Not that it will be brand new; Catholic Charities USA has been receiving government funds for years. But the ambition for this plan and its ultimate scope could be quite sweeping.

There are problems to address, of course, and the usual secular humanist and First Amendment crowds will be out in droves. My concern would be more about the corruption or impairment of the mission of the faith-based organizations by government than any church-state or proselytization problems. In fact, some of the latter will no doubt be beneficial in the often necessary behavior modification of the recipients. And there are operating details to be worked out, but we should not fear innovations that have the power to transform lives if they are well structured and offered as an option to public programs on a competitive basis. This is compassionate, but also empowerment conservatism, much like school choice, because it is bottom-up driven, not top-down. Alexis de Tocqueville noted more than 160 years ago that the genius of America lay not in its government, but in its free associations. To a large extent we have allowed government to supplant independent charities and have come to rely on a coercive one-size-fits-all approach to treating social pathologies that usually creates dependence. We often have forgotten that many of these pathologies have as their root cause a spiritual void that must be filled, that behavior matters, and that true welfare reform requires more than money.

Religion and the Public Square

April 3, 2001

In a recent editorial in *The Weekly Standard*, William Kristol writes that the distinctive legacy likely to be left by George W. Bush will be an end to government hostility to religion and a new era in which pluralism and faith are no longer at odds. This is a striking comment. Certainly no area of public life over the past several decades has been as divisive as the debate over the proper role of religion in public policy. Last year, two symposia on the subject caught my attention. One was the March 2000 convocation of The American Assembly on "Matters of Faith: Religion in American Public Life" and the other was a July 2000 American Enterprise Institute symposium emphasizing Alexis de Tocqueville's views on the subject. The American Assembly convocation of 57 business, civic, and religious leaders produced a statement of general, albeit not unanimous, agreement that "...religious voices are a vital component of our national conversation and should be heard in the public square. We reject the notion that religion is exclusively a private matter relegated to the homes and sacred meeting places of the faithful..." The AEI meeting highlighted Tocqueville's thoughts on the threat of tyranny, not from the guillotine or the gulag, but from a form of "perpetual childhood" brought about by a Faustian bargain – the state assures affluence and contentment in exchange for power over our lives. He believed this condition would reign when materialism and individualism led to power seeking through government. Ultimately, he believed this society would be forced to make a choice and that the only bulwark against this tyranny would be our voluntary, private associations informed by religious faith.

Norman Podhoretz has written of the "curious fear and loathing" of religious conservatives by the liberal elite. Their talk of fascism has been replaced by the sincere conviction that if the Christian Right ever got into power behind a Republican President, we would face an updated version of the Salem witch trials. (Incidentally, he finds a clue here as to how Bill Clinton survived impeachment.) He dismisses this paranoia by pointing out that the religious conservative communities have served as a reminder of the religious foundations of the country and the (rapidly depleting) moral capital on which the democratic system still draws.

Remember that the mantra of "separation of church and state" comes from a judicial perversion of the religion clause of the First Amendment, which was designed to limit what the state can do, not what the church can do. With any luck, this President, with his public faith witness and his emphasis on private, faith-based social initiatives, can introduce a neo-Tocquevillian era and replenish our moral capital. Politically, this may be what the liberals fear most of all.

Useful By-Products Of War

January 4, 2002

Let me be clear: war is never a positive good. However, a just war can produce useful by-products, and this one is no exception. For instance, I have no doubt that this country is in the midst of a soul-searching experience and dialogue like no other in at least a century, if not since the Civil War. In coffee breaks, chat rooms, talk shows, churches, schools, boardrooms, and on op/ed pages, we are re-examining the American idea and the sources of moral authority in ways that will produce renewed purpose in our society. For "wonks" like me, this is great, and I particularly like the fact that, for a change, we're being forced into serious national debates about our convictions in matters other than material progress or the size of our 401(k)s.

When we begin again to think in these terms there follows a re-evaluation of our priorities in life and the grounding of our values. I am reminded of a remark by Lynne

Cheney, whom George Will has called our "secretary of domestic defense:" "A people cannot be expected to defend what they do not understand." This is a direct reference to our higher education system and the degree to which it has distanced itself from grounding in our founding ideas. In many instances, this has been manifest in anti-Americanism, pure and simple. A reversal of this trend would be another useful by-product, as well as a beneficial restoration of the mission of higher education in the transmission of our cultural heritage.

The dialogue on religion has been instructive, and I hope that another by-product will be to dispel this notion of equivalence between Islamic fanaticism and Christian fundamentalism (see "The Bin Laden Tapes" above). Bill Moyers, in his recent Middleton Lectures address, seems to think that religion will be this century's biggest problem and that we should put our "faith" in democracy, which he feels is threatened by religious believers. In fact, democracy, properly understood, doesn't stand a chance outside a moral order and the rule of law, which are well informed by the Judeo-Christian tradition.

Finally, as I have mentioned previously, another useful result of the war would be a transformation of the Arab world to a secular governing paradigm based on consent of the governed and the rule of law. This will no doubt be impossible without an Islamic "Reformation," and truly will be a battle of ideas and theology that may have more to do with the shape of the world in this century than any other conflict. We in the West cannot be a direct participant, but we can encourage it by facing up to the duplicity of these regimes and our complicity with them, and by forcing states like Egypt and Saudi Arabia to make choices. It will not be pretty, but the battle should be fought to a conclusion, because there is no room for the "Islamism" that preaches nihilism in the name of Allah. There are many cultures, but only one civilization, and the leaders of responsible Islam must decide whether or not they want their people to join it. This will be the most significant by-product of all.

Thoughts on the Pledge

July 3, 2002

In a previous issue, I posed the question as to whether or not the second paragraph of The Declaration of Independence ("all men are endowed by their Creator," etc.) could be ratified by Congress today. It's a rhetorical question, but one that again resonates in the wake of the Ninth Circuit Court's decision on the Pledge of Allegiance. In the flurry of opinion essays that have followed, I have been amused at the secular left's spin on the Pledge and other enunciations of our creed, such as "in God we trust" and "so help me God." E. J. Dionne and others call the customary use of these invocations "ceremonial deism," the idea that they are used without reference to context and are therefore meaningless, merely backdrops in American life. Behind much of this kind of commentary, however, I sense a nervousness that these judges have forced the issue and that the anti-religion elites, particularly those holding public office, will now be called into a serious debate on their hostility to religion in the public square. As Michael Medved noted in a *USA Today* opinion piece, the secular worldview that dominates American elites insists that all religions deserve identical respect or similar dismissal, either as paths to the same God or to violent, anti-intellectual, intolerant tendencies. It's time we dispensed with this theory along with the historical revisionism that the Constitution is "Godless." Some religions are better or worse than others. Ours is represented by the "under God" in the Pledge – the creator God of The Declaration of Independence and the source of our rights. But let's have the debate; it's long overdue, and what better timing than in an election year!

The Courts and the Pledge

November 4, 2003

Here are my thoughts on the ridiculous decision of the Ninth Circuit Court of Appeals prohibiting the use of the "under God" phrase in the Pledge of Allegiance and other assaults on the presence of religious and other faith-based symbols and practices in our public square:

Neutrality as to the diversity of sectarian practices and particular religious beliefs or the absence thereof is consistent with the intent of the American Founders. But, if by our current definition of neutrality we have come to mean neutrality on the validity of the ideas espoused in the second paragraph of the Declaration of Independence; if we mean neutrality on the question of the validity of the foundational belief in a moral order undergirded by natural law with its origins in divine law; or if we mean neutrality on the validity of the premise that the freedoms and equality we champion can be sustained only within this moral order; then our civic republican ideal of ordered liberty under the rule of law cannot survive.

The Coming Islamic Reformation

February 4, 2004

I previously have commented on the fact that the war on terror will be a major transforming event for the Arab Middle East, and I was reminded of the degree to which this is well underway by the report of a recent interfaith conference in which the father of slain journalist Daniel Pearl conferred with leading Arab scholars about the necessity of communication and reconciliation across religious barriers. A key point in the dialogue was that, despite the regret expressed for Pearl's death, not a single Islamic imam has publicly denounced his murder as a sin under religious law. I mention this anecdote, because it is instructive of the oft-mentioned need for an Islamic Reformation, which I believe will be necessary to resolve the split-mindedness in the Muslim world. Frankly, we cannot hope to live in long-term peace in an environment with one-sixth of the world's population suffering from an intellectual/philosophical/theological schizophrenia – in which none of the mainstream religious leaders of Islam can bring themselves to condemn such an act in religious terms. Some will say that this is evidence of a clash of imperialist religions that has been looming for 1,400 years, but I believe it has been brewing for only about 100 years, or since the radical elements of Islam were hijacked by thugs and the ideologies of national socialism, and more recently fueled by even more radical totalitarian Islamist theology. Regardless of its lineage and the desirability that the coming reformation be conducted on theological and philosophical grounds, it, as with the Reformation in Western Christianity, probably will not be completely resolved without a civil war (or wars) to be waged within Islam, and we are already seeing some portents of this in the Palestinian and Saudi Arabian societies. Needless to say, the U.S. will not be able to remain a completely idle spectator, if for no other reason than that the Bush Doctrine will probably have been the catalyst.

Gibson's Passion

March 3, 2004

Well, I saw Mel Gibson's "The Passion of the Christ" on opening night, and one thing that should be said is that it was not oversold. It was at once probably the most compelling and repelling movie experience of my life. Entertaining it probably isn't, in the sense that term is ordinarily used. I could see *Casablanca* 15 more times; I probably won't see this one again. Anti-Semitic? Only if you believe that the Gospels are. As Gibson has said, there were only Jews and Romans in the courtyard; no

Norwegians were there. He also has said, which I believe to be true, that substantially all the criticism he has received is not mainly about him, but about the New Testament. Violent? To the extreme, but purposefully, and not gratuitously so, as with much exploitative violence in the movies today, which I will not watch. All in all, it is a great movie, and I recommend it to people of all faiths.

Religion and Spirituality

August 2, 2004

A recent lead article in the "Weekend Journal" section of *The Wall Street Journal* caught my attention. It was another one of those surveys of the tendency that has been prevalent in the past 20 years or so in America toward "do it yourself' religion. At least anecdotally, this seems to me to be a condition primarily of the now late middle-aged baby boomer generation, frustrated with traditional religion and its institutions, striving for meaning in their lives, and the struggle by their former clergy to woo them back into the mainstream. The common mantra of these religious groups is their preference for "spirituality" in an environment in which, as one group founder put it, "dogma doesn't get in the way." Another common attribute among these groups seems to be the tendency toward "personal growth" over "fixed creed," as David Brooks has described it. In a country that remains the most religious in all the free world, save possibly India, and which alone has sustained a competitive marketplace for religious beliefs almost since its founding, this phenomenon is not surprising, and it is probably good evidence of the tolerance that has made us immune to religious wars. I'm all for the search for personal meaning, but I'm not sure that this movement from religion to spirituality, personal growth over fixed creed, and its accompanying anti-theological "bonding" and pop-psychology is entirely healthy for our religious life as a nation, particularly to the extent that it is in some ways tied to the concerted effort by many to remove from the public square all evidence of America's Judeo-Christian heritage, which is, after all, the foundation of our common adherence to a distinctive American creed.

God and Tsunamis

February 2, 2005

Of all the immediate responses to the enormous tragedy of the Southeast Asian tsunami catastrophe, the two most misguided were: 1) the silly allegations that the U.S. was not responsive enough in timing or financial commitment, and 2) the continuing questions, "where was God?" or "why would God allow this to happen?" To the first of these, suffice to say that any critics of American response should now have been entirely silenced, if not embarrassed, by the now obvious fact that the U.S. totally is dominating the relief and recovery effort, and, in fact, has shown that its logistical capabilities to do so effectively dwarf all other humanitarian relief capabilities, most conspicuously those of the United Nations. And, incidentally, where is the Islamic world in this effort? The last time I noticed, the Arab countries were virtual "no shows" in relief of this devastation, which was primarily centered on Muslim populations. So much for Islamic solidarity.

As to the question of God's role, this is probably one of the most enduring mysteries of faith, entangled as it is with the issue of theodicy, or the problem of evil in a world created by a benevolent, loving Creator. Although it is human to wonder why bad things happen to innocent people and what sort of God would let a thing like this happen, our postmodern intellectual climate has damaged our capacity to respond. To this question, two Jewish Rabbis had the best responses I have seen. Jonathan Sacks recalled the teaching of Maimonides that natural disasters have no explanation other than that God, by placing us in a physical world, set life within the parameters of the physical. Nature is not benign in this world – sometimes innocents die – and we are called upon to be "partners in the work of creation." Daniel Lapin reminds us that God runs this world with as little supernaturalism as possible, and gave us the intelligence and commanded us to make ourselves less vulnerable to nature. And, while the casualties cannot be blamed on human actions, many of them can be blamed on human inactions, such as failure to provide warning systems or, I would add, the failure to allow countries like Sri Lanka to participate fully in the global trading system by eliminating tariffs and other impediments so that they and other developing nations can have an opportunity to build better infrastructure and fend for themselves against nature.

There is in these questions, I sense, an element of what the ancient Greeks called acedia, the fear of things spiritual, or, in more current terms, fear of a transcendence that our all-seeing and all-powerful science cannot and will not ever fully explain. In this world, there are no guarantees.

Back to the "Real War" in America

March 2, 2005

Meanwhile, on the domestic war front, we owe Texas Attorney General Greg Abbott our thanks for defending the religious freedoms enshrined in the U.S. Constitution by forcefully arguing before the U.S. Supreme Court the case for keeping the Ten Commandments monument on the State Capitol grounds.

To illustrate the point to be made, last year *The American Enterprise* magazine ran a very interesting picture "tour" of several of Washington, D.C.'s major federal buildings that included: Moses with the Ten Commandments in the rotunda of the Library of Congress; the Ten Commandments in the floor of the National Archives; the "Liberty of Worship" statue with the Ten Commandments outside the Ronald Reagan Federal Building; Moses with the Ten Commandments tablets on the rear façade of the U.S. Supreme Court; Moses with the Ten Commandments inside the Supreme Court's hearing room; and an excerpt from Lincoln's Second Inaugural Address, with its multiple references to God, carved into the interior of the Lincoln Memorial. We could add many other examples in that city, but you get the point.

Some will make the argument that the only way these icons on government grounds, along with such of our heritage expressed in the mottos of "in God we trust" and "so help me God," can be justified is by confirming their role in a kind of "ceremonial deism," carefully avoiding any representation that their subject actually informs our creed. In other words, we should pursue a kind of "don't ask, don't tell" policy as to any religious presence in the public square. Au contraire. Listen to James Madison: "We have staked the whole of our political institutions on the capacity of mankind to govern themselves according to the Ten Commandments of God," or note the argument of Michael Novak: "...the specific right of religious freedom guaranteed by the U.S. Constitution is based on Judeo-Christian concepts not replicated in any other religion."

As to sectarian religion we must be neutral, but if by that neutrality we mean neutral on the validity of the foundational belief in a moral order undergirded by natural law with its origins in divine law, then our civic republican ideal of ordered liberty under the rule of law cannot survive.

By Their Fruits Ye Shall Know Them

September 1, 2006

In recent weeks, we have been treated to an intellectual discussion on the nature of our enemy that, frankly, is long overdue. More often in his public appearances, President Bush has referred to them as "Islamic fascists," setting aside at least momentarily the characterization of our conflict as a "war on terror," a term which I believe has been a mischaracterization from the outset, referring to a tactic, not to the essence of the enemy. So, what is a fascist regime? Any objective reading of the usually reliable dictionary sources and popular historical usage reveals common threads of definition – totalitarian, imperialistic, strict ideological control, xenophobic, dictatorial, typically racist, and belligerently nationalistic. Are these traits recognizable in any current movements? Now, for those such as the Saudi government or the Council on American-Islamic Relations who have objected to the connection of the religion of Islam with movements so characterized, let's add additional context. One of the widely read and still ardently followed founders of modern jihadism was the Egyptian radical and leader of the Muslim Brotherhood, Sayyid Qutb, whose writings clearly indicate the linkages of radical jihadist Islam with the intellectual roots of fascism as practiced by the Nazis in the 1930s. Qutb roundly denounced all secular law as blasphemous and considered Sharia law the only legitimate ordering of society. Have we heard any leading moderate or mainstream Muslims denounce the widespread teaching of this ideology or deny its fascistic tendencies? Do we see evidence of any meaningful introspection on these points at all? If so, it hasn't been very often or very loud. In his book, *Salt of the Earth,* Joseph Cardinal Ratzinger (now Pope Benedict XVI) includes some very candid comments about Islam: "…the interplay of society, politics, and religion has a completely different structure in Islam as a whole… which simply does not have the separation of the political and the religious sphere, which Christianity has had from the beginning. The Koran is a total religious law… Islam has a total organization of life that is completely different from ours; it embraces simply everything… One has to have a clear understanding that it is not simply a denomination that can be included in the free realm of a pluralistic society." Not much room for the Western ideal of liberty of conscience here and, although he doesn't use the word, it is clear that the term totalitarian fits rather well with the Pope's description. In this characterization, President Bush has been very clear since the attack of 9/11 – "we have seen their kind before." The first essential of successful warfare is moral clarity, but a close second is to know your enemy and call it by its proper name.

Last month I posed the question – what will it take to convince the West that the war on Islamofascism is World War III and every bit the equivalent of the global conflicts, including the Cold War, that preceded it? Here's hoping that the recent disruption of the plot to arm as many as 10 commercial airlines as WMDs on America can be the tipping point for the skeptics, the appeasers, and those who still have lingering doubts about the nature and intentions of the enemy.

Enter Benedict with the Tough Questions

October 3, 2006

I've often thought that Pope Benedict XVI has his current job primarily because he was far and away the best choice to lead the Catholic Church's primary mission of this century – to salvage Europe for Christendom – and because this mission cannot be separated from its corollary, which is to determine how Western Christian culture can coexist with fundamentalist Islamic culture. In his recent lecture at Regensburg University, he entered the fray, and not a moment too soon. Here's hoping that there is much more to come, for this brilliant theologian/philosopher has much to say in depth about the historic relationship between faith and reason (Jerusalem and Athens, if you will) over the centuries, and important questions that must be addressed by the intellectual classes of all faiths, as well as secularists, agnostics, and atheists, if the age of right reason, properly understood, is to survive this century. In the book, *Salt of the Earth*, then Cardinal Ratzinger speaks of the essence of Islam, noting that it does not have the separation of the political and the religious sphere that Christianity has had from the beginning. The Koran is totalitarian – sharia law shapes everything in society. Consequently, Islam is "not a denomination that can be included in the free realm of a pluralistic society." In other words, the liberty of conscience, so integral to the belief system of the West, is not embodied in Islam. Nor is there in Islam a "teaching authority" that openly pursues errors and inconsistencies, as well as promotes dialogue and public introspection among Islamic scholars and laymen. For these attributes, the West owes a debt to the Greeks beginning with Socrates with his discipline of critical self-examination and the subsequent assimilation of the reason of Athens to the faith of Jerusalem that formed the basis of the Western intellectual tradition, a tradition based on the right reason of a law-ordered universe discoverable by man. It is about the future of this tradition of reason wherein Benedict's questions are so timely.

The most insightful commentary on the Pope's speech that I have seen came from Lee Harris in *The Weekly Standard,* to wit: At Regensburg he was reminding us that "the encounter between Biblical faith and Greek philosophical inquiry was an event of decisive importance, not only for religion, but for world history. Further, this is a legacy that we in the West are duty-bound to keep intact, yet it is a legacy that is under relentless attack, both from those who do not share it, namely Islam, and from those who are its beneficiaries, namely, Western intellectuals."

So, according to Harris, the critical challenges in the form of questions (more directed to Western elites than to Islam) posed by Pope Benedict are these: Is it really a matter of subjective choice whether men follow a religion that respects human reason and that refuses to use violence to convert others? Can even the most committed atheist be completely indifferent to the imaginary gods that the other members of his community continue to worship? If modern, scientific reason cannot persuade men to defend their own communities of reason against the eruption of disturbing pathologies of religion and reason, then what can persuade them to do so? Shall we delude ourselves into thinking that the life of reason can survive without courage and character? And, most decisively, shall we be content with lives we refuse to examine, because such examination requires us to ask questions for which science can give no definite answer?

In his book, *The Universal Hunger for Liberty,* Michael Novak begins the final chapter by asking whether Islam can come to terms with democracy, but as with Benedict's challenge, ends up with questions directed primarily to the West, such as:

- Why in a world without purpose, resulting from blind chance, should human beings follow reason?
- Of what avail is reason in a reasonless world?
- What legacy of reason are we left by the secular West's fundamental right to the individual's untrammeled freedom of choice?

I am more convinced than ever that Islam is in the midst of a long period of reformation and that we in the West are its unwitting catalysts. However, the Muslim community is not alone in its need for introspection in dealing with the post-9/11 world, and our own intellectual leaders had best listen seriously to the questions posed by the philosopher Pope. The final exam will come soon enough.

What Has Atheism Ever Produced?

November 1, 2007

Like many observers, I have wondered at the motivation for the rash of atheistic books that have achieved bestseller status over the past year or so. All of a sudden, they are everywhere, and the electronic media has picked up the lead with follow-up interviews and debates pitting their author/celebrities against surrogates for the Judeo/Christian tradition. Of course, much of it is political in motivation, but as Harvey Mansfield has noted, these atheistic attacks are no longer limited to the personification of "organized" religion, the institutional church, but attempt to reach more deeply into religion itself as manifest in the faith of the believer.

Well, the jury is still out on all of this, I suppose, but in spite of my bias, the defenders seem to have the upper hand. For one thing, the atheists clearly hold believers to a much higher standard than for non-believers. After all, the sole source of tyranny, whether religious or secular, is human, and there clearly has been much more tyranny led by atheistic secular humanism just in the past century alone than all of it that has been led by religious zealots in history combined – if you doubt it, count the bodies. For another and more important point, what has atheism ever produced for the benefit of mankind that even remotely compares with the beauty, hope, faith, and perseverance instilled and nurtured over the years by the religious impulse and religious sources? Not to mention the contribution of religion to the greatest achievements of human culture, including most of the values and virtuous human attributes revered by the authors of these atheist tracts.

I think Hitchens, Dawkins, and their ilk would be well advised to be on the winning side of Pascal's "wager" – it's a good bet and one I wouldn't want to lose.

American Genius

March 7, 2008

A recently released study from the Pew Forum on Religion and Public Life, contrary to the analysis offered by some observers, should give Americans renewed comfort in the founding concept that has, probably more than any other single element, fostered American exceptionalism among the nations. This concept, based on the dual U.S. Constitutional guarantees of anti-religious establishment, along with the free exercise thereof, has produced a healthy free market dynamism of religious tolerance and practice that is unique in world history.

According to the study, 60 percent of Americans consider religion "very important," compared to 12 percent for the French, for example, and 84 percent of Americans claim one of a broad range of religious institutional affiliations. So, what of its finding that 44 percent of American adults have switched religious affiliations at some point in their lives? Although this might smack of "cafeteria-style" religion to suit a lifestyle without doctrinal commitment, it seems attractively dynamic to me and describes the competitive religious marketplace free of coercion, which the founders envisioned, except that they no doubt could not have forseen the amazing number of choices that would be available. One more thing that is distinctive about America that has produced a "public" religion is the second paragraph of the Declaration of Independence, which begins "We hold these truths to be self-evident…" This is the real source of American genius and exceptionalism, however it is practiced.

On the other hand, among many in our establishment elite, this element of exceptionalism is not necessarily an asset or a characteristic to be praised, and this view is particularly evident among our foreign policy officials. Writes Angelo Codevilla in the *Claremont Review*, "Having concluded that mankind is outgrowing religion, our experts react to religion's presence in the Islamic world – and in America – by inventing the distinction between "moderate" religion, acceptable, because not taken seriously, and "fundamentalism," i.e., actually believing in God and His commandments." This view inevitably leads to the conclusion that religion is the mother of all strife and the enemy of all progress in world affairs, and precludes an intelligent and honest discussion about why certain religious beliefs and expressions are preferable to others. Unfortunately, this growing attitude among our elite that the prominence of religious faith in the public square is an American anachronism, which the rest of the West has moved "beyond" is destructive to the very genius that underpins our exceptionalism, as well as a significant foundation of our moral authority.

A Regensburg Moment

April 2, 2010

The recent release of the book, *Son of Hamas*, by Mosab Hassan Yousef, has caused quite a stir across the Middle East. Yousef is the son of the founder and leader of the Palestinian terrorist group Hamas, and in his book he discloses that he has served as one of the top spies for Israel's internal security organization. Needless to say, a shocking revelation for the hard-core Islamic jihadists.

As I understand from reviews of the book, his basic premise is that Muslim fanatics are in need of liberation from their god. In fact, he says in an interview that his father "is not a fanatic, he's a very moderate, logical person. What matters is not whether my father is a fanatic or not, he's doing the will of a fanatic God… At the end of the day, a traditional Muslim is doing the will of a fanatic, fundamentalist, terrorist God… The problem is not in Muslims. The problem is with their God. They need to be liberated from their God."

Previously, I commented at length on the views of Pope Benedict XVI as they pertain to the dangerous ideas that the Muslim faith presents to civilization, the most dangerous of which is the idea that God approves violence in his name. In his 2006 lecture at Regensburg, Germany, much maligned in the Muslim world for its alleged blasphemy, the Pope outlined how the choices made by Islamic theological and intellectual leadership over the centuries have resulted in an inability to reconcile the truths of their religion with those of reason, a critical ingredient that has produced the dominance of the West in economic and scientific development. And it's not simply all about the radical swamps of Islam; even mainstream Islam has no real concept of tolerance, plurality, or true introspection. Their God is pure will, and their mission is the rule of sharia law. Obviously, these views resonate with young Yousef, and his courage should be a beacon for responsible Muslims.

Strangely (or maybe it's not so strange) missing in response to Yousef's revelation and conspicuously absent from any of the speeches by President Obama in Cairo or other venues where Middle Eastern leadership is focused is any reference to the need for a recognition of this obvious disconnect by responsible Muslim leaders. The Pope could use a little help here, and it would be nice if it came from the political leader of the free world.

I am reminded of the words of Alexander Solzhenitsyn in his Nobel lecture of 40 years ago: "The timid civilized world has found nothing with which to oppose the onslaught of a sudden revival of bare-faced barbarity, other than concessions and smiles… a sickness of the will of successful people, it is the daily condition of those who have given themselves up to the thirst after prosperity at any price, to material well being as the chief goal of earthly existence."

The Perversion of Religious Freedom

July 4, 2010

Let's take a quick look at the "religion clause" of the First Amendment to the U.S. Constitution: "Congress shall make no law respecting an establishment of religion, or prohibiting the free exercise thereof."

The genius in this phrase is striking and it is a major foundation of the idea that produced American exceptionalism. No established church, but free religious exercise. This has resulted in a competitive marketplace of religious preferences that has allowed many flowers to bloom along with the weeds, and the resulting outlet for expression of belief has spared us from untold grief and conflict, while making us the most religious nation on earth.

There is a growing problem, however. We are now being informed in myriad ways that the protection of free exercise has a meaning much different than intended, and this is producing a perversion of the purposes of religious freedom. Some examples: the substitution of "freedom to worship" by officials such as Hillary Clinton in place of religious freedom, as she did in a speech at Georgetown University; the limitation of religious freedom to private expressions of faith and the proscription of religiously grounded convictions from public expression, as with healthcare providers who object to certain medical procedures; and the constant public intimidation to accept the radical gay/lesbian rights agenda.

Some of these encroachments are more subtle than others, but all of them offer what George Weigel calls "a diminished view of religious freedom." Further, he suggests that religious freedom, properly understood, cannot be reduced to freedom of worship. If this were the case, there is religious freedom in Saudi Arabia, where expatriots can attend Mass. No, religious freedom, rightly understood, includes the right to make religiously informed moral arguments on public policy in the public square without interference from the state. If this is not the common understanding derived from a reading of the First Amendment, then let's have the debate before we wake up and find that the right to free exercise has been taken away.

Religious Liberty Watch

September 26, 2011

The staff of the Manhattan Declaration, a non-partisan statement of conscience in defense of human life, traditional marriage, and religious freedom, to which I am a signatory, does a good job of tracking trends in religious liberty in America and lately they report a rash of transgressions – teachers being removed from classrooms for expressing opposition to same-sex marriage on their personal time, the Governor of Kentucky considering forcing a Catholic hospital to perform abortions, a group of atheists suing for removal of a cross from the 9/11 Memorial and Museum, etc. And as the Presidential campaign picks up speed, the Christophobes have begun to pour out of the woodwork, led by *The New York Times* executive editor Bill Keller, who wants assurance that "religious doctrine does not become an excuse to exclude my fellow citizens from the rights and protections our country promises" and proposes that all candidates be asked "tough questions about their faith," whatever that means.

Of course his colleague Paul Krugman is not far behind with an essay on "Republicans Against Science." Probably the most egregious transgression lately, however, is the decision by New York City Mayor Michael Bloomberg that religious leaders and themes have no part or presence in the 10th anniversary commemoration of the 9/11 attack at Ground Zero. The free exercise of religion, the free market in religious belief, the tolerance of all faiths, and the role of religious faith in the public square informing the deepest values and commemorating the most sacred moments in our history are at the core of American life as we have known it. We disturb this tradition at our peril.

Pope Francis

April 6, 2013

From what I have seen and read, I like the new Pope. I am not a Catholic, but I recognize the significant leadership potential that resides in the papacy, and I have been a huge fan of the last two incumbents, who have each in their own way had enormous influence on world events.

Obviously, John Paul II was a rock star and a huge player in the defeat of Soviet communism, but I applauded his intellect more than his celebrity, particularly his encyclical *Fides et Ratio*, which gave new meaning to me in the assimilation of faith and reason.

Pope Benedict XVI was not so much a celebrity, but was also a great intellect, and his lecture at Regensburg in 2006 was a definitive crystallization of the philosophical issues dividing the West and the Islamic world, as well as a call to the West to mend its ways in terms of its drift toward "the dictatorship of relativism."

Pope Francis is a Jesuit, but defied the move of many of his colleagues to liberation theology. He also has confronted the leftist Argentine regime and he clearly was selected as a reformer, particularly of the Vatican Curia, which is obviously long overdue. It remains to be seen whether he has the intellectual depth of his immediate predecessors, but he has shown that he will be a man of the flock and will, according to Catholic scholar George Weigel, advance the concept of Christ-centered evangelical humility, devoid of willfulness, self-absorption, and careerism. Good for him.

The Church and Secular Policy

November 8, 2013

"Give to Caesar the things that are Caesar's, and to God the things that are God's." – Matthew 22:21.

Last month, the National Council of Churches, the U.S. Conference of Catholic Bishops, and the National Association of Evangelicals, along with a few other religious organizations, sponsored a "Faithful Filibuster" to encourage Congress to protect programs "that meet the essential needs of hungry and poor people at home and abroad. As evidenced by the comments of various leaders of the constituent groups, this would include "adequate funding" of anti-poverty programs, including raising revenues (taxes) and the elimination of "unnecessary" military spending.

Likewise, in Houston, local clergy including Cardinal Daniel DiNardo and other denominational leaders were prominent in publicly joining with activists for immigration reform in rallying support for comprehensive immigration reform and encouraging Congress to reject the SAFE Act, which would allow the states to enact more stringent border control by local authorities.

I always will be one to support the role of religion in the public square, which informs and enriches American civic life, but this engagement should be limited to the championship of liberty, religious freedom, and the dignity of each human being and should not include direct engagement in politics or specific government policy, both of which are outside the competency or purview of the church.

In the case of the needs of the poor and otherwise disadvantaged, these activist religious leaders seem to have no hesitation about lobbying for government intrusion into what should be the subject of private philanthropy (think the Good Samaritan) and, which as they should be well aware, otherwise breeds and sustains crippling government dependency. This is a very disturbing trend.

ObamaCare v. the Nuns

January 4, 2014

How would you like to be the attorney who is directed to sue the Little Sisters of the Poor? Not a fun assignment and it's interesting that Obama's Attorney General has chosen this particular organization as the opponent in the enforcement of the mandate for abortion and contraception coverage under ObamaCare. I think it illustrates the arrogance of this crowd, who want to roll back the principle of religious liberty that is firmly embedded in the free exercise clause of the First Amendment. It is an old objective of progressivism to want to dissolve the "little platoons" of voluntary organizations embodied in religious institutions that have been the backbone of social services since the founding in favor of government monopoly of delivery of these services and to have the state completely engulf the public square of community life.

The first sign of trouble in this administration came in 2009 when then Secretary of State Hillary Clinton, in narrowing the definition of religious liberty, spoke not of "religious freedom," but of "freedom to worship" in describing U.S. human rights policy. This characterization of religious liberty and freedom of conscience is more like a privacy right, or something that one does for an hour on Sunday, as opposed to a life's calling.

The administration is offering "accomodation" here and is saying that the nuns' claims have no legal basis, but the Little Sisters are not buying it. Let's hope they hang tough, because this issue reaches far beyond ObamaCare implementation and goes to the heart of one of the most fundamental rights in our Constitution.

Religious Freedom Prevails

July 5, 2014

The Supreme Court took a necessary step to preserve one of the most basic foundations of our liberty in its 5-4 decision in favor of Hobby Lobby and the Green family. At the same time, it severely damaged the Obama administration's push to very narrowly restrict our First Amendment right to religious liberty to non-profit religious organizations.

Make no mistake, contrary to those who think that the ObamaCare contraception mandate was simply inadvertent regulatory overreach, the administration knew exactly what it was doing here with the ObamaCare law – going directly to the heart of religious liberty to gut the Religious Freedom Restoration Act of 1993, which was adopted by large bipartisan majorities in both houses and signed by President Clinton specifically to protect this right. Why? Because, the left knows that the religious liberty embedded in the First Amendment and spelled out in the RFRA is the firewall that not only slows the sexual revolution, but damages the century-long progressive dream of the transformation of the Constitution from a document of "negative" liberty (things the government can't do to us) to one of "positive" liberty (things that government must provide for us or mandate that others do so).

The spin on the decision from the left already has been over the top, unfortunately led by Justice Ruth Bader Ginsburg's dissent in the decision, which was more of a rant than a legal brief, and the coming demagoguery on women's "rights" will be deafening through 2016. But, the frightening thing about this decision is that four justices voted against religious freedom and how close we are to a tipping point in this country.

The True Face of the Intolerant Left

April 5, 2015

"The free exercise of religion has been called the first freedom, that which originally sparked the development of the full range of the Bill of Rights... What this law basically says is that the government should be held to a very high level of proof before it interferes with someone's free exercise of religion. This judgment is shared by the people of the United States, as well as by the Congress. We believe strongly that we can never be too vigilant in this work." – An excerpt from President Bill Clinton's remarks upon signing the Religious Freedom Restoration Act at the White House on November 16, 1993.

In addition to this federal law signed by Bill Clinton more than 20 years ago, 20 states now have similar versions of this legislation on their books, which became necessary primarily because in 1997 the Supreme Court ruled that the federal RFRA was too broad and could not be applied to the states. The Texas version of the law was signed by Governor George W. Bush in 1999 and, when the bill's sponsor, then state representative Scott Hochberg (D-Houston), was recently asked about its impact by a Dallas Morning News reporter, he was hard-pressed to remember one insignificant case in which it has been invoked. Of course, the most recent addition is Indiana, and what a firestorm and what a different atmosphere than the one that existed in 1993.

You ask why? It's simply for two reasons: One, the radical gay rights community and their fellow travelers have become so aggressive that tolerance of the LGBT lifestyle is no longer acceptable; there must be unexceptional affirmation of it in every social aspect, and two, because the political left in this country has become so hardened in its intolerance that any cultural dissent or deviation from its secular progressive dogma must be met with all-out war.

If you have any doubt about the radical gay rights agenda, note this: A leading gay rights advocacy group, the Human Rights Campaign, recently released a lengthy document, "Beyond Marriage Equality: A Blueprint for Federal Non-Discrimination Protections," in which it outlines an agenda that advocates the application of the full range of current civil rights law to sexual orientation and gender identity. In other words, a complete emulation of the racial civil rights campaign of the 1960s, as if there is any analogy of today's militant sexual identity politics with that noble cause of a half-century ago that makes sense.

It is clear that the sweeping changes in public opinion on gay rights have been unlike any such phenomenon we have seen in our lifetimes and that, in all likelihood, for example, same-sex marriage ultimately will be validated by the Supreme Court, a major turnaround in attitudes in a relatively short period of time.

But, there is no more important current story or anything to match in all of its implications the lynch mob mentality that has permeated the hard-left totalitarianism that has greeted the new Indiana law. There is nothing else to call it, and the most disappointing aspect is the stampede of weak-kneed corporate CEOs and business associations, who are supposed to be among our most reasoned policy leaders, willing to throw our foundational right to free religious exercise under the bus of the intolerance of the secular progressives. One of the most egregious examples of selective indignation is Apple CEO Tim Cook, who condemns the Indiana law while investing heavily in countries like Saudi Arabia, which stones homosexuals, and China, not exactly a model for human and civil rights. Walmart is another disappointing embarrassment, among others.

Of course, much of this issue boils down to the long-standing objective of the secular left to squeeze the religious freedom guarantee down to freedom of worship confined to private faith commitments limited to exercise in religious institutions; in other words, "the naked public square." And the reason we can't come together on key wedge social issues in this country is illustrated by this very issue – we are required by the rules of the "procedural republic" that we have become to bracket any moral issue from public policy debate and to deal with it as autonomous players unencumbered by choices we have not made for ourselves. Unfortunately, the courts have made it almost impossible for representative democracy, or even majoritarian democracy, to find our way out of this procedural box and restore the civic republic we once were. But we had better choose some leaders who won't be intimidated and are willing to find a way, and soon.

The Pope's Visit

October 6, 2015

It's pretty simple – I will just have to get used to the fact that, as attractive and engaging as he is in many ways, Pope Francis is not John Paul II or Benedict XVI. He obviously is not cut out to be the philosophical intellect or to man the barricades of challenge, confrontation, and resistance against state tyranny. I wish he was, and for example had been more confrontational with the Castros in Cuba, but he is a different leader for a different need that his flock currently has, and that's OK. And, although I have my concerns about some of the "over his head" comments about capitalism, the environment, colonialism, and immigration, some of which are consistent with those of the new "sustainability" movement, I can pass much of this off as gaffes that are ill-informed, while well-intentioned.

I agree with David Brooks that Francis' approach is personal, intimate, and situation-specific, not about the application of abstract rules, which he believes is the right balance of rigor and compassion. And on balance, I liked his speech to Congress, which was delivered without too much pointedly political rhetoric, and I particularly liked his choice to single out for a visit the Little Sisters of the Poor in lieu of lunch with members of Congress, which sent a good message.

I think we all learned something from his U.S. tour and he is a great listener, so I hope he learned something about us as well. But, overall the visit was positive if for no other reason that millions of people were mesmerized with his presence and the goodness of spirit that he represents. We need all of that we can get.

Pope Francis is Loose Again

August 5, 2016

Pope Francis is reaching Donald Trump levels with some of his "back of the plane" media commentary. On his return flight to the Vatican from Poland last week, just days after extremists slit the throat of an elderly priest celebrating Mass in a French church, he was asked why he doesn't identify such violence with Islamic terrorism. His quoted response was, "I don't like to talk of Islamic violence, because every day when I go through the newspapers, I see violence," in reference to crime news in Italy. "And these are baptized Catholics. If I speak of Islamic violence, then I have to speak of Catholic violence." Later, he said, "I believe that in every religion there is always a little fundamentalist group."

There is no evidence of any Catholic fundamentalist group of which I am aware, or Protestants for that matter, who are involved in sponsoring organized violence. He is just wrong not to differentiate between random acts of violent crime committed by people of all faiths or none and the organized terrorist violence committed in the name of political Islam, often under state sponsorship.

No doubt Pope Francis is a good shepherd, but I miss the intellectual depth of Pope Benedict XVI, who was deeply insightful and instructive on the issues surrounding the crisis of Islam and the West, as evidenced by his Regensburg Lecture in 2006, which set a high standard that Francis doesn't seem equipped to reach.

A Trump Teaching Moment in Warsaw

August 5, 2017

Say what you want about President Trump's lack of intellectual and policy depth and the fact that, like other presidents, he doesn't write his major speeches, but he delivered a major teaching moment in his Warsaw speech in early July. Here is a sample: "Our defense is not just a commitment of money, it is a commitment of will… The fundamental question of our time is whether the West has the will to survive. Do we have the confidence in our values to defend them at any cost? Do we have enough respect for our citizens to protect our borders? Do we have the desire and the courage to preserve our civilization in the face of those who would subvert and destroy it? … If anyone forgets the critical importance of these things, let them come to one country that never has, let them come to Poland and let them come to Warsaw…" This was definitely a "let them come to Berlin" moment, and it doesn't end there.

He evoked John Paul II's 1979 visit that prompted the chants of "we want God" from the assembled crowd when he said "With that powerful declaration of who you are, you came to understand what to do and how to live." And by doing so, he clearly aligned himself with Pope Benedict XVI in his warning to Europe at Regensburg in his 2006 lecture on the preservation of Western Civilization that its turn to secularism is a threat to its survival and he warned of a lack of pride and confidence in our values.

Of course, as Daniel Henninger noted, if Donald Trump recited "The Star Spangled Banner" before a baseball game, it would be criticized as an alt-right dog whistle, and many from the left consider Western Civilization code words for Christian white nationalism. And sure enough, William Galston asked, "what does Trump mean by the West?" as though this is some reference to a strange culture. Well, Galston knows, but just to be sure, this is a culture and a region informed by Greece and Rome, forged by Judeo/Christian heritage that once was called Christendom, which formed the basis for what became Western Civilization. Yet, Galston suggests that the chant of "we want God," while comfortable in Poland, would now be offensive to most of Europe, and of course this is a big part of the problem Trump addressed.

Even *National Review*, certainly no friend of Trump's, had this to say: "What struck a new note was Trump's insistence that these values arose in the West and required defense. Any history-minded universalist must recognize that, while all men deserve liberty as men, only one civilization – ours – has worked with any consistency to identify and secure it. This Trump boldly and clearly did."

This speech would have been a great inaugural address. For all his flaws, let's give the guy the credit he is due.

22
Social Issues

Genetic Considerations

July 3, 2000

The recent announcement of breakthrough progress in mapping the human genome reminded me of a lecture on bioethics at Rice University I attended several years ago. It became clear to me then that our 27-year-old war over abortion and the *Roe v. Wade* decision is just the tip of the iceberg compared to the ethical/moral dilemma we will certainly face as the genetic map reveals itself. In the May/June 1996 issue of *Society* magazine, Toby Huff describes genetic engineering as the fourth great scientific revolution, after the Copernican, the Darwinian, and the Freudian. In fact, the previous three upheavals in self-understanding now seem to pale in comparison to the genetic possibilities that were formerly, not only impossible, but unimaginable. Man now is poised to alter the human genetic endowment – once thought to be irrevocably the purview of God. That means that increasingly what is "natural" is in doubt.

Peter Singer, who holds the chair in bioethics at Princeton University's Center for Human Values, says we need a newly defined ethic, because the old one of the sanctity of human life based upon man created in God's image has collapsed. This brand of opinion leadership in the bioethics community is fairly widespread. In order to have influence in this community, one must subscribe to the paradigm – those whose advocacy is rooted in religion and the Judeo-Christian ethic are usually ignored. According to Wesley J. Smith in his *The Culture of Death*, mainstream bioethics reached a consensus long ago that religious values are divisive in a pluralistic society and thus have little place in the formulation of public policy. As we grapple with the bioethical issues that unfold, we should be mindful that an era of genetic manipulation is upon us and many agendas will be at work. We should pay careful attention to those who would make public policy and remember that, as Horace Busby cautioned me many years ago, government is never a benign institution, that the purposes of those close to power and authority are never, innocently, to be trusted.

The belief that human behavior could be shaped by social engineering has had terrible consequences, particularly during the past century. The institutions of our liberal democratic order are based on the realities of human nature. As George Will has so eloquently put it, "If we treat moral scruples impatiently, as inherently retrograde in a scientifically advancing civilization, we will not be in moral trim when, soon, our very humanity will depend on it."

A final point: It has been suggested by some, including Jeremy Rifkin, that the human gene pool and related intellectual property be held in trust as a "commons" for all mankind. I disagree in two respects – one, my genes are mine, they don't belong to the state or the United Nations, and two, excluding the genes and the sequence itself, we must allow incentives and protection for private property rights for the proper future development of the spin-off intellectual property.

Promoting Fatherhood

July 1, 2001

One of the programs that has a nice fit with President Bush's faith-based initiative is the promotion of responsible fatherhood, and one particular organization, the National Fatherhood Initiative, has done a good job of leading a movement toward restoration of traditional concepts of family, marriage, and fatherhood. Recent U.S. Census statistics reflect that one-third of American children live apart from their biological fathers, 83 percent do not see their fathers more than once per week, and 40 percent have not seen them in at least one year. Frightening, and consistent with Daniel Moynihan's famous 1965 report: "A community that allows a large number of men to grow up in broken families, dominated by women, never acquiring any stable relationship to male authority, never acquiring any rational expectations about the future – that community asks for and gets chaos, and it is richly deserved."

Bush has committed significant resources through grants to community and faith-based organizations whose mission includes promoting responsible fatherhood. It is emblematic of our times that his nominee to lead the initiative, Wade Horn, is being opposed by feminist groups, because of his outspoken advocacy of traditional marriage and fatherhood. And it is instructive that in a recent interview, when pressed, Patricia Ireland, President of the National Organization of Women, wouldn't answer the simplest question about the preference of marriage between a man and a woman over other family structures. Census figures show that fewer than 25 percent of American households are comprised of a married couple with children and that this percentage has been steadily declining. Should we care? Should we support public policy that favors family structures that are in the minority? It is well understood by leading family sociologists that fathers bring cultural influences to families and children more than mothers, whose biological commitment is more compelling. Consequently, the involvement of fathers must be supported and influenced by laws and societal norms. Traditional marriage is the most basic public institution of a self-governing society. It changes goals, behavior, obligations, and priorities in ways that enhance civil society and make the good society possible. Studies show that the leading indicator of family and child dysfunction and poverty is the absence of a father. Moynihan also said "...politics can change a culture and save it from itself." Traditional marriage and fatherhood should hold a privileged place in our public policy and our politics.

The Stem Cell Debate

September 1, 2001

After studying this issue for several weeks, it's clear to me that we will not resolve it or other issues involving genetic research, not to mention abortion, until we resolve as a society what is meant by being human and at what point human life begins, with its automatically attached and inalienable rights. This is obviously a moral question, but the answer can be grounded philosophically. Until we answer it, the debate will be pointless. When we do, we should return to the time-honored principle that human beings are never to be considered as means, only as ends. I'm sorry, folks, but it's either a life or it's not a life, and the argument that an embryo is going to die anyway won't wash. Whose principle is that?

I suppose President Bush made the right decision on federally funded research, and the only feasible one under the circumstances. And he provided significant leadership as the "teacher-in-chief" in his TV address announcing the decision. But much more will be needed, for the larger question now is, what happens next, particularly in an age in which, as Tom Wolfe has suggested, science and the inexorable march of "progress" are courts from which there seem to be no appeals. The debate has really just begun.

Humanity in the Balance

February 4, 2002

Consistent with the soul-searching experience and dialogue that I discussed in the January issue as a "useful byproduct" of the war on terrorism will be the debate orchestrated by the President's Council on Bioethics over the next couple of years. Leon Kass seems the ideal choice to lead this panel and, if reports of the Council's first session in January are an indication, we are indeed in for some morally serious deliberations. As Kass himself said, "one feels a palpable increase in America's moral seriousness, a fresh breeze of sensible moral judgment, clearing away the fog of unthinking and easy-going relativism." Wow! I can't wait. As Andrew Ferguson reports in *The Weekly Standard,* it is the second of two Council charges that is unprecedented – "to undertake fundamental inquiry into the human and moral significance" of recent advances in genetic science. One gets the distinct feeling that there are critical issues at stake – like what it means to be human – and that there are grown-ups in the room deliberating them. It's about time.

If you want some insight into the thought of Leon Kass and the direction in which he might lead the Council and the country in this regard, I recommend his article "The Meaning of Life-In the Laboratory," in the Winter 2002 issue (No. 146) of The Public Interest. One quote will give you a flavor: "The current boundaries defining protectable human life, gerrymandered for the sake of abortion – namely, birth or viability – may now satisfy both women's liberation and the U.S. Supreme Court and may someday satisfy even a future Pope, but they will not survive the coming of more sophisticated technologies for growing life in the laboratory." In *The Abolition of Man*, C. S. Lewis says that human nature will be the last part of nature to surrender to man. There is now serious work underway examining the possible repercussions. Let's pay close attention.

Morality and the Public Interest

June 5, 2002

Two recent events involving public standards of morality were instructive to me. In one, the director and cast of a Conroe, Texas production of *The Best Little Whorehouse in Texas* resigned, because of the censorship of parts of the script involving curse words and the portrayal of teenage actresses as prostitutes. The other was the Supreme Court decision ruling unconstitutional a law banning "virtual," or computer-generated, child pornography. What is the common thread here? There are two. One is that for most of our history the Constitution has protected a community's prerogative to establish standards of public morality. The Conroe case has not, to my knowledge, been litigated and, so far, the community's prerogative has been sustained. In the virtual porn case, the Court is continuing its disdain for this community prerogative and the democratic process. The second point is that, until recently, the courts recognized a public interest in the moral and ethical development of youth and generally found no objection to the legislating of limitations on exposing minors to pornographic materials. In fact, no less a liberal than Justice William Brennan supported the long-standing view that the principal harm of pornography is its capacity to corrupt and deprave and that there is a government interest in preventing this moral corruption. For an enlightened and perceptive take on these issues, as well as other aspects of our natural law heritage and how it has been undermined by our judiciary, I recommend *The Clash of Orthodoxies: Law, Religion, and Morality*, by Robert P. George.

Roe v. Wade Redux

April 2, 2003

I have often noted my view that the ill-decided Supreme Court decision in *Roe v. Wade* in 1973 will have been our generation's version of the 1857 decision in the *Dred Scott* slavery case in terms of its divisiveness for our social fabric. Now pending is another invitation to further ideological warfare – the case of *Lawrence v. Texas*, challenging the state law prohibiting homosexual sodomy. In a recent very perceptive letter to an editor, Gary L. McDowell writes from London that the Supreme Court, in overturning the remaining such state laws, might well do for homosexual rights what *Roe v. Wade* did for abortion – take it from the states and turn it into a national firefight. I admit that, as one who believes in the supremacy of natural law, it would please me to see a reversal of *Roe*, but my better judgment tells me that natural law is better applied in the legislative arena through the various state legislatures, a bottom up approach much preferable to top down imposition from an over-active judiciary in search of new "rights."

Same-Sex Marriage Confusion

August 3, 2004

In the battle over the definition of marriage, there are many confusing currents, but as usual, we can depend on Thomas Sowell to sort through them and cut to the heart of the matter, as follows:

"Love affairs are personal relations. Marriage is a legal relation. Sexual relations are between consenting adults, but now the gay activists are taking the view that they are government's business. Then there are those strained analogies with the civil rights movement. Martin Luther King was a private citizen who did not put himself above the law; neither did he wield the power of the law. The Massachusetts judges and the mayor of San Francisco are using their authority under the law to subvert the law. The last refuge of the gay rights activists is that this is a matter of equal rights. But marriage is not an individual right. Otherwise, why limit marriage to unions of two people, or people at all? Marriage is a social contract, because the issues involved go beyond the particular individuals. Unions of a man and a woman produce the future generations on whom the fate of the whole society depends. Society has something to say about that." Note that Sowell did not use religious terminology in the above passage. And I would suggest that the moral considerations surrounding this issue that are informed by our Judeo-Christian heritage cannot, and should not, be excluded from the discussion. I also would add to Sowell's argument against the use of the civil rights analogy that there is a big difference between civil rights denied based on race and those that are created based on behavior.

The real question from a public policy standpoint is, "who decides?" Here we are in a box from which there may be no escape, short of a constitutional amendment defining marriage. It is sad that it has come to this, but our Founders could naturally conceive of no situation that might arise that would represent such a frontal assault on natural law and the moral order. The only alternative to such a divisive battle is for Congress to take its rightful place in the democratic process and deny jurisdiction to the judiciary in deciding this question. If not, we are one step closer to the end of democracy.

Two Landmark Battles

February 1, 2005

Two huge domestic policy battles are now underway that will transform the social contract in ways that will have enormous consequences for the American experiment far into this and probably the next century. One, the President's push to repair the Social Security system, has been given high visibility and top domestic priority in his second term; the other, healthcare reform, is also high on his list, if not quite so visibly at present. Both of these issues involve the same philosophical conflicts and divergent worldviews that seem to drive much of our domestic policy – more government or more individual responsibility, more socialism or more capitalism, more market-based allocation of resources or more top-down, one-size-fits-all solutions. Writing in the January/February 2005 issue of *Foreign Policy*, Kenneth Rogoff notes that "the next great battle between socialism and capitalism will be waged over human health." I agree, and I would add the Social Security system to his prognosis. In both cases, the question is not if government will have a role, for, as Rogoff suggests, the case for some government intervention and regulation in both policy areas is compelling on the fairly well settled grounds of efficiency and moral justice (I would add, much more settled as to the latter than the former), but the issue is precisely how much redistribution of income and government intervention is warranted.

At the heart of both issues is the fact that they are central to America's "entitlement mentality," in the case of Social Security, because of a particular promise made in another world 70 years ago, and for healthcare, because of the employer-based finance system, which was an expedient also devised for another world and different time. Both of these commitments have become deeply embedded in the social contract, but they should be revisited and significantly revised. Many of the solutions being floated are variations of a theme that involves better use of government, on the theory that the public good can be better (or only) served through public sector direction and oversight, while the focus should be on empowerment – how to reverse this entitlement mentality and get many more individuals involved in and committed to personal responsibility for their personal and family welfare. There is a wide gulf between the "entitlement society" and "ownership society" mentalities. President Bush understands this, and I also think he knows that the old paradigm will die hard and not without a huge fight. In fact, his prescription for solutions in both cases would, over time, completely transform the dynamics of the welfare state, which the left cannot abide. But it's a fight worth having now, for the sake of our economic viability and, more importantly, for the sake of our experiment in self-government.

The Schiavo Debacle

April 2, 2005

In the tragedy that has played out over the past month in the Terri Schiavo case, one has to look very hard to find any redeeming legacy. However, there is one possible legacy that may assure that this woman will not have died in vain, and that is a heightened sense that there is something truly amiss in the constitutional confusion between the legislative and judicial branches at the state and federal level and the process by which we resolve questions of life and death, as well as other moral issues. Let's set aside the true facts of this case, which are known only to a few (possibly excluding even the trial judge in the case), and focus instead on the seat of responsibility for its resolution. In the absence of specific written instructions from the victim, to the extent that government has any role at all in personal judgments on moral values, it is the legislative branch, Florida's in this case, expressing the consent and will of the citizens, that is the proper venue. In the scheme of our founding principles, no court should have the jurisdiction or authority to substitute its values for this consensus. Therefore, aside from the trial judge's complete reliance on the representations of a "husband" with glaring conflicts of interest, the biggest mistake here was the ruling of the Florida Supreme Court that the will of the people in the form of "Terri's Law" authorizing the replacement of her feeding tube is unconstitutional.

This case provides clear evidence of the point to which the advent of the "procedural republic," so well described by Michael Sandel in his book, *Democracy's Discontent*, has brought us over the past half century – process trumps civic virtue in almost complete contravention of the civic republic we once were. We have so contorted our legal system that it has become almost impossible to overrule the will of the judiciary in the absence of egregious procedural errors or legal malpractice. Common sense, as exercised by the norms of the civic republic expressed through its elected representatives and executive, is more often than not set aside in favor of "due process" and the value judgments it produces. Ask yourself, what kind of regime denies a mother the right to give her starving child food and water? It is true that we are a nation of laws, not of men, but "erring on the side of life," as the Bush brothers have so pointedly and rightly preferred in this case, requires moral judgments that are outside the purview of legal procedure and belong in the political arena. And I can't help noting the unusual political configurations and strange bedfellows this case has produced, or wondering when was the last time I found myself on the same side of an issue with Ralph Nader and Jesse Jackson!

We are a society increasingly possessed with power struggles over the issues of life and death, intensely personal issues that also have enormous implications for the health of our polity. Make no mistake: we know the definitions at stake here – our science knows when human life begins and when it ends. The question is whether or not the Schiavo debacle will awaken us to the damage that already has been done by the procedural republic and the quest for unfettered personal autonomy unencumbered by a moral order and a duty to life.

The Continuing Creep of Same-Sex Marriage

July 3, 2005

From the Institute for American Values comes word that its leadership is considering a major conference on the crisis of parenthood and related issues. It couldn't come too soon or at a more critical juncture. The Institute also reports that Canada is seeking to erase the term "natural parent" from federal law, replacing it with the term "legal parent," and in New Zealand an influential commission recommended that children conceived by donors should in some cases have three legal parents. And just recently, Spain has legalized same-sex marriage. The encroachment from this insidious worldwide movement to undermine the basic family unit is palpable. In the U.S., this movement is manifest in the trends in family law. For example, the American Law Institute, an association of America's elite legal scholars, judges, and lawyers, published a report proposing to sideline what it calls "traditional marriage," resituating marriage as merely one of many possible and equally valid family forms. In addition, it seeks to break the ties between biological and functional parenthood and recommends full legal marriage rights for same sex couples. In the courts, a recent pronouncement by a California superior court judge struck down the state's traditional marriage laws, which had been reaffirmed in a referendum in 2000, and there is no indication that the political leadership there will attempt to overturn the decision with a constitutional amendment.

In an October 2004 essay, Mary Ann Glendon makes an important point about where the recent history of all this has led: "With widespread acceptance of the notion that behavior in the highly personal areas of sex and marriage is of no concern to anyone other than the 'consenting adults' involved, it has been easy to overlook what should have been obvious from the beginning – individual actions in the aggregate exert a profound influence on what kind of society we are bringing into being… affluent Western nations have been engaged in a massive social experiment, an experiment that brought new liberties and opportunities to adults, but has put children and other dependents at considerable risk."

There are those, like David Blankenhorn of the Institute for American Values, who would like to eliminate the issues of social justice and "rights" from this debate and focus on the purposes of the institution of marriage and the reasons human beings founded it in the first place. But given the current environment, it seems pretty foolish to assume that the proponents of transforming the institution of marriage have any interest in such a dialogue, nor in any compromise resolution of this enormously important issue through the give and take of democratic politics. It has become increasingly clear that the only viable option is a federal constitutional amendment.

The One Percent Difference

August 2, 2005

This summer, the folks in Dayton, Tennessee are no doubt at least recognizing, if not celebrating, the 18th anniversary of the Scopes Trial, sometimes popularly dubbed the "monkey trial," which largely because of the mythology that has been built around it by Hollywood and the larger than life personalities who were involved, has become the ultimate historical confrontation between the "evolutionists" and the "creationists." Most people probably don't remember that the prosecution won the case, and Mr. Scopes was found guilty of violating Tennessee law by teaching Darwin's theory of the evolution of species. What is vivid with most people as the mythology of the trial has grown and been embellished is its caricature of the buffoonery of the argument of the case made on behalf of the state by the "creationist" counsel, William Jennings Bryan. And for the past 80 years, the relative positions have been solidified in the public mind and in the culture war – the evolutionists as the progressives, enlightened by the scientific method and unburdened by faith-based biblical creation myths, versus the creationists, retrograde medievalists who would roll back the scientific revolution and infect the teaching of biology with religious mythology.

In fact, in this confrontation, as with much else in our public square today, the two camps are talking past each other, because both arguments have long ago become much more about worldviews than about science, and worldviews, as someone before me has said, are essentially all about how one feels about two things – human origins and human consciousness. Tell me what you believe about how we got here and how human consciousness was developed and I will tell you what you believe about the large majority of the hot button social issues that permeate today's public debates. How do Americans divide on these questions? The closest proxy for an answer comes from a series of polls conducted by the Gallup organization from 1982-1998, that asked people, which of the following statements best describes their point of view: 1) Creationist – believes God created humans in their present form within the last 10,000 years, 2) Theistic Evolutionist – believes that God guided the process of evolution over millions of years, or 3) Darwinist – believes that God played no role in evolution. The poll results remained virtually unchanged over this period, as follows: Creationists – 44 percent, Theistic Evolutionists – 39 percent, Darwinist – 10 percent, Don't Know/ Other – seven percent.

Whatever your personal view of human nature or human origins, it is pretty well accepted that Darwin rejected the traditional view that had been dominant in Western thought for many centuries before him, which is that man significantly differs in kind, not in degree, from all other animal life. Since his time, with the enormous advances in the biosciences, it has become popular to note that, at the level of DNA, humans and chimpanzees differ by only one percent. But it is more than just a little obvious that this seemingly small difference accounts for an enormous gulf in the respective potentialities of humans and the other animals. Why? As Mortimer Adler has so clearly explained over the years, it boils down to man's intellect, which in simplest terms is the exclusively human attribute that allows man an imagination, or as Adler put it, "to understand what certain kinds of objects are like both: a) when the objects, though perceptible by the senses, are not actually perceived, and b) also when they are not perceptible at all, as with the conceptual constructs we employ in physics, mathematics, and metaphysics. There is no empirical evidence whatsoever that such concepts are present in animal behavior. Their intelligence is entirely sensory."

Russell Kirk approaches the question from a slightly different direction: "The moral imagination is the principal possession that man does not share with the beasts. It is man's power to perceive ethical truth, abiding law, in the chaos of many events. It is a strange faculty – inexplicable if men are assumed to have an animal nature only – of discerning greatness, justice, and order, beyond the bars of appetite and self-interest." Obviously, what we have known as Western Civilization would have been impossible without this human capability that Kirk describes.

Many may continue to wonder and debate about the source of this human consciousness, but we're all still waiting for either evolutionary biology or evolutionary psychology to satisfactorily explain it within a strictly materialist worldview.

At Long Last, a Veto

August 1, 2006

"I think modern science is a religion for many of its practitioners, by which I mean they have utter faith in the sufficiency of their concepts to give full account of life. But science cannot be a source of wisdom. By design it is morally neutral and indifferent to the pursuit of wisdom about human life... If modernity went wrong, it was in taking partial truths of science to be the whole truth about the world... no purely biological account of man ever will be able to do justice to our lived experience as human beings." – Dr. Leon Kass, Founding Chairman, President's Council on Bioethics.

"When the traditional ethic of the sanctity of human life is proven indefensible at both the beginning and end of life, a new ethic will replace it... We will understand that even if the life of a human organism begins at conception, the life of a person – that is, at a minimum, a being with some level of self-awareness – does not begin so early." – Dr. Peter Singer, Professor and Chair, Department of Bioethics, Princeton University.

These two points of view help to illustrate the difficulty of finding consensus in the scientific research and bioethics communities on the proper limits of science as it pushes us ever more rapidly and intensely into the debate on the nature of what is meant by being human. There are those like Singer and many others of a utilitarian persuasion who cannot seem to find any moral limits to this pursuit. And there are those like Kass, Charles Krauthammer, and others who are scientists by training, but who maintain a certain awe and reverence for the mysteries of life and the wisdom of the ages, however humanly limited they may be in their own wisdom about how it should be specifically applied to today's scientific breakthroughs.

President Bush's veto of the bill that would have overturned his executive order imposing limits on federal funding of stem-cell research should not have been his first. I can think of a handful of others that should have preceded it, such as the McCain-Feingold campaign finance bill, the atrocious agriculture subsidy appropriation of 2002, which is now helping to scuttle the Doha free trade talks, and the Medicare "reform" bill, to name a few. And there even might have been a better answer for the research funding limits he imposed or a different place to draw the moral line. But at least he is willing to draw the line somewhere and, if only in that respect, the veto was appropriate, because the proposed law contained no meaningful limits.

We need to get beyond the notion of "if it can be done, it will be done" in the name of scientific "progress," and, as Krauthammer suggests, get to a serious discussion of the real threat, which is "not so much the destruction of existing human embryos… the real threat to our humanity is the creation of new human life willfully for the sole purpose of making it the means to someone else's end… The real Brave New World looming before us is the rise of the industry of human manufacture…"

Despite claims to the contrary, with the exception of the overwhelming opposition to human cloning, the polling on this issue is far from conclusive on a public consensus, so the President's veto serves the purpose of sending us back to the drawing board. There has been some high quality work done by Dr. Kass and his colleagues, including specific legislative recommendations that have languished because of "embryo politics" from both the left and the right. We now have a President who is as sympathetic as we are ever likely to have to the concerns of human dignity we should all share, who has been presented with a meaningful body of work to move us forward in establishing wisdom in policy in an area that ranks with national security and public education as the most urgent of the early 21st century. We should get on with it.

An Early Look at Two Critical Issues for the GOP

June 3, 2007

Let's talk about two issues that no one wants to discuss in Presidential politics, particularly in the Republican Party – abortion and religion.

First, abortion. Rudy Giuliani says that "abortion is morally wrong, but a woman should have the right to choose," and that he would appoint strict constructionist judges, presumably to render decisions that would ultimately restrict, if not eliminate, abortion rights. Let's apply his approach to an analogous moral and public policy crisis in our nation's history, that of slavery. Imagine this response – I'm personally opposed to slavery, but if someone wants to own slaves, I will support their right to do so, or if a state votes to legalize slavery, that's their sovereign right to do so. (Come to think of it, this is very close to the position of Stephen Douglas in the famous Lincoln/Douglas debates of 1858). Abraham Lincoln had an answer for this perverse thinking – no one has a right to commit a wrong. And he publicly and forcefully condemned the notorious Supreme Court decision upholding slavery in *Dred Scott v. Sanford.* Rudy, you need a better answer to this question. And, by the way, we also should be asking all the candidates how, if elected, they will respond to any future Congressional moves to expand federal funding for abortion, embryonic-destructive research, or cloning.

Now, religion. Here we involve the Mitt Romney campaign. The last time I saw a poll on the issue, about 36 percent of people say that his Mormon faith will preclude their voting for him. Meanwhile, he has continued to move up in the Republican primary polling and appears to be a competitive candidate for the nomination. Does this mean that he should stage a major speech to address the issue of his faith, just as John Kennedy was compelled to do to explain his Catholic faith in 1960? Some say this is critical to his chances. I would advise otherwise. Romney doesn't need a "Kennedy speech" on his religious views; he needs to allow his faith to drive a candid conversation with the voters on the relevant questions about who we are. Radical doctrines of separation of church and state in the decades since Kennedy's speech have gone much too far in dictating the removal of faith-based convictions from the public square, to the point where any political views that are informed by religious conviction are unwelcome and the very expression of moral truths are verboten. Romney can engage in a teaching moment and begin to turn this around, and it will not only be refreshing, but its boldness will be politically profitable for him.

Only in California (Let's Hope)

February 8, 2009

California Attorney General Jerry "Moonbeam" Brown is asking the California Supreme Court to declare unconstitutional, seemingly on natural law grounds, the constitutional amendment approved last November by the voters of that state defining marriage as a relationship between a man and a woman. The perversity of this is mind boggling – as Kenneth Starr notes in response to Brown's petition, the consequence of it would be that the people can never amend the Constitution to overrule judicial interpretations of inalienable rights.

I am a natural law devotee. In giving birth to the "second founding" at Gettysburg, Lincoln merged the natural law espoused by the Declaration of Independence with the negative rights and positive law of the Constitution. But nowhere in natural right/natural law philosophy is the **right** to marriage, which is a convention based on the concept that the union of one man and one woman is the most successful means by which children are nurtured and continuity provided to social order.

Darwin and the Texas State Board of Education

February 8, 2009

Count me among those who believe that the State Board's recent debate over a short phrase in the Texas science curriculum standards was an unfortunate waste of time. It was not, however, without importance, and it did not deserve the ridiculously slanted coverage that it received by the uninformed media. The phrase in question currently reads as follows: "The student is expected to, a) analyze, review, and critique scientific explanations, including hypotheses and theories, as to their **strengths and weaknesses,** using scientific evidence and information." The offensive language, in place for 20 years, is in bold type. The Board narrowly voted to remove the phrase and replace it with similar, but "more scientific" language, due to the fear that the current phrase has become an opening to challenge Darwinian evolution of species and other elements of the theory.

Here is my problem. Far from simply supporting science, the Board has now succumbed to the fallacy of scientism in the paranoid fear that somehow the investigation of any weakness in Darwin's theory will lead directly to teaching creationism. It is important for both sides in this debate to make a distinction between the two types of evolution. Microevolution, change within species, and macro-evolution, change from one species to another, are different theories. Critics of Darwinism must understand that microevolution is factual and clearly happens; supporters of Darwin must acknowledge that macroevolution remains very much a theory that should be subject to scientific critique. Let's don't take this issue down the path of the environmental totalitarians with their notion that the "global warming debate is over." More importantly, let's don't close the minds of our kids.

The Repoliticization of Stem-Cell Research

April 2, 2009

"If human embryonic stem-cell research does not make you at least a little bit uncomfortable, you have not thought about it enough." – James A. Thompson, the first scientist to isolate human embryonic stem cells, as quoted by Charles Krauthammer.

Krauthammer served as a member of President George W. Bush's Council on Bioethics and has recently characterized Bush's widely vilified stem-cell policy announced in 2001 as having been thoroughly vindicated. How so? First, because he had the courage of his convictions that a moral line had to be drawn; and second, by supporting research that might lead to the production of stem cells of adult origin, thereby bypassing the need for creation of human embryos for research purposes. The successful result of this research having now been achieved, there is now a plentiful and, according to reliable scientific authorities, an even more productive source of stem cells. Thus, the complete vindication of Bush's courage and confidence, which not so incidentally, was articulated by him at the time in a speech that was delivered with fairness, balance, and due respect for the moral seriousness of the issue.

Now comes President Obama, who delivered on one of his campaign promises by reversing the Bush policy on federal research on embryonic stem cells and, by so doing, returned the issue to the political arena in a way that is disingenuous at best and anti-democratic at worst. First, he has not only needlessly reversed the policy restricting embryo-destructive research funding, but he has reversed the order that encourages the National Institute of Health to further pursue non-embryo-destructive sources of stem cells. Of course, this is exactly the kind of "in your face" rejection of Bush policy that is red meat for Bush-haters and food for Obama's leftist base.

But second, and at least as important, as Robert George so well described in a recent article, far from "removing politics from science" as he has claimed, Obama's decision is simply anti-democratic. The question of whether to allow the destruction of human embryos for research purposes is fundamentally a moral and civic question about the uses and limitations of science, not a scientific question. On this most basic of considerations on this issue, Obama has nothing to say. He leaves full discretion to the scientists, a complete abdication to scientism.

So, the politics of the issue will continue and, in fact, will escalate; the question now is whether it will play out in an orderly fashion through a deliberative democratic process. (On this last point, I am pleased to note that the Texas Legislature is taking on the issue through healthy debate on legislation now pending.)

Obama's decision almost certainly will provide new incentives for taxpayer funding of federal stem-cell research, which will in turn produce new incentives for destruction of human embryos, a huge supply of which will be the "leftovers" from in vitro fertilization (IVF) clinics, an issue which has acquired significant prominence, as highlighted by such extremes as the recent case of the "octomom."

Leon Kass, the former Chairman of President Bush's Council on Bioethics, warned as early as 1972 that IVF one day would pose almost insoluble dilemmas, the most consequential of which is the changing conception of ourselves, what it means to be human, and "the erosion of our idea of man as something splendid or divine, as a creature with freedom and dignity; and clearly, if we come to see ourselves as meat, then meat we shall become."

As Ramesh Ponnuru has noted in a great essay on the IVF issue, the problem of mass creation and destruction of "excess embryos" illustrates that some slopes are indeed slippery. And it's not as though some very thoughtful people haven't warned us. As the man said, if this doesn't bother you, you need to think again and more deeply.

The Proper Role of Science

January 1, 2010

"What of the 'why' of the world? Of course the question has no scientific answer. It is the question beyond science, the question left over when all of science has been written down. It is a philosophical question." – Roger Scruton, *An Intelligent Person's Guide to Philosophy.*

Recently, I have been exploring the phenomenon of "scientism," a concept suggested by the quote above. There are several suitable definitions, but one by Kierkegaard is about as short and precise as it gets: "the inability of the mind in its thinking to rise above the absolute reality of time and space." Two books have greatly expanded the issue for me. One is *Toward a More Natural Science: Biology and Human Affairs*, by Leon Kass, who served as George W. Bush's Chairman of the President's Council on Bioethics, and the other is *The Restitution of Man: C. S. Lewis and the Case Against Scientism*, by Michael D. Aeschliman.

President Obama has said that he wants to "restore science to its rightful place." We should agree that science certainly has a rightful place, although I am not sure that he and I would agree on exactly what that role should be. These two books explore that role, how it has been distorted by scientism, how it should relate to its counterpart in human knowledge, which Lewis calls *sapientia*, or metaphysical wisdom, and how to achieve a restoration of proper balance between science and philosophy.

Patenting Life?

April 3, 2010

Recently, a fairly obscure court decision caught my attention. A Federal judge in Manhattan struck down some of a company's patents on genes linked to breast and ovarian cancers. This decision no doubt will revive the debate as to whether human genes, or any living thing for that matter, should be subject to patent protection.

The guiding precedent in these matters is the 1980 Supreme Court decision in the case of *Diamond v. Chakrabarty*, wherein the Court ruled 5-4 that engineer Chakrabarty's patent of a bacterium capable of breaking down crude oil be upheld. The decision was very narrowly structured, however, and the Court emphasized that it is the responsibility of Congress to decide the limitations of patent law as they pertain to living things.

The recent New York decision will be appealed and this is a rare instance in which I agree with the American Civil Liberties Union – it should be upheld. Further, the Court should have no role in determining whether such patents *ought* to be approved, only whether or not they are permitted by law. Congress should do its job and definitively outline what constitutes "patentable matter" under the law.

Significantly at issue here is language used by the Patent Office in granting the Chakrabarty patent: "…the fact that microorganisms are alive is without legal significance for purposes of patent law" and, as Leon Kass has made clear, the principle used here seems to be that there is nothing *in the nature of a being* that makes him immune to being patented.

This is erroneous thinking. There is potentially considerably more to a living organism than a "composition of matter," a term coined by the Court as synonymous with a "manufacture." Human consciousness cannot be separated from its embodiment. Congress needs to make this clear before we get much farther down this trail.

This is Getting Very Old

September 6, 2010

I am getting very tired of reading and listening to accusations of my intolerance, bigotry, racism, sexism, and nativism in my objections to the construction of the Ground Zero mosque, support of the Arizona illegal immigration law, and support for the California anti same-sex marriage law, among other cultural issues on which I share the views of the substantial majority of Americans. I'm sorry, Americans have absolutely nothing to prove to anyone, including Jeremiah Wright, as to their record as the most generous, benevolent, unselfish, tolerant, and welcoming society in world history. Jonah Goldberg has it right – those Americans who are in the majority on these issues are the real victims of hate, directed I would add by a totalitarian left that cannot win a democratic majority on any of these issues. Of course the response from my President is that my refuge from this brand of "progressivism" is to "cling to guns or religion or antipathy to people who aren't like me." And of course, according to the progressive elite and their fellow media travelers the only people who could hold views like mine are ignorant bigots or political panderers. The demonization of its opponents is a well-honed tactic of the left and a very effective one over the years. Well, I have news. This time the totalitarian left has overplayed its hand. For about half a century, it has relied on the good will of Americans coupled with the guilty instincts of many in the majority in pursuing the progressive agenda, but it has now overstepped its bounds and overestimated the size of its mandate and it is about to be rolled back.

Most of the media analysis of the upcoming election characterize the central issue as the economy and jobs, and this is to a large extent reflected in the polling, but I have a different take. The issues raised by the mosque, the Arizona law, and the gay rights issue are about who we are, and we are manifestly not the bigots the left would have us believe. The guilt trip is over.

We're Missing the Point in the Same-Sex Marriage Debate

July 10, 2011

National Review notes that a lot of wealthy Republicans in New York helped to fund the same-sex marriage campaign, which recently resulted in the adoption of a state law permitting them, and it quotes one hedge fund manager saying, "I'm a pretty straight down the line small government guy, but this is an issue of basic freedom." No, it's not, but give credit to the radical gay rights advocates who are winning the hearts and minds of Americans with this notion that it's a civil rights issue. I have discussed the phenomenon of the "procedural republic" in a number of instances. It occurs to me that the same-sex marriage issue is the procedural republic at work at its best (or worst).

The procedural republic is best defined by Michael Sandel, who wrote *Democracy and Its Discontents*, the seminal work on the subject, as the public life that is informed by the liberal notion that asserts the priority of fair procedures over particular ends. It further asserts that citizens are free and autonomous selves, unencumbered by moral or civic ties they have not chosen. Its rival public philosophy is republican political theory, which asserts that citizens cannot be neutral towards the values and ends its citizens espouse. It regards moral character as a public, not merely private concern, while the procedural republic requires that morality be omitted from public policy deliberations. The classic expression of the procedural republic is the so-called "mystery passage" in the 1992 Supreme Court decision in *Planned Parenthood v. Casey*: "At the heart of liberty is the right to define one's own concept of existence, of meaning, of the universe, and of the mystery of human life."

The conflict between these two political philosophies is essentially the story of the culture war of the past several decades, in which same-sex marriage is but one manifestation of the battle (the recent Supreme Court decision on videogames is another, about which more later), and it will not come as a shock that I am of the republican political theory persuasion.

Years ago, I had a dialogue with a subscriber that was one of the most rewarding since I began the publication. He and his grown son, who is homosexual, wrote a thoughtful response to my essay on same-sex marriage (Same-Sex Marriage Confusion, August 2004), to which I responded as follows, which helps to frame what I believe to be the core issues in this debate:

You are correct that I cannot find any compelling argument that homosexuality is an innate and irreversible condition. I have read extensively on this question, and I have found no source that makes the case that the condition is deterministically genetic, nor do I know of any report of the discovery of the "gay gene." I am persuaded that, as with many other conditions, there exists a genetic predisposition to homosexuality to varying degrees in many people, and that this predisposition is either nurtured, enhanced, and accommodated, or discouraged, repelled, rejected, and overcome, as the case may be, by temperament, environment, consultation, and preference. If I stand corrected on this point by evidence I have missed, please inform me.

This characterization is useful primarily for distinguishing a set of rights based on sexual orientation and preference from those natural and civil rights claimed by all persons irrespective of race and ethnicity, but has no bearing for me on the question of same-sex marriage except to counter the analogy to the battle for civil rights on the part of racial minorities. My position here would apply even if the homosexual condition was proven totally genetic. Remember that Martin Luther King was not asking for new rights that were not already entrenched in our founding principles, but rather the restoration and actualization of these rights.

Marriage is, as your son suggests, about love, but it's also about much more than love. It's about procreation, and many have suggested that marriage would not exist if the conceiving of children were not a regular consequence of heterosexual sex. In fact, the decline of heterosexual marriage seems to coincide with the acceptance in society of the separation of sex from procreation and marriage from parenthood, not positive developments for the institution of marriage or for children. The institution of marriage ennobles the biological bonding of a relationship that at least holds forth the potential for procreation and, if for no other reason, deserves the protection of the law to avoid further removal from its orientation toward the rearing of children. As a conservative, I am tempted by the contention that same-sex marriage would be a positive development for the institution of marriage, but this ignores the philosophical argument, particularly the Aristotelian theory of natural teleology that has stood the test of time – that the function of something can be ascertained by what it exclusively does. Thus human sexuality cannot be understood apart from procreation. This is a philosophical argument, not a theological one. The biological unity that is the foundation of marriage derives its value and significance from this purposeful function, whether or not children actually result from it; no matter how loving the relationship, homosexuality cannot aspire to this unique relationship.

Further, as Maggie Gallagher of the Institute for Marriage and Public Policy notes, historically, marriage was not just a matter of private taste, or a values issue, or even a religious issue in America, it was one of the handful of core social institutions that make limited government possible. In this view, shared family norms enshrined in law were at least as vital to the republic as norms about property rights and democratic government. Think about the case of Utah, which was obliged to revoke its laws permitting bigamy in order to join the union.

As with so many of the battles in the contemporary "culture war," the Founders saw no need to directly infuse the Constitution with the moral order, which is so necessary for its sustenance, because they assumed that it was a given that the republic they were founding could not possibly survive without a grounding in natural law, natural right, and the nature of man (including the teleological nature) that they took for granted. They could not have conceived of the "mystery passage" of the Planned Parenthood v. Casey decision of 1992. Such an unencumbered, autonomous individual would have been a stranger to them.

This leads to the second part of the issue – who decides? I have often written of the threat to democracy posed by the hyperactive "rule of judges" and its potential for judicial tyranny, and I wish that this issue could be decided by the people in the several states, just as I have suggested that the abortion question be returned to the state legislatures. Alas, Roe v. Wade rendered the latter impossibility for the foreseeable future (the recent vote in New York notwithstanding), just as I feared and warned that the Lawrence v. Texas decision might begin to circumscribe the democratic process for the homosexual rights issue. And, sure enough, it didn't take long for four Massachusetts judges to pre-empt the democratic process on same-sex marriage. The problem this time is the "full faith and credit" clause of the Constitution, which will ultimately force the U.S. Supreme Court into jurisdiction unless it is precluded by the limitation of its jurisdiction by Congress or a constitutional amendment.

As for civil unions, although this seems to be a reasonable compromise, I tend to agree to some extent with Charles Murray, who notes that these constructs would have the effect of further undermining marriage by allowing heterosexuals the benefits of marriage without the covenanted commitments, compounding the problems created by the advent of "no fault" divorce laws. However, I must add that I haven't as thoroughly thought through this, I don't feel as strongly about civil unions as marriage, and I suppose that I could be convinced of their utility as a compromise by a properly structured law permitting them. Natural law scholar Robert George offers a possibility in the form of certain forms of domestic partnerships that could be authorized by the states, available to people based on needs, not on sex (widowed sisters living together, etc.)

In short, this is not about equal rights, but about whether or not we can sustain a federal republic under the rule of law, or whether or not we will allow the critical issues involving who we are to be determined by judicial fiat. This is why we conservatives can make exception to our normal aversion to amending the constitution in the case of defending the institution of marriage, because the creation of a "right" to homosexual marriage undermines a major element of the order necessary to sustain republican principles. I wish there was another answer.

Science Marches On

October 8, 2011

Comes now word that Einstein's theory of relativity is under review. This theory in turn depends on the "bedrock" theory of physics that nothing in the universe can travel faster than light. But the latest experiments in Europe indicate that a fired beam of neutrinos (whatever those are) has exceeded the speed of light. Of course, further validation will be necessary, and obviously this would be a stop-the-presses moment, if ultimately validated. But for now it simply validates another fact, which is that no theory is carved in stone. So, the theory of our universe developed by Copernicus succeeded that of Ptolemy, Einstein's theory updated Newton's mechanics, etc. And as science mercilessly pursues its truths through repeated experimentation, can it be surprising that Darwin's theory of macroevolution and the theory of man-made global warming, among others, are still open and subject to this process? There are no sacred cows, but, as I indicated in a previous essay, we need to be mindful that science depends on philosophy for the validity of its terms and procedures and the determination of the uses or ends to which scientific knowledge will be put.

The Counterrevolutionary Century?

June 3, 2012

Mary Eberstadt of Stanford University's Hoover Institution wrote a very insightful essay for the April 2, 2012 issue of *National Review* entitled "Sexual Counterrevolution," which I highly recommend. In it she contends that it is not unthinkable that the range of conflicts now raging over the social issues, in which the conflict over who will decide the final legacy of the now half century of sexual revolution, will in the end result in a counterrevolution. If she is at least partly correct, it goes without saying that this will have momentous implications for our politics, the economy, and the entire public and private sphere. She believes that the intellectual struggle over all these imponderables has only just begun, for after all and needless to say, there are those who think this revolution has been a benign force in the world and those who think otherwise.

As Eberstadt emphasizes, nothing arouses distaste in reasonable people, those she calls the "voices of reason coalition," quite as efficiently as the "social issues," of the advocates on all sides of which the voices of reason ask, "can't they just go away?" and "why are we talking about this stuff when the economy is in the tank?" Well, they won't go away, they shouldn't go away, and Eberstadt makes it very clear why this is so. First of all, the revolution isn't over by a long shot and its premises are not settled doctrine; second, and more important, with the passage of time, it has become increasingly clear that the sexual revolution has imposed significant costs on individuals and society that no one predicted when it was started.

And please understand that this is not a theology matter, but one of secular social science. The bottom line here, from a purely secular perspective, is that the fruit of the sexual revolution, which since its inception has been a corollary of the question of what is human nature, is the destruction of the basic foundation of society, the family. In fact, we know that the best predictor of youth problems is no longer poverty, but family structure. And, as Charles Murray notes in his recent work on the subject, "I know of no other set of important findings that are as broadly accepted by social scientists who follow the technical literature, liberal, as well as conservative, and yet are so ignored by network news programs, editorial writers, and politicians of both major parties."

The most frustrating part of this phenomenon, as Eberstadt notes, is that the bane of the "voices of reason coalition" – the rampantly expanding welfare state – is a direct consequence of the family crisis engulfing the entire Western world, but they don't want to talk about it. In fact, statism and family breakdown feed off and nurture each other. Just think of all the infrastructure that has been put in place to replace the broken family. This is the ugly truth. Yet when Pope Benedict spoke on the sanctity of the family based on the marriage of one man and one woman before more than a million people during Mass at the 7th World Meeting of Families in Milan, there was not a word from the mainstream media. Imagine the media response to a rally of one million for same-sex marriage!

Ten years ago, I asked readers of the Pilgrim to focus on the major themes that would dominate the 21st century and to send me their thoughts on them. I received some interesting responses and then formulated my own thoughts, which basically proceed as follows: As important as the daunting geopolitical issues are, there is an issue that will trump even those of worldwide war and peace, the transformation of the Middle East, the configuration of the American role in the world, the rise of China and India, and the reformation of radical Islam. It is the looming cultural, philosophical, and religious conflict on the question of the meaning of human nature, or what it means to be human. And this, of course is largely centered on the issue of human sexuality, which is the primary focus of Eberstadt's essay.

And yet the issue is even much broader. The advances in the biosciences and neurosciences have for the first time provided man with the capability to transform his very nature. As a result, we will be forced to return to the questions of who we are and why are we here in a way that has been too long absent from public discourse. If this be a counterrevolution as Eberstadt suggests, it can't come soon enough. There will be political decisions on these issues of enormous impact and complexity under deliberation over the next several decades. To hope that these decisions can be made in a morally neutral vacuum without being judgmental is a delusion, and to delegate these decisions to the scientists and professional bioethicists (or worse, the judiciary) would be a dereliction of duty in a democratic republic.

The Genesis Particle?

July 6, 2012

A very intriguing story is unfolding this week with the announcement of the probable discovery of the Higgs boson by the scientists managing the European Organization for Nuclear Research (CERN), made possible by its Large Hadron Collider on the French-Swiss border. I'm way over my head here in the physics, but I have read enough to know that this is a very big deal, probably one of the great moments in scientific history, because it will provide new insights into what the universe was like in the trillionth of a second after the Big Bang. For the long sought-after Higgs bosons are the particles responsible for the conversion of the energy of the Big Bang into the mass of the universe. With this discovery, a new chapter in physics opens, leading to who knows what next.

I was not very well exposed to sub-atomic physics in school, but I have encountered it since, most prominently in philosophy, where the concept of "theoretical constructs" was first introduced to me by Mortimer Adler in his exploration of what we can know beyond that which is perceptible to the senses. In explaining the notion of theoretical constructs in his terrific book, *Ten Philosophical Mistakes*, he notes that "many of the conceptual constructs that we employ in scientific and philosophical thought concern objects such as black holes and quarks in physics, as well as God, spirits, and souls in metaphysics. These are objects about which it is of fundamental importance to ask about their existence in reality… The real existence of instances of such objects can be posited only on the grounds that, if they did not exist, then observed phenomena could not be adequately explained… The idea of God, for example, and the idea of the cosmos as a whole are not concepts derived from sense experience. They are instead theoretical constructs… (which) apply to some of the most important ideas in 20th century theoretical physics."

Adler would probably agree that it is premature to think that the discovery of the Higgs boson will lead to our theoretical constructs becoming empirical, but this major breakthrough seems almost certainly to have moved us to the next threshold. And I'm convinced that whatever we find there will be orderly for, as Albert Einstein said, "God does not play dice."

Newtown

January 5, 2013

Aside from the horror of the evil in the act, what is most disturbing about the Newtown, Connecticut school shooting is the immediate reaction to want to understand "why," followed by the inevitable call for a political response centered on more gun control. As to the "why," we've been attempting to answer that question about these kinds of events for centuries, and while religious faith can provide some comfort and even a kind of sanctuary, many of life's troubling aspects forever will remain inscrutable to mortals. As for a political solution, Charles Krauthammer is correct: everything should be on the table – guns, more assertive involuntary commitment of those needing mental treatment, and the entertainment culture.

Of these, more gun control is the least likely to have significant impact. We've tried it and it hasn't worked. The only instances in which gun control has been significantly effective involved confiscation of all guns, which would spark an immediate revolution in this country.

Without treading on the first amendment, we need to seriously examine what passes for innocent entertainment in the movies, on the internet, and with video games, much of the violent content of which is deadening and hollowing out the souls of our kids.

Steve Forbes has said that "the shutting down of most of our institutions that treat people with severe mental problems beginning in the 1960s was one of the most deplorable, if not barbaric, moves the U.S. has made in the last half-century." It is the reversal of this misguided deinstitutionalization policy at the state level that seems to have the most promise.

So while we're having yet again another "conversation" about this issue and calling out the NRA, let's also call out the ACLU and our friends in Hollywood to get serious about something we can do about it that might work.

Federalism Seems to be Alive and Well

April 7, 2013

I always have believed that, like slavery, for reasons grounded firmly in science, as well as the natural law tradition, the abortion issue rises above resolution through the concept of "popular sovereignty" so famously debated by Lincoln and Douglas. But, since the Supreme Court completely removed the issue from the democratic process with the deeply flawed decision in *Roe v. Wade* 40 years ago, I look for any signs of hope that the issue can find a way back into the political debate that might lead to a better outcome, even if it must be on a state by state basis.

It appears that this is beginning to happen through the wonder of our system of federalism. While New York Gov. Andrew Cuomo wants to further liberalize abortions in his state with a bill permitting late term abortions, the North Dakota and Arkansas legislatures have voted to outlaw abortions after six and twelve weeks, respectively, and the Kansas legislature is considering an abortion-related bill including a phrase declaring that life begins "at fertilization." Of course, all of this activity will ultimately be subjected to judicial review, and it's possible that another reaffirmation of *Roe* will result, but it's refreshing to know that there are plenty of people who are not going to let this 40-year-old mistake go unchallenged. So, good for popular sovereignty!

Speaking of Federalism…

April 7, 2013

What an obviously preferential process within which to resolve the same-sex marriage question. Hopefully, this Court will not make the same mistake here as with the abortion issue by completely cutting off the very productive national debate now underway on this issue, which would inflame the losers and further poison the body politic. Thankfully, I heard encouraging remarks and questions during oral arguments from several of the Justices. For me, this issue is much different from the abortion issue, which is about who is and who isn't a human being with the unalienable right to life guaranteed by the state. Legal questions just don't get any bigger than that. Long time *Pilgrim* readers know that I have a clear preference as to the outcome of the marriage conflict, but it is more important that it be determined through the democratic process, even if this happens on a state by state basis.

The Gosnell Case

May 6, 2013

Anyone who has stopped to listen to the description of the criminal charges against abortion practitioner Dr. Kermit Gosnell and is not totally repulsed is either amoral or completely numb. Of course, one could be excused, because until recently, no media outlet other than Fox News was giving any air time to the case, a subject of journalistic malpractice that has become all too commonplace.

This case is a vivid illustration of the corruption that has been enabled by the notorious *Roe v. Wade* decision. It permeates every corner of our jurisprudence and our politics and, worse, it eats at our soul, because we can't reconcile that horribly misguided ruling with the repugnance at the practice that it sustains, in spite of its violation of human dignity.

The best commentary on this case comes from Leon Kass in a *Wall Street Journal* interview entitled "The Meaning of the Gosnell Trial." No surprise here. He was masterful in his chairmanship of President George W. Bush's Council on Bioethics. It is at his suggestion that I use the word "repugnance," the preferred reaction of Dr. Kass to the details of the Gosnell trial. This term reflects a kind of deep moral intuition, as "pain is to the body so repugnance is to the soul," and he fears that Americans are becoming indifferent to this impulse.

He laments the tendency that we no longer see a child as a gift but as a product of our will to be had by choice only and that this makes human choice the basis of all value. And this tendency leads to "other things that are threats to human dignity in its fullness," such as cloning and genetic engineering.

Methinks that Leon Kass is worth listening to and that we should also be attentive to those pangs of repugnance that are "written on the heart."

Detroit is a Very Big Deal

August 4, 2013

The bankruptcy of Detroit should be watched very closely, not simply, because of its immediate financial impact on the country and the pain of its citizens, which are important, nor even, because it will be the model for probably many more such reorganizations to come, but, because it will be a major turning point for the social compact that has been in place since the end of World War II. This compact was the model and Detroit was the primary face and the embodiment of the collaboration of big government/big business/big labor in the structure of American domination of postwar economic leadership, which for a time served the country well. But it has been for some time a badly broken system predicated on an unsustainable base of unrealistic commitments and entitlements across the board in the public and private sectors alike. The model must be scrapped, and the critical question to be answered is what will replace it. Will we face the fact that it is truly in need of "creative destruction" or will we be intimidated by the vested interests in the bankrupt system in an attempt to politically manage the pain and sustain the entitlement and dependency culture? The answer will help define the future of the country for the remainder of the century.

A Big Problem in Arizona

March 5, 2014

The problem highlighted by the recent veto by Gov. Jan Brewer of an Arizona bill that would have allowed business owners to deny service to customers based on the owners' religious beliefs will not go away anytime soon, because the issue strikes at the heart of religious liberty and freedom of conscience, among the bedrock principles that define American exceptionalism.

The intervention of corporate America from every sector, backed by the intimidation of the gay rights lobby and the related media attention, was brutal and ultimately no doubt decisive in Brewer's decision, serving to demonstrate once again that economic interests and demagoguery too often prevail over matters of principle. But in this case, we need to be very careful not to jump to conclusions about the nature of the issue.

We seem to want to continually conflate the LGBT movement with the civil rights movement of the 1950s and 1960s. They are not the same. There is no analogy here to the Jim Crow South or the civil rights of blacks which were in many cases specifically excluded by state laws. And this issue is not the same as the public accommodation clause of the Civil Rights Act of 1964 – can you imagine a restaurant owner asking a patron about his or her sexual orientation prior to admittance or service? A Christian baker in Colorado faces charges for refusing to bake a wedding cake for a same-sex couple. Are you kidding? This is not analogous to racial discrimination; it's about whether or not a business can exercise the right to religious liberty in deciding not to provide services or products to events connected to same-sex marriages or "commitment ceremonies."

The constitutional rights to religious liberty and freedom of conscience, which are absolutely critical to the genius of the no establishment and free exercise clause of First Amendment, are at stake here. And, while being committed to the human and civil rights of all citizens, we must preserve these basic foundations, and not just for religious institutions, but for businesses and individuals, as well.

Corporate America is out of line here and should be part of the solution, not a force for special interest pressure tactics borne out of cowardice in the face of intimidation. This is a difficult issue not easily resolved and will no doubt require considerable work by Congress, because there are more Arizona-type bills in the pipeline.

The Posthuman Century Question Revisited

June 8, 2014

More than 10 years ago, I invited readers to submit their thoughts as to what grand themes will dominate the 21st century and highlighted some of the responses. My own view at the time was that, despite the specter of radical Islam and the usual issues of war and peace, there was one issue that would trump them all, and I still feel the same. It is the looming cultural, philosophical, and religious conflict on the question of the meaning of human nature, because of the growing capability for man to transform his very nature due to the advances in the biosciences and neurosciences. As a result, we will be forced to return seriously to the questions of who are we and why are we here in a way that has been too long absent from public discourse. And I fear that our public intellectual leadership has been so undermined by the postmodern drift away from the discipline of philosophical pursuit of moral truth that we will not be equal to the task.

For example, this week I watched a segment of CBS *Sunday Morning*, which explored the phenomenon of young children who are challenging their sexual identity. In other words, they came into this world as either boys or girls, but want to reverse that identity and their parents, while hesitant, are generally sympathetic. And these are children of ages four to 12! *National Review* reports that Facebook gives its users 51 genders to choose from and that we have accepted the notion that sex is biology, but gender is what we choose for ourselves. This is a manifestation of the "mystery passage" in the Supreme Court decision in *Planned Parenthood v. Casey* in 1992: "At the heart of liberty is the right to define one's own concept of existence, of meaning, of the universe, and of the mystery of human life," the ultimate in what has been called "postmodernist jurisprudence." Brave new world, indeed.

There are implications for this trend that go far beyond the same-sex marriage debate and will make the abortion wars of the past 40 years mild by comparison. There will be political decisions of enormous impact and complexity on these and related issues over the next several years. As I said then, to hope that these decisions can or should be made in a morally neutral vacuum is a delusion and to delegate them to the scientific and professional "bioethicists" (or worse, the judiciary) is a dereliction of duty in a democratic republic.

If you want a good read on why the American body politic seems so polarized and dysfunctional, look no further for a leading indicator. It's the culture, stupid.

Of Flags, Monuments, and History

August 7, 2015

The flap that has ensued in the wake of the church shootings in Charleston, South Carolina has, it seems, brought an old debate to another level of intense discussion, one that I think can be productive and has so far been mostly civil. Here is my take on it.

Despite the often benign use of it in many cases, the abuse of the Confederate battle flag and what it has grown to represent in its worst context has obviously pushed it to the same status as the Nazi swastika. I applaud South Carolina Governor Nikki Haley in taking the overdue lead in removing it from the state capitol grounds. Throughout the South, it needs to be moved to a museum where it belongs.

Monuments, school names, other memorials to the Confederacy and its leaders are another matter. What is most important here is to get the history right and to teach it properly, a job that, in my experience, is insufficiently done. In American history, particularly as it pertains to the slavery issue and the causes of the Civil War, we need to understand the U.S. constitutional debates, the Federalist Papers, the Lincoln/Douglas debates, Lincoln's First Inaugural Address, the *Dred Scott* Supreme Court decision, the ideology of the so-called southern "lost cause," etc. In Texas history, as in the case of the other former Confederate states, there should be full disclosure of who these people are that are memorialized in our school names and on our capitol grounds and other public venues. And, in cases where the inscriptions on the memorials are incorrect or misleading, let's add a plaque explaining the full story with all the warts. I'm all for a special commission to lead and supervise this effort.

But beyond getting the history straight, are we then going to airbrush the visible symbols out of history? Where do we stop? What about the founders who owned slaves, most prominently Washington and Jefferson? How many thousands of name changes would that entail, not to mention their respective memorials in Washington? What about Statuary Hall in the U.S. Capitol, which includes statutes of nine Confederate statesmen and military leaders, including President Jefferson Davis? And was Robert E. Lee a traitor? In what way did he differ from the founders who rebelled? I have already seen some quite intriguing discussions on that point and we should keep having them. But to wipe the record clean as some kind of atonement for our sins is not the answer. These monuments, memorials, symbols, and their legacy should be used as learning tools, understood in full and not removed. Let's get the history right and learn to live with it, warts and all.

HERO Goes Down

November 7, 2015

My confidence in the judgment of my fellow Houstonians has taken a giant leap with the decisive 61-39 defeat of the Houston Equal Rights Ordinance (HERO). The fact that the people of Houston, among the most diverse in the nation, were able to withstand the intimidation of the onslaught of elite opinion brought to bear from across the country and from local business and social institutional leadership is validation of the innate common sense of Americans, particularly Texans.

In the first place, this ordinance was a solution in search of a problem. What was it designed to fix? Where is the evidence of discrimination against any of the supposed targeted groups? If there is no evidence of discrimination, then the initiative could be nothing more than "politically correct" pandering to the radical lesbian/gay/bisexual/transgender agenda. And let's be clear – the installation of the rights demanded by these activists was what this ordinance was all about.

The opposition framed the issue as the "bathroom ordinance," as though it would allow sexual predators posing as transgendered to have access to women's facilities, which was a winning strategy, but although the ordinance would have established a defense for such incursions, I never thought that this was the primary problem with it.

The larger problem for me was that the ordinance included no protection for religious liberty. It made businesses that serve the public subject to the law, with religious "institutions" exempt. There are two points to be made here. First, the decision made by the Supreme Court to recognize same-sex marriage in *Obergefell v. Hodges* is in no way analogous to the Civil Rights Act of 1964, particularly as to its public accommodations clause. There is no comparison between a black patron denied service in a restaurant with a same-sex couple denied service by a facility, floral, photography, or wedding cake provider that makes the vendor a participant in the marriage ceremony. Second, the exemption for religious institutions did not include individuals or non-religious organizations, including business owners, acting on their conscientious objections to becoming, in effect, a participant in the ceremony.

We have a long way to go in this country on this debate. Just because five justices have decided that same-sex marriage is legal is not definitive, nor is it final. And this notion that gender identity can be based on a personal whim, however deeply held, with a new set of enforceable "rights" attached, is nonsense. The courts will be very busy with all of this over the next several years. But, come to think of it, they deserve this burden, because they gave this ideology and line of thinking a substantial share of its credibility in the first place. Remember the "mystery passage" from the majority Supreme Court decision in *Planned Parenthood v. Casey* in 1992?: "At the heart of liberty is the right to define one's own concept of existence, of meaning, of the universe, and of the mystery of human life." The author of this opinion was Justice Anthony Kennedy, who also wrote this in the majority opinion in *Obergefell v. Hodges*: "The Constitution promises liberty to all within its reach, a liberty that includes certain specific rights that allow persons, within a lawful realm, to define and express their identity." Ideas have consequences.

Have We Gone Completely Nuts?

March 6, 2016

The U.S. Department of Education has warned public schools that under its reading of Title IX, the 1972 law that bans sex discrimination in education, it is illegal to deny transgender students access to the restrooms and locker rooms of their choice. Many schools around the country have yielded to the guidance, but a backlash is now brewing. South Dakota is leading the pushback with a bill that would require transgender children and teenagers to use the school facilities that correspond to their chromosomes and anatomy at birth. Lawmakers in 22 other states have introduced similar legislation, so the battle is engaged, but it will be a long fight.

The LGBT community is committed to the acknowledgement of sexual identity as a matter of choice, not biology, and nothing less than full acceptance of their autonomy in this regard will be acceptable to them. This issue relates to, but extends beyond the issue of religious freedom legislation and is more about the meaning of human nature that I have discussed in previous issues. Who are we? Are we free to determine our own identity in what has been termed "postmodern jurisprudence" – the right to define one's own concept of existence, meaning, and the mystery of human life? This is dangerous territory and the answers should be determined by democratic processes under natural law, not by the judiciary.

Where is the Work Ethic?

March 6, 2017

In a recent *Forbes* magazine article, Rich Karlgaard summarizes the Trump economic blueprint as laid out in a white paper by Commerce Secretary Wilbur Ross and trade advisor Peter Navarro entitled "Scoring the Trump Economic Plan: Trade, Regulatory and Energy Policy Impacts." As he describes it, the major underlying premises are:

- The "new normal" is a political excuse for poor growth.
- Fix trade, regulation, taxes, and energy – in that order.
- Excessive regulation is killing business.
- Manufacturing has the best wealth and job multiplier effect.

Pretty hard to disagree with these priorities and one would have to say that Trump is serious about the campaign promises he has made about them and is moving forward as he promised.

But, I haven't heard enough from the administration about what has become a very serious underlying economic and social issue that will have an undermining impact on any economic plan and which has been the subject of a lot of attention by people like Nicholas Eberstadt at the American Enterprise Institute. As he has noted in his recent book, *Men Without Work*, and in recent essays, the 21st century so far has been in his words miserable, because despite the fact that unemployment has been cut by half since the Great Recession and household net worth has grown substantially, there has been a continuing collapse of work, especially among American men. Several data points reflect serious underlying problems that do not bode well for Trump's plan or future American prosperity:

- The work rate for American men aged 25-54 was slightly lower in 2015 than in 1940 at the end of the Great Depression and has been steadily declining for the past several decades.
- Almost one in six prime working age men has no paid work at all and almost one in eight is out of the workforce entirely, neither working nor looking for work.
- For every man between ages 25-54 that is counted among the unemployed, there are three who are neither working nor looking for work, nor are they doing charitable work.

This is much more than an economic issue, it is a social pathology of enormous proportions. Who are these men? How are they spending their time? What are the implications for America and its ideals? Eberstadt calls this issue "America's invisible crisis." His colleague Charles Murray also has done considerable work in this area, as well as other aspects of the rending of the social fabric, and it needs to be much higher on the administration's list of priorities for long-range strategy. This is not a problem that can be solved with an executive order or even the admirable list of policy priorities outlined by Trump's economic plan. It will require an in-depth analysis of the dysfunctional social and cultural attributes at work here, as well as the disincentives to work that have become embedded in our social contract.

Bathroom Politics in Texas

August 5, 2017

I've made every attempt to distance myself from the so-called "bathroom bill" issue during the regular and special sessions of the Texas Legislature, but it has more legs than it deserves and that I originally thought it might, so here goes.

First, we don't need a state law that preempts local ordinances governing access to public restrooms by the transgendered. We're perfectly capable of dealing with the issue locally, as we did in Houston two years ago with the decisive 61-39 percent defeat of the Houston Equal Rights Ordinance (HERO), which would have opened a set of access rights based on "gender identity." I strongly supported this outcome and I don't see any significant conflicts in other communities in the state that warrant a state law of preemption of similar ordinances. It's a solution in search of a problem.

Second, I have followed the various lobby efforts and statements of opposition to this bill by the major business organizations and leading corporate CEOs and while I agree with their opposition, I do so for a different reason. Their opposition is based on the threat they perceive of the economic damage that such legislation would have to Texas and the message of discrimination that it might send and they point to the experience of North Carolina, which suffered from conference and sports events cancellations due to the enactment of anti-HERO-type legislation there that was considered discriminatory. Although convention officials opposing the Texas bill estimate that some damage has already been done with the debate on the bill, I think this threat is overblown and primarily the product of intimidation by and pandering to the LGBT activist lobby. In the two years since HERO was voted down, I am not aware of any significant cancellation of a major event or corporate relocation to Houston. And, incidentally, substantially all of the Houston business groups and leaders opposed to the current bill were in support of the HERO initiative.

My third point is simple: For me, the transgender issue is all about chromosomes. While I am fully aware that a predisposition to identify with a gender other than biological can be in evidence as early as age three and I sympathize with the psychological problems that might pose for some, to my knowledge there is no "transgender gene." Human genetic sex is determined at the time of conception. A female has two X chromosomes, a male has one X and one Y. That is definitive enough for me.

Extreme Caution in Gene Editing Warranted

August 5, 2017

A brief recent report of a gene editing breakthrough caught my attention, but so far I have seen no follow up reportage on the event. *The Wall Street Journal* reported that an international group of researchers reported that they have edited viable human embryos to correct a disease-causing defect using the gene-editing tool named Crispr-Cas9. The embryos, created for research, were not implanted in a woman, according to the researchers in an article in the journal *Nature*.

The new tool Crispr-Cas9 has been approved by regulatory agencies for testing treatments for diseases in individuals, but the U.S. Food and Drug Administration is prohibited by law from using funds to accept applications for research using gene editing of the human germ line, the genes of sperm, eggs, or embryos, or, in lay terms, the modification of the individual that would be carried to future generations. Need I say more about the critical issues at stake?

I have written before of the need for serious transparency and oversight in the development of these technologies that have the potential to alter what it means to be human. There will be political decisions under deliberation on these issues of enormous impact and complexity over the next several decades. To hope that these decisions can be made in a moral vacuum is a delusion. Sixteen years ago, President George W. Bush appointed the President's Council of Bioethics under the leadership of Leon Kass, which produced a masterful survey of the then current biosciences technology, its future prospects, and recommendations for policy. Maybe it's time for a renewal and update of that project to reflect on the current status of the capabilities.

As I have said before, the rationality of man in the era of scientism doesn't have a very good historical record on these issues. One century of mass murder perpetrated by totalitarian regimes driven by the utopian notion of the denial of human nature should have been enough to convince us that just because man can doesn't mean he should. Beware the false promise of scientism and utility in the name of progress.

Reaping What We Sowed

December 2, 2017

The sexual harassment avalanche now has reached a level that is difficult to get one's head around to make sense of any of it and I don't doubt that there is much more to come. Those of you who have been subscribers for any length of time know that one of my mottoes is "ideas have consequences," a phrase I borrowed from Richard Weaver, whose major work carries that title. Recently, in that context, a friend sent me a recent article from *Front Page* magazine by Bruce Thornton of Cal State and the Hoover Institution entitled "Sow the Free Love Wind, Reap the Sexual Debasement Whirlwind." It's the best I have seen so far on this whirlwind of events. Thornton's essential point is that, like many of our social pathologies today, our sexually saturated public culture and the unleashing of sexual predators are the bitter fruit of the free love movement of the 1960s. As he notes, one has to be of a certain age to remember how things were before that decade and how quickly and significantly our mores were transformed. And it wasn't accidental, as he makes clear – "…that change was encouraged by certain species of dubious pop-Freudian psychological ideas that had been combined with left-wing theories of political revolution (see Herbert Marcuse). This synthesis was predicated on the delegitimization of the 'bourgeois' virtues, morals, and values that had created the "false consciousness" empowering capitalist oppression." So, you get "if it feels good do it." Thus sexual liberation became an instrument of political "liberation," and these two revolutions merged to enable personal liberation in the Marcuse model, which we are living with today in many aspects of our public and civic squares. There is no telling where this all ends, but it won't be pretty.

Once Again We Must Do Something

March 2, 2018

Now we have a Parkland and a Nikolas Cruz to add to the litany of disturbed young men who have committed mass murder of other young men and women and, as usual, the cry is that "we must do something." But the something almost always begins with more control of guns that would not have prevented the event. This is not exactly the case here, because this deranged young man, given the mounting evidence of failure of local police and FBI follow up in advance of and even during the shooting, should never have been in a position to commit a crime to this extent. So, the argument about changes in gun control policy in this case is moot.

But, other parts of the "something" are still in play here. First, the lack of aggressive supervisory intervention in lives that are obviously tormented and oriented to violence must be corrected and there should be a bias for action regardless of privacy and civil rights concerns. No, I don't mean "take the guns first" without due process, as the President has clumsily suggested, but I do mean a revisit to serious levels of coerced treatment, including involuntary institutionalization. Second, the fact that we now have plenty of evidence that these random shooting events primarily take place in "gun free zones," an obvious opening and incentive for these disturbed young men to have free rein in their aggression, should prompt us to remedy this defenseless situation by arming well-trained educators and security officers in these buildings to shoot back. Third, and maybe most significant, we must get serious about the cultural inputs that drive a sense of hopelessness and meaninglessness in many of our youth, particularly young men who, because of family breakdown, do not have father figures in their lives. They have a dark vacancy in their souls, yes souls, that cannot be filled by the cultural constructs produced by our media and entertainment outlets or other secular substitutes. This last and most important point is not one we will hear much about in the debates over Parkland, but it is probably the one to which we should devote the most attention.

Kissinger on Artificial Intelligence and Its Threats

June 5, 2018

In a recent provocative article in *The Atlantic* entitled "How the Enlightenment Ends," Henry Kissinger provides much-needed context and definition to the issues and concerns around the explosive growth of artificial intelligence (AI) that includes warnings that we ignore at our peril. To cut to the chase, he makes the case that – philosophically, intellectually, in every way – human society is unprepared for the rise of AI.

He applies a very broad range to what fits the AI category and it includes a lot more than various types of robots, the most transformational of which he calls the "self-learning" variety – machines that acquire knowledge by processes particular to themselves and apply that knowledge to ends for which there may be no category of human understanding. Yes, we already have these, and he has questions about them the implications of which we haven't yet even begun to pose, much less answer, such as: Would these machines learn to communicate with each other? How would choices be made among emerging options? Was it possible that human history might go the way of the Incas, faced with a Spanish culture incomprehensible and even awe inspiring to them?

He views this period as the equivalent of the invention of the printing press in the 15th century, the technological advance that most altered the course of modern history, which allowed the search for empirical knowledge to supplant liturgical doctrine, and the Age of Reason to gradually supersede the Age of Religion.

But this period of innovation is even more dramatic, for it goes far beyond automation as we have known it. He notes that automation deals with means; it achieves prescribed objectives. By contrast, AI deals with ends; it establishes it own objectives.

Kissinger sees three areas of special concern: 1) that AI may achieve unintended results, mainly by misinterpreting human instructions due to lack of context; 2) that in achieving intended goals, AI may change human thought processes and human values; it knows only one purpose-to win; and 3) that AI may reach intended goals, but be unable to explain the rationale for its conclusions. The bottom line is his most difficult yet important question about the world into which we are headed: What will become of human consciousness if its own explanatory power is surpassed by AI, and societies are no longer able to interpret the world they inhabit in terms that are meaningful to them?

The most compelling questions for me about the threats he describes are: Who decides? Who is responsible for the actions of AI? How should liability be determined for their mistakes? These questions are about accountability, and for that discussion he suggests a high-level presidential commission, which I would liken to the President's Council on Bioethics under President George W. Bush, with leadership comprised of the best philosophers and other disciplines in the field of the humanities along with religious advisors and advisors in the sciences and relevant technologies to begin to formulate a national vision. And as he also suggests, the developers of these particular AI technologies should begin right away to incorporate these questions and answers into their developmental paradigm and engineering.

I have written several times over the years about the grand themes that will dominate the 21st century. My own view has consistently been that, despite the specter of radical Islam and the usual issues of war and peace, there was one issue that would trump them all. It is the looming cultural, philosophical, and religious conflict on the question of the meaning of human nature, because of the growing capability for man to transform his very nature due to the advances in the biosciences and neurosciences. Well, after reading Kissinger's very compelling essay, I'm about ready to add the advancement of AI technology as a close second on my list.

The "Resilient City" Aspiration

October 4, 2018

A recent essay in the *Houston Chronicle* by Brett Perlman, CEO of the Center for Houston's Future, prompted me to revisit a few previous posts on the characteristics and distinctiveness of my hometown. Perlman is rightly proud of the fact that Houston was recently added to the Rockefeller Foundation's 100 Resilient Cities program, the members of which are "prepared to deal with both acute shocks (such as hurricanes or terrorist attacks) and chronic stresses (such as mobility and affordable housing), the sort of ills that over time corrode our day-to-day quality of life." The potential of such an affiliation, according to him, is "that it is this broad work on resilience that could transform our community into a region that competes globally with places as diverse and powerful as New York, San Francisco, Singapore, and London."

I'm all for working with those urban areas around the world that have unique perspective on resiliency from which we can learn. But I would caution – some of our would-be peers have models and are pursuing ideas that are not to be emulated, so we should be careful what we wish for – there are good and bad strategies even among these elite cities. And, I also think that Houston has a lot to offer others in this regard and it has much to do with characteristics I have noted many times that highlight our city's organic culture, as well as some cautions about how not to mess it up, as follows:

- The future belongs to those regions like the Houston area that are attractive to capital and where it is well-treated, so those attributes, particularly those that are friendly to enterprise and opportunity and that have made Houston attractive to capital should be emphasized.
- A large part of Houston's attractiveness is that there is "no price of entry" in terms of class, origin, race, or family wealth. Houston is a place where people come from all over the world to pursue whatever version of the American dream they bring with them.
- Our city's accessibility and openness should be celebrated. We don't need "image" campaigns or consultants, which are often fronts for transforming our image to

one of "urbanity" or "globalism" and the commensurate lifestyle that fits the preference of many so-called "smart growth" advocates.

- Houston can continue to be what *The Wall Street* Journal once called "the Hong Kong of the Western hemisphere" only if it can avoid the tendency to embrace "progressive" ideas, such as zoning and its cousins, land use planning and smart growth theories, along with publicly financed hotels and transit plans that are insufficiently user-financed.

- It will be of increasing importance to take a critical look at the role and proper functions of government at every level and to be receptive to marketization opportunities wherever they present themselves. The competition for capital will demand this.

- Race- and ethnic-based contract set asides and other group preferences, whether to correct perceived past injustices or promote race or gender "diversity," will have a long-term negative impact on social relations.

- The most threatening area of risk to our success at resiliency is the performance of our institutions of public education and Houston's top priority should be a model elementary and secondary education system. This will not be possible until a declaration of war is declared on childhood illiteracy and when competition and post-secondary readiness accountability become fully integrated into education delivery.

So let's work with our peers to improve our response to pressing needs, but remember – Houston is unique in many ways and if we didn't have a Houston, we'd want to build one, so let's take care of the one we have, and I believe that our response to the Harvey disaster is plenty of evidence that we will.

A Very Shameful Truth

February 6, 2019

As I write, it remains to be seen whether or not Virginia Democrat Governor Ralph Northam will be able to keep his job after the exposure of photos from his medical school yearbook showing him either in blackface or in KKK robes. But if he resigns, he should receive going away thanks for exposing a very shameful truth about the abortion industry. For in his comments in advocating for a bill in the Virginia legislature that would have allowed abortions through the third trimester and as a practicing pediatric neurologist, he has ripped the covers off of the details of this horrendous practice, already permitted under the law in eight states, and exposed it for its true nature – infanticide, pure and simple.

The reaction to the Governor's description of the procedure from Senator Ben Sasse (R-NE) was spot on and spoke for many: "In just a few years pro-abortion zealots went from 'safe, legal, and rare' to 'keep the newborns comfortable while the doctor debates infanticide.'" The bill later failed in the legislature, but the Governor's remarks will live in infamy and serve to greatly heighten the abortion debate and energize the pro-life community of activists. It should also give new impetus and visibility to Gosnell: The Trial of America's Biggest Serial Killer, the documentary film about the murder case of Philadelphia abortion doctor Kermit Gosnell that had not previously received the coverage it deserves. Ironically, the Governor has done a great service to the country and the unborn.

23
Sports

The "Student-Athlete" Myth

August 3, 2001

If you care at all about college athletics or its relationship to the mission of higher education, I urge you to read the "Report of the Knight Foundation Commission on Intercollegiate Athletics," released in June. This report is a follow-up to the Foundation's report of 1991, which proposed what it called a "one plus three" approach for intercollegiate athletics – presidential control directed toward academic integrity, financial integrity, and independent certification of athletics programs – to rectify what it considered widespread abuses that were undermining the integrity of the sponsoring institutions.

In its recent report, the Commission finds that, despite considerable progress with its previously recommended reforms, "…the problems of big-time college sports have grown rather than diminished. The most glaring elements of the problems outlined – academic transgressions, a financial arms race, and commercialization – are all evidence of the widening chasm between higher education's ideals and big-time college sports." It recommends a new "one plus three" model – a Council of Presidents directed toward an agenda of academic reform, de-escalation of the athletic arms race, and de-emphasis of the commercialization of intercollegiate athletics. In short, the goal should be "the reintegration of college sports into the moral and institutional culture of the university."

After reading the report, I cannot find one aspect of it with which I disagree, either in its findings or recommendations. In fact, I would have made some of the latter even stronger. My support of and involvement with college sports has been lifelong, but I have been greatly disappointed over the past couple of decades in the obvious trends in college athletics in which most major universities have been willing and often, no doubt, unwilling participants. At the major college level, we are, in effect, complicit in a lie – the myth of the student-athlete – and have become totally beholden to, and corrupted by, the professional sports leagues, particularly the NFL and NBA, in the management of our major men's athletic programs.

No one wants success on the field and the court for my alma mater more than I do, but make no mistake – the trustees and alumni of our major universities are the only sources of leadership that can reverse the trends, which I believe we must do before the integrity of the mission of higher education is permanently undermined.

A Profile in Academic Courage

November 2, 2003

My hero of the month is Gordon Gee, Chancellor of Vanderbilt University. Recently he announced that Vanderbilt is eliminating the position of athletic director and replacing its traditional athletic department with a new body that is more connected to the mission of the university and more accountable to the institution's academic leadership. As he said, Vanderbilt is making a clear statement that the "student-athlete" belongs back in the university as a step in the much-needed reform of intercollegiate athletics. To me, the most important points he made are the fact that many athletic departments exist as almost autonomous fiefdoms and serve as semi-professional "farm" systems for the professional sports franchises. I also was encouraged by an editorial by Duke University President Nannerl Keohane in which she echoed many of the same comments. Of course, the Vanderbilts and the Dukes of the world are unique, have much different constituencies and missions than most big-time flagship universities, particularly those with top-rated football programs, and their leaders can get away with such boldness. But I think it is a leadership step in the right direction. A couple of years ago, I wrote of the report of the Knight Commission on Intercollegiate Athletics, from which I repeat this passage: "...the problems of big-time college sports have grown rather than diminished. The most glaring elements of the problems outlined (in the report) – academic transgressions, a financial arms race, and commercialization – are all evidence of the widening chasm between higher education's ideals and big-time college sports." The myth of the student-athlete in the most successful athletic programs is the "emperor with no clothes," and I believe those courageous college administrators who want a return to the integrity of their mission deserve the support of active and influential trustees and alumni.

Baseball Has Now Lost Me

January 6, 2008

The Mitchell Report might have been the last straw. I long ago abandoned professional football – haven't watched a game live or on TV since the Houston Oilers fired Bum Phillips and traded Earl Campbell – and professional basketball put me to sleep long before that, in both cases more for the on and off field culture they helped promote and reward than the quality of the play. But major league baseball always has been my first love as a professional sport and I continued to have respect for its intricacies as the "thinking man's game," the strategic drama, the poetry of it all – *The Natural, Field of Dreams, Casey at the Bat*, etc. – and the great traditions of the game. True, it has over the past 30 years or so succumbed to many of the same corruptions as the NFL and NBA, but it had managed to maintain a certain nostalgic attraction for me that even George Steinbrenner couldn't completely destroy. But the Mitchell Report on the widespread use of performance-enhancing drugs may do it. I'm not naive. Intuitively, I knew that the drug problem was more widespread than had been reported publicly, but I guess I wanted to believe that substantially all players were above it, if not ethically, at least in terms of its destructive potential. I've just watched Mike Wallace interview Roger Clemens on *60 Minutes* and I would like to believe that he is being truthful in his denials of the reports of his usage of steroids, but it's difficult to know what or who to believe, and that's the problem for me – we almost have reached the point that to assign complete credibility to anyone in such cases where the incentives are so compelling, one must choose to be totally cynical to avoid being guilty of extreme naiveté.

Of one thing I am sure. Our society will not purge itself of this corrupting imagery for our children until we take a no tolerance attitude with those who are proven guilty and not only condemn these practices, but completely remove the financial incentives for the perpetrators by removing them from their profession and stripping them of their records and awards. I totally disagree with George Mitchell's suggestion that past infractions not be prosecuted. In fact, if there are criminal referrals for drug use to be made, they should be made, and whether or not laws have been violated, major league baseball should deal harshly with those who violated the public trust by using these substances. That's the only chance they have to get me back.

College Athletics in Turmoil

July 4, 2010

Like many enthusiasts of college sports, I monitored closely the daily drama of the near implosion of the athletic conference alignments that recently unfolded over a period of several weeks involving several major football conferences, with primary focus on the Big 12 and its potential dismantling. I won't belabor all the various cross-currents; I will simply say that I am generally pleased with the outcome for the time being, although I believe that it is merely a transition to another round of contention in just a few years.

Obscured by the headlines that followed these high-profile machinations was the announcement of the third report of the Knight Commission on Intercollegiate Athletics, entitled "Restoring the Balance: Dollars, Values, and the Future of College Sports." This report was not as provocative as the first two, but it was certainly timely, dealing as it did with the impact of the enormous and rapidly increasing funding of college sports that seemingly overwhelms all other considerations in the strategies of these programs and the deliberations on conference affiliations. In fact, in the release of the report, the Commission noted that recent events give "new urgency to the finding of a survey in which a majority of university presidents agreed that current spending trends cannot be sustained."

The recommendations offer three principles for reform: 1) require that financial reports be public and transparent; 2) reward institutions that make academic values a priority; and 3) treat athletes as students first and foremost – not as professionals. The Commission further recommends that the financial reports filed by each institution with the NCAA be made public and include an additional measure comparing spending in athletics and academics, with athletic revenue distribution more closely tied to academic values and standards.

I am on record in this publication in agreement with almost every conclusion and recommendation of the first two Knight Commission reports (see "The Student-Athlete Myth," August 2001 and "A Profile in Academic Courage," November 2003) and I certainly have no problem with the current recommendations, although some of them seem to require significant transformation of human nature. But here is the immediate problem: Of 119 colleges with NCAA Division 1-A football programs, only 19 were profitable in 2009 and only six have been profitable for five consecutive years, so the "arms race" in college athletics is producing a clear demarcation between the "haves" and the "have-nots," and the gap is becoming more pronounced with every passing year.

In the interest of full disclosure, my alma mater, The University of Texas, is one of the six and leads the nation in annual gross athletic revenues at $138 million, a fact that gives me no great cause for celebration, but I will add this – although I am no fan of the current system, until we fix it, UT has no intention of unilateral disarmament. And I also should add that UT athletics is one of the very few programs that not only doesn't require any subsidy from its parent, but rather distributes significant funding to the academic side of the institution on an annual basis. Common sense dictates that sustainable coexistence by UT and others among the "haves" in the same conference with schools on the other end of the financial spectrum is problematic at best.

So what will be the outcome? I certainly don't know and I'm not sure anyone can predict. But I fear that if the leadership of the schools at the upper end of financial success do not take aggressive action soon, there is a risk of government intervention on issues such as tax exemption, compensation of student-athletes, and antitrust considerations, not to mention intervention in matters of conference membership, none of which will be productive for college athletics or academics.

Penn State – the Shame and the Legacy

August 5, 2012

Readers who have been with *The Texas Pilgrim* for awhile know that I have shared a love/hate relationship with college athletics in several essays, primarily surrounding the issues raised by the reports of the Knight Commission on intercollegiate athletics. I have been a huge fan of college sports and close follower and supporter of The University of Texas for most of my life and no one wants success for my alma mater more than I. That's the "love" part. The "hate" part that is so well described by the Knight Commission in its reports has to do with the corrupting elements – the out-of-control commercialization, the undermining of the academic mission, the myth of the "student-athlete," and related problems, mainly involving football.

Now we have the Penn State/Sandusky child abuse case, and in my mind nothing in the Knight reports remotely touches the deep-seated corruption here. Some say it is about the money. Wish it were so, it would be easier to fix, and maybe it is a factor. But this is primarily about the breakdown of authority and the corruption of moral judgment by a system that favors procedure over substance. Hillsdale College President Larry Arnn said it well: "You can't write prudence and judgment into a code… When a code tries to cover every possibility, it ends up shifting power from the college president and trustees to the compliance officers." Simply put, the "cops" in the form of the NCAA are incapable of dealing with this kind of breakdown.

Many say that competitive sports build character. I have always disagreed with that. Sports don't build character, they reflect it. Similarly, many say that colleges and college athletics reflect the nature of the society and the culture. That may be so, but it shouldn't be; they should be better than that, they should rise above it with much higher standards.

Legacy? Penn State will never be the same, or let's hope so. Same for college athletics across the board. We'll see.

The Real "Johnny Football" Issue

September 5, 2013

Let me begin by admitting that, as a fan of college athletics, I followed the autograph signing case of Texas A&M quarterback Johnny Manziel pretty closely, but I don't have anywhere near all the facts and I couldn't care less about the recent eligibility settlement of the case with the NCAA. However, there are larger issues here that concern me, as follows.

A large portion of the commentary on this case maintained that, whether or not Manziel was guilty of receiving compensation for his autographs, the NCAA rule prohibiting such compensation is antiquated and should be repealed. In fact, significant opinion over the past several years has it that college football players should receive compensation for their efforts that produce significant revenues for their school, and that this unfair exploitation should be ended. For at least a beginning to the resolution of this issue, we await the judgment of the court in the now pending case filed by former UCLA basketball star Ed O'Bannon and co-plaintiffs, which pleads for a share of the revenues in college athletics to be shared with the players. Needless to say, a ruling for the plaintiffs in this case would result in a massive transformation of college sports as we know it. In fact, of the 125 Division I football programs, only 20 of them were profitable in the past year, and only about a half dozen of them were profitable over the past five years, so it is not difficult to forecast the impact that player compensation would have, even at a nominal level. Quite simply, the top division of college football would quickly shrink to 30 or 40 schools. Moreover, the entire concept of the student/athlete, which already has been rendered a joke, would disappear along with the NCAA itself, and the top division of college football, possibly along with basketball, would become simply a farm system for the professional leagues, finalizing their prostitution that has been underway for several decades.

The proponents of compensation for college athletes have a point, however. We have for some time defended the notion that players receive sufficient compensation in the form of four years of free tuition and a college education, along with various perks, notoriety, etc. But the numbers have become so overwhelming that this argument has lost its relevance. My alma mater leads the nation in its athletic budget, which now approaches $200 million and nets $60 million or so annually, pays its head football coach $5 million, and affords me a tax deduction for the football seating option I purchase (go figure). So, the balance between the compensation to the players and their value-added to the enterprise has become grossly distorted.

NCAA President Mark Emmert poses the question, shouldn't Texas A&M have a share of the value-added to Johnny Manziel when he enters the NFL, and this is where I believe the changes need to be made. Some think that the outstanding player does more for the school than the school does for the player. I disagree, but I think this is an empirical question. If I could be "czar" for a day, I would dictate the following: 1) After signing a college letter of intent and registering, no college player could be drafted by the NFL or NBA before their 21st birthday; and 2) For each player drafted and signed by the NFL and NBA, the drafting team would pay compensation to the college of the draftee the amount of, say, $100,000 or some percentage of the first year's salary, with appropriate escalation clauses. This certainly and swiftly would result in a lawsuit, but bring it on. If the professional leagues want to continue to exploit the colleges as their farm system and corrupt the academic mission, at least they should pay for the privilege.

A Tipping Point for College Athletics

September 1, 2014

Mark the date: The recent court ruling against the National Collegiate Athletic Association (NCAA) in the O'Bannon case combined with a decision by the NCAA in effect creating a division of "superconferences" will serve as the impetus for the acceleration of the downward spiral of the highest levels of college athletics into farm systems for the National Football League and the National Basketball Association.

The decision in the O'Bannon case could have been worse for the NCAA. There could have been a huge settlement for retroactive compensation of the plaintiffs with unlimited stipends going forward, as well as major antitrust violations, but by simply banning the prohibition of cost-of-living stipends in addition to scholarships, the student-athlete myth is now completely dead and the dam is broken on fully professionalizing the two primary revenue-producing college sports.

And the related decision by the NCAA to recognize in scholarship policy the obvious gulf between the "haves" (the five major conferences) and "have nots" (everyone else) in the college sports arms race will incentivize the hastening of these outcomes.

This bargain with the devil has been coming for quite some time and, as I was told by a prominent university leader a number of years ago in response to several of my recommendations for reform, to have reversed this process would have required an almost complete overhaul of human nature.

As a consolation, at least now those institutions that either can't afford or prefer not to join in this bargain can move strategically in a different direction, toward athletic programs that are consistent with and do not undermine their academic mission.

The NCAA as Social Justice Cop

October 4, 2016

As if it doesn't have enough to worry about in its primary mission to govern college athletics, the National Collegiate Athletic Association (NCAA) now has discovered a new addition to its purpose in life – the policing of local cultural norms in its administration of college sporting events. In this new role, it recently has pulled seven major athletic events out of North Carolina, closely followed by the Atlantic Coast Conference, because the State of North Carolina, in its hateful temerity, has passed a bill requiring its citizens use the public bathrooms that correspond to their biological sex.

It seems to me that it is in no way the role of the NCAA to intervene in such matters involving contentious social change, which is otherwise being pursued through public deliberation, as well as the judicial system, particularly in the employment of its considerable economic power derived from its member institutions to influence public policy and, worse as in this case, without consulting its member institutions.

There are many ramifications here. For 5,000 years we have held that gender is fixed in human nature. Now, just in a very short period of time, we are busy determining that gender is a self-selecting choice and are making sweeping decrees, without serious debate, with total disregard for our system of federalism, and with threatened penalties for failure to immediately comply. In addition, in so doing, in education we are using Title IX, which was written to address sex discrimination, in a perverse way that erases sexual differences altogether.

I warned about this more than 10 years ago in another context, but the bottom line and my caution then and now is that the underlying question in these and related issues that will torment us in this century is: what does it mean to be human?

The Kaepernick Phenomenon

October 4, 2016

I wasn't going to write about this, but it has dragged on far beyond the one 24-hour news cycle it deserved, so I can't ignore it. Let's acknowledge the obligatory nod to San Francisco 49er Colin Kaepernick's civil right to protest his grievances in whatever peaceful way he chooses, even in so ignorant and ungrateful a manner as he chose – to disgrace the anthem recognizing the symbol of the regime that makes possible this and other rights unprecedented in human history and those who fought and died to defend them.

With that out of the way, let's get to the response. First, if I owned an NFL franchise, I would go to the locker room before the next game and say this:

"Gentlemen, you are about to take the field to play a game for which you are paid by me as your employer a significant amount of money. When you do so, you are representing me, my team, and my city. Your grievances are your business, but your job is my business, so if the airing of your grievances of whatever type extend to ignoring or otherwise disgracing the flag of this country and the anthem that pays homage to it while on this field, you will not play another down for my team, beginning today. Effective immediately, the applicable team rule is that when the national anthem is played, you will stand straight and salute with your hand over your heart. Singing is optional, but preferable. Any questions?"

As for other, non-employer/employee relationships, The University of Texas System Chancellor Bill McRaven had the most comprehensive response in the form of a letter sent to the presidents and athletic directors of all University System schools. This was a follow-up letter to one sent earlier prescribing the proper conduct of college athletes during the playing of the national anthem, and in it, in part, he said this: "I spent 37 years defending freedom of speech and freedom of expression. Nothing is more important to this democracy. Nothing! However, while no one should be compelled to stand, they should recognize that by sitting in protest to the flag they are disrespecting everyone who sacrificed to make this country what it is today – as imperfect as it might be… The flag rode with the Buffalo Soldiers. It was carried by the suffragists down the streets of New York City. It flew with the Tuskegee Airmen of WWII. It was planted in the fields where Cesar Chavez spoke. It marched with Martin Luther King, Jr… It is a flag for everyone, of every color, of every race, of every creed, and of every orientation, but the privilege of living under this flag does not come without cost. Nor should it come without respect."

The editors of *National Review* remind us that freed slave Frederick Douglass wrestled with a similar problem in a July 4th speech in 1852, when slavery was in full flower, and he said "the existence of slavery brands your republicanism as a sham," but then went to say that the Constitution was a "glorious liberty document. Read its preamble, consider its purposes. Is slavery among them? Is it at the gateway? Or is it in the temple? It is neither." I suggest that Douglass had a much deeper understanding of the stakes than anyone today kneeling during the playing of the national anthem before an NFL game, yet for America and its ideals he did not despair.

It has been said that this is a "teaching moment." Well, yes, but I consider it a "teaching repair" moment. Over the past several weeks these protests have reached a number of copycat high school and even middle school games. This is a tragedy, unfortunately led by adults who should know better. But a big part of the problem is in education, where there has been major emphasis over the past several decades on the pathologies of our history over its ideals and where multicultural ideologies value class, racial, gender, and ethnic identities to the detriment of our national civic identity. This is a problem that is chipping away at our civic cohesion and it deserves much more of our attention than it is currently receiving.

The Anthem and the NFL

October 3, 2017

The "take a knee" salute to our national anthem during NFL pre-game ceremonies hit a new level after President Trump weighed in with his comments in a campaign speech in Alabama, as players across the country have generally acted in solidarity with their colleagues in protest of his suggestion that any player taking a knee should be fired and that any team owner doing so would likely be considered a hero. And of course NFL Commissioner Roger Goodell chimed in with his support of the players by calling out Trump's comments as "divisive." One might expect some leadership from the league, for after all they are quick to enforce a number of other behavioral rules, but with the racial implications involved here, it is not surprising that the political correctness of "unity" with the players has priority, even though one of their rules requires that all players stand at attention during the national anthem. We should understand that this is where we go when our culture is poisoned by "progressive" identity politics and it has infiltrated a popular spectator sport, because the left has made heroes out of its perpetrators.

Although the President's ill-advised input certainly inflamed the issue unnecessarily, this issue didn't start with him, having been with us since last season when now-unemployed quarterback Colin Kaepernick initiated this form of protest and, frankly, should have ended there, were it not for the total capitulation by the feckless team owners and the failure of leadership on the part of the Commissioner. One of the best responses I have seen on this failure comes from a recent letter to the editor of The Wall Street Journal, in which a reader wrote:

"Mr. Goodell should have issued a statement like this when Kaepernick first knelt: The NFL is a business providing sports entertainment for our customers. Actions that are offensive to a majority of our customers will not be tolerated. Players are employees of the teams and league. A requirement of the job is to stand and show respect during the national anthem. This isn't a free speech issue. This is a job requirement."

Amen.

24
Travels

Letter from Central Europe

November 3, 2007

My wife and I just returned from a very busy three-week tour of Rome and Central Europe, including stays in Warsaw, Krakow, Budapest, Vienna, and Prague, as well as other interesting stops between in places like Auschwitz and Birkenau, Czestokova, and the Slovak Republic. Lots of history here, and it was greatly enhanced with several cultural events, as well as commentary from our tour guide, who holds a graduate degree in European history, in addition to the very knowledgeable local guides.

Impressions? There were several. First, in all this history of the various founding tribes and their many conflicts over the centuries, one important characteristic of European history and culture stands out, particularly in contrast to American culture. This is that European (particularly continental Europe) loyalty is mainly expressed in terms of two aspects – religion and language – and that citizenship is not an important factor in this mix. I have often commented about American exceptionalism, and here is an area in which I think it is most manifest. Uniquely among the world's nations, citizenship is a primary element of American cultural loyalty to a set of ideas, and this has made a huge difference in our development.

Second, after witnessing almost constant daily anti-American demonstrations in London last year, I expected at least some of that phenomenon in continental Europe. To my pleasant surprise, in all our travels, there was not one incident of anti-Americanism or any physical evidence of it, either in the streets or in the media. In fact, the only criticism of the U.S., in English at least, was in the editorial pages of the *International Herald Tribune*, a publication of the *New York Times.*

Third, we probably toured or at least visited about 50 churches, cathedrals, and synagogues, and all of them were fascinating. Of course, it was no surprise that many of them are now operational mainly as museums – revered for their beauty, but also for their quaintness, almost as relics from a world that many in the last two generations no longer recognize. This was true to a greater or lesser extent in all places we visited, but

Poland was an exception in many ways. In fact, Soviet assimilation, collectivization of agriculture, and other totalitarian measures didn't work with the Poles very well. It's therefore no surprise that they led the purge of Communism in the 1980s. This is part of the same resilience that caused them to persevere as a culture while not even being on the European map for 123 years. It's no coincidence that the church remains strong here.

One final point. It was well noted that the Slovak Republic approved a flat income tax rate almost immediately upon achieving independence in 1993, and that their average annual per capita income has increased almost 450 percent since then. Poland and even Russia are currently considering the adoption of a flat tax. When will we learn?

Great trip, good to be back home, lots to be thankful for as Americans.

Letter from China

April 11, 2008

Anyone who is reasonably perceptive on the broad sweep of public affairs would be hard pressed to challenge the case that the massive economic, political, and societal transformation of China and, in particular, the future of its relationship with the United States, is the leading geopolitical issue of the 21st century. The only other issue that seems reasonably close is the final resolution of the worldwide conflict between the West and radical Islam, which will likewise occupy most of the remainder of this century.

It is very unlikely that I will be called upon for involvement at any close and personal level with the resolution of our problems with Islamofascism, for which I probably should be thankful, but I recently had a great opportunity to get a reasonably good feel for the former issue when I was invited to accompany a delegation of seven to visit China for dialogue with senior representatives of the Central Party School (CPS) of the Chinese Communist Party. This trip was a continuation of conversations and exchange visits that began about two years ago between that institution and The Texas Lyceum Association, an organization of which I was a founding Director and Past Chairman, to seek areas of common ground across a range of cultural, economic, and political subjects.

For those not familiar with the CPS (and I wasn't before the trip), it was founded in the early 1930s by the Party as the primary institution for development of its future leaders and, in addition, now serves as the "think tank" for strategic issues facing the Party and the country. Its main campus is in Beijing, which accommodates about 3,000 students in both an undergraduate and graduate mode, and it has branches in each of China's 30 provinces.

The meetings with our CPS hosts were fairly formal, conducted through very capable translators, and very open and candid. Much of the discussion revolved around the objectives of the two parties in the relationship going forward, and a significant development was the tentative agreement, subject to final arrangements, of a return trip to Texas by the senior CPS representatives for an extended visit later this year, to include forums with civic and business leaders and field trips to key institutions, as well as the publication of a journal of essays originated by the counterparts.

In addition to the meetings in Beijing, our hosts guided our visit to the amazing infrastructural development underway in the port city of Tianjin and meetings with the economic development leadership in that area. Mealtimes were businesslike, but very festive, and included many varieties of food and drink, almost none of which were on my diet! After the "official" part of our trip, several of us spent a few days touring significant sites in the cities of Xian and Shanghai, meeting business leaders on an informal basis, and getting a good introduction to Chinese life, at least in the eastern provinces, all of which to me was a big highlight of the trip since this was my first to the country.

Now for some observations:

- The Texas Lyceum has taken a major leadership step in developing and nurturing this relationship. Whatever your views about China and its problems and challenges, and there are many, or their relationship with the U.S., which has many moving and tricky parts, it remains an incontrovertible fact that we must deal very forthrightly with a country that constitutes 20 percent of the world's population, occupies a very significant trade relationship with us and holds more than $1 trillion of our debt, will no doubt soon pass the U.S. as the world largest economy at least in aggregate terms, will continue to expand its power and reach from both economic and military standpoints, and expects to command the respect and even deference that normally accompany such a configuration. The Lyceum's leadership should be commended for bringing this relationship to this point and encouraged in its efforts to move it forward.

- Clearly, the future relationship with America is a very important consideration with Chinese leadership. They want to know everything about us, but primarily from a cultural perspective, and this was the most distinctive part of our dialogue on this trip. I heard the words "cultural context" about 50 times in two days of talks. They want lists of readings that treat American cultural heritage and political philosophy, they want to know about our religious institutions and habits, and to explore the possible cultural common ground between our country and theirs. In fact, although this project is **somewhat** about economic and business exchange, it is not **primarily** about these things, and anyone who pursues a meaningful dialogue beyond the surface without understanding this point will not succeed.
- The Chinese Communist Party clearly is struggling mightily to "stay ahead of the curve" and preserve its relevance so as to maintain power in a society changing at warp speed, and their leaders know that to do so they must continue to allow transformation of civic life on a parallel with economic life. In fact, Li Junru, the most senior CPS official who hosted our delegation, was quoted in *China Economic Review* while we were there as follows: "China's economic reform has reached the stage in which it becomes a must to deepen the political system reform. The market economy has met many obstacles, and the majority of these obstacles have to do with the political system."
- The primary tenets of communist ideology, for all practical purposes, have been totally undermined except in name only. While in Shanghai, I visited the Memorial House of the First National Congress of the Chinese Communist Party and read the founding Marxist/Leninist creed posted on the wall. With the exception of some remaining limitations on ownership of private property, all of the critical elements of this creed have been rendered obsolete. The fact only awaits the acknowledgement in official policy, which is sure to come. It's a matter of time. Remember that Marxism is a product of Western philosophy, it is alien to their culture in the first place, and in the grand sweep of Chinese history will appear only as a blip on the screen.
- I was somewhat surprised at the continuing reverence for Chairman Mao Zedong, even among the younger generation who, although their reverence doesn't reach to the divine status held by their grandparents, still project a certain veneration. His image is visible everywhere. I was asked by one of my guides, who is college educated and very knowledgeable, how Chairman Mao is treated in U.S. history books. My response was, not extensively, but fairly and appropriately harshly. I sense that in China, as in Russia, there soon will be a need for much more

transparency about their history, particularly that of their regimes of the 20th century.

- In their pursuit of the relationship with the U.S. that offers the optimal outcome for them, as well as a peaceful transition to a more open and democratic polity, I sense that they have an opportunity to be much more successful than the Soviet Union in their transition. Much of this is because the Chinese went to school on Russia's mistakes, but more of it is, because of the discipline produced by many centuries of the tradition of the Tao, an approximation of the natural law tradition of the West, as well as the Confucian philosophy of discipline and the primacy of the family unit. My judgment is that these are very aggressive, talented, and disciplined people who will take the time necessary to "get it right," and when they do, look out, for they will be fierce competitors for world leadership in every respect. And in the interim they will vigorously defend their strong sense of sovereignty over domestic affairs and their nationalism.

I have serious concerns with various aspects of our relationship with China and its conduct in domestic and world affairs – human rights, political rights, Tibet, Darfur, Taiwan, growing nationalism, the war with Islamofascism, etc. – and I have big problems with their 20th century regime, but there is symmetry in the relationship and it behooves us to do what we can to help make their transformation a peaceful one that respects human and civil rights and one that preserves American values and interests to the extent possible.

Rethinking Outdated Institutions

October 11, 2008

My wife and I just returned from a delightful 12-day tour of New England, one of the stops on which was the beautiful old Mount Washington Hotel in Bretton Woods, New Hampshire, which of course was the site of the international monetary conference in 1944 that established the world monetary system that lasted until 1971 and several of its institutions that are still around. I won't belabor the details of how the system came unwound, but my point is that in walking the hallways of this magnificent old place, it occurred to me that here was spawned several of the institutions reflecting the reality on the ground at the end of World War II that are now functionally obsolete. Others include the United Nations, or at least its Security Council, and probably NATO. There are several reasons, all of which have been provided high relief by the events of the past decade, most recently the Russian intervention in Georgia. The UN is worthless as a security forum, as has been well documented. With a few exceptions, notably Great Britain and the former Warsaw Pact members, Europe is no longer a serious player in world security matters, and is easily intimidated or blackmailed by rogue states, including Putin's Russia. Candidly, on this point the U.S. presently has no realistic policy for dealing with situations like the Russian intervention in Georgia, nor with a resurgent Russia generally.

What all of this means is that we need to seriously consider abandoning these obsolete institutions in favor of new multinational organizations, some of which could be organized on regional bases, both for security issues as well as trade. The new format and criteria for membership should be those of a league of democracies, not the nominal ones, but those whose leaders and institutions are truly responsive to the consent of the governed under the rule of law. Incidentally and not surprisingly, I have heard nothing of this kind of thinking from either of our presidential nominees.

"Civilization" Revisited

May 5, 2012

Recently I revisited the masterful 1970 BBC production, "Civilization: A Personal View by Lord Clark," a sweeping, approximately 12-hour DVD tour of the historic places, structures, artifacts, and legacy of the evolution of Western Civilization in Europe from the collapse of the Roman Empire to the 19th century, as guided and described by the eminent art historian Lord Kenneth Clark. I highly recommend it for its quality of presentation and for the often provocative commentary by Lord Clark along the way. Much of the commentary struck me as sad in a way in the sense that it described a world from which, to a significant extent, we have become alienated and no longer recognize. And why is this so? Primarily, because the foundational linchpin of the development of this civilization in all of its manifestations was the Christian religion, a heritage which has now been hollowed out in Europe and has not been sustained by the dominant culture for at least five or six decades.

I have made three trips to Europe in the past six years and have visited a number of the places and viewed many of the structures and artifacts highlighted in the Clark tour. These are awesome places, with enormous implications for the historical development of Christendom, which was synonymous with Western Civilization. Many of these places are now mostly museums and tourist stops. Who will sustain their viability in the story of the development of the greatest civilization in world history in the absence of their grounding in the worldview that produced them? And, more importantly, who and what will follow in a next phase of civilizational evolution? I wonder and I worry.

In an essay in *The New Criterion*, Charles Murray writes that a major stream of human accomplishment is fostered by a culture in which the most talented people believe that life has a purpose (*this is what I was put on this earth to do*) and that the function of life is to fulfill that purpose. Further to his point, the characteristics of nihilism are at odds with the zest and life-affirming energy necessary to produce great art, architecture, and cultural artifacts, not to mention a broad range of other manifestations of human accomplishment, the kind that is demonstrated in the tour by Lord Clark. If life is purposeless, no one kind of project is intrinsically more important than any other kind. And what is the most direct cause of the belief that one's life has a purpose? Belief in a personal God who wants you to use your gifts to the fullest, a belief that has been in constant decline in Europe for about a century. There is a secular counterpart to this in the form of Aristotle's pursuit of "the good," a concept which also has been out of style for many years.

Can we turn around this sense of purposelessness? Murray is optimistic, probably more than I am. He believes that humans are ineluctably drawn to fundamental questions of existence and purpose and that the elites that have shaped culture in America and the West have avoided thinking about these fundamental questions for too long and will inevitably return to them. I hope he is right before it's too late.

Book Reviews

Introduction

In the mid-1970s I became a voracious reader to make an attempt to fill a void that I had created in my education when I didn't take full advantage of my opportunities in the core literature and humanities courses in high school and college. This objective was expanded when I helped to organize a great books discussion group focused on political philosophy and I began to seek out other venues for book discussions, such as seminars at the Aspen Institute and St. John's College. These experiences prompted even more immersion in the humanities, primarily in biography, history, philosophy, and political philosophy, and I began to build a sizable library in these subjects. So when the idea for *The Texas Pilgrim* was conceived, the inclusion of space for book reviews was an obvious complement to the theme of the publication, that "ideas have consequences." And over the past 20 years, I have written more than 150 reviews, selections of which are included as follows.

Faith, Reason, and Wisdom

May 1, 2000

One of my heroes of the 20th century is Pope John Paul II. He not only has been a great leader for his church and his faith, but a significant statesman and one who provided critical political (yes, political in the philosophical sense) and moral conviction during the momentous final years of Soviet and Eastern European Communism. His 1994 book, *Crossing the Threshold of Hope*, offers insight on the great theological concerns of our times on an accessible level: the existence of God, the dignity of man, pain and suffering, evil, and the relationship among the various Christian faiths and between Christianity and other faiths. Most of all it is about hope for all mankind in his motto, "be not afraid." Recently, I completed a second reading of his September 1998 encyclical to the Catholic bishops, *Fides et Ratio*, on the relationship between faith and reason. Here is his magnum opus, a broad sweep of 90 pages of distilled wisdom from a life of philosophical and theological study. In it, he traces the historical relationships between and among faith and reason, philosophy, science, revelation, and empiricism, pointing out many of the false philosophical idols and sophistries along the way, many of which are with us today in the forms of the various postmodern ideologies. Finally, he calls for a return to true, speculative philosophy as "an inquiry that can help greatly to clarify the relationship between truth and life, between event and doctrinal truth, and above all between transcendent truth and humanly comprehensible language." I have often thought that our intellectuals have failed us in leading us away from this inquiry over the past century. Hopefully, John Paul II has helped redirect us.

More Wisdom From Thatcher

July 2, 2003

Regular readers know that Margaret Thatcher is one of my heroes, and her latest book, Statecraft, did not disappoint. In fact, it added to my appreciation of her depth and common sense approach to policy. The book's subtitle, *Strategies for a Changing World*, is appropriate, for it is a sweeping tour of the world's conflicts and policy challenges, with insights that are not available to the average observer. There are chapters on every region, outlining the critical issues and players, each followed by the definitive policy recommendations one would expect from this lady of so much depth of conviction. Of particular attraction are the chapters on the European Union and her battles over the years over the related issues of the delegation of British sovereignty; her recollections on the final victory in the Cold War for which she deserves so much credit; the Russian "enigma;" the Balkan Wars; and her postscript on the historical British legacy of freedom and the rule of law as originated with the Magna Carta. But she is at her best in expressing her admiration for "the American achievement" and the leadership role the United States has played and must continue to play in world affairs. No surprises here – the book is dedicated to Ronald Reagan.

Who Are We?

July 5, 2004

Before reading Samuel P. Huntington's book, *Who Are We? The Cultural Core of American National Identity*, I read several reviews of it, some of which were highly critical of what they characterized as his tones of racism, xenophobia, and cultural elitism. These focused almost entirely on the aspects of the book that describe the massive wave of post-1965 U.S. immigration from Hispanic, primarily Mexican, sources. And it is the case that Huntington spends a lot of space describing his concern with the very different nature of this most recent phase of immigration to this country and what it means for our values, our culture, and our future national identity. But the book is much more than that. In fact, it is a grand survey of American cultural roots, the exceptionalism of its founding as an Anglo-Protestant settlement, and the tangled relationship of these attributes with what Huntington calls the American Creed. I have long been interested in the question of whether America is primarily a "culture" or an "idea," and this book speaks to this issue, as well as anything I have read. It is also cautionary in many ways. Huntington (who, incidentally, identifies himself as a liberal Democrat) outlines in great detail the powerful forces among American elites that have mounted a sustained effort over the past several decades to "deconstruct" American national identity, he makes it very clear that the overwhelming bulk of the American people do not support this effort, and he offers the alternatives we have in shaping our future. Although he doesn't say it, the strong suggestion is that we had better decide soon if the deconstructed vision of our future is the one we want before we find ourselves strangers in a country we don't recognize.

Witness and Judgment

January 4, 2005

During the past few weeks, I have revisited two classics – one, a book, *Witness,* by Whittaker Chambers, and the other, a movie, *Judgment at Nuremberg*, with an all-star cast directed by Stanley Kramer – and I was struck by a profound thought: that you can't fully understand the 20th century unless you understand the issues raised so penetratingly by these works. *Witness,* of course, is the life story of a former Communist and active member of the CPUSA underground, who left the party and later provided crucial and very controversial testimony in the famous Alger Hiss Case before the House Un-American Activities Committee on the Communist infiltration of high levels of the U.S. government during the 1930s and 1940s. *Judgment at Nuremberg* (1961) tells the story of the trial and conviction by the post-World War II American tribunal of high-ranking members of the Nazi German judiciary during the Third Reich.

Nothing I have read captures the essence of the Communist mind and socialist threat as Chambers does, and he weaves his tale in 1954 in a way that is eerily prescient of many of the conflicts we still face today, for the crux of the Communist faith, which is that salvation by society in a world without God is the only solution to the crisis of history, is alive and well in the progressive remnants left behind under other names, both here and abroad, by the discrediting of institutional Communism. And it is amazing how complicit in this faith and the relentless pursuit of power based on that faith were and are the American fellow-travelers, up to the point of complete denial to this day, despite incontrovertible evidence gleaned from KGB files since the fall of the

Soviet Union, and how willing to ignore or rationalize the pervasiveness of this evil our major cultural institutions were and are.

Judgment at Nuremberg is a must-see in understanding the true corruption of the Third Reich, because it focuses not on the military war criminals, but on those whose insidious corruption of the rule of law undermined what was at the time the most advanced intellectual society in the world. I was particularly struck by how easy it might have been to rationalize, as defense attorney Rolfe (portrayed by Academy Award winner Maximillian Schell) did, the compromises of the rule of law as temporary expedients to salvage a nation and a culture. It is also a classic treatment of the conflict, very much at issue today, between the positive law and natural law in the prosecution of crimes against humanity, and how, in fact, our distinctively American philosophy of pragmatism as expressed in key U.S. court decisions during the progressive era was thrown back at us in defense of Nazi eugenics policy.

These are timeless works with messages to match, and I was reminded of C. S. Lewis's line about the "magician's bargain" from *The Abolition of Man:* "Give up your soul, get power in return. But once our souls, that is, ourselves, have been given up, the power thus conferred will not belong to us. We shall in fact be the slaves and puppets of that to which we have given our souls."

Enlightenment Options

May 1, 2005

From time to time, I have commented that the Middle East that we are in the process of transforming, never had the experience of either a Reformation or Enlightenment and therefore did not have the same cultural reference points as the West for a successful transition to the modern world. As we contemplate a possible "enlightenment" of the Islamic Middle East, hopefully in parallel with a belated reformation of Islam itself, we might reflect on the question of which enlightenment model we wish for – the popular and romanticized French model of "liberty, equality, fraternity" or the less exalted, but profoundly more successful British and American models. Now comes Gertrude Himmelfarb and her book, *The Roads to Modernity,* with very useful perspective on the differences among the three Enlightenments – French, British, and American – and the difference they have made. And, although she doesn't specifically speak to the question to which I allude here, she clearly answers it without serious doubt.

For Himmelfarb, the key differentiation is the driving force for the three "roads" – for the French, it was the ideology of reason as the enemy of, and to completely supplant, religion; for the British, it was the "social virtues" or "social affections" of the moral philosophers; and for the Americans, it was "the politics of liberty." Unlike the French model, which attempted to transform human nature itself, the British and American models recognized the innate similarity in human nature across cultures and social status. And, critically for the success of the latter two, reason was an instrument for the attainment of the larger social end, not the end itself, and religion was an ally, not an enemy, in this pursuit. So as we observe and help guide the transformation of the Middle East, it is helpful to remember which models have produced true human freedom and productivity and which one, notwithstanding its popular appeal, has produced human strife. Himmelfarb's book provides helpful insights.

The Bush Doctrine and History

May 4, 2005

Those who criticize the Bush Doctrine in dealing with world terrorism and Islamofascism, as well as others who wonder about its place in historical perspective would benefit from a small book by John Lewis Gaddis, *Surprise, Security, and the American Experience*. Gaddis places George W. Bush in a context that reaches back to John Quincy Adams' term as Secretary of State under President James Monroe to find that Bush's strategy is more consistent than not with the American tradition of foreign policy. Adams' innovation at the time was to introduce the notion of national expansion as the basis of providing the necessary security for the relatively new country. And his methods for pursuing this expansion were preemption, unilateralism, and hegemony. Sound familiar?

Gaddis traces these concepts through the next two centuries and finds that they were consistently applied, albeit in different ways in different situations, in every foreign policy crisis until World War II and the Cold War, when more of a multilateral approach came into vogue and the concept of American exceptionalism was diluted, while American hegemony overseas was justified and accepted because there existed "something worse" in the form of Soviet domination. The question Gaddis poses is whether Osama bin Laden is enough of this "something worse" to permit the same degree of American hegemony, and he wonders if the part of the Bush Doctrine that is at odds with Adams, that of the deliberate American expansion of liberty and democracy abroad, is sustainable. This is a very provocative historical perspective on critical foreign policy issues and I highly recommend it.

Soft America Meets the New Realities

June 1, 2005

Previously, I commented on Michael Barone's book, *Hard America, Soft America,* which portrays the two different worlds occupied by those in our country who are products of the demands of competition (hard) versus those who have avoided or have not been subjected to such rigors in education, employment, and other walks of life (soft). Now comes Tom Friedman with his new book, *The World is Flat: A Brief History of the Twenty-First Century*, which vividly outlines the new realities of what he calls Globalization 3.0, a phenomenon, which has, in a very brief period, not only shrunk the world from "a size small to a size tiny," but has flattened the playing field at the same time. By flattening, he means that this latest phase of globalization is not being driven by the West, nor by governments, but by non-Western, non-white individuals, led by the mass of entrepreneurs and empowered individuals in China and India. For whether intended or not, and most of it wasn't, the "dot com" boom and bust of the late 1990s wired the world with the technologies and infrastructure that has empowered and enabled many millions, if not billions, of these folks to be fully competitive with the West at all levels of the production and value-added chain. We're not talking low-wage, labor-intensive outsourcing here, we're talking high value-added from very high speed knowledge-based industries conducted by very competitive and capable people and, as Friedman notes, "the Indians and Chinese are not racing us to the bottom, they are racing us to the top." In addition, one of the most important factors to note is that, unlike America and Europe, they are not burdened by the sunken costs of old delivery systems; they can leap immediately into the new systems enabled by the new technologies.

It should be pretty obvious how this scenario relates to the notion of "soft America." We are decades behind in restructuring our education system, both at the secondary and higher education levels. But more importantly, we are nowhere near the mindset and the sense of urgency necessary to make such a commitment. Even the use of the word "competition" is shunned by most of our education establishment. The current mindset of "leave no child behind" is noble, but not good enough. Access should be a high priority, but should not be accomplished at the expense of proficiency and excellence. A recent letter to the editor in *The Wall Street Journal* said it well: (In considering the trade-offs), "the interests of this country will be determined by whether we can meet the challenges of China, India, and other nations by producing large numbers of graduates who exceed our expectations as engineers, scientists, and scholars, and who can meet competition for world leadership and hegemony with innovation in science and commerce." In the new "flat earth" environment, this objective will not be accomplished by a soft America.

Bloom Revisited

May 2, 2006

Thinking about various recent events and spectacles in higher education – the Ward Churchill fiasco, the shameful dismissal of President Larry Summers at Harvard, affirmative action marketing to the LGBT community at my own alma mater, Yale admitting as a student a former ambassador-at-large of the Afghan Taliban, and the deliberations of the Department of Education's higher education commission – led me back to a classic of almost 20 years ago. Allan Bloom stunned the academic world in 1987 with his *The Closing of the American Mind: How Higher Education Has Failed Democracy and Impoverished the Souls of Today's Students*, not just because of its sweeping indictment of our elite institutions of higher learning, but also because of the unusually resounding commercial success of a scholarly work by such an intellectual. No doubt it is an extraordinary analysis of the state of the American university and the mind of the students who populate the most elite of the institutions. It is also an in depth survey of the intellectual history leading to the present condition, which is difficult slogging, but very instructive and rewarding for the effort. Essentially, the crisis of liberal education and American intellectual life, according to Bloom, who was certainly no right-wing reactionary, is that no one is prepared to ask or answer the big questions about the nature of man and of good and evil. We have so "closed" the mind of the American student to these philosophical pursuits that we have impoverished their minds, as well as their souls and rendered them incapable of determining the nature of man and moral truth. The result is that the large majority of students are "unified only in their relativism and their allegiance to equality, and their greatest fear is not error, but intolerance…openness, and the relativism that makes it the only plausible stance in the face of various claims to truth, is the great insight of our times, and the true believer is the real danger."

The American system of higher education is the envy of the world in engineering, business, and professional education, but in the humanities, where we pursue the answers to the question, who are we, there clearly has been a relentless hollowing of our core. According to Bloom, more than a century of evolution in higher education standards brought us to this point, but the great ungluing came in the late 1960s, when university governance completely capitulated to the forces of postmodernism, "openness" was victorious over natural rights, civic education turned away from concentrating on the Founding and the result was the denigration of the core curriculum and the pursuit of philosophical truth. The trend since then, which no one save groups like the Association of College Trustees and Alumni and the National Association of Scholars are doing anything to change, has been anything, but encouraging and Bloom, who died about five years ago, would say he told us so. A great read, but not for the beach.

Einstein: His Life and Universe
by Walter Isaacson
September 6, 2007

This book has been on *The New York Times* best seller list for many weeks now, to no surprise. It is a very well written chronology of the life of a man whose exploits have become larger than life and the stuff of near-mythology for many among the generations who shared the past century. But more than that, it is a fascinating study of the life of a mind in pursuit of the elusive independent and objective reality in which he passionately believed exists and is destined for man's discovery. One quote from his writings that illustrates the humility and reverence he brought to the task: "A spirit is manifest in the laws of the universe – a spirit vastly superior to that of man, and one in the face of which we with our modest powers must feel humble."

The Regensburg Lecture
by James V. Schall
September 6, 2007

In September 2006, Pope Benedict XVI ignited a firestorm among fundamentalist Muslims with a passage from a lecture he delivered at the University of Regensburg in Germany. This is an excellent study of the lecture and its context by a Catholic theologian and professor of government at Georgetown University. Dr. Schall writes in his introduction that he believes this lecture to be the first of its kind that speaks to "the fuller dimensions of what our time is intellectually about." After reading the lecture in its entirety and the accompanying analysis, I have no doubt that this might very well be the case. It is a compelling critique of the current predicament of the West and what must be done to repair the disorders of our public life.

What Went Wrong?
by Bernard Lewis
September 6, 2007

Dr. Lewis is generally acknowledged as the dean of Islamic and Middle Eastern studies, and his reputation certainly precedes him. I have read a number of his essays and articles, but just now caught up with this bestseller, which was released just prior to the attacks of 9/11. The subtitle is *The Clash between Islam and Modernity in the Middle East*, and it is a widely acclaimed treatment. I must say, however, that I was somewhat disappointed. There is certainly much to be learned from his overview of the history of the Islamic cultures and their clash with modernity, but I expected more depth in his answer to the question he poses in the title. Pope Benedict has delved deeper and is more revealing on the philosophical wedges between Islam and the West and the cultural differences they have produced that are much more instructive on the question.

Leo Strauss and the Theologico-Political Problem
by Heinrich Meier
September 6, 2007

If you get the idea that this is not a "beach read," you're correct. I hesitated to include it, but Leo Strauss is one of my favorites, and the subject of this book by one of the leading interpreters of his work, the juxtaposition of religion and philosophy, revelation and reason, is one of the oldest and most important debates in Western civilization. Strauss was a master of these issues and this is a great treatment of his thought on them.

The Inevitable Showdown
March 5, 2009

Joint Chiefs of Staff Chairman Admiral Mike Mullen moved us one step closer to reality recently with his statement that Iran now has enough enriched uranium to build a nuclear bomb, thus confirming a similar report by the United Nations nuclear weapons agency. Secretary of Defense Robert Gates was quick to add that "there is some time," but how far are we from the day when we will be forced to confront a nuclear-armed fanatic that has pledged to eliminate us and our strongest and only true Middle East ally? Everything we have attempted has failed – talks conducted by the Europeans, sanctions, economic and diplomatic pressure – and in fact, much of it has served to embolden Iran's Ahmadinejad, who knows very well that we will not get help in the form of pressure on him from Russia, even if we concede on every contentious point with Putin – Georgia, Ukraine, the Eastern European missile defense shield, etc. And he also knows that the United Nations Security Council will veto any proposed resolution of military force against them. President Obama's team is "studying" the management of relations with Iran, and evidently remains committed to diplomacy in an international configuration as an end in itself. Meanwhile, this is not a rhetorical exercise for Israel; it is life or death. And the new Israeli government being organized by Benjamin Netanyahu will not be bashful about moral clarity on the issue. Nor should we.

I have just read a short, but compelling book, *Faith, Reason, and the War Against Jihadism,* by George Weigel. In it he reminds us that the war we are in (and have been since at least 1979) requires first, that we understand our enemy. In describing Ahmadinejad, he distinguishes his mission from that of the Sunni jihadists like Osama bin Laden, who want to restore the Islamic caliphate. Shiite jihadists, like Ahmadinejad, have an entirely different objective: to hasten the return of a messianic figure, the Twelfth Imam, who will cleanse the world. Hence, the mission is of an apocalyptic cast of mind and he and his cult believe that they are obligated to do whatever they can to hasten this age, including incinerating Israel and its allies, even if it means self-destruction. Not exactly the symmetry in a relationship that makes it anywhere close to analogous to our Cold War with the Soviets. So I wish our President well in his diplomatic attempts, but meanwhile, we'd better be well prepared, militarily, as well as emotionally and politically, for the next step, which might come sooner than we think.

Soft Despotism, Democracy's Drift: Montesquieu, Rousseau, Tocqueville, and the Modern Prospect **by Paul A. Rahe**

September 7, 2009

In 1989, when the Cold War ended, many intellectuals expected the "end of history" or the ultimate triumph of liberal democracy. However, this hasn't materialized as expected, and the fact that there remains much discontent in democratic societies has been widely discussed. In fact, as Rahe demonstrates, the uneasiness that has prevailed among the modern republics and the drift toward "soft despotism" was anticipated by thinkers well represented in the history of the development of the

American experiment. In this volume, he outlines their thought as it pertains to how this condition arises within a democracy when paternalistic state power expands and gradually undermines the spirit of self-government. A good analysis, well researched, but not long on solutions at this late date.

Beyond the Revolution: A History of American Thought from Paine to Pragmatism
by William H. Goetzmann
September 7, 2009

This is a pretty broad sweep of American intellectual history which tells the story of America's greatest thinkers, writers, and other creators, showing how they built upon and battled one another from 1776 to 1900. I found the book to be a very helpful overview of the evolution of American political philosophy, however, some reviewers have been critical of its single-minded adherence to what is called the "Harvard Narrative." This is a pejorative term for the standard rendition of the path of American political thought from the founders to a pragmatism that many believe is devoid of ideas and moral grounding, but seeks only acceptable results. I agree with some aspects of this criticism, but the book is good history, and it is what it is.

Woodrow Wilson and Roots of Modern Liberalism
by Ronald J. Pestritto
September 7, 2009

From his early days as a political scientist through his term as President of Princeton University and Governor of New Jersey to his election as President of the United States, Woodrow Wilson was a central figure in the development of progressivism and its successor, the liberalism that dominated 20th century political life and public policy in America. Wilson was totally committed to Hegelian historicism and the Social Darwinism of Herbert Spencer as organizing philosophies, and these of course were completely antithetical to the natural rights constitutionalism of the American founding. You wonder where we get the notion of the "living constitution?" Here's your man. And this book has been described as the deepest and most comprehensive treatment to date of Wilson's political thought. Very well done.

Living Constitution, Dying Faith: Progressivism and the New Science of Jurisprudence
by Bradley C. S. Watson

September 7, 2009

Legal historian Watson examines how the contemporary embrace of the "living" Constitution has arisen from the radical transformation of American political thought, particularly since the Civil War. He also traces the history of why our jurisprudence has become so alienated from the constitutionalism of the American founders. All of this is rooted in progressive legal theories, historicism, Social Darwinism, and pragmatism, and it significantly has undermined Americans' faith in the eternal truths, as well as the limited Constitution of our founding. Some of the book is redundant with the Wilson book, but the approach is much different, as Watson focuses more on the evolution of our jurisprudence.

Sovereignty: God, State, and Self
by Jean Bethke Elshtain

September 7, 2009

I enjoyed a new book by Jean Bethke Elshtain, *Sovereignty: God, State, and Self,* which was the central theme and grew out of her Gifford Lectures at the University of Edinburgh. In it she examines the origins and meanings of sovereignty as they have evolved over the centuries and as they relate to the ways in which we attempt to explain our world: God, state, self. She intertwines theology, philosophy, and psychology in a unique approach to understanding a concept that is absolutely essential in defining who we are, and she invites us to reflect on the toll that a narrow secularism is taking on human values and dignity. Not a light read, but worth the effort.

Financial Suicide

January 1, 2010

Of all the misguided initiatives to revive "industrial policy" currently underway, none is more foolhardy and risky than the massive intrusion into the financial markets under the guise of the rollback of the financial deregulation that has been officially designated the leading culprit in the meltdown of the past two years. It will lead to massive domination by government and increasing distortion of the capital markets as a result. And all of it could be avoided by looking at history, using common sense about what truly has been successful, and getting serious about our role as the keeper of the world's reserve currency. We could start by reading a great book, *Econoclasts*, by Brian Domitrovic, which outlines the formulation, rationale, and history of the application of supply-side economic theory, with emphasis on the people who sparked the supply-side revolution beginning in the early 1970s. Essentially, the story is about monetary policy at least as much as about tax and fiscal policy, because the policy mistakes there have been the primary culprit in most of the crises of the past century, including this one. The most recent irony here is that the world's champion of capitalism is now being lectured on monetary policy by a communist country that happens to be its leading creditor. The Chinese are not stupid – they hold $1.3 trillion of our debt and they know that the only way we can repay it is to inflate our way out of the problem and defraud the bondholders. Again, as the keeper of the world's reserve currency, we have a higher obligation.

A Tragedy Even Worse than it Appears

February 5, 2010

"The central conservative truth is that it is culture, not politics, that determines the success of a society. The central liberal truth is that politics can change a culture and save it from itself." — Daniel Patrick Moynihan.

I have used this quote before, but it has never been more appropriate than in the context of the recent earthquake disaster in Haiti. It is also the underlying theme of a very good book, *The Central Liberal Truth,* by Lawrence E. Harrison. It was given to me several months ago, but I had not read it before the disaster in Haiti. As it happens, the book features the island of Hispaniola, comprising Haiti and the Dominican Republic, as a case study of how much culture really does matter and the concept of the necessity of cultural change in order to save certain societies. Why is this island such an ideal place in which to study this concept? Because, as the book describes, it is the best location in the world to analyze two adjoining nations under conditions in which a number of the usual variables – geography, climate, history, etc. – can be controlled so that cultural influences can be isolated. And the result is striking.

Here are two nations that share an island discovered and claimed for Spain by Columbus in 1492, both of which were exploited by European powers through plunder and slavery over three centuries that today display a remarkable divergence in human development indicators. A few samples from the United Nations Human Development Report of 2003: an 18-year gap in life expectancy at birth; a 33 percent gap in adult literacy; a 20 percent gap in school enrollment among school-age children; a four to one ratio in per capita GDP based on purchasing power parity; and a gap in the overall human development index ranking among nations, combining health, education, and prosperity factors, of 56, where one is best and 173 is worst. If you guessed that the Dominican Republic is on the higher end of these indicators in every case, you are correct. Why is this so?

In a word, it's the culture. After controlling for all the other factors to which I previously alluded, there is no other explanation. In fact, in research conducted over the years by Harrison and his colleagues, the result is that Haiti is much closer culturally to Africa than to its neighbor on the island they share. What are the critical cultural factors that produce this remarkable result? Based on research conducted over the years and detailed in the book, there have been identified 25 key cultural factors that determine whether a society is driven by a "progress-prone culture" or a "progress-resistant culture." These factors have been validated by subsequent studies of cultural values in countries comprising 85 percent of the world's population. The upshot is that human progress or lack thereof is primarily determined by these cultural factors that fit into four categories – worldview, values and virtues, economic behavior, and social behavior – the most important of which seems to be worldview, which is in turn informed and shaped over the years by religion.

In brief, religions that nurture rationality, achievement, material pursuits, optimism, and pursuit of scientific truth are progress-prone; those that nurture irrationality, inhibit material pursuits, focus on the "other" world, emphasize fatalism, discourage punctuality, and emphasize abstract truth are progress-resistant. From these basic differences in religious worldview, otherwise seemingly compatible cultures take on widely divergent ideas about their destiny, values, and economic and social behavior.

Much has been made of Pat Robertson's unfortunate remark in the wake of the earthquake that the disaster was a judgment of God on the Haitian people because of their "pact with the devil" more than 200 years ago. This refers to a speech made by the leader of the Haitian slave revolt that ultimately led to independence in the early 19th century, the actual words of which have been a subject of controversy since then. This strain of conversation is a distraction at best. But what is incontrovertible is that the practice of the animist religion of Voodoo has been widespread in Haiti for centuries, mainly among the poor who comprise the vast majority of the population, but not without its significant influence among the upper classes.

Voodoo has many features that fit the worldview of the progress-resistant cultural factors discussed above. It is not a religion that concerns itself with ethical issues. It is a fatalistic religion; the destinies of its followers are believed to be controlled by hundreds of human-like spirits who require constant nurturing. It is a species of the sorcery and witchcraft that are prevalent in Africa. And it discourages initiative, rationality, achievement, education, and other progress-prone factors. All of these factors are antithetical to the worldview propagated by the Judeo-Christian tradition and, although Catholicism has had its problems with assimilation with democracy and capitalism over the centuries, the embrace of its essential teachings in the heritage of the Dominican Republic have clearly produced a much more progress-prone culture.

So, to return to Moynihan and Harrison, what should be done in Haiti? Well, first, we are doing about all we can do in response to the current disaster, as only America is capable. Second, after the physical rebuilding, Haiti needs to be rebuilt socially from the ground up – more of the same of the past couple of generations will lead to more of the same human tragedy. Someone suggested a "Marshall Plan" for Haiti. That would be a total waste. Europe could accommodate one, because Europe was not in need (then, at least) of a cultural transformation. Haiti is in such need, but so it has been for many decades. Harrison makes some suggestions as to how to put Moynihan's truths to work, probably the two most important of which are the premise that the fix cannot be imposed from the outside and that the ideology of cultural relativism so firmly embedded in the institutions of social change must be confronted and refuted. I won't belabor the rest of them here, but suffice to repeat, it's all about the culture, and add that there is a real opportunity here to change the paradigm.

No Victory, No Peace

February 4, 2011

A review of the new book, *Between War and Peace*, a collection of essays edited by Matthew Moten, resonated with a great book I am now completing – *The Shield of Achilles*, by Philip Bobbitt. This is a sweeping, 800-plus page history of war and peace over five centuries, highlighting the impact of war, its preparation, and its aftermath on the structure and strategy of the state. Both the review and Bobbitt's book emphasize the fact that, in essence, there is no substitute for victory. Bobbitt says that strategic success in war certifies the constitutional form adopted by the winning state and spreads to the constitution of the society of states as a whole, thus while violence and war initiate change in the constitutional order, peace and law ratify the results. In other words, without victory there is no peace, and the world moves on to the next phase of the war. I have long maintained that real victory in this context is possible only with unconditional surrender. Think about it: Every conflict in which America has been engaged that had an unconditional victor resulted in the resolution of the underlying issues; those that didn't left the issues unresolved, many of them to this day.

James Q. Wilson, RIP

March 7, 2012

Wilson was a favorite essayist and political and social scientist, and his book, *The Moral Sense*, was an important one for me. In it, he identifies our moral sense, what some have described as "written on the heart," as a fact of human nature, the primary enemy of moral relativism, and an essence that statist regimes of all stripes must defeat in order to attain sovereignty. He could not be described as a political conservative, but he certainly had conservative instincts, as evidenced by remarks, such as these which resonate in current issues: "Our freedom does not depend on eliminating acknowledgements of the power of religion; it relies instead on the fact that for many generations we have embraced a secular government operating in a religious culture. That embrace will be weakened, not strengthened, by silly attacks on religiosity, stimulating the spiritual to question the seriousness of people who profess a concern for civil liberties."

Repeating History in Syria and Iraq?

July 6, 2012

The Spanish Civil War of 1936-39 always has been somewhat a mystery to me, very often misunderstood, more often mischaracterized, and the players and factions were very confusing. It was, of course, a precursor to the main event, World War II, with Germany and the Soviet Union using it as a proxy for their respective interests, but beyond that I didn't understand it very well until I recently read *The Last Crusade – Spain: 1936*, by Warren Carroll. This is an admittedly Nationalist partisan treatment, but it lays out the background, the detailed history of the conflict, the factions, and the issues very well.

The book also gave me the insight to understand a couple of essays on recent and current conflicts in the Middle East, comparing the contemporary conflicts with the Spanish Civil War. Stephen Schwartz writes in 2006 of the Iraq war being a harbinger of bigger things to come and takes the analogy further by suggesting that there is another lesson, because the Spanish Civil War was the first major example of the modern proxy wars, in which local conflicts are exploited in the pursuit of global or regional interests. In this context, it anticipated the Communist-incited civil wars of the last half of the 20th century.

Pat Buchanan follows in June 2012 with an essay analogizing the Spanish Civil War with the current conflict in Syria and commends, both FDR and the current U.S. administration, respectively, for maintaining neutrality, but worries that the Syrian conflict could yet become what he calls a "dress rehearsal for a Mideast War." He likens the configuration of the various factions, religions, allies, and strategic interests in the Middle East that are manifest in Syria today with similar characteristics in Spain in the late 1930s.

These comparisons with history could be appropriate, and time will tell. But, what bothers me is the response to the current situation, and Schwartz and Buchanan have very different ideas about what that should be. Buchanan is well known for his isolationism, and I can't agree with that for a variety of reasons, not least of which is that, as the leader of the free world, we have a responsibility to confront tyranny and support freedom, particularly when it is in our interest to do so. As George W. Bush recently said, "We do not get to choose if a freedom revolution should begin or end in the Middle East or elsewhere; we only get to choose what side we are on."

We have possibly already undermined the long-term success of democracy in Iraq with our premature withdrawal and I worry that we are squandering an opportunity to make a significant difference in the outcome in Syria by relying on the feckless United Nations and not more directly confronting Iran and Russia on their support for the murderous incumbent regime. Stephen Schwartz ends his essay by suggesting that "by winning the battle of Iraq, and by fostering real change in Saudi Arabia, Syria, and Iran, the democratic nations may save the world from a later, longer, bloodier, and more terrible war." This is the analogy with the Spanish Civil War that we want to avoid.

Who We Are, According to Dionne

September 3, 2012

I often at least scan E. J. Dionne's syndicated newspaper essays, because although I don't often agree with him, I do respect his insight and intellectual honesty. There really are intellectually honest leftists out there! His recent book, *Our Divided Political Heart,* was true to form – I greatly enjoyed his insight and analysis on our deeply divided political culture, but disagreed with his conclusions on the core problem and the solution.

Let's begin with his major premise – that we Americans can't agree on who we are as a nation and a people, because we can't agree on who we have been. And he says that who we have been in our history and tradition is a nation not of radical self-reliance and self-interest, but of a commitment to a balance between love of individual freedom and devotion to community. This insight is right out of the "communitarian" playbook, not a particularly radical notion nor outside the mainstream. But he makes an all too frequent mistake in his approach to communitarianism, properly understood in American history.

David Brooks makes the same mistake in a recent essay critical of what he calls the "hyperindividualism" in the current Republican message coming from their recent national convention. He laments that there was no talk of community and "compassionate conservatism," the latter I always have considered to be a duplication of terms since Bush 43 coined it.

The major mistake here is to conflate "community" with "government." When Edmund Burke spoke and wrote of the "little platoons" of community activists and the organic nature of community service, he wasn't referring to government intervention and bureaucracy. When Alexis de Tocqueville lauded the American structure of "voluntary associations" that permeate every aspect of life as the backbone of our brand of communitarianism, he wasn't talking about government administration of social programs. At most, what they had in mind for government services was based on the principle of subsidiarity, or government that is close to the people it serves and is bound up in a web of custom, habit, and local accountability.

This is the community best understood in our history. Dionne provides a historical survey of our tradition in this regard, but seems to want to have the definition of community begin with the progressive movement of the late 19th and early 20th centuries, which was an attempt to reverse the model envisioned by the Founders. He calls the period since the advent of Populism, Progressivism, the New Deal, and the Great Society the Long Consensus. And he vilifies the Tea Party movement, which in fact, wants a return to the founding principles, as a radical element that is borderline anarchist in nature and wants to roll back this "consensus."

I don't deny that throughout our history there has been a delicate balancing act between our love of liberty and our striving for equality of opportunity, along with major battles over the role of government in fostering both. Tocqueville was explicit in pointing this out. Nor do I deny that government has played a major role in providing the infrastructure and public works that have made the American success story possible. Think where we would have been without the intercontinental railroad, the Erie Canal, the interstate highway system, or even the GI Bill, which financed a different kind of infrastructure.

But, these partnerships and major national projects have been beneficial to community, properly understood, and are much different in nature from what now passes for community – the intrusiveness of government paternalism, which is too often coercive, creates dependency, and feeds an entitlement mentality that is corrosive to our character and moral fiber and in many respects destructive to community. David Brooks says that "what matters is not whether a program is public or private but its effect on character." I agree, but the result of "community" read as "government" too often has a negative impact on our character.

For all my issues with Dionne's conclusions, this book is a good read and pretty accurately identifies the wedge points in the American "divided political heart," and this conflicted vision about who we are is what watershed elections like this one are all about.

Special Edition – Top Ten Books

December 3, 2013

Since inception of *The Texas Pilgrim* almost 14 years ago, I have reviewed more than 100 books and recently my son-in-law asked me to list for him my top 10 books, which gave me the idea to publish this special December edition. To do so, I considered not only those books I have reviewed, but essentially all the books I have read over the past 35 years or so, some 500 books. The selection involved some difficult choices. Getting to the top 50 was not a problem, but the eliminations down to 10 were tough, and I left some very good ones off the list. You will no doubt note an absence of fiction in the list and I admit that my post-college exposure to great fiction has been limited, an obvious shortcoming. In any case, I thought that Pilgrim readers might have interest, so here is the list, in alphabetical order by author.

Ten Philosophical Mistakes
by Mortimer J. Adler (1985)
The author himself writes in the preface that a more accurate, if cumbersome, title would have been *Ten Subjects About Which Philosophical Mistakes Have Been Made*. *Time* magazine described it as "a provocative look at the errors of modern thought by America's "philosopher for everyman," and it is certainly that, covering a wide range of issues on which Adler believes that errors have been compounded over the years, resulting in a number of seriously misguided conclusions that have had consequences. The range of issues he discusses include human consciousness, the intellect, knowledge and opinion, moral values, freedom of choice, and human nature, society, and existence, among others. I have found it to be the book I have most often referred to in the 20 years since I first read it.

The Closing of the American Mind: How Higher Education Has Failed Democracy and Impoverished the Souls of Today's Students
by Allan Bloom (1987)
Bloom stunned the academic world with this book, not just because of its sweeping indictment of our elite institutions of higher learning, but also because of the unusually resounding commercial success of a scholarly work by such an intellectual. No doubt it is an extraordinary analysis of the state of the American university and the mind of the students who populate the most elite of the institutions. It is also an in depth survey of the intellectual history leading to the present condition. Essentially, the crisis of liberal education and American intellectual life, according to Bloom, who was certainly no right-wing reactionary, is that no one is prepared to ask or answer the big questions about the nature of man and of good and evil. We have so "closed" the mind of the American student to these philosophical pursuits that we have impoverished their minds, as well as their souls and rendered them incapable of determining the nature of man and moral truth. The result is that the large majority of students are "unified only in their relativism and their allegiance to equality, and their greatest fear is not error, but intolerance." A classic.

Witness
by Whittaker Chambers (1952)
I often have said this is one work without which you can't fully understand the 20th century. It is, of course, the life story of a former Communist and active member of the CPUSA underground, who left the party and later provided crucial and very controversial testimony in the famous Alger Hiss Case of the late 1940s. Nothing I

have read captures the essence of the Communist mind and socialist threat as Chambers does, and he weaves his tale in a way that is eerily prescient of many of the conflicts we still face today, for the crux of the Communist faith, which is that salvation by society in a world without God is the only solution to the crisis of history, is alive and well in the progressive remnants left behind under other names, both here and abroad, by the discrediting of institutional Communism. And it is amazing how complicit in this faith and the relentless pursuit of power based on that faith were and are the American fellow-travelers, up to the point of complete denial to this day, despite incontrovertible evidence gleaned from KGB files since the fall of the Soviet Union, and how willing to ignore or rationalize the pervasiveness of this evil our major cultural institutions were and are.

A New Birth of Freedom
by Harry V. Jaffa (2000)
This is a masterful analysis of American political philosophy as defined by the Founders from its roots in the classical and Judeo-Christian traditions and as refined (or "re-defined" as some would say) by Lincoln in the re-founding years leading up to the Civil War. Jaffa is a natural right enthusiast out of the Leo Strauss school and his debates with strict constitutional constructionists like Robert Bork and William Rehnquist are legendary. The issues he confronts and the ideological conflicts he illuminates are critical to our understanding of the exceptional nature of the American idea and are as current as today's conflicts, both domestic and foreign.

The Abolition of Man
by C. S. Lewis (1944)
As so well noted in a recent essay by Joseph Pearce, this small book is Lewis's masterful critique of the relativism that was rampant in his day as in ours, and represented the culmination of the author's quest for the quintessential meaning of man's being and purpose. In it, he confronts the great question of post-modernity – can we live well without moral truth? His answer, supported by convincing logic, is no. His foundation is the Confucian concept of the Tao (The Way), known in the West as the natural law, which is to Lewis not one of among a series of possible systems of value, but the sole source of all value judgments, a principle which we violate at our peril. His fear is the conquest of nature by man, particularly when human nature itself surrenders to man, and he cautions about the end game of this conquest: "What we call man's power over nature turns out to be a power exercised by by some men over other men with nature as the instrument."

Democracy's Discontent: America in Search of a Public Philosophy
by Michael J. Sandel (1996)
Sandel is the Harvard professor whose course, "Justice: What's the Right Thing To Do?" is the most popular lecture series on campus. This is another book that I frequently revisit for its insight into the badly damaged state of affairs in our republic, which was designed to settle contentious issues through our system of federalism and the mediating power of thousands of voluntary associations and institutions, which are a primary source of American exceptionalism. This is the "civic republic" well-described by Sandel, but it has been corrupted by what he calls the "procedural republic," which essentially demands that we move foundational cultural and moral considerations off the table in our deliberation of public policy and focus exclusively on "fair procedures." And where has this taken us? To an imperial judiciary and deep divisions in the body politic, because it has been denied political resolution to a number of issues nearest and dearest to our core. An in-depth discussion of this problem and possible solutions is the central focus of this book.

A Conflict of Visions: Ideological Origins of Political Struggles
by Thomas Sowell (1987)
Columnist Tom Friedman has a concept of what he calls "systemic misunderstanding," a condition of debate or conflict between or among parties in disagreement wherein the conflict cannot be resolved with more facts or information. With Thomas Sowell, among my favorite essayists, such a condition is even more deeply seated in what he has named "a conflict of visions." For Sowell, the intellectual origins of the sides of debate on essentially all public policy issues can ultimately be traced to the degree to which the opposing parties are of the "constrained" or "unconstrained" vision. Consequently, the very meaning of words like "freedom," "rights," "equality," and "power" may be drastically different, depending on their context within different worldviews, or visions of man. Put simply, the unconstrained vision allows for considerably more knowledge, morality, virtue, and fortitude on the part of human nature to successfully accomplish its objectives than are thought humanly possible by the constrained vision. A profound study that has had a big impact on my thinking for 25 years.

Democracy in America, by Alexis de Tocqueville
Edited by Richard D. Heffner (1956), originally published in 1835 and 1840
The New York Times wrote this: "No better study of a nation's institutions and culture than Tocqueville's Democracy in America has ever been written by a foreign observer; none perhaps as good." My only quibble with this analysis would be that I would

possibly omit the word "foreign." What else is there to say? This is the classic treatise on the American way of life written as a result of Tocqueville's visit to the United States in 1831-32. A must read for anyone who wants to understand the American culture, American exceptionalism, and the pitfalls of and internal threats to American democracy.

Ideas Have Consequences
by Richard Weaver (1948)
From the outset, one of the underlying themes of *The Texas Pilgrim* has been the notion that "ideas have consequences," and one of the thinkers who inspired that notion in me is Richard M. Weaver, whose book of that name has been an invaluable source of the wisdom of that aphorism. Weaver diagnoses the ills of the age as the culmination of an evolution of thought that began with a major change in philosophy when, in the 14th century, man's conception of the reality of transcendentals was first seriously challenged. In short, the issue involved whether or not there is a source of truth higher than, and independent of, man. Thus was born the philosophy of nominalism – the idea that the only reality is that perceived by the senses. Once this concept took hold, the rest, as they say, is history. From there, we proceeded beyond the careful scientific study of nature to the denial of anything transcending experience, to rationalism elevated to the rank of a philosophy, to the materialistic idea of man explained only by his environment, and to psychological "behaviorism" and the abolishment of free will. And from there it was not a great leap to the postmodern abandonment of timeless moral truth and the attendant moral relativism that plagues our age. Needless to say, the consequences abound.

Faith, Reason, and the War Against Jihadism
by George Weigel (2007)
This is simply the most compelling explanation that I have encountered of the evil we face in radical Islamism and its sources. Weigel draws on 25 years of experience in moral argument and its intersection with public policy to paint clearly the threat posed by global jihadism. He explores the ideology's theological, social, cultural, and political roots and offers a new direction for public policy and interreligious dialogue. One point is driven home relentlessly: that our first step in understanding this enemy and achieving moral clarity is to overcome the powerful prejudice, grounded in progressive hope and naiveteé, that religious belief is disappearing as a factor in world politics.

Coming Apart: The State of White America, 1960-2010 by Charles Murray

January 1, 2015

This book had been on my short list almost since it was published a couple of years ago, and I had read so many reviews of it that I almost felt I had already consumed it. Then my friend Adam Meyerson of the Philanthropy Roundtable gave me a copy and I am pleased that he did so. Because, despite all that has been written and said about American cultural decline, this book is the most enlightening and frightening analysis of it that I have seen. Of course, Murray is no stranger to being out on the leading edge of provocative analyses of American social life and I'm sure he has the scars to prove it. In this analysis, he identifies the domains through which human beings achieve deep satisfaction in life as only four – family, vocation, community, and faith – and proceeds to demonstrate with compelling data the degree to which these foundations have collapsed among white adults in their prime years of 30 to 49 over the past half-century. The result is that the Founders' vision for the "pursuit of happiness" has been severely damaged. He offers alternative outcomes, but his final warning is that this trend away from the qualities necessary for this pursuit will not be reversed by incremental victories by specific items of legislation or elections or specific court cases, but "only when we are talking again about why America is exceptional and why it is so important that America remain exceptional. That requires once again seeing the American project for what it has been: a different way for people to live together, unique among the nations of the earth, and immeasurably precious." Should be required reading for anyone in a leadership role in America.

Kissinger and World Order

February 4, 2015

I'll open by saying that, although I always thought he was brilliant and I enjoyed meeting and visiting with him more than 30 years ago, I didn't always agree with Henry Kissinger's conduct of foreign policy, particularly the notion of detente that he and Richard Nixon practiced in policy with the Soviets. But his new book, *World Order*, which I just read, is a masterful survey of the evolution of political power in the world, beginning for the West, including Russia, with the Treaty of Westphalia at the end of the Thirty Years' War in 1648. From there it sweeps through the past three centuries plus and picks up the Eastern counterparts in China, Japan, and India as they become relevant. In the process, he relates this evolution in comparison with the principles established in Westphalia, which he evidently considers foundational, and I thought this to be the unique thread in the book. His analysis is insightful, his range is encyclopedic, and his scholarship is deep. There is a lot to think about here.

I thought it was particularly timely that Kissinger recently appeared along with former Secretaries of State George Schultz and Madeleine Albright before the Senate Armed Services Committee to discuss current conditions and American foreign policy. All agreed that the defense spending sequester must be ended and that "national defense should have a strategy-driven budget, not a budget-driven strategy," said Kissinger. He added that in the last two wars "withdrawal became the principal definition of strategy; we have to know the objective at the start and develop the strategy to achieve it." Finally, "foreign policy is not a series of discrete events, it is a question of continuous strategy in the world." The depth of this thinking is sorely missed. We don't have his equal on the scene.

The Future of War

April 5, 2015

I finally caught up with Philip Bobbitt's 2009 book, *Terror and Consent: The Wars for the Twenty-First Century,* a follow up to his masterful 2003 work, *The Shield of Achilles: War, Peace, and the Course of History*, which traced the evolution of warfare from the Italian city-state up to what he calls the modern market state and which I have previously reviewed.

Terror and Consent picks up with the development of the market state, which Bobbitt says has superseded the nation state in the conduct of war just as it has done so in the development of the globalization of markets. He applies this concept in a provocative analysis of the West's battle against terror, and he boldly advances the notion that the primary driving force of terrorism is not Islam (a point on which I disagree to an extent in a way that deserves longer explanation), but rather the emergence of market states, producing a form of globalization of warfare in which weapons of mass destruction will be commodified.

Bobbitt quotes Henry Kissinger, who praises the Bush administration for recognizing the global threat posed by terrorism, but was critical of that administration for having not been able to "operationalize a response or develop a language to discuss it." On the other hand, I believe that, properly defined and implemented, nationalism coupled with universal democracy was the object of Bush's version of neo-conservatism, which failed both in definition and implementation, but should be revisited and revised. To me, this is the task that Bobbitt sets out to accomplish, and his approach is well-informed by history, law, and military strategy. If you're interested in where all of this is leading, this is a very good read.

An Interesting and Instructive Constitutional Analysis

July 9, 2015

For years I have been fascinated by the similarities between the Supreme Court decisions in the 1857 *Dred Scott* case involving slavery and the 1973 *Roe v. Wade* case involving abortion rights. My interest to date has been more about the cultural similarities rather than those involving legal and constitutional principles, because I have felt and said a number of times that in many ways, *Roe v. Wade* is "our *Dred Scott*" in terms of the political and culture clashes that they both produced.

Now comes a book that brings the similarities to light in a very instructive analysis. *Slavery, Abortion, and the Politics of Constitutional Meaning*, by Justin Buckley Dyer, provides a scholarly treatment of the parallels between slavery and abortion in American constitutional development and he comprehensively explains how slavery and abortion are historically, philosophically, and legally entangled. And the analogies extend to current considerations of the constitutional principles driving recent Supreme Court decisions, highlighted by extensive analysis of the origin and history of the concept of "substantive due process," a controversial principle, which allows federal courts to protect certain rights from governmental interference under the due process clauses of the Fifth and 14th Amendments to the Constitution. A very enlightening read.

Shame: How America's Past Sins Have Polarized Our Country

by Shelby Steele

February 4, 2016

Shelby Steele has long been a big favorite and his essays have provided me the most insightful penetration of the issue of race in America, possibly equaled only by Thomas Sowell in his worldwide analyses of race and culture. And the impact of this book, which at 198 pages is really a long essay, has changed my perspective on the race issue, particularly as it has been shaped and portrayed by the activists from all persuasions over the past half century. In fact, I have a long-standing habit of underlining key passages in non-fiction books that I read to which I want to return for a second reading and to internalize the thoughts, but this book is so rich with insight that I found myself wanting to underline almost every sentence!

Essentially, Steele believes that the root of our current political polarization originates in the decade of protest of the 1960s, when in the act of dismantling what he calls our national hypocrisies of racism, sexism, and militarism, liberals adopted the posture that there was something inauthentic and probably evil in the American character that rendered the entire regime essentially illegitimate. This conclusion has sustained the notion of "poetic truth," a certain license for race-based activism in which facts have no bearing. And this has resulted in a half-century of well-intentioned, but ill-advised government social programs, fueled by white liberal guilt that in his estimation have not only failed, but have done harm to the very minorities they were designed to help.

As I read this book and explored its insights, it occurred to me that the concepts necessary to understand Barack Obama, what brought him into power, what informs him and the constituency that sustains him, are spelled out in this book. It also helps one to realize how badly he failed the black community during his administration, a fact that I believe most thoughtful blacks understand.

I don't agree with every point he makes, particularly on our "militarism," but Shelby Steele has performed groundbreaking work here and this book deserves the attention of all who genuinely want to address American race relations.

The Continuing Relevance of the Election of 1896

March 6, 2016

I have just read *The Triumph of William McKinley: Why the Election of 1896 Still Matters* by Karl Rove and I was struck by the continuing relevance of that election.

For me, when I thought about it at all, the election of 1896 always has been associated with the William Jennings Bryan "cross of gold" speech at the Democratic National Convention, but I had never delved deep enough into the details or the depth of issues to understand what this election really meant and how important it has been and still is.

Rove has done a masterful job of combining the blow by blow of the election year, including meticulous details of strategy and tactics which are his stock in trade, with the underlying currents of the transforming American political body and its driving issues. And the electoral tactics of this election were groundbreaking, for McKinley steadfastly refused to actively travel to campaign, to "take to the stump" as he said. His was the "front porch" campaign conducted literally from his front porch in Canton, Ohio, with hundreds of thousands of voters from across the country trekking there to meet with him and hear him speak on the issues. Another critical element of his victory also broke new ground, at least for a Republican. McKinley ran as an "outsider," breaking the stronghold of the "bosses" and their election "machine" politics in the urban areas and going directly to the people with his message, both for the party nomination and the general election, and Rove calls it the first modern primary campaign.

As for the critical issues in this election, there were primarily only two, but they were big ones: the protection of U.S. business interests with the tariff and the currency issue – free silver coinage and convertibility vs. a gold-backed currency. On the first issue, McKinley and the Republican Party had been consistently supportive of tariffs to protect American manufacturing interests and employment, a major difference with the current Republican position, but one that produced national political dominance with few exceptions from the end of the Civil War until 1932. On the currency issue, McKinley initially vacillated, but very late in the campaign moved the issue to the forefront and came down solidly against free silver coinage and for "sound money" backed by gold. In the end it was, of course, a winning issue for him as he soundly defeated Bryan and his demagoguery on it.

Interestingly, Milton Friedman writes extensively about the currency issues of the late 19th century in his 1992 book, *Money Mischief,* including the debates of the 1896 election, and I referred to it during my reading of Rove's discussion. Friedman actually (and surprisingly to me) writes that he would have favored the free coinage of silver at the time of its elimination in 1873, believing that it would have avoided the damaging deflation of the recession of the early 1890s, but under conditions in 1896 believes that McKinley's position on a gold-backed dollar was correct.

Fast forward to today and we find that these two key issues are still very much with us. On the tariff, we have the leading Republican candidate for President who would return his party to the support of protectionist trade policy for the first time since the early 20th century, which would abdicate our world trade leadership. On the currency issue, we have a Federal Reserve that has so inflated its balance sheet with fiat money and so exceeded its primary mission of dollar price stability in micromanaging interest rates that it no longer has the leverage to engage in meaningful monetary policy.

Rove's book is a good place to catch up on the history of these critical issues that still resonate.

A Path Forward From the Gridlock?

July 4, 2016

Without doubt, America is more seriously polarized and anxious than at any time at least since World War II, and there appears very little hope that these maladies will be in any meaningful way cured by the results of this election year; in fact, they are likely to be exacerbated, whatever the outcome.

There has been no shortage of books, essays, and commentary on this condition, but none more perceptive and ambitious than the recent book by Yuval Levin, *The Fractured Republic: Renewing America's Social Contract in the Age of Individualism.*

Levin's major theme is that America, across the political and ideological spectrum, is in what he calls a trap of competing nostalgia and that this condition is preventing any meaningful discussion across partisan lines. He is from staunch conservative instincts, but he says that both right and left have been blind to how America has changed over the past five decades. The left is nostalgic for the middle of the 20th century, when unions were strong, big government made huge promises to solve social problems, and the civil rights movement was prominent. The right looks back at the Reagan era of deregulation, lower taxes, cultural traditionalism, and American optimism and confidence. Both sides mistakenly think that a return to their respective "golden age" would solve our problems and Levin is convinced that this politics of nostalgia is failing Americans of the 21st century. Of interest, in a recent article in the Washington Examiner, Michael Barone also uses the nostalgia angle to describe the same problem, while using somewhat different eras that attract the nostalgia of right and left.

For Levin, the path forward must avoid both radical individualism and centralized statism and seek to revive the Tocquevillian institutions of voluntary association in the private middle layers of society – schools, churches, civic organizations, chambers of commerce, trade associations, charitable organizations, etc. This, along with the re-establishment of the principle of subsidiarity, the entrusting of power and authority to the lowest and least centralized institutions capable of using them well, will reinforce the return to community-based governance.

Levin provides a perceptive analysis of the history of how we got here and an ambitious plan for how we proceed to get out of this seemingly unending cycle. And he is not naive about the daunting challenges in reviving these traditions, which have been undermined by overreaching government at every level over the past 80 years. There really is no better alternative. I just wish I could be more optimistic.

Two Books That Changed My Thinking

July 5, 2017

This year marks the 30th anniversary of the publication of two books that have had an enormous impact on my thinking about education policy across the board, from elementary to secondary to higher, not to mention completely changing the conversation among intellectuals and others involved with education policy.

The first was *The Closing of the American Mind: How Higher Education Has Failed Democracy and Impoverished the Souls of Today's Students*, by Allan Bloom, which I mentioned several years ago as part of a survey of my top ten books. Bloom stunned the academic world with this book, not just because of its sweeping indictment of our elite institutions of higher learning, but also because of the unusually resounding commercial success of a scholarly work by such an intellectual. No doubt it is an extraordinary analysis of the state of the American university and the mind of the students who populate the most elite of the institutions. It is also an in depth survey of the intellectual history leading to the present condition. Essentially, the crisis of liberal education and American intellectual life, according to Bloom, who was certainly no right-wing reactionary, is that no one is prepared to ask or answer the big questions about the nature of man and of good and evil. We have so "closed" the mind of the American student to these philosophical pursuits that we have impoverished their minds, as well as their souls and rendered them incapable of determining the nature of man and moral truth. The result is that the large majority of students are "unified only in their relativism and their allegiance to equality, and their greatest fear is not error but intolerance."

Recently, in commemoration of its 30th anniversary, the Witherspoon Institute hosted on their website "Public Discourse" a symposium on Bloom's book, featuring among others Paul Rahe, who was one of Bloom's students during the campus revolutionary period of the late 1960s. He has this to say about the relevance of Bloom's thinking today: "There is nothing that has happened in American higher education in the last few years that would have surprised Bloom. The demand for "trigger warnings" and "safe spaces," the offense taken at so-called "micro-aggressions," and the resort to violence are a parody of the rougher stuff that happened in Germany in the mid-1930s. Bloom believed that the cowardice displayed by university administrations and faculties in the face of thuggery back in the late 1960s portended an end for the life of the mind in the United States. Recent events at Yale University, the University of Missouri, Claremont McKenna College, the University of California at Berkeley, Middlebury College, and elsewhere suggest that he was right. On most campuses, the most important questions can no longer be posed and students, as well as faculty members engage in self-censorship."

Needless to say, this does not bode well for higher education or for our country and Bloom was prescient in his forewarning.

The second book from 1987 was *Cultural Literacy: What Every American Needs to Know*, by E. D. Hirsch, Jr., one of the most brilliant minds in education reform of the past half-century. Again, the commercial success of such a book was stunning, steeped as it is in pedagogical concepts and teaching and learning methodology. As the cover jacket indicates, it is essentially a book about reading, but it is much more – it has much to say about how students learn to read, what they read, and how badly that flawed education policy has crippled our students over the past 60 to 70 years. From a public policy standpoint, it is a scathing indictment of the pedagogical upheaval foisted on our education system since the mid-20th century by so-called "progressive" educators that succeeded in completely gutting the coherent grade-by-grade curriculum that had made American elementary and secondary education the envy of the world. This system was replaced by methodologies based on the romantic theories of child development dating from the 18th century thought of Jean-Jacques Rousseau as adapted by John Dewey in the 20th century, which were based on the notion of "constructivism," that children should dispense with "mere facts" and "construct their own knowledge," with the teacher as a mere guide and facilitator. By the 1960s, this ideology had penetrated the depths of the American school system, resulting in "learner-centered" methodologies in every state. In his work on analyzing this debacle, Hirsch has shown that the early damage appears in reading proficiency, because of the poor quality of teacher training and that it is most severe in its harm to the most disadvantaged children.

Also, very significantly, he notes that this failed pedagogy disrupted the transmission of civic values and traditions from generation to generation, a reversal of the valuable insight that a nation's schools must follow a common curriculum soaked in cultural literacy, that there is no such thing as "mere facts," and that this cultural factual immersion is critical for students' ability to read and comprehend advanced texts. In a recent essay, "A Sense of Belonging," Hirsch has this to say on this point: "The recent scientific consensus about the role of unspoken shared knowledge in the language transaction has implications for educational policy that American educators have not yet been willing to draw. If shared background knowledge is essential for effective reading, writing, speaking, and listening in a nation, the schools of a nation need to be common schools that teach this shared knowledge of the public sphere. They must do so if all students are to be literate." And I would add that it goes without saying that this shared common heritage is absolutely necessary to sustain a democratic republic.

At 88, he has recently published his fifth book on these subjects and I wish I could say that we are closer to a complete reversal of the failed policies that he has so insightfully analyzed. Thanks to him some progress has been made, but alas, the progressive ideological barricades are still firmly entrenched.

Both of these books are classics, even more relevant now than when I first read them 30 years ago, and still in print. They will change the way you think about some important things.

The Nature and Roots of the American Left

February 5, 2018

What is fascism and what is a fascist? I'll bet that, even among those who are well read in political philosophy and who have occasion to use these words, a very large percentage of people would say that these are characterizations of those from the political right, in fact, the extreme political right. Think Benito Mussolini, for sure, and Adolf Hitler, along with any number of authoritarian rulers of the 20th century.

George Orwell once said, "Those who would change a culture, corrupt its language, particularly by hiding the reality of an evil they desire behind a less revealing name." This observation probably never has been more appropriate than in the use of the word fascism. Two books will completely expose the fallacy and the lies of this mischaracterization. One of them is *Liberal Fascism: The Secret History of the American Left from Mussolini to the Politics of Meaning*, by Jonah Goldberg; the other is *The Big Lie: Exposing the Nazi Roots of the American Left*, by Dinesh D'Souza.

I read and reviewed the Goldberg book about 10 years ago and the subtitle pretty much sums up its content. He does a brilliant job in fully documenting the history of this word as it applies to the regimes of the 20th century and, more importantly, the degree to which it has been corrupted by the left to disguise policies they desire, while condemning the political right for aiding and abetting fascist tendencies. His basic argument is that early 20th century progressivism, the forerunner of the liberalism of today, has its emotional and doctrinal roots in European fascism, which is essentially and has always been an ideology of the left, not the right as the mythology has presented it.

The D'Souza book is more recent and covers much of the same ground, but with a slightly different approach and more of a partisan edge. He starts with identifying the patron saint of fascist philosophy, largely unknown now even to political philosophy students, although he was one of the world's most influential philosophers of the first half of the 20th century. He was the Italian Giovanni Gentile and, in effect, he is to fascism what Karl Marx is to communism. He was very much a committed socialist who was diametrically opposed to liberal democracy as being "too centered on liberty and personal rights" and therefore selfish. And for Gentile, fascism is a form of socialism, indeed to him its most workable form is the centralized state popular with progressives. In fact, when Mussolini, who converted fascism into an action plan, made his most famous quote, "all is in the state and nothing human exists or has value outside the state," he was merely paraphrasing Gentile. In addition, fascism also is socialism with a national identity, hence, for example, Nazi is a contraction of the term "national socialist."

D'Souza follows this thread and how it has been manifest in leftist parties, including the U.S. Democratic Party, and their policies and fellow travelers in our elite institutions through the rest of the 20th century to the present day Antifa movement, which, contrary to its name, is arguably the most virulent of fascist elements active today.

Orwell was right: Words matter. The truth matters.

Lone Star Nation

May 3, 2018

After it sat on my shelf for several years, I finally got around to reading *Lone Star Nation*, by H. W. Brands, and quickly discovered what a treat I had been missing. I guess I thought I knew all I wanted to know about the formative history of Texas, particularly since I consumed the late Ted Fehrenbach's classic, *Lone Star: A History of Texas and the Texans,* and had the opportunity to meet and discuss it with him during the Texas Sesquicentennial period more than 30 years ago. And it is a great book, but it is in many ways complemented by Brands and I learned a lot and understood much more by having experienced both books.

There are differences: Fehrenbach covers more historic ground, from the early 16th century through the early 1970s, when 20th century urbanization and globalization were beginning to take their toll on the culture of the "days of the republic." Brands on the other hand takes us from the 1820s and the beginning of the colonization of Texas through the trials of the Civil War in 1861-65, and his story is more tightly focused on, as he says, "how a ragged army of volunteers won the battle for Texas independence and changed America."

Brands also does a really good job of explaining the struggle from colonization through independence from the standpoint of Mexico and its leaders, particularly Santa Anna, covering significant internal debates on competing Mexican systems of governance after its independence from Spain, much of which was a new perspective to me and one that added a lot of depth to the story. The same applies to his treatment of the issues involving U.S. expansion, the Indian conflicts, and slavery during the turbulent period leading to Texas independence and statehood from the perspective of the American leaders of the time – J. Q. Adams, Jackson, Clay, Webster, Calhoun, et al.

And then, of course, there are the personalities – Austin, Houston, Bowie, Travis, Crockett, and a host of lesser names. Brands goes in depth on all of them, including the lives they left behind to come to Texas, with a few surprises of which I was not previously aware.

Like many of you I'm sure, I have seen the 1962 movie *How the West Was Won* more than once, and it's a pretty good movie, but one part of it is deficient in the extreme and that is in the portrayal of the role that the battle for Texas played in the completion of "manifest destiny" and the winning of the American West. I think it was allotted about a minute or so of background narrative without enough explanation and no significant scenes that are memorable. Among other important elements of this history, these books remind us of this crucial episode that, as both authors know, drastically changed America, arguably as much or more than the Louisiana Purchase. It really is pretty simple – no Alamo, no San Jacinto; no San Jacinto, no Texas; no Texas, no Mexican

War; and no Mexican War, no California. So if you liked *Lone Star*, you will like *Lone Star Nation*. And if you haven't read either one, I recommend them both.

Jordan Peterson's Rules

September 4, 2018

After seeing him on almost every talk show for months and reading a number of reviews and essays on his work, I finally caught up with Jordan Peterson's best seller, *12 Rules for Life: An Antidote to Chaos*, and I can say without hesitation that it is one of the more unusual works I have encountered. I'm not much into "self-help" readings and pop culture "to do" lists, but this one was different.

In *Plato's Apology*, at his trial for impiety and corrupting the youth of Athens, Socrates supposedly uttered his famous dictum, "the unexamined life is not worth living," for he believed that philosophy, the love of wisdom, was life's most important pursuit and this was manifest in his life's work asking questions, such as "what is virtue," "what is justice," and "how can one live the good life." Peterson's book offers an existential route to such an examination and I use the term existential, because rather than a more politically correct characterization, what he offers are not suggestions or guidelines, but rules. And the overriding rule is that you must take responsibility for your own life.

He starts by defining the parameters of consideration, which take place between life's elements of chaos and order, where chaos is unexplored territory and what he calls the place you end up when things fall apart, but also when challenging opportunities present themselves. By contrast, order is explored territory, the hundreds of millions of years of hierarchy, place, position, and authority – the structure of society and also of biology. His dozen rules help to traverse between these two elements as he takes you through various aspects of philosophy, religion, case studies from his clinical practice, and personal life experiences.

There is a little something for everyone here: There is a little too much of Heidegger's "Being" to suit me, but he makes good use of Nietzsche, rejecting his atheism, but acknowledging his belief that the so-called "death of God" was a huge disaster for mankind. He doesn't deny Marx's charge that culture is an oppressive structure, but he says it's always been that way and he thinks the benefits outweigh the suffering involved in conforming to tradition. And, although the exact nature of his religious faith is unclear, he believes that it is necessary and beneficial for religions to have a dogmatic element. And when the 12-chapter tour has concluded, there is no doubt that

Peterson has forcefully made the case that not just freedom, but order is a basic human need and one that is too often being neglected.

There are numerous nuggets of wisdom here and much to chew on, and I believe that he has made a serious contribution to the discussion we need to have in the re-founding of a conservatism that needs restoration for the 21st century.

Has Liberalism Failed?

October 4, 2018

Patrick Deneen has written a very ambitious book, *Why Liberalism Failed*, in which in several respects he makes a compelling case that its founding ideology was destined to fail, because it was built upon a foundation of a number of contradictions. He opens the book as follows: "A political philosophy conceived some 500 years ago, and put into effect at the birth of the United States nearly 250 years later, was a wager that political society could be grounded on a different footing."

This wager was contingent on the success of rights-bearing individuals under a social contract to which newcomers could subscribe, ratified by free and fair elections of responsive representatives under limited government, the rule of law, and an independent judiciary. In other words, a bet on the validity of a regime grounded in the second paragraph of the Declaration of Independence.

Most observers would say that the wager on this regime, in spite of all of its sins and flaws, has been a rousing victory in what it has meant to the advancement of mankind. But then he says this: "Liberalism has failed – not because it fell short, but because it was true to itself. It failed because it succeeded… it has generated pathologies that are at once deformations of its claims, yet realizations of liberal ideology, including titanic inequality, forced uniformity, material and spiritual degradation, and the undermining of freedom."

He actually agrees that the fundamental wager was a winning one, which he describes as follows: "The replacement of one unequal and unjust system with another system enshrining inequality that would be achieved not by oppression and violence, but the the population's full acquiescence, premised on the ongoing delivery of increasing material prosperity, along with the theoretical possibility of class mobility." In this success he believes is grounded the failure of the liberal faith.

His chapters cover a lot of ground in exploring the successes and resulting failures of the various aspects of the liberal order that our founders put in place – the impact on liberty of technology and globalization; encroaching statism; the degradation of citizenship; the breakdown of particular cultures; what he calls the "new aristocracy;" the relentless conquest of nature; and the rise of the autonomous self. But his chapter on education provides the centerpiece of his argument and the one that resonated most with me, in which he says that liberalism "undermines education by replacing a definition of liberty as an education in self-government with liberty as autonomy and the absence of constraint. Ultimately it destroys liberal education, since it begins with the assumption that we are born free, rather than that we must learn to become free." This is the area described in his argument in which we are threatened the most, because it is the means by which we convey our heritage and our culture to the next generation and in which we desperately need and should be able to fashion a repair and recovery project to rescue us from liberalism's deficiencies.

This is a complex book and one that demands at least a second reading to fully understand his message. On balance, he makes a number of insightful arguments on the current fragility of the republic on which there are reasons to be pessimistic, but I believe he sells our founders short in their genius and the compelling arguments that they have made in the grounding of the republic and that what we need is more implementation, not less, of the founding ideals.

What is Nationalism?

November 11, 2018

Since the Brexit vote in the UK and the election of Donald Trump, the theme of nationalism has been thrown around like some 20th century disease that grew out of Nazism and with movements rife with xenophobia and worse, racism. Well, there are some nationalists who might harbor such instincts, but it is an unfair characterization of nationalism as a general proposition. I have used this quote before, because I believe it is a good description of the concept as we seem to use it currently, particularly in comparison to its opposing view, globalism. It is from an essay entitled "Why Historians Get It Wrong," by Jeremy Black in *The New Criterion:* "There is no greater gulf than between, on the one hand, those who identify primarily with their nation, and are concerned at what globalization might be doing to it and to them personally, and on the other hand, those who identify with wider abstractions and are more concerned with retaining the benefits that globalization has brought them."

At a recent campaign stop in Houston, Donald Trump proudly announced that of the two choices, he is definitely a nationalist. No surprise here for one whose entire campaign over the past three years has been about "America First," but I wonder if he realizes the full spectrum and implication of that identity. If not, I hope he will read a great book on the subject, *The Virtue of Nationalism*, by Yoram Hazony.

Hazony lays out a compelling case that nationalism as a political theory comes from the principled standpoint that regards the world as governed best when nations are able to chart their own individual course, cultivating their own traditions and pursuing their own interests without interference. He opposes this theory with that of imperialism, which in various forms including global institutions, seeks to bring peace and prosperity to the world by uniting mankind, as much as possible, under a single political regime. He recounts how, beginning in the 16th century and through the Treaty of Westphalia ending the 30 Years' War in 1648, English, Dutch, and American Protestants revived the Old Testament's emphasis on national independence, leading to the founding of the first nation states.

He laments that nationalism has been unfairly characterized by the internationalists as the cause and home of racism and hatred, largely because of its association with Nazi Germany, a view he rightly says is misguided, because the Nazis were nothing if not imperialists to the core. The answer offered by the internationalists – global governance – is well-intentioned he maintains, but misses the point that all of us are inevitably shaped by the bonds tying us to our families, communities, and nations, the true source of our identities and our strength. But he is quick to acknowledge the argument most commonly made against nationalist politics that it encourages hatred and bigotry and takes on the issue by suggesting and offering evidence that pushing for universal political ideals as with global organizations like the European Union invariably generate hatred and bigotry to at least the same level as nationalist movements.

This is an important book, deeply philosophical, and one that could be very useful in the hands of opinion leaders who need to better understand the deeper history and meaning of the words they use.

Leading a Worthy Life: Finding Meaning in Modern Times
by Leon R. Kass
January 2, 2019

As some introductory comments point out, although Leon Kass is best known as a bioethicist, at heart he is a humanist. I first came in contact with his work when he was appointed Chairman of the President's Council on Bioethics by George W. Bush, and I was immediately impressed with the introduction he wrote to the Council's report to the President, which included this important observation: "...the President's decision (to create the Council) established, or re-established, the precedent that scientific research, being a human activity, is primarily a moral endeavor..." But of course at St. John's College and the University of Chicago for many years he has been helping students and colleagues seek out the most important questions on the issues of life through the study of the great works of literature, philosophy, and science. This book covers a wide range of these issues written over several decades, all of which are timely and on point – they speak to what the title suggests: finding meaning in modern times.

After an overview, the essays are organized into four sections, some written with his wife, Amy, as follows: "Love, Family, and Friendship;" "Human Excellence and Human Dignity;" "In Search of Wisdom;" and "The Aspirations of Mankind: Athens, Jerusalem, and the Gettysburg Address." There are jewels in each section, but I should point out that the essay on the Gettysburg Address is a classic, the best of many I have read on the subject.

If I had to pick a theme or a common thread throughout the book it would be a critique of the ideology of scientism as the foundation of meaning, a critique that is much needed and well-articulated by Kass in a number of contexts in the essays. He doesn't wear a religion on his sleeve, but in a number of instances I was reminded of a passage from the Bible, 2 Corinthians 4:18: "So we fix our eyes not on what is seen, but on what is unseen. For what is seen is temporary, but what is unseen is eternal."

A great read.

ABOUT THE AUTHOR

JAMES M. WINDHAM

Jim's professional career includes more than 35 years in public accounting, commercial and investment banking, and investment portfolio consulting, including six years as chief executive officer of a major Houston bank and 15 years as managing principal of Windham Capital Advisory Services and its predecessor firm.

He has had board level involvement in the banking, investment management, life insurance, venture capital, and title insurance industries, as well as leadership positions in local, regional, and statewide organizations, including service as chairman of the Texas Association of Business; founding director of the Texas Public Policy Foundation; founding director and chairman of the Texas Lyceum Association; member of the Board of Regents, Stephen F. Austin State University; member of the Executive Committee of the Houston Livestock Show and Rodeo; and member of the State Board for Educator Certification. He founded and served for 12 years as chairman of Texas Aspires Foundation, a statewide non-profit organization of business and education leaders advocating public education reform.

A native of Livingston, Texas, he is a graduate of The University of Texas at Austin. He and his wife, Lela, live in Houston and have two daughters and four grandchildren.

Find more online at www.TexasPilgrim.com.

www.ingramcontent.com/pod-product-compliance
Lightning Source LLC
Chambersburg PA
CBHW081322120626
46546CB00011B/3188
* 9 7 8 1 9 5 6 6 4 2 7 8 0 *